THROUGH
THE GLOBAL LENS

Dorothy Blackmon, Ph.D
Cuyahoga Community College
Sociology and Social Science

THROUGH THE GLOBAL LENS

AN INTRODUCTION TO THE SOCIAL SCIENCES

MICHAEL J. STRADA

West Liberty State College
and West Virginia University

PRENTICE HALL, UPPER SADDLE RIVER, NEW JERSEY 07458

Library of Congress Cataloging-in-Publication Data

STRADA, MICHAEL J.
    Through the global lens: an introduction to the social sciences
by Michael J. Strada.
    p. cm.
Includes bibliographical references and index.
ISBN 0-13-614538-8 (alk. paper)
1. Social sciences. I. Title.
H85.S77 1999
300—dc21   98-5442
                                                     CIP

Editorial Director: Charlyce Jones Owen
Editor-in-Chief: Nancy Roberts
Creative Design Director: Leslie Osher
Interior and Cover Design: Anne DeMarinis
Marketing Manager: Christopher DeJohn
Photo Researcher: Beaura K. Ringrose
Photo Research Supervisor: Melinda Reo
Image Permission Supervisor: Kay Dellosa
Electronic Art Creation: Asterisk Group (graphs)
                                        Carto-Graphics (maps)
Cover Art: "Save the World," Diana Ong/SuperStock

Line Art Coordinator: Guy Ruggiero
Page Layout: Matthew S. Garrison and Mirella Signoretto
Acquisitions Editor: John Chillingworth
Managing Editor: Sharon Chambliss
Director of Production and Manufacturing: Barbara Kittle
Editorial/Production Supervision: Rob DeGeorge
Copyeditor: Virginia Rubens
Buyer: Mary Ann Gloriande
Manufacturing Manager: Nick Sklitsis
Director, Image Resource Center: Lori Morris-Nantz

This book was set in 10/12.5 Berkeley Book by Prentice Hall Production Services
and was printed and bound by RR Donnelley & Sons Company.
The cover was printed by Phoenix Color Corp.

 © 1999 by Prentice-Hall, Inc.
Simon & Schuster/A Viacom Company
Upper Saddle River, New Jersey 07458

Printed in the United States of America
10 9 8 7 6 5 4 3 2 1

ISBN 0-13-614538-8

PRENTICE-HALL INTERNATIONAL (UK) LIMITED, *London*
PRENTICE-HALL OF AUSTRALIA PTY. LIMITED, *Sydney*
PRENTICE-HALL CANADA INC., *Toronto*
PRENTICE-HALL HISPANOAMERICANA, S.A., *Mexico*
PRENTICE-HALL OF INDIA PRIVATE LIMITED, *New Delhi*
PRENTICE-HALL OF JAPAN, INC., *Tokyo*
SIMON & SCHUSTER ASIA PTE. LTD., *Singapore*
EDITORA PRENTICE-HALL DO BRASIL, LTDA., *Rio de Janeiro*

FOR SHAUN
AND DYLAN

BRIEF CONTENTS

CONTENTS

PART II   POLITICS IN A CHANGING WORLD

PART III   LIVING IN GROUPS

PART IV   SUBJECTIVE ASPECTS OF THE HUMAN DRAMA

PART V   ECONOMIC BEHAVIOR

PART VI SPATIAL AND ECOLOGICAL ISSUES

PART VII   CONCLUSION

PREFACE

This introductory-level textbook brings a global perspective to the tasks of the six social science disciplines: sociology, anthropology, political science, economics, psychology, and geography. Some social science texts prefer a strong American flavor coupled with a taste for sociology as the ripest fruit of the tree of social sciences. This text's interdisciplinary menu encourages a more varied palate.

In addition to offering an interdisciplinary palate of tastes, it seeks a complementary range of visual hues emanating from the spectrum of internationalism. All the traditional social science concepts are examined, but through a modern prism. The world now opening up to you is a more colorful place than the one that existed when your parents' generation was coming of age. Not only is our world shrinking in time and space, but the emerging global milieu features new actors, as humanity struggles to cope with a vexing array of global issues. To follow the most exciting action in the social sciences today, we must look beyond our traditional boundaries and embrace more complex ways of seeing.

While these two themes—interdisciplinary studies and globalism—set the intellectual *breadth* for our journey into the land of the social sciences, another theme adds depth to this endeavor. In both substance and method, the approach here speaks to the indebtedness of the social sciences to their dual progenitors in knowledge: the natural sciences *and* the humanities. This approach requires a balanced appreciation of both the natural sciences and the humanities in the development of six modern social sciences. With these goals in mind, what can sociology, anthropology, political science, economics, psychology, and geography tell us about human behavior in the contemporary world?

SUPPLEMENTS

A carefully prepared supplement package is available to users of this text.

Instructor's Resource and Testing Manual

Prepared by the author, this comprehensive manual includes core objectives, thematic questions, synopsis, annotated documentary filmography, list of feature films discussed, and case studies for each chapter. Also included are multiple choice, true/false, and matching questions.

Prentice Hall Custom Test

This computerized version of the test questions allows instructors to construct tests, create alternative versions of the same test, edit existing questions, and add their own questions. Available for DOS, Windows, and Macintosh computers.

Internet Guides

Sociology on the Internet

Anthropology on the Internet

Political Science on the Internet

Psychology on the Internet

Each of these brief guides introduces students to the origin and innovations behind the Internet and provides clear strategies for navigating the complexity of the Internet and World Wide Web. Exercises within and at the end of the chapters allow students to practice searching for the myriad of resources available to the student. Your choice of one of these 96-page supplementary books is free to students when packaged with *Through the Global Lens*. See your local Prentice Hall sales representative for packaging details.

Study Guide

This carefully written guide helps students better understand the material presented in the text. Each chapter consists of a chapter summary, key terms with definitions, and practice tests keyed to the text.

Acknowledgments

Any human creation owes much to the catalysts who spawned it. And when it comes to writing, inspiration usually trumps perspiration. A top ten list of scholars whose ideas motivated my synthesis of the social sciences include Hayward Alker, Benjamin Barber, Carol and Melvin Ember, Stephen Gould, Garrett Hardin, Abraham Kaplan, Sam Keen, Sophia Peterson, Dennis Pirages, and John Rourke.

I would like to thank the following people for their thoughts and suggestions during the preparation of the text: Morita Bailey, Oakton Community College; Brian Barry, Rochester Institute of Technology; William E. Deibert, West Virginia Northern Community College; Thomas Everett, Middlebrook School; Tim Garner, Franklin College; Susan Herrick, West Liberty State College; Arthur J. Jipson, Miami University–Ohio; Kevin T. Leicht, University of Iowa; Kooros M. Mahmoudi, Northern Arizona University; Peter Makuck, East Carolina University; Michael Marshall, West Liberty State College; Pamela S. Meyer, Texas A&M University; Scott Meyer, Plymouth State College; and Nancy Horak Randall, Wingate University.

I'll chalk it up to good kharma that two gems—managing editor Sharon Chambliss and production editor Rob DeGeorge—shone brightly enough to bring this project to fruition. Research grants from the West Virginia Humanities Council and the West Liberty State College Foundation also helped a great deal. Logistical support from David Brooks, Peter Freeman, Ed Jacobs, David Javersak, Ann Levine, Peter Makuck, and Allan Ramsey is greatly appreciated. To Hesh Troper I am indebted for reminding me that not only is life intended to be fun, but so is writing about it. Finally, I nominate my wife, Linda, for academic sainthood. Only librarians can find obscure sources, edit verbose text, and keep the computer performing its magic.

THROUGH
THE GLOBAL LENS

CHAPTER **1**

A Global Window on the Social Sciences

Thematic Questions

- In what sense have global issues unrelated to the collapse of the Soviet Union or the end of the Cold War more subtly and gradually achieved status as crucial to the future of our species?

- Why do metaphors serve as useful illustrators of the shrinking effect of global interdependence?

- If competition and cooperation represent fundamentally different social processes in the repertoire of human behavior, in which of these directions do the new realities of interdependence seem to be pushing us?

- Sovereign independence of the nation-state may have dominated the ordering of human affairs for the last 350 years, but what kinds of forces threaten it today?

- Why is it particularly important today to enlist all six social sciences in the complex endeavor of studying human behavior?

CORE OBJECTIVE

To establish how the palpable reality of modern global interdependence affects the content and methods of the social sciences.

The crucial theme recently dominating world affairs is easy to identify: profound change. Some changes have occurred very rapidly. The collapse of communism in the former Soviet satellite countries of eastern Europe from June to December 1989 and the reunification of east and west Germany in 1990 represent incredibly speedy change. Other changes, however, like the end of legally sanctioned racial segregation in South Africa and the development of democratic institutions in Russia—while equally intriguing—have been slower in developing.

INTERDEPENDENCE

Alongside these highly publicized world events, more subtle, but equally important global transformations have been underway. Foremost among such quieter changes is the emergence of forms of global **interdependence** unimaginable a generation ago. In various economic, political, cultural, and social ways, the world has been shrinking; everyone's fate has become linked to that of others around the world. The popular recording artist Khaled crosses regional, racial, and religious boundaries and symbolizes globalism. In the mid-1990s, corporate giant IBM's main television advertisement depicted **indigenous people** as computer nerds to draw attention to its computers with this slogan: "IBM: solutions for a small planet."

Global Issues

Simultaneously, the emergence of a set of problematic **global issues**—particularly environment, population, food, energy, the nuclear dilemma, and human rights—has greatly changed the world. These two mutually reinforcing, long-term transfigurations (global interdependence and the agenda of vexing global issues) represent the essence of our examination here of the vibrant, complex modern world. Evidence of global interdependence is all around us.

The IBM corporation tweaks the web of global interdependence in this advertisement depicting rural Irish shepherds logging onto the Internet with a laptop computer.

International travel has sky-rocketed at airport terminals like this one in Frankfurt, Germany.

As tourism has become the world's largest industry, one million people cross borders every day, and you probably know someone who has recently traveled to another country, since United States residents make up 40 percent of international travelers and 56 million of us travelled abroad in 1997. Among them are 100,000 American college students annually destined for **study abroad** programs in all regions of the world. Even students who remain in the United States to study are influenced by the wave of internationalization of curricula that has swept over higher education during the last two decades.

Made in Hong Kong

Examine the labels on your clothing. Almost certainly, most of it was made in far-off places such as China, Brazil, or Malaysia. If you drink coffee, it likely comes from Latin America. The number of Americans working for foreign firms doubled between 1980 and 1997 to more than 5 million. While you may drive a car with an American name, much of it was probably assembled outside of the United States. The Honda Accord is made in the United States, but the Dodge Stealth is not. Incredibly, my Mazda 626 is officially classified as a United States domestic car while my friend's Ford Crown Victoria (a "tuna clipper" of a giant car) qualifies as a foreign vehicle. The American Automotive Labeling Act of 1994 defines an American car as one with 75 percent of its parts made in the United States.

Borderless Athletes

If you are a basketball fan, you probably know that Lithuania's Aruydas Sabonis, Croatia's Toni Kukoc and Vlade Divac, Germany's Detlef Schremp, and Nigeria's Hakeem Olajuwon rank among the top players in the NBA. United States college coaches now actively recruit European players by means of scholarships. The National Hockey League is filled not only

Los Angeles Dodgers star pitcher Hideo Nomo symbolizes the growing number of borderless athletes.

with Canadian hockey players, but with more than a hundred Europeans, almost half of whom hail from what Ronald Reagan once referred to as the "evil empire"—Russia. The influx of talented European players has brought parity to the NHL, leading to immediately competitive expansion teams such as the Florida Panthers and the Phoenix Coyotes. Even baseball, the quintessentially American sport, opened its 1995 All-Star game with Japanese pitcher Hideo Nomo on the mound for the National League. The Florida Marlins, 1997 World Series champions, included more Latin American Hispanic players than United States-born Caucasians. In *The Global Sports Arena: Athletic Talent Migration in an Interdependent World,* John Bale and Joseph Maguire explore the wide-ranging economic, social, and political consequences of highly paid international athletes on the move.[1]

A Cottage Industry in Metaphor Making

Common metaphors such as "the global village," "spaceship earth," or "our shrinking world" come alive most poignantly via the fruits of the global communications revolution. In 1980 fewer than 2 million computers existed in the world, and nearly all of them were mainframes. By 1995, 150 million computers had come into usage, more than nine-tenths of them personal computers.[2] Not only were there a lot more computers around, but companies like Andrew Grove's Intel were making them much faster and more powerful than before. All of this new computer hardware needed smart software programs to tell it what to do. Enter Bill Gates. By the mid-1990s, as the head of the prototypical software company named Microsoft, Gates had become the richest person in the world. His 1997 total worth? About $40 billion.

MINI-CASE 1.1
The Internet: Cyberspace Pros and Cons

The Internet was developed in the late 1960s at the initiative of the U.S. Department of Defense. Its intent was to enable scientists and engineers working on military contracts to share computers, resources, and ideas—the latter through "e-mail," a way of sending messages electronically. Designed to survive a nuclear war, information was transmitted in small "packages" through the different routes, making it difficult to eavesdrop on the data and messages sent.

The popularity of the Internet spread slowly throughout the academic world, which by the mid-1980s was its principal user. Two innovations then revolutionized the ease with which the Internet could be used, propelling its popularity beyond academe. One was the invention by Swiss software engineer Tim Berners-Lee of the World Wide Web and "hypertext" to link documents with one another. The other was a software program known as Mosaic (written primarily by Marc Andreesen, an undergraduate student at the University of Illinois), which provides user-friendly access to the "Web" and the "Net."

In 1994 commercial companies surpassed universities as the leading users of the Internet. Today it is the functional equivalent of the "information superhighway" telecommunications specialists have long anticipated and promised.

As the use of the Internet has grown—fueled by the growth of personal computers in homes and businesses—concerns about its uses and abuses surfaced, and questions about whether and how governments might exert control over the "Net" inevitably have followed. Here are contrasting viewpoints about the culture and concerns cyberspace poses.

The Ethos of Independence and Individuality

The [Internet] classic user takes a libertarian stance, is suspicious of government, disdainful of politicians, and actively hostile towards those who would screw up his paradise with indiscriminate advertising, stupid questions and "newbie" (naive newcomer) behavior....

Fundamental to the Internet credo are the protection of free speech and the right of every group to be heard... Enthusiasts see the Internet as a sort of digital Utopia, not because everything on it is admirable, but because it is there at all. The Internet defies centralized authority; its mantra is "do your own thing."

—The Economist 336 (July 1, 1995): 14

The Internet Elite

Theoretically, anyone can post information, but the reality is that the main content of the Internet.... is controlled by governments, corporations, and academic institutions.... The ease with which it is possible to alter information—or merely to shade the truth by selectively culling out unfavorable information—is a real concern.... Who will be the custodians of the world's information?

Although the Internet supposedly is available to anyone with a modem and the will to use it, the profile of users is skewed by race, gender, income and age.... Access may be unlimited in theory, but it is restricted by the cost of technology and the steep learning curve for computer neophytes.... If electronic communication is the future, what will become of the vast majority of people who can only stand by and watch the worldwide exchange of electrons?

...There are disturbing social implications of a future in which human communication increasingly takes place through electronic media.... Work will be done at home and transmitted by modem; shopping will be done over the World Wide Web and paid for by debits to our electronic bank accounts. Even entertainment will take place through the computer screen.

...No one is examining the question of whether a world split between an elite minority of information-empowered people interacting electronically and a majority mired in information poverty is in anyone's best interests. Do we really want to choose between a "successful" but soulless electronic existence and disenfranchisement?

—H.W., "The Internet Elite," Bulletin of the Atomic Scientists
51 (July/August 1995): 44-45

Source: Charles Kegley and Eugene W.H. Kopf, *World Politics: Trends and transformation* (St. Martin's , 1977), p.252

For ordinary consumers, never has it been as easy, or as inexpensive, to pick up a telephone and call someone in Asia, Africa, or Europe. Furthermore, electronic mail allows hundreds of millions of users to communicate instantaneously, regardless of location. In 1995 an amazing 6 billion e-mail messages were sent over the Internet. (If you want to make it six billion and one, then send me your impressions of this book: stradamj@wlsvax.wvnet.edu.) CNN International, brainchild of communications mogul Ted Turner (also owner of the Atlanta Braves baseball dynasty), is available via satellite transmission and keeps the world abreast of current events. Almost incidental, wondrous fax machines also permit us to transmit print communications anywhere that phone lines exist.

Global interdependence, however, consists of much more than the technological wizardry of the information age. Our pocketbook may be our most vulnerable body part in alerting us to this insight. When the next Middle Eastern dictator seizes someone else's oil supply, watch the price of a gallon of gas increase almost immediately. It may surprise you that four of five new manufacturing jobs in America result from trade, and that fully one-third of all United States farmland produces goods for the export market. Any thought today of **isolationism** as a viable policy for the United States may be a quaint throwback to earlier and simpler days, but it fails to make very solid contact with reality.

Competition or Cooperation

Some optimists see this web of interdependence as aiding humanity's efforts to resolve the **ecological global issues** (environment, population, food, and energy) confronting us. For most of recorded human history we have relied on competition and a growth model to solve difficult problems. National competition, however, has led to frequent conflicts. During most of recorded history humans have been fighting wars, resulting in 3.5 billion deaths—111 million in this past century alone.[3] These numbers suggest that humorist Ambrose Bierce's sardonic statement that peace is a period of cheating between two periods of fighting is not too far off the mark.[4]

In the last three and a half centuries the **nation–state** system has enshrined national **sovereignty** and competition as its central features. Pessimists point out that in recent decades sovereign competition has proven unsuccessful in dealing with global issues. These problems are serious not only because they affect everyone, but also because they belie humanity's growing tendency to bump its head against the global ceiling.

Never before have humans needed to think about limits to growth and expansion. Never before have humans had to consider shifting to more cooperative behaviors. But, then, never have such perplexing global issues defiantly stared humanity in the face. Since global cooperation is something our species has not been very good at, no one can guarantee that problems such as ozone depletion, deforestation, global warming, overpopulation, and nuclear proliferation will provide a sufficient slap in the face for humanity to come to its collective senses. Interdependence, however, may enhance our ability to find heretofore elusive solutions to global issues.

This interdisciplinary text borrows concepts, data, and analytical tools from all of the social sciences, introducing you in the process to the world beyond the United States from a global perspective. Sociology, anthropology, political science, psychology, economics and geography all have derived largely from two earlier bodies of knowledge: the natural sciences and the humanities. The substantive and methodological debts that the social sciences owe to the natural sciences and humanities are taken up in Chapter 3, an **epistemological** chapter covering the history and philosophy leading to the modern social science six.

THE SOCIAL SCIENCE SIX

Sociology gives us ways to comprehend human behavior in a group context. *Anthropology* uses cross-cultural analysis, often involving remote societies, for insights into humanity's journey up the developmental ladder. *Political science*, concerned with power and authority, asks how societies determine "who gets what, when and how?" *Psychology* offers insights into human subjective (inner) experience, trying to unravel what leads individuals to behave as they do. *Economics* examines the production, distribution, and consumption of goods and services in domestic and international contexts. *Geography* provides a systematic spatial perspective on humanity's relationship to the physical environment. While these disciplines have separate academic identities, they also share a common subject: human behavior.

A World Stage Analogy

Each social science makes unique contributions to understanding of the human drama played out on the world stage. Sociology's interest in society translates onto the world stage as the players, or actors, whose organized interaction provides the action of the drama. The *content* of social life—its lifestyle or culture—falls mostly within the domain of anthropology and is comparable in a stage play to the script followed by the actors.

Political science looks at human relationships in regard to power and authority. This interest converts to the stage as the behavior of the directors and producers, who exercise authority by making tough decisions. Many performers have acting coaches who try to coax, cajole, or inspire the best performances from their actors. This coaching effort involves a keen appreciation of the subjective inner life of the individual actor. The acting coach seems in many ways similar to the psychologist in modern society.

It not only takes human resources to bring a stage play to life; it also requires material resources, especially the financing needed to rent the theater, pay the actors, and advertise the finished product. The collection and distribution of these material resources is what economists spend their time studying. Material resources also come into play as part of the physical backdrop to the drama. The success or failure of a stage play can be greatly affected by the setting in which it is presented. Are the critics in the audience comfortable? Is the room temperature pleasant? Does the theater have good acoustics? Is the stage large enough to hold the action of the play? These physical and spatial issues are comparable to those addressed by geographers examining the relationship between human behavior on the world stage and the physical realities of planet earth.

The contemporary global drama is fast paced and exciting. However, its complexity also can be confusing. Both individually and in concert, the six social sciences provide us with **theories, concepts,** and **data** with which to judge and evaluate the human drama playing itself out on the world stage. With these bodies of knowledge at our disposal, a vast panorama of additional information and technique spreads out before us. Without such tools, we are fenced in by common sense and our very limited personal experience. For example, if you have a ninety-year-old grandfather who has smoked two packs of cigarettes for sixty years, you might be tempted to conclude that you can likely do the same thing. But an impressive body of scientific research suggests otherwise. The statistical probability of your engaging in heavy smoking and surviving to age ninety is small.

As Harvard professor Stephen Jay Gould argues in a recent book, our unchallenged assumptions based on common sense can seriously distort our understanding of reality. In addition to being a respected scientist, Professor Gould is a passionate baseball fan; he freely uses baseball illustrations, like the one in Mini-case 1.2, to make a point.

MINI-CASE 1.2
Where Have all the .400 Hitters Gone?

Between 1901 and 1930 a total of seven major league baseball players managed to record batting averages of .400 or better. Ty Cobb and Rogers Hornsby each did so three times. These impressive feats, however, have not been duplicated since 1941. The only close calls occurred in 1980 and 1977 when George Brett and Rod Carew hit .390 and .388 respectively.

For more than half a century, pundits have tried to explain the disappearance of .400 hitters. The consensus has been that the phenomenon of hitting among major league ballplayers has experienced a general deterioration, resulting in the specific manifestation of no batters hitting over .400 for a season. The Boston Red Sox's splendid splinter, Ted Williams, who stroked base hits at a .406 clip in 1941, shares this view. He stated in a 1992 interview that "I don't think today there as many smart hitters,"[5] a thesis he expands on in his book, which he had the temerity to call, *The Science of Hitting:*

> After fifty years of watching it I'm more convinced than ever that there aren't as many good hitters in the game.... There are plenty of guys with power, guys who hit the ball a long way, but I see so many who lack finesse, who should hit for average and don't. The answers are not all that hard to figure. They talked for years about the ball being dead. The ball isn't dead, the hitters are, from the neck up.[6]

This commonsensical consensus seems plausible enough on the surface, especially when touted by the last great .400 hitter—that is, until someone like paleontologist Stephen Jay Gould subjects the numbers to exhaustive statistical scrutiny. What Gould reports is that, over a century of major league play, mean batting averages for all hitters have remained amazingly constant at about .260 per season. While short-term dips and spikes have occurred, the norm continually heads back toward a base of .260 per season.

Success at hitting, then, has not gotten worse, but has remained constant. What has occurred is a shrinking variation from the arithmetic mean: fewer very high averages as well as fewer very low averages. The reasons for this shift could not be gleaned without statistical analysis and scientific techniques of inquiry. Paradoxically, hitting and pitching have *both* steadily improved over the years, essentially balancing each other out. The seemingly unassailable commonsensical assumption that an historical trend exists toward worse hitting is actually false, as Figure 1.1 suggests.

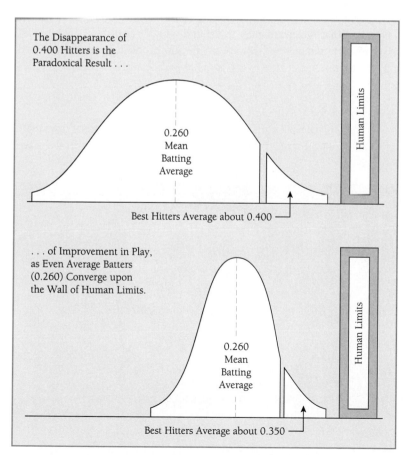

Figure 1.1

Four hundred hitting disappears as play improves and the entire bell curve moves closer to the right wall of human limits while varition declines. Upper chart: early twentienth-century baseball. Lower chart: current baseball.

Source: Stephen Jay Gould, *Full House* (Crown Publishers, 1996), p.119.

Baseball makes a wonderful laboratory for testing propositions scientifically. First, it is awash in statistics. Slower paced than other major sports, baseball allows its fans to talk about baseball during the many lulls in the action. What those fans often chat about is baseball history and baseball statistics. Trivia buffs seem to gravitate toward baseball's cornucopia of numbers.

Second, although baseball is a team sport, its moments of drama come from individual confrontations between two players—most notably pitcher versus batter. These distinct events provide endless statistical profiles for every player to an extent alien to other major sports.

Third, the actual game of baseball has changed remarkably little over its century of existence. The ingenius physical dimensions of its diamond remain a thing of beauty. Its pristine rules have remained relatively sacrosanct. Basketball needed to add a shot clock to prevent stalling tactics and the three-point shot to give shorter players a chance against the thunder-dunks of seven-footers who now play for every team. More problematic for basketball is that the skill level, especially as measured by vertical leap, has so exceeded the ten-foot basket that almost every pro player now operates above the rim.

Football began changing rules often, with the advent of the forward pass sixty years ago, and hasn't stopped since. Soccer-style kickers have forced a redefinition of the field goal almost yearly. Rules against spearing, clotheslining, clipping, hitting a vulnerable quarterback in the grasp of a player, and unnecessary roughness have all been added in response to the sharp rise in serious injuries to high-priced players. What has historically transpired on a baseball field, by contrast, has changed little. Baseball could ultimately be doomed by the shortsighted greed of its owners and/or players, but not by the time-tested nature of the game played between the white lines.

CHALLENGE TO AMERICA

And what special role does the United States play in this effort by social scientists to explain human behavior on the world stage. Americans face new and different challenges in the post-

How the Earth looks from space.

Cold War era. The intellectual resources of all the great bodies of knowledge—natural sciences, humanities, social sciences—become increasingly crucial to success in this new era. Whether the United States meets the challenges provided by the age of complex interdependence depends greatly on its citizens and their understanding of new opportunities. To comprehend global realities, Americans need flexibility to see the world through more complex lenses. We also must engage in anticipatory thinking, not reactive thinking, for problem solving. The very first step in this direction is recognizing the **paradigm** of globalism: earth as a web of fragile interacting parts, as elegantly depicted by NASA's satellite photos of "spaceship earth."

Chapter Synopsis

Profound change, in the form of the collapse of the Soviet empire and the end of the Cold War, came about in very speedy fashion. Other, subtler forces have evolved more slowly but also contribute mightily to global interdependence. Among these are six major global issues: four fall under the rubric of ecological issues (environment, population, food, and energy), one deals with security (the nuclear dilemma), and one focuses on the relatively new idea that all people automatically ought to enjoy certain freedoms which their governments cannot trample (human rights).

The image of a borderless world has gone from fantasy to reality in recent decades. Scratch the surface of the clothes you wear, the car you drive, or the sports and entertainment heroes you admire, and you will discover the stuff of global interdependence. The communications revolution has produced e-mail, fax messages, and satellite television transmissions that link the all the world's continents in ways unimaginable a generation ago. These new ways of communication treat borders as obsolete by forging linkages based on shared interest and information, not physical proximity. They also facilitate cooperative human endeavors at variance with the competitive mind-set of the traditional nation-state.

Collectively, the social sciences represent one of the three great bodies of knowledge (along with the natural sciences and the humanities). They provide us with both methods and substance in our efforts to comprehend the varied nuances of human behavior. While sociology looks at human behavior in a groups context, anthropology relies on cross-cultural analysis often related to remote cultures, and psychology quests after insights into subjective human questions such as motivation. Political science looks to issues of power and authority in assessing how societies order their public affairs; economics examines the production, distribution, and consumption of goods and services; and geography provides a systematic spatial perspective on how societies relate to the physical world. All these disciplines want to unravel the enigmas of human behavior. By conceiving of the complex human drama as unfolding on a world stage, we have a recurrent motif broad enough and clear enough to integrate the efforts of all social scientists—sociologists, anthropologists, psychologists, political scientists, economists, geographers—as they bring data, concepts, and theories to their tasks.

For Digging Deeper

Bale, John, and Joseph Maguire. *The Global Sports Arena: Athletic Talent Migration in an Interdependent World.* Frank Cass, 1994.

Brown, Lester R., et al. *State of the World 1996.* W. W. Norton, 1996.

Cvetkovich, Ann, and Douglas Kellner. *Articulating the Global and the Local: Globalization and Cultural Studies.* Westview, 1996.

Gould, Stephen J. *Full House: The Spread of Excellence from Plato to Darwin* Harmony Books, 1996.

Hamilton, John M. *Entangling Alliances: How the Third World Shapes Our Lives.* Seven Locks Press, 1992.

Mittelman, James H. *Globalization: Critical Reflections.* Lynne Reinner, 1997.

Pirages, Dennis C. *Global Technopolitics.* Brooks/Cole, 1989.

Rockwell, Richard C. *"The Case of the Sociologist Who Untangled Himself from the Web."* ASA Footnotes, March 1997, pp. 5-6.

Stares, Paul B. *Global Habit: The Drug Problem in a Borderless World.* Congressional Quarterly, 1996.

World Development Report 1996. Oxford University Press, 1996.

Internet

International News Sources

CNN   *http://www.cnn.com/*

The New York Times   *http://www.nytimes.com/*

The Washington Post   *http://www.washingtonpost.com*

World Education News and Reviews   *WENR@wes.org*

World News Connection   *http://wnc.fedworld.gov*

Search Engines

Alta Vista   *http://www.altavista.digital.com*

Council of European Social Science Data Archives   *http://www.nsd.uib.no/cessda*

Info Seek   *http://www.infoseek.com/home/internetsearch.html*

My Virtual Reference Desk   *http://www.refdesk.com/*

New American Global Dialogue   *http://globetrotter.berkeley.edu:808*

Research Engines for the Social Sciences   *http://www.carleton.ca/~cmckie/research.html*

Social Sciences Information Gateway *http://sosig.esrc.bris.ac.uk/*

World Game Institute Global Data Manager   *http://www.worldgame.org/~wgi*

Yahoo   *http://www.yahoo.com*

Key Glossary Terms

concepts
data
ecological global issues
epistemology
global issues

indigenous people
interdependence
isolationism
nation-state

paradigm
sovereignty
study abroad
theories

CHAPTER **2**

Patterns of Social Identity

Thematic Questions

- To what extent is spatial analysis necessary for identifying world regions?

- In what ways can nation–states be said to be unique?

- Why is the emergence of three trade-driven super-regions a decidedly modern and contemporary phenomenon?

- Is dividing the world into North versus South too broad a dichotomy to be useful for analysis by social scientists?

- What factors contributed to the potency of the West (capitalist) versus East (communist) schism during the Cold War era?

- Is the delineation of First, Second, Third, and Fourth Worlds somehow unfair and prejudicial?

- Is the concept of a civilization too vague and broad for meaningful application in today's world?

- Can modern humans realistically be expected to identify with one another as a single global community?

CORE OBJECTIVE

To conceptualize the human family according to the main patterns of social identity competing for popular loyalty during the twentieth century.

Given the human family's size and complexity, it is helpful to conceive of the world's people as divided into groupings of shared identity. Social scientists are accustomed to applying at least eight such conceptions of identity: regions, nation–states, three economic super-regions, north/south (rich/poor) hemispheres, rival types of economic systems, worlds of development, civilizations, and one global community.

WORLD REGIONS

Identification of world regions is based on a **spatial** synthesis of physical, political, social, and historical factors. No consensus exists among geographers on how to divide the world into major regions, but many of them identify eight main areas: Europe, the former Soviet Union, the Middle East, Asia, the Pacific Rim, Sub-Saharan Africa, Latin America, and Anglo-America.

Europe

The 1989 collapse of communism in the eight Eastern European countries rendered the distinction between Western and Eastern Europe anomalous. Europe consists of 0.5 billion people in thirty-eight countries. They look increasingly similar politically, economically, and culturally as the ex-communist nations emulate the Western model.

Varied economic and security organizations—such as the **European Union (EU)**, the **North Atlantic Treaty Organization (NATO)** and the **Conference on Security and Cooperation in Europe (CSCE)**—constitute the world's most advanced regional cooperation. Since Europe was the site of many bloody wars over the last five centuries, an underlying objective of the European Union was to reduce the likelihood of war there. Today war between EU members seems inconceivable, because of economic, political, and social interdependence among its affluent members.

The 1990 reunification of Germany created a country of 81 million people boasting the world's third largest economy. German unification frightened some Europeans, who remember the devastating Second World War, unleashed by Adolf Hitler's Third Reich. But if regional integration serves as an antidote to aggressive behavior, staunch German support for rapid EU consolidation provides reason for optimism concerning a peaceful German role in Europe.[1]

Europe no longer enjoys the dominant position in world affairs that it held in previous centuries. Nevertheless, Europeans continue to marshal the human resources required to compete successfully in the modern world. Western European countries make up fourteen of the top twenty nations in the world on the **Human Development Index (HDI)**, which measures overall quality of life. Wealth in this peaceful and influential part of the world runs about triple the world average, while life expectancy averages an impressive seventy-five years of age.

In a continent that is smaller in size than the United States but more densely populated, three of four Europeans live in urban areas. Most European countries educate their people well, preparing them for the postindustrial age of computer-generated information. Protestantism, Catholicism, and Judaism are the region's principal religions.

Figure 2.1

Former Soviet Union

Prior to fracturing in December 1991, the Soviet Union encompassed one-sixth of the earth's landmass. A global nuclear superpower, it had a population of 285 million, ranking third after China and India. It was the only country to take up an entire world region.

Its fifteen Union Republics have broken apart into independent countries, with Russia as the largest and most important successor state to the Soviet Union. A Eurasian nation en-

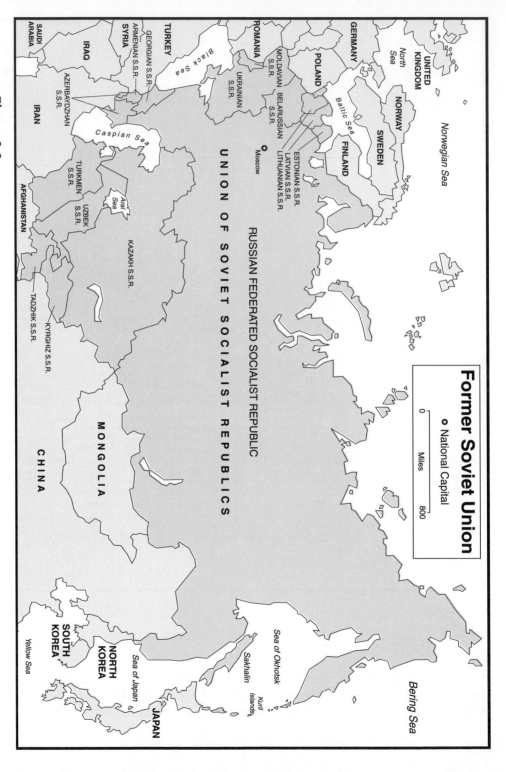

Figure 2.2

compassing both European and Oriental characteristics, Russia has trailed its Eastern European counterparts in slowly shedding its communist heritage and moving toward **democracy** and **capitalism**. It continues dangling in an uncertain limbo between seventy-four years of communism and an uncertain future.

Russia's 150 million people overshadow their ethnic **(Slavic)** brothers in neighboring Ukraine (52 million) and Belarus, formerly Byelorussia, (10 million). The average Russian income is only about 10 percent of that in the United States, and Russia's HDI (quality of life) index ranks fifty-second out of 174 countries worldwide.

Besides Slavs, three other main groups comprise successors to the Soviet Union. The small Baltic nations of Estonia, Latvia, and Lithuania (1.5, 2.5, and 3.5 million population, respectively) have many traditional ties to Europe and were forcibly annexed by Soviet dictator Joseph Stalin in 1940. These Baltic republics were the first Soviet republics to achieve independence, in 1991.

The three countries south of the Caucasus mountains—Armenia, Georgia, and Azerbaijan—have experienced the worst ethnic and religious violence in the former Soviet Union. Georgia, a small country of 5 million people, has been embroiled in civil war as ethnic minorities such as the Abkhazians and South Ossetians have sought independence. Christian Armenia (4 million) and Islamic Azerbaijan (8 million) have conducted an extended war over a disputed piece of territory within Azerbaijan called Nagorno-Karabakh (inhabited 85 percent by ethnic Armenians).

The final sector of the former Soviet Union (FSU), Central Asia, consists of five Islamic countries inhabited by 50 million Muslims with much closer ties to Turkic and Asiatic nations than to the Russians who dominated them for a century and a half. The largest of these, Uzbekistan, has 23 million people.

Each group of nations from the FSU harbors resentment against previous Russian and Soviet domination by Moscow. When the Soviet Union fell apart in 1991, these nations experienced emotional ethnic renaissances, seeking to sever all links with Russia. But these new nations have yet to prove their economic or military viability. Like a recoiling rubber band, their emotional rush to independence shows signs of abating, exposing underlying economic ties to the Russians.

Middle East

The Middle East region, a desert and semiarid grassland at the confluence of northern Africa, southwestern Asia, and southern Europe, runs from Morocco in the west to Pakistan and Kashmir in the east. Human settlements in this part of the globe cluster around scarce fresh water sources. Most countries' economies rely on primary products extracted from the earth, generally a formula for poverty.

The glaring exception? Oil: the earth's most lucrative **primary product**. King oil divides the region's nations into those fortunates who have it and those unfortunates who don't. Huge disparities separate rich countries like the United Arab Emirates (GNP per capita $20,000) or Qatar (GNP per capita $16,000) from poor neighbors such as Syria (GNP per capita $990) or Yemen (GNP per capita $550). The majority of the region falls below the world average on the HDI measuring quality of life, with only Bahrain and the United Arab Emirates scoring in the world's top forty-five HDI rankings.

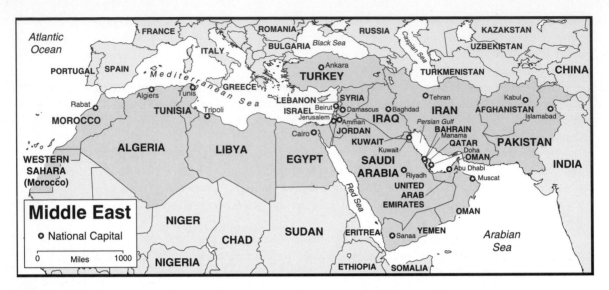

Figure 2.3

Although oil politics tends to split the region, the dominant Islamic religion provides a unifying foundation. Real differences exist between **Sunni** and **Shiite Muslims**, and between liberal and conservative Muslims, but Islam nevertheless constitutes a crucial binding force in the area. About 175 million inhabitants of the Middle East also share an ethnic identity as Arabs. It has been a millennium since the glory days of undisputed Arab unity, but **ethnicity** remains another important regional unifier. Notable minorities in the region are the Jewish state of Israel and the Persian Shiite Muslims prevalent in Iran.

The borders separating many Middle Eastern countries, arbitrarily drawn by European powers during the days of **colonialism**, remain in dispute today. For example, when Saddam Hussein's Iraq invaded Kuwait in 1990, Saddam complained that the British colonists' borders, drawn in 1921, had cut Iraq off from the Persian Gulf; he intended to rectify the situation.

Long considered the world's most volatile region, the Middle East has experienced recent hope for peace, owing to agreements between Israel and Arab neighbors such as the Palestinian Liberation Organization (PLO), Jordan, and Syria. Nevertheless, the democratization that has spread across other regions in recent decades has not found its way to the Middle East. Israel continues to be the region's only viable democracy.

Asia

Many observers predict that the twenty-first century will be the Pacific century. Why so many upbeat prognoses for the health of Asia? A virtual economic explosion has been underway, particularly in east Asia. Japan's GNP per capita ($27,000) ranks among the world's highest, and in recent years Japan has ranked among the top three countries in the HDI quality of life ratings.

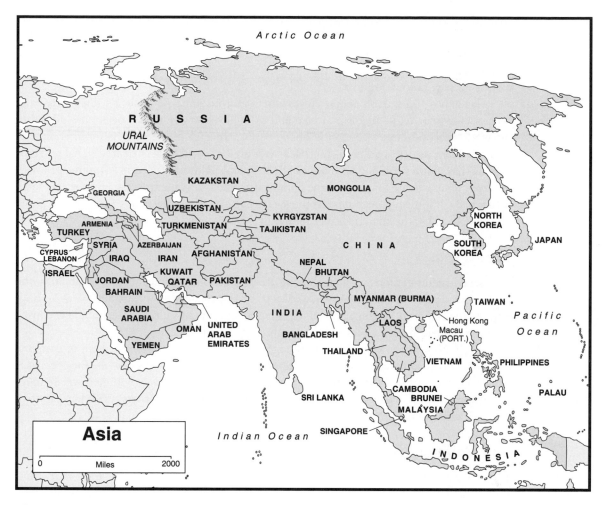

Figure 2.4

Only a decade or two ago scholars considered Japan's "economic miracle" an aberration not replicable elsewhere in Asia. But the recent success of the **newly industrialized countries (NICs)**—Taiwan, South Korea, Singapore, Malaysia, and Hong Kong—has generated a new optimism. Following Japan's example of an export-driven, **managed economy**, the NICs have demonstrated impressive growth in recent years. All these NICs rank among the top one-third of nations on the HDI index and have life expectancies averaging over seventy years. In 1996, 125 of the world's 450 billionaires came from Asia, as did 25 percent of global economic output, compared with only 17 percent fifteen years earlier.[2]

Equally impressive, China's liberalized **command economy** has produced double digit growth rates—the highest in the world. The Asian region stands out among former colonies for finding ways to grow its economies substantially, making it the envy of the other once-colonized regions: the Middle East, Latin America, and Africa. Asia warrants special attention for another reason: one-half of humanity resides in this region. Fully one-fifth of the world's people (or 1.2 billion) live in China, although India's 925 million are reproducing more rapidly, a growth leading to predictions that by the year 2020 India will replace China as the world's most populous country.

Japan has 125 million people crowded into four resource-poor islands smaller than the state of Montana. Yet its highly educated and culturally **homogeneous** society has produced the world's second-largest economy. Japan's performance in the second half of this century would warrant its designation as comeback actor on the world stage. The traditional religions in Japan have for a very long time been Buddhism and Shintoism. Japan's economic prowess, however, tempts some to joke that the dominant religion in contemporary Japan seems to be hard work! Hinduism constitutes the prevalent religion in heterogeneous India, while China remains officially atheistic under its communist government.

Pacific Rim

As isolated island–nations with small populations, economies, and military capabilities, the Pacific Rim represents the most overlooked region. The area includes Australia, New Zealand, Fiji, Micronesia, and Western Somoa. Geography, more than culture or economics, constitutes the cement for the diverse world region of the Pacific Rim.

Only 28 million people live in the region. In general, these nations tend to combine traditional, pre-industrial cultures of indigenous peoples with the ways of white European settlers. Australia dwarfs the other nations in most comparisons, with its 3 million square miles of territory, 19 million inhabitants, life expectancy of seventy-six years, GNP per capita of $18,000, and ranking of eleventh in the world in quality of life.

Sub-Saharan Africa

The largest of the world's geographic regions, Sub-Saharan Africa, contains forty-four countries. African countries south of the Sahara Desert, former European colonies all, have gained political independence since the 1960s. Most have barely begun the process of nation building, largely because their boundaries—drawn by European colonial powers—bear little resemblance to traditional patterns of African tribal identity.

Many hundreds of languages are spoken. The world's very poorest people exist in countries such as Ethiopia ($120 GNP per capita), Tanzania ($120 GNP per capita), and Mozambique ($80 GNP per capita), leading some pessimists to call this region the **Fourth World**, or never-to-be-developed area. The region's mean GNP per capita is a meager $520, accompanied by a life expectancy of fifty-two years. Nine of the ten lowest countries on the HDI index are Sub-Saharan.

Guarded optimism has sprung up recently in the southern cone of the continent—in the Republic of South Africa—previously condemned by the international community as a bastion of racial segregation. A peaceful transfer of power from F. W. de Klerk's white National Party to Nelson Mandela's African National Congress occurred in 1994, representing a positive development in the broader picture of the African continent.

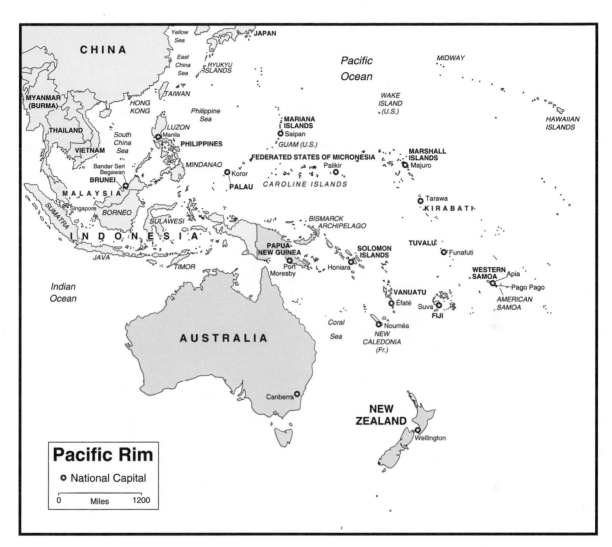

Figure 2.5

Latin America

The region of Latin America includes both Central American countries such as Guatemala, Panama and, Nicaragua as well as South American states such as Brazil, Colombia, and Argentina. The South American continent is much larger and its population is double that of Central America. Per capita GNP and average life expectancy are very similar in both areas.

Since European colonization wiped out more indigenous populations in Latin America than in Africa, the Middle East, or Asia, the influence of the Iberian (Spanish and Portuguese)

Figure 2.6

cultures remains crucial to an understanding of Latin American countries, especially South America. Overwhelmingly Roman Catholic in religion, with the Spanish language dominant in most countries other than Portuguese Brazil, Latin America possesses a regional glue similar to that discussed for the Middle East. Yet, again like the Middle East, real divisions of import exist just below the surface.

Latin America

National Capital

0 — Miles — 1,000

Figure 2.7

Figure 2.8

Brazil stands out as the region's giant, with 3.3 million square miles of territory and a population of 160 million. Its GNP per capita of $2,700, life expectancy of sixty-five years, and HDI ranking of sixty-third in the world place it in straits comparable to Thailand, Turkey, or Colombia. In 1992 Rio de Janeiro was selected to host the United Nations **Earth Summit**, because of global concern over the fate of Brazil's Amazon Basin, where half of the world's rain forests are under serious pressure by land developers and cut-and-burn subsistence farmers.

The region's climate, tropical and subtropical, contributes to the emphasis of many economies on primary product extraction: natural resources such as oil, copper, tin, and silver as well as agricultural products such as coffee, bananas, and sugar. Beginning in the 1970s, a wave of **democratization** swept elected leaders into power in the region, leaving only communist Cuba as the glaring contemporary exception.

Anglo-America

The last region, Anglo-America, consists of the United States and Canada. With passage of the 1994 **North American Free Trade Agreement (NAFTA)**, Mexico's classification gets complicated. Mexico's historical, cultural, economic, and political identity has been with Latin America. It is uncertain whether NAFTA ties with the United States and Canada will offset Mexico's traditional southern orientation.

Canada and the United States, already the world's largest trading partners, both enjoy moderate northern latitudes, rich arable lands, abundant natural resources, and sophisticated human resources. The U.S. population of 260 million towers over Canada's 30 million. The average of their economies ranks among the world's most productive, with GNP per capita around $22,000, life expectancies averaging at seventy-six years, and both HDI rankings among the top three in the world.

NEARLY 200 NATION–STATES

The world political map provides the most powerful image of how the world is divided up. The nearly 200 existing **nation–states** delineate how humanity orders its public affairs, and these countries continue to command strong loyalty from the majority of their citizens.

When a large group of people identifying with one another (**nation**) combines with an entity recognized by its peers as their legitimate representative (**state**), they form the modern nation–state (**country**). Far too many popular national identities exist for all to have their own nation-state, or country. Among extant nations unable to achieve their dream, we think of peoples like the Kurds and the Palestinians in the Middle East, the Chechens and the Tatars in Russia, or the Tibetans in China.

In 1648 the **Peace of Westphalia** ended the European struggle between religious and secular authority known as the **Thirty Years War**. The modern nation–state system evolved from this affirmation of secular national autonomy three and a half centuries ago.

One of the most cherished attributes of the nation–state to develop under traditional international law—sovereignty—gave theoretical independence to each nation–state, freeing it to conduct internal affairs without outside interference. Since World War II, however, traditional international law, challenged by new legal assertions of individual **human rights**, has acceded to limits on the sovereign authority of nation–states in dealing with their citizens.

The world community has delved into internal matters recently in places such as Somalia, Haiti, South Africa, and Bosnia when human rights or peace has been threatened by domestic events. While the sovereign independence of nation–states today is much more limited than in the past, the nation–state remains the foremost means of human political organization.

The number of nation–states has increased dramatically in the twentieth century, particularly since the end of World War II. **Decolonization**—European powers giving up control of colonial possessions in Asia, Africa, Latin America, and the Middle East—contributed most to this increase. For example, when Great Britain ended its colonial administration of India in 1947, not only did the "new" sovereign state of India emerge; civil war between Hindu and Muslim religious forces led to the separation of India from what became Pakistan and, later, Bangladesh. When the United Nations was founded in 1945, it had fifty-one members. Today it includes more than 185 and continues to grow.

As nation–states proliferate, so does their diversity. There are huge countries such as Canada, Russia, and Brazil, as well as tiny ones like San Marino, Monaco, and Seychelles. Populous countries like China, India, and Indonesia balance off sparse ones such as Dominica,

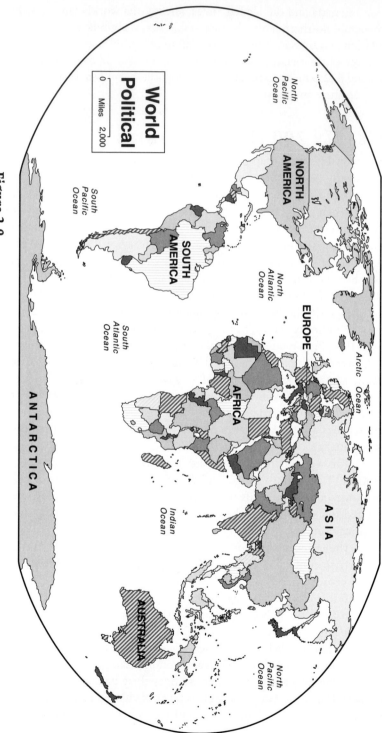

Figure 2.9

Saint Lucia, Micronesia, and Andorra. The United States, Russia, and France possess nuclear weapons, whereas Costa Rica has no standing army whatever. Iran is a Shiite Muslim theocracy, China is officially atheistic, and the United States encourages religious freedom while prohibiting any official state religion, while Russia gropes to find a model of church–state relations fitting its postcommunist era.

Which nation–states have social scientists studied most carefully? The powerful states that are able to get what they want in a world of scarcity. There is no easy way to measure a country's power; the **power** of nation–states exists relative to other countries. But factors such as size, human resources, natural resources, industrial capacity, military prowess, and economic strength certainly contribute to national power.

During the Cold War—from World War II until the collapse of the Soviet Union—nuclear weapons were the key element of power, with the United States and Soviet Union considered superpowers. Recently economic prowess in the trade-oriented world of interdependence has elevated Japan and Germany to the forefront as America's new competitors for world leadership.

THREE TRADE-DRIVEN SUPER-REGIONS

The last quarter-century has seen the volume of international trade increase by 1,000 percent to $5 trillion per year. First Japan, and then the newly industrialized countries (NICs) of east Asia, stunned the world with impressive economic growth based on **neomercantilist** practices fostering trade in an increasingly open global economy.[3]

In Europe, modest regional cooperation began in 1951 with the **European Coal and Steel Community (ECSC)** and gained momentum in 1957 with the construction of the **European Community (EC)**. Gradually moving beyond a free-trade zone into economic union, with plans for further political integration under the 1992 Maastricht Treaty, European integration represents the prototype of an incipient triad of super-regional blocs: Japanese-led cooperation in east Asia, German-led cooperation in Europe, and U.S.-led cooperation in North America.

Americans now consider competitive regional blocs in Europe and in Asia as inevitable. They also see these blocs as threatening America's position as a global economic superpower. This **perception** contributed to a sense of urgency in United States efforts to construct a comparable trading bloc in North America (NAFTA).

Creation of the **European Union (EU:** successor to EC) required four decades of incremental trust-building. The United States hopes to accomplish similar regional cooperation—but more rapidly. In 1989 the United States and Canada signed a bilateral trade agreement. This arrangement was expanded in 1992 with the NAFTA agreement signed by the United States, Canada, and Mexico. In 1994 President Bill Clinton announced that Chile would be the first country admitted into an expanded NAFTA which might eventually encompass the entire hemisphere.

Our rapidly changing world requires the successful competitor to think ahead. The psychology of the trilateral economic competition (U.S.-led North America, Japan-led Asia, German-led Europe) allows no side to idly watch the others embark on a new path of development which, in the future, could leave it odd actor out. In this regard, the United States is currently concerned over exclusion from a global economy dominated by powerful regional free-trade zones. The psychological dynamics in this situation resemble those that drove the spiraling arms race to massive levels during the U.S.–Soviet Cold War.

Figure 2.10

GNP per Capita, Atlas Method, for Low-, Medium-, and High-Income Countries, 1982—1992, in Current Dollars.

Source: Joan Spero and Jeffrey Hart, *The Politics of International Economic Relations* (St. Martins, 1997), p.150.

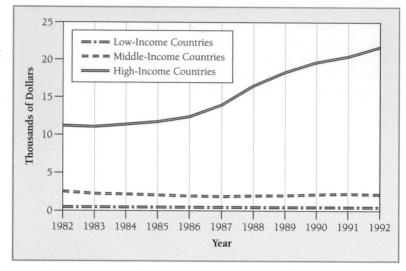

NORTHERN HEMISPHERE VERSUS SOUTHERN HEMISPHERE

The primacy of economic concerns in the post-Cold War emphasizes the dichotomy between the more developed countries (MDCs) and the less developed countries (LDCs). The MDCs, located mostly in the northern hemisphere, enjoy an average GNP per capita of $17,900 and a life expectancy of seventy-four years. The vast majority of roughly 130 southern hemisphere LDCs have a GNP per capita of only $810 and an average life expectancy of sixty-three years.

Only 1.2 billion people live in MDCs, and the annual population increase there is a modest one-half of one percent, while 4.4 billion crowd into the LDCs, which have a 2 percent rate of growth. Making matters worse, the gap between MDCs and LDCs continues to widen, as attested to by Figure 2.10. Obviously troublesome for the LDCs, this north–south split is also potentially dangerous for the MDCs in an age of interdependence—especially if poor peoples become sufficiently desperate to do desperate things.

Poor southern hemisphere countries like Somalia and Haiti blame **neocolonialism** for their problems, demanding special privileges aimed at making them more competitive in the global economy—roughly akin to **affirmative action** programs in the United States. Rich northern countries, say France or Japan, suggest that LDCs remain poor because of their internal inefficiency and corruption, not their colonial legacy.

The LDCs, more numerous and more agitated about the north–south gap, bring more radical solutions to the international agenda. The MDCs, not only wealthier, but also more militarily powerful, proceed very cautiously in the dialogue over poverty issues. Nevertheless, even northern countries realize that complex interdependence has swept away the luxury of assuming world poverty to be their problem.[4] It's now everyone's problem, but precious little agreement exists between rich and poor over how to deal with it.

Most of the contentious issues in the north–south dialogue were at one time looked upon as soft issues: assumed less important than Cold War military issues. Often subjective or intangible in nature, soft issues did not seem to national leaders as compelling as Cold War military confrontation.

Objective comparative economic data—such as **gross national product**, **national balance**, and **trade balance**—prove useful in contrasting rich and poor countries. But other, less tangible cultural and psychological factors, although more difficult to measure, also contribute to the north–south chasm. The end of the Cold War now allows the world community to focus on these long-ignored problems. Understanding the world's people as being deeply divided between northern and southern hemispheres will become more and more vital to fleshing out the skeletal features of the post-Cold War world.

WESTERN (CAPITALIST) VERSUS EASTERN (COMMUNIST)

For roughly forty-five years (1945–1991) the Cold War prism represented the most important conception of the world. Deadly serious in nature, the struggle between the American bloc and the Soviet bloc developed very differently than did the current north–south economic confrontation. Cold War competition was driven by political, military, and ideological differences.

Fortunately, the Americans and Soviets did not directly fight each other during the Cold War. Each worked through **surrogates**, or proxies, to weaken the enemy. In practically every corner of the globe, the United States and USSR supported opposing sides in local conflicts, pouring massive amounts of aid into regional struggles.

If the Soviets supported India, then the United States would back neighboring Pakistan. If the Americans helped South Korea, then the Russians would aid North Korea. If the Soviets befriended the Nicaraguan Sandinista government, then the United States would arm the Nicaraguan Contra rebels. Such combat by proxy helped avoid nuclear war between two superpowers, whose combined nuclear missiles peaked at about 50,000, with roughly 17 trillion tons of TNT equivalency. The downside? While preferable to nuclear war, these surrogate conflicts produced casualties in the tens of millions, and dollars in the trillions. This rivalry also encouraged the superpowers to get involved in practically every local conflict.

An interesting aspect of the Cold War military conflict was its quasi-religious, holy war quality. Each side saw the other as more than an enemy—it was also a **heretic**. American and Soviet mental images of each other, simplistic and dichotomous, featured black and white coloration with little appreciation of the gray hues that add depth and realism to national assessments of an adversary.

The deeply ingrained assumptions of the Cold War conflict resembled something almost hypnotic in nature. Even today, with the Cold War long over, its powerful imagery—East versus West, communist versus capitalist, bad versus good—still lingers in the thinking of people who lived through that intense era. American foreign policy, seeking a coherent role in a world where **containment** of communism no longer makes sense, struggles to rid itself of reflexes forged by half a century of East–West tension.

FIRST, SECOND, THIRD, AND FOURTH WORLDS

Another means used to conceptualize humanity's division in the world also derives from the powerful imagery of the Cold War. It refers to the First World, Second World, Third World, and Fourth World. The term **First World** identifies the Western democracies of North America, Europe, Japan, Australia, and New Zealand.

The Cold War rival of the Western democracies—Eastern-bloc communist countries led by the Soviet Union—constitutes the so-called **Second World**. It includes the eastern European countries taken over by the Soviet Union after the defeat of Germany in 1945; but not the four other communist countries of China, Vietnam, North Korea, and Cuba, which are more properly seen as part of the **Third World**.

Poverty and shared colonial experience create common identity among Third World countries. In general terms, the Third World refers to much of Latin America, Africa, Asia, and the Middle East. Many areas of Asia and Latin America experienced agricultural growth under the "Green Revolution" begun in the 1960s. Unfortunately, this revolution of scientific and technological innovation did not take hold in the impoverished countries of Africa, who also have the world's highest birthrates. Falling further behind economically, Sub-Saharan Africa has become known as the **Fourth World**, distinguished from the rest of the Third World.

CIVILIZATIONS

Another way to conceive of the world is that of civilizations. Land and location created the conditions for the great ancient civilization of Egypt more than 4,000 years ago. Originating in Ethiopia, the Nile River is one of the world's great arteries of life. It facilitated the consolidation of Lower Egypt and Upper Egypt into a great civilization based on agricultural surplus. Neither ancient Egypt's wealth nor high civilization (pyramids, kingship, art, religion, military) could have occurred without the blessings of the Nile River. Two technological innovations that revolutionized farming along the Nile were the shadoof, a device for irrigation, and the waterwheel. Grains like millet and wheat, as well as barley and flax, were enjoyed by the ancient Egyptians.[5]

While most international conflict in recent centuries has been caused by either ideological or economic forces, Harvard political scientist Samuel Huntington predicts that future global conflict will spring from the clash of modern **civilizations**. The cement holding large civilizations together consists of common culture: shared values, beliefs, and lifestyle. Quite often religious conviction represents the highest expression of shared cultural identity.

Huntington reasons that as modern communications spread Western civilization's secular and materialistic tendencies worldwide, traditional civilizations will feel threatened and will fight back, and the result will be a confrontation of "the West with the rest."

The Nile River contributed to wealth in ancient Egypt, resulting in impressive monuments like the Temple at Luxor.

He sees future local conflicts occurring at the fault lines between civilizations, such as Bosnia, lying between Western (European) and Islamic (Middle Eastern) civilizations. Huntington predicts that future world wars will occur between civilizations, not between nations or regions. He considers seven religiously based civilizations as likely to confront one another: Western, Confucian, Japanese, Islamic, Hindu, Slavic-Orthodox, and Latin American.[6] Other scholars, while accepting Huntington's basic premise of confrontation between civilizations, consider only three of his seven as truly autonomous civilizations likely to come into conflict: Western civilization, Islamic civilization, and Confucian (Chinese) civilization.[7]

ONE GLOBAL COMMUNITY

Some scholars describe human history as a progression of psychological identity from smaller to larger units: individual → family → tribe → nation → region → civilization → planet. According to this view, humans are moving toward the ultimate global identity: the human species in all of its colorful hues. Howard Rheingold believes that the electronic information highway, with its instantaneous global communications, leads not to Samuel Huntington's nightmare of clashing civilizations, but rather to the **virtual community:** a world of shared interests and benefits contributing to cooperation among people of all kinds.[8]

Mr. Rheingold's Neighborhood

Rheingold's idealistic perspective considers today's global interdependence not as the culmination of a process, but rather as its beginning. People, all members of the same human species, will recognize centrifugal forces that pull us together as being more compelling than centripetal ones that separate us. His Website, Electric Minds (www.minds.com), is intended to "lead the transformation of the Web into a social Web."[9]

Perhaps the most popular musical expression of a global community was ex-Beatle John Lennon's 1970 song "Imagine." It reflects the communal spirit and invokes visions of a more peaceful world.[10]

If Howard Rheingold turns out to be right and the Internet facilitates a global community, it will be ironic, since the Internet began in the 1960s as a Pentagon-funded means of post-nuclear war communication between military generals. The idea was to create a decentralized system, a fishnet, which an enemy attack could not destroy. By the 1980s the Department of Defense had dropped out of the Internet to set up its own system, leaving the Internet to the universities. In 1991 Mark McCahill invented a user-friendly, point-and-click Internet service provider, Gopher, at the university of Minnesota. By 1993 an easier-still service provider called Mosaic was created at the University of Illinois by a student named Mark Andreesen. Mosaic spawned the explosion of the worldwide web by bringing hypertext to the screen, and its commercial adaptation, Netscape, brought the world of the Internet to corporations.

Although today's access systems are simpler to operate, you can still take a wrong turn on the information superhighway. Humorist Dave Barry tells a story about a message that he posted on the Internet to a British writer, whom he labeled in the message Mr. Chuckletrouser's. Because of Barry's inexperience on the Internet, he mistakenly sent the Chuckletrouser's message to tens of thousands of people, who found it hilarious and began rerouting it to still

Personal space at work.

more thousands of their friends. Ironically, however, Barry had failed to send it to the writer for whom it was intended, who heard indirectly from others that his name was circulating in cyberspace via a funny letter entitled "Mr. Chuckletrousers."[11]

Idealism has exerted only sporadic influence in American foreign policy, but political scientist Jerel Rosati argues that the essence of United States president Jimmy Carter's 1970s foreign policy vision consisted of nothing less than a "quest for global community." Although sidestepped by events and obstacles, Carter's idealistic foreign policy beliefs represented an agenda to further the same concept of global community that inspired John Lennon in the 1960s and Howard Rheingold in the 1990s.[12]

Territoriality

Optimistic one-world images of human harmony offer encouraging projections for the future. But good reasons can also be given for doubting that a single global community of shared interests is likely to materialize. Illustrative of such nay-saying is humanity's historical penchant for **territoriality**. Some scholars argue that as individuals, we carry about "as an extension of ourselves an envelope of territory called our personal space." While the dimensions of personal space differ from culture to culture, it seems that all humans have a sense of portable territory that we carry around with us.[13]

Humans also have a sense of territory in groups. Some scholars compare expressions of social space, such as street gangs using graffiti or sports teams performing better in home games than away games, as analogous to dogs urinating on trees or deer using glandular secretions to establish territorial boundaries. Scientific scholars of human territoriality, called **ethologists**, dip freely into the rich pool of data provided by biology. Modern ethologists such as Robert Ardrey consider *Homo sapiens* an animal very much like its primate cousins. Therefore they think that an excellent way to learn about humans is to study scientifically animals like apes and chimpanzees. Ardrey boldly claims that "the territorial nature of humanity is genetic and ineradicable."[14]

More humanistic social scientists, such as Mel Gurtov, point to unique *Homo sapiens* qualities—for example, symbolic communication through language, artistry, spirituality, and conceptual mental abilities—as refutations of the ethologist's belief that humanity exists as merely another species in the animal kingdom.[15]

Territoriality sometimes manifests itself in the form of excessive psychological attachment to relatively worthless bits of turf. Every piece of land on the globe is claimed by someone, regardless of its value. At times humans have engaged in seemingly irrational violence to secure or maintain unimpressive territorial spoils. A study by political scientist Kal Holsti concludes that more than half of the conflicts since World War II had a significant territorial dimension, and that since the Peace of Westphalia in 1648 "the territorial aspect of international conflict remains fairly constant."[16]

Throughout this text movies are used to make various points. The reason is that film is the most accessible art form; movies blend effortlessly into the human landscape; they are both interesting and instructional. Concerning the age-old question of whether movies shape society's attitudes or vice versa, the untidy answer is neither and both: the relationship between films and society is too complex for causation to be defined, and it is best understood as associative rather than direct. But movies do matter, especially U.S. films, which historian Arthur Schlesinger, Jr., once labeled as America's only great contribution to the arts.

Kevin Costner's expensive movie, *Waterworld* (1995), seems to mock the exaggerated human lust for land cited above. It portrays a futuristic hell-on-earth where dirt is the rarest of valuable commodities. Why? Because only endless stretches of ocean can be seen from horizon to horizon. The degradation and violence to which the humans of *Waterworld* resort, just to get their hands on a little soil, seems disgusting. No believers in one-world unity are to be found in this bleak futurist scenario.

Humans periodically engage in short, emotional outbursts of turfmanship. At least these cases of impulsive violence seem comprehensible from the ethologist's perspective as some primordial urge briefly run amok. An example is the 1983 Falklands War between Great Britain and Argentina. The Falklands Islands, over which the war was fought don't amount to much strategically, militarily, economically, or geographically. The two sides' emotional attachment to the symbolic status of this area—or of any object fought over—seems understandable as an ephemeral flight from reason.

The Falklands controversy was all over very quickly, almost before its implications could be pondered. More perplexing are those cases of stubborn, long-term territorial fixations maintained in the face of serious, even self-defeating, costs, such as the Kurile Islands, discussed in Mini-case 2.1.

MINI-CASE 2.1
The Kurile Islands—Still Stubborn After All These Years

When the war in the Pacific was coming to an end in 1945, the United States expressed a strong desire for the Soviet Union to assist in the Allied effort to defeat Japan. Although the Soviets declared war against Japan and entered into the fray only a few days prior to Japan's surrender, the Soviet Union benefited from some of the spoils of war. Among these were the Kurile Islands, a small island chain just northeast of the four Japanese home islands, a mere three miles from Japanese Hokkaido, and nearly as close to the Kamchatka region of Siberian Russia. A treaty formally ending the war was never signed between the two neighbors because of Japan's unwillingness to accept losing the Kuriles.

For decade after decade these minor islands remained a part of the USSR. Then, with the breakup of the Soviet Union in 1991, Japan became more assertive about its claim to the Kuriles, which are called the "Northern Islands" by the Japanese. During the long Cold War between the United States and the Soviet Union, Japan acted as a loyal supporter of America's foreign policy, and so the Soviet refusal to return the Kuriles seem like an aspect of the Cold War chasm. The West saw the Soviets as evil, and the Kuriles appeared to be one more example of the Soviet Union's acting its part in the Cold War drama: unreasonable, but in character with its role.

Then, in rapid succession, Eastern European and Soviet communism died, democratic reforms became the norm among America's former enemies, and Russia and the other successor states suddenly became allies and trading partners. With Cold War animosities relegated to history's dustbin, the Japanese believed their reasonable request for a return of the Northern Islands would be honored in a spirit of reconciliation.

Also contributing to these expectations was the condition of the two countries' economies: Russia as a postcommunist basket case, Japan as one of the two richest countries on earth; Russia as resource rich, Japan as resource poor; Russia as needing foreign assistance, Japan as the world's number one giver of foreign aid. Such would seem the stuff of which deals are made—extensive Japanese development assistance for the expendable Kurile spoils.

In 1990 the Japanese offered then-President Mikhail Gorbachev a $26 billion swap for the disputed islands, including badly needed exploration of Russia's eastern Siberian natural resources, help in building the region's infrastructure, and extensive purchases of raw materials. When the Soviets balked, the patient Japanese waited two more years before proposing a similar package to Gorbachev's successor, Boris Yeltsin.

However, Yeltsin had earlier pledged that Russia would never consider the transfer of "one square meter" of Russian territory, and he too backed away from the incentives dangled before his eyes by Japan. The growth of Russia's huge but isolated eastern Siberian territory remains hostage, as the largest country in the world clings to "four rocky specks" of turf with only 50,000 residents, and while Russia enviously observes the world-class economic boon occurring in the near-by Pacific region.

What seems intriguing about the Kuriles saga is that more than fifty years have passed since World War II ended, yet for the Japanese, this issue remains a significant one. As for the Russians, they have had plenty of time to consider the proposition that no particular benefit has accrued to Russia by possessing them. Japan is a very important player on today's world stage and it seems that warmer relations would be in Russia's economic and political interests. Yet well after the Soviet collapse Russo-Japanese relations still resemble the Cold War deep freeze. How does one account for such apparent intransigence on the part of the Russians?[17]

Figure 2.11

Chapter Synopsis

The size and complexity of the human family leads social scientists to conceive of groupings based on shared identity. Eight such conceptions compete for prominence: regions, nation–states, economic super-regions, north–south hemispheres, rival types of economic systems, worlds of development, civilizations, and a global community.

World regions include Europe, former Soviet Union, Middle East, Asia, Pacific Rim, Sub-Saharan Africa, Latin America, and Anglo-America. Nearly 200 nation–states today face challenges more serious than any encountered during the three centuries when nation–states monopolized humanity's ordering of its public affairs. The economic success story of the Eu-

ropean Union in recent decades has spurred development of rival trade-driven regional blocs in North America and in East Asia. Possibly the most ominous global division is the widening chasm between the countries of the rich north and the poor south. For about half of the twentieth century the internecine confrontation between the capitalist West and the communist East pervaded every nook and cranny of world affairs. Deriving largely from the Cold War legacy is the vision of the world as essentially four worlds: First, Second, Third, and Fourth. Loosely tied civilizations, encompassing shared values and belief systems, and often larger than nation–states, formed the first great social organizations thousands of years ago and some scholars predict a revitalization of civilizations. Finally, intense debate rages over whether the human family might be moving toward a genuine family—a global community—although disagreement exists about whether this would be good news or bad.

Optimists and pessimists among social scientists differ concerning the implications of such an emerging identity among people seeing themselves as global citizens. Humanity's historical penchant for territorial attachment raises some caveats regarding rosy one-world future scenarios. The Kurile Islands mini-case illustrates how a nation–state can continue following a seemingly outdated policy of highly emotional attachment to a marginal piece of turf at the expense of more pressing and real contemporary imperatives of economic development. The country acting in ways describable as self-defeating is Russia. The dubious land to which it continues to cling is the Kurile Islands, taken from a defeated Japan at the end of World War II. Russia, a postcommunist economic basket case, could benefit greatly from Japanese economic aid, which is being withheld by Tokyo pending resolution of the Kuriles issue.

For Digging Deeper

Barry, Dave. *Dave Barry in Cyberspace*. Crown, 1996.

DeBlij H. J., and Peter O. Muller. *Geography: Regions, Realms, and Concepts*. John Wiley and Sons, 1994.

Frederick, Howard H. *Global Communication and International Relations*. Wadsworth, 1993.

Glassner, Martin Ira. *Political Geography*. John Wiley and Sons, 1993.

Gurtov, Mel. *Global Politics in the Human Interest*. Lynne Reinner, 1994.

Hahn, Harley, and Rick Stout. *The Internet: Complete Reference*. Osborne McGraw-Hill,.1995.

Huntington, Samuel P. *Political Development and Political Decay*. Irvington Books, 1993.

Rheingold, Howard. *The Virtual Community: Homesteading on the Electronic Frontier*. Addison-Wesley, 1993.

Schiller, Herbert I. *Information Inequality*. Routledge, 1996.

Wresch, William. *Disconnected: Haves and Have-Nots in the Information Age*. Rutgers University Press, 1996.

Internet

Citing Information from Electronic Sources   http://www.usu.edu/-polisci/ps/cite.html
Babel: A Glossary of Computer Oriented Abbreviations and Acronyms   http://www.access.digex.net/-ikind/babel96b.html

Key Glossary Terms

affirmative action	command economy	country
capitalism	Conference on Security and Co operation in Europe (CSCE)	democracy
civilization		democratization
colonialism	containment	Earth Summit

ethnicity
ethologists
European Coal and Steel Community (ECSC)
European Community (EC)
European Union (EU)
First World
Fourth World
gross national product
heretic
homogeneous
Human Development Index (HDI)
human rights
managed economy

nation
nation balance
nation–states
neocolonialism
neomercantilism
newly industrialized countries (NICS)
North American Free Trade Agreement (NAFTA)
North Atlantic Treaty Organization (NATO)
Peace of Westphalia
perception
power
primary product

Second World
Shiite Muslim
Slavic
sovereignty
spatial
state
Sunni Muslim
surrogates
territoriality
Third World
Thirty Years War
trade balance
virtual community

CHAPTER **3**

The Evolution of Social Science Disciplines and Methods

CORE OBJECTIVE

To establish the historical, philosophical, and methodological foundations on which contemporary social sciences are based.

Thematic Questions

- What is the relationship among the three great bodies of knowledge?

- What characterized the great ancient civilizations?

- In what ways do the ancient Greeks influence modern civilization?

- How do scientism and humanism undergird inquiry by the social sciences?

Social Science Roots

Three Great Bodies of Knowledge

Humanity's long struggle to understand itself and the world it inhabits has resulted in the emergence of three great bodies of knowledge: natural sciences, humanities, and social sciences. The natural sciences consist of physics, chemistry, biology, geology, and astronomy, all of which deal with laws related to nature. These disciplines experienced tremendous advances during the European Renaissance from the middle of the fifteenth century to the end of the seventeenth century.

The humanities are made up of history, philosophy, literature, ethics, comparative religion, and criticism of the arts. Each of the humanities involves a personalized quest for insight into the human condition, particularly its aesthetic, spiritual, and emotional aspects. Their contributions to knowledge can be traced back 2,500 years to ancient Greece.

The social sciences, by contrast, have emerged as the six separate disciplines of political science, economics, sociology, anthropology, psychology, and geography only during the last two centuries. As more recent disciplines, they have freely borrowed insights, techniques, and information from their progenitors in both the natural sciences and humanities. Together the social sciences undertake the daunting task of studying the complexities of human behavior.

Modern-Day Social Sciences

One way to define the contemporary social sciences is to examine what today's social scientists do. To do this, we must look at the site of the largest concentration of social scientists—the United States—where higher education is big business. Nearly all of America's 3,200 colleges and universities have departments housing social scientists who spend their time teaching, researching, writing, and consulting about myriad aspects of the human drama. In defining themselves professionally, most identify with a specific social science discipline. Typically, separate departments of political science, economics, sociology, anthropology, psychology, and geography establish lines of administrative demarcation.

Studying people becomes very complicated. This division of mental labor allows scholars to approach human studies from a variety of perspectives. These disciplinary boundaries, however, do not prevent social scientists from pursuing topics that spill over into related disciplines. Human behavior represents the crux of the social sciences. Given such a broad and elusive mandate, cross-fertilization is common among social scientists. If you ask your professors about their specialties, you are likely to uncover social psychologists, political geographers, economic psychologists, economic geographers, psycho-anthropologists, political sociologists, and anthropological geographers.

Political scientists often examine topics related to issues of power, authority, or government—as one observer put it, trying to answer the question of who gets what, when, and how? The interests of political scientists sometimes overlap with those of *economists* studying how people make a living. The production, distribution, and consumption of goods and services occupies much of the attention of modern economists. *Sociologists* deal with human interaction in various groups, as do their intellectual cousins in *anthropology*, who often specialize in preliterate societies while exploring the origins of various human characteristics. The individual's subjective realm of inner experience—including elusive topics such as mind, motivation, and perception—intrigues today's *psychologists*. Finally, *geographers* trace the link between humans and their physical environment and concentrate on spatial analysis.

If you are tempted to take for granted this portrait of well-established, distinct, stable, and Americanized social science disciplines—don't. Its canvass has been painted mostly during the last century, which is like the blink of one eye when compared with the long haul of human history.

Prequel to the Human Drama's Lengthy Script

About 35 million years ago humanlike creatures, *hominids*, climbed down from the trees in which they lived and began gradually to walk upright. Roughly 2.5 million years ago *Homo erectus* (erect man) lived simultaneously with a number of other similar *hominid* species, but a larger brain and more upright posture seem to have provided an edge over competitors. *Homo erectus*, whose time line runs from 2.5 million to 100,000 years ago, was also one of the first to utilize fire and to make basic stone tools. Hunting animals, eating meat, and foraging for berries and nuts provided subsistence. Hunting not only provided protein-rich meat and cut down on time spent eating, it also aided the development of planning and social organization, which were important catalysts to communication via language. Only humans use the symbols of language to communicate. However, studies of the African bonobos ape suggest its use of physical signals to communicate with other bonobos. Bands of about 100 apes travel miles during the day but reunite nightly at a new site by using trail markers.

According to the theory known as "out of Africa," *Homo erectus* migrated from African origins toward both Europe and Asia around one million years ago. The most important skeletal find of *Homo erectus*, Peking man, occurred in China. Philosopher Joseph Bronowski pinpoints a most intriguing yet elusive question in this evolutionary saga: "How did hominids come to be the kind that I honor: dexterous, observant, thoughtful, passionate, able to manipulate in the mind the symbols of language and mathematics both, the visions of art and geometry and poetry and science?"[1]

Skeletal and fossil evidence, "bones and stones," provides us with clues about the species from which modern humans evolved: *Homo sapiens* (thinking humans), earthly inhabitants from 300,000 to 100,000 years ago. Tool-making and weapons-making advances, division of labor according to gender, and the beginning of family identities characterize early *Homo sapiens*. The first modern humans, who appeared nearly 100,000 years ago, engaged in social rituals such as burying their dead. Extensive evidence in Europe depicts two species tantalizingly similar to our species: the Neanderthals and the Cro-Magnons, both of whom benefited from the social glue provided by the use of language.

The Neanderthals, named after the region in Germany where they lived, thrived from 100,000 to 40,000 years ago. With a three-pound brain the size of a modern human's, Neanderthals used tools to make clothing from animals they hunted. Scholars have also long known that Neanderthals lived in loose settlements, retired to caves for safety when necessary, and decorated their dead with flowers. However, only in 1997 was it discovered by German paleontologist Oscar Todkopf that Neanderthals also made musical instruments, including a six-foot long tuba-like instrument with sixteen holes carved out of a mastadon tusk. This 50,000-year-

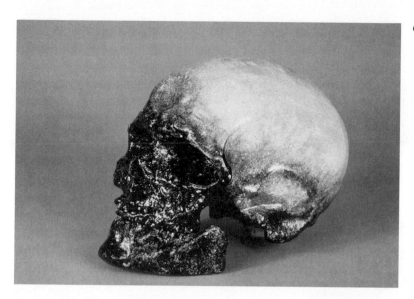

Cro-Magnon skull.

old instrument was found near a cave featuring wall paintings of it.[2] Neanderthals were apparently swept aside 40,000 years ago by early humans in both Europe and Asia.

Living not far from the Neanderthals, in what is now France, were the Cro-Magnons (40,000 to 10,000 years ago). These humans expressed aesthetic sensitivity via elaborate cave paintings and seem to have experienced a spiritual dimension to their lives. However, like their predecessors over the previous one million years, they survived as nomadic hunters and gatherers. Skeletal DNA evidence reported in a 1997 issue of the scientific journal *Cell*, suggests that Neanderthals were not our ancestors, but Cro-Magnons were. The Cro-Magnons had already become extinct by the time the agricultural revolution sprang up in regions as diverse as Mesoamerica, China, and the Fertile Crescent near the Tigris and Euphrates rivers in the Middle East, roughly 10,000 years ago.[3]

In most parts of the world where agriculture took root, human foragers gave up their roaming to settle down and plant grain in order to make what must have seemed tantamount to a miracle: bread made from unleavened cakes of ground grain and baked on red-hot stones. A 1997 article in *Science* contends that while the domestic cultivation of plants was taking place in several places 10,000 years ago, only in the Americas did agriculture precede villages—elsewhere settlements predated agriculture.[4]

Most anthropologists agree that breadmaking motivated the rapid growth of agriculture. However, at least one of their colleagues clings to a minority viewpoint. Soloman Katz argues strenuously that the agricultural revolution was generated as much by a taste for the elixir of beer as for bread. His research on the Sumerians of Mesopotamia (present-day Iraq) reveal proficient brewers and enthusiastic consumers of beer before 3000 B.C.[5]

Whatever motivated the creators of the agricultural revolution, few developments have so dramatically transformed humanity's prospects. Myriad spillover effects included such milestones as population concentration in settled communities, storage of surplus crops, the invention of pottery, cloth making, trade with other groups, domestication of animals, and record keeping.

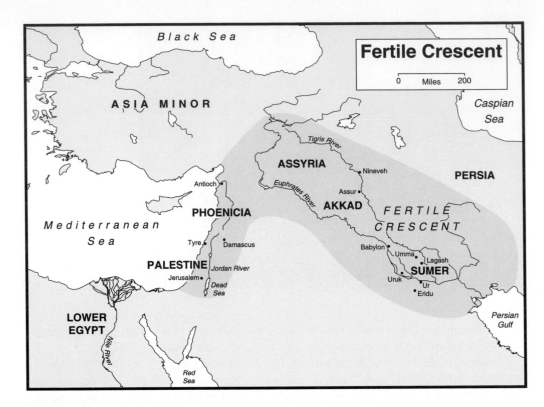

Figure 3.1

The advent of written records ended the mute days of human prehistory, ushering in the chorus of voices known as recorded history. Dogs had already been domesticated by humans prior to the agricultural revolution; then came goats, sheep, oxen, and eventually horses.

A serendipitous set of natural and human factors combined to trigger the agricultural revolution. An explosion of new vegetation accompanied the end of the last Ice Age. The most crucial genetic piece of this puzzle was the creation of a fertile wheat hybrid resulting from a cross between wild wheat and a natural goat grass. Humans first benefited from harvesting this new strain of wheat, then learned the secret of planting it themselves.

Ancient Civilizations and Recorded Human History

Up until this point, humanity's ascent consisted mainly of a biological evolution lasting millions of years. The gradual progression of this early script for humanity's performance on the world stage stood in contrast to the rapid transmutation which has dominated the last ten millenia. It is almost as if a videotape of the human drama has been cranked up to a fast-forward speed during our most recent 10,000 years. The grandeur of humanity's relatively recent social take-off can be understood only in the context of emerging civilizations.

The first civilizations followed on the heels of the agricultural revolution, prior to 5000 B.C., in the Middle East, where the nations of Iran and Iraq now exist. Between 4000 B.C. and the time of Christ, major civilizations also arose in Egypt, India, China, Greece, Rome, and Japan. Each ancient civilization advanced the cause of humanity immeasurably by organizing its residents into social classes, creating governments led by divinely inspired rulers, facilitating the emergence of commercial trade through fledgling market forces overseen by the government, and providing for the defense of the civilization. Such civilizations were to develop much later in the New World of the Western hemisphere than they did in the Old World of the Middle East, Europe, and Asia.

Humanity's creative juices worked overtime in establishing many of the great ancient civilizations well before the birth of Christ. Some historians believe that no other advance in the human script has resulted in such a profound expansion of our species' imagination. Yet a dark side to this rapid social, political, and economic ascent also demands recognition. Part of the human legacy distinguishing us from other higher order species is that humans seem always to have devoted time and energy to killing one other.

For the one million years spent as hunters and gatherers, however, humans were relatively inefficient in this endeavor. With the advent of complex social organization, economies producing a surplus of goods, and powerful as well as legitimized political elites—the stuff of civilization—warfare expanded in both scope and intensity. Many of the bloodiest and most brutal early wars were fought between representatives of the two contending models for human social organization at the time: nomadic social customs versus the settlement as a more orderly social existence.

Despite their military successes, many nomadic invaders rode horseback from their Central Asian homelands into Europe only to find that, after hard won victories, their proud way of life possessed little staying power and was absorbed over time by the peoples whom they had defeated. The Huns of Attila and Genghis Khan's Mongols both experienced such ignoble fates; the civilized way of life had gradually taken center stage in the human drama and relegated nomads to bit parts.

The age of ancient civilizations came to an end with the military defeat of the Roman Empire at the hands of Franco-Germanic tribes in the fifth century A.D. Much of the Roman way of life, however, continued to pervade the growing societies of northern Europe, which were long on power but short on culture. One of the most pervasive influences of the late Roman Empire was the monotheistic religion of Christianity.

The Middle Ages

The thousand years between the fifth-century demise of Rome and the consolidation of modern civilizations in the fifteenth century is referred to as the Middle Ages, an era characterized by **feudalism**. The feudal manors were run by privileged feudal lords. **Serfs,** who were bound to the land ruled by their feudal lords, lived a near-slave existence as farm laborers holding no real rights.

Two levels of authority vied for power during the Middle Ages: (1) the feudal lords, running the local estates loosely referred to as principalities, kingdoms, or fiefdoms; (2) the Papal Church and Holy Roman Empire at the pan-European level, with all their centralized organization, impressive wealth, and monopoly of moral authority. Throughout the Middle Ages these rival levels of authority alternately cooperated and competed with one another as

German reformer, theologian, and originator of the Protestant Reformation, Martin Luther (1483-1546), shown in a reflective mood.

varying circumstances dictated different strategies at different times.

Few such circumstances can match the perception of an external threat to a group's spiritual and physical survival. When the other competing monotheistic religion, **Islam**, captured a city (Jerusalem) that was sacred to both religions, the Pope begged, threatened, and bribed Christians to take up arms in defense of their faith. The result? A recurring wave of **Crusades**, begun in 1095 and repeated eight times over the next two centuries. All this carnage on an unprecedented scale left Christians and Muslims essentially where they had begun: stalemated in a bitter power struggle.

As to the power struggle between local feudal lords and the Papacy, neither side won that long battle either. A new form of human organization appeared in the form of the nation–state, which operated midway between the feudal lords at the local level and the Church at the pan-European level. After a millennium, the Middle Ages were finally giving way to modern civilizations. Symbolizing this process were these newly emerging nation–states, such as Sweden, Spain, and France. Possessing a secular authority largely independent of the Church, and able to provide its residents with a sense of security stemming from its size and resources, the nation–state ushered in the modern form of social organization.

Rationalism and the Renaissance

This latest twist in the human script brings us to modernity. Yet even the briefest review of humanity's drama ought to pay homage to the pivotal role of the **Renaissance**. Literally "rebirth," the Renaissance spark was lit in fourteenth-century Florence, swept across northern Italy, then engulfed Europe by the seventeenth century. The Renaissance emphasized **rationalism**, newly unearthed by scholars by way of ancient Greek civilization. This classical revival expressed itself in two main areas of learning: natural science and moral philosophy.

Critical thinking was a linchpin of Greek rationalism, and one person who epitomized it was Martin Luther, a free-thinking Augustinian monk. Luther ushered in the **Protestant Reformation** when he nailed his "95 Theses" to the cathedral door in Wittenberg, Germany. With unquestioned obedience to Papal authority now a relic of the Middle Ages, critical thinking settled deeply into the minds of men, and later, of women.

A final irony to the story goes back to the bloody Crusades fought between Christians and Muslims. Critical thinking, the intellectual backbone of today's world, entered modern consciousness through the Renaissance, which took it from the rationalism of ancient Greece. When

Greek civilization fell in 500 B.C., most of its way of life disappeared with it, but that which managed to survive eventually became an influential contributor to Western civilization.

The Greeks believed that reason could produce the "good society," which Plato (427–347 B.C.), in his manual *Republic*, outlined for enlightened politicians. Aristotle's (384–322 B.C.) *Politics* provided a more general blueprint for a **utopian** society. What we know today of Greek philosophers like Plato and Aristotle comes mostly from unlikely middlemen: Persian (soon-to-be Muslim) conquerors of the Greeks who preserved ancient Greek knowledge for more than 1,000 years. Greek rationalism was replanted in European intellectual soil by Christian Crusaders returning from the Middle East. Slowly taking hold during the late Middle Ages, Greek rationalism failed to capture the philosophical soil of Europe's oases of learning until the Renaissance.

INTELLECTUAL HISTORY OF THE SOCIAL SCIENCES

European Enlightenment

The ideal Renaissance scholar was expected to cultivate every grain of knowledge and eventually collapsed from intellectual fatigue, leading gradually to scholarly specialization during the period of the **Enlightenment** (1700–1800). The first disciplinary earthquake severed philosophy from physics and the natural sciences; others soon followed.

Social theorizing during the Enlightenment became increasingly sophisticated and well regarded. Influenced by the powerful ideas of Enlightenment scientists like Sir Isaac Newton, social thinkers mechanistically conceived of society as part of the order of nature, thus bending to inexorable natural laws. Early European "system-builders" like Auguste Comte, Herbert Spencer, and Karl Marx tried to account for all social phenomena; they represented social commentators of the broadest sort. By the eighteenth and nineteenth centuries these theories had all firmly accepted a basic assumption: the historical inevitability of social progress. From these philosophically oriented theories of history spring modern social sciences.

This optimistic notion of historical progress fits neatly with the traditional German faith in history as the grand unifying discipline of human studies. Broad-based theories of optimism dotted the German intellectual landscape right up until the outbreak of World War I in 1914. What we now conceive of as the discrete humanities disciplines of philosophy and history were then inseparable contributors to the way Europeans theorized about human affairs. When eighteenth- and nineteenth-century European scholars theorized about political matters, for example, they engaged mostly in political philosophy.

Political Philosophy: Hobbes, Locke, and Rousseau

Three great political thinkers stand out as pioneers. British political philosopher Thomas Hobbes (1588–1679) argued in his book *The Leviathan* that life prior to the formation of the political state (leviathan) was "solitary, poor, nasty, brutish, and short." Humans, in other words, need a government to protect them from their own worst impulses. He viewed government not as something alien imposed from above by divine authority, but rather as a rational alternative that was beneficial to its citizens.

Hobbes' countryman John Locke (1632–1704) emphasized the importance of the rights of the individual citizen. Today these are called civil liberties, epitomized by the freedoms spelled out in the first amendment of the U.S. Constitution: freedom of speech, press, religion, assembly, and petition. John Locke was the first to argue systematically that the rights of individuals take precedence over the rights of the government in certain circumstances, and that government forfeits its right to rule if it violates the public trust. Leaders of the American Revolution of 1776 took Locke's philosophical musings very seriously.

The Swiss philosopher Jean-Jacques Rousseau (1712–1778) began his political analysis with an assumption diametrically opposed to that of Thomas Hobbes: humans are essentially good at heart. Rousseau believed that the tendency of absolutist governments to abuse power must be opposed and that ultimately the power to rule needs to be traced back to the people. It did not take very long for Rousseau's ideas to be applied to real-world conditions close to home in the French Revolution of 1789–1799.

Today most social scientists think of the realms of politics and economics as separate. To European philosophers of the time they seemed as complementary as symmetrical sundials. However, while Hobbes, Locke, and Rousseau emphasized the relationship between government and its citizens, others zeroed in on the relationship between government and the economy.

POLITICAL ECONOMY: ADAM SMITH AND KARL MARX

The father of classical economic theory was the Scottish philosopher Adam Smith (1723–1790). His enormously influential book, *The Wealth of Nations* (1776), argued that government should keep its hands off the economy—a laissez-faire approach, sharply critical of the tendency for government to use the economy as a vehicle for accumulating wealth for itself. Smith held that an "invisible hand" guided "the rules which men naturally observe in exchanging goods either for money or for one another." These self-adjusting market exchanges, according to Smith, tend to produce the greatest good for the greatest number over time if governments will only stay out of the way.

Not all those who theorized about free-market economics offered interpretations as confidently optimistic as Adam Smith's. Sitting atop the list of nay-sayers would have to be Karl Marx (1818–1883). When Marx looked at contemporary European economies, he saw abject poverty for the masses while the rich got much richer; he saw political systems catering exclusively to the needs of the rich elites; he saw ethical issues of social justice buried in a rush to accumulate wealth; he saw the growing inequities of market economics, leading to an inevitably violent revolution being carried out by the many against the few. Karl Marx's theories can be linked to the Russian Revolution of 1917 just as profoundly as those of John Locke to the American Revolution and those of Jean-Jacques Rousseau to the French Revolution.

Social Philosophy: Comte, Durkheim, and Weber

The French philosopher Auguste Comte (1798–1857) was the first to treat society as a "system" of interacting parts. He thought that the politically oriented thinkers failed to understand

The French scholar Auguste Comte (1798-1857) argued for an independent discipline of sociology using scientific methods.

Émile Durkheim (1858-1917), pioneer French sociologist who laid the foundation for studying how social systems affect individual behavior.

the importance of the "interconnections" between aspects of society existing apart from the political economy. While political philosophers had remained transfixed by the big picture of human studies, Comte preferred to examine interacting parts of the social system. In the 1830s Comte proposed a "positive science of society," opening the door to a sociology both independent as a discipline and increasingly scientific in its methods.[6]

Two later scholars agreed with Comte's plea for a separate sociology, but they epitomized the tension underlying his scientific aspirations for the discipline. Frenchman Émile Durkheim (1858–1917), a philosopher turned sociologist, objected to the historical analysis prevalent in European social thought and became one of the founders of quantitative sociology.

Durkheim's special interest was the conflicting tendencies of cohesion versus alienation among members of society. As the holder of the first endowed academic chair in sociology, in 1896, he soon published his landmark statistical study entitled, *Suicide: A Study in Sociology* (1897). In it he tried to show that even highly personal and individual acts, such as the decision to commit suicide, are influenced by what he called "collective reality," or social factors.

The German belief that historical analysis stands as the linchpin of all social analysis was expressed best in the work of Max Weber (1884-1920).

Like Karl Marx before him, Max Weber (1884–1920) was a German theorist of general historical trends whose voluminous writings often lacked clarity. Unlike the view of Marx, Weber's analysis of contemporary conditions emphasized a faith in the progressive nature of the existing European sociopolitical order. Where Max Weber parted company with sociologist Durkheim, as well as with the emerging center of gravity among new sociologists, was over the growing rift between **historicism** and **scientism**. Weber remained true to the traditional German ideal of history as the vehicle for social analysis par excellence. In one book, he asks pointedly, "Can this project [science] be expected to produce useful new insights germane to their concrete problems?" His answer is highly skeptical concerning the prospects.[7]

The Americanization of the Social Sciences

The evolution of the social sciences in the United States followed a markedly different course of events. According to intellectual historian Dorothy Ross, the formative decades of the social sciences in America were 1870 to 1929. Unlike their European counterparts, American scholars steered the social sciences sharply away from their historico-philosophical roots and in the direction of science. The new scientific mission to discover laws of society meant ignoring subjective phenomena such as emotions, applying rigorous research methods, and remaining neutral on ethical and/or public policy questions.[8]

During the Gilded Age following the U.S. Civil War, rapidly expanding wealth, urbanization, the founding of many American colleges and universities, and a growing specialization of knowledge ushered in separate and viable social science disciplines in the United States. America's mostly sectarian colleges had been teaching a curriculum heavy on moral philosophy for nearly a century. What America sorely lacked, however, was the system of universities to be found in Germany, France, Britain, and Italy.

U.S. Universities and the Paradigm of Science

Not until Baltimore's Johns Hopkins University opened its doors in 1876 could the United States boast of an American university. Even then no domestic university or its professoriate could dream of rivaling the status of venerable European institutions like Cambridge, Oxford, Berlin, or the Sorbonne. But philosopher Peter T. Manicas points out that while American universities lacked tradition as a source of authority, they did not lack "science," which they came to see as their passport to respectability.[9]

The millennial newness of America, its freedom from tradition, allowed American universities to reinvent themselves as paragons of progressive ideas—with science heading the agenda. Also, in sharp contrast to the French Revolution, Americans considered their own revolution to have been a resounding success. This viewpoint added to a growing suspicion among Americans that their land was an exceptional place able to accomplish exceptional things.

In the latter part of the nineteenth century the action in American higher education moved swiftly and decisively away from its older undergraduate colleges to its spanking-new universities. The key feature of new universities like Johns Hopkins, New York University, University of Chicago, and the public land-grant universities in every state was their introduction of graduate programs. The first such program in the social sciences was begun in political science, at Columbia University in 1880, by German-trained scholar John Burgess. Within a decade Columbia's model graduate school also had departments of economics, geography, and sociology (which included anthropology at that time). A crucial innovation of U.S. graduate programs was the graduate seminar, which encouraged specialized instruction and research and which was based on the laboratory model already operating in the natural sciences.

Professionalization of the Social Sciences

American social scientists were intent on professionalizing higher education, a goal that necessitated the creation of professional associations publishing their own specialized journals. First the American Academy of Political and Social Science appeared in 1889, then the American Economic Association and the American Psychological Association in 1892, the American Political Science Association in 1903, the Association of American Geographers in 1904, and the American Sociological Society in 1905. Keenly interested in separating themselves from the curriculum of moral philosophy taught in America's small colleges, the new graduate programs in U.S. universities seized upon the scientific method as their intellectual Holy Grail; "Science began to appear not only as the most authoritative modern knowledge, but as a courageous source of free inquiry, as against an authoritarian, outmoded religion."[10]

It has also been argued widely that a form of sexism contributed to American social science's fixation on scientism: at a time when almost all leading scholars were male, science seemed more acceptable to a macho-oriented, frontier-era America than did historical or philosophical analysis. A final factor that likely contributed toward putting the "science" into the social sciences a century ago is that, as a very complex and diverse new nation, America needed a unifying symbol around which to rally, and science was it.

Before long the top social scientists were advocating scientific approaches to the study of humans. In 1919 sociologist Luther Bernard proclaimed that "We are so definitely launched upon the trend toward objectivism and definiteness of method that it is needless to argue in its defense."[11] Two years later American Political Science Association President Charles Merriam issued a clarion call for the scientific study of politics, which he believed would enable scholars to exercise intelligent influence over governmental affairs. Merriam urged his colleagues to borrow the statistical techniques already in use among psychologists.

In economics, the transition to a quantitative social science was facilitated by the nature of its subject matter, and less exhortation was required. When necessary to do so, however, major economists such as Thorstein Veblen challenged their colleagues to become more rigorously objective. The final imprimatur sealing the success of scientism arrived in the 1920s in the form of large financial contributions for scientific research from charitable organizations with deep pockets, like the Rockefeller and Carnegie foundations.

Philosophical Dialogue in the Social Sciences

It seems remarkable how little some of the underlying issues affecting the American social sciences have changed over the last seventy years. Although much of our knowledge about human behavior has derived from humanities disciplines, especially from history and philosophy, the prevailing methodology continues to favor scientific objectivity and quantification over analytical and experiential insights. The history of these two rival schools of thought in the American social sciences—scientism versus humanism—has remained one of confrontation over cooperation, isolation over engagement, emotionalism over reason.

Two Contending Camps

Except for occasional expressions of antipathy, scientism and humanism have generally attempted to ignore each other. Modern social sciences owe debts to each progenitor (the natural sciences and the humanities), but only grudgingly do the proponents of either scientism or humanism even acknowledge the existence of the other. I applaud advocates of a more roomy definition of the social sciences: one involving a synthesis of scientism and humanism.

Insights and methods from both the natural sciences and humanities are needed. Why? Because the social sciences are still very young in comparison with their more experienced brethren. They also face the daunting task of comprehending the behavior of a species as perplexing as modern humans. As social science philosopher Kenneth Hoover succinctly put it: "There is no particular sense in limiting the facilities of the mind in any inquiry."[12]

Scientism   Before a clear image of a roomy social science can be painted, however, the contrasting features of scientism versus humanism must be sketched in. As the prevailing approach in twentieth-century America, scientism deserves first crack at presenting its case. Scientism assumes that the differences between the natural and social sciences are a matter of degree, not of kind. Two scholars provide texture to this argument: "Just as the seventeenth and eighteenth centuries saw the maturing of the physical sciences, and the nineteenth that of the biological sciences, so the twentieth century marks the coming of age of the behavioral [social] sciences."[13] While people as subjects of study may prove more irascible than atoms, paramecia, or ozone gas, all remain ultimately amenable to the same methods of study: science is science is science.

Science gathers **facts** which help to answer the *what* type of questions. When facts are organized, they can be more abstractly analyzed to answer the complicated *why* type of questions. These general explanations of specific factual realities are known as **scientific theories**.

The approach to knowledge known as *science* has been defined variously as an objective system for providing the truth, finding a pattern in a set of phenomena, insistence on systematic and methodical study, a language transporting humans to new countries of the mind, and the freeing of inquiry from bias and prejudice.[14] Philosopher of science Carlo Lastrucci says that the scientist makes basic assumptions about her work. For example, the assuption that all objective phenomena are knowable in a world of underlying order and uniformity, and that truth must be demonstrated objectively, since nothing is self-evident.[15]

The rules of the scientific game are provided by a loosely structured set of procedures known as the scientific method. Most Ph.D. dissertations in the social sciences emulate these guidelines:

Scientific Method
- Selection of an area to be researched and a review of the existing literature on the subject
- Definition of the problem: formulation of a specific researchable question (hypothesis) within the framework of a more general explanatory theory
- Construction of the research design: the methodological task of identifying a technique for measuring data relevant to the hypothesis of the study
- Data collection: observation and recording of information intended to test the hypothesis
- Classification and organization: after data are gathered, a proper ordering of them for maximum usefulness
- Conclusions: evaluation of hypothesis based on data on hand, an attempt to generalize from the results of the study, and recommendations for further research

If an objective method represents the heart of science, then its soul consists of a certain attitude—one of skepticism; science believes that things are not always what they seem to be, rendering commonsensical understanding inadequate. Common sensory perception alone may suggest to us that the earth is flat, that the sun revolves around the earth, that heavy bodies always fall faster than light bodies, and that ships made of iron must head to the bottom of the sea. Yet humanity has long known all these expectations to be false.

As a leading social science methodologist has argued, relying on common sense risks making inaccurate observations, overgeneralizing about the significance of our own anecdotal experiences, and making observations selectively on the basis of human desire to see what we want or expect to see.[16] In 1633 the Catholic Church condemned the Italian astronomer Galileo (1564–1642). His crime? Galileo had relied on science to argue that the sun serves as the center of the universe. Both common sense and, not coincidentally, Church doctrine then held that the earth, not the sun, functioned as the center of our universe.

The marriage of objective methods and a skeptical attitude produce three main scientific offspring: verifiability, systematic inquiry, and generality. *Verifiability* aims at proving the truth or falsity of statements by testing them enough times to feel confident in the results. *Systematic inquiry* consists of sorting and organizing bits of information into coherent patterns—putting the oranges with the oranges, and the bananas with the bananas. *Generality* calls for gradual movement from specific levels of explanation to broader levels. Once scientific inquiry can explain things by means of laws at a general level, it then should proceed to the most challenging task of all: predicting the workings of similar phenomena in the future.

Research Designs   What kinds of research designs do scholars use when they study humans scientifically? The first is **survey research**. Social scientists rely on survey instruments more than any other technique to gather data about human subjects. Surveys can be easily mailed to subjects or conducted in an interview. They allow researchers to tap subjective states of mind such as attitudes and beliefs in an objective fashion and to analyze the results statistically. Voter studies by political scientists have achieved sophistication through sample surveys. While surveys usually provide accurate readings, they are time bound, since some people have a way of changing their minds, such as concerning for whom they intend to vote. The results of surveys also can be influenced by the way in which questions are phrased; furthermore, researchers must exercise caution to limit their personal biases.

Second, when possible, social scientists may use **experimental design**. As the technique most directly borrowed from natural sciences such as chemistry and biology, experiments are eminently rigorous, controllable, and verifiable. Psychologists have pioneered in the use of in-laboratory experiments, but geographers and sociologists sometimes use more loosely constructed field experiments. The popular image of the social scientist dressed in a long white coat, with clipboard in hand, furiously scribbling notes about human subjects, best fits the experimental research design. Critics point to the ethical dilemmas raised when experiments are conducted on unwitting human subjects, and conversely, to the possibility of self-fulfilling prophecies, a phenomenon known as the "Hawthorne effect," when subjects know they are under investigation.[17]

The third most rigorous research design involves the social scientist directly in **participant observation**. Rather than the researcher's aloofly analyzing survey statistics or observing an experiment in progress, participant observation places the scholar in the midst of the action. Anthropologists like Margaret Mead, who went to live with and study preliterate groups in Samoa in 1925, have opened a range of creative research options to fellow social scientists. There simply is no other practical way to gather information about such remote groups of people.

The fact that both similarities and dissimilarities can be found among lifestyles around the globe makes participant observation a flexible tool for comparing human societies. How-

An anthropologist discussing local plant-life with villagers in rural Cameroon.

ever, if science demands objective neutrality, participant observation suffers when the scholar becomes too personally involved with the subjects. Under such circumstances, the observer may either alter the course of events among the subjects or become biased enough to interpret the results of the investigation inaccurately.

A fourth example of social science research design is **content analysis**. This technique uses oral or written communication as a basis for insights concerning the person or group expressing a viewpoint or opinion. Like the sample survey, content analysis allows for the quantification of subjective aspects of human experience: thus it is attractive to advocates of scientism. In international studies, speeches made by inaccessible leaders of foreign countries are often scrutinized via content analysis for repetitive patterns or for hidden meaning.

By systematically quantifying certain characteristics of a speech, a researcher can produce insights not apparent to the casual reader. The simple act of counting (although often complexly via computer programs) can provide clues regarding the state of mind of an important leader. In an era known as the age of communication, this device offers a scientific handle for us to grasp the communication process. Although very amenable to quantification, content analysis encounters problems of **validity**; is the scientist really measuring what he thinks he or she is measuring?

Finally, much less quantifiable and systematic is the research design known as the **case study**. A case study usually revolves around a particular historical event or lesson, which is used to generalize beyond its narrow confines to a wider truth. Cases can serve a long-range purpose as building blocks for broader theories to be developed at a later date; they also represent immediate illustrations of important phenomena. Their beauty stems from their concreteness.

Social scientists are sometimes criticized for getting lost in abstraction, and case studies require them to ground their theoretical musings in real events. The watchword of the social scientist browsing for good case studies might be summed up by the question, "Of what is this an instance?" Professional graduate schools of business were the first to popularize the case study method of teaching. The expansion of case studies into the social sciences has been facilitated by a major effort from a philanthropic organization known as the Pew Charitable Trust. This case study described in Mini-case 3.1 shows how scientific investigation can be applied to certain questions of historical fact.

MINI-CASE 3.1:
Good Science and the "Real Anastasia"

One of the crucial events of the twentieth century took place around the 1917 Russian Revolution. For more than 300 years the Russian monarchy had been controlled by the Romanov family. Whereas monarchical rulers in Britain, Sweden, Spain, and The Netherlands found ways to compromise with fledgling democratic movements in their countries—thereby continuing in a role of symbolism rather than power—a much different fate befell the last Romanov ruler, Tsar Nicholas II, and his family.

The turn of the century witnessed ever worsening conditions for rural peasants and the growing numbers of urban workers. Strikes, demonstrations, and demands for political reform became commonplace. But Tsar Nicholas II would hear none of it for the Russia he inherited from his Romanov predecessors. By nature a cautious traditionalist, he interpreted demands for change as treasonous.

Nicholas insisted on continuing Russia's disastrous fight against Germany in World War I; he isolated himself further and further from real conditions in the country and refused to listen to advisors who counseled political and economic reform. His procrustean character rendered him incapable of creative insight or flexibility at a time when only such adaptation could save the crumbling dynasty. The besieged, weary tsar finally abdicated power on March 13, 1917, in the tiny rail town of Dno, which means "the bottom."

Within a matter of months, under the leadership of Vladimir Lenin, the Communists had seized the government and brutally tried to eliminate all rivals. Widespread opposition to Lenin's government organized itself into an armed force, and a full-scale civil war ensued between the Reds (Communists) and Whites (Monarchists). The Russian civil war was to rage for nearly three years before the Reds emerged as victors. Neither Nicholas II nor his family of royal Romanovs lived to witness this culmination of events.

After the March 1917 abdication, Nicholas and his entourage of Romanovs resided for six months at his Tsarskoye Selo palace. Many observers expected that they would be sent to England to reside with royal relatives. British King George V even hastily offered to host the Romanovs but then reneged under pressure from British labor groups. As the civil war heated up, Nicholas and his entourage were sent by Lenin first to Siberia and then to Ekaterinburg in the Ural Mountains—supposedly for safety.

Here they lived for many months under guard in the home of a merchant named Ipatiev. It was suggested by some Communist leaders that Nicholas ought to be tried publicly for crimes committed during his reign. Although the Romanovs were under armed guard during the civil war, the Communists saw them as a potential threat to their shaky government. Nicholas' family symbolized the past order. The Romanovs also represented an alternative government which many saw as more legitimate than the Communist rulers.

In the summer of 1918 it looked as though Ekaterinburg might be taken by the Whites, meaning that the Reds could lose custody of the Romanovs. Lenin's orders were unequivocal: kill the royals. The eleven victims who were awakened and led to the basement at one o'clock A.M. on July 17 included the Tsar, his wife, son, four daughters, their doctor, cook, valet, and housemaid. The victims unknowingly walked into a clumsy execution. Diamonds that the Tsar's daughters had hidden by sewing them into their corsets deflected some of the bullets, forcing the executioners to use bayonets to finish off the young girls.

Personal identification in those days was imprecise. Throughout Russian history the appearance of pretenders to the throne occurred often after the death of royal figures. True to form, pretenders did appear for decades after 1917, but few seemed credible. One persistent rumor, however, had staying power: that Nicholas' youngest daughter, Anastasia, had miraculously escaped the massacre. Royal emigres living in Paris complained of requests for interviews from women claiming to be the "real" Anastasia. The case that captured the fancy of journalists on both sides of the Atlantic was that of Anna Anderson. From the time she first turned up in Berlin in 1920 until her 1984 death, Anna insisted that she was the youngest Romanov daughter.

This scenario of Anastasia the escapee caught on in various fictional venues. First in the form of a French play by Marcelle Maurette, then as successfully adapted to the Broadway stage, then in Hollywood's *Anastasia* (1956), featuring Ingrid Bergman in the title role. Bergman's sympathetic portrayal won her an Oscar for best actress. In addition to its doing well at the box office, the *New York Times* named it one of the year's ten best films. Finally, the story of Anastasia re-surfaced in 1997 as an animated film.

Fueling the rumor mill over the years was the fact that the location of the Romanov bodies remained unknown during seven decades of Communist rule. Then in 1989 a team of researchers uncovered the skeletons outside of Ekaterinburg. Traditional means of skeletal examination of the remains proved inconclusive. But then into the story entered modern science in the form of DNA testing. Could an application of cutting-edge science identify the remains and settle the "Anastasia" question?

A new method of analyzing mitochondrial DNA (found in cells outside the nucleus, it holds up well over time) was used to test the bones at the British forensic science laboratory. By comparing the mitochondrial DNA with blood samples donated by living relatives of the Tsar's family, the 75-year-old mystery was solved. The bones examined do, in fact, constitute the remains of the members of the royal family, including Anastasia. Furthermore, tests done on hair samples of Anna Anderson proved that she was *not* a blood relative of the Romanovs.[18]

The application of DNA testing to forensic science has also begun to affect the outcome of many criminal cases. A total of twenty-eight murder and rape convictions were overturned on the basis of new DNA evidence in American courts between 1989 and 1996, and the use of DNA testing is increasing. In one case, three Northwestern University journalism students conducted a class project which resulted in the release of three men wrongfully imprisoned for a 1978 murder. Northwestern professor David Protess, who specializes in investigative reporting of possible wrongful convictions, unleashed his students—Stacy Delo, Stephanie Goldstein, and Laura Sullivan—on this eighteen-year-old case. Three months later they had uncovered enough evidence challenging the conviction for the prosecutor's office to order DNA testing of the three prisoners, and the DNA evidence exonerated the prisoners.[19]

Conversely, DNA science came to the aid of society in a murder mystery played out in Newtown, Connecticut. In 1986 an airline stewardess named Helle Crafts disappeared without a trace. With no body found, the police remained stymied for a decade. Then forensic scientist Dr. Henry Lee broke the case. Although Helle Crafts' husband had shredded her body with a wood chipper, enough hair was recovered by Dr. Lee for DNA testing and a conviction.[20]

Another worthwhile application of modern science and technology lies in the quest for new ways to disarm the 100,000 land mines that have outlived wars from Angola to Afghanistan. The methods currently practiced resemble those employed by beachcombers looking for lost coins; they will also require 100 years to disarm the kinds of mines that have robbed one of every 134 residents of Cambodia of at least one limb. The luck of thousands of others has been even worse. Researchers at Fort Belvoir and in Berkeley's Lawrence Livermore lab are striving to come to the rescue by testing more than twenty new technologies, including mass spec-

Nervous duty: a technician for the Halo Trust society searching for land mines.

trometry of chemical signatures similar to those used in airport security, bacterial triggers for fluorescent locating, microchips coded to detect vapors from disintegrating mine components, and ground-penetrating radar.

But the issue of dangerous land mines also illustrates how science and humanism overlap. For years efforts to ban land mines went nowhere fast at international conferences. One of the few celebrities to champion the fight against them was Princess Diana of Britain, who was motivated by compassion for the many victims claimed annually. Few emotions come as close to the essence of humanism as that of compassion. Princess Diana's death in a bizarre 1997 car accident ironically generated global interest in the case against land mines almost overnight. Within weeks of her death, a little-known long-time anti-land mine activist named Jody Williams received the prestigious Nobel Peace Prize (worth $1 million in cash) for her efforts. A new international treaty to ban land mines also gained a new lease on life.

Humanism   If all such applications of science to human affairs proved as laudable as those cited above, critics of scientism would likely be few. But the complexity of human behavior creates all manner of problems, opening the door to an alternative vision of the social sciences—humanism. Scientism and humanism each makes contributions to both the content and method of the modern social sciences.

Humanism emphasizes humankind's aesthetic and experiential sides as providing meaningful knowledge. The National Endowment for the Humanities (NEH) considers the humanities to include history, philosophy, linguistics, literature, jurisprudence, comparative religion, and the criticism and theory of the arts. Humanism offers a more personalized mirror of social reality than does scientism. The humanities feature ideas on how to live, providing depth, texture, and meaning to sometimes routine human existence. As social beings, people face troubling moral dilemmas which venues such as literature, film, and theater can help to resolve. Life presents *Homo sapiens* with cloudy paradoxes which the humanities seek to illuminate.

Humanists believe in the value of fresh insights into the human condition as something akin to chicken soup for the spirit. They argue that the search for meaning and enjoyment serves as a palliative to overreliance on cool, detached rationality. Humanistic appreciation of a piece of music, a painting, a film, or a ballet connects directly to human emotions. To some extent, the humanities relate to what many traditional societies considered feminine traits, such as spirituality, emotion, and intuition.

Advocates suggest that the humanities help people to keep their values in proper perspective, a task made difficult by the materialism characteristic of Western civilization today. Like the supporters of scientism, humanists see their expressions of subjective experience as means of communication among all peoples. The key difference, however, is this: for the last century scientism has held center stage in the American social sciences, with humanism relegated to a supporting role.

No comparable triumph of scientism over humanism transpired in Europe, where historical and philosophical analyses have remained paramount. One humanistic scholar decries the American divorce of history from the social sciences as being responsible for a contemporary "United States of Amnesia."[21] Since star billing has gone to scientism, advocates of a more humanized social science have had to serve as the critical opposition. Unlike scientism, humanism considers the differences between natural and social sciences to be a serious matter of *kind*, not of degree. Much of what falls under the rubric of quantitative social science, say the humanists, is better described as **pseudo-science**, practiced by those whom British philosopher of science Bertrand Russell sarcastically caricatures as "slaves of routine who would rather die than think."

Humanistic Critics of Social Science   It would be difficult to find a more persistent and articulate critic of scientism than sociologist Stan Andreski, who claims that "even the old and valuable insights inherited from our illustrious ancestors are being drowned in a torrent of meaningless verbiage and useless technicalities." He considers the rush to quantification responsible for creating a methodological trap of the trivial: in order for human affairs to be measured, only sterile and unimportant questions get asked.[22]

The result can be an "ends/means distortion": what is first valued (methodological complexity) only as a means to a greater end soon becomes valued for its own sake, with the original end (social explanation) getting lost in the shuffle. Humanists consider such methodological exoticism to spring from a mistaken belief that if certain kinds of data can be quantified and analyzed by computer, then these must be more important than those not quantifiable; this is an article of scientistic faith accepted without proof. British statesman Benjamin Disraeli, with tongue in cheek, once described "three kinds of lies: lies, damned lies, and statistics." The social sciences seek the nearest approximation to the truth under the circumstances of the real world. Sometimes that search involves quantification, often it does not.

One of the strongest criticisms of scientism has to do with human free will. Scientific method inherently seeks to uncover regular and predictable patterns of behavior. Science seeks the discovery of underlying laws to explain such recurrent patterns. When the object of investigation is electricity, freon gas, or a spider, all seems right with this method. People, on the other hand, frequently do not follow predictable scripts. They have free will, meaning that they can change their minds, act irrationally, or behave differently than they have in the past. As mixtures of both rational and emotional motivation, humans can choose to experiment with new ways of doing things, even if these fail to make sense to an outside observer. As eighteenth-century German philosopher Immanuel Kant more colorfully put it: "Nothing straight from human timber shall ever be constructed."

The realm of human feelings is one in which humanism claims a special interest. While scientism appeals to the human proclivity toward order and precision, the humanities focus on humanity's equally important penchant for emotional and experiential meaning. Nobel Peace Prize winner and Holocaust expert Elie Wiesel has said that all of his professional activities—including thirty books, hundreds of lectures, university teaching, and the creation of international organizations—boil down to one purpose: helping people to experience *feelings* about the World War II Holocaust in which 6 million innocent Jews died at the hands of the Nazis.[23] Few lives stand as such eloquent testimony to the spirit of humanism.

MINI-CASE 3.2
Pseudo-science Dressed in a Gray Lab Coat:
The Stanley Milgram Experiment

O f the various research designs discussed earlier, none matches the potential scientific elegance of the experimental method. The link between the natural and social sciences never appears stronger than when social scientists are able to apply the controlled conditions of the laboratory experiment. But the practical problems of social experimentation do not exhaust its liabilities. A host of ethical issues bubble to the surface when the subjects are human beings. One intriguing but troubling case is the Stanley Milgram Experiment, named after the Yale University social psychologist who designed it in 1965.

Professor Milgram was interested in testing the thesis that German citizens possess an unusual readiness to obey authority. His plan was, first, to conduct a laboratory experiment concerning obedience to authority in the United States as a control study, and then to take the same experiment to Germany, where he expected to find subjects to be more obedient. He recruited a cross-section of volunteers who were told, falsely, that the experiment had to do with testing a method for teaching people more effectively.

The only ones not informed of the real nature of the experiment were the "teachers," who were told that they were to administer increasing levels of electric shock to "learners," the supposed subjects of the educational experiment. None of the "teachers" knew that they, in fact, were the real subjects of the experiment. The so-called "teachers" were each told by a "scientific researcher" in a laboratory coat to administer what they believed to be live electric shock to "learners" in an adjacent room. The shocks were not real, although the "learners" feigned responses of pain and fear. The experiment was designed to see how far the "teachers" would go in delivering what they believed to be painful electric shock to the "learners."

The results of the experiment actually did shock Professor Milgram in one respect. While he expected only a few isolated subjects to continue administering the supposed jolts beyond the point when "learners" began to groan, scream, and demand to be released, in fact almost two-thirds of the subjects obeyed the authority figure completely and applied the highest, clearly dangerous, level of shock available. Milgram had uncovered such unexpected obedience to authority in Americans that he abandoned plans to move the experiment to Germany.

This experiment, and others like it, have contributed to an ethical firestorm in social science research which rages on today. Professor Milgram lied to the so-called "teachers," who were the real guinea pigs in his experiment within an experiment. Some of them reported being deeply upset by the ruse. Can researchers justify deceit in the quest of knowledge?

Milgram also placed the "teachers" in a highly stressful situation where they had to choose between two unpleasant alternatives: disobey a scientific authority figure or apply increasing levels of shock to the recipients. Could such trauma be damaging to them? Does the experiment violate the human rights of the subjects so badly as to make the master scientist legally culpable? Is deception in the name of scientific method an abuse of the image that the public associates with science?[24]

Negative publicity from such cases as the one described in Mini-case 3.2 has led professional associations such as the American Psychological Association (APA) to adopt voluntary codes of ethics for their members. Further, governments have begun passing legislation specifying rules for the protection of human subjects. Since much research depends on funding from governmental grants, controlling the purse strings is an effective means of getting the attention of insensitive researchers.

MINI-CASE 3.3
Dr. Edward Saenger and "Dual-Use" Experiments

*U*nfortunately, violations of the rights of subjects sometimes go way beyond the moral squirming to which Stanley Milgram exposed his "teachers" (see Mini-case 3.2). In the deadly serious struggle known as the Cold War, American citizens, often without consent, were exposed to high levels of radiation in tests conducted by their own government. From the 1940s to the 1970s more than 4,000 radiation experiments were conducted on tens of thousands of unwitting subjects.

In 1995 the Presidential Advisory Committee on Human Radiation Experiments found that one-third of 125 government-funded human research proposals were "ethically unacceptable." Even more disquieting was the panel's analysis of previously secret Cold War radiation experiments, most of which employed "dual-use" modalities, colloquially referred to as "twofers": (1) radiation as medical treatment for sick patients, and (2) collection of data for the U.S. government on the effects of radiation exposure.

An egregious case cited by the presidential panel is that of Dr. Edward Saenger, a radiologist at the University of Cincinnati, who the Pentagon paid $650,000 from 1960 to 1971 for Total Body Irradiation (TBI) research. Saenger was the only doctor in the United States using TBI on human tumors known to resist radiation, and a recent medical assessment of his work concludes that "he was looking to experiment—not treat their disease." The 1995 presidential panel similarly decries Saenger's research as "morally unconscionable."

Edward Saenger's eighty-eight TBI patients were almost all poor and uneducated, most were black, and their average IQ was 86. Saenger refuses all interview requests but, through his lawyer, claims that the TBI was intended to treat his patients' cancers. His critics counter that his motivation was to supply new information to military planners concerned about the effects of radiation in a possible nuclear war with the Soviet Union.

About half the families of Saenger's patients have sued him for failure to inform the TBI subjects of the gap between risks and benefits in the experiments. The Nuremberg code, adopted worldwide in 1949, as the first international moral expression on the rights of human subjects, condemns experiments on humans without their explicit consent. Like all other expressions of the international conscience, it remains difficult to enforce in an imperfect world.[25]

Summarizing Scientism versus Humanism   Reducing complex phenomena such as the views of scientism and humanism to dichotomous pairs of characteristics carries a risk of oversimplification. Nevertheless, the following list, derived from the preceding discussion, may help to summarize these divergent vantage points on the social sciences.

Scientism	Humanism
quantitative	qualitative
methods	content
verification	insight
experimental	experiential
objective	subjective
reality is absolute	reality is relative
reality is discovered	reality is created
world is orderly	world is paradoxical
rational/logical	emotional/aesthetic
detached	engaged
predictable humans	human free will
descriptive	normative
specificity	generality
physicality	spirituality
impersonal	personal
common sense limited	common sense useful
value-neutral	value-laden
human senses suspect	human senses trusted
newer	older
U.S.-based	European-based

Synthesis: "Roomy" Social Sciences

> There is a community of scholarship between the humanities and the behavioral
> sciences, and the validity of one does not depend upon alienation from the other.
> —Leonard Broom American philosopher

My vision of the social sciences is eclectic: one beholden to both the humanities and the natural sciences. The essence of the social sciences consists of understanding and explaining human behavior, endeavors monopolized by no single approach. Such a roomy definition of the social sciences requires the peaceful coexistence of scientism and humanism, despite their differences.

Many great monuments to human ingenuity point to the fusion of these two tendencies of human nature: scientism and humanism. Consider the marriage of precision and beauty embodied in the 4,500 year-old pyramids of Egyptian civilization or the classic Coliseum of ancient Rome, whose inspiration came partly from the mathematics of numbers then considered divine and partly from emulation of nature.

Architect Frank Lloyd Wright's masterpiece "Fallingwater," built during the 1930s for the wealthy Kauffman family in western Pennsylvania, is considered one of the twentieth century's works of genius. Constructed of sandstone quarried on the property, the stone functions as separate reinforced concrete trays producing three levels of rooms. The whole structure is boldly candilevered over a stream and anchored on a natural boulder: part scientific precision, part aesthetics. The beauty of Fallingwater stems largely from the seamless way in which living space blends into its gorgeous natural surroundings. Only by experiencing Frank Lloyd Wright's creation can you fully understand the way it works both functionally and aesthetically.

It is certainly easy to split scientism and humanism into opposites: verification versus insight, objective versus subjective realities, experimental versus experiential design, and so on. Synthesizing these impulses into cooperative endeavor is much harder. Yet, as the Egyptian pyramids, Roman Coliseum, and Fallingwater suggest, when successfully blended, scientism and humanism can produce a dynamic synergy, tapping the best of both worlds.

Three decades ago philosopher of science Abraham Kaplan advocated a middle position in the social science confrontation between scientists and humanists—not as a "golden mean" compromise to avoid strife, but rather because of the intrinsic value of the synthesis.[26] A recent book by well-known international studies scholar Hayward

The Sphinx, in front of one of the Great Egyptian Pyramids at Giza.

Alker mines this same idea of synthesis. He describes the essence of his intellectual quest as a "philosophical, methodological, and disciplinary preoccupation as a social scientist with somehow voyaging between, connecting up, or finding a bridging place between the humanities and sciences."[27]

The world stage on which the human drama plays itself out has changed at breathtaking speed in recent decades. This mind-bending pace of global change is one of the principal themes repeated throughout these pages. The content of the social sciences certainly has changed toward greater internationalization in recent years. Particularly in the United States, where social scientists have historically exhibited more parochialism than their European counterparts, the shrinking world of interdependence has increased awareness of how each social science discipline is affected by modern global interactions. Beginning with the 1979 presidential commission on international studies and foreign languages, many studies have advocated curricular internationalization; few more potent winds of change have swept across American higher education in the last two decades.

Yet concerning the relationship between scientism and humanism, the social sciences seem frozen in time. During the one-third of a century between the clarion call for a more integrated social science by Abraham Kaplan and Hayward Alker's echo of that plea, many social scientists continue to conduct their business with so little shared between scientism and humanism that they might as well be speaking Greek and Latin to one another. But in those instances where knowledge and insight from these two schools are shared, good things tend to happen. This textbook sows a few seeds in this elusive but fertile middle ground.

Chapter Synopsis

To know who we are as a species, we must have some idea of where we came from. Our relevant prehistory runs from the time when humanlike *hominids* climbed down from trees and maximized their prospects for survival by beginning to walk upright. Then roughly 10,000 years ago the agricultural revolution led nomadic hunters and gatherers to settle down in one place. This time of great change soon led to the first written records. Within a few thousand years of the agricultural revolution humans created ancient civilizations in advanced places like China, Egypt, and Persia. With the fall of the Roman Empire in the fifth century A.D. the ancient civilizations gave way to the 1,000-year period known as the Middle Ages, in which the Church played a central role in all aspects of European life. The last 500 years is referred to as Modernity and began with the Renaissance—an

intellectual rebirth of the rationalism and critical thinking deriving from ancient Greek scholars. While both Greek scholars such as Plato and Aristotle and Renaissance giants such as Copernicus and Martin Luther often addressed issues of social, political, or economic import, they did so from the perspectives of historical or philosophical analysis, not in the way that we think of social scientific inquiry today.

Even today the social sciences in Europe emphasize the time-honored tradition of historico-philosophical analysis of human affairs. It is primarily in America, where higher education in the social sciences is uniquely big business, that discrete professional disciplines emphasizing scientific methods have developed during the past century. Prior to the 1880s, higher education in the United States occurred entirely in small liberal arts colleges funded and influenced by religious organizations. As universities sprang up at the end of the nineteenth century, new graduate programs in the nascent social sciences (first sociology, political science, and economics) emulated the laboratory techniques and seminar discussions modeled by natural sciences like chemistry and biology. Massive growth has characterized the Americanized social sciences in the last 100 years.

The roots of the social sciences reach deeply into the fertile soil provided by the older natural sciences and humanities. From these sources come two competing philosophical schools of thought affecting the social sciences in their study of human behavior: scientism and humanism. Scientism emphasizes quantification, empiricism, systematic inquiry, verifiability, and a skeptical attitude concerning commonsensical beliefs. Humanism values historico-philosophical analysis as well as the wisdom of insights derived from personal experience and aesthetic appreciation. Scientism has been the majority viewpoint and humanism the loyal opposition during the last 100 years when the social sciences have been effectively Americanized in their methods. While these two camps have often denied each other's legitimacy, this text seeks a roomier definition of the social sciences which recognizes the debt they owe to both sets of intellectual progenitors.

For Digging Deeper

Alker, Hayward R. *Rediscoveries and Reformulations: Humanistic Methodologies for International Studies.* Cambridge University Press, 1996.

Andreski, Stanislav. *Social Science as Sorcery.* St. Martin's Press, 1973.

Babbie, Earl. *The Practice of Social Research.* Wadsworth, 1995.

Bannister, Robert C. *Sociology and Scientism: The American Quest for Objectivity, 1880–1940.* University North Carolina Press, 1987.

Campbell, Bernard. *Humankind Emerging.* Little, Brown, 1988.

Cuba, Lee. *A Short Guide to Writing about Social Science.* Longman, 1997.

Davis, Kenneth C. *Don't Know Much About History.* Avon Books, 1996.

Eastoy, David, and Corrine Schelling. *Divided Knowledge Across Disciplines, Across Cultures.* Sage, 1991.

Edel, Abraham. *Relating Humanities and Social Thought.* Transaction, 1990.

Hoover, Kenneth R. *The Elements of Social Scientific Thinking.* St. Martin's Press, 1992.

Kirsch, George B., et al. *The West in Global Context: From 1500 to the Present.* Prentice Hall, 1997.

Kishlansky, Mark, Patrick Geary, and Patrick O'Brien. *The Unfinished Legacy: A Brief History of Western Civilization.* Addison Wesley Longman, 1997.

Kuhn, Thomas S. *The Structure of Scientific Revolutions.* University Chicago Press, 1970.

Lastrucci, Carlo L. *The Scientific Approach.* Schenkman Publishing, 1967.

Leakey, Mary. *Disclosing the Past.* Doubleday, 1984.

Manicas, Peter T. *A History and Philosophy of the Social Sciences.* Blackwell Publishers, 1987.

Rosenberg, Alexander. *Philosophy of Social Science.* Westview, 1995.

Ross, Dorothy. *The Origins of American Social Science.* Cambridge University Press, 1991.

Tarnas, Richard. *The Passion of the Western Mind.* Ballantine Books, 1991.

Wells, H. G. *An Outline of History.* Doubleday, 1971.

Internet

Humanities on Line (H-Net) http://h-net.msu.edu

Key Glossary Terms

case study	historicism	scientism
civilization	Islam	serf
content analysis	participant observation	survey research
Crusades	Protestant Reformation	theory
Enlightenment	pseudo-science	utopia
experimental design	rationalism	validity
fact	Renaissance	
feudalism	scientific theory	

CHAPTER **4**

Rise and Decline
of the Nation–State

Thematic Questions

- In what ways do domestic and international politics differ?

- What is the meaning of realism versus idealism?

- How is the contemporary international scene heterogeneous?

- From what origins does the nation–state system spring?

- How has humanity attempted to control the ravages of war?

CORE OBJECTIVE:

To examine
the evolution
of the
nation–state
system,
how realism
and idealism
serve as
meta-theories
of international
relations, and
what legacy
of war
humanity
has inherited.

Political scientist Harold Lasswell's definition of politics as the study of "who gets what, when, and how" speaks to the essence of competition in the political process. Similarly, when Robert Dahl describes the "authoritative allocation of values" and Michael Sego asks, "who gets the cookies," the core to which they all refer is *power*—the currency of politics.[1] Austin Ranney observes that "politics everywhere involves conflict.[2]" But since world affairs operate in less controllable circumstances than domestic politics, the use of power to achieve international goals is especially vital in that more chaotic milieu. The competitive stakes also become magnified in a world where scarcity is the norm, adding to the willingness of actors on the world stage to exercise whatever power they find at their disposal.

Returning once more to our world stage metaphor: if geography represents the physical props, and society constitutes the company of players, and culture is the coherent script, then political decision making expresses itself in the authoritative roles of director and producer of the drama. As the social science that concentrates on power, authority, and conflict, political science contributes much to our traditional understanding of the nation–state system. One of the discipline's four subfields, international relations, specializes in studying how nations interact. However, political scientist James Rosenau argues in his *Turbulence in World Politics* that a new troupe of actors has emerged parallel to the nation–state. These actors deal mostly with global issues in an age of interdependence—an entirely new realm to which political scientists have only slowly adapted.[3]

REALISM VERSUS IDEALISM

Two broad theories, **realism** and **idealism**, underpin most people's views on specific issues of world affairs. Personal preferences regarding these theories help shape our day-to-day opinions about the complex world in which we live. In skeletal form, realism and idealism can be contrasted on various dimensions:[4]

Idealism	Realism
optimistic about human nature	pessimistic about human nature
focus on values and ethics	focus on pragmatism
see cooperation as key to human interaction	see competition as key to human interaction
belief in power of ideas	belief in power of action
human rights central to foreign policy	human rights tangential to foreign policy
religion relevant to policy	religion separate
national interest = doing what is right	national interest = power maximization
minority U.S. view since World War II	majority U.S. view since World War II
favors arms reductions	favors security through strength
patience of long-term view	short-term view
famous proponents: Woodrow Wilson, Quincy Wright, Jimmy Carter, Cyrus Vance	famous proponents: Hans Morgenthau, Richard Nixon, HenryKissinger, George Shultz

These descriptions represent **ideal types**. Most people are unlikely to fit either category any more perfectly than they would the ideal types of liberalism and conservatism in American domestic politics. But this qualification does not preclude their usefulness in analyzing either context. Humanistic social scientists probably lean in the direction of idealism's hopefulness, social conscience, and penchant for subjectivity, while scientific colleagues feel more comfortable with realism's skepticism, action orientation, and objectivity. Like **yin and yang**, we need both in order to see the full horizon of human experience.

Traditionally, realism has been the prevailing outlook, both globally and in the United States. Idealism has proven resilient, however, and gained the ascendancy for short periods, particularly after the devastation of major wars has encouraged pacifist perspectives. In the United States, twentieth-century idealism first flourished under President Woodrow Wilson's Fourteen Points and during the anti-war feelings in the 1920s following World War I. Its spirit of cooperation later helped launch the United Nations after World War II, then thrived when Jimmy Carter emphasized human rights in his late-1970s presidency, and has more recently rebounded after the Cold War's demise.

Former Secretary of State, and spokesman for Realpolitik in foreign policy, Henry Kissinger.

Henry Kissinger's Realism

The most authoritative modern proponent of realism, Henry Kissinger, former secretary of state under Presidents Richard Nixon and Gerald Ford, contends in his massive tome *Diplomacy* (1994) that America needs less idealism and more *Realpolitik*. According to Kissinger, the United States must define its vital interests conservatively, set clear priorities, and avoid getting bogged down in most of the ethnic and religious conflicts of the post-Cold War: "Not every evil can be combated by America, even less by America alone." While recognizing that the world has changed significantly, he suggests that the basic determinant of world order does not change. World order will always spring from the "balancing of competing national interests," says Kissinger.[5]

Woodrow Wilson's Idealism

No comparable spokesperson epitomizes modern idealism. However, this century's first idealist voice was also its greatest—that of Woodrow Wilson. He once claimed that "America is the only idealistic nation in the world."[6] "Making the world safe for democracy," in his memorable phrase, demands much of the United States. Wilson favored a world system of **collective security** to maintain the peace. The first such experiment, the League of Nations, was Wilson's brainchild, but it ended in failure. Its post-World War II successor, the United Nations, benefited from the earlier experience of the League of Nations and provided the international community with a viable global forum.

Woodrow Wilson also believed that, for global democracy to succeed, the United States needed to support ethnic **self-determination**. The self-determination of peoples is a laudable principle, but one that is sometimes difficult to implement; it has become especially problematic amid the uncertainties characteristic of the post-Cold War. Equally optimistic was Wilson's belief in an evolving international body of law, whereby nation–states would come to accept universal rules of the game as meaningful and desirable.[7] Among recent prominent political scientists recognizing the importance of idealism is Charles Kegley, whose 1993 presidential address to the International Studies Association suggests that "classical realism to the contrary, human nature is subject to modification and not permanently governed by an eradicable lust for power."[8]

NATION + STATE + COUNTRY = NATION–STATE

Like a **culture**, a *nation* consists of a group of people with shared characteristics and a common identity. But the nation is a group with an attitude—a political attitude. Members of a nation want their identity recognized in official ways by similarly constituted groups. Under international law, the entity empowered to represent the nation and to extend recognition to other actors is the *state*. As a juridical concept, the state is abstract rather than concrete. The term generally used to identify the turf or the physical space of a legally recognized nation is the *country*.

In a perfect world a distinct nation of people would blend smoothly with a legally recognized state and exist neatly in a specific physical country. Taken collectively, these pieces add up to what we call the *nation–state*, the dominant actor on the world stage in recent centuries. In relatively rare nation–states, including Japan, France, China, and Poland, nation, state, and country fit snugly together in this manner as homogeneous entities.

A Mostly Heterogeneous World

Unfortunately, the fit between nation, state, and country seldom works as smoothly as in Japan, France, China, or Poland. Many nations of people, like the Kurds, Palestinians, and Chechens, desperately wait for legal recognition as states entitled to representation in world affairs; they wait in vain. These dissatisfied peoples live in nation–states where they feel like repressed minorities. The 25 million Kurds in Iraq, Iran, Turkey, and elsewhere make up one of the largest such groups. Many Palestinians live as legal aliens in Jordan, Syria, or Egypt. The Chechens in the Caucasus mountains of southern Russia have been so disgruntled as to fight a civil war against the huge Russian army. The great majority of nation–states today consist of heterogeneous mixtures, as in Malaysia, the United States, India, and Brazil. The Japans, Frances, Chinas, and Polands of the world are rare exceptions.[9]

Mel Gibson's popular, Oscar-winning film *Braveheart* (1995) poignantly recounts the crosscurrents of loyalties that beset the movement for Scottish nationalism in the thirteenth century. In it, director Gibson also stars as the steadfast Scottish nationalist, William Wallace, who is subjected to humiliation, treachery, torture, and execution for his defiance of an English king intent on subjugating the Scots. While clearly identifying themselves as a nation, the Scots have never managed to make it on the world scene as a bona fide nation–state. Rather, in one form or another, they have typically had to settle for minority status in a larger union led by an English majority. What, exactly, is the nature of the modern nation–state that was referred to as England until 1800, then as Britain, and more recently as the United Kingdom? (See Mini-case 4.1.)

MINI-CASE 4.1
The United Kingdom: Four into One

What is properly known as the United Kingdom consists of four nations of people with a total population of 58 million: England, Wales, Scotland, and Northern Ireland. The largest and most powerful nation, England, managed by military and diplomatic means over many centuries to consolidate the four into one nation–state. For citizens of the minority nations, this situation meant maintaining dual loyalties: (1) the ethnic, religious, and linguistic identities lying closest to their hearts, and (2) the economic and security loyalties to a necessary evil in the form of the United Kingdom. People may not be capable of holding directly conflicting loyalties, but we are clearly capable of feeling divided identities to two or more groups.

In the southwest, Wales was the first to be formally linked to England, in 1284; Scotland to the north officially joined the union in 1707; the entire island of Ireland to the west was subdued by the 1800 Act of Union and remained so until 1921. Then, badly shaken by its losses in World War I, London decided to accord independence to the lower three-quarters of the Irish island. The northern quarter has remained part of the U.K. as Northern Ireland. While most Welsh and Scots would like their nationalities to enjoy more independence from English power, no serious threat of violence toward that end has materialized in many decades. But the saga of Northern Ireland has followed quite another script.

What local residents refer to innocuously as the "Troubles" has been a quarter-century cycle of bloodshed, recrimination, and retaliation between Catholic and Protestant factions. The Protestant majority in Northern Ireland are mostly Loyalists, meaning loyal to the British government and favoring Northern Ireland's staying in the United

Figure 4.1

Kingdom. The Glorious Revolution (1688–1689) officially elevated Protestantism as the religion of Britain. By American standards, 300 years probably seems the equivalent of national eternity. For the British it seems more like yesterday: witness the violence annually accompanying the celebratory parade down the streets of Belfast, Northern Ireland, in which the Protestants remind Catholics of their defeat in 1689.

Predictably, the Catholic minority in Northern Ireland feels much more natural affinity with their co-religionists to the immediate south in the independent Republic of Ireland. Many Northern Ireland Catholics are poor and consider themselves a repressed minority. Not surprisingly, some believe they have little to lose and consider any change likely to bring improvement. The Irish Republican Army (IRA) finds such minds fertile soil for planting their seeds of violent solutions to the problems of the Catholics.[10]

So if most nation–states are heterogeneous, and even the most successful and affluent ones, like the United Kingdom, are subject to prolonged domestic violence threatening their sense of unity, in what kind of general condition does that leave the nation–state? The health of this aging actor—the most important actor on the world stage for 350 years—cannot be considered in any way a trivial matter. Some political scientists, such as Seyom Brown, see the present nation–state in a "crisis of incongruence" and unlikely to emerge in decent shape.[11] Others, such as Hendrik Spruyt, consider the nation–state to be more adept than other actors on the scene at dealing with the complex changes required by an interdependent world.[12] Such widespread disagreement characterizes the discipline's prognosis for the nation–state. Describing where it came from is much easier than prescribing where it is going.

Emergence of the Nation–State System

To our contemporaries, the nation–state's domination of the world stage seems tantamount to forever. Yet when contrasted with the long-running human drama, the nation–state is a relatively recent phenomenon. The nation–state system evolved out of European experience, beginning loosely in the fifteenth century and coalescing around the 1648 Peace of Westphalia, which brought closure to the bloody Thirty Years War, as was mentioned in Chapter 2.

Beginning with the fall of the Roman Empire in 476 A.D., power was exercised on two separate levels in Europe for 1,000 years. At the pan-European level, the Pope's Catholic Church represented the most important source of political as well as spiritual power. On the local level, feudalism reigned in the guise of fiefdoms, baronies, and principalities—all run by minor royalty who were quite independent within their limited sphere.

By the fourteenth century, however, both Papal central authority and the power of local royalty began weakening. Small fiefdoms could no longer provide safety in light of new military inventions, especially gunpowder. Then during the Renaissance (1350–1650) a new idea, individual freedom, swept across Europe like a tornado, challenging the central autocracy of the Catholic Church. These opposing forces culminated in the Thirty Years War (1618–1648). The 1648 Peace of Westphalia established the legitimacy of secular political authority and ended the Catholic Church's political dominance of Europe. From these humble beginnings sprang the consolidation of fiefdoms and principalities into the modern nation–state.[13]

The major nations conducting the negotiations at Westphalia and agreeing to respect each other's sovereignty were Sweden, France, Spain, and the newly emergent Netherlands. The nation–state's autonomy within its territorial borders, or sovereignty, enabled it to operate as an independent actor. The weakening of the Catholic Church as a pan-European force led to intense nation–state competition in this newly decentralized political environment. With sovereignty in hand and no central authority above it, the nation–state could compete at will over pieces of territory, economic assets, trade routes, or, later on, colonial possessions. Although these European nation–states worked out agreements to promote peace, power was really what counted most. All nation–states spent power as the main currency to pursue their interests. Those having less tried to increase their power as best they could. Competition for power has characterized nation–state behavior in the international system since the seventeenth century.

The nation–state system was a European invention and this region has always benefited most from its creation. Peoples of the African region have probably identified least with the nation–state, partly because it was imposed upon them by colonial oppressors and partly because the nation–states created there are grossly at variance with traditional ethnic and tribal loyalties among nomadic African peoples. Latin America probably falls roughly in the middle of these two extremes: benefiting from the nation–state system far less than Europeans, but not faring as abysmally as the nations of Africa. What is the point? The history of the nation–state system has been one of extremely uneven winners and losers.

War's Devastating Legacy

International competition has seen dramatic increases in both the number and severity of **wars**. About 1,000 wars (minimum 1,000 deaths) have been counted over the last 1,000 years, forming an odd confluence of death around the number 1,000. At least 150 million people have died in those wars, 75 percent of them, or 111 million, in the twentieth century alone.[14]

An incredible 53 million died in World War II, 27 million of whom were Soviet citizens. America's greatest losses were incurred in its Civil War, where it lost more than in World Wars I and II, Korea, and Vietnam combined. International relations scholar George Kohn lists more than 1,700 entries in his *Dictionary of Wars*, which covers the time from 2000 B.C. to 1980.[15] Another study, measuring somewhat differently, concludes that during fifty centuries of human "civilization," war has been raging somewhere on earth 94 percent of the time. Since World War II many smaller wars and internal conflicts have exploded, with a total of 127 wars from 1945 to 1991, an average of 2.8 per year, leaving only six years when a new war did not begin.[16]

Particularly since the breakup of the Soviet empire, civil disturbances have increased in number, with about thirty going on in 1997. One study identifies almost 150 significant ethnic, religious, or cultural conflicts from 1958 to 1976 alone.[17] The decade between 1985 and 1995 saw 2 million children die in wars, one million others were orphaned, and 12 million were left homeless, in an era when an unbelievable 90 percent of war deaths were made up of civilians, up from 50 percent a few decades before. From 1980–1988 the African countries of Angola and Mozambique lost 33,000 and 490,000 children respectively to war-related caus-

Figure 4.2   890 Years of War Death, 1110-1993

This figure shows the long-term trend in the rise of both the frequency and severity of war. Beginning in the year 1100, the number of wars in each century has usually increased. The total for the twentieth century has declined from that of the nineteenth century, but new wars have increased this century's total since Eckhardt's study, which only went through the end of 1989. The soaring death toll of this century's wars, which account for 75 percent of the millennium's total, is truly a alarming figure.

Source: John T. Rourke, *International Politics on the World Stage* (Dushkin, 1995), p. 389. *Data Sources:* William Eckhardt, "War Related Deaths since 3000 B.C.," *Peace Research*, 23 (1991), 80–85; author. Eckhardt defines a war as a conflict that (1) involves a government on at least one side and (2) accounts for at least 1,000 deaths per year of the conflict.

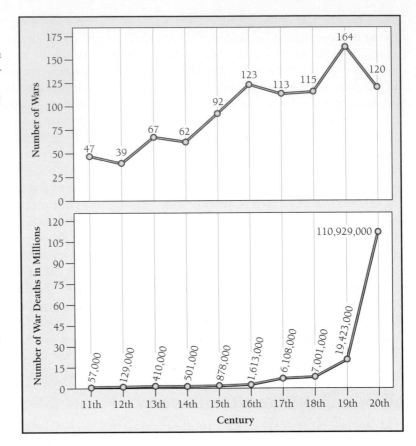

es.[18] Such figures lend credence to Karl von Clausewitz's famous dictum, "war is a continuation of political commerce by other means."[19] Equally discouraging is the Morgenthau proposition, named after a well-known realist scholar, which says that "Nations active in international politics are continuously preparing for, actively engaged in, or recovering from organized violence in the form of war."[20]

Religion and State Violence

War wasn't always accepted as a routine endeavor. Strong pre-Christian **pacifist** sentiments can be clearly identified, such as the passage from Isaiah in the Hebrew Scripture which advocates nations "beating their swords into plowshares and their spears into pruning hooks." More directly relevant to the European experience, however, is the moral imperative expressed by Jesus Christ in his Sermon on the Mount:

> You have heard that they were told, "You must love your neighbor and hate your enemy." But I tell you, love your enemies and pray for your persecutors, so that you may show yourselves true sons of your Father in heaven, for He makes the sun rise on the bad with the good alike, and makes the rain fall on the upright and the wrongdoers.[21]

Until the fourth century these passages carried great weight among Christian thinkers protesting against acts of war by the state. However, the Christian conversion of emperor Constantine, establishing a Roman unity of church and state, greatly changed the role of Christianity. Christian theologians gradually buried the fifth Commandment's ("thou shalt not kill") application to wars, coming gradually to settle upon a distinction between two separate categories of war: **just wars** and unjust wars.

History of Just War Doctrine

Of course, those wars waged on behalf of Christendom's empire against infidels represented just wars. This evolution of the Church's position on war greatly facilitated most subsequent wars, especially the eight Crusades (1095–1291) fought to recapture the Holy City of Jerusalem from Muslims, and then the bloody religious wars unleashed by the Protestant Reformation (1517), pitting Protestant against Catholic for a century prior to the Peace of Westphalia in 1648.[22] Catholicism, Protestantism, Judaism, and Islam all developed a "just war" concept. Principles gradually incorporated into the body of international law included **discrimination** (no hostilities between civilians and combatants), **proportionality** (violence not to exceed injury suffered), **just cause** (good reason), and **option of last resort** (options exhausted).

Traditional international law evolved into two separate bodies, the laws of war and the laws of peace, with a declaration of war necessary to activate the rules of war. The father of international law, seventeenth century Dutch jurist Hugo Grotius, in his landmark work, *On the Law of War and Peace*, considered resorting to just war as a normal means of redressing grievances once other approaches had failed. The 1991 Persian Gulf War was noteworthy for the time and effort devoted to framing it within the confines of just war doctrine (see Mini-case 4.2).

MINI-CASE 4.2
1991 Persian Gulf War: Just Another Just War?

After stockpiling arms during his stalemated war with Iran (1980–1988), Iraqi dictator Saddam Hussein possessed the world's fourth largest conventional military force, boasting a million troops. Apparently believing that the United States would not intervene against him, on August 2, 1990, Saddam unleashed his experienced military forces against the tiny but affluent neighbor of Kuwait, crushing its weak defenses in a matter of days. This action put Saddam in control of 20 percent of the world's oil reserves; it also placed him in a strategic position for a possible invasion of oil-giant Saudi Arabia.

Saddam Hussein rationalized his aggression by claiming that Kuwait had violated limits on oil drilling set by the Organization of Petroleum Exporting Countries (OPEC). He said that Kuwait had engaged in oblique-line drilling, illegally stealing Iraqi oil from the Rumali oil field; he argued that Kuwait was the long-lost nineteenth province of greater Iraq, now returning home. The real reasons for his attack, however, had to do mostly with oil, Iraqi access to the Persian Gulf, and enhanced power for Saddam in the Middle Eastern balance of forces.

The United States had sold military hardware to Iraq during the Iranian war. Presidents Ronald Reagan and George Bush had subtly tilted toward Iraq with a policy of mixed messages: expressing neutrality in official statements but leaning toward Iraq with aid and private assurances of common interests. The United States had gone so far as to look the other way and say precious little when in 1988 Saddam Hussein unleashed illegal chemical weapons against Kurdish citizens in a northern Iraqi town, killing over 5,000 innocent people.

Making matters worse, the U.S. ambassador to Iraq, April Glaspie, had been conveying vague messages to Saddam Hussein concerning the U.S. position on tensions mounting between Iraq and Kuwait during the summer of 1990. Saddam decided to gamble: given the absence either of any clear U.S. criticism of Iraq's provocations, or of statements of commitment to Kuwaiti sovereignty, he assumed President Bush would reluctantly accept an invasion of Kuwait as a *fait accompli* and do nothing more than complain about it. He assumed incorrectly.

President Bush, energized in ways not otherwise apparent during his presidency, reacted with determination. With North America, Europe, and Japan all dependent upon Persian Gulf oil, Bush and his advisors believed that Saddam could not be allowed to remain

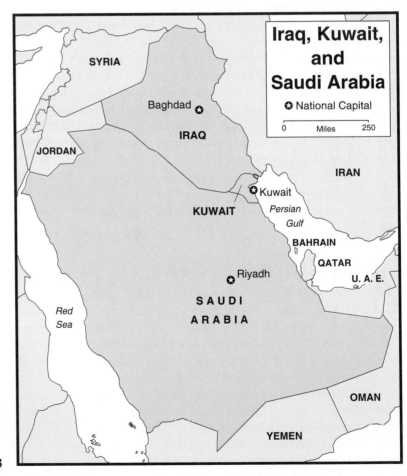

Figure 4.3

atop so much oil. Another danger was the sudden proximity of Iraqi troops to Saudi Arabia; its capture would give Saddam about half of known global reserves. The economic effects of the Iraqi invasion quickly rippled across all the world's oceans. Affluent financial investors took a beating as the Wall Street stock market plunged in response to the invasion; average Americans felt like they had been hosed when gas prices jumped at pumps across the U.S.

While it seemed clear to President Bush that Saddam's seizure of Kuwaiti real estate and its oil could not be tolerated, he knew only too well that leading a democracy into war requires deft salesmanship, particularly with searing memories of the Vietnam debacle still vivid in America's consciousness. What could Bush do to generate support for a war against Iraq? One thing he did early and effectively was to involve the United Nations directly in the decision making, making it the world community against Iraq, not simply the United States versus Iraq. With the Cold War over, no real Russian opposition to his efforts materialized, despite Russia's thirty-year alliance with Iraq. Numerous U.N. Security Council resolutions provided global legitimacy for Bush's efforts. The U.N. also imposed an economic **embargo** against Iraq as punishment.

The most direct effects on Americans were economic. Bush's Secretary of State, James Baker, tried to sell a war against Iraq on the basis of the price of gas at the pump, and what he called, "jobs, jobs, jobs." These were vital issues, but somehow not the stuff of which American wars are made. Americans generally want a loftier justification for war than the obvious economic one. Clear majority support for a U.S.-led war to liberate Kuwait did not materialize until President Bush carried the argument beyond self-interest and provided a moral imperative for action. That moral imperative rested squarely on the concept of just war, which Bush referred to often in public statements. He also brought Christian evangelist Billy Graham physically to his side while making his case. The President's message? The bully, Saddam Hussein, had engaged in naked aggression against a helpless ally in Kuwait. As in the past, America would make sacrifices to do the right thing: it would lead a war effort based upon Christian just war principles.

While a small minority in Congress and elsewhere continued to advocate economic sanctions instead of military action, once Bush had demonized Saddam Hussein as "the worst dictator since Hitler" and had justified war in Christian terms, momentum built toward the crescendo of Operation Desert Storm. From January 17 to February 27, 1991, the U.S.-led Gulf Coalition battered Iraq in two stages: (1) a massive bombing campaign comprising tens of thousands of sorties, and (2) a 100–hour ground attack begun on February 24 which out-flanked the Iraqis and easily compelled their surrender.

THE NUCLEAR DILEMMA

As if humanity's legacy of conventional war were not enough, the Cold War arms race created an **overkill** capability in nuclear weaponry. The superpower combined stockpiles peaked at roughly 17 trillion tons of nuclear TNT equivalency, in the form of 33,000 warheads. Such firepower

US. Civil Defense drills at the peak of the Cold War used a catchy song called 'Duck and Cover' to teach school children how to react to a nuclear attack.

amounted to one billion times the U.S. atomic bomb dropped on Hiroshima in 1945.[23] Most of those missiles carried one, three or, five-**megaton** bombs; however, the Soviets actually tested a mammoth fifty-megaton bomb in 1954.

To provide such mega-numbers with some contextual feel, consider this. The Hiroshima **A-bomb** of August 6, 1945, a twenty-**kiloton** bomb, killed roughly 100,000 people. This twenty-kiloton bomb represents a mere one-fiftieth of a one-megaton hydrogen bomb—relatively small by modern **H-bomb** standards. With U.S. and Soviet Cold War arsenals possessing about forty times overkill capacity, British statesman Winston Churchill once asked, with tongue in cheek, "How many times do we need to make the rubble bounce?"

Balance of Terror

The bizarre psychology of the nuclear standoff amounted to a mutual suicide pact. This **balance of terror** was meant to deter each side from attacking the other, because any nuclear attack would be met by in-kind retaliation. In one crucial sense this superpower understanding, called **mutually assured destruction (MAD)**, worked: no nuclear war occurred between the Americans and Soviets during the Cold War. In another sense, this fact may contribute to the illogical belief on the part of many people that because it hasn't happened yet, it won't. With the Cold War now safely tucked away in the annals of history, it is tempting to forget about nuclear war as a serious global dilemma.

It is also easy to forget just how deadly seriously Americans and Soviets took nuclear war back in the 1950s and 1960s. They built fallout shelters and practiced civil defense drills to ease their fears. Schoolchildren were taught songs telling them to "Duck and Cover" if they heard the fateful siren of nuclear war. I remember a hopelessly inadequate fallout shelter in the basement of my parents' home. Documentary films like *Atomic Cafe* (1982) convey the palpable terror, as well as the absurdity, of many popular reactions to the threat.[24]

Nuclear Avoidance

As much as possible, Americans tried to avoid thinking about the subject of nuclear war. The Hollywood film industry, often a sensitive barometer of popular attitudes, ignored nuclear war for the twenty tensest years of the Cold War. A few films in the 1950s, such as Arch Oboler's *Five* (1951) and Peter Kramer's *On the Beach* (1959), were brave enough to imagine a post-holocaust world, although not actually nuclear war itself. Not until 1964, two years after the

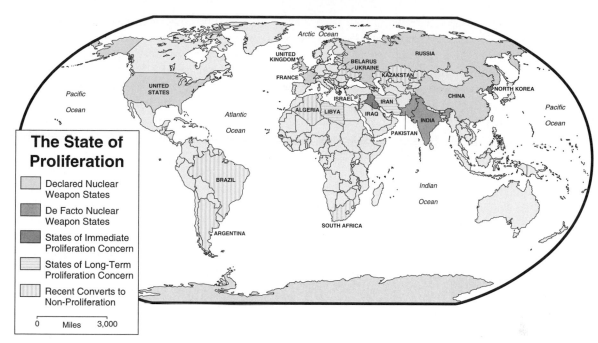

Figure 4.4   Nuclear States and the States Likely to Join the Nuclear Club

A number of countries are capable of producing nuclear weapons on short notice and are regarded as probable candidates for joining the "nuclear club" of declared nuclear weapon states. Others, such as Sweden, have long possessed the capability, but few experts consider them likely to seize the option. This map pictures the state of nuclear proliferation in June 1996.

Source: Charles Kegley & Eugene A. Wittkopf, *World Politics: Trends and Transformation* (St. Martin's, 1997), pp. 396-97. Projections based on predictions provided by the Arms Control Association in June 1996.

real-world warning provided by the Cuban missile crisis, did Hollywood dare look directly into the nuclear fireball. Looking to the arts likely seems too subjective a technique for scientifically oriented professors. But to humanistic social scientists, turning to the arts for insights into the human condition makes sense. Stanley Kubrick's *Dr. Strangelove* and Sidney Lumet's *Fail Safe* broke Hollywood's nuclear taboo in 1964.

Dr. *Strangelove* did so with unrelenting sardonic humor, making a mockery of the logic underpinning nuclear deterrence through MAD. Its ending? Totally insane nuclear destruction. *Fail Safe*, on the other hand, dissected the topic more coolly and hopefully, allowing rational heads to prevail. Although escalation to total annihilation was averted, the cities of Moscow and New York were destroyed by an unintended attack unleashed by a mechanical failure: pretty awful, but at least *not* total Armageddon.

Nuclear Proliferation and the Post-Cold War

The superpowers—and the world—made it through the Cold War without a comparable real-world calamity. Since the demise of the Soviet Union and end of the Cold War, fear of nuclear confrontation has been eased by amicable American–Russian relations, treaties reducing nuclear warheads, and the status of the United States as the only superpower with a global military reach. Most people do not worry about nuclear war between China, France, Great Britain, Russia, or the United States today. Yet good reasons seem to exist for concern over the prospects of **nuclear proliferation** at the regional level. While Ukraine, Kazakhstan, and Belarus (of the former Soviet Union) have pledged to turn their nuclear weapons over to the Russians or to destroy them, several regional rivalries could escalate to nuclear confrontation: India and Pakistan, Israel and her Arab neighbors, North and South Korea, China and Taiwan, Brazil and Argentina.

Figure 4.4 describes the status of the world's nuclear and near-nuclear states. India became the first undeclared nuclear nation in 1974. Neighboring Pakistan, then Israel, soon followed suit. In the 1990s Iraq, North Korea, and Iran have tried to develop nuclear bombs. The latter three countries are undemocratic and hostile toward the West. To many nuclear experts, this is the crux of the post-Cold War problem: how to keep nuclear weapons out of the hands of unpredictable dictators in countries like Iraq, North Korea, and Iran. What can be done about this problem? There are two main groups of responses: (1) direct approaches taking the issue head-on, usually via international treaty, and (2) indirect approaches, based on the belief that the proliferation problem will take care of itself if other more basic issues are resolved.

The Direct Approach to Peace

The emphasis of the direct approach has been to seek a permanent extension for the Nuclear Non-Proliferation Treaty (NNPT), which was established in 1970 for a 25-year period and signed by 90 percent of all countries. The NNPT requires nonnuclear powers to pledge not to seek these weapons, but it does allow nuclear states to share resources for the peaceful use of nuclear energy, and it binds nonnuclear states to allow unannounced inspections by the International Atomic Energy Agency (IAEA). In 1995, the Clinton Administration led a successful campaign for permanent extension of the NNPT.

World leaders gathered in New York City in 1995 to sign the permanent extension of the Nuclear Non-Proliferation Treaty (NNPT).

Another part of the treaty binds the nuclear states to work toward setting a date for eventual nuclear disarmament. That has not yet happened. Even if something as unlikely as total nuclear disarmament were to occur, humanity would not cease being burdened with a genuine dilemma: we can never unlearn the nuclear secret; we are stuck with this knowledge as irrevocably as any other once unknown to us, like how to vaccinate against polio. The capability to destroy itself will accompany the human race into the future. Idealists among us favor exploring all creative avenues to defuse the nuclear risk: arms control treaties, disarmament talks, international organizations addressing the issue, or grass roots efforts to change popular attitudes. Realists, however, skeptical of so-called do-gooders, believe that such efforts are pointless, since people and nations use power to enhance their own interests, not some abstract vision of the global good.

The Indirect Approach: Richard Rosecrance on Nuclear Abstainers

Many indirect ideas on beating the nuclear proliferation problem have also been advanced. Some argue that if the north–south economic gap can be reduced, much of the impetus for proliferation will be removed. Others suggest that encouraging democracy worldwide will help. An interesting idea has been developed by political scientist Richard Rosecrance, who believes that countries who could possibly build a bomb will decide that doing so is not in their national interests. His reasons for arriving at this conclusion warrant a closer look.

According to Professor Rosecrance, "the genie is not yet out of the bottle" concerning nuclear proliferation, and a variety of factors, other than the NNPT, work against new countries taking the nuclear plunge. First, he says, there are the many examples of "nuclear abstainers"—countries who could have developed nukes but didn't—like Canada, Switzerland, Sweden, Germany, Italy, Japan, Australia, Taiwan, and many others. They did not see it as in their interests to undertake the expense and risk of nuclear weapons production. Equally notable is the case of South Africa, a recent demobilizer of its nuclear stockpile consisting of six bombs, which have since been converted to civilian power projects.

Rosecrance believes that thinking about the utility of nuclear weapons has undergone a massive change since the height of the Cold War. Although it was once believed that nuclear weapons would deter not only nuclear attacks but conventional ones as well, the history of the past five decades reveals that nuclear weapons have not effectively deterred conventional attacks.

The new thinking, then, is that the possession of nuclear weapons is of greatly "diminished utility." Threats to launch nuclear weapons are no longer credible, and with every passing year what can only be called a "nuclear taboo" has taken firmer and firmer hold. In other words, if rival nations don't believe you will use nuclear weapons, they are of little value to you. This leads to the conclusion that direct action to prohibit nuclear proliferation is unnecessary because nuclear weapons are no longer particularly valuable to possess.[25]

One fly in the ointment of Rosecrance's analysis may be its assumption that nuclear proliferation will fade because national leaders will make the rational calculation that such weapons are not in the best interests of the nation. Can you think of national decision makers who have made important decisions arguably quite irrational? On a scale of one to ten, where do you think these national leaders would score on a rationality test: Muammar Khadafy of Libya; Saddam Hussein of Iraq; Kim Jong Il of North Korea; and "dictator for life" in Uganda during the 1970s, Idi Amin?

THE DEMOCRATIC PEACE: REASONS FOR HOPE?

The best reason to think that the nation–state's future may outshine its war-torn past stems from studies positing a link between democracy and peace. These studies follow on the heels of a distinct wave of democratization sweeping many of the world's regions in recent years. Samuel Huntington's *The Third Wave: Democratization in the Late Twentieth Century* traces more than thirty democratic transitions from 1974 to 1990, in what he calls the "third wave" of democratization in the world. Huntington is encouraged by both the diverse regions in which this has occurred and its peacefulness. U.S. State Department analyst Francis Fukuyama's optimistic 1989 essay, "The End of History," argued that the great twentieth-century ideological battle between dictatorship and democracy has ended, democracy has won, and no other viable competitor exists.[26]

In the 1970s and 1980s democratic elections swept military dictators out of many Latin American countries, including Augusto Pinochet in Chile and Alfredo Stroessner in Paraguay. Communist President Daniel Ortega also peacefully stepped down from power in Nicaragua when rejected by voters in 1990. In Africa the 1990s saw unprecedented free elections in Benin, Cape Verde, Chad, Gabon, and Mauritania, not to mention the huge democratic changes introduced in the Republic of South Africa.

East Asian countries such as Taiwan and South Korea have also made democratic strides. In addition, Spain, Portugal, and Greece—the southern tier of the European Union—have strengthened the foundations of their democracies. An accusing finger sometimes is pointed at the Middle East as impervious to this global trend. However, a book by three Canadian professors thoroughly addresses democratization in the Middle East and concludes that, while civil strife has caused democratic failures in Sudan, Algeria, and Yemen, notable democratization is underway in Egypt, Lebanon, Jordan, and Kuwait.[27] The most cataclysmic change, however, has occurred in Eastern Europe (late 1989) and the former Soviet Union (1991), where communism buckled like overly ripe watermelons when squeezed by popular demands for free elections.

Fall of the Berlin Wall in November 1989.

But why should a wave of democratization augur well for peace? Because according to numerous recent studies, the historical record strongly demonstrates that democracies almost never fight with democracies.[28] Scientific scholars find heartening the rigorous methodologies used in many of these studies, and political scientist Bruce Russett's extensive survey concludes that this notion of a democratic peace is "one of the strongest conclusions that can be made about international relations."[29] For the first time in history, democracies have most of the military and economic power; fully 92 percent of the world's wealthiest countries are currently democracies.[30] Therefore it is hoped that if democracy continues to spread, fewer wars will occur in the future.[31] *New York Times* columnist Thomas Friedman adds an entertaining wrinkle to the peace argument with what he calls the McDonald's factor: no two countries with McDonald's fast food restaurants have fought one another. In 1997 Belarus became the one hundredth country to host the McDonald's chain.

New Thinking about War's Legitimacy

Other scholars argue that the very idea of war is gradually being rejected and the result is an antiwar culture. The most eloquent such voice belongs to historian John Mueller, who brands war as a "thoroughly bad and repulsive idea, like dueling or slavery, subrationally unthinkable and therefore obsolescent."[32] Mueller attributes much of the new thinking about war to the end of the Cold War, equating the collapse of the Soviet Union to the "functional equivalent of World War III"—transfiguring both the balance of power between states and human thinking about war.[33]

Similarly, mathematician and peace researcher Anatol Rapoport suggests that many ideas lie dormant in human consciousness until the "ideational environment" becomes receptive to their germination. He claims that the time for peace has arrived.[34] The great physicist Albert Einstein, whose 1939 letter to President Roosevelt started the nuclear avalanche rolling, once quipped that "The unleashed power of the atom has changed everything except our modes of thinking."[35] While once undoubtedly true, a recent book suggests that Einstein's observation may be less true than in the past. Creative new ways of thinking about war and peace seem to be springing up all over the world.[36]

Political scientist Donald Snow says that another hopeful development consists of the redefinition of **security** taking place today. In the past, especially during the Cold War, security was conceived strictly in terms of military defense. Today a wider "psychological sense of safety"—incorporating such global issues as environment, population, and hunger—fit into the equation of security.[37]

MINI-CASE 4.3
The Indomitable James Earl Carter

*F*ormer President Jimmy Carter has broken new ground since 1982. His Carter Center at Emory University, a nonprofit center that specializes in resolving disputes, protecting human rights, and fighting hunger, is unique. As a maverick diplomatic troubleshooter, Carter has been seen less as a blessing than as a curse by the Clinton administration's foreign policy team.[38] In 1994 Carter interceded to break a stalemate between the United States and North Korea over the latter's nuclear weapons program, but not before embarrassing President Clinton by criticizing American plans to levy economic sanctions against the North Koreans.

Carter's other highly publicized mediation occurred in Haiti, where he managed to get military dictator Raul Cedras to resign in exchange for safe passage out of the country—allowing the democratically elected president Jean-Bertrand Aristide to return and thus succeeding where the Clinton administration had not. Carter's efforts to resolve disputes in Somalia, Sudan, and Bosnia have generated fewer headlines but remain equally unpopular among foreign policy analysts in the State Department. In 1995 the presidents of Tanzania, Uganda, and Zaire—all African countries straining from the displacement of one million **refugees** fleeing from 1994 civil wars in Rwanda and Burundi—asked Jimmy Carter to mediate at a conference. No one can accuse the former president of cherry picking, for these dislocations are among the most complex and intractable of any in the world.[39]

The ex-president's negotiations in international trouble spots employ conflict resolution methods similar to those spelled out in a book by Roger Fisher and colleagues at Harvard University. In *Beyond Machiavelli: Tools for Coping with Conflict*, Fisher et al. provide step-by-step procedures to deal with complex disputes through international conflict management.[40] Citizens seem more and more involved in work done only by governments in the past. This spirit of individual empowerment also finds expression in writings by James Rosenau, who sees the information age contributing to "people power" where previously passivity had existed.[41]

Similarly, political scientist John Rourke cites instances of involvement by humble individuals as global players of consequence in the information age. For example, Rigoberta Menchu is a Guatemalan of Mayan descent who led a campaign to protect the human rights of indigenous peoples in her country. In 1992 her efforts were recognized with the Nobel Peace Prize. In Africa an auto plant worker named Michael Werikhe has been conducting walkathons to protect the endangered black rhino. Sometimes wearing his pet python, Survival, he has collected over $1 million, used to achieve international agreements aimed at saving the black rhino.[42] Of course, the rich have always been influential, but Hungarian-American philanthropist George Soros must have set some kind of record when he surpassed even the U.S. government by giving $500 million in aid to Russia in 1997.

Four Traditional Prescriptions for Peace and Security

But what if the democratic peace fails to materialize, and nuclear abstainers become nuclear bullies, and Jimmy Carter can't keep up with increasing numbers of civil disturbances? What becomes of the human condition if some of the encouraging early post-Cold War trends prove ephemeral? What tools has the international community built up over the centuries to cope with war and violence?

Traditionally, four methods have been advanced in behalf of international peace and security, two popular with realists and two favored by idealists. The two realist approaches, **balance of power** and **collective security**, share some conceptual underpinnings. Both emphasize a configuration of national power as the crux of deterring aggression. The older of the two, balance of power, seeks to create a fluid system of alliances used by members to countervail the power of any country, or group of countries, becoming strong enough to upset the peace. Potential aggressors are deterred by countries committed enough to the system to join together to discourage aggression. The longest and most successful balance-of-power system occurred for a century from the end of the Napoleonic Wars (1815) until the outbreak of World War I (1914).

The second realist formulation, collective security, entails an alliance not of balanced power, but rather power so overwhelming as to deter aggression. Collective security was first attempted by the League of Nations after World War I but quickly lost credibility when it failed to act against a tide of militarism sweeping over Germany, Japan, and Italy in the 1930s. The concept of collective security received a second chance under the United Nations, which was constructed on top of the ashes of World War II in 1945. The five Allies of World War II, the United States, Britain, France, Soviet Union, and China, formally carried their partnership over into the Security Council of the United Nations.

Idealists, however, think that their realist colleagues are trying to navigate today's international waters using a rear-view mirror focused on outdated lessons. The idealists believe there is a need for new visions. Their two recipes for order and peace are **arms control** and **international law**. Both seek to use various forms of agreement between nations as the basis for promoting international understanding. Whereas the realist methods share the notion for peace through strength, these idealist approaches lean toward peace through mutual obligation.

Proponents of arms control believe that the greater the number of sophisticated weapons available to a country, the more tempted it will be to use them. Idealists suggest that we are better off agreeing with rival nations to get rid of some of these sources of temptation. The executive director of the Institute for Defense and Disarmament Studies, Randall Forsberg, contends that as much as $100 billion annually could be cut from the U.S. military budget without endangering national security.[43] Some advocates of arms control go all the way to suggesting the abolition of all weapons of mass destruction, or total **disarmament**.

The other idealist construct for peace, international law, is based on an analogy to domestic politics and the rule of law within nations. Proponents of international law argue that a similar set of rules are gaining credibility in the global arena. International law may trail domestic law in its evolution, but nations generally tend to obey the rules of the international game as spelled out in international law. Richard Falk claims that the international community needs to revise its ideas of sovereignty, democracy, and security and aim toward a "vision of humane governance."[44]

Both of these idealist concepts invite derision from realist scholars as causing us to let down our guard. Peace through strength, say the realists, continues as an immutable principle of statecraft.

The most poignant case study of the last half-century incorporates elements of both realist and idealist thinking in coping with what could have degenerated into global thermonuclear war: the 1962 Cuban missile crisis.

President Kennedy relaxes with three Army generals after the resolution of the Cuban missile crisis.

HIGHEST DRAMA ON THE WORLD STAGE:
The Cuban Missile Crisis

Protagonists

John F. Kennedy—U.S. President

Nikita S. Khrushchev—Soviet General Secretary

Fidel Castro—Cuban prime minister since 1959 revolution, which overthrew the Batista regime

"Executive Committee Hawks"

General Maxwell Taylor—Joint Chiefs chairman

Dean Acheson—former secretary of state

John McCloy—Wall Street lawyer

Paul Nitze—State Department official

Douglas Dillon—secretary of treasury

"Executive Committee Doves"

Robert Kennedy—attorney general

Robert McNamara—secretary of defense

George Ball—undersecretary of state

Ted Sorenson—presidential advisor

Adlai Stevenson—ambassador to U.N.

Llewellyn Thompson—Soviet expert; ambassador at large

Charles Bohlen—State Department Soviet expert

Role Players

Valerian Zorin—Soviet ambassador to the U.N.

Anatoli Dobrynin—Soviet ambassador to the United States

Nicholas Katzenbach—deputy attorney general; formulator of the legal arguments justifying a blockade

William Knox—Westinghouse president in Moscow—used by Khrushchev as a conduit to U.S. government

Rudolph Anderson—U-2 pilot shot down over Cuba on October 27, 1962

Prologue

Democrat John F. Kennedy won the 1960 presidential election partially by trying to out-Republican the Republicans: he demanded a "get-tough" policy with the Soviet Union, complaining of a supposed missile gap, with the United States behind. When he took over the presidency, however, the inexperience of America's youngest president clashed with his tough campaign rhetoric.

Mere months after assuming office, Kennedy supported the disastrous attempt to liberate Cuba from Fidel Castro's control—the Bay of Pigs invasion. Then at their first summit meeting in Geneva, Switzerland, young Kennedy allowed an aggressive Nikita Khrushchev to lecture him on U.S. policy; the news media portrayed it as J.F.K. being bullied and badgered by Khrushchev.

In reality, the United States maintained a sizable nuclear advantage over the Soviets at the time. However, having won an election partly on the basis of a "missile gap," Kennedy could not credibly reassure an American public which hadn't stopped worrying since the Soviets launched the world's first orbiting "sputnik" capsule in 1957. In the international psychological milieu, Americans felt themselves in retreat while the Soviets, epitomized by Khrushchev's "we will bury you [economically]" 1960 speech at the U.N., considered themselves the wave of the future. Against this backdrop of the American people's considering Kennedy to be on the defensive, exploded the Cuban missile crisis.

Dramatic Plot

It all had to do with the offensive missiles placed secretly in Cuba by the Soviets. The crisis lasted thirteen days for the Executive Committee (October 16 to October 28, 1962), an intentionally diverse group of advisors convened by the President to deal with the crisis. The public phase lasted only six days (October 22–28, 1962). After a week of secret Ex-Comm discussions, Kennedy went public with a televised speech explaining that the Soviets had put "offensive nuclear missiles in Cuba" along with 20,000 of their troops.

A total of six response options had been considered by the Ex-Comm: (1) inaction (wait-and-see), (2) private diplomatic advances in search of a solution, (3) expressions of public outrage at the U.N., (4) a naval blockade around the island of Cuba, (5) a surgical air strike intended to wipe out missile sites only, and (6) a full-scale invasion of Cuba. After many days of heated debate, the surviving alternatives in the Ex-Comm were the air strike (favored by the "hawks") and the naval blockade (favored by the "doves"). On October 20,

Figure 4-5
Source: Herblock, *The Washington Post* (November 1, 1962).

1962, the Ex-Comm presented its views to the President: a majority favored the blockade, but a sizable minority preferred the air strike option.

A day later Kennedy decided in favor of the naval blockade, issuing an Executive Order for action. Nicholas Katzenbach of the State Department developed the legal rationale for the blockade, justifying it with Article 51 of the U.N. Charter (collective self-defense) and with an Organization of American States (OAS) vote in support of the blockade. Katzenbach suggested use of the less belligerent term "quarantine," since a blockade technically represents an act of war under international law.

By October 24, 1962, American naval forces began the actual blockade, ringing Cuba with U.S. vessels. That day the world looked over the "edge of the precipice," as twenty Soviet ships with submarine escorts approached the quarantine line. With possible nuclear war hanging in the balance, eyeball-to-eyeball over missiles in Cuba, Khrushchev blinked: Soviet ships stopped in the water and, fortunately, headed back to the Soviet Union. The world released a large collective breath of relief, as is suggested in the Herblock cartoon in Figure 4.5.

For the next four days negotiations occurred between the two sides, in an attempt to end the crisis without undue humiliation for the Soviets. The final agreement involved dismantling the missile sites under the supervision of U.N. inspectors and returning them to Russia. Castro stated publicly that no new missiles would be accepted by Cuba, and the United States pledged never again to support an invasion of Cuba. A secret protocol also called for America to remove its missiles from Turkey as a quid pro quo for the Soviet missiles in Cuba. Kennedy instructed his government not to present the outcome as a victory for the United States or as a surrender by Khrushchev.

Critical Analysis

President Kennedy believed in the importance of "process," the structuring of decisions according to rational procedures, and he has been credited with adhering to his principles in this crisis. He gathered an eclectic set of advisors in the Ex-Comm; he listened carefully to all suggestions; he avoided overreaction; he tried to place himself in Khrushchev's shoes as he worked his way through the tensest of situations. He also learned from earlier mistakes in the Bay of Pigs invasion, when he blindly accepted the advice of military experts.

Virtually all contemporary analysts agree that only disaster could have resulted if Kennedy had followed the advice of "hawks" like Dean Acheson, General Maxwell Taylor, and John McCloy, who demanded an air strike against Cuba. Assuming that an air strike would have killed some of the 20,000 Soviet troops but missed some of the numerous missiles operational in October, Khrushchev would have been pressured at home to escalate the crisis, and the United States would have been left more vulnerable than before.

Yet while the President and the Ex-Comm deserve credit for keeping cool heads, they fare less well in modern assessments of their interpretation of Soviet motivations for placing missiles in Cuba in the first place. Kennedy and his advisors believed that Khrushchev was again testing Kennedy's mettle, as he had done at the Geneva summit, and that he was using the missiles to gain a strategic advantage over the United States. However, new materials now show that Khrushchev was motivated mainly by fear of a second American attempt at invading Cuba—or as he put it, "protecting the Cuban revolution."

Cuban intelligence had penetrated the CIA and obtained a memo stating that if the United States could not "get rid of Castro by October of 1962, more drastic action would have to be taken." When Khrushchev received this information, he believed it presaged a U.S. invasion of the island. The U.S. analysts had rejected, out-of-hand, that Khrushchev's motivation could have been defensive in nature; believing (incorrectly) that the United States had conveyed to Moscow that it had no intention of invading Cuba.[45]

What long-term effects emanated from the Cuban crisis? Two major types of changes occurred: one psychological in nature, one more policy oriented. In a psychological sense, the crisis forced the world to examine what it was loathe to behold: the possibility of nuclear Armageddon. Staring into the nuclear fireball, humanity came to grips with the bizarre nuclear dilemma as the greatest of all earthly enemies. Suddenly the Soviets and Americans came to their senses about each other: they may not have liked each other's systems, but both were hostages to a form of mirror-image nuclear blackmail. The bomb—not the Soviets—was the most serious threat. On the policy front, this mental realignment quickly manifested itself in the form of the communications hotline, a Partial Nuclear Test Ban, regular summit meetings, expanded trade and cultural contacts, and a Nuclear Non-Proliferation Treaty. The most dangerous phase of the acute Cold War era had ended with the world still in one piece.[46]

* * * * * * *

Chapter Synopsis

Comprehending international affairs is complex enough that we often rely on ideological predispositions to simplify the world before us. Two broad meta-theories, or intellectual umbrellas, helpful in this respect are realism and idealism. The realist viewpoint values pragmatism, sees competition as healthy, believes in the potency of action over ideas, and equates security with strength. Idealism, conversely, emphasizes ethics, regards cooperation as healthy, considers ideas as crucial as action, and favors arms reduction as a path to national security. In much the same way that the ideological lenses of conservatism and liberalism help to explain political behavior in the domestic arena, realism and idealism assist us in ordering information about international politics.

The assumptions and purposes of the nation–state system are largely Eurocentric, since Europe is where it originated about 350 years ago. The most direct catalyst enabling nation–states to supersede the authority of principalities and fiefdoms at the local level, and the authority of the Papacy at the pan-European level, was the termination of the bloody Thirty Years War via the Peace of Westphalia in 1648. Nation–states such as Sweden, Spain, Denmark, and France began to agree on rules of the political game—like the core principle of nationhood: sovereignty.

The human legacy respecting warfare is bleak indeed. Owing to the enhanced lethality of weapons of war, the twentieth century alone witnessed more than 100 million war deaths. Historically, two re-alist approaches (balance of power and collective security) and two idealist approaches (international law and arms control) have led efforts to control warfare. Fortunately, there are some hopeful trends regarding war in today's post-Cold War world. For example, the theory of the "democratic peace" goes to great lengths to support two contentions: (1) the historical record shows that democracies do not fight one another, and (2) a wave of democratization has been sweeping the globe in recent decades. From the happy confluence of these two propositions, it is argued that the next century should prove more pacific than the last.

For Digging Deeper

Brown, Michael E., Sean Lynn-Jones, and Steven Miller, Eds. *Debating the Democratic Peace.* MIT Press, 1996.

Brown, Seyom. *New Forces, Old Forces, and the Future of World Politics.* HarperCollins, 1995.

Dahl, Robert A. *Modern Political Analysis.* Prentice Hall, 1984.

Danziger, James N. *Understanding the Political World: An Introduction to Political Science.* Longman, 1996.

Forsberg, Randall, William Driscoll, Gregory Webb, and Jonathan Dean. *Non-Proliferation Primer: Preventing the Spread of Nuclear, Chemical, and Biological Weapons.* MIT Press, 1995.

Kagan, Donald. *On the Origins of War and the Preservation of Peace.* Anchor Doubleday, 1995.

Moore, Barrington. *Social Origins of Dictatorship and Democracy.* Beacon Books, 1993.

Mueller, John. *Retreat from Doomsday: The Obsolescence of Major War.* Basic Books, 1989.

Parrish, Thomas. *The Cold War Encyclopedia.* Henry Holt, 1995.

Pierson, Christopher. *The Modern State.* Routledge, 1996.

Ranney, Austin. *Governing: An Introduction to Political Science.* Prentice Hall, 1996.

Rosenau, James N. *Turbulence in World Politics: A Theory of Change and Continuity.* Princeton University Press, 1990.

Skocpol, Theda, and John Campbell. *American Institutions.* McGraw-Hill, 1994.

Vanhanen, Tatu. *Prospects of Democracy.* Routledge, 1997.

Key Glossary Terms

A-bomb
arms control
balance of power
balance of terror

collective security
country
Crusades
culture

democratization
disarmament
discrimination
embargo

H-bomb	(MAD)	realism
ideal types	nation	refugees
idealism	nation–state	security
international law	nuclear proliferation	self-determination
just cause	option of last resort	sovereignty
just war	overkill	state
kiloton	pacifist	Thirty Years War
megaton	power	wars
mutually assured destruction	proportionality	yin and yang

CHAPTER **5**

New Actors Challenge the Nation–State

CORE OBJECTIVE

To render comprehensible the competitors (NGOs, IGOs, MNCs, IFIs) threatening the nation–state's starring role on today's world stage.

Thematic Questions

- What sort of dynamic tension between competition and cooperation ripples through human consciousness in global affairs?

- Why have NGOs gained prominence so quickly, and how has the end of the Cold War affected the operation of IGOs?

- What is paradoxical about MNCs seeming invisible, and in what ways are IFIs unique?

- How do these other actors threaten the nation–state?

Much of the new sense of personal and group empowerment discussed at the end of chapter 4 comes at the expense of the nation–state. Gradually, almost imperceptibly, a parallel set of actors has emerged to challenge its leading role on the world stage. At one time nation–states provided security for their citizens well enough to warrant undivided loyalty. No longer. For one thing, the underlying insecurity of the nuclear age has shattered the once impermeable shell of the nation–state. Furthermore, modern definitions of human security have expanded beyond the military dimension to incorporate wider global concerns.

In addressing troublesome global issues, the nation–state system has proven ineffective. Citizens have begun looking elsewhere for solutions to such problems as population, environment, food, energy, human rights, and the nuclear dilemma. The discipline of political science has also been perplexed by these global issues, performing less well here than in its traditional role of examining the nation–state system. Both the nation–state and political science have been forced to make some changes in response to global realities.

COMPETITIVE NATURE OF THE NATION–STATE SYSTEM

One thing that has not altered appreciably, however, is the inherently competitive nature of the nation–state. Nearly 200 countries compete for power and influence in a world of scarcity, often maximizing their interests at the direct expense of their rivals. Realists point out that this **quasi-Darwinian** model of international behavior has served humanity well for 350-odd years: progress has been energized by international competition, often resulting in technological solutions to vexing human problems. The nation–state system's record may not be perfect, but it has enabled more rapid and pervasive progress than in any previous era of human history. They warn against throwing out the baby with the bath water.

GLOBAL ISSUES AND COOPERATIVE IMPERATIVES

What, then, do idealists see as the problem? The short answer: today's **global issues** require greater international cooperation—something nation–states have not been good at. The longer answer: nation–states and their leaders see the world through international lenses—to them, the important relations in the world exist between powerful countries like France, China, Russia, or Japan. From their perspective, pleas for cooperation conceal efforts by poorer countries to steal the good life from affluent countries.

While such thinking may have worked fifty or a hundred years ago, idealists believe it works poorly today. Contemporary global issues do not respect national boundaries. Deforestation, global warming, ozone depletion, and nuclear radiation affect *everyone*, not single nations or regions. In an age when aerosol spray cans and air-conditioning units in North America can cause skin cancer 12,000 miles away in Australia, we find ourselves in new territory. Idealists, claiming that international competition has failed to solve global issues, maintain that only **cooperative global endeavors** can succeed.

Greater cooperation could come from existing nation–states, if they were to get global "religion" soon enough. If they do not, the nation–state's days as the dominant force in world affairs may be numbered. Already many people have begun shifting their loyalties to new actors arising to combat these complex global problems. Who are these new, more globally oriented actors appearing on the world stage?

NONGOVERNMENTAL ORGANIZATIONS (NGOs)

Nongovernmental organizations (NGOs) are **transnational** entities, meaning that they engage in activities that cross national boundaries and involve private, not public (governmental) participants. They usually focus only on one or two issues, bringing together people from around the world who think similarly on that issue. Strictly speaking, their activities are not considered international (*between* nations), but rather transnational (*across* nations). The recent global communications revolution provides hardware in the form of fax machines, the Internet, e-mail, improved telephone services, satellite transmission, and video recording—each serving to increase contact between like-minded people in different areas of the world. Expanded communications have contributed to the proliferation of NGOs: there were 5,000 in 1995, whereas only 795 existed in the year 1945, and 69 in 1900.[1]

However, four other factors have increased the importance of NGOs as players on the world stage: (1) failures of nation–states, (2) growing citizen concerns over human rights and environmental issues, (3) the end of the Cold War as the dominant force in world affairs, and (4) the fact that while the demands on international organizations like the United Nations have grown, their funding has not.[2] These NGOs, often loosely structured, prosper and grow because they meet people's needs in ways that traditional nation–states do not.

Most have grass roots origins: they grow out of individual-level (micro) contacts rather than national-level (macro) initiatives. They reflect a new sense of individual global empowerment, detailed by scholars such as David Cortright, David Korten, and Craig Comstock.[3] Variously referred to as citizen summitry, track II diplomacy, or transnational participation, all relate to private individuals and groups taking part in the dialogue over world affairs. Their actions may be aimed at influencing governments, the United Nations, or private corporations—often by using publicity to embarrass the perpetrators of illegal or unethical behavior.

A unique institution which some scholars classify as an NGO is the Papacy of the Roman Catholic church. It really is an anomaly left over from the Middle Ages, when the Pope was not only a pan-European spiritual leader, but a pan-European political authority as well. One legacy of that medieval political role is the continued existence of "Nuncios," or Papal diplomatic representatives to the 150 states with which the Papacy maintains diplomatic relations (almost like a nation–state). Although the Vatican is supposedly not a political actor, many examples of political activism belie that assumption: (1) at the 1994 Cairo Conference on Population the Papacy exerted great influence on the abortion issue; (2) the Vatican was among the first to extend diplomatic recognition to the new state of Croatia when it broke away from Yugoslavia in 1992; (3) in the 1980s Pope John Paul II and President Ronald Reagan secretly conspired to support the Solidarity labor union then battling the Polish communist party. Citing a few examples of NGOs with more typical profiles than the Papacy may be instructive. (See Mini-cases 5.1 to 5.5.)

MINI-CASE 5.1
The "Flipper" Factor

The "Dolphin Safe" logo is now a routine fixture on tuna cans.

Dolphins are graceful and intelligent mammals for which many people feel empathy. They are also an endangered species. For some reason that scientists have yet to determine, dolphins swim above the great schools of tuna that thrive in the tropical Pacific area. Unfortunately, many commercial fishing ships use narrow-gauge, **purse seine** nets in an effort to catch the lucrative tuna fish, which is much in demand by consumers throughout the world, often trapping dolphin in the process.

Throughout the 1980s both animal rights activists and environmentalist NGOs, like the Sierra Club, agitated against the large tuna-processing companies to end **purse seine** netting techniques. In 1986, 130,000 dolphins died in such nets. Protests, demonstrations, adverse publicity, and economic boycotts were used to put pressure on the guilty corporations to mend their ways. Nervous companies, experiencing slumping sales and bad press, responded to grass roots pressures in 1990. StarKist, Chicken of the Sea, and Bumble Bee all created a bright red "dolphin-safe" logo signifying that their suppliers no longer use narrow-gauge netting. In 1992 Congress made the "dolphin-safe" logo a condition for sale in the United States, and by 1995 annual dolphin deaths had dropped to 3,200. Chalk up one for NGOs (and for the dolphins).[4]

MINI-CASE 5.2
The Rainbow Warrior

Continued testing of nuclear weapons in the post-Cold War period has become very controversial. Given the risks of radiation poisoning, many scientists have argued against nuclear testing. France, one of the five declared nuclear powers, has conducted 130 atmospheric and underground tests since 1966 on the French Polynesian Pacific island of Mururoa Atoll. In the mid-1980s the NGO Greenpeace was one of many groups protesting France's nuclear testing. The founder and leader of Greenpeace, Canadian real estate developer David McTaggart, had a long-running feud with French nuclear tests going back to 1972, three years before the creation of Greenpeace.

In 1972 McTaggart sailed his ship, the *Vega*, into the nuclear blast zone and was rammed by a French naval vessel for his interference. The next summer McTaggart was back again, joining other peaceful protest ships.

By the summer of 1985 David McTaggart had been head of Greenpeace for ten years. He founded the organization with the goal of nonviolent disruption of activities that threatened either the environment or world peace. McTaggart now had the 145-foot Greenpeace sailing ship, *Rainbow Warrior*, at his disposal. After a series of high-profile passes intended to embarrass the French government, the world was shocked by a bizarre event on July 10, 1985: scuba divers from the French secret service quietly boarded the *Rainbow Warrior* in Auckland harbor, New Zealand, and set two time bombs, which exploded and sank the vessel. Tragically, Greenpeace photographer Fernando Pereira was aboard and drowned with the sinking ship. It was also revealed that the French military had been spying on Greenpeace and infiltrating its operations for months.

An even louder explosion of world public opinion condemned the French attack against these peaceful protestors, and contributions to Greenpeace tripled in the wake of the incident. The French also lost a big court battle which cost them $5 million in reparations. David McTaggart gave up leadership of Greenpeace in 1991, amidst charges of financial mismanagement and other criticisms. Greenpeace had become much larger (5 million members), wealthier ($150 million budget), more bureaucratic (offices in twenty-seven countries and a staff of 1,000), and establishmentarian than anyone could have anticipated in 1975.

Many accused the organization of unproductive "hit-and-run" tactics with little follow-up activity. Poor people in countries like Argentina and Chile argued that Greenpeace was causing unemployment through its efforts to ban tuna fishing. Right-wingers described it as radical enough to threaten capitalist economies, while left-wingers claimed

The Greenpeace NGO's ship "Rainbow Warrior."

Greenpeace had sold out to mainstream interests to get more power. This influential and visible NGO had generated considerable opposition to its efforts. It was forced to look inward and reassess its mission, tactics, and global image in light of its rapid rise to international stardom. In a sense, Greenpeace became a victim of its very success.

Despite organizational soul searching and David McTaggart's departure, relations with the French continued to be contentious. A new Greenpeace ship, *Rainbow Warrior II*, once again confronted the French at Mururoa in 1992. This time French commandos arrested its crew and impounded the ship. Another storm of criticism resulted in French President François Mitterand's declaring a moratorium on further nuclear testing.

The saga continues, however. On the heels of a 1995 French announcement by its new president, Jacques Chirac, that it would resume nuclear tests at Mururoa, Greenpeace responded by sending *Rainbow Warrior II* into French territorial waters on the tenth anniversary of the 1985 explosion. The French in turn sent 150 commandos aboard the vessel to remove its two dozen protesting passengers. Clear-cut winners and losers are difficult to pinpoint in this case, but the ongoing Greenpeace–French tension symbolizes a broader international struggle underway today: that between NGOs and nation–states for the hearts and minds of humanity.[5]

MINI-CASE 5.3
"Perzent"—Women's Health in Uzbekistan

The collapse of the Soviet Union created scores of problems for people in many of its areas. In Uzbekistan, suddenly an independent nation–state, the fledgling government has been able to fund only minimal social services for its citizens. In one entire region of Uzbekistan, irresponsible Soviet agricultural practices around the Aral Sea district left a sad legacy: salinization of soil and water resources, desertification from a fast-shrinking Aral Sea, and dangerous levels of pesticide residue.

Local residents suffer from unusually high levels of digestive illnesses, and the women, 50–60 percent of whom normally become pregnant before age twenty, experience pregnancy complications. Into this bleak scenario has stepped local gynecologist Oral Ataniyazova and the grass-roots NGO Perzent (progeny), which she formed to cope with her community's health crisis. In the absence of governmental assistance, Perzent conducts scientific research on pollution and women's health, educates young women about alternative health practices, and provides public service information as well as direct medical services.

Attending the 1994 Cairo Population Conference as an NGO representative, Dr. Ataniyazova was able to take part in the global debate over family health issues. International contacts forged in such meetings have enabled her and her NGO to pursue funding sources outside of impoverished Uzbekistan.[6]

MINI-CASE 5.4
Tigers, the EIA, China, and Taiwan

During the twentieth century nearly 95 percent of the world's 100,000 tigers have disappeared, leaving fewer than 7,000 on the planet. The main reason is simple: in the poor countries that tigers happen to inhabit—India, Indonesia, China, Russia, Kenya—poachers can make big money very quickly, often a year's average salary in a single day. The annual black-market trade hovers around $25 million. In East Asia, especially China, Taiwan, and Korea, many people believe that tiger parts possess medicinal powers. Tiger penises are placed in soups and sold as a remedy for flagging libidos. The highly valued leg bone of the tiger can fetch more than $500 per pound.

But to the world's governments this issue seems a relatively minor one compared with economic prosperity or military security concerns; consequently, they tend to look the other way. Since most slaughtered tigers end up in China, Taiwan, Korea, or a few affluent Mideastern oil states, animal rights activists would seem to have a manageable number of countries to work on. However, unlike the case of Greenpeace's efforts to embarrass the French government over nuclear testing, east Asian countries have proven impervious to publicity campaigns in the past.

In 1989 the London-based Environmental Investigation Agency (EIA) and The African Wildlife Foundation were among concerned NGOs urging a different approach: they beseeched Western nations to apply trade sanctions against China and Taiwan for allowing rampant black markets in endangered species to prosper on their soil. Not surprisingly, no nations responded quickly to the call for action.

Then with a new administration in Washington, Interior Secretary Bruce Babbitt, known as an unusually ardent environmentalist, began lobbying within the Clinton administration for a stronger stand against poaching of endangered species. Pointing to the heretofore overlooked Pelly Amendment to the 1978 U.S. Fishermen's Protective Act, Babbitt advocated leveling American trade sanctions against offending countries. While the Clinton administration has often talked a better environmental game than its predecessors, President Clinton has also been known to place high priority on free trade as a vehicle for growing the U.S. economy, and few pundits thought Babbitt's efforts within the administration would succeed.

Then in April 1994 President Clinton announced that the United States would be the first country to impose trade sanctions against Taiwan for its continued tolerance of the trade in endangered tigers. Most observers credit Interior Secretary Babbitt with energizing the administration to respond, making this a case illustrating lobbying from within government as well as from external NGOs.[7]

MINI-CASE 5.5
Waste Technologies Industries (WTI)

*I*n the 1980s the Von Roll corporation of Germany searched for a site on which to build a hazardous-waste disposal incinerator. The burning of hazardous waste is an activity most communities prefer not to engage in, and so companies like Von Roll target communities on the downside of the prosperity curve. Industry analysts showed no surprise when Von Roll sought to build its $160 million hazardous-waste plant along the Ohio River in East Liverpool, Ohio, where coal and steel industries once reigned supreme.

A large and powerful corporation promising new jobs to a small city down on its luck: seemingly the stuff of which rapid deals are made. Not if nurse, mother, and housewife Terri Swearingen can help it. Arrested nine times in the process, she has conducted a decade-long campaign to prevent WTI from burning hazardous wastes in her community, actually within a few hundred feet of a public elementary school. Court cases, congressional hearings, and federal studies have resulted in a moratorium on future incinerators in Ohio, as well as tightened regulation of dioxin and other dangerous emissions. Although the WTI plant is now constructed, it is restricted to burning only at a level known as "limited commercial operations," pending further tests and court cases.

In 1994 *Time* magazine named Terri Swearingen to its list of "Fifty for the Future: a Roster of America's Most Promising Leaders, Age Forty and Under." Noting that President Clinton had been named to a similar list in 1979, Swearingen hoped that "the attention might cause his administration to take another look at the incinerator."[8] Swearingen later received the Goldman Award for environmental activism in North America in 1997. In her own words, the award showed how "an ordinary person can get involved in an issue like this and make a difference."[9]

INTERGOVERNMENTAL ORGANIZATIONS (IGOs)

IGOs are international bodies set up by nation–states to operate in their behalf and for their common good. Unlike NGOs, these are public organizations. They vary in scope, yet most tend to be either regional or global. Their functions also differ, although most concentrate either on military/defense issues or economic/social issues. The **North Atlantic Treaty Organization (NATO)** is a regional military/defense IGO, the **North American Free Trade Agreement (NAFTA)** is a regional economic IGO, The United Nations' Security Council is a global military/defense IGO, and the **World Trade Organization (WTO)** is a global economic IGO.

Political scientist Craig Murphy provides a comprehensive history of IGOs, concluding that, over the long haul, they have benefited humanity by fostering industrial change under capitalism, facilitating transportation and communications developments, and promoting the

Figure 5.1 Expansion of International Organization, 1900–1993

The number of IGOs and NGOs has expanded rapidly. Moreover, the rate of growth has been faster than the also significant increase in the number of countries. This figure shows the growth, in percentages, of the number of countries between 1900 and 1945 and overall between 1900 and 1993. The growth of international organizations results from many factors, especially the need felt by countries to cooperate to regulate the ever-more-complex and interdependent international system.

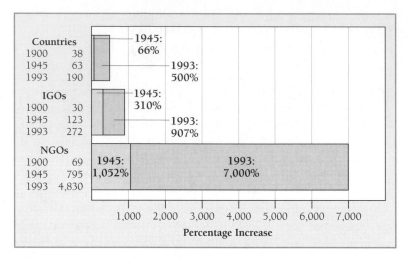

Source: John Rourke, *International Politics on the World Stage,* (Dushkin,, 1995), p. 343. *Data Sources:* Feld & Jordan (1988) for 1900 and 1945; Union of International Associations (1994) for 1993. The 1992 figures include only the most significant IGOs and NGOs as classified by the UIA.

ideals of internationalism.[10] During the Cold War era military IGOs held center stage, but they have been shuffled aside in the post-Cold War amid new attention to economic IGOs.

Similar to NGOs, IGOs have grown in number and importance during the twentieth century, as is shown in Figure 5.1. The 1815 six-member Central Commission for the Navigation of the Rhine is the oldest continuous IGO. The Universal Postal Union (1874), another IGO tracing its roots well into the last century, includes all the nations on earth. The World Health Organization and the International Criminal Police Organization (INTERPOL) also boast high participation, with about 180 and 170 members respectively. In the year 1900 thirty IGOs existed, that number grew to 123 by the end of World War II, and an astonishing 272 by the early 1990s.[11]

From EEC to EC to EU

Regional economic cooperation is all the rage in the post-Cold War, and Europe represents the prototype that everyone wants to copy. But how did Europe get to this seemingly enviable position? The answer can be found mostly amid the burning rubble which was Europe at war's end in 1945. In addition to the carnage of more than 50 million war deaths, Europe's cities and their economies were decimated by World War II. As the culmination of many centuries of bloody wars, the Big One caused creative thinkers to look for new ways to avoid a reprise.

Among the new ideas was **functionalism**, best elucidated by David Mitrany.[12] Direct approaches to averting war, like the idealistic 1928 Kellogg-Briand Pact attempting to outlaw war by treaty, or the collective security alliance known as the League of Nations, had failed. So why not try an indirect approach, asked the functionalists? If European nations could begin cooperating modestly on a piecemeal basis over cultural, economic, and social matters, then maybe these cooperative habits would eventually spill over to more important political and military issues. Frequent interaction might improve relations and conflict might become less likely, ran the functionalist logic. In the late 1940s and early 1950s such idealistic thinking was derided by many

Robert Shuman speaking in favor of European integration in 1954.

Jean Monnet, the other half of the team crusading for a united Europe, more than forty years ago.

realists as pie-in-the-sky. However, today Europe is prosperous and pacific—in fact, war seems inconceivable among Western European nations—and idealists believe this situation vindicates the functionalist vision. But how did Europe get to this condition?

It did so largely in three installments, issued in 1957, 1967, and 1986: the EEC, EC, and EU. Installment number one was the Common Market of the 1957 Treaty of Rome. Two Frenchmen, Robert Schuman and Jean Monnet, spearheaded cooperation between France, West Germany, Italy, Belgium, The Netherlands, and Luxembourg—the inner six—creating a customs union called the Common Market, or European Economic Community (EEC). Modest in scope, the EEC reduced tariffs and other trade barriers among the inner six and set common policy for trade with outsiders. The EEC of the Treaty of Rome was in many ways the prototype for North America's NAFTA in the 1990s.

Not only did the European Economic Community succeed by growing successful economies among the inner six, it also fostered a desire to build on its cooperative foundation. In 1967 the EEC merged with the European Coal and Steel Community (ECSC) and European Atomic Energy Agency (EURATOM), forming a bigger and better European Community (EC). Faced with stiff economic competition from the United States, and military competition from the Soviet Union, the European countries, all much smaller by comparison, had arrived at a keen insight: only through cooperative effort could they maintain their role as a global player of stature. Expanding to twelve members, the EC in the 1960s and 1970s also created quasi-governmental institutions, like the European Parliament, Council of Ministers, and The Commission.

The momentum of European cooperation continued to mount into the 1980s, culminating in the Single European Act of 1986, whereby members pledged to create what some called "borderless Europe" and others referred to as a "United States of Europe." Europhoria reigned as the EC pointed to 1992 as the date for an expanded European Union (EU) to replace the EC—creating all-European passports, completing economic integration, setting common foreign and defense policy, and eventually establishing a European currency and European Bank.[13]

Since every act of conceding authority to a central European body in some way reduces the sovereignty of member states, problems continue to frustrate the achievement of these ambitious goals. But the strategy of European cooperation has been a resounding success story. By 1996 the GNP of the European Union ($6.2 trillion) exceeded that of the United States by 20 percent ($5.3 trillion), and at least fifteen other European countries are pleading to gain entrance to this glamorous club. With such a centralized organization, some bureaucratization has, of course, been inevitable. Trying to get fifteen different nations to agree to standardized ways of doing things will invariably cause conflict—sometimes over the big questions, like whether to intervene militarily in Bosnia, but sometimes over things as simple as defining chocolate (see Mini-case 5.6).

MINI-CASE 5.6
Wee Willy Wonka It Ain't!

If only the EU melodrama over chocolates were as idyllic and calm as Walt Disney Studio's *Willy Wonka and the Chocolate Factory* (1971), the film version of Roald Dahl's classic children's novel, *Charlie and the Chocolate Factory*. But rather than the "G" rating of the Disney film, the European Union's headlong plunge into the chocolate vat would seem, by comparison, to warrant an "R." The EU's members have been able to agree on some complex forms of standardization, such as universal use of the metric system of measurement. Not so on the question of what in the EU may be called chocolate.

The EU Commission, a Brussels-based administrative body which makes most trade regulations for the EU, wrestled with this issue for nearly two years in the mid 1990s. A total of eight purist commission members insisted on strict control of the ingredients of chocolate: that it be made entirely of cocoa butter derived from beans imported from West Africa. The Belgians led this faction; David Johnston, head of Belgium's Godiva Chocolates, argued that only 100 percent pure chocolate should bear that name and that another name can be found for imitations.

The British head the rival faction, which advocated a looser set of standards, and Richard Frost, spokesman for Cadbury Chocolates, urged the EU to "celebrate Europe's regional diversity" by allowing for different types of chocolate. The seven countries expressing this position currently allow manufacturers to substitute up to 5 percent of the cocoa with cheaper vegetable oils, which they claim make a shinier, crisper, and more heat-resistant product.

Lobbyists from outside of the EU also tried to influence the Commission's decision. The West African nations of Ghana, Cameroon, and Ivory Coast claimed that earnings from cocoa account for 25 percent of their total exports, and that a 5 percent increase in use of vegetable fats across Europe would devastate their fragile economies. The food-aid NGO known as Oxfam backed the view of the West African nations in arguing against allowing vegetable fats in Euro-chocolate. The director of a group of candy makers called Coabisco, Arnold van Hecke, probably spoke for many other people when he groaned that "The whole thing is driving us completely berserk." What do you make of this brouhaha? Whose side do you find more convincing in the debate? Does this relatively small issue before the Commission symbolize any broader issues facing the EU?[14]

The United Nations Faces Crossroads

Because of U.S.–Soviet tension from the late 1940s to the late 1980s, the United Nations was unable to act as decisively as its founders intended. The threat of either a Soviet or American veto in the Security Council crippled the world body's role as an enforcer of the peace. Then, as communism suddenly disintegrated in the Soviet Union and Eastern Europe, peace began breaking out all over, with the U.N. playing a pivotal role.

While the U.N.'s biggest and boldest action occurred in 1991, authorizing the U.S.-led forces to liberate Kuwait from Saddam Hussein's Iraqi invasion, many other key U.N. actions occurred: twenty-one new peacekeeping actions were undertaken between 1988 and 1994, almost twice as many as from 1948 to 1987. In 1995 U.N. peacekeeping troops operated in twenty countries, with more than 70,000 soldiers, fully six times the number active in 1992. Pakistan led the list with 7,000 troops, India was second, France third, and Bangladesh and the United Kingdom fourth and fifth respectively. The United States ranked thirty-third, with 754 U.N. peacekeepers in uniform.

Almost drunk with feelings born of relevance, the U.N. was nagged by a problem while it enjoyed this heady brew: increased demands for its services were not matched by increased funding from member nations. In fact, its largest benefactor, the United States, was complaining about its financial burden (25 percent of the U.N. budget) and was threatening to cut its contributions. Secretary-General Boutros Boutros-Ghali reminded members that the U.N. consists of the sum of its parts—an IGO capable of doing only what its members empower it and fund it to do—that it is neither a world government nor a sovereign body above the nation–states that comprise it. If members will not fund new activities, then they must accept a U.N. scaled back to earlier levels.[15]

The U.N. celebrated its fiftieth birthday in 1995. In addition to receiving praise for some of its past successes, however, the world body also took a pummeling from rich and poor countries alike. What topped the minimalist agenda of the wealthy countries? They think that the U.N.'s biggest problem is that it spends too much money. More important to the maximalist agenda of the poorer members, on the other hand, is an increase in its various services as well as payment of dues by nations (like the U.S.) in arrears. While nearly everyone attending the gala event agreed that some kind of reform was needed, a huge gulf separated the rich and poor countries' suggestions for reform.

The great-power criticisms revolved around the theme of administrative waste and inefficiency at the U.N. To them, the world body at Turtle Bay, with its 15,000 employees, has become a bloated Third World bureaucracy. In what sounded much like a reprise of American electoral

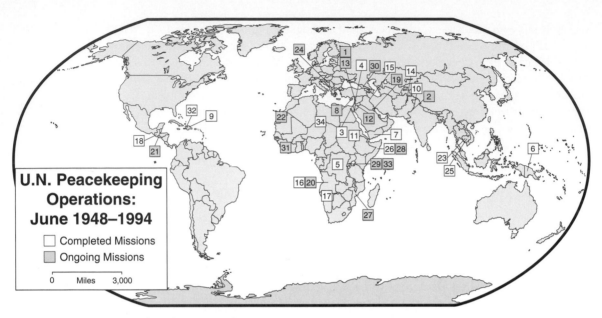

Figure 5.2   UN Peacekeeping Operations: June 1948-1994

1. UN Truce Supervision Organization (UNTSO), June 1948-Present
2. UN Military Observer Group in India and Pakistan (UNMOGIP), January 1949-Present
3. First UN Emergency Force (UNEF 1), November 1956-June 1967
4. UN Observation Group in Lebanon (UNOGIL), June 1958-December 1958
5. UN Operation in the Congo (ONUC), July 1960-June 1964
6. UN Security Force in West New Guinea (West Iran) (UNSF), October 1962-April 1963
7. UN Yemen Observation Mission (UNYOM), July 1963-September 1964
8. UN Peacekeeping Force in Cyprus (UNFICYP), March 1964-Present
9. Mission of the Representative of the Secretary-General in the Dominican Republic (DOMREP), May 1965-October 1966
10. UN India-Pakistan Observation Mission (UNIPOM), September 1965-March 1966
11. Second UN Emergency Force (UNEF II), October 1973-July 1979
12. UN Disengagement Observer Force (UNDOF), June 1974-Present
13. UN Interim Force in Lebanon (UNIFIL), March 1978-Present
14. UN Good Offices Mission in Afghanistan and Pakistan (UNGOMAP), April 1988-March 1990
15. UN Iran-Iraq Military Observer Group (UNIIMOG), August 1988-February 1991
16. UN Angola Verification Mission I (UNAVEM I), January 1989-June 1991
17. UN Transition Assistance Group (UNTAG), April 1989-March 1990

18. UN Observer Group in Central America (ONUCA), November 1989-January 1992
19. UN Iraq-Kuwait Observation Mission (UNIKOM), April 1991-Present
20. UN Angola Verification Mission II (UNAVEM II), June 1991-Present
21. UN Observer Mission in El Salvador (ONUSAL), July 1991-Present
22. UN Mission for the Referendum in Western Sahara (MINURSO), September 1991-Present
23. UN Advance Mission in Cambodia (UNAMIC), October 1991-March 1992
24. UN Protection Force (UNPROFOR), March 1992-Present
25. UN Transitional Authority in Cambodia (UNTAC), March 1992-September 1993
26. UN Operation in Somalia I (UNOSOM I), April 1992-April 1993
27. UN Operation in Mozambique (ONUMOZ), December 1992-Present
28. UN Operation in Somalia II (UNOSOM II), May 1993-Present
29. UN Observation Mission in Uganda-Rwanda (UNOMUR), June 1993-Present
30. UN Observer Mission in Georgia (UNOMIG), August 1993-Present
31. UN Observer Mission in Liberia (UNOMIL), September 1993-Present
32. UN Mission in Haiti (UNMIH), September 1993-Present
33. UN Assistance Mission for Rwanda (UNAMIR), October 1993-Present
34. UN Aouzou Strip Observer Group (UNASOG), May 1994-June 1994

Includes Forces in Bosnia and Herzegovina, Croatia, the Federal Republic of Yugoslavia (Serbia and Montenegro), and the former Yugoslav Republic of Macedonia.

Data from United Nations Department of Public Information, "United Nations Peacekeeping Update: May 1994," July 1994.
Source: John Spanier and Robert Wendzel, *Games Nations Play.* (Congressional Quarterly Press, 1996), p. 454a.

themes during the 1990s, "leaner and meaner" could have been the buzzword of the powerful countries. Consolidating various U.N. agencies, reducing staff, cutting back on travel expenses, setting realistic and measurable goals, and establishing an internal auditor to ferret out corruption were all prominently mentioned. These wealthy nations pay the lion's share of the annual budget, which their cost-cutting mind-set succeeded in reducing by 4 percent beginning in 1996.

A clear majority of U.N. members today are small, poor, and reform minded. Most of the changes they favor entail a more aggressive role for the world body, which means more expensive programs funded mostly by the wealthy countries. Heading their list of complaints at the half-century celebration was the U.N. debt crisis; the organization was in the red to the tune of $3 billion, more than a third of which resulted from what the United States owed in 1995. A decade earlier, with 5,000 blue-helmeted U.N. troops, the peacekeeping budget amounted to $600 million annually, but by 1995 those figures had risen to 60,000 troops at $3.6 billion annually. The Bosnian situation alone was costing $6 million a day. In addition to wanting the big states to pay up, Third World countries also argued for greater representation in the U.N.'s most powerful organ, the fifteen-member Security Council, whose permanent membership has not changed since its inception in 1945. For example, despite their contemporary importance, Germany and Japan are not Security Council members. When the U.N. began, it had fifty-one members; in 1995 it contained 185. The smaller countries want restructuring to meet new realities.[16]

Which do you find more compelling, the cost-cutting efficiency argument of the large countries, or the debt resolution and restructuring priorities of the small members? Currently at a crossroads in its history, the world body can expand, or it can contract. Like clay in the hands of member nations, the U.N. can be shaped and molded to fit a wide variety of purposes. Generally speaking, most idealists within the United States tend to support a more robust U.N. role and increased funding toward that end. Realists, often seeing the U.N. either as ineffectual or as too beholden to Third World critics of the United States, prefer to see a less ambitious and less expensive world body in the future.

MULTINATIONAL CORPORATIONS (MNCs)

Like NGOs and IGOs, **multinational corporations (MNCs)** have grown recently in number, expanding their reach and extending their operations, often at the expense of nation–states. Technological revolutions in transportation and communications have enabled the MNC octopus to spread its commercial tentacles into every conceivable global nook and cranny. Subaru Motors, Chrysler, Shell Oil, IBM, Texas Instruments, Samsung, and Fuji Film are examples of the seemingly endless list of global actors in this category. The essence of the MNC has been described as

> a firm with production, marketing, and distribution facilities located in several countries, and highly flexible in moving around capital, goods and technology to match market conditions. It also "thinks globally," or has no specific [national] loyalty in making decisions.[17]

The MNC does, however, respond to one paramount motivation: profits. This is the undisputed fuel driving the MNC engine. The MNC's constant shifting of its resources in quest of the profit motive leaves it vulnerable to criticism by proponents of social justice. Humanistic values such as altruism, charity, fair play, and compassion can be overwhelmed by a corporate fixation on the bottom line.

The MNC's Critics

The most scathing publicist of the MNC's global role has been David C. Korten of the People-Centered Development Forum, a social justice NGO. Korten complains that nation–states have allowed MNCs, often larger and wealthier than many countries, to function irresponsibly, with little or no public accountability. Of the world's 100 largest economies, half are corporations. Economic globalization has resulted in the reduction of antitrust actions taken by governments, in turn allowing huge corporations to merge to the point of monopolization.

David Korten says that any industry in which five firms control 50 percent of the market constitutes a monopoly and that five firms do in fact control more than half the market in aerospace, automobiles, airlines, electronics, consumer durables, and steel. Five firms control over 40 percent of global markets in oil, personal computers, and communications media. Korten sees all of this as damaging to individual human rights and to the environment.[18] Defenders of MNCs counter by arguing that their expansion contributes to improved global prosperity, economic efficiency, and the dissemination of democratic ideas to new areas. Do you consider it possible that one day MNCs would replace nation–states as the dominant actors on the global stage? How do you think that structure would affect, in specific ways, the kind of world in which you would live and work?

Gargantuan Actors

While Table 5.1 shows that controversy swirls around MNCs, which can operate in the service of good or ill, what is beyond debate is the impressive growth of MNCs. One of the 25 largest MNCs, General Motors, boasted sales of $134 billion in 1993, larger than Indonesia's Gross Domestic Product (GDP) of $122 billion, and more than twice Israel's GDP of $55 billion. But as Table 5.2 indicates, GM is far from alone as a giant MNC. A staggering total of 10,000 MNCs now exist; 2,000 of these function in more than six countries, while 8,000 are of a smaller variety.

A total of 90,000 subsidiaries operate under the control of these 10,000 parent MNCs. Most remain based in a few locations: 90 percent of the top 500 MNCs operate out of North America, Japan, or Europe.[19] Many corporations that were once thought to be identifiable with one country have merged with firms from other countries, adding to the interdependent look of the global landscape. Examples are Ford Motor Company and Mazda, and US Air and British Airways. An example of the long-term proliferation of one of the less visible MNCs might be helpful (see Mini-case 5.7).

MINI-CASE 5.7
Going Global with ICI

Imperial Chemical Industries (ICI) was created in 1926 when four British chemical companies decided to pool their resources. For many decades it remained a relatively modest corporation based primarily in Britain. Until the 1970s fully two-thirds of ICI's capital and its labor force were strictly British. Then a series of domestic economic pressures, including a

Table 5.1   Multinational Corporations in World Politics:
A Balance Sheet of Claims and Criticisms

MNCs have been praised and condemned alternatively, depending on how their performance is viewed. The record is mixed and can be evaluated differently in terms of different criteria. Below is a "balance sheet" summarizing the major arguments, pro and con.

Positive	Negative
• Increase the volume of world trade.	• Give rise to oligopolistic conglomerations that reduce competition and free enterprise.
• Assist the aggregation of investment capital that can fund development.	• Raise capital in host countries (thereby depriving local industries of investment capital) but export profits to home countries.
• Finance loans and service international debt.	• Breed debtors and make the poor dependent on those providing loans.
• Lobby for free trade and the removal of barriers to trade, such as tariffs.	• Limit the availability of commodities by monopolizing their production and controlling their distribution in the world marketplace.
• Underwrite research and development that allows technological innovation.	• Export technology ill suited to underdeveloped economies.
• Introduce and dispense advanced technology to less-developed countries.	• Inhibit the growth of infant industries and local technological expertise in less-developed countries while making Global South countries dependent on Global North technology.
• Reduce the costs of goods by encouraging their production according to the principle of comparative advantage.	• Conspire to create cartels that contribute to inflation.
• Generate employment.	• Curtail employment by driving labor competition from the market.
• Encourage the training of workers.	• Limit worker' wages.
• Produce new goods and expand opportunities for their purchase through the internationalization of production.	• Limit the supply of raw materials available on international markets.
• Disseminate marketing expertise and mass-advertising methods worldwide.	• Erode traditional cultures and national differences, leaving in their place a homogenized world culture, dominated by consumer-oriented values.
• Promote national revenue and economic growth; facilitate modernization of the less-developed countries.	• Widen the gap between the rich and poor countries.
• Generate income and wealth.	• Increase the wealth of local elites at the expense of the poor.
• Advocate peaceful relations between and among states in order to preserve an orderly environment conducive to trade and profits.	• Support and rationalize repressive regimes in the name of stability and order.
• Break down national barriers and accelerate the globalization of the international economy and culture and the rules that govern international commerce.	• Challenge national sovereignty and jeopardize the autonomy of the states.

Source: Charles Kegley and Eugene Wittkopf, *World Politics: Trends and Transformation*, (St. Martin's, 1997), p. 192.

prolonged battle with England's active labor unions as well as a lengthy economic downturn, caused corporate executives to look to the international venue for solutions to ICI's problems.

The prospects of globalization provided some excellent opportunities to energize ICI's lethargic bottom line. By holding assets in many countries, an MNC can move the location of its manufacturing operations, shift to the production of new products, or diversify into money-making activities quite unrelated to its original menu. In a world of rapidly changing consumer demand, wildly fluctuating labor costs in various parts of the world, and tax incentives from countries anxious to attract a job-creating MNC, it takes little imagination to understand why corporations seek to globalize their operations. By the 1980s ICI had shifted both its production and sales to countries where research suggested the highest profits were possible.

Today ICI runs factories in over forty countries and sales offices in every part of the globe. Its original chemicals portfolio has been expanded to include plastics, fibers, explosives, agriculture, oil, paints, and pharmaceuticals—all nicely balanced to limit exposure, with no more than 17 percent profits from any one area of sales. Annual sales of about $25 billion include ICI among the elite one hundred economic entities on earth, with its annual production exceeding that of 65 percent of nation–states. Over seven decades ICI has quietly grown into a genuine giant among giants.[20]

Can Such Giants Seem Invisible?

To the great majority of the world's people, the growth of MNCs like ICI not only has been quiet, it has been nearly invisible. For most, the activities occurring in corporate boardrooms might as well be on another planet. Distant, inscrutable, and elitist, MNC decision makers could not be further removed from the lives of most citizens. Compared to NGOs or IGOs, we just don't read as much about MNCs.

Having precious little contact with their world, where do our images and assumptions about such people come from? Popular culture fills in the blanks on topics about which we have no hard information. One medium in particular, the Hollywood film, influences our thinking disproportionately. As the world's most popular form of entertainment, movies subtly provide us with more than mere distraction: their images convey attitudes, beliefs, and assumptions, especially on subjects about which we know little. The most powerful images of huge corporations emanating from Hollywood have been negative ones.

Sleazy Cinematic CEOs

In Robert Wise's *Executive Suite* (1954) a fierce battle for control ensues when the president of a large corporation dies, apparently of overwork. Corporate values, all upside down here, are exposed as trivial, as when an employee not wearing a tie is sharply ordered to "get dressed." More inhumane is the corporate environment portrayed in *Patterns* (1956), written by Rod Serling (of *Twilight Zone* fame) and directed by Fielder Cook. The publicity tag originally promoting the film read, "Inside the skyscraper jungle! Ruthless men and women clawing for control of a billion-dollar empire!" Everett Sloane plays a tough boss of a New York firm who orchestrates a sneaky showdown between an ambitious young

Table 5.2 The World's Twenty-five Largest Public Companies

Rank 1994	Rank 1993	Company (Country)	Market Value	Fiscal 1993 Sales	Fiscal 1993 Profit
1	1	NTT (Japan)	$130,344	$58,277	$1,505
2	5	Royal Dutch/Shell (Netherlands/U.K.)	97,170	95,173	4,497
3	4	General Electric (U.S.)	86,005	60,562	4,424
4	14	Toyota Motor (Japan)	78,788	91,483	1,581
5	6	Mitsubishi Bank (Japan)	75,029	444,649	563
6	3	Exxon (U.S.)	73,899	99,160	5,280
7	2	AT&T (U.S.)	73,875	67,200	4,260
8	8	Industrial Bank of Japan (Japan)	70,890	378,298	367
9	10	Fuji Bank (Japan)	65,254	504,395	522
10	7	Sumitomo Bank (Japan)	63,339	501,913	188
11	11	Sanwa Bank (Japan)	62,542	495,874	851
12	9	Dai-Ichi Kangyo Bank (Japan)	59,190	475,893	421
13	13	Coca-Cola Co. (U.S.)	57,575	13,957	2,188
14	12	Wal-Mart Stores (U.S.)	57,469	55,483	1,994
15	17	Philip Morris (U.S.)	48,235	60,901	3,568
16	15	Sakura Bank (Japan)	47,363	481,340	517
17	20	Nomura Securities (Japan)	43,295	75,877	32
18	16	Tokyo Electric Power (Japan)	40,515	42,104	661
19	23	Roche Holding (Switzerland)	40,459	9,651	1,669
20	24	Dupont (U.S.)	40,231	37,098	566
21	21	Procter & Gamble (U.S.)	38,008	30,433	269
22	18	Merck (U.S.)	37,148	10,498	2,166
23	25	General Motors (U.S.)	36,990	119,600	2,465
24	34	IBM (U.S.)	36,018	62,716	-7,987
25	—	Singapore Telecom (Singapore)	35,723	1,715	625

Note: Ranked by market value as of July 31, 1994, as determined by Morgan Stanley Capital International Perspective (in millions of U.S. dollars; financial data at December 31, 1993, exchange rates; percentage changes based on home currencies).
Source: *Wall Street Journal,* September 30, 1994.
Source: John Spanier and Robert Wendzel, *Games Nations Play.* (Congressional Quarterly Press, 1996), p. 67.

executive and a "dead-wood" old-timer whom the boss wants to get rid of. At one point, boss Everett Sloane growls that his firm "can't be run like a welfare comfort station."

"I'm mad as hell and I'm not going to take it any more!" With these provocative words, actor Peter Finch sums up the little person's frustration amid corporate greed and bloodlessness in Sidney Lumet's angry film, *Network* (1976). Finch won a posthumous Academy Award for his portrayal of Howard Beale, a television anchorman who threatens an on-air suicide when heartless executives fire him because of a drop in his ratings. The foil to Finch's vulnerable humanity appears in the form of Ned Beatty, playing an amoral power broker pulling corporate strings behind the scenes. He is as distasteful as he is frightening in this role that garnered him an Oscar nomination.

You would be hard-pressed to find a more seductively corrupting corporate model than Michael Douglas's depiction of financier Gordon Gekko in *Wall Street* (1987). Double-dealing and utterly unscrupulous, Douglas's Gekko lures a Wall Street novice, played by Charlie Sheen, into emulating his financial skullduggery. Gordon Gekko epitomizes corporate irresponsibility when he declares, unabashedly, that "greed is good!" Shameless, selfish, and unprincipled, Gordon Gekko oozes the slick image so often associated with Hollywood's corporate shadows.

For every cinematic Gordon Gekko there seems to be a real-world counterpart. The moguls we hear about are the likes of Michael Milken and Ivan Boesky, both convicted of insider trading. Negative screen images do not need to stretch credulity. When research-scientist-turned-whistle-blower Dr. Jeffrey Weigand released documents in 1995 showing how the U.S. tobacco industry had systematically concealed scientific data about the health hazards of smoking as part of a thirty-year conspiracy to hide the truth, a barrage of public criticism was directed at tobacco's CEOs.

Filmic Conscience

Films can also prick the social conscience on hidden issues, triggering a public response. Such seems to have been the case with the Indian film *Salaam Bombay* (1988). Director Mira Nair's finger found the hidden pulse of child labor in Indian corporations, and the success of her award-winning picture provides the world with a glimpse into this "gritty urban netherworld." *Salaam Bombay* tells the story of a ten-year-old boy who runs away to the city of Bombay. To earn money, he becomes a *chaipau*—one who delivers tea and bread to inhabitants of Bombay's seedy red-light district. His plight tugged at the heartstrings of audiences worldwide, and considerable action in behalf of child laborers in India has ensued. This event serves as the cue card for Mini-case 5.8.[21]

MINI-CASE 5.8
Indian Child Labor

For most of the long Cold War, India sidled up to the Soviet Union as its benefactor while the United States supported India's neighbor and rival, Pakistan. One of the by-products of a close Soviet–Indian liaison was a suspicion of capitalist free enterprise, resulting in the Indian government's ownership of most large industries and close regulation of those remaining in private hands. As with most other countries that turned their backs on capitalism, India's economy suffered: its annual GNP per capita (about $200) ranked it among the poorest countries. But as the end of the Cold War highlighted flaws inherent in socialist economics, India moved its quasi-socialist econo-

Child laborers in Dindi Gui, India.

my in the direction of market capitalism. In many areas competition spurred growth and prosperity. On the down side, however, it also worsened the long-standing problem of abusive child labor in India. With economic expansion, labor shortages shoved more children into poor working conditions.

India's 1991 census reported that minors make up 8 percent of the laboring population. A Bangalore-based NGO, Concern for the Working Child, estimates that a whopping 100 million children labor in agriculture, brick kilns, carpet weaving, stone quarries, and diamond cutting. The U.N.'s International Labor Organization (ILO) found five-year-olds and ten-year-olds among the 80,000 workers in the match and fireworks industries. A labor ministry official estimates that 300,000 children work in India's carpet industry alone. The sad conclusion reached by the ILO? "Children are required to work beyond their physical and psychological development, for long working hours, mostly for less than meager wages (33 cents per day)."

NGOs such as the South Asian Coalition on Child Servitude, ChildRight Worldwide, and Butterflies join forces with the main IGO in this area (the ILO) to lean on offending MNCs, the Indian government, Western consumers, and the U.S. government. Aided by publicity from the film *Salaam Bombay*, signs of progress exist. A grass-roots boycott by German consumers against carpets woven by children has cut into the profits of offending MNCs. Senator Tom Harkin (D–Iowa) has introduced legislation to bar U.S. entry to products made by children. Recently a historic first occurred when a group of children, aided by the NGO Butterflies, took a case all the way to the Indian Supreme Court, and won. The Court ordered the Indian government to explain why children should be allowed to work like adults but not be entitled to unionize to defend themselves legally.

Many corporations operating in India are feeling the heat; more than 130 carpet makers have signed on to a "Rugmark" logo campaign, akin to the tuna industry's "dolphin safe" logo discussed earlier. The child labor situation in India and other south Asian countries remains grim, but improvements can be cited.[22] A thirteen-year-old Canadian student named Craig Kielburger has been conducting a public crusade against child labor practices in India, Pakistan, and Sri Lanka. He garnered national, then international, attention when he raised enough money to make a fact-finding trip to south Asia. The Canadian prime minister, Jean Chretien, just happened to be in India when Craig Kielburger was visiting rug factories there. Craig's dogged determination got him an interview with his PM, whom he lobbied strenuously to take a stronger stand against abusive child labor in the Third World. Relying on information gleaned from dozens of interviews conducted on his tour, Craig now visits schools across Canada drumming up support for youngsters toiling in south Asian sweatshops. Craig Kielburger's efforts demonstrate how a single determined person, even a thirteen-year-old, can make a difference in the world.

INTERNATIONAL FINANCIAL INSTITUTIONS (IFIs)

The all-purpose United Nations is made up of six main organs and scores of ancillary institutions, covering practically every area of human endeavor. Increasingly, however, institutions with more specific agendas are gaining attention at the global level, among them the **international financial institutions**, or **IFIs**. Three main areas of economic and financial need arose after World War II, producing three major bodies focusing on global coordination. These relatively new activities—in the areas of *monetary policy, development lending*, and *trade*—have risen like silent Phoenixes. Believing that the Great Depression of the 1930s and Germany's aggression in World War II resulted partly from unregulated economic trench warfare, the world's leaders gathered in 1944 at Bretton Woods, New Hampshire, to set up cooperative bodies, described in the following sections.

Monetary Policy—The International Monetary Fund (IMF)

Early on, the main function of the **International Monetary Fund (IMF)** was currency stabilization—bringing order to the process whereby dollars, marks, yen, lira, or pounds fluctuate in value vis-à-vis one another. By the 1960s the IMF turned more toward lending money to countries with **balance-of-payments** problems resulting from trade deficits or heavy loan payments. The IMF generally imposes stiff **austerity measures** as a requirement for lending, making its demands unpopular with many people in countries experiencing the budgetary pinch. In addition to the IMF's operation at the global level, there are similar regional institutions, such as the European Monetary System and the Arab Monetary Fund.

Development Lending—The World Bank

Whereas the IMF has been likened to a fire brigade, the World Bank functions more like a global construction company. The **World Bank**, involving all countries except North Korea and Cuba, has emerged as the leading source of long-term finance and policy advice for **less-developed countries (LDCs)**. It consists of three divisions: (1) the International Bank for Reconstruction and Development (IBRD), which makes loans to medium-range countries;

(2) the International Development Association (IDA), which specializes in low-interest loans to the poorest countries; and (3) the International Finance Corporation (IFC), which helps private economic ventures in developing nations. The evolution of the World Bank is capsulized by its director, Lewis Preston, who relates that it initially operated toward the reconstruction of Europe and Japan at the end of World War II. The World Bank later shifted toward lending for infrastructure development, then into adjustment lending when the 1980s debt crisis hit Latin America (see Mini-case 5.9). In the 1990s its mission focused on rebuilding the former Soviet states.[23]

Trade—The General Agreement on Tariff and Trade (GATT)

GATT, also a post-World War II phenomenon, has functioned as the central mechanism regulating world trade. Its purpose is to promote **free trade** by reducing **protectionist** measures, such as **tariffs**. American leadership in behalf of free and open trade has produced eight rounds of talks, each expanding the role of the GATT. The latest—the Uruguay Round—created an expanded World Trade Organization (WTO), which superseded the GATT on January 1, 1995. More than 120 countries participate in the WTO, comprising over 90 percent of world trade.

MINI-CASE 5.9
The 1980s Debt Crisis, Mexico, and the IMF

During the 1970s the Organization of Petroleum Exporting Countries (OPEC), for the first time in its decade-and-a-half existence, achieved agreement on oil production. By restricting the flow of black gold to the **more-developed countries (MDCs)**, OPEC created panic in the West as the price of a barrel of oil rose from about $3 early in the decade to more than $38 in 1979.

Panic also struck the less-developed countries (LDCs), who needed oil to fuel their development programs. The oil price increases resulted in a massive influx of revenues—so-called petrodollars—into OPEC countries like Saudi Arabia, Kuwait, and the United Arab Emirates. What did these countries do with these billions of petrodollars? They invested most of them in Western banks. And what did the banks do with them? With their coffers bulging with surplus money, they aggressively pursued potential borrowers, among them many Third World countries with dubious repayment prospects.

One of these countries was Mexico. Given the rapid oil price increases of the 1970s, Mexico assumed that it could borrow heavily, invest in its growing oil exploration industry (PEMEX), and reap big profits by selling new-found oil, especially to the United States, which was then quite nervous about the reliability of Persian Gulf oil. However, the Mexican government had gambled and lost. Rather than continuing to rise, oil prices dropped from their high of $38 to the mid-teens. To make matters worse, OPEC saw its disciplined unity of the 1970s dissipate, and countries like the United States began conserving energy in unexpected ways, including one way not anticipated by Detroit: consumers began buying smaller, fuel-efficient cars. The dilemma for Mexico became known as the *scissors crisis:* mounting foreign debt at a time of shrinking export earnings. With its foreign debt ballooning from $6 billion in 1970 to $88 billion in 1982, Mexico shocked world markets by announcing itself unable to pay these debts. Similar events in other countries triggered the international debt crisis of the 1980s. For U.S. banks like Citicorp, with more than 10 percent of its assets loaned to shaky Third World countries, analysts feared that the ripple effects of insolvency would reach deep into the American heartland.

Enter the IMF. Only global lending agencies could mount the relief—in the form of more long-term loans, at lower interest rates—required to stem the tide of crisis and panic. Acting as a kind of international credit union, the IMF provided the assistance that enabled the debtor nations to avoid defaulting. As always, however, the IMF exacted a price for its help: it required governmental spending cuts, lower government **subsidies** to businesses, and higher interest rates charged by the nation's banks. Such IMF conditions invariably prove painful; often countries aided by the IMF cannot stay the course in the face of protesting citizens hurt by such austerity measures.

Fortunately, however, Mexico bit the political bullet. Two successive presidents, Miguel de la Madrid Hurtado (1982–1988) and Carlos Salinas de Gortari (1988–1994), managed to stick to responsible fiscal policies, resulting in a slow-but-steady economic recovery. They reduced governmental spending and **privatized** the heavily subsidized economy with growth rates impressive enough to gain entry into a NAFTA treaty with the United States and Canada in 1994.[24]

POLITICAL SCIENCE AND WORLD AFFAIRS

Two intersecting axes of choice confront political scientists regarding their contributions to the future study of world affairs. One choice is between the traditional nation–state and the newer range of interdependent global issues; this issue forms the key intellectual division of this chapter. The other choice relates to methodological options, personified throughout this text by the competing social science philosophies of scientism and humanism.

The first choice raises the question of what political science should study. The latter deals with how it should go about doing so. Since the late 1960s a tension has existed between scholars who believe in rigorous quantitative methods of science, and their colleagues committed to more qualitative and analytical approaches. However, regardless of the specific substantive and methodological directions pursued by political scientists examining world affairs, they will continue to focus on questions of power, security, and the authoritative allocation of scarce resources as the conceptual glue binding their discipline together.

Chapter Synopsis

The quasi-Darwinian model of international relations as quintessentially competitive in nature has dovetailed nicely with humanity's attachment to the idea that progress results from expansion—particularly economic and technological expansion. However, the realist belief in international competition as inevitable is being eroded by many of these new actors who do not buy into traditional notions of power politics. This is especially true of the many NGOs and IGOs which have blossomed from the seeds of popular discontent over the failure of nation–states to deal creatively and aggressively with global issues like environment, population, food, energy, human rights, and the nuclear dilemma.

It is no exaggeration to state that these newly empowered actors are locked in a struggle with nation–states to win the hearts and minds of global citizens. No longer is it a given that nation–states must ultimately claim the first loyalty of John and Jane Doe. None of these global issues will simply go away. While nation–states have damaged their standing through inertia concerning all of these global issues, their failure to cope with the environmental issue has proven most unforgivable among the educated populations of northern hemisphere affluent countries. Many NGOs and IGOs offer agendas emphasizing cooperative ventures much more attractive to educated global citizens communicating more freely in the post-Cold War electronic age.

For Digging Deeper

Cederman, Lars-Erik. *Emergent Actors in World Politics: How States and Nations Develop and Dissolve.* Princeton University Press, 1997.

Edwards, Michael. *Beyond the Magic Bullet: NGO Performance and Accountability in the Post-Cold War World.* Kumarian Press, 1996.

Krieger, Joel. *The Oxford Companion to Politics of the World.* Oxford University Press, 1993.

Mingst, Karen A., and Margaret P. Karns. *The United Nations in the Post-Cold War Era.* Westview Press, 1995.

Nathan, Richard P. *Social Science in Government: Uses and Misuses.* Basic Books, 1988.

Owen, Richard. *The Times Guide to World Organizations: Their Role and Reach in the New World Order.* Westview Press, 1996.

Parrish, Thomas. *The Cold War Encyclopedia.* Henry Holt, 1995.

Rourke, John T. *International Politics on the World Stage.* Dushkin, 1995.

Spruyt, Hendrik. *The Sovereign State and Its Competitors: An Analysis of Systems Change.* Princeton University Press, 1994.

Zartman, I. William, and J. Lewis Rasmussen, Eds. *Peacemaking in International Conflict: Methods and Techniques.* U.S. Institute for Peace Press, 1997.

Key Glossary Terms

austerity measures
balance-of-payments
cooperative global endeavors
free trade
functionalism
global issues
intergovernmental organizations (IGOs)
international financial institutions (IFIs)

less-developed countries (LDCs)
more-developed countries (MDCs)
multinational corporations (MNCs)
nongovernmental organizations (NGOs)
North American Free Trade Agreement (NAFTA)
North Atlantic Treaty

Organization (NATO)
privatization
protectionism
quasi-Darwinian
subsidy
tariff
transnational
World Bank
World Trade Organization (WTO)

CHAPTER **6**

Society and Culture

Thematic Questions

- Where does sociology end and anthropology begin?

- What fundamental relationships exist between the phenomena of society and culture?

- What is the link between symbolic communication as language and the existence of culture?

- What social institutions are fundamental?

- What do we know of cultural universals and cultural differences in our world?

CORE OBJECTIVE

To demonstrate how society and culture represent the structure and content of living in groups.

I n the family of social sciences, sociology and anthropology are particularly close siblings. Much like geography, which spun off from geology late in the nineteenth century, anthropology emerged from departments of sociology early in the twentieth century. Professor Franz Boas of Columbia University mentored the first wave of anthropology graduate students in the 1920s; his star pupils included Margaret Mead and Ruth Benedict, harbingers of a female majority of the 7,000 professional anthropologists now working in the United States. Impressive as anthropology's growth has been, sociology's professional directory remains the second largest in the social sciences after psychology: 15,000 practitioners in the United States.

SOCIOLOGY

Sociology deals with human behavior in the context of social groups. The discipline came of age in a Europe trying to fathom the unending social effects of the Industrial Revolution. As was discussed in Chapter 3, sociology's early shining lights were theorists like Karl Marx, Émile Durkheim, Auguste Comte, and Max Weber, all of whom engaged in broad historical comparisons. With the twentieth century Americanization of the discipline, there emerged a new breed of specialists with a preference for studies of American social topics.

The first sociology department opened in 1893 at the University of Chicago, which eventually nurtured prominent scholars such as George Herbert Mead, John Dewey, and William F. Ogburn. The founder of American sociology, Lester Ward, served as first president of the newly formed American Association of Sociologists in 1905. Harvard University started a department in 1930, but Chicago led the profession until the end of World War II. Survey research questionnaires and personal interviews form the methodological basis for most modern sociological research. However, some contemporary sociologists, such as Joan Ferrante, bemoan the loss of vision characteristic of their discipline's classical European scholars, as well as the disproportionate modern emphasis accorded to studying the United States.[1]

Irrespective of where sociologists study them, social groups are usually divided into either **primary** or **secondary** ones, and they vary greatly in size from a few people to millions. Primary groups consist of the relatively few people with whom we have close relations, whereas secondary groups are comprised of a larger number of people with whom we are acquainted. Most often, sociologists look at humans in large, complex, and modern **societies**. Behavior in societies is influenced by prevailing social **norms**, which are standards of what is considered acceptable. The existence of **status** positions in the group—such as scientist, parent, minister, judge, or salesperson—provide both a division of labor and a ranking of positions in the group. A person's **role**, or what he or she does to carry out the expectations of a status position, adds to the organizational function of social status.

Roles can exert a powerful influence on personal behavior. I have conducted many model United Nations Security Council sessions, and it constantly amazes me how quickly and completely students lose themselves in the roles of the delegates whose nations they represent. My own anecdotal experience in different roles confirms to me that societal expectations subtly influence behavior: junior faculty (deferential), senior faculty (opinionated), parent (authoritative), son (rebellious), grandparent (patient), husband (loving), friend (tolerant), shopper (impatient), medical patient (obedient), public speaker (entertaining), spectator (enthusiastic), traveler (urbane), counselor (empathic), student (spontaneous), consultant (observant), administrator (decisive), athlete (humble), author (pensive), researcher (persistent), coach (supportive).

ANTHROPOLOGY

While the disciplines of sociology and anthropology comfortably overlap, the study of preliterate groups, the origins and variety of human evolution, and the workings of faraway social bands are generally left to the latter. Traditionally, anthropologists have been most interested in non-Western ways of life; today they can be found searching for the typical characteristics of groups, both preliterate and literate, in what might be likened to a quest after a definition of the psychology of social groups. Anthropology often relies on participant observation or informant reporting as a basis for the field research which enables it to stimulate what is probably the broadest comparative analysis in the social sciences.

Members of this discipline are usually divided into **physical anthropologists** and **cultural anthropologists**. Ever since Charles Darwin's work in the nineteenth century, we have known that, as biological organisms, humans also evolved via the slow process of natural selection, or survival of the fittest. The physical evidence for the ascent of *Homo sapiens* presents itself largely in the form of fossils (impressions etched into rocks in an earlier geological age) and human skeletal remains. By unearthing such clues to human prehistory, physical anthropologists can transport social science back more than 2 million years into our distant past. They also try to understand why human populations have developed different physical features, such as skin color or height, in different parts of the world.

In addition to varying *biologically*, humans also differ *culturally*. The lifestyle taught in a society is what piques the interest of cultural anthropologists. For a very long time Ethiopians have eaten with their fingers and Koreans with chopsticks, not because of genetic transmission, but as part of a group's culture. The ability to teach a new generation how to start a fire, fix a flat tire, program a computer, or complete a double play in baseball adds up to **socialization**—teaching a way of life, a culture.

When three American professors filmed children in American and Chinese kindergartens, they were recording aspects of socialization largely overlooked by the natives but meaningful in comparative perspective. For example, when American preschoolers go to the bathroom, they do so alone and at a time of their choosing. When Chinese youngsters go to the bathroom, they do so as an orderly group at a specified time. Thousands of such vignettes add up to depict greater individualism in America and greater collectivism in China.[2] In such subtle ways, society conveys a host of important **values** about distinguishing the acceptable from the unacceptable, right from wrong. As was aptly put long ago by anthropologist Ralph Linton, "The last thing a fish would ever notice is water."[3]

Something that is easily noticed, however, and that sets humans apart from other species is that only we can use language to communicate preferred ways of living from one generation to the next; only we can teach others in this way what we ourselves once learned. Since most other cultures in the world are distant both in their lifestyle and location, in order to compare and contrast cultures, anthropologists probably lead all other social scientists in frequent traveler miles.

Both sociology and anthropology bring a variety of conceptual tools to the study of human affairs. Sociology provides diverse concepts like status, role, norms, society, race, ethnicity, gender, crime, socialization, stratification, institutions, bureaucracy, class, social processes—all contributing to our understanding of what is foreign (i.e., within other societies), what is **international** (between countries), and what is **global** (involving everyone). Anthropology likewise contributes important notions such as culture, cultural universals, ethnocentrism, evolution, holism, taboos, culture shock, artifacts, and cultural relativism. Probably no two other social sciences blend together more naturally than sociology and anthropology; this fusion leads to much sharing of concepts, methods, and insights.

CORE CONCEPTS
Society and Culture

The subject matter of sociology and anthropology deals with both social structure (**society**) and social content (**culture**). Although pretty much inseparable in their day-to-day workings, society and culture do not mean exactly the same thing. They can be contrasted for closer analysis. The dichotomous pairs listed below are intended to give a better sense of how society and culture are both similar and dissimilar. Keep in mind, however, that most concepts relating to human behavior cannot be defined with the precision afforded objects like automotive mufflers, carburetors, or windshields.

Physical anthropologists conducting an excavation in Olympia, Greece.

Society:	Culture:
structure	content
organization	lifestyle
concrete	abstract
objective	subjective
formal	informal
social building blocks	social codes
people on a territory	psychology of a people
more direct	more indirect
practical	ideational
framework	process
social interaction	social thought

Since we normally observe societies and cultures operating in tandem, we tend not to notice the nuances uncovered by analysis of these two important social science concepts. There

Quintessential Mexicana: festival
celebrating the Virgin of Guadalupe.

seems to be an inner logic possessed by the people who, over time, construct a society and its culture. The two combine as easily as bread and butter, so that differences between structure and content generally elude the casual observer.

For example, if you visit Mexico, you will notice many things that seem different from the United States, despite physical proximity. Various elements of society and culture contribute to this quality of Mexicanness. But rather than separating these elements of society and culture, we tend to integrate them into a coherent whole. The spicy foods, the siestas taken by many people after a lengthy lunch, people gesturing with hands and standing close enough to touch while conversing, friends embracing in public, the brightly colored visual art in public display, and the **homogeneous** nature of its people all seem quintessentially Mexican.

Types of Societies

While societies like Mexico have unique characteristics, they are so numerous that we categorize them to study them in more than a casual manner. The most basic distinction scholars make delineates societies that are **simple** from societies that are **complex**. In recent centuries many simple societies have either disappeared or been absorbed into more complex societies, creating a powerful trend toward consolidation. However, enough simple societies remain to make them much more than mere historical curiosities.

Simple societies are generally isolated from others, small in size, homogeneous, and comprised of preliterate peoples who interact on a personal basis with their peers. The extended family is vital to the continued existence of the society and the personal security of its denizens. Technology is primitive, little economic surplus gets accumulated, and a clear set of traditional customs direct human behavior. Word of mouth represents the prevalent form of communication. People in such contexts share a sense of vulnerability vis-à-vis the external physical world and they exhibit a high level of sharing based on reciprocity: I am willing to help you today because I believe that you will be willing to act similarly tomorrow. Religious beliefs invariably play a powerful role in explaining the mysteries of life and guiding behavior in simple societies. Kevin Costner's Oscar-winning film *Dances With Wolves* (1990) comes as close as any Hollywood movie to portraying life in a Native American simple society.

German sociologist Ferdinant Tonnies referred to such simple societies with the term *Gemeinschaft*, or "traditional society." To describe their opposite type, he coined the phrase *Gesellschaft*. Complex *Gesellschaft* societies feature literate peoples living impersonal lifestyles in more formalized and specialized ways. They have frequent but brief contacts with outsiders and become accustomed to fast-paced social change. Such large, often heterogeneous societies utilize industrial production to create economic surpluses and unevenly distributed wealth. They also lean toward secularism rather than religiosity and nuclear rather than extended families. Again, by contrasting pairs of characteristics we can sharpen the focus of the social science prism:

Simple Societies:	Complex Societies:
small	large
homogeneous	heterogeneous
personal	impersonal
isolated	contact with others
preliterate	literate
low tech	high tech
religious	secular
subsistence	surplus
slow social change	rapid social change
monocultural	subcultures
extended family	nuclear family
education via family	education separate
work for generalists	work for specialists
egalitarian	stratified

A World Stage Metaphor

Consider a broader drama as transpiring on the world stage. Geography's basic building blocks represent the physical props, such as the stage, curtain, scenery, and climatic environment of the theater. Any play needs a company of players: actors and actresses to carry out specific roles. They are analogous to society—organized and predictable, yet expressing the dynamism of human creativity. Finally, the players in this global drama require the substance of culture—the dialogue of a script, giving direction to the story.

This human saga is anything but a new one. Evidence of the first humans on earth goes back more than 2 million years. Anthropologists trace human organization back at least 10,000 years to the advent of agriculture, while recorded human history has been part of the script for well over 5,000 years. Setting, plot, roles, and players have all evolved during this story on the world stage.

The discovery of agriculture about ten millennia ago served as a vital catalyst to greater social organization than what had existed in hunting and gathering societies. The agricultural revolution created wealth, social differentiation, human settlements, record keeping, and group decision-making authority. From that point on, the players, the script, and even the physical environment began changing more rapidly. We humans became better educated, more affluent, and capable of shaping the contours of the world in which we live.

Means of Subsistence

Another widely used classification scheme derives from the work of sociologists Gerhard and Jean Lenski. They argue that the historical record reveals a progression from simple societies gradually evolving into more complex ones. What drives this process in the Lenskis' viewpoint? Changes in a society's "means of subsistence," or what we think of as making a living. The Lenskis describe a social evolution spanning six types of societies: hunting and gathering, pastoral, horticultural, agricultural, industrial, and postindustrial.[4]

Humans spent roughly one million years on earth as hunters and gatherers living off the land. They hunted wild game and foraged for whatever roots, nuts, and fruits blossomed from their environs. Although far less than one percent of the earth's 5.7 billion global inhabitants support themselves this way today, until about 10,000 years ago everyone did. Nomadic bands probably not exceeding fifty members existed at the precipice of death—very much at the mercy of nature's bounty. Stone-age tools and weapons provided them with an important advantage against competitive species.

Then some of these bands developed a pastoral way of life, built around the herding of domesticated animals such as cattle, goats, and sheep. Pastoral benefits included dairy products and meat, as well as skin and bone for making garments. While still small by our standards, these societies proved able to support much larger groups than had the hunting and gathering life. As pastoralists accumulated surplus goods, their societies expanded into the thousands. Some remained nomadic, following migratory animals like northern caribou. Others in more forgiving climates settled into restricted grazing for their domesticated animals.

At roughly the same time, horticultural societies sprang up when humans figured out how to plant and grow seeds obtained from nature. This small-scale, hands-on primitive gardening enabled humans to settle down and develop a relationship with a tract of land. The potential for expansion of the social group and for creation of surplus wealth was severely limited by small digging sticks, small plots, and small harvests.

Before long, genuine agricultural societies honed the earlier skills of horticulture into something bigger and better. Animal-drawn plows suddenly expanded productivity, opening up all kinds of vistas for their inventors in agricultural societies, as described in Chapter 3. Since huge surpluses meant great wealth for only a few privileged souls, unprecedented inequities burst forth in these larger and more complicated societies. Even today, most of the southern hemisphere consists of societies that are primarily agrarian.

But the modern world as we know it in the West becomes much more recognizable in the Lenskis' next evolutionary stage: industrial society. Spreading from its origins in England during the mid-eighteenth century, the Industrial Revolution quickly captured the human imagination. Its mechanized mass production created **economies of scale**, enabling industrial entrepreneurs to make barrels of money. With first wood, then coal, and later petroleum to fuel the Industrial Revolution, mass production's influences have always been more than merely economic. For better or worse, urbanization, bureaucratization, impersonalization, and stratification have all gathered momentum from the avalanche known as the Industrial Revolution.

The last stop on the Lenskis' odyssey through societal history is one inhabited by only a few of today's most advanced competitors. Postindustrialism refers to those industrial societies that have gone beyond the manufacture of goods and leapt into a brave new world of high-tech communications. They rely on computers for information, and the emphasis is on providing services rather than manufacturing goods. These societies nourish well-educated white-collar workers who are more likely to deal in law, trade, finance, tourism, health, or science than in agriculture or construction. Some observers describe these cutting-edge societies as **technetronic**: combining high technology with electronic communication to create synergistic forces seemingly greater than their component parts. Recent trends in these societies include high levels of inequality, leaving the poor further behind the rich in education, health, and opportunities. In some ways, technetronic societies like Japan, the United States, Canada, Germany, and Singapore are linked together in a borderless world of free-flowing services, information, and financial resources.

STRUCTURE AND SOCIAL INSTITUTIONS

To live together in social settings, humans require a certain amount of predictability. **Social institutions** therefore become essential. Regardless of whether people live in simple or complex societies, agricultural or industrial ones, a few basic human needs must be met in any case.

Social institutions like the family, religion, education, government, and the economy are created by societies to satisfy their most essential needs. They do so not by exerting extraordinary or special effort, but rather by establishing patterned, repetitive, and habitual ways of getting things done: they create expectations of normality. The family provides security and affection, religion speaks to our spiritual longings, education formalizes what one generation decides to teach to the next, government makes authoritative social policy decisions, and the economy gives us a system within which to make a living.

The Bedrock Social Institution: The Family

Which of the social institutions listed above is the oldest? Which is the most important in the socialization process? And which is found in all societies throughout human history? The family, the family, the family! Among primate species, *Homo sapiens* take the longest time to mature, making us extraordinarily dependent for years on end. Given such multifaceted vulnerability, humans require a nurturing learning environment: the family.

Most cultures celebrate the passage to creating a family with some form of ceremonial marriage leading to mutual obligations. For some, like the Pukapuka of Polynesia, the ceremony typically elicits ritual insults between the yet to be united families. Among the Taramiut Inuit Eskimos, however, parents arrange marriages around puberty, at which time the young male moves in with his companion; if a child is produced, the couple then move in with the boy's family and are regarded as married.[5]

Shinto marriage scene in Japan.

Anthropologists Carol and Melvin Ember cite the nineteenth-century southern Indian caste known as the Nayar as an equally rare exception. Nayar marital unions required no consistent or exclusive sexual activity, or binding economic responsibilities, as part of their loose arrangement. Since males of the Nayar caste were military specialists who were frequently away from home, the Nayar bride was expected to entertain surrogate sexual partners, as long as they were members of the same caste and approved by her family.[6]

As an extremely heterogeneous society, India is teeming with interesting subcultures. In the northeastern part of the country operates one of the last remaining matrilineal groups. In the land of 800,000 Khasi, only women inherit property, own land, run businesses, and lead clans. The Khasi way has for centuries required the youngest daughter to inherit the family's property and have her husband move in with her family. But the times are changing, and a group of disgruntled Khasi men have recently organized for more equal life chances. The group's leader, A. Swer, is quoted as saying, "We are sick of playing the roles of breeding bulls and baby-sitters."[7]

In Western cultures, when we talk of marriage, we think of a union of one man and one woman, or **monogamy**. Yet the majority of global societies allow for the possibility of **polygamy**, or plural marriage. This usually involves multiple females and one male (**polygyny**), and only rarely multiple males with one female (**polyandry**).The Sinhalese of Sri Lanka, the Toda caste of India, and some Tibetan tribes have practiced something called fraternal polyandry, in which the plural husbands are brothers.[8]

Since marriage usually creates a union both sexual and economic, it is to be expected that family members have a vested interest in the outcome of mating decisions. The selection of partners occurs either through **arranged marriage**, whereby the respective families play the key role in matchmaking, or **choice mating**, in which prospective mates have the discretion to choose their own partners. Advocates of arranged marriage believe that romantic infatuation can cause young lovers to miss the more subtle considerations that make for a good long-term relationship, and that family members know best. Questions of class, religion, politics, family relations, wealth, and property might not be appreciated by the inexperienced.

In Sri Lanka not only are marriages arranged, but the key consideration for matchmaking is the compatibility of the candidates' horoscopes; decisions are based on astrology. While arranged marriages continue to thrive in India, Morocco, Sri Lanka, Saudi Arabia, and elsewhere, the more liberated lifestyles prevalent in complex industrial societies emphasize freedom of personal choice. In the United States, for example, which prides itself on individual liberty, young people find it incongruous for society to tell them that they are free to vote for whomever they want at the ballot box but that they ought to accept a marriage arranged by their families.

The form of family we find natural in the Western world consists of parents and their children, or the **nuclear family**. While most North Americans or Europeans take this form of small, intimate family for granted, in a majority of cultures studied by anthropologists a larger form of family predominates. In most simple societies the **extended family** is the norm. While nuclear families consist of only parent–child links (husband, wife, offspring), extended families also involve sibling links (brothers or sisters, their spouses and children); therefore such families are much larger. The extended family has some built-in advantages: it allows children to forge close relationships with several people, it spreads out the difficult tasks of child rearing, it provides a child with more role models, and the incidence of child abuse or neglect is lower than in nuclear families.

As societies become more complex, people become more mobile, and therefore more likely to move away from the traditional family home—often to pursue educational or career opportunities. Social mobility helps to account for much of the shift from extended to nuclear families. In complex societies such as France, Canada, or Australia the nuclear family has also suffered from increasing divorce rates, with about one-half of all marriages ending

One large extended family.

fractiously. While families in traditional societies have often been disrupted by the death of a spouse, the phenomenon of divorce remains the exception in those places.

As difficult as divorce in complex societies can be for the spouses, the emotional and economic burdens placed on the children often lead to great stress and confusion. With divorce comes an increased incidence of single-parent families. Many recent Hollywood pictures have reflected tensions inherent in the modern American family, among them *Kramer vs. Kramer* (1979), *Ordinary People* (1980), *Postcards from the Edge* (1990), and *Hoop Dreams* (1993). Despite these new pressures facing the family in both simple and complex societies, it remains the single most important social institution constructed by humans.

How can we account for the staying power of the family institution? Here we look to the school of thought in sociology known as **functionalism**, which concentrates on social order and stability as motivating forces and considers society as a set of interrelated parts. Functionalism suggests that social processes enshrined as institutions are those that work—or *function*—well enough to satisfy human needs. Like other animals, humans possess a sex drive. Unlike other animals, however, humans have created restrictions concerning the expression of the sex drive. Marital relationships help to regulate human sexual behavior. The central imperative of the human species is to replicate itself through procreation; this function too is facilitated by the family, since the family restricts and limits sexual competition. Another function of the family is that it compensates for the lengthy infant maturation process by socializing children to learn what they must know to survive in a complicated world. Finally, the family creates an environment where the human need for affection has a good chance of being met.

Religion as a Social Institution

Just as the family is found in all societies, so too is religion. Although religions vary tremendously worldwide, they all entail beliefs relating to some form of **supernatural** power. Most often, this involves an image of a supreme spiritual being, notions of an afterlife, ethical codes of conduct, and a sacred place where religious rituals transpire. Hunting and gathering societies seem to have believed that all natural objects have a soul or spirit. Their nature worship featured the sun, moon, or mountains as reverential objects; we refer to this type of belief as **animism**. Horticultural societies more often practiced various forms of ancestor worship.

With the agricultural revolution and the emergence of ancient civilizations in places like Egypt, Persia, Greece, and Rome, these societies shifted to worshiping a more abstract pantheon of gods: they practiced **polytheism**. None of the gods inhabiting the heavens of polytheistic religion is considered supreme. Some of these gods—like Vishnu, the creator god in Hinduism, or a vague supernatural force called *mana* among Polynesians—are impersonal. In some cases, however, polytheistic gods began taking on a decidedly **anthropomorphic** (human) countenance. This anthropomorphic tendency was later to dominate the development of the three great **monotheistic** religions of modernity: Judaism, Christianity, and Islam.

Anthropologists are fond of asking vexing "why-type" questions. One of the most intriguing is this fundamental query: Why is religion found—not just sometimes but *always*—across divergent cultures? As was discussed earlier in chapter 3, the Crusades from 1095 to 1272 provide ample evidence of how religion can contribute to fanaticism, bloodshed, and

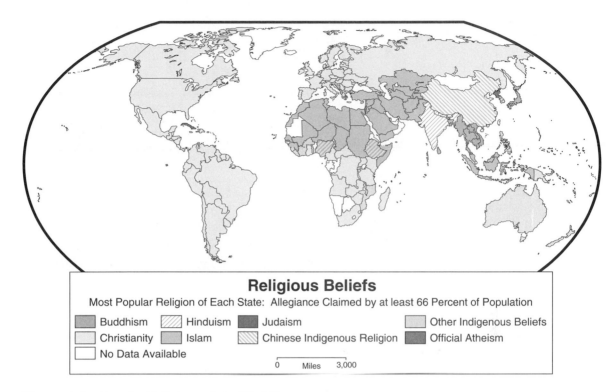

Religious Beliefs

Most Popular Religion of Each State: Allegiance Claimed by at least 66 Percent of Population

Buddhism	Hinduism	Judaism	Other Indigenous Beliefs
Christianity	Islam	Chinese Indigenous Religion	Official Atheism
No Data Available		

0   Miles   3,000

Figure 6.1   Popular Religions of the World*

*In more than 80 percent of the world's states at least two thirds of the population claim allegiance to a single faith. For Christians in Europe this is no indication of regular church attendance.

Source: Joanne O'Brien and Martin Palmer, *The State of Religion Atlas* (New York: Touchstone, 1993), pp. 16–17. Copyright © Myriad Editions, London. Text copyright © 1993 by Joanne O'Brien and Martin Palmer. Maps copyright © 1993 by Myriad Editions Limited, London. Reprinted by permission of Simon & Schuster, Inc.

warring cycles. The flip side of the religious coin, however, is that in many societies, especially simple ones, beliefs relating to the supernatural can perform an integrative function binding believers into a coherent social whole.

The pioneering French sociologist Émile Durkheim suggested that by contributing to this coherent whole, religion was helping meet one of the basic human needs: the need for community. Durkheim felt that the genuine object of religious worship was really the social unity responsible for giving people feelings of confidence.[9] Edward Tylor expressed a more direct answer in arguing that it is a basic human need for intellectual understanding that underlies human religious experience: people desire to know what life is all about.[10]

An alternative interpretation by Bronislaw Malinowski emphasizes humanity's fear of death, rather than a curiosity about life, and our ultimate inability to achieve immortality in the physical realm. Since we can do nothing definitive about our physical mortality, says Malinowski, we cope with our death anxieties by creating the therapeutic institution of religion to soothe our fragile psyches. This viewpoint attaches great significance to religion's inclusion of a spiritual afterlife.[11]

Chamulans from Mesoamerica celebrating their patron saint San Juan.

Sometimes spiritual rituals combine parts of seemingly disparate religions, at times even mixing animistic or polytheistic ones with monotheistic practices. Among the Chamulas of Mesoamerica it is common to borrow the worship of celestial objects from their ancient Mayan Indian ancestors and merge it with the worship of Jesus Christ, taken from the Roman Catholic Spanish conquistadors who invaded the indigenous culture. In the Chamula version of an afterlife, most human souls (except those of murderers and suicides) are transported to a pleasant underworld, earthlike existence, replete with cyclical sunlight. However, one area of human pleasure does not exist for these otherwise fortunate souls: engaging in sexual relations is believed to be not possible.[12]

Not far from where the Chamula live today once thrived the proud Aztec civilization. Like many of the most advanced ancient civilizations of both the Old and New Worlds (Mesopotamian, Greek, Viking, Celtic, Incan, and Mayan), the Aztecs engaged in a religious practice considered by Western civilization as barbaric: ritual human sacrifice (see Mini-case 6.1).

MINI-CASE 6.1
Humans Sacrificed at the Altar of Aztec Gods

The Aztec state originated with a community of Nahuatl-speaking Amerindians in the Valley of Mexico during the early fourteenth century. Tenochtitlan developed into the grandest city in the Americas as the capital of this large, powerful state, located in what today remains the heart of modern Mexico. The Aztec irrigation system supported organized agriculture, producing huge surpluses. The inventive Aztecs connected many of the Mexican lakes by canals, establishing regular canoe traffic which brought agricultural products like corn, sweet potatoes, tomatoes, beans, and tobacco to cities genuinely deserving of that designa-

Figure 6.2

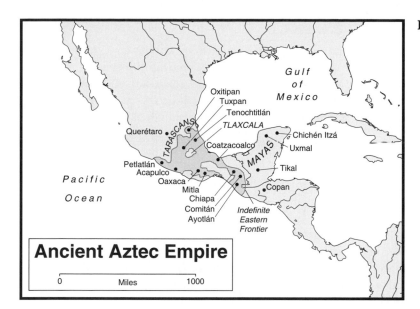

Ancient Aztec Empire

tion—cities with specialized and skilled labor forces and well-organized economic and political institutions. An efficient bureaucracy collected taxes, delivered mail, and enforced the law. World-class science, art, architecture, and writing were also produced by this thriving empire.

But another characteristic of Aztec society was its extreme militarism, its intent to conquer most of its neighbors, especially those toward the east and south. From these subjugated neighbors they extracted heavy taxes and tribute. As religious polytheists, the Aztecs had plenty of gods whom they believed needed appeasing, and many unfortunates defeated in war were slated for sacred rituals of sacrifice. The protection of the gods of the sun, earth, and rivers stood at the pinnacle of Aztec beliefs and required payment in human blood. At their peak, they led about 30,000 hapless victims per year to the sacrificial stone in Tenochtitlan. Many had their heart and vital organs cut or torn out while still conscious and breathing.

As brutal and unnecessary as this sacrificial carnage seems to Western civilization, it made logical sense to the Aztecs: their religious gods required regular appeasement as the price for this empire's continued success. What seemed utterly without sense in Aztec logic was their own rapid butchery from 1519 to 1522 at the hands of Spain's Hernando Cortez, with his horses and thundering artillery.

An Aztec prophecy had predicted that "white gods" would appear, and at first it was believed that the arrival of the conquistadors ought to be heralded. The Aztecs were disabused of any such illusions when Cortéz unleashed a holy war against religious idolatry and human sacrifice. While the Spaniards found Aztec religion heretical and barbaric, many Aztecs did not find Catholic doctrine all that strange. Some of them reportedly considered the sacrifice of Jesus Christ as the path to human salvation quite congenial with their own notions of the relationship between salvation and sacrifice.[13]

WINDS OF SOCIAL CHANGE

The impetus for social change can come from within or from without a given society. Cultures seldom remain static for long, particularly when they come into contact with outsiders. The most potent external force stimulating social change over the last 500 years has been that of Western society, which has managed to spread its influence to every region of the globe. The forces of change can occur either peacefully or violently, and not all indigenous societies were ripped asunder by the colonial sword as quickly or bloodily as the Aztecs.

The winds of social change can arrive in the wake of a new idea like democracy or socialism; they can blow in more concretely through inventions like the steam engine or the personal computer. Cultures such as the Aztecs, North American Sioux Indians, and African Zulus were decimated by Westerners. Stronger and more resilient cultures, like the Japanese and Chinese, were able to blend aspects of Western influence into their traditional lifestyles. External influence can also result in useful adaptation, as with our contemporary system of numbers, which did not originate in Europe but rather came to Western civilization from India, by way of scholars in the Arab world. It would be very difficult to make a case for the old Roman numerical system as equal to the modern one adapted from the Arabs.

Most theories attempting to explain the nature of social change tend to approach the issue from one of two directions: (1) assuming that change occurs in a linear, progressive, and evolutionary manner, with an "onward and upward" view of humanity; or (2) assuming that change occurs in a cyclical, repetitive, and lateral fashion, resulting in life continuing as more similar than dissimilar to our past. Do you think scientific and humanistic social scientists might vary in their preferences regarding these two sets of assumptions about social change?

In sharp contrast to the rapid and violent change forced upon the Aztecs half a millennium ago, contemporary anthropologists have examined cases of slower and more peaceful change up close and personally. Among these is one African tribal band whose hunting and gathering lifestyle remained stable for 10,000 years but that now finds itself struggling to maintain a semblance of its former independent identity (see Mini-case 6.2).

MINI-CASE 6.2
The Fading of the Kalahari !Kung

Formerly known as the Kalahari Bushmen, the nomadic !Kung were the first people to populate southern Africa. Short in stature, nimble, and with light brown skin, they seemed well suited to the Kalahari Desert where they hunted and foraged for a living. In small bands of thirty to forty members, the !Kung males hunted more than sixty animal species while the women worked with about a hundred edible plants. These native speakers of Khoisan, like all those of the San-group, have a distinctive clicking pattern to their speech. Although they possess no written historical record, much oral history continues to pass from generation to generation. The !Kung also appear in the annals of other tribal groups and leave a visual legacy in the form of numerous but faded cave paintings.

It has often been said that while the Zulus epitomize the warrior tradition among southern African tribes, the other end of the spectrum is populated by the philosophical and spiritual !Kung. Much of the world became familiar with the !Kung via South African filmmaker Jamie Uys's movie *The Gods Must Be Crazy* (1980). In this strange picture, an errant Coca-Cola bottle falls from an airplane; it is found by Bushmen who interpret it as a sign from the gods and assign one of their members the task of getting rid of it. One little Coke bottle ends up causing all kinds of havoc in the lives of the bewildered foragers.

While most other foraging societies in the region were disappearing during the nineteenth and early twentieth centuries, the !Kung held to the essence of their nomadic existence of group sharing. A long-term anthropological study, the Harvard Kalahari Project, which began in 1951 and ran officially until the 1970s, provided considerable data about the process of change within this society. Anthropologists Richard Lee, Irven DeVore, John Yellen, and Lorna Marshall studied the group intensely. Professor Yellen's long-term analysis reveals that, as of the 1950s, they were still almost entirely hunter-gatherers, kept a leaderless group without anyone designated to adjudicate disputes, and remained committed to a highly reciprocal culture of unselfishness.

Kalahari !Kung woman and child.

In the 1960s many more domesticated goats and cattle were being consumed than previously and traditional animal skin clothing was starting to give way to garments from outside, yet the males still set out to hunt with poison arrows and females still foraged for plants and roots to dig on a daily basis. The 1970s, however, witnessed much more profound social changes: marriages with members of the neighboring Bantu tribe, enlisting the Bantu chiefs for adjudication purposes, families planting fields of crops and eating more domesticated cattle, fewer young boys learning bow-and-arrow hunting skills from their fathers, people hoarding material goods rather than sharing them, and more people seeking privacy rather than their traditional social intimacy. What explains these far-reaching changes to a society that was for so long impervious to external forces?

About 60,000 Bushmen still exist in Botswana, Namibia, South Africa, Angola, and Zambia. But a fundamental transformation has occurred among the !Kung in recent decades and their future seems in peril. According to John Yellen, the shift from a foraging to a mixed form of subsistence occurred not because of external force and not because of the failure of traditional foraging to feed the !Kung adequately.

An uncharacteristic hunger for **materialism** had begun eating away at the basis of !Kung culture: once they experienced regular access to material goods from outside, they began hoarding rather than sharing. Since such attachment to objects was alien to the traditional beliefs of !Kung society, people felt ashamed for not living up to their ideals of sharing and unselfishness. As the !Kung felt more embarrassed, they increasingly sought solace in privacy. Burgeoning materialistic values, so familiar to Western civilization, seem to have led the !Kung into the land of profound cultural change, and probably closer to the cultural graveyard. *The Gods Must Be Crazy* is another example of art imitating life imitating art imitating life.[14]

CULTURAL UNIVERSALS, CULTURAL DIFFERENCES

Cultural differences jump out at us because they often seem odd. More subtly shared cultural elements usually go unnoticed. Thus we tend to exaggerate the differences and underestimate the similarities. Under the surface, there are many more ways in which cultures resemble one another than ways in which they diverge. Sometimes cultural differences even challenge our definition of reality.

On a group trip to Taiwan some students returned from a rural visit with film footage they had taken of Buddhist fire walkers. We viewed the action and it was vividly described to us by our fascinated students. About fifteen Buddhists had worked themselves into a meditative state by chanting and dancing, then repeatedly walked, quite slowly, across a large pit of burning coals at least ten feet square. None was harmed in any way. A physician from our group was present and examined the white-hot bed of coals as closely as possible, but he reported that they were too hot for him to get close. Every student present was excited over this experience yet confused by it. They wanted to talk about it in great detail, partly to relieve the disorientation associated with witnessing something they considered physically impossible. This reaction represented an *intellectual* dilemma. How do you explain such an experience?

Not easily, I assume. Such factors as personality differences along with cultural and professional differences account for individual reactions to such an anomaly. The unshakeable consensus among our group was that they had in fact witnessed fire walking over extremely hot coals. One possible response is to regard the fire walking as mere trickery, akin to an after-dinner magical act of deception, albeit a very clever one. Scientific adherents might consider this fact, by definition, impossible—therefore outside the bounds of serious consideration. Skepticism is one of the core attitudes of science, and anyone with a scientific bent would likely cast a dubious eye in the direction of anything like fire walking.

More humanistic individuals would be more likely to consider this as a case of mind over matter: the untapped potential of the human mind is so vast as to be capable of producing phenomena well beyond the current consciousness of most people. They might point to countless other examples of well-chronicled feats considered impossible by scientific reckoning.

None of these opinions is patently irrational or demonstrably false. How do you account for this fire-walking experience? What kind of explanation makes the most sense to you? Does the type of explanation most plausible to you tell you anything about your general outlook on the world?

Political scientist Marshall Singer conducts sessions in cross-cultural communication at the University of Pittsburgh. In them he sometimes tells a story of a cocktail party he once hosted for his graduate students. Among the items he put out were fried caterpillars which an Asian student had given to him. Well into the party, one American student approached the professor, remarking that she enjoyed the shrimp on the table in the corner. Singer then informed her that she had in fact eaten an Oriental delicacy, namely fried caterpillars. The student immediately turned away and vomited on the living room carpet. The fried caterpillars had not made her sick, her culture-bound perceptions produced that result. The majority of peoples throughout history have eaten insects, grubs, toads, and worms—all as nutritious as they are unappetizing to us.

Many of my students travel to other countries via study abroad programs. They often return speaking of **culture shock** as part of adjusting to new ways of doing things. Simple things that we take for granted—mealtimes, sleep patterns, language, foods consumed, leisure activities, religious rituals—may be done quite differently elsewhere. An instructive documentary film by Regge Life, *The African American Experience in Japan*, describes day-to-day difficulties confronting the few black Americans living and working in the world's most homogeneous large country, where more than 99 percent are ethnic Japanese and immigration is strictly limited. In Japan social and professional life are more intertwined than in the United States, a practice that can be disconcerting to Americans more accustomed to a separation

"Look, everyone here loves vanilla, right? So let's start there."

Figure 6.3

Source: Drawing by P. Steiner, © 1980 The New Yorker Magazine, Inc.

between the two.[15] Occasionally exposure to novel cultures can be even more devastating. Consider the Panara wilderness tribe of Brazil, whose first contact with Caucasians in 1971 resulted in death by disease for 90 percent of its people within four years.

Cultural universals, also called *cultural traits*, consist of less sensational but equally important things. These universals exist because all humans have similar basic needs. Each society finds its own ways of dealing with these needs—but deal with them it must. Humans need something to link their existence to a divine or natural order, and societies find ways of addressing these ontological questions. People need to learn how to function effectively in their social milieu—thus institutions of education. People require membership in a basic social group to assist them in life, and a form of family exists in all cultures. Medical attention in some form is needed by all peoples, regardless of setting. Official rules of the social game must provide order and stability; hence some form of political decision making appears in all cultures. People must have some regular way of engaging in the production, distribution, and consumption of goods and services, and so every society is forced to develop its own variant of an economy. All societal cultures also include some means of artistic expression, play, and hospitality.[16]

Chapter Synopsis

The professionalization associated with graduate education did not emerge for the discipline of anthropology until after World War I, when modern anthropology separated from the broader discipline of sociology as part of the Americanization of the social sciences. For about two centuries, inquiry into what we now think of as sociological and anthropological issues in European academe occurred under the wider intellectual net of historico-philosophical discourse. The analytical net among European scholars was applied in no small part to comprehending the social and cultural implications of the Industrial Revolution which reverberated throughout the European experience from 1750 onward. Only with the Americanization of the social sciences one century ago did scientific inquiry come to pervade sociology and did anthropology break free as a viable discipline in the new universities of the United States.

At its most basic level, sociology studies the human experience of living in groups, with society—the structures and institutions of group life—comprising the stuff of sociology. In the analogy of the world stage, society represents the company of players who populate and give life to the drama. Simply by virtue of being human, all people have certain basic needs. As organized groups of people called societies pool their resources to establish patterned, regular, predictable, and recurrent ways of meeting these needs, social institutions like the family, religion, and education are established. Societies vary greatly in this diverse world. In order to compare and contrast societies, sociologists have devised classification schemes. One very basic one delineates between simple and complex societies. Another more sophisticated one focuses on means of subsistence as a key element in the historical evolution of societies.

Similarly, the discipline of anthropology studies the group experience with an emphasis on culture—the content, or script—of the human drama. Anthropology's fixation on culture often leads to cross-cultural comparison in this discipline possessing a healthy aversion to parochialism and ethnocentrism. Since humans remain humans regardless of how they choose to live their lives, cultural universals (traits) can be found in every culture. Yet, because there are many rooms in humanity's home of cultural habitation, cultural differences often jump out at us when we study another culture. They sometimes seem strange, even bizarre, to the casual observer. Anthropologists, however, are trained to see beyond the titillating uniqueness of a culture in quest of the inner logic that dictates cultural behaviors—behaviors so unassailable to the residents as to preclude serious examination.

For Digging Deeper

Ember, Carol, and Melvin Ember. *Cultural Anthropology.* Prentice Hall, 1996.

Ferrante, Joan. *Sociology: A Global Perspective.* Wadsworth Publishing, 1995.

Heider, Karl G., and Carol Hermer. *Films for Anthropological Teaching,* AAA Special Publication #29, 1996.

Jones, Brian, Bernard Gallagher, and Joseph M. Falls. *Sociology: Micro, Macro, and Mega Structures.* Harcourt Brace, 1995.

Lenski, Gerhard, and Jean Lenski. *Human Sociology: An Introduction to Macro-sociology.* McGraw-Hill, 1987.

Mills, C. Wright. *The Sociological Imagination.* Oxford University Press, 1959.

Murdock, George Peter. *Social Structure.* Macmillan, 1949.

Key Glossary Terms

animism
anthropomorphism
arranged marriage
choice mating
complex societies
cultural anthropology
cultural universals
culture
culture shock
economies of scale
extended family
foreign
functionalism

global
homogeneous
international
materialism
monogamy
monotheism
norms
nuclear family
physical anthropology
polyandry
polygamy
polygyny
polytheism

primary group
role
secondary group
simple societies
social institutions
socialization
society
status
supernatural
technetronic
values

CHAPTER **7**

Comparing Cultures

Thematic Questions

CORE OBJECTIVE

To appreciate the resiliency of the key concept of culture by examining cultural universals and cultural differences in varied contexts.

- How is culture a nebulous concept, and what levels of analysis enter into its examination?

- What similarities and differences characterize Japanese and Chinese cultures, how is Russian culture Eurasian, can broad civilizations such as Islam be understood as cultures, and how does Morocco fit into Islamic culture?

- What is the nature of subcultures, and how do the Baka and Arara peoples illustrate this concept?

- What kinds of classification schemes help us to categorize and compare different cultures?

The concept of culture, though vital to the social sciences, is also a nebulous one. Defined quite variously, it defies precise dissection. Another issue that arises in a study of cultures is the level-of-analysis question. We often refer to large societies—like Spain, Brazil, or India—when comparing cultures, since they are interesting, well organized, and easy to examine. But what about the endless variety of **subcultures** within these societies? Hare Krishnas, Jews, liberals, free-trade advocates, right-wing militia, hockey fans, Polish-Americans, Gypsies, Dead Heads, and the Amish warrant attention in their own right.

If we think of cultures as possessing personalities, then awareness of cultural characteristics can aid in our comparing them. In comparing cultural patterns, we reduce the confusion created by their multiplicity. Comparing cultures also enriches understanding and appreciation of our own culture. Philosophers have long argued that knowledge of the self occurs partly through knowledge of others.[1]

Cultural diversity is endless. Germany, for example, tends toward an active lifestyle, while Sri Lanka feels comfortable with greater passivity. Some Western cultures focus on the present, whereas many Oriental cultures have more of a sense of history. Cultures based on the Judeo-Christian religious heritage consider humans to stand above nature, while most indigenous peoples, like Native Americans, see humanity as part of a cyclical natural order. Islamic cultures directly involve religion in public life, while most Western countries are more secular.

The culture of the United States is imbued with an optimistic sense of efficacy, while Italians are more pessimistic in general outlook. Heterogeneous cultures like India vary much more than do homogeneous ones like Korea. Some, like Australia, are quite egalitarian, while England remains more stratified. Some can stay fairly static, like Tibet, but others, such as Malaysia, are quite dynamic. The Persians of Iran constitute an ancient culture, while Canada's is relatively young. Such generalizations simplify reality—a price we pay to translate global complexity to human comprehension. Let's look more closely at some of the details.

JAPANESE CULTURE

Japan holds a unique paradoxical position in being both crucial to the U.S. yet fundamentally different from it in lifestyle. It is the second leading trade partner of the United States, and thus the Japanese–American economies are inextricably linked and co-dependent; yet, misperception and resentment constantly lurk beneath the surface of trade issues. Robert Christopher's book *The Japanese Mind* explores the many ironies pervading this relationship between what he calls the "oddest couple."[2]

When hurricane Andrew struck southern Florida in 1992, multimillion-dollar looting added to the natural devastation. Years later the Federal Emergency Management Agency (FEMA) was still seeking to recover $209 million from suspected false insurance claims.[3] In striking contrast, the 7.2 magnitude earthquake of 1995 which rocked the Japanese port city of Kobe, killing more than 6,000 people, resulted in almost no looting of goods, or fraud, by local residents. If you visit Japan, you will surely notice some of the 3 million bicycles daily left unlocked at rail stations in this nation of commuters. They almost never get stolen. Would you advise leaving bikes unlocked all day long in Memphis, Scranton, Boise, or Phoenix?

Is this merely anecdotal reporting, unreliable and meaningless, as scientifically oriented social scientists would probably insist? Or are valuable insights generated by juxtaposing

Bikes parked at a train station in suburban Tokyo.

the young, heterogeneous culture of the United States with the 2,000-year history of homogeneous Japan, as humanities-oriented professors might suggest? In sifting through information to analyze human behavior, how do we decide which comprises the wheat and which the chaff? Or are all data somehow useful in their own unique ways?

Some comparative generalizations about Japan and the U.S. can surely be made more confidently than others. Few would argue with the observation that Japan, an extremely homogeneous culture, is more exclusionary and closed to outsiders than the United States, one of the world's most heterogeneous and open societies. Similarly, not many social scientists would dispute the potency of group responsibility in Japan. Whether at the level of the family, the corporation, or the nation, Japanese willingness to sacrifice personal interests to those of the group confounds Americans, who are noted for rugged individualism.

Attendance at a Japanese baseball game is a marvelous way for Americans to appreciate the impact of cultural differences on a game that is technically the same but under the surface operates quite differently. For example, consider the group-versus-individual contrast cited above. Cheering by the crowd at a Japanese ball game seems more akin to a high school football game in the United States: organized cheers complete with cheerleaders armed with megaphones, and a band backing them up. The emphasis is on inspiring team effort and cohesion, not on individual heroics. By contrast, North American baseball crowds cheer more as individuals than as a group, and their cheers are aimed at individual star players to live up to their exalted billing (and salaries). North Americans also resort to jeers when cheers fail, booing or verbally skewering their fallen heroes. Such emotionally negative behavior in public would seem crude to the Japanese. The documentary film *Baseball in Japan* (1994) is the next best thing to seeing a game in Tokyo or Kobe.[4]

Consensus also exists over the Japanese penchant for long-term planning and patience in all areas of life, but especially in business matters. By contrast, it requires no degree in rocket science to see that in American culture, immediacy—instant gratification—rules the roost. In the business world this attitude expresses itself in corporate preoccupation with the bottom line for the current quarter; planning for ten or twenty years hence simply does not enter into computations. In negotiations, Americans consider a formal agreement as final, with implementation resulting as a natural consequence, while their Japanese counterparts see a negotiated solution as merely part of an ongoing process during which implementation will require future negotiation.[5]

Other observations about the two cultures get decidedly more contentious. Some scholars believe American culture to be more confrontational and direct and Japanese to be more subtle and evasive, attributing the latter partly to the inherent complexity of the Japanese language. America has one lawyer for every 440 citizens, but Japan has only one lawyer per 10,000 people. Never intimately wed to restrictive ideologies or religions, the Japanese are considered by some to be highly pragmatic and flexible: living in harsh circumstances, they do what is needed to survive and prosper.

Some observers go so far as to describe the use of guilt as an important social lever in Japan, getting people to conform to society's norms. As loyal group members, they are more susceptible to manipulation by guilt. Fitting in is imperative; it manifests itself symbolically in the school uniforms worn by all students. In contrast, guilt seems much less potent as a social motivator in America. A closely related idea is that honor and obligation are endemic to Japanese culture but rarer among defiantly individualistic North Americans. A more certain observation: that the Japanese know much more about Americans than vice versa—partly because more than 40,000 Japanese students attend U.S. colleges and universities each year.

While Japan's higher education system suffers from an inability to accommodate all those wishing to attend college in the modern democratic era, its public education system features some impressive qualities. Parents, students, and teachers work hard to meet the expectations of a culture that considers success in school and success in life as nearly coterminous.[6] Student discipline, study habits, and time spent both in school and doing homework might make some North American educators visiting Japan drool with envy. But one negative consequence of this driven mentality is palpable in Japanese schools: the pressure it places on young people wanting not to disappoint family and society. The comprehensive tests taken after high school are dreaded as "examination hell" by students competing for very few university slots.[7]

Smaller in area than the state of Montana, Japan's four islands would constitute 4 percent of U.S. territory, yet they support a population half that of the United States: 125 million people. Nearly half are packed into Tokyo, Osaka, and Nagoya in a country with a high population density of 860 per square mile. An unbelievable 99 percent are ethnic Japanese, with a small number of Chinese and Koreans making up most of the remainder.

Over half of Japan's land is mountainous, of which only 13 percent is arable, and so the country imports nearly half of its food. Farming efficiency is stretched by terracing of steep slopes, mechanization among the 8 percent of its people who farm, heavy irrigation, development of hybrid rices, and multiple cropping. Its vibrant fishing industry provides protein by taking one-seventh of the world's total catch. To top it off, Japan has few natural resources, no oilfields, and very little coal.

But Japan has created the world's second largest economy, making its remarkable twentieth-century success story seem reminiscent of another small archipelago nation prominent in the previous century: Great Britain. Japan's GNP per capita is about $26,000, and, most impressively, it usually ranks first or second out of more than 170 countries on the Human Development Index.[8] Japanese people weigh less than those in any industrialized country, and average life expectancy has reached the eighty-year plateau, the highest in the world.

Japan's economic miracle is not simple to explain. However, efficient use of human resources has compensated for its physical weaknesses. There can be no doubting the Japanese work ethic. Author Michio Morishima attributes economic success mostly to cultural values. A well-educated, hard-working, loyal, and unselfish work force obviously counts for a great deal—as do Japan's close management–worker relations, managed economic policies, and U.S. assistance since 1945 (Japan's average defense expenditure: a miniscule 1% of GNP).[9]

CHINESE CULTURE

Just as individual people differ in personality, leading them to perceive reality somewhat differently, cultures possess personalities which serve as giant lenses through which they see the world. From the U.S. perspective, Japan and China, as Asian cultures, seem quite similar. However, viewed from inside the Japanese or Chinese cultural prisms, they exhibit quite different style and substance.[10] What do North Americans tend to notice when considering Japan and China? Old cultures with strong group identities, homogeneous peoples, and certain values. We might observe formal and conservative rituals, such as bowing to show deference or discomfort at being touched by strangers, or possibly respect for the elderly and an aversion to losing face (honor). Oh yes, both eat with chopsticks. Roughly the same number of Chinese and Japanese students attend American higher education institutions. Our cultural lenses magnify all these genuine similarities.

Contrarily, Chinese and Japanese cultural lenses highlight equally real, but quite different qualities. For example, compare the situation in Japan to these Chinese realities: China's rural populace, its authoritarian communist government, less developed economy, official atheism, Confucian conservatism, moral puritanism, rudimentary education system, and attempts by the government to weaken family loyalties. On such issues, no divining rod is required to locate significant differences. The question about a glass being half full or half empty is instructive here. Depending on your point of view, you can make an interesting case that Chinese and Japanese cultures are very similar; the student who sits next to you might also make an interesting case that Chinese and Japanese cultures are very different.

As one of the world's oldest civilizations, China has long been influenced by a conservative philosophy valuing social stability and order—**Confucianism**, which dominated Chinese life for over twenty centuries. One of Confucius's most famous observations was that "The cautious seldom err." Confucius (551–479 B.C.) wrote during China's classical Zhou dynasty and urged the emperor, who was more than autocratic—he was considered divine—to encourage education by using meritocracy based on national examinations to select ministers to advise him. He stressed the role of the family and respect for parents and the elderly as the crux of Chinese culture.

Since 1949, however, China's communist leaders have tried to weaken Confucian influences by creating a system revolving around two Chinese leaders: first Mao Zedong, who was in power from 1949 until his 1976 death, then Deng Xiaoping, the most influential post-Maoist leader. What has resulted bears little resemblance to the stability associated with a traditional

Confucian culture. Mini-case 7.1 looks to communist-era China to illustrate a topic that modern sociologists study often, namely, how societies deal with what they define as social **deviance**.

MINI-CASE 7.1
The Great Proletarian Cultural Revolution

The notion of social deviance becomes particularly easy to apply in any highly **ideological** context. In the Crusades, discussed earlier, Christians could rely on Church doctrine to brand the Muslims as heretics, and therefore expendable. Communism represents one of the few social ideologies that has often equaled world religions in ideological fervor among its adherents. And nowhere did communist ideological fervor overachieve the way it did in China. As Communist China's supreme ruler for almost three decades, Mao Zedong held the power to set any policies he desired. Converting them to social reality proved more difficult. Put simply, Mao tried to replace millennia of Confucian influence with communist ideology. He grossly underestimated the staying power of conservative Confucian principles, which weighed heavily on the failure of his socioeconomic programs.

Mao hated Western influences and sought to turn China's efforts inward, hoping to propel the country into the industrial era. A veritable "bamboo curtain" separated the Chinese people from the outside world as Mao touted "self-reliance" as China's salvation. Part of what Mao disliked about the West was its technological complexity and what he considered as its undisciplined decadence. Ideological purity was to sanctify the people's sacrifices in building a communist paradise, and this purity was personified by Mao's *Little Red Book*, a compendium of his most cherished sayings. Anyone daring to question Mao's orthodoxy was immediately branded with the label of "revisionist." Religious analogies flow easily concerning Mao's China, and comparing his infallible book to the Koran among Muslim fundamentalists, or the Bible for fundamentalist Christians, does not represent an imaginative stretch. Not only was Mao's thought considered unquestionably true, but it was also to be memorized and publically recited.

The cacophony of devoted voices praising the "Great Leader" reached a crescendo from 1966 to the early 1970s, during the heyday of the Great Proletarian Cultural Revolution. In this period the social definition of deviance became incredibly narrow, with only overt devotion to Mao deemed acceptable. At the vanguard of the Cultural Revolution were the strident paramilitary Red Guards, millions of zealous youth ready to humiliate anyone seemingly not loyal enough to the "Great Helmsman."

> During this period any person who held a position of authority, worked to earn a profit, showed the slightest leaning toward foreign ways, or had academic interests was subject to interrogation, arrest, and punishment. Included in this group were scientists, teachers, athletes, performers, artists, writers, private business owners, and people who had relatives living outside China, wore glasses, wore make-up, spoke a foreign language, owned a camera, or a radio, or had traveled abroad.[11]

Reliable figures on the costs of the Cultural Revolution are hard to establish. Some observers suggest that 10 million people may have perished in the mayhem.[12]

Members of China's Red Guard, wearing armbands and carrying books containing the sayings of Mao Zedong, parade through the streets of Beijing during the Cultural Revolution. The portraits they carry also pay homage to Chairman Mao.

Undoubtedly, the human toll was enormous, as individuals and families suffered under abject conditions. The number sent into rural exile for "reeducation" ran into tens of millions. Social institutions, like hospitals and schools, were closed for arbitrary reasons. Economic productivity plummeted, doctors did not graduate from medical schools, and welders did not get trained during China's lost generation. The hangover from this ideological binge lasted beyond Mao's death, creating massive headaches for the leaders who later attempted to catch up with the rest of the world, which was engaged in powerful technological advances while China convulsed in spasms of self-absorption over political deviance.[13]

Contemporary China, slightly larger in area than the United States, similarly experiences seasonal climates. The majority of China's 1.2 billion people live in the fertile and temperate eastern region. During the Maoist era, population control was seen as a Western imperialist plot to weaken China's world power, and Mao encouraged the birth rate to stay at about three children per family. Deng Xiaoping interpreted this rate of growth differently. He considered it as a brake against economic development and introduced strong population control measures, which resulted in the birth rate dropping to only 1.2 per family by the mid-1980s.

The dominant ethnic group, Han Chinese, makes up 92 percent of China's population, whose literacy rate stands at a modest 73 percent; the main educational goal for the 1990s is to provide an elementary education for all citizens. Fully 60 percent of China works in agriculture, GNP per capita barely reaches $2,000 per year, and China ranks low on the Human Development Index: 111 of 174 countries. More impressive is the double-digit economic growth rate in the mid-1990s and an average life expectancy of sixty-nine years. Most of China's recent economic growth has emerged from a ring of experimental regions along China's east coast. A variety of tax breaks, investment incentives, and foreign dealings, which are not permitted in the rest of the country, are allowed in these Special Economic Zones (SEZs).[14]

The idea of a single overriding Chinese culture sometimes confuses students, since it can be directly associated with three places: the People's Republic of China, the Republic of China, and Hong Kong. The People's Republic of China (PRC), usually called Communist China or China, amounts to one-fifth of the world's population and has nuclear weapons, a Red Army of 4 million strong, and a rapidly growing economy. All of these considerations make it easy for China to get the attention of other countries.

Such has not always been the case with the Republic of China (R.O.C.), also referred to as Taiwan or Formosa, which has been overlooked often on the world stage during the last fifty years. This is an island nation the size of West Virginia, located 120 miles off China's coast, where Kuomintang Party leader Chiang Kaishek fled in 1949 when defeated by Mao Zedong's communists in the Chinese civil war. Considered by Communist China to have no legal right to exist as a nation–state, Taiwan continues to have a diplomatic presence, which can be attributed largely to U.S. financial and military support. How-

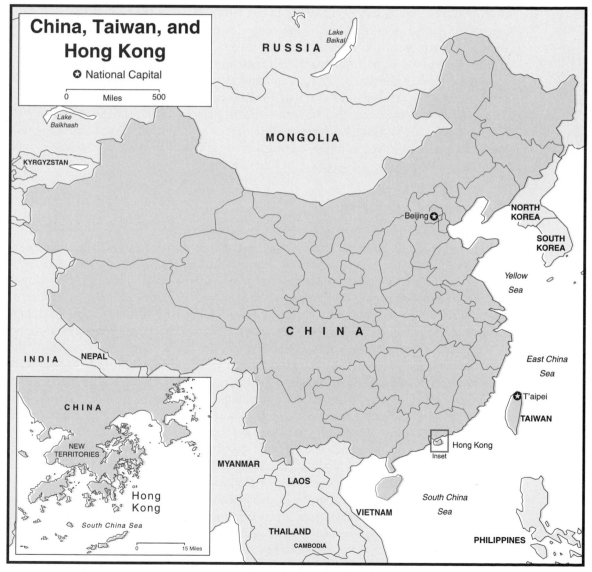

Figure 7.1

ever, during the 1980s and 1990s Taiwan has achieved new status as a role player in world affairs. Why? Because it is one of the east Asian NICs who have followed the Japanese path of **neomercantilism** to economic prosperity.

Another of the NICs, Hong Kong, is even more intriguing. A city–state jutting out from the Chinese coast, it was ceded to the British in 1842 under the Treaty of Nanking, because of Chinese losses in the devastating Opium War. Hong Kong's 7 million polyglot inhabitants lived in the world's most wide-open laissez-faire economy—and an affluent one at that, with a 1996 GNP per capita of almost $11,000—at least for those who survived its cutthroat economic competition.

It also became a very nervous city in the 1990s, because the United Kingdom had agreed to return Hong Kong to Chinese control, which occurred officially in 1997. Although China promised to allow Hong Kong to keep its own political and economic system for fifty years, many residents do not trust the Chinese communist leaders. Fresh memories of what happened in China's capital city of Beijing on June 4, 1989, haunt many Hong Kong residents. On that date the Chinese government massacred many hundreds of peaceful demonstrators from the student democracy movement in Tienanmen Square. Many affluent Hong Kong residents fled, mostly to Canada. Most Hong Kong residents, however, remained at home, hoping that the glitter of their economic success will result in the Hong Kong tail wagging the Chinese dog.

RUSSIAN CULTURE

Both Japan and China, as group-oriented Asian cultures, strike many North Americans as exotic. Russia is a Eurasian society with a mixed culture, approximately halfway between collectivist Oriental cultures and the Western belief in individual liberty. Russia is more than twice the size of either the United States or China, and its Siberian region alone, with only 15 million people, dwarfs the United States. But the term "Eurasian" culture misleads, suggesting a smooth comingling of East and West. The Russian historical drama has featured violently clashing opponents, with the pendulum swinging from one extreme to the other, seldom coming gently to rest in the center.

The two main irreconcilable forces in Russian culture are **Slavophilism** versus **Westernization**. The Slavophiles love that which is Russian, glorifying the dignity of Russia's proud 1,000 years of culture. Deeply rooted in the traditions of the Russian Orthodox Church, they see "Holy Russia" as morally superior to Western materialism and expediency. Suspicious of Western individualism, their collectivist preferences show through in an old peasant proverb: "It is the tall blade of grass which first gets cut." The Russophiles have traditionally dominated both the inner sanctums of power and the hearts of the simple peasants. Conservative and status-quo forces in the society have generally supported Slavophilism.

The gradual change characteristic of, say, British or Swedish history finds virtually no harbor in the stormy sea that has been Russian culture for a millennium. The Westernizers, also known as Reformers, find themselves swimming against the dominant tides in Russia. Russia missed out on the European Renaissance and Enlightenment and therefore was left a step behind its neighbors to the west in science, education, politics, and the arts. Russia has always faced this dilemma: change or fall behind your rivals. Little in Russian culture, however, facilitates gradual change: not autocratic political systems; not weak agrarian economies; not a church under the thumb of dictators; not fatalistic popular attitudes.

Like a teakettle, Russia lies dormant for long periods of time, suddenly erupting when enough steam builds to blow off the top. These eruptions have been the intermittent, violent rebellions littering the landscape of Russian history. In addition, change sometimes is imposed from above. Reform leaders like Peter the Great, Catherine the Great, Alexander II, or Mikhail Gorbachev—trying to pull Russia up by its bootstraps—meet stiff resistance from both the masses and the entrenched elites.

Similar to European countries like Britain, Germany, and France, Russia expanded into a colonial power in earlier centuries—except that while the Europeans used sea lanes to subjugate a colonial empire, the Russians traveled only the vast expanses of the Eurasian territory. Under both the Romanov tsars and communist commissars many diverse ethnic groups fell under Russian and Soviet control. Even today there are twenty-one republics and seventy other ethnic groups within Russian territory agitating for greater freedom. If the 1995 rebellion-turned-civil-war in Chechniya were emulated in other parts of Russia, the map of this sprawling country could begin to look like Swiss cheese.

MINI-CASE 7.2
Subculture of Musical Herders:
The Tuvan Throat Singers

One of the least militant and most unique of the many subcultures in Russian society can be found in the southern republic of Tuva, located near the Mongolian border in what is called Russian Central Asia. Most of its 320,000 Turkic-Muslim people still live an ancient pastoral lifestyle based on herding animals, a lifestyle essentially unchanged by a long line of outside political rulers: Chinese emperors, Mongolian warriors, Russian tsars, and Soviet commissars.

One of the inescapable facts of life on these steppes of southwestern Siberia has always been loneliness for the hunters and herders able to survive by making the most of the lean resources available in a harsh physical environment. From the depths of Tuvan pastoral loneliness developed a unique form of self-expression, one based on the people's relationship to the animals they herded and the environment that tolerated them both. Called throat singing, or biphonic singing, it allows the herder to produce two-to-three different melodic tones at once.

Journalist David Brown notes that Tuvan throat singing produces high and whistling sounds like birdcalls. The songs mostly have to do with nature as Tuvans experience it. In ordinary singing, the tongue remains flat in the mouth, but in throat singing the tongue touches the palate, thus dividing the throat and mouth into separate resonating chambers, contributing to what Brown calls "multiple-pitch effects." Most of the larger Russian culture is unaware of even the existence of the Tuvan sub-culture tucked away in a remote corner of this huge and diverse land.[15]

As a heterogeneous, Eurasian culture, Russia bursts with paradoxes. One noted by journalist Hedrick Smith in *The Russians*, the best-selling book ever written on Russia, is the contrast between the "public Russian" and the "private Russian." In public places—lectures, concerts, markets, or buses—Russians tend toward the self-restraint and formality of many Orientals. But then a metamorphosis frequently occurs around the kitchen table, where they become warm and emotional, informal and outgoing, in many ways like North Americans. A generous spirit causes Russians to love having guests and giving gifts. Hedrick Smith says this split makes them "both stoics and romantics," or in the words of the late Russian emigre poet Joseph Brodsky, "like the Irish—in their poverty, their spiritual intensity, their strong personal relationships, their sentimentality."[16]

Although 120 ethnic groups coexist, 82 percent of the 150 million citizens are ethnic Russians. Three-quarters of the shrinking population consists of urban dwellers. Education is free and compulsory, with pockets of true excellence in theoretical sciences, math, language instruction, and engineering. Some very creative reforms have enlivened public education since the demise of the communists, to whom creativity was anathema. The literacy rate is 99 percent, making almost every Russian able to read about how poor current living conditions are for most citizens.

Among the worst situations is a health care system that has essentially disintegrated. Anyone nostalgic for the days of communism in Russia finds plenty of fodder to criticize in the present unavailability of medical facilities and services. But the poor state of public medical attention cannot alone account for a most startling fact: Russia is the only country in which a precipitous drop in life expectancy has occurred. Many studies show that for males it has fallen from 65 years in 1980 to 57 years in 1995. For years U.S. sociologist Maury Feschbach was accused by critics of hyperbole when describing health conditions in Russia. Professor Feschbach has stated that he now feels vindicated by many other sources of data corroborating his dire assessments.[17] Environmental degradation, pollution, poor diet, excessive smoking, lack of exercise, obesity, rampant alcoholism, increased criminal violence, and the stress produced by a rapidly changing society have proven lethal for many Russians.

Russia's economy is heavily industrial, with GNP per capita of about $7,000, and its Human Development Index of .849 ranks it 52 out of 174 countries.[18] Communism's legacy has left Russian leaders with environmental, nuclear, economic, social, and political messes to clean up.

One key question, however, confronts postcommunist Russia: Can it make a successful transition to Western-style democracy and capitalism? The dynamics of this issue amount to a modern variant of the age-old Westernizers versus Slavophile's conflict. Somewhat of a split seems to exist among groups of scholars handicapping the odds. Many academic historians look to Russia's peasant-dominated past; most find little there to predict successful westernization. Few go as far as Daniel Rancour-Laferriere, whose book *The Slave Soul of Russia* paints a portrait of a national psyche caught up in self-defeating suffering—stemming largely from a failure to put its peasant past to rest.[19]

Yet numerous political scientists and sociologists, marveling at how much Russia has changed peacefully in recent years, argue that this is a new Russia—a "civil society"—for the first time. According to this view, Russia's increasingly sophisticated urban population will not accept the antiquated ways of a peasant culture. These social scientists express more hope for westernization than do their historian colleagues. It is hard to imagine Russia returning to autocracy or to communism. Yet it also stretches credulity to envision Russia as the kind of capitalist democracy that we know in the West. On balance, something approximating a Russified compromise between these alternative scenarios seems most plausible. Predictions are always risky for the social scientist, but predicting conditions in Russia's volatile context could easily be mistaken for foolishness. The sage counsel of British statesman Winston Churchill is as instructive today as when spoken in 1939: "I cannot forecast to you the action of Russia. It is a riddle wrapped in a mystery inside an enigma."[20]

ISLAMIC CULTURE AND MOROCCO'S MIXED BAG

Some identities even larger than the nation–state serve as the basis for a culture. Among religiously based civilizations, the specter of a renascent Islam has triggered a flood of journalistic and academic ink in the West. Many Western writers have suggested that the disappearance of the Soviet Union as a psychological enemy has elevated the Islamic world as the gravest threat to Western civilization. The United States, in particular, seems to be on the lookout for villainy. This apparent search for a post-Soviet enemy coincides with a period of Islamic revivalism, which historically has occurred in broad cycles. The new revival, however, differs from the old in two important ways: it is global in scope and polycentric in organization.[21]

One thing remaining constant in Islamic civilization is its fusion of religion and politics; as was put by medieval Muslim philosopher Al-Ghazali, "Religion and temporal power are twins." Not surprisingly, this concept confuses many Westerners, who were socialized under the quite different Christian dictum, "Render unto Caesar the things that are Caesar's and unto God the things that are God's." Nevertheless, like Christians and Jews, Muslims believe in a monotheistic God and a day of judgment. They accept most biblical prophets, but consider Muhammad as the final prophet.

Mir Husain elucidates six world events in recent decades that help to explain why Islam has risen to the forefront of Western awareness: (1) Iran's 1979 Islamic Revolution (spilling

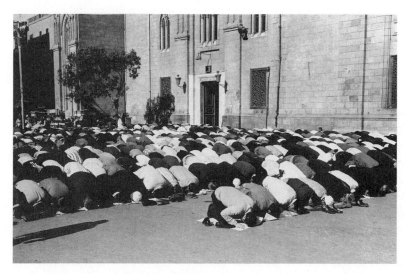

Muslim worshipers in Cairo, Egypt.

over to Pakistan and Sudan); (2) Islam's role in the mayhem of Lebanon's fifteen-year civil war; (3) the religious fervor of the Muhajedin rebels who inflicted 15,000 deaths on the Soviet Red Army, driving it out of Afghanistan in 1988; (4) its role in the 1981 assassination of Egypt's President Anwar Sadat, in retaliation for his peace agreement with Israel; (5) its being a constant thorn in the side of Israeli–Palestinian relations in the Middle East; and (6) the hostility toward democracy expressed by Islamic factions in Algeria's domestic violence.[22]

The world Muslim population equals that of China—about one-fifth of humanity. The 100 million Muslims in India are the world's largest minority. Muslims represent a majority in fifty countries and a significant minority in sixteen others: mostly on the Asian continent, where Muslims constitute two-thirds of the population, and in Africa, where they are more than one-quarter. Their locations place Muslim countries in proximity to seven strategic sea routes as well as much oil—they possess two-thirds of the world's known reserves. They represent ten of twelve members of the Organization of Petroleum Exporting Countries (OPEC). The spread of Islam was often achieved by the sword; two scholars, however, evoke images of its commercial impetus, claiming "Islam was the religion of the marketplace, the bazaar, the caravan."[23]

All these factors suggest that the West must recognize Islam as a key player on the world stage. In the United States, however, overreaction has sometimes occurred. Sensational press reports, focusing on a small number of violent Islamic fundamentalists, blow the realities of Islamic militance out of proportion. Much of the resultant diatribe has been reminiscent of similar exaggeration of a monolithic communist threat during the Cold War. Both print and electronic media embellish the dimensions of a unified global threat, this time colored green for Islam rather than red for communism.[24]

The Islamic world actually contains significant diversity. Professors John Esposito and John Voll analyze the unique Islamic experiences in Algeria, Egypt, Iran, Malaysia, Pakistan, and Sudan to argue that Islam is no monolith.[25] Some countries are modernized, others traditional; a few enjoy riches while many struggle in poverty; some interpret the Koran strictly, others more loosely; some are pro-Western, but a few see the West as the Great Satan; a few are urban, most others rural. No consistent pattern exists over the legality of selling alcohol, which the Koran forbids consuming. No Islamic country stands out as truly typical. Morocco, however, is intriguing for the great diversity within its national culture—an Islamic microcosm of sorts.

Roughly the size of California, Morocco enjoys a strategic location: sitting atop the Strait of Gibraltar, participating in the Arab League of the Middle East, resting on the African continent, but a mere twelve miles from Spain and accessible to the Americas via the Atlantic Ocean. Its earliest known settlers, the Berbers, were overwhelmed in the seventh century by Arab invaders, who brought Islam with them. In 711 A.D. an Arab–Berber alliance, known as the Moors, invaded Spain, where they remained for nearly seven centuries. The sunny Andalucian region of southern Spain still glistens with the cultural grandeur of the Moors, especially in places like the Alhambra in Granada and the Great Mosque in Cordoba.

Morocco's 27 million people, most of them either Arab or Berber, speak Arabic as the official language. But the country is cosmopolitan for the region: many city dwellers speak French (because of French colonization until 1956), Spanish is widely used because of proximity, and English is quite common—the United States and Morocco have honored one of the first U.S. friendship treaties since 1787, and Morocco staunchly supported U.S. Cold War leadership.

Half the population, urban and young, follow the Islamic religion rather loosely, while in rural areas a stricter traditional approach remains prevalent. Moroccans often brush cheeks when greeting one another, and in the countryside they touch their hearts with the right hand after shaking hands.

Especially in those rural settings, the extended family dominates Moroccan social life; people there feel a strong obligation to support family members spiritually and materially. Dating among rural young people does not occur as in the West, the youngsters do not socialize openly with the opposite sex, marriages are generally arranged, and men expect women to bring virginity to the marital bed. According to Islam, polygamy up to four wives is allowed, but the husband must take care of each equally and receive permission from current wives to take another.

Moroccans eat with their fingers from a communal dish after washing hands. As in many traditional societies, they use only their right hands, reserving the left for basic bodily functions—an awkward convention for your left-handed author.

Half of Moroccans engage in subsistence farming, and most of their children do not regularly attend school, a situation contributing to the country's modest literacy rate of 50 percent. In modern cities like Casablanca, Rabat, or Tangier, however, students attend schools based on the French system much more regularly than their rural counterparts. The country's main natural resource, phosphate, ranks as the world's third largest supply. Standard of living reflects significant gaps between urban and rural locations, but Morocco's GNP per capita averages out at only $3,000 and its Human Development Index ranks it 117 out of 174 countries measured.[26]

BRAZIL AND THE ARARA TRIBE OF ITS RAIN FOREST

The concept of culture, flexible as a rubber band, stretches beyond the borders of the nation–state to encompass large civilizations such as Islam. Conversely, it also contracts to surround countless subcultures such as the Arara tribe, inhabitants of the Brazilian rain forest near the Uriri River. Like many other indigenous peoples, the nomadic Arara attempted for three centuries to elude the enslavement of Brazil's Portuguese colonists. The Arara proved more successful than most. However, in 1950, after repeated efforts to find traces of the Arara tribe, the Brazilian government officially declared them extinct, seemingly closing the books on another irretrievable culture.

Then, twenty-six years later, the Brazilian news media jumped all over a most bizarre event. Three government mineral prospectors were killed by wilderness tribesmen, and parts of their bodies were eaten by the killers. The arrows used against the prospectors were examined and believed to be those of the long-lost Arara tribe. Representatives of Brazil's Indian Affairs Agency (FUNAI) were sent to investigate. In 1981 they returned with detailed information about the Arara, including the first extensive film footage of Arara daily life.

The Arara complained to FUNAI anthropologists about decades of harassment and murder at the hands of whites; they also expressed concern about rapid encroachment upon the rain forests on which the Arara depended. Only when cornered on an island, with nowhere to flee, did the Arara turn and attack the Caucasian prospectors. Although normally pacific, the Arara believe they have a duty to defend themselves. It is also part of their traditional beliefs that eating the organs of slain enemies will increase strength, and that severing their heads will prevent foes from going to heaven. In this situation, then, the Arara were not only killers, but cannibals. It takes little imagination to envision the news media squeezing every ounce of drama from this haunting clash of cultures.

But the detailed FUNAI report also reveals a tribal culture notably harmonious and generous, at least within the confines of its own inner logic. The sixty-person Arara tribe can survive its nomadic hunting and gathering lifestyle only through cooperation of two types: (1) comity between all tribal members, and (2) oneness with nature's rain forest. The FUNAI team found no evidence of serious internal strife during many months of studying the Arara.

This cooperative ethic is socialized into tribal members via a powerful myth of atonement which teaches that their ancestors once engaged in greed and selfishness, which led to a huge fight. The gods of the forest, greatly displeased, then imposed a severe punishment—not only on the perpetrators but on their progeny as well. As penance, all tribal members are bound to cooperate unselfishly; also, all Arara ancestors must become jaguars after death. To pay respect to the jaguar forever more, the Arara paint their bodies with jaguar spots and cause no harm to any jaguar in the rain forest.

As in many animist religions, the Arara shaman fills a crucial role, mediating between the tribe and the spirit world, seeking balance and harmony. When animals are killed for food, rituals must be performed to appease the jungle spirits. The tribe also takes on any slain animal's offspring to raise as honored tribal pets. The Arara understand life as a series of exchanges, seeking natural balance as they blend into the rain forest, leaving hardly a trace to reveal their presence. In a modern world struggling after sustainability to offset centuries of human ecological abuse, this simple lifestyle contains some elements worth examining.

Certainly the FUNAI delegation subjected the Arara to unprecedented examination, and their official report provides balance to the sensationalist 1976 news reports concerning cannibalism. FUNAI's conclusions in no way condone any element of killing or of cannibalism. Yet these Brazilian anthropologists do manage to appreciate the desperately defensive nature of the Arara's act of violence. A sincere, possibly naive, but internally consistent set of beliefs among the Arara comes through in the FUNAI report, providing a more complete picture of the Arara tribal culture than do journalistic accounts of this tragic violence.[27]

Many members of the FUNAI team were well educated, cosmopolitan individuals. This assessment would hold true especially for the anthropologists in the delegation. But despite having open-minded attitudes about indigenous peoples, they also worked for the Brazilian government. As civil servants, they answered to officials who were subject to the political pressures found in any popularly elected system. Governments tend to be keenly aware of public opinion and tend to respond to its preferences. So in what kind of a larger Brazilian culture did this Arara case transpire? In what type of society did citizens wake up one morning to read newspaper accounts of cannibalism in their midst?

In some fundamental respects, Brazil's national culture parallels that of the United States: both are large, ethnically and racially heterogeneous societies successful in forging unified national identities. In the United States, the ideas of American exceptionalism, moralism, and world leadership, coupled with the English language, serve as centrifugal forces to offset the country's many centripetal social differences. In the Brazilian melting-pot the Catholic religion,

Figure 7.2

Portuguese language, historical sense of relative racial tolerance, a strong musical tradition, and passion for the sport of soccer all perform a similar role.

No nation in the world has as many Catholics as Brazil. Its population of 156 million ranks fifth in the world and exceeds the rest of South America combined; one percent of Brazil's people are indigenous peoples like the Arara, 11 percent are black descendants of slaves arriving prior to 1880, 44 percent are of European ancestry, and 44 percent are racially mixed. Its open immigration policies have resulted in many other nationalities moving to Brazil's shores, including the largest Japanese community (one million) outside of Japan. Half of the national population is under twenty years of age, 90 percent crowd onto 10 percent of the land, including the 15 million who live in the two great cities of São Paulo and Rio de Janeiro. A high rate of population growth has been brought under control since the mid-1980s without direct governmental programs toward that end.[28]

Brazil is equally impressive in natural resources as in human resources: its 3.3 million square miles of territory place it fifth globally and allow it to border on every South American country except Chile and Ecuador. Almost one in three Brazilians works in an agricultural sector; it leads the world in coffee, oranges, and bananas and is second in soybean and cocoa production. Overall, Brazil's economy is the world's ninth largest, and it appears capable of advancing to a higher level after decades of troublesome high inflation and debt.[29]

As in both the United States and the world in general, distribution of wealth trends in Brazil have been toward "the rich getting richer and the poor getting poorer." While the World Bank lists Brazil among the lower-to-middle-income countries, its riches are maldistributed. A mere 2 percent of its people hold 70 percent of the land and earn more income than the total earned by two-thirds of their fellow citizens. The percentage share of income for the poorest 40 percent is only 8 percent. Some estimates put chronic malnutrition in the country at one-half of the populace.[30] The HDI index similarly reflects weaknesses in the profile of this nation aspiring to regional leadership, ranking it 63 out of 174, including life expectancy of sixty-six years and a literacy rate of 82 percent.[31]

Although caution should be exercised in using Brazil to typify the Latin American region, there are qualities of the broader Latin culture that influence Brazilian life. What are referred to as **machismo, militarismo, caudillismo**, and **personalismo** represent common patterns in Latin American cultures and cannot be ignored. These respective images of proud and strong male leaders (*machismo*); a historical legacy of military men as cultural heroes (*militarismo*); the consolidation of unbridled power (*caudillismo*); and paternalistic relationships grounded in feudal agriculture, when the patron took care of the needs of his *peones* (*personalismo*)—continue to affect the mental outlook of Brazil's elites as well as its masses.[32]

Brazil's leaders have the awesome responsibility of trying to avert two forms of extinction; one we hear debated loudly in the West, the other barely gets whispered. The one currently emblazoned into Western consciousness is Brazil's stewardship over the world's largest rain forest, including the richest concentration of biodiversity. The other endangered resource—human rather than natural—is Brazil's comparable stewardship over indigenous cultures threatened with extinction.

While massive pressure has been put on Brazil to treat the rain forest as a global/ecological resource rather than as a national/economic resource, no international campaign exists to view tribal groups as global cultural resources. Other than its history of accepting interracial marriage for those socialized into the values of the dominant culture, little in the broader Brazilian culture seems to augur well for tolerating the lifestyles of Amerindians like the Arara. Thus neither from within Brazil nor from the international community does help for the Arara seem likely. Anthropology and sociology, as the conceptually broadest social sciences, provide tools to appreciate the links involved in the bigger global picture, or what humanistic sociologist C. Wright Mills referred to long ago as the "sociological imagination."[33]

THE BAKA TRIBE OF THE ITURI RIVER FOREST

A continent and thousands of miles away from Brazil live the Baka people, or the "Pygmies," in southeast Cameroon's rain forest. Located on the west coast of what is called Equatorial Africa, Cameroon is a sparsely populated nation of 12 million people, 1.1 million of whom live in Yaoundé, the capital city. Some oil has recently been found, and exports have increased for timber and some light industry, boosting Cameroon ahead of its neighbors in this poorest region of Sub-Saharan Africa.

The adult literacy rate of 59 percent barely exceeds numerically the average life expectancy of fifty-six years. GNP per capita is just over $2,000, and Cameroon's HDI quality of life index ranks it 127 out of 174 countries.[34]

Cameroon was a German colony from 1884 to 1916, was divided into British and French protectorates after World War I, and gained final independence in 1961. It has been relatively more stable than most countries of Equatorial Africa, and in 1996 it had the distinction of hosting the annual meeting of the 53-member Organization of African Unity (OAU).

Although the Baka people live within Cameroon and are citizens of that country, they have no more identity with Cameroon than the Arara feel toward Brazil. The Arara and the Baka peoples possess loyalty to their tribal groups of two- or three-score people. No larger social reality seems relevant to their traditional consciousness. As a seminomadic hunting and gathering society, the Baka exhibit many cultural similarities to their Arara tribal counterparts from the Amazon Basin of South America. Most obvious is that the Baka and Arara rely on extended families to organize their small societies. Critical to the functioning of these simple societies is a deeply held belief in the necessity of cooperation, compromise, and harmony. Possibly most intriguing to observers from modern societies is that the Baka and Arara find it quite natural to blend into nature rather than subjugating it. Closely tied to these cyclical and harmonious cultures is an animistic sense of fear and need to appease the spirits of the forest.

When it comes to socializing young people into the values and conventions of their unique lifestyles, each relies heavily on mythological storytelling, which provides entertainment as well as ethical codes of conduct. Among the Baka and the Arara, the taking of life—animal or human—

The Baka tribe lives a peaceful, sustainable existence in the Uturi River forest of Cameroon.

occurs only when deemed necessary by these peoples who are otherwise quite reluctant to do so. As in any society, simple or complex, a division of labor leads to differing social roles for various individuals, although roles are much less specialized among the Baka or Arara than in complex societies. When the great labor of a successful hunt is completed, both hold celebrations with singing, dancing, and intoxicating beverages. The Baka and Arara live completely sustainable lives.

At least four major differences, nevertheless, exist between these two tribal cultures. The Arara atonement myth, based on their ancestors' perceived sin of greed, imposes a burden of guilt and includes punishment, which the more carefree Baka do not share. While both tribes are internally pacific, the Arara have a greater proclivity for violence under siege, including the kind of ritual cannibalism—under extreme circumstances of conflict with outsiders—discussed earlier.

The Arara also take more varied sexual partners, making paternity uncertain in many cases. This custom places an even greater emphasis on the role of the extended family, and weakens the immediate family, in child-rearing responsibilities. Finally, while both engage in subsistence hunting and gathering on a seminomadic basis, the Arara supplement these practices with horticulture, whereas the Baka do not.[35] As was noted with regard to Japan and China, the human mind allows us to focus either on the similarities or on the differences between the Arara and Baka tribes; the path chosen by the observer can lead to quite different conclusions, because in addition to social reality having a discoverable objective dimension, it also has a subjective dimension which we help shape through our perceptions.

DIGGING FOR CULTURAL ESSENCES

Intercultural training specialist L. Robert Kohls has adapted a complex framework for comparing cultures—originally known as the Kluckhohn Model—facilitating its application to our present analysis. It involves five central questions aiming at the essence of any culture's value system, resulting in five cultural orientations:

Figure 7.3 *This chart, an adaptation and simplification of one developed by Kluckhohn and Strodtbeck, indicates the range of possible responses to the five orientations. It is intended to be read horizontally, each horizontal box relating to one of the five orientations.*

Source: Florence Kluckhohn and Fred Strodtbech, *Variations in Value Orientation* (Row, Peterson, 1961); from L. Robert Kohls, *Survival Kit for Overseas Living* (Intercultural Press, 1984), p. 22.

Orientation	Beliefs and Behaviors		
Human Nature	Basically Evil	Mixture of Good and Evil	Basically Good
Relationship of Man to Nature	Man Subjugated by Nature	Man in Harmony with Nature	Man the Master of Nature
Sense of Time	Past Oriented	Present Oriented	Future Oriented
Activity	Being (Stress on Who You Are)	Growing (Stress on Self-Development)	Doing (Stress on Action)
Social Relationships	Authoritarian	Group Oriented	Individualistic

Table 7.1 Six Cultures Applied to Kohls Model

	Human Nature	Person–Nature	Time	Activity	Social
Japan	mix	master	future	doing	group
China	evil	harmony	past	being	auth
Russia	mix	master	present	being	group
Morocco	evil	harmony	past	being	auth
Arara	evil	harmony	present	being	group
Baka	good	harmony	present	being	group
U.S.	good	master	future	doing	indiv

Orientations of six cultures:

Five Questions and Orientations

1. What is the character of innate human nature?
   (human nature orientation)

2. What is the relation of persons to nature?
   (person–nature orientation)

3. What is the temporal focus (time sense) of human life?
   (time orientation)

4. What is the mode of human activity?
   (activity orientation)

5. What is the mode of human relationships?
   (social orientation)[36]

Any model purporting to describe social reality in a given culture runs the risk of **reductionism** if the inherent limits of explanatory models are not appreciated. An abstract model comparing social reality in several cultures is especially capable of abusing its function. Yet, if applied cautiously, conceptual frameworks like the Kohls Model help us to describe, analyze, and contrast the essential tendencies of diverse cultures, and perhaps to create new insights and heuristic explanations along the way.

The Kohls Model provides a range of three answers to each of the five questions deemed essential to defining any culture. In the model shown in Figure 7.3, three physical boxes cover a continuum of likely options. For the human-nature orientation, the range includes the views that human nature is: (1) basically evil, (2) a mixture of good and bad, or (3) basically good. Similarly, for the person–nature orientation, people are seen as either (1) subjugated by nature, (2) in harmony with nature, or (3) masters of nature. With the time orientation, the choices suggest a culture that is (1) past oriented, (2) present oriented, or (3) future oriented. When it comes to the activity orientation, we are looking for an emphasis on (1) being, (2) growing, or (3) doing. Finally, the social orientation can take the form of (1) authoritarian, (2) group oriented, or (3) individualistic. The obvious question, then, is what does the Kohls Model do for us in summarizing our comparative analysis of the six cultures examined, along with the United States as a commonly understood baseline culture?

If nothing else, a quick perusal of these summary comparisons ought to dispel notions of the United States as a cultural archetype. This point comes through most poignantly on the social relationships dimension, where only the United States can be classified as individualistic. The only other culture that can be characterized as doing-oriented is Japan.

Japan, and to a lesser extent Russia, defy facile categorization in some orientations. Japan presents a problem on the time dimension, because of the seeming anomaly of an ancient culture of great historical depth blending rather harmoniously with a future-oriented and pragmatic work ethic. It would be difficult to find another large society that has so elegantly married such disparate cultural partners.

Much more problematic today is Russia's perennial battle between its Westernizers and its Russophiles, a battle in which compromise and evolution appear much less often than strident militancy. Russia is changing rapidly; it may be heading in the direction of the United States (future, doing, and individual oriented), but it is too early to tell.

As small, animistic, hunting-and-gathering societies, the Arara and Baka share a sense of harmony with nature and with their fellows. The Arara atonement myth, however, casts a deep-seated spell of guilt and penance over its members which would appear quite alien to the more optimistic, secure, and carefree members of the Baka tribe.

Chapter Synopsis

Flexible as a rubber band, the concept of culture can contract to include small subcultures of a few score persons, then expand to incorporate civilizations covering entire regions of the globe. However, in the present world of nation–states, social scientists most frequently examine culture at the level of the society (nation–state). Some societal cultures, like the collectivist-oriented cultures of Japan and China, are homogeneous. From the Western perspective, such Oriental cultures seem highly similar, as we notice lifestyles appearing ancient, group oriented, formal, socially responsible, respectful of elders, and abhorring the loss of face. Yet when viewed from within either of these cultures, differences seem more compelling— for example, China's rural populace, authoritarian communist government, less-developed economy, official atheism, Confucian traditionalism, moral puritanism, rudimentary educational system, and efforts by the government to weaken family loyalties.

Relatively few national cultures are as homogeneous as Japan and China. More common are cultures of a heterogeneous nature. Russia's thousand-year-old Eurasian culture bursts with paradoxes born of striking diversity. Two competing philosophies have nearly always vied for dominance in this vast national space: Slavophilism (Russian tradition is best) and westernization (modernity is best). In the postcommunist era, westernization has gained the ascendancy as Russia struggles in the direction of political democracy and an economic free market, but the traditional forces of Slavophilism continue to oppose wholesale westernization. The Arab world is another region where westernization remains controversial, and the resurgence of Islamic culture here creates another area with a confluence of strong cultural forces. One Islamic country that epitomizes cultural diversity is Morocco. History, geography, colonialism, religion, and economics have all contributed to a diverse cultural landscape defying Western stereotypes of a monolithic Islamic Middle East.

While culture can stretch beyond the level of the nation–state to encompass civilizations like Islam, it can also contract to the level of the myriad subcultures present in most nations. The Baka culture (Cameroon) and the Arara culture (Brazil) illustrate the diversity of subcultures present in the world. Each relies on extended families, socializes its small society through storytelling, believes deeply in a spirit of social cooperation, blends seamlessly into the natural environment, and seeks to appease animistic spirits of the forest. As with the case of Japanese and Chinese cultures, it may seem to outsiders that these are remarkably similar hunting and gathering cultures. However, real differences exist: an atonement myth among the Arara people leads to a burden of guilt not present among the carefree Baka; when under seige, the Arara have a proclivity toward violence not exhibited by the Baka culture; the Arara take more varied sexual partners than do the Baka, contributing to a wider sense of extended family responsibility; the Arara supplement their hunting and gathering subsistence with horticultural activities alien to the Baka people.

For Digging Deeper

Christopher, Robert C. *The Japanese Mind.* Fawcett Columbine, 1984.

Esposito, John L. *Islam and Democracy.* Oxford University Press, 1996.

Fogel, Joshua, A. *The Cultural Dimension of Sino-Japanese Relations.* Mitchell E. Sharp, 1994.

Husain, Mir Zohair. *Global Islamic Politics.* Harper-Collins, 1995.

Mills, C. Wright. *The Sociological Imagination.* Oxford University Press, 1959.

Morishima, Michio. *Why Has Japan Succeeded? Western Technology and the Japanese Ethos.* Cambridge University Press, 1984.

Rancour-Laferriere, Daniel. *The Slave Soul of Russia: Moral Masochism and the Cult of Suffering.* New York University Press, 1995.

Smith, Hedrick. *The Russians.* Ballantine, 1976.

Smith, Hedrick. *The New Russians.* Random House, 1990.

Tobin, Joseph J., David Wu, and Dana Davidson. *Pre-School in Three Cultures: Japan, China, and the U.S.* Yale University Press, 1993.

Key Glossary Terms

caudillismo	machismo	reductionism
Confucianism	militarismo	Slavophilism
deviance	neomercantilism	subculture
ideology	personalismo	westernization

CHAPTER **8**

Cultures: Rough Around the Edges

Thematic Questions

- In what sense is anthropology a discipline with a holistic mission?

- What is the nature of the complex relationship between ethnocentrism and cultural relativism?

- How is cultural imperialism both similar to and different from more traditional manifestations of imperialism and colonialism?

- What is unique about the global role of U.S. popular culture?

Cultural identity serves an important function by integrating individuals into groups that become societies. Chaos would seem the likely alternative to structured living in societies. But the very act of psychological identity—creating an "in-group" mentality—makes inevitable the existence of "outgroups." From this basic reality spring a host of problems. Hypothetically, it might seem that cultures ought to fit as snugly as so many pieces in a jigsaw puzzle. But cultures are not that neat and smooth. Rough around the edges, they rub up against one another, often producing sparks.

For example, in Denmark it is a commonly accepted practice for parents to leave their babies in strollers in the fresh air and sunshine outside of a restaurant while the parents eat inside. On a nice spring day in 1997 Danish citizen Xavier Wardauer and his wife did exactly that—but where they did it was not in Denmark, but rather in New York City. While they were in the restaurant, their infant was picked up by city police, and the parents were ushered into jail, where they spent the next two very frantic days. The Wardauers were arrested for child endangerment, an offense punishable by both a fine and jail time. Incredulous over the entire incident, they claimed they loved their child and considered no danger to exist for the baby, since they did this often at home. New York mayor Rudolph Giuliani defended the actions of the police and refused to intervene on behalf of the Wardauers. With whom do you agree in this situation?

ETHNOCENTRISM VERSUS CULTURAL RELATIVISM

People are so accustomed to the circumstances in which they are socialized that they tend to take them for granted. Anthropologists possess the clearest understanding of a phenomenon stemming from this comfort level in regard to one's own culture: **ethnocentrism**. It produces a skewed sense of reality rising from the assumption that because other cultures are different

Danish parents commonly leave their infants in the sunshine while eating in restaurants.

from ours, they are inferior or at least bizarre. Ethnocentrism has been called "a rigidity in the acceptance of the culturally alike and in the rejection of the culturally unalike,"[1] and the ethnocentric person has been accused of "following the path of least intellectual and psychological resistance."[2] Joan Ferrante points out that ethnocentrism can occur at quite harmless levels, such as Hindu vegetarians' considering eating of beef to be sacrilegious, but it also can appear in more virulent forms, such as **cultural genocide**, as when Japan tried between 1910 and 1945 to destroy Korean culture.[3]

According to anthropologists such as Carol and Melvin Ember, the main antidote to combat ethnocentrism is **cultural relativism**: "a society's customs and ideas should be described objectively and understood in the context of that society's problems and opportunities."[4] What is sometimes referred to as anthropology's **holistic** perspective is relevant here; in this approach, bits of foreign cultures are considered only in conjunction with their broader milieu rather than piecemeal. Cultural relativism speaks to the scientist in all of us, imploring us to seek objectivity, as challenging a task as that may be. It also asks us to respect cultural diversity and the right to be different. Anthropologist Dorothy Lee warns particularly against the insidious effects of the ethnocentric myth that humans are necessarily better off in modern cultures.[5]

Each culture does, in fact, make sense when viewed from inside its private logic. Only when outsiders make value judgments about cultures do those cultures seem strange. Few concepts in social science are more defensible than cultural relativism. It carries the force of both moral suasion and logical analysis. It represents the cultural counterpart to "you do your thing and I'll do mine"—that most North American aphorism of individual freedom. Conversely, it would be a rare social scientist indeed who would care to argue in favor of ethnocentrism as a general principle.

Difficulties can arise, however, in translating an important concept like cultural relativism from the abstract level to concrete application. Human beings hold deep-seated beliefs, and sometimes we feel like traitors if we think we have abandoned them, even in the face of good causes like cultural relativism. The obvious moral dilemma here arises when our ethical judgments about practices in other cultures come into direct conflict with a desire to adhere open-mindedly to cultural relativism. Does cultural relativism require us to set aside our moral beliefs? Is there no way to remain true to our values while respecting other cultures' right to march to the beat of their own drummer? Can we be good, objective social scientists while remaining true to our ethical beliefs?

In our culturally diverse world, great variations exist in what is deemed acceptable and unacceptable. Every society has ethical codes, but not necessarily the same ones. Among the Ik tribe in Africa, for example, the legitimacy of wife beating is well established, with very specific procedures followed. In Iraq, daughters who shame the family by illegitimate pregnancy can be put to death. Drunk drivers can share the same unpleasant fate in Bulgaria. In India, ultrasound tests are used to identify unwanted female fetuses as candidates for abortion. The Anasazi Amerindians of the Southwest practiced cannibalism. In some parts of China, men gather around a monkey clamped into a tabletop so they can eat its brains while it is still alive, as was graphically depicted in the popular movie *Indiana Jones* and the *Temple of Doom* (1984). Eskimo mothers regularly strangled daughters who, unlike sons, were seen as a burden to society. Each of these practices represents a serious challenge to the sensibilities of almost anyone socialized in the Western world. Consider the similar ethical dilemmas raised in greater detail by mini-cases 8.1, 8.2, and 8.3.

MINI-CASE 8.1

Lydia Oluloro's Daughters: A U.S. Court Decides Their Fate

*I*n 1994 Lydia Oluloro appeared before Judge Kendall Warren in a Portland, Oregon, court of law. A Nigerian by birth, Lydia Oluloro had been married, given birth, and then divorced in the United States. What did Mrs. Oluloro want from the court? Cultural asylum in the United States for her and her two young daughters. Why? Because the U.S. Immigration Service was trying to deport them to Nigeria. She argued that her five-year-old Lara and her six-year-old Shade would be subjected to a form of extreme hardship if deported to Nigeria: clitoridectomy, sometimes called female genital mutilation. It is intended to encourage female premarital chastity by removing the clitoris and thereby reducing the pleasure of sex. Nigeria is one of twenty-five African countries where clitoridectomy is commonly practiced.

Some African traditionalists contend that this ancient practice is the female counterpart to circumcising adolescent males and that the development of healthy and normal masculine and feminine traits are dependent upon these procedures. It is believed that a failure to do so will result in the unfortunate person's being disinclined toward procreation.[6] A well-educated Kenyan anthropologist-turned-president, Jomo Kenyatta, argued that those who condemn clitoridectomy do so from ignorance and prejudice and should be pitied more than condemned.[7] Another defender of this ritual, Somali-born Washington pediatrician Dr. Asha Mohamud, suggests that Westerners should mind their own business and stop interfering in cultural matters that they cannot understand.[8]

Contemporary American feminists express a decidedly different set of opinions about clitoridectomy. Robin Morgan and Gloria Steinem called it an "international crime" which the world would eradicate if it affected men.[9] Syndicated columnist Ellen Goodman has periodically written pieces attacking this practice, which she equates to "child abuse," claiming that 6,000 adolescents are subjected to it daily around the globe. In a column devoted to the case of Lydia Oluloro's daughters, Goodman's deeply felt feminist values are unmistakable:

> Shade and Lara would have their genitals attacked with a blade. One and then the other would have her clitoris cut out along with her labia minor. One and then the other would be stitched together with barely room for urinating and menstruating. They would be mutilated in the name of tradition.[10]

Back in that Portland courtroom, in the first decision of its type, Judge Warren ruled that forced genital mutilation constitutes a human rights abuse; he allowed Lydia Oluloro's family to remain in Oregon. A documentary film and book, *Warrior Marks*, co-authored by Alice Walker, have mobilized many concerned citizens to speak out against this practice. Colorado Representative Pat Schroeder (D-CO) introduced legislation in 1995 to outlaw genital mutilation in the United States and advocated trade sanctions against countries who allow its practice.

Where does this issue leave thoughtful citizens socialized in Western cultures? Most of us believe in the global applicability of basic human rights, which makes it difficult to express tolerance about seemingly abusive practices like clitoridectomy. Where does this leave feminists who feel a responsibility to liberate sisters around the world who may not even comprehend the nature of their subjugation and unequal treatment? Where does this leave you in balancing one valid concept (cultural relativism) against a conflicting one (global human rights)?

MINI-CASE 8.2
The Execution of Gui Bingquan

T he London-based human rights group Amnesty International reported evidence that there were 1,419 executions in China during 1993, fully 70 percent of the world total. In 1994 that figure rose even higher, to 2,500. A very large portion of these executions were for what in the West would be considered "white collar crime"—corruption—mostly in the form of bribing governmental officials.

Although its communist economy was restricted for three decades under Mao Zedong, China later loosened things up under Deng Xiaoping, unleashing considerable economic growth in the process. The motto of the 1980s seemed light years from the days of Mao: "to get rich is glorious"; but not much was said about doing so honestly or legally. One Communist Party official stated at a 1994 press conference that "Corruption is very serious and threatens reforms, liberalization, and the socialist market economy."[11]

The government's crackdown on corruption certainly seemed serious and threatening to Gui Bingquan, grain bureau director in the northeastern Liaoning Province. He was arrested and charged with embezzlement and accepting bribes totaling $33,000—not a huge crime by Western standards. His sentence was death! What is striking about the Bingquan case is that it is more typical in China than aberrational.

Chinese officials bristle at Western criticism of China's criminal justice system, arguing that Western notions of the primacy of individual rights don't fit China's Oriental emphasis on protecting the group. As was seen in the last chapter, Chinese culture in some respects goes beyond simply a group emphasis and approaches authoritarianism. All this sounds too much like convenient rationalization to Western human rights organizations like Human Rights Watch and Amnesty International, both of which have leveled criticisms at the human rights record of Chinese criminal justice. For them, the case of Gui Bingquan represents merely the tip of a very large, but well concealed, iceberg.

What do you make of this continuing saga on the world stage involving China and Western human rights groups? You may not identify completely with one view or the other, but do you find yourself leaning in the direction of cultural relativism and China's right to operate according to its own cultural values, or do you feel more partial to the universal sense of moral outrage expressed by Amnesty International over cases of seemingly perfunctory execution such as that of Gui Bingquan?

American teenager Michael Fay leaves the Queenstown Prison in Singapore following his release.

MINI-CASE 8.3
Michael Fay's Vandalism—Never in Singapore

L ess severe in human consequences, but more dramatically portrayed by the news media, was the 1994 case of Michael Fay. This eighteen-year-old native of Kettering, Ohio, who was living in Singapore with his mother and her husband, pleaded guilty to charges brought against him in a Singapore court. Of what crime was Michael Fay accused? Vandalism, in the form of spraying paint and throwing eggs at some cars.

A typical U.S. cultural reaction to such an incident might be that "boys will be boys"—that it was certainly not anything good or smart to do but it was a relatively small matter. A global controversy developed, however, over the nature of the sentence the Ohio youngster received: four months in prison, a fine of $2,215, and most controversially, six strokes to the bare buttocks with a split bamboo cane. The latter punishment generated much public discourse and seemed to symbolize the deeper gulf separating Oriental and Western conceptions of societal versus individual rights.

Heavy publicity surrounding the case got politicians on two sides of the Pacific involved, including both national leaders. In a *Time* magazine interview, Senior Minister Lee Kuan Yew emphasized that "to govern, you must have a certain moral authority. If we do not cane him because he is an American, I believe we'll lose our moral authority and our right to govern." President Bill Clinton also got publicly involved, making a direct appeal to Minister Lee for clemency. Michael's family claimed leniency was warranted because of medical hardship, reporting that he became so depressed over the case that he required a two-week stay in a psychiatric hospital.

Figure 8.1

Source: Lukovich, *The Atlanta Journal Constitution*

Singapore represents what some observers project as the model for twenty-first-century Asia: a seeming paradox involving impressive economic growth and a dictatorial political system. To others, it seems ominously comparable to George Orwell's nightmare vision in his novel *1984*. In this southeast Asian city state, three-quarters ethnic Chinese, the rights of the individual count for relatively little. The general needs of society take precedence over individual rights, a philosophy that leads some critics to describe it as more regimented than a U.S. marine boot camp. The minor case of Michael Fay created major headlines because it stood for a growing clash of values—a growing clash of cultures—East and West.

Singapore's initial response was the same as that of China whenever the United States has complained about human rights abuses in the People's Republic of China: mind your own business. After the intervention of lawyers, parents, priests, and politicians, Singapore's cabinet lowered the punishment from six to four lashes with the cane, but the prison sentence and fine remained intact. To Singaporeans, this seemed like a significant concession, involving a loss of face endured in the interests of cordial relations with the United States. Many North Americans, however, saw the reduction as trivial, continuing to believe that the caning of a person's bare buttocks equals barbarism. Do you share the moral outrage felt by the majority of Americans over the caning of Michael Fay for vandalism? Or do you feel more comfortable with the view taken by only a minority of U.S. citizens: that the punishment was not egregious enough to erase Singapore's right to operate its legal system according to its indigenous values?

In all three cases, adherence to cultural relativism becomes complicated by the messiness of the real world. Most North Americans, if forced to consider these cases, would brand genital mutilation (Nigeria), execution for white-collar crime (China), and caning for vandalism (Singapore) as international human rights abuses. Does that mean, however, that we should abandon the goal of cultural relativism?

Most scientifically oriented social scientists would probably cling to the long-term validity of cultural relativism, despite troublesome short-term problems in its application. The scientific attitude favors acting intelligently, with the big picture in mind, while trying to limit the influence of personal feelings and values. While it may not be possible to follow cultural relativism completely, social scientists attempt to do so as much as possible—tolerating things we dislike in other cultures whenever we can, opposing them only when we feel we must.

Many humanistic colleagues, believing in a higher-order moral imperative, consider scientism devoid of ethics and possibly even spiritually bankrupt. Some humanities-oriented social scientists might argue that they cannot condone the evasion of ethical responsibility, quoting philosophers and religious scholars to make the point that, without personal morality, humans remain but animals. In their opinion, genital mutilation, routine death sentences, and caning for vandalism are all acts of depravity demanding vocal opposition from human rights advocates.

CULTURAL IMPERIALISM AND GLOBAL COMMUNICATIONS

One good reason why social scientists remain cognizant of cultural relativism is that human history has consistently witnessed groups with power inflicting their will upon the weak. Western civilization's history of colonialism bristled with the imposition of its religious, social, and economic values on most of the rest of the world. Today the powerful country most often accused of acting as global bully is the United States.

U.S. power stems from a wide variety of factors. One that sometimes is overlooked is its position at the heart of global communications in an interdependent world. The hardware for the instantaneous information age has been provided by satellites, fax machines, videotape, e-mail, and the Internet, which have been conceived and constructed in many different east Asian, European, and North American countries. But the United States supplies the software. Whether in news coverage, films, television programs, music, fashion, or food—the marketing of American **popular culture** as global mass culture either frightens or angers defenders of domestic cultural traditions in many countries.

Not surprisingly, this phenomenon can be witnessed in almost every poor southern hemisphere nation, many of which feel overwhelmed by the volume and slick character of well-financed American artifacts of popular culture. The U.S. influence has become so pervasive that even in old, secure, and sophisticated countries like France, intense criticism of American cultural imperialism has reached fever pitch. Despite its long and proud history, the viability of the French film industry has been challenged by what many French citizens see as an onslaught of marketing for mediocre Hollywood action films starring cardboard characters like those invented by Sylvester Stallone. Hollywood films also typically cost ten to twenty times more to make than the average French film. It's no wonder the French have developed something akin to a David and Goliath complex over this issue.

Fast food restaurants now dominate the landscape of North American cities.

On the news front, a comparable strain of cultural imperialism can be diagnosed. Here the United States has traditionally felt comfortable advocating the global free flow of information, based on the American belief in individual freedom of expression. The American idea is that, theoretically, freedom to participate in the system is equally available to all parties. The real-world situation, according to many Third World peoples, operates quite differently. From their vantage point, the powerful interests in the United States, Europe, and Japan dominate the content and form of the flow of information, blithely replicating their minority snapshots of global reality as if they were the only ones.

And in the United States, higher forms of cultural expression have been in retreat for many years, much to the chagrin of lovers of ballet, live theater, art, opera, poetry, and orchestral music. Public funding for arts and letters has been cut as a symptom of shrinking budgets at all levels of government. As has been suggested by sociologist George Ritzer in his provocative book, *The McDonaldization of Society* (1995), what thrives today is a commercially driven popular culture dominating the scene: less news analysis, but more sensational violence; few documentaries or serious feature films, but an avalanche of Arnold Schwarzenegger movies; miniscule philharmonic music, but loads of rap. Now so pervasive that we hardly even notice them are the fast-food chains like McDonald's, Pizza Hut, and Burger King, which have made distinctive family-owned restaurants about as rare as dinosaur steaks.[12]

The origins of this superficiality represent no mystery to journalist David Rieff. He describes America as "ahistorical," meaning essentially two things: (1) the United States has relatively little historical depth when compared with most great national cultures, and (2) what history the United States does have is largely ignored by Americans, who are much more future oriented than past oriented. Not to worry, says Rieff, because its more rootless character fits comfortably with the current global condition of change, change, change—in ways that elude Tibetans, Brazilians, and Spaniards, all products of more historically grounded cultures. Rieff's analysis speaks to the pervasiveness of popular culture when he refers to the "dream-scape," an easy blending of reality and fantasy, as the U.S.'s major contribution to the twentieth century.[13]

Because this country's influence is global in scope, the vagaries of its cultural attitudes matter a great deal. A case that hints at how excesses of the American national psyche can manifest themselves in emotional overreaction occurred in the late 1980s and involved the U.S., Japan, and Norway.

 DRAMA ON THE WORLD STAGE:
Ronald Reagan, Public Opinion, and the TTAC

Protagonists

William Casey—CIA director and Reagan confidante who established TTAC in 1981, with mission to "stanch the flow" of classified information to communist countries

Duncan Hunter—Conservative Democratic congressman from southern California who led a well-publicized smashing of a Toshiba radio on the Capitol steps on June 30, 1987, and sponsored a bill to ban Toshiba products

Dan Rostenkowski—Democratic congressman from Illinois and chairman of House Ways and Means Committee, whose efforts to ease trade restrictions for economic development were killed by publicity over Toshiba

Kongsberg Vapenfabrik—Norway's only defense contractor, accused with Toshiba of selling submarine technology to Soviets

Toshiba—Japanese firm accused [along with Norwegians] of selling to the Soviets technology for quiet sub propellers

Prologue

President Ronald Reagan's agenda, when he took office in 1981, included getting tough with the Soviet Union. One objective in his military competition with the Soviets was to "stanch the flow of military secrets" which he believed were making their way through the Iron Curtain. He soon appointed CIA Director William Casey as head of a new Technology Transfer Assessment Center (TTAC). Casey proceeded to unleash a variety of efforts toward the goal given him by the president. Most of Reagan's first term in office featured harsh rhetoric aimed at the Soviets.

After Reagan's 1984 reelection, relations with the Soviets improved greatly, but competition over military matters continued right up until the collapse of the Soviet Union in 1991. Also during Reagan's second term, William Casey's TTAC efforts bore fruit, with the discovery of illegal transfer of technical information to the Eastern bloc.

Potentially most damaging was evidence of the sale of technology enabling Soviet submarine propellers to run quietly enough to avoid detection by U.S. naval sonar equipment, a capability that would, in effect, give the Soviets a "stealth" submarine. William Casey and his investigators uncovered two companies, one Norwegian (Vapenfabrik) and one Japanese (Toshiba), which had sold these classified secrets to the Soviet Union. How would you expect American public opinion to react to this fact? Would you expect the U.S. government to take action? If so, what kind of action and against whom?

Dramatic Plot

Much of the public response to this situation could hardly have been embellished by Hollywood scriptwriters. Early in 1987 information about the TTAC's investigation of these illegal transfers began leaking to the press. A firestorm of verbal attacks ensued all aimed at the Japanese.

On June 30, 1987, Congressman Duncan Hunter and a few colleagues summoned the congressional press corps for a photo opportunity replete with caustic sound bites. Using a large sledgehammer, they took turns smashing a portable radio made by the Toshiba corporation of Japan. The reason? The congressional delegates were expressing anger over the Japanese sale of strategic submarine technology to the Soviets. Cameras rolling, Congressman Hunter took the opportunity to call for support of his bill to ban the import of Toshiba products.

About the same time, Congressman Dan Rostenkowski, powerful chairman of the House Ways and Means Committee, was holding hearings to jump-start economic development through the easing of U.S. trade restrictions. The idea was to increase the U.S. economy by expanding trade with other countries, and part of that effort involved reducing barriers that discouraged foreign countries from trading with the United States. Despite his political clout, powerful position, and desire to boost America's economy in time for the 1988 elections, Congressman Rostenkowski abandoned his plan. Why? Because of the wave of "Japan-bashing" sweeping the country, and his desire to avoid being seen as working in behalf of Japanese trade interests, something that could land him on the wrong side of a very emotional issue.

And what about Congressman Duncan Hunter's bill to ban imports by Toshiba: it squeaked by in the House on a vote of 415 to 1. A similar measure easily passed the Senate by a 92 to 5 vote. These bills merged and became law, establishing a three-year ban on such imports.[14]

Critical Analysis

This case involves public opinion, the U.S. government, Japan, Norway, and the Soviet Union. But what does it have to do with the analysis of cultures? The glaring inconsistency that jumps out of this case is the hard line taken by the U.S. public, and some of its representatives, against Japan's Toshiba, as contrasted with the velvet-gloves approach accorded the equally culpable Vapenfabrik corporation of Norway. This disparity raises some interesting questions about the relationship between cultural attitudes and public policy.

• • • • • • •

A consensus exists over the undeniability of an American double standard on this issue in 1987–1988. But what does this tell us? A rigorous social scientist would point out that no causal connection can be established from such loose bundles of evidence. Rather than U.S. cultural attitudes having produced differential responses toward Japan and Norway, these events may be merely coincidental; other more powerful forces may be at work here. From the perspective of this social scientist, this case amounts to no more than anecdotal information; the scientific establishment of cause and effect requires more stringent methods of testing a hypothesis. That the facts of this case may seem interesting affords no presumption of validity from a scientific stand-point. Social scientists would better expend their energy asking more tangible questions.

A humanities-oriented social scientist might hold a different view. Granting that nothing has been proven here, this social scientist could argue that the subjective nature of much human experience simply defies direct quantitative examination, and that being invisible does not keep forces like cultural attitudes and biases from exerting a powerful influence. Such a scholar may suggest that public attitudes in this case probably were affected by frustration felt by North Americans because of their giant trade deficit with Japan, and that hostile feelings toward Japan bled over to color this case of massive overreaction based mostly on emotion. By this logic, we had no comparable agenda of discontent vis-à-vis Norway, and consequently we did not overreact in the direction of the Atlantic. Although this thesis cannot be proven, says our humanist, it exhibits a logical consistency worthy of attention.

Aside from the validity of any conclusions drawn from the TTAC case, one thing does seem clear: our world is a very complicated place in which to operate. To render it simpler, humans make generalizations based on stereotypes—assumptions about groups of people and organizations. These stereotypes may sometimes contain a kernel of truth. However, they often become exaggerated and lead to inappropriate action based on shaky assumptions. The case of differential response toward Japan and Norway shows how humans can easily get the apples mixed up with the oranges in our mental sorting process, apparently causing a spillover of overreaction.

Chapter Synopsis

Most humans assume that the cultural circumstances in which they live represent the correct style of living. These unexamined beliefs of cultural superiority result in the pervasiveness of ethnocentrism. Such a cultural in-group mentality can lead to out-group hostility against those practicing different lifestyles. But the fact that ethnocentrism is about as common as the flu bug in December does not mean that we must accept it as inevitable. Social scientists almost universally caution against the hidden traps involved in blithely accepting our culture's biases and habits. It may not be possible to obviate the effects of ethnocentrism completely, but it is reasonable to struggle against its more insidious manifestations. How? Largely through the tool of cultural relativism: regarding other cultures as different rather than inferior, intriguing rather than bizarre. At the heart of cultural relativism is the effort to afford other cultures the right to live their own lifestyles according to their own inner logic.

Like many good ideas, putting into practice the laudable intentions of cultural relativism is often easier said than done. Human history is replete with strong societies subjugating weak ones via varied forms of imperialism or colonialism. Today the United States is often accused of a somewhat subtler form of cultural imperialism deriving from its great size, wealth, power and the appeal of its popular culture. Cultural relativism uses moral suasion in arguing against such forms of unfair domination and advocates a "live and let live" ethos. However, as is seen in three poignant case studies in this chapter (genital mutilation, execution for white-collar crime, caning as punishment) cultural relativism can unearth dilemmas wrought by other cultures' behaving in ways we believe to be immoral. The unsettling question is raised: how do we resolve increasing cases of conflict between the noble sentiment of cultural relativism and tolerance of activities in foreign cultures that violate our ethical standards?

For Digging Deeper

Ember, Carol, and Melvin Ember. *Cultural Anthropology*. Prentice Hall, 1996.

Kenyatta, Jomo. *Facing Mt. Kenya*. Secker and Warburg, 1953.

Lee, Dorothy. *Valuing the Self: What We Learn from Other Cultures*. Waveland Press, 1995.

Ritzer, George. *The McDonaldization of Society*. Pine Forge Press, 1995.

Key Glossary terms

cultural genocide
cultural relativism

ethnocentrism
holistic

popular culture

CHAPTER **9**

Psychology and Human Motivation

Thematic Questions

- From what historical sources does the discipline of psychology emanate?

- Which two psychological theories dominated the twentieth century?

- What major challengers have emerged as alternatives to the mainstream theories of motivation?

- In what venues and with what results have psychological theories been applied to the real world?

CORE OBJECTIVE

To understand the major theoretical accounts of human motivation and their application to social discourse.

Anwar Sadat (1918–1981), Egyptian president who became the first Arab leader to recognize the state of Israel.

In 1977 Egyptian President Anwar Sadat journeyed to Israel to make a historic speech in the heartland of his traditional enemy. In it he expressed the startling judgment that "problems between these two nations are 70 percent psychological."[1] A significant amount of what happens on the world stage results from intangible and subjective forces. Since it is always people who run the institutions that we have been discussing—nation–states, NGOs, IGOs, MNCs, and IFIs—we cannot ignore what motivates those people: their attitudes, values, perceptions, religious beliefs, habits, drives, fears, and mind-set. This is the stuff of psychology's effort to unravel the complexities of human behavior.

If anthropology is the broadest social science in conceptual terms, psychology surely is the largest in size, with more than 140,000 members of the American Psychological Association. There are 60,000 licensed therapists in the English-speaking world, and probably twice that many practicing professionals.[2] This breadth led Dennis Coon, author of a widely used psychology text, to observe, "Psychology has become such an enormous and colorful beast that no short description can do it justice." Although unwilling to provide a pithy definition, Coon succinctly identifies psychology's goals as describing, understanding, predicting, and controlling human behavior.[3]

THE DISCIPLINE OF PSYCHOLOGY

Professor Keith Stanovich's overview of the discipline, called *How to Think Straight about Psychology*, provides some useful insights concerning psychology's strengths and weaknesses. With at least forty-eight recognized subfields, this vast and diverse area of study, he says, cannot rely on its content to provide the glue to bind it together. He believes that if all college psychology departments were magically disbanded, his colleagues would easily integrate into other related departments, such as sociology, education, social work, business, or biology. In his view, only the rigorous application of scientific methods of investigation can overcome the discipline's significant "image problem," deriving largely from the volumes of amateur psychology to which the general public is exposed by the mass media. "Psychology probably more than any other science, requires critical thinking skills that enable students to separate the wheat from the chaff that accumulates around all sciences."[4]

Psychology differs from the other social sciences in another way. In addition to being an academic discipline which conducts basic scientific experiments to accumulate a body of knowledge, it is also an

applied discipline: its theories and methods are used by society to deal with practical problems. The main applied specialties include:

- clinical and counseling psychology
- community psychology
- industrial/organizational psychology
- engineering psychology
- environmental psychology
- educational psychology
- consumer psychology
- legal psychology
- sports psychology[5]

The History of Psychology

Like all modern social sciences, the study of human psychology can be traced to the ancient Greeks. Plato implored his students to "know thyself," acknowledging our species' unique introspective capabilities. The *Confessions of Saint Augustine* (351–425 A.D.) were the first truly autobiographical writings that dwelt on analysis of the inner self as an independent consciousness. Augustine's work not only served as a precursor to psychology, but also contributed mightily to the development of the novel as a form of literature.

Much later on, during the Renaissance, psychological questions of mind, motivation, character, and human consciousness became intimately bound up with the master discipline of philosophy. The first to attempt systematically to divorce psychology from philosophy was the German scholar Immanuel Kant (1724–1804). By the middle of the nineteenth century the term "psychology" was coming into general use, but Auguste Comte, the Frenchman who founded sociology, argued against disciplinary status for psychology, believing that "mind, ego, and the like were but useless abstractions," meaning that they could not be readily observed and measured.[6] It was not until the start of the twentieth century that psychology did indeed emerge as a discrete discipline.

In 1875 the first psychology course was offered by the U.S. scholar William James, who developed an approach related to the functionalist school in sociology, asking how the mind operates to enable us to adapt to our environment. The first American Ph.D. in psychology was conferred three years later. However, it was at the University of Leipzig, in Germany, in 1879, that Wilhelm Wundt (1832–1920) earned the status of father of psychology by establishing the first laboratory. Wondering how sensations and images are formed, he developed a technique of experimental introspection, which combined structured introspection with objective measurement techniques.

With the legitimacy of the discipline finally established, two main psychological theories appeared, side by side, at the turn of the century. The first school, psychoanalysis, was based on observations made in the private practice of Viennese physician Sigmund Freud (1856–1939). The other, behaviorism, first developed by John B. Watson (1878–1958), derived much of its approach from the laboratory techniques used by biologists to study animals. It is to these amazingly different theories of mind, personality, and therapy that we now turn.

Psychological Theories

Psychoanalysis   Charles Darwin's nineteenth-century theories of natural selection suggested the revolutionary idea that *Homo sapiens* were subject to the same developmental laws as other species. Humans were now viewed not only as less unique than once believed, but also as legitimate objects of scientific study. One of those greatly influenced by Darwin was Sigmund Freud, who thought that humans are driven by the conflicting demands of underlying impulses, some of which we are not even aware. Freud was looking deep down under the skin of the human animal for the fundamental causes of behavior. Within each of us, he suggested, rages a battle among three dynamic mental forces: the **id**, the **ego**, and the **superego**.

The id consists of an impulsive, pleasure-seeking well of energy stemming from biological instincts. The ego, by contrast, is more rational. It operates according to principles of reality, not fantasy, with practical planning as part of its repertoire. The superego is the judge, or censor, for the plans of the ego, and it represents the morality of a conscience, rendering it susceptible to feelings of guilt. A constant tug-of-war takes place, with the ego in the complex position of trying to balance two irreconcilable forces. Freud believed that the individual is highly susceptible to the long-term effects of childhood trauma and that she or he must develop through a series of psychosexual stages by age five in order to avoid unhealthy consequences in adulthood. Personality, Freud reasoned, is set in concrete very early in life. For those carrying ill effects of childhood trauma into adulthood, Freud created the so-called "talking cure." He coaxed patients into lengthy dialogues in which he would guide the client ever closer to insightful recollections intended to resolve painful buried memories.[7]

Hollywood's most entertaining window on the vagueness, self-absorption, and absence of closure associated with psychoanalysis is epitomized by the angst-ridden characters who populate the films of Woody Allen. Rent the video for any of Allen's following movies, fast-forward randomly to any segment of the picture, and chances are you will witness the personalized, bittersweet humor and pathos of characters stuck on a treadmill of therapeutic introspection and self-doubt (especially characters played by Allen himself): *Take the Money and Run* (1969), *Everything You Wanted to Know about Sex but Were Afraid to Ask* (1972), *Annie Hall* (1977), *Interiors* (1978), *Manhattan* (1979), *Stardust Memories* (1980), *Zelig* (1983), *The Purple Rose of Cairo* (1985), *Hannah and Her Sisters* (1986), *Mighty Aphrodite* (1995), *Deconstructing Harry* (1997).

Freud was interested mostly in the storm that he observed raging within the individual psyche. His fullest exploration of the social implications of the battle of id versus superego found expression in his *Civilization and Its Discontents*, which analyzed the struggle of culture versus the raw-boned state of nature. Typically, his prognoses ranged only from grim to grimmer to grimmest.

Freud's theories are followed today by less than 10 percent of psychologists in the American Psychological Association. Nevertheless, Keith Stanovich laments what he calls the "Freud problem" in his profession: for most laypeople, some version of Freudian theory represents the core of what they think psychology is about, despite the profession's having essentially abandoned Freudianism.[8] Freud's theories were based on case studies of mental problems presented by his patients and lacked basic scientific guidelines. Somewhat like Karl Marx's analysis of social causation, Sigmund Freud's analysis of psychological causation was eclectic, brilliant for its time and place, and creative. For both Freud and Marx, however, what was widely taken 100 years ago for scientific discovery generally fails to hold water under contemporary scrutiny.

Behaviorism In 1906 Russian physiologist Ivan Pavlov began publishing accounts of his **conditioned response** experiments on animals. Extrapolating some of the principles Pavlov was applying to dogs, John B. Watson's behaviorism caught on quickly after World War I. Reacting against the subjective dreamworld of Freud's psychoanalytic school, behaviorists committed themselves to operating scientifically: observability, verifiability, and quantification became their watchwords.

But behaviorists believed they were armed with more than scientific methods; they believed they understood the importance of the environment's influence on individual behavior. Through their methods they sought to demonstrate the powerful mechanics of positive and negative conditioning, or rewards and punishments. Environmental **stimuli (S)** cause behavioral **responses (R)** by the subject under examination, and it was considered the scientist's job to record these observations. A conditioned response is nothing more, or less, than a learned reaction to a given stimulus.

Less concerned than the Freudians about childhood trauma, behaviorists think that behavior patterns can change, since they remain subject to modification by outside influences. Unraveling personality is no mystery to them: individual personality consists of observable behavioral habits forming the structure of who you are. One of the discipline's major contemporary branches, learning psychology, derives from behaviorism's scientific penchant and leans toward the natural sciences in both method and content.

The most important behaviorist of the second half of the twentieth century, B. F. Skinner (1904–1990), focused more on macrolevel societal issues than did his more micro-oriented predecessors, and spoke of using conditioned response for social engineering purposes—that is, using carefully distributed rewards and punishments to get people to do the things we want them to do, thereby creating the good society. First broaching the idea in fictional form via his novel *Walden Two*, then addressing it more directly in *Beyond Freedom and Dignity*, Skinner attacked as outmoded Western society's attachment to the primacy of individual rights and freedoms.

Modern forms of social problems (including the global issues discussed elsewhere in this book) call for modern solutions of social engineering based on the application of conditioned response. If you apply these prescriptions to Mini-case 8.3, the caning of Michael Fay in Singapore, do you think Prime Minister Lee Kuan Yew has read Skinner? Two more congenial peas would seem hard to find in any pod—although in fairness to Skinner, he has expressed a preference for positive reinforcement as more effective in encouraging desirable behavior than punishment in discouraging undesirable behavior.

Behaviorism satisfied the desire for a psychology that is more observable and measurable than psychoanalysis, but it accomplished these scientific objectives at a considerable price. Behaviorism's entire edifice rests on the questionable assumption that what we know about animals is transferrable to humans. It also treats humans as if we were robots, completely ignoring the inner life of symbolic contemplation that characterizes only our species. Behaviorism is very deterministic in outlook, presenting a problem for those who believe that humans have free will to think their way through a situation rather than merely reacting to it. Many scholars consider the questions addressed by behaviorists too far removed from real-world experiences to identify closely with their research agenda.

Humanistic Psychologies   In neither of psychology's two leading theories were humans accorded any real sense of **efficacy**. In the Freudian model, we find ourselves at the mercy of deep, dark forces inside us that we don't even understand. Deterministic behaviorism seems no better, since it considers our robotic behavior to result from external forces once again well beyond our control. For anyone with a more optimistic sense of the human condition, little theoretical ammunition was provided by the discipline's big guns.

A key characteristic of America's revolutionary heyday in the 1960s was its feeling of efficacy, its sense that anything is possible. At this very time, a "Third Wave" of **humanistic psychologies** engulfed the country. In no other social science do we find a chasm between scientism and humanism wider than that separating behaviorist and humanistic psychologies. Although the latter are quite numerous, all of them conceive of human personality as developing continuously over a lifetime.

Probably the earliest to argue that "Man is the origin of his actions" was the Greek philosopher Aristotle.[9] More than anyone else, psychologist Erik Erikson's "Eight Ages of Man" developed this concept, which also filtered into popular consciousness through Daniel Levinson's *Seasons in a Man's Life* and Gail Sheehy's *Passages*.[10] According to Erikson, we face eight common psychosocial dilemmas which we must seek to resolve for ourselves in the course of a lifetime, and how we deal with them shapes much of who we become. The long-standing Freudian principle that personality was set by age five was being taken apart.

A belief in untapped human potential also made many humanistic theories attractive. For a 1960s generation which believed it could change society, the idea of individuals changing themselves was not hard to accept. Fritz Perls's Gestalt therapy, Eric Berne's Transactional Analysis, Albert Ellis's Rational-Emotive Therapy, Abraham Maslow's Self-Actualization, and Carl Rogers's Client-Centered Therapy all offered venues to cast aside self-defeating habits and embrace new patterns of behavior. Humanists generated interest in those areas of human experience that had been overlooked by the psychoanalytic and behavioral approaches: the need for love, self-esteem, belonging, self-expression, creativity, and spirituality.[11]

Bio-psychology   By the 1990s a new form of therapy had arisen in psychology which was shaking up the balance of forces in the age-old question of **nature versus nurture**. Almost no psychologists dispute that some combination of nature (biology and heredity) and nurture (socialization and life experiences) makes us into the unique individuals that we are. The tough part, of course, lies in assessing the relative weight of each factor: is it 50/50? 75/25? 25/75? 90/10? 10/90?

For most of this century the psychoanalytic emphasis on nature and the behaviorist emphasis on nurture remained essentially stalemated. Then, with the advent of the humanistic psychologies in the 1960s and 1970s, the balance of forces clearly tilted toward the nurture side of the equation. Now, in the 1990s, we find an entirely new body of evidence lending credence to the relative importance of nature. These studies come largely from biology and entail discoveries related to the human brain, findings tied to the exploration of DNA as the building block of life, and genetic engineering research.

What is the practical result of these areas of laboratory research? An entirely new generation of prescription drugs for ailments such as **anxiety, depression**, and **obsessive-compulsive disorder** has taken over the discourse in clinical psychology. Psychoactive drugs are not new. They have been around for decades, but they have to live down a forty-year perception of causing serious side effects while offering limited relief to the sufferer. Symptomatic of the fast-paced world in which we live today, that assessment seems to have changed remarkably quickly. New drugs have raised hopes for "better living through chemistry"; the evidence reported in studies thus far is that they work more effectively and more selectively than their predecessors, thus causing fewer side effects. Suddenly biological considerations seem to be generating more sustained interest than early-childhood trauma, environmental conditioning, or self-actualization as the tool of choice for those in psychological pain, especially in a frugal era marked by managed health care. However, many mental health traditionalists believe that a pill will never adequately replace human compassion.[12]

So, we have defined psychology as the most diverse social science discipline in a multifaceted manner: (1) by its vast content, spilling over into far-flung disciplines such as education, biology, business, sociology, and philosophy; (2) by its huge number of practitioners spanning forty-eight-plus subfields (which include areas known as peace psychology and environmental psychology) within psychology's broad parameters; and (3) by its functioning both as a science of knowledge concerning behavior and as an applied science aiming to solve practical problems confronting society. Yet, despite its diversity and its status as an applied science, relatively few of its principles have been applied to the dynamics of the world stage featured in this book—namely, that which is international, that which is foreign, that which is cross-cultural, and that which is global. One exception is the work of Canadian political psychologist Blema Steinberg. In a recent book she applies principles of psychoanalytic theory to presidential decision making in the Vietnam War, and she asks, "Why did Lyndon Johnson and Richard Nixon choose to escalate the conflict in Vietnam, while Dwight Eisenhower desisted?" See Mini-case 9.1.

MINI-CASE 9.1
The U.S. in Vietnam: To Escalate or Not to Escalate?

One of France's colonial possessions was the southeast Asian nation of Vietnam. Like most other colonial peoples, the Vietnamese conducted a campaign after World War II for their independence. Like many other colonial powers, France resisted, and a prolonged war of independence ensued. Finally, in 1954, France lost the decisive battle of Dienbienphu and retreated in defeat. The leader of Vietnamese independence was Ho Chi Minh, whom the Western countries considered to be a communist. At the height of the Cold War, the issue of communist influence among Vietnamese independence fighters converted the struggle within Vietnam to the level of the global battle between communism and capitalism. As the military leader of Western capitalism, the United States had a decision to make

Figure 9.1

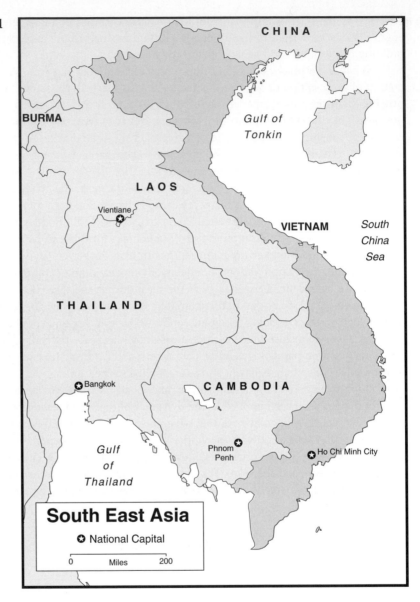

in 1954: whether to fill the power vacuum left by France's withdrawal with a sizable American presence. President Dwight Eisenhower decided against such an escalatory move.

What then developed was a civil war fought between the North Vietnamese (with material support from China and the Soviet Union) and the South Vietnamese (with material support from the United States). For years this domestic battle raged without any external powers directly participating. This condition was characteristic of regional struggles during the Cold War: the major powers remained in the background, leaving military confrontation to the local forces whom they supported materially. But then, by the middle of the 1960s, the North Vietnamese gradually but surely began winning the war. The United States had been supplying military hardware and military advisors to South Vietnam, which nevertheless failed to keep the North from gaining the ascendancy.

In 1965 President Lyndon Johnson was faced with a momentous decision: should he actively "Americanize" the war by sending large numbers of U.S. combat forces to fight? Or should he more passively continue to allow the South Vietnamese to fight their own war? Johnson chose the former path, which soon resulted in more than 500,000 combat troops in Vietnam, but still no victory in sight. His policies failed so badly that in 1968 he decided not to run for a second presidential term, retiring instead to his Texas ranch. Succeeding Lyndon Johnson was President Richard Nixon, whose campaign pledged "peace with honor" in Vietnam: a gradual U.S. withdrawal without abandoning its South Vietnamese allies.

But Vietnam proved a military and political quagmire for Nixon as well. In 1970 U.S. losses continued at an alarming pace, generating massive public protest in America's streets. Making matters worse, Nixon had not managed to coax the North Vietnamese, as promised, to the peace table for ne-

Figure 9.2

Source: Herblock, *The Washington Post,* (April 23, 1967)

gotiations. He then decided to gamble. Nixon upped the ante, expanding the war in secret, bombing and invading North Vietnamese supply routes through neighboring Cambodia.

What Blema Steinberg wanted to know was whether psychoanalytic theory helps us comprehend why Eisenhower chose not to escalate U.S. military involvement in 1954 but Johnson and Nixon chose the opposite path in 1965 and 1970. To seek such answers in the psychoanalytic garden, she needed to dig into the personalities of the three presidents, using as her trowel the concept of **narcissism** and looking especially for the impact of feelings of shame and humiliation common to narcissistic personalities. She argues that these cases are ideally suited to examining the effect of personality profiles on foreign policy decision making because of the absence of strong public opinion or advisory influences: these presidents were relatively free to act as they chose.

Her sketch of narcissistic personalities draws a picture of riveting self-involvement and exaggerated concern with the achievement of success and fame, compensating for love and affection not received in childhood. Being singled out as "special" convinces such children that love depends on performance. The self-absorption of narcissists makes it difficult for them to see life through the eyes of others or to experience intimacy with other people. They need to accomplish things and to be acclaimed for their successes; they need the feelings of grandiosity that accompany achievement. Believing they are not likeable for themselves but only for their worldly accomplishments, they are also subject to the opposite feelings of inferiority—especially shame and humiliation—when they cannot live up to their lofty expectations.

After a careful examination of their formative years, Steinberg says that Lyndon Johnson and Richard Nixon each had mothers who conveyed to them that they were special; therefore much was expected of them. Johnson and Nixon also shared the experience of fathers who were angry, impatient, and discounted by wives who were more sophisticated and intelligent. Not surprisingly, neither Johnson nor Nixon made many good friends in their childhood. In sharp contrast, Steinberg's analysis of Dwight Eisenhower's childhood reflects a poor but loving environment that encouraged stability; young Dwight also blended in comfortably with his five brothers. He held a healthy self-concept and felt loved for who he was rather than for anything that he might do. Professor Steinberg's comparative psychological assessment of Nixon and Johnson on the one hand, and Eisenhower on the other, is succinctly capsulized in these words:

> Lyndon Johnson and Richard Nixon were two highly narcissistic individuals who suffered from painful feelings of shame and humiliation. It was these feelings, in the overall context of their narcissistic character structures, that played an important part in shaping their presidential decisions on Vietnam. Dwight Eisenhower, in contrast, was not a narcissistic personality. As a confident, psychologically well-adjusted individual, his political decision-making in 1954 was less colored by his psychological needs and fears.[13]

It is important to note that Professor Steinberg's analysis is intended as one explanation of presidential decision making on Vietnam, but not the only one. Such matters are complex, and social scientists are careful to avoid what philosophers refer to as the fallacy of single cause, or treating one factor in a multicausal situation as if it were the only one. Certainly Presidents Eisenhower, Johnson, and Nixon were subject to a host of political, military, economic, and social influences on their decisions. Nevertheless, psychological factors have sometimes been ignored in studies of international relations, and Blema Steinberg's work serves as a reminder that doing so represents an intellectual loss. Political scientist John Stoessinger's studies of U.S. foreign policy share the view that the personality of a president is important in shaping American policy.[14] This concept leads us to a more general consideration of the idea of limits to the appropriate use of psychological concepts in world affairs.

Limitations   The other five social sciences (geography, sociology, anthropology, political science, and economics) operate mostly at either the macro (national) level or the mega (global) level. Only psychology deals primarily with human behavior at the micro (individual) level. Given this basic reality, it seems obvious that the applicability of psychology's micro-level concepts to the dynamics of behavior at the macro or mega levels is subject to limits. While it is always the behavior of humans that social scientists study at all three levels of analysis, the milieu confronting us differs markedly from the micro to macro to mega levels.

Therefore, it is prudent to exercise caution when crossing levels of analysis, especially the giant step between the micro and mega levels. Yet this concern does not mean that we cannot jump these intellectual barriers when appropriate. The value of interdisciplinary studies has been widely touted in recent years, and the use of psychological concepts at the international level symbolizes the synergistic nature of interdisciplinary studies in general. Since psychologists have been slower than other social scientists in internationalizing their curricula, the initiators of such cross-fertilization have often been anthropologists, economists, or political scientists. However, a brief example of one social psychologist's skillful application of psychological concepts to world affairs might be instructive (see Mini-case 9.2).

MINI-CASE 9.2
From David Lee Rice to Nuclear Numbing

I n 1986 psychologist Sam Keen went to a Seattle prison to conduct extensive interviews with an inmate convicted of murdering an innocent family of four. What intrigued Keen was not the gruesome crime itself, which is distressingly common in U.S. society. Rather, it was the mind-set of the murderer, David Lee Rice, that haunted Keen as he questioned the inmate.

It would seem that nothing could be more irrevocably grounded in the face-to-face reality of micro-level behavior than the murder of a model family in its home by an intruder. That is, until Keen begins unraveling the rhetoric, beliefs, and defense mechanisms of David Lee Rice, who did not commit murder for revenge, robbery, money, or lust for power. Rice actually believed, concludes Keen, that he was a soldier fighting a deadly war against global communism. He killed, Rice said, only when he had to in order to defeat the communist menace.

It seems quite absurd that this convicted murderer would use the global communist menace as a justification for murdering four law-abiding family members. While they were not even communists, Rice had been told that they were, and apparently simple-mindedly believed it. Even the most anticommunist citizens, however, do not go around killing people, and Keen in no way offers to defend the unalterable evil committed by Rice.

But after many sessions with the subject, Keen was struck less by the admittedly bizarre aspects of Rice's thinking than by how Rice's beliefs about communism reflected some generally held societal attitudes about communism as expressed in the mass media. The Cold War was still raging when Rice committed the murders, and in his skewed thinking he considered this mega-level conflict of conflicts as legitimizing his personal fight against communists. It can be said that both Rice and society generally shared simplistic Cold War black/white lenses, symbolic imagery depicting the enemy as subhuman, and a moral imperative justifying our side's righteousness.

In his documentary film *Faces of the Enemy*, Keen acknowledges the limits to skipping across levels of analysis. Yet he thinks that such efforts provide insights into international behavior not otherwise possible. Among those that can be gleaned from his case study is this conclusion: it is dangerous for humans to numb themselves into an unfeeling avoidance of reality. His examination led him to marvel at how Rice had become an unfeeling, virtual automaton. The path of least resistance for Rice was that of avoiding feelings associated with his crime. While Rice likely would never "heal" in any psychological sense without coming to grips with his feelings, numbness represented the short-term easy way out.

Keen applies this micro-level insight to humanity's penchant for a comparable psychic numbing against feelings generated by the nuclear arms race. It is relatively easy to avoid confronting the realities of the nuclear dilemma in an age of overkill, but by doing so we become less likely to come to grips with the true nature of the problem. We can't hope to resolve the nuclear dilemma if we fail to assess its dimensions realistically. Like David Lee Rice, we numb ourselves to avoid powerful feelings associated with fully exploring the frightening problem of nuclear weapons.[15]

PERCEPTUAL ANALYSIS AND WORLD AFFAIRS

During the past quarter-century, the study of world affairs has been enhanced by the systematic study of **perceptual analysis**.[16] Examination of the process of human perception suggests that in addition to the objective dimension of reality that we encounter, a subjective dimension also operates: what we *think* exists can be as vital to our behavior as what, in fact, *does* exist. The human mind does not work like an organic photocopying machine, absorbing images of everything crossing its path. Rather, the mind engages in **selective perception**. Your five senses are capable of internalizing many different impressions from your present environment, storing them away for future use. While reading this sentence, you may be unaware of other stimuli available to your senses at this moment: possibly the sound of an air-conditioner, sight of a fly buzzing around the room, the smell of wet socks thrown into the corner, or the vibration from a stereo down the hall. By perceiving one thing (this sentence), you exclude other things from your attention.

When we perceive social phenomena more complex than buzzing flies or vibrating stereos, the human mind responds in a more sophisticated fashion. For one thing, selective perception does not occur randomly; it is influenced by our underlying beliefs and expectations. Once again we turn to the ancient Greeks to trace an important insight. Demosthenes said: "Nothing is easier than self-deceit. For what each man wishes, that he also believes to be true."[17] Furthermore, it is not only the individual who is subject to selective perception—members of societies also share cultural prisms comprised of common values and historical memories.

While aspects of selective perception often pertain to specific cultures, John Rourke summarizes what he calls five universal perceptual tendencies that can affect decision makers and citizens alike: (1) we believe that people in other cultures see and interpret events pretty much as we do; (2) other countries are seen as more hostile than is ours; (3) the behavior of adversaries is often believed to be more efficient than our own; (4) we assume that our sincere intentions are so self-evident as to defy their being doubted by our adversaries; and (5) two countries intensely involved with one another tend to see each other as either positive or negative mirror images of one another.[18]

The conditions for misperception in international affairs are particularly ripe—the stakes are high, cultural differences between actors are often great, and communication between the players is made difficult by distance, multiple languages, and competing interests. Our earlier case study of the Cuban missile crisis gave President Kennedy high marks for sticking to a rational decision-making process but flunked him for completely misinterpreting Khrushchev's motivation for placing missiles in Cuba. The outbreak of World War I is often cited as the classic example of a war triggered by widespread misperception. When the players are global superpowers, the consequences of distorted perceptions can be especially serious. In two examples from the tense Cold War days of the 1960s (Mini-case 9.3), the Americans and Soviets conveniently flip-flopped their interpretive arguments to suit their shifting interests in the Dominican and Czechoslovakian crises.

MINI-CASE 9.3
Perceptual Role Reversal in the Czech and Dominican Crises

Neither the United States nor the Soviet Union had any incentive to question the validity of its Cold War mission. The enemy, by definition, was an aggressor and an international scoundrel. Perceived facts and events all had to be filtered through these general Cold War prisms. Given such firmly held convictions, discovering that the superpowers might exhibit polar opposite interpretations of two serious 1960s crises can hardly be surprising.

In 1965 U.S. President Lyndon Johnson received intelligence reports that the Dominican Republic's government, headed by Juan Bosch, had fallen under the control of communists. Johnson responded by sending American marines to the tiny Caribbean nation to overthrow its leftist government and secure a regime seen as more friendly to the United States. He defended his action with an argument known as "regional sphere of influence," citing the 1823 **Monroe Doctrine** and other actions taken by U.S. presidents to protect American interests in the Western hemisphere. He considered the Dominican invasion a local matter occurring in America's backyard, and certainly not the business of powers from other regions.

The Soviets begged to differ. Rather than viewing the Dominican crisis as local in nature, the Soviet Union interpreted it as a matter of global proportions. Taking a "universal international law" approach, the Soviets branded the invasion a violation of the sovereign independence of the Dominican Republic. Soviet eyes perceived nothing short of naked aggression violating the United Nations Charter and other international legal standards of conduct. Accordingly, the Soviet Union condemned the United States at the U.N. and elsewhere.

Fast-forward three years to the Czechoslovakian crisis: same players, complete role reversal. With Czechoslovakia one of the East European countries occupied by the Soviet Union after Germany's defeat in World War II, the Czech Communist Party had long walked a tightrope. Czech ties had historically been to the European West, not to the Soviet East. Culturally, politically, and economically, its people felt kinship with the West, and most of them hated the control over their lives resulting from Soviet armed forces on Czech soil. Czech party leaders hoped to exercise some freedom from Moscow. They knew, however, that if they made Kremlin leaders nervous about changes to their political and economic system, they could be crushed like puppets.

Czech leader Alexander Dubcek cautiously fashioned what came to be known as the "Prague Spring": allowing certain limited pockets of freedom of expression and economic freedom which deviated from the Soviet model of a highly authoritarian system. Dubcek wanted to create what he called "communism with a human face," that is, one more humane and flexible than the rigid form pushed by the Russians. In 1968 euphoria swept through the capital city of Prague. Citizens enjoyed freedom of speech; religion was practiced quietly; farmers improved their income with profits earned from the sale of privately grown produce. It all seemed too good to be true—and it was. Stanley Kauffman's bittersweet film, *The Unbearable Lightness of Being* (1987) re-creates a slice of life from Prague at this exciting time.

Fearing that Czech freedom could spill over not only to other East European countries, but even to the Soviet Union itself, in August 1968 Soviet leader Leonid Brezhnev sent tanks into Prague and brutally smashed Alexander Dubcek's breath of fresh air, replacing it with a regime that kow-towed to the Soviet line. Espousing the new **Brezhnev Doctrine**, the Soviets warned other East European communist states that no deviation from the Soviet path to communism would be tolerated. Brezhnev invoked the argument of "regional sphere of influence," calling this a local socialist drama in which outsiders had no role. The parallels between the Monroe Doctrine and the Brezhnev Doctrine are multifaceted.

The United States perceived the invasion of Czechoslovakia quite differently. As had the Soviets in the earlier Dominican crisis, America invoked the language of "universal international law" in criticizing Brezhnev's Czech invasion as a gross violation of the territorial integrity of a sovereign nation–state. The United States blasted Soviet aggression in every possible public forum.[19]

Only three years separated these two superpower crises, and so the key decision makers were in place for both. To outside observers with any semblance of objectivity, the overt behavior involved in the U.S. invasion of the Dominican Republic and the Soviet invasion of Czechoslovakia shared much in common. In each case, a superpower invaded a small country in its regional sphere of influence to further that superpower's perceived national interest. The parallels between the two situations are striking. Yet the influence of official American and Russian Cold War prisms was very potent. Each prism so skillfully filtered reality to fit that nation's belief system, that if you were to take at face value the words spoken by U.S. and Soviet leaders, you would think that the two cases consisted of completely unrelated elements.[20]

MINI-CASE 9.4
Textbook Spin, U.S. and Japanese Style

Important events in world affairs sometimes acquire symbolic meaning layered onto their more literal or factual meaning. One prime candidate for getting lost in symbolic meaning is a society with some painful past experience. In such a case, selective perception often contributes to a form of **cultural mythology**. The content of public school textbooks can provide a window on the role of selective perception in coping with a society's psychic scars. Comparing American and Japanese textbooks' treatment of the August 6,

Memorial cenotaph in a Japanese Peace Park reminding the world of the devastation of atomic weapons.

1945, dropping of the atomic bomb on the city of Hiroshima by the United States allows us to peek through such a window.

This critical event has been widely studied by many scholars. While much factual information has been produced, interesting differences of emphasis exist in textbook accounts of the Hiroshima bombing. Read the following two excerpts; then reread them, making two lists: *identical* elements versus *different* elements in the information reported.

Excerpt from American textbook

On 6 August the first atomic bomb was dropped on Hiroshima, killing nearly eighty thousand people and reducing four square miles of the city to rubble and ashes. Still, Tokyo did not surrender, and three days later the only other bomb that had thus far been produced was dropped on Nagasaki with similar dreadful consequences. At the same time, Soviet Russia declared war on Japan. On 14 August the Japanese at last accepted the Allies' terms of surrender, provided only that the Emperor be permitted to remain on his throne.

Excerpt from Japanese textbook

On 6 August America dropped the world's first atomic bomb on Hiroshima. On the 8th of August the Soviet Union, breaking the Japan–Soviet Neutrality Treaty, declared war on Japan and invaded Manchuria. On the 9th, America dropped an atomic bomb on Nagasaki as well.

The atomic bombs took about 200,000 lives in Hiroshima and 100,000 in Nagasaki. Not only were there victims of the high heat and the shock wave, but also many of those exposed to radiation died within a few weeks. Moreover, for more than 20 years afterward, people continued to fall ill and die. The damage from these A-bomb after-effects shows people even today the dreadfulness of nuclear weapons.

On 14 August Japan finally decided to accept the Allies' terms of surrender, and the nation was informed the next day by the Emperor's radio broadcast.[21]

Are you struck more by similarities or differences in these two textbook accounts? Why do you think this is so? Of what value is perceptual analysis in explaining the nature of these accounts and your observations about them? How is it possible for nations like Japan and the United States to switch so rapidly from adversaries in the 1930s, to enemies in the 1940s, and then allies after World War II?

THE PSYCHOLOGY OF ENEMY MAKING

Our discussion in Chapter 4 makes clear that wars have played an integral role in human history. Since all societies express taboos against killing—many on the basis of religions forbidding the taking of human life—how is it that we have managed to kill 111 million members of our species in this century alone?

If social taboos condemn killing but wars require it, we would seem to be in a genuine pickle. The psychodynamics involved in creating the concept of "enemy" help explain how humans have resolved this dilemma. The trip wire that allows nations to shift—as did Japan and America—from being allies to enemies and back again, consists of the process of **dehumanization**. Societies use dehumanization as a simple but powerful tool by convincing themselves that the enemy is subhuman. The enemy is a monster, vermin, beast, madman, or demon; all decidedly different from us, all inhuman.

By examining diverse cultures at various times, Sam Keen has described the dehumanization process as a universal psychological process used by countries preparing to fight wars. In comparing their visual imagery from posters, films, cartoons, and paintings, he marveled that it was "almost as if they all went to the same art school." Keen is not arguing for pacifism. It would be unrealistic to think that societies should never have any enemies or that we never need to kill in war. However, greater awareness of the enemy-making process may enable us more accurately to assess our enemies. By so doing, we can identify those who really deserve to be our enemies, rather than accepting any who show up to play that role. Societies might find options other than killing their enemies in war. Accuracy in our perceptions of nations is the basic building block needed to begin constructing such alternative ways of dealing with nations whose interests differ from ours.[22]

America: Behold the Ugly Face of International Terrorism

The revolution in global communications has enabled obscure groups to gain instantaneous worldwide notoriety for their grievances in ways impossible to imagine a generation or two ago. Former British Prime Minister Margaret Thatcher once passionately urged the communications media to "starve terrorists of the oxygen of publicity!"[23] A nice sentiment, but not likely to happen. Technological improvements have also made the assembly and delivery of ever more lethal weapons of terror increasingly easy.

Something else that makes terrorism especially difficult to deal with is the mind-set of those who engage in acts of public violence. Terrorists usually believe themselves to be martyrs in a political or religious crusade. Their lack of fear of death renders the task of stopping such human geodes extremely complex, if not impossible. The interminable list of international terrorist acts grows daily. Frustrated Westerners look on in dismay—their governments almost never able to act proactively, and only occasionally successful in apprehending perpetrators after the fact.

Only in rare cases have captured terrorists proven to be **clinically insane**. The knee-jerk reaction that all terrorists are insane is not supported by available evidence. Walter Reich's *Origins of Terrorism*, examining the motivations of terrorists, finds that they seldom act without purpose and a consistent inner, albeit private, logic. They conduct what they see as specific battles of overt violence, but their war is ultimately a covert one aimed at global attention for their cause. Terrorists have goals, although they select decidedly reprehensible means of achieving them in the opinion of most of the world's people.[24]

International terrorist attacks have been most frequent in number in and around the Middle East, but they have also been common in Latin America, Europe, and South Asia. At one time some North Americans may have worried about terrorism when traveling abroad but few considered it in their home context. Those halcyon days consisted of either complacency or wishful thinking, since transportation routes into the United States are virtually limitless, American security is inadequate, and miniaturization allows devastating weapons to be readily concealed. Nevertheless, most Americans have thought of terrorism as something that happens elsewhere—in Tel Aviv, Rome, Bogota, or New Delhi—but not in the United States. For many decades they were correct.

Then, on February 26, 1993, a rented yellow Ryder truck delivered terrorism to America's doorstep. The truck carried 1,200 pounds of fertilizer topped with three cylinders of hydrogen gas. When detonated, it tore a five-story hole in New York City's World Trade Center,

International terrorism washed onto America's shores, not far from the Statue of Liberty, when a bomb left rubble, death, and trauma in its wake at the World Trade Center in New York.

killing six and injuring more than 1,000, filling Manhattan's financial district with scorched survivors. Its psychological shock waves reverberated across a stunned nation. Such was America's rude awakening to the world of international terrorism.[25] The World Trade Center disaster was, nevertheless, at least comprehensible to Americans as the work of Islamic fundamentalists from the Middle East, probably acting with the support of America's 1991 enemy, Saddam Hussein of Iraq. Much more difficult to digest was what happened two years later in Oklahoma City.

When the Enemy Becomes the State

A growing number of disenchanted right-wing groups have gained notoriety in the United States during the 1990s. Some describe themselves as part of a loosely defined Patriot movement advocating grass-roots activism against the power of the federal government. Others belong to similar groups who emphasize defense of the Second Amendment's right to bear arms and are engaged in preparation for what they see as an inevitable military confrontation with the federal government. Most of the **Patriots** and the **Militias** believe that a United Nations-based international conspiracy aims to steal America's sovereign independence.

The defining moment of their mission crystalized on September 11, 1990, when President George Bush proclaimed the Gulf War coalition as the realization of a "new world order" under the auspices of the U.N. What President Bush had in mind with these words was generating public support for a war against Iraqi aggression in Kuwait. But the words "new world order" have been interpreted by right-wing activists as confirmation of a global conspiracy to invade the United States. During the Cold War, right-wing extremists worried about international communism taking over the United States. Now with world communism in shambles, their international conspiracy has acquired a new look: the global threat is no longer ideological (communism), but racial; Third World peoples of color are believed to manipulate the U.N. as a conduit to the North American heartland.

Precise numbers are elusive when one is discussing North America's right-wing extremists. One reason is that they intentionally avoid clear organizational structures, relying mostly on "leaderless cells," thus leaving few footprints in the wake of their activities. Estimates suggest that only about 100,000 of them are armed-to-the-teeth militia members but as many as 12 million may see themselves as disaffected antigovernment patriots, mostly in rural America.[26] When such figures are placed alongside those describing "America's bomb culture," the combination seems ominous. FBI data reflect a huge increase in bombings over the course of one decade: only 442 in 1983, but up to 1,880 in 1993. Part of the problem is bomb know-how, now more widely disseminated through the Internet, fax machines, and mail-order publishing companies like Paladin Press of Boulder, Colorado, whose catalog lists forty books and videos on making explosives, including *Homemade C-4: A Recipe for Survival.*[27]

In the 1980s, right-wing extremists drew inspiration from Hollywood movies glamorizing grass-roots heroes rising up to defend America against communist invaders. In John Milius's *Red Dawn* (1984), a band of down-jacketed Colorado teenagers came to the rescue as resourceful guerrilla fighters to shoot, bomb, and knife foreign forces occupying the United States. A weak and unsuspecting America was again easily invaded in *Invasion, USA* (1983), starring vigilante Chuck Norris as a retired FBI agent who almost single-handedly unleashed a trail of bloody vengeance against the evil foreigners. In *Amerika*

(1986) a complacent United States again is invaded and occupied by consummately bad outsiders. Feature films in the 1990s shifted to reflect the sharp increase in domestic bombings, in movies like *Speed* (1995), *Blown Away* (1994), and *The Specialist* (1994). The start of Bruce Willis's action-adventure, *Die Hard with a Vengeance* (1996), features the bombing of a department store. In Chuck Norris's *Top Dog* (1996) neo-Nazis bomb an apartment building to begin the action.

MINI-CASE 9.5
Oklahoma City and Timothy McVeigh

What may pass for entertainment on the silver screen disintegrates into horror and chaos in real life. At 9:00 A.M. on Monday morning, April 19, 1995, the work week in Oklahoma City was over before it began. A massive explosion in front of the Alfred P. Murrah Building killed 168 people, physically and psychically injuring well over 500 more. The Murrah Building wasn't just any building, it was a federal government building. Almost overnight the prime suspect was arrested, but unlike the case in the World Trade Center bombing, this was not an Islamic fundamentalist from the Middle East, or anywhere else. Rather, he was an American army veteran, a recipient of the bronze star and combat infantry badge for service in the Persian Gulf War. The pieces to this bizarre puzzle did not add up to a clear picture for a U.S. public looking for foreign villains.

Timothy McVeigh came from suburban Buffalo, New York, where he grew up in an Irish-Catholic divorced family. He was known by his teachers as a computer buff and a gun aficionado. As a self-described survivalist, in his teen years he often paraded around with bandoliers of shells, "Rambo-like." He was considered by friends and neighbors as a quiet

The north side of Oklahoma City's Alfred P. Murrah Federal Building, after the truck bomb detonated by Timothy McVeigh in 1995.

and introspective young man. After high school he landed his first regular job as an armed guard. His favorite movie was *Red Dawn*, which he watched many times.

Before long he enlisted in the army; he was described as a good soldier: quietly efficient and dedicated. In 1990, at the age of twenty-two, he was in the midst of trying out for Army Special Forces when his unit was sent to Saudi Arabia to prepare for the Persian Gulf War. His service in the 1991 war was recognized with a bronze star and combat infantry badge. His fellow soldiers reported that he bragged about his first kill, a rifle shot which tore off an Iraqi soldier's head at 1,000 feet. Upon returning from the war to Fort Bragg, North Carolina, he was reportedly very excited about a chance to try out for the elite Green Berets. However, his Saudi duty had taken its toll on him and he was not in adequate physical condition to pass the screening test.

Wracked with feelings of failure and deeply embittered, McVeigh withdrew into himself, reading and rereading *The Turner Diaries* (1978), a novel that demonizes the U.S. government and advocates violence in pursuit of racial separation. Slowly turning toward right-wing conspiracy theories, he quit the army. When he returned home, he wrote letters to a local paper criticizing big government in America, especially as a threat to the Second Amendment right to bear arms. He drifted out to the Midwest, where he had some army friends.

The marker event for Timothy McVeigh's antigovernment beliefs occurred on March 19, 1993, when the FBI and the Bureau of Alcohol, Tobacco, and Firearms raided the Waco, Texas, camp of Branch Davidian religious leader David Koresh. McVeigh later commented that the Waco raid seemed to him very similar to China's Tienanmen Square massacre of 1989. He also said of the federal government, "When they govern by the sword, they must reckon with protest by the sword." Waco appeared to validate what had become his political Bible, William Pierce's fictional *The Turner Diaries*. And just who is this guru of so many right-wing extremists?[28]

Former Oregon State University physics professor William Pierce now lives on 400 acres in rural West Virginia, where he heads an organization called the National Alliance, distributes a newsletter, writes revolutionary fiction, and schedules speaking engagements. Each of these activities is in service of one goal: spreading his ideas of white supremacy and revolution. His writings frequently encourage violence against the U.S. government and against racial minorities. *The Turner Diaries* put him on the revolutionary map and made him a hero to people like Timothy McVeigh. The 1995 bombing in Oklahoma City is a virtual carbon copy of a truck bombing of FBI headquarters on page 31 of Pierce's book—one more example of life imitating fiction. Another passage in the *Diaries* observes, "There is no way we can destroy the system without many thousands of people dying."[29]

How do some people become so committed to something so ugly as this extremist movement? It is undeniable that the complicated world in which we live contains real dangers. It is also both reasonable and healthy to fear some of those things that might actually threaten us individually or socially. The difficult thing to comprehend is the mental process of those who go beyond rational fear and enter into the violent, nether world of irrational **paranoia**, with its gross distortions of judgment. The paranoid personality is generally not insane but has fallen much further out of touch with reality than the common forms of misperception to which we are all susceptible, as discussed earlier in this chapter.

Most of us have felt some grievance against the large and impersonal bureaucracy at the core of modern government. Reasonable people can recognize a kernel of truth in complaints against big government and even empathize with brief emotional outbursts of antigovernment sentiment. Precious few, however, allow a grievance to take over their lives to the point where they massively arm for a fight to the death. How do some cross the line into rampant paranoia and violence?

One brick apparently often loose in the foundation of the paranoid person relates to isolation. Alone and alienated, he finds the acceptance of radical groups attractive. By joining a group with a siege ("they are out to get us") mentality, the member loses any remaining contact with those who hold different views. Psychiatrist Robert Jay Lifton suggests that paranoids who commit violence often consider themselves fragile and "experience feelings of falling apart."[30]

The paranoid militiaman's psychological identity has become increasingly group based rather than individually based. With an in-group identity comes peer pressure to conform to the beliefs on which the group is founded. Frequent repetition of the content of the alarmist message reinforces its volume and intensity. By this time, the paranoid perspective has been routinized into seeming conventional. Yet even after absorbing all this group mentality, most militia members remain in a defensive posture (if the government attacks, we're ready), and only rarely do they switch to an offensive mode of violent attack. Sometimes it is those who have been ejected from the group who are pushed over the edge to commit violence.[31]

This is not to suggest that armed insurrection is never warranted. For example, we have no trouble seeing the American Revolutionary War against Great Britain as heroic resistance to oppression by freedom-seeking colonists. Separating legitimate rebellion by people aiming to protect human rights from irrational paranoid violence against legitimate governmental authority is not always a simple matter. And when social scientists grapple with these issues, the tools provided by psychology can be as relevant as those offered by political science or sociology.

THE CROSS-CULTURAL PERSPECTIVE

For its 100 years of existence, the discipline of psychology has studied individual and social-psychological behavior almost exclusively in the context of Western societies, assuming that whatever it discovered would be universally applicable. In other words, when it comes to psychology, people are people—period.

Not quite so fast, says psychologist Otto Klineberg. He recounts a 1974 experience with colleagues from cultural anthropology which he says influenced him "like a religious conversion" and which speaks to the potency of the interdisciplinary sharing advocated in this textbook. As Klineberg aptly puts it, "How could psychologists speak of *human* attributes and *human* behavior when they knew only one kind of human being?"[32] After surveying the cross-cultural research literature, anthropologists Carol and Melvin Ember conclude that the preliminary evidence indicates that a few psychological universals exist, but significant psychological differences from one culture to another are also well established. More cross-cultural research is necessary.[33]

Donald Brown catalogs research that points to some psychological universals found in all cultures. Among the most interesting ones are the concept of the self, inferring a person's intentions from his or her paralinguistics (nonverbal cues), trying to imagine the thoughts of other people, empathy with others' feelings, and the facial communication of emotions such as sadness, happiness, fear, and surprise. Evidence also supports the theory that human development universally proceeds according to a predictable sequence of stages featuring new mental skills in each stage.[34]

As early as Margaret Mead's Somoan field research in the 1920s, anthropologists have been challenging the assumption that human psychology is universal. Her early studies of adolescent psychology in Samoa contradicted the belief that adolescent psychology was universally a volatile one of "storm and stress" owing to the biological effects of puberty.[35] Subsequent cross-cultural research has corroborated Mead's thesis that adolescent psychological experience is more varied than was previously thought.[36]

A captivating cross-cultural contrast between a society of psychologically timid people and a society of psychologically aggressive people is provided by Carol and Melvin Ember. In Malaysia live the Semai people, well-known for their meekness and absence of hostility. In the words of one Semai, "We do not get angry." Their child-rearing practices involve no physical punishment and convey nonviolence through the absence of any violent behavior on the part of adults.

In bold relief to the Semai stand the Yanomamo people of Brazil's Amazon Basin. Child rearing among the Yanomamo encourages youngsters to express feelings of anger physically, including hitting another child or an adult. Parents not only tolerate such behavior but even goad children into violent outbursts. Punishment for striking others with a fist or an object is very rare. Not surprisingly, wife beating, bloody fights, and verbal abuse are common within

The socialization process among the Semai tribe of Malaysia encourages gentle behavior among its young people.

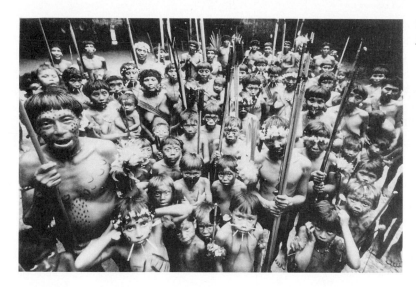

Yanomamo Indians, in tribal dress, from western Brazil.

the Yanomamo tribe. Adversaries from outside the tribe fare even worse; the Yanomamo are feared for the fierce way they fight their chronic wars.[37]

Timidity versus aggressiveness represents about as fundamental a psychological dividing line as we can identify. If peoples like the Semai and the Yanomamo can diverge so greatly in this respect, we need to exercise caution in assuming that Western psychology's theories and explanations apply to all places at all times.

Chapter Synopsis

With forty-eight officially recognized subfields, psychology includes more content areas than any other social science. It also boasts the greatest number of practitioners. Its size and popularity contribute to a vexing image problem exacerbated by loose, amateurish psychological speculation common in much of the mass media. Its academic practitioners warn that critical thinking skills are required to separate wheat from chaff in the psychological discourse to which most citizens are exposed. Ancient Greek philosophers like Plato struck a psychological chord in advising students to "know thyself," but a bona fide discipline of psychology did not materialize until one century ago. By then Charles Darwin had legitimized the idea that humans obey the same developmental laws as other species, making humans fair game for scientific study. Psychological laboratory experiments

borrowing heavily from natural sciences were first conducted in Leipzig, Germany, in 1879.

A Viennese physician named Sigmund Freud was much influenced by the Darwinian model of uncovering explanatory laws via scientific inquiry. Freud believed that humans are driven by conflicting demands stemming from underlying impulses about which we have no conscious awareness. He believed that psychosexual childhood trauma leads to adult dysfunctions that are hard to cure, since he considered personality set in stone by age six. His psychoanalytical school emphasized a talking cure of free association as the road to resolving painful buried memories. The subjective character of psychoanalysis bred its chief competitor: behaviorism. Striving for a more rigorously scientific theory, behaviorists stressed observation of overt and measurable human behavior, relying on conditioned response as a lever for encouraging desirable behaviors. In sharp contrast to the two major theories have been two challengers. The first was humanistic psychology, which emerged from the efficacious and confident days of the 1960s in the United States. It stressed human free will and the lifelong evolution of human personality, thus rejecting Freud's notion that the die is cast at an early age. Finally, in the 1990s stunning research advances in brain and genetic research have brought bio-psychology to the forefront. Breakthrough chemical discoveries have resulted in many new and improved drugs earmarked for those in psychological pain.

Formulating theories about human behavior is one thing; applying them beneficially to real people is quite another. Psychology has nine applied specialties, suggesting that extending a helping hand to people in psychological need is big business. Psychological theories are also applied as intellectual explanations of human motivation at the micro, macro, and mega levels. Various case studies are used in this chapter to show how psychological concepts generated primarily for use at the micro (individual) level can be shifted to other levels of analysis, providing fresh analytical insights to questions confounding social scientists.

For Digging Deeper

Barber, James David. *The Presidential Character.* Prentice Hall, 1985.

Brislin, Richard. *Applied Cross-Cultural Psychology.* Sage Publishing, 1990.

Coates, James. *Armed and Dangerous: The Rise of the Survivalist Right.* Hill and Wang, 1996.

Coon, Dennis. *Introduction to Psychology: Exploration and Application.* West Publishing, 1995.

Ember, Carol and Melvin Ember. "Psychology and Culture," in *Cultural Anthropology* Prentice Hall, 1996.

Janis, Irving L. *Groupthink.* University of Illinois Press, 1981.

Keen, Sam. *Faces of the Enemy: Reflections of the Hostile Imagination.* Harper and Row, 1986.

Mead, Margaret. *Coming of Age in Samoa.* Morrow, 1961.

Myers, David G. *Social Psychology.* McGraw-Hill, 1995.

Ornstein, Robert. *The Evolution of Consciousness: Of Darwin, Freud, and Cranial Fire: The Origins of the Way We Think.* Prentice Hall, 1991.

Reich, Walter. *Origins of Terrorism: Psychologies, Ideologies, States of Mind.* Cambridge University Press, 1990.

Segall, Marshall H., et al. *Cross-Cultural Psychology: Human Behavior in Global Perspective.* Brooks/Cole, 1979.

Stanovich, Keith E. *How to Think Straight About Psychology.* Harper Collins, 1996.

Steinberg, Blema S. *Shame and Humiliation: Presidential Decision Making on Vietnam.* University of Pittsburgh Press, 1996.

Veitch, Russell, and Daniel Arkkhelin. *Environmental Psychology: An Interdisciplinary Perspective.* Prentice Hall, 1995.

Key Glossary Terms

anxiety
applied discipline

Brezhnev Doctrine
clinically insane

conditioned response
cultural mythology

dehumanization
depression
efficacy
ego
humanistic psychology
id

militias
Monroe Doctrine
narcissism
nature versus nurture
obsessive-compulsive disorder
paranoia

patriots
perceptual analysis
response (R)
selective perception
stimulus (S)
superego

CHAPTER 10

Ethics and Human Rights

CORE OBJECTIVE

To consider the relevance of ethical and humanitarian influences

on human behavior.

Thematic Questions

- How does the domain of ethics interface with the social sciences?

- What sort of a relationship exists between religion and ethical questions?

- How is the concept of human rights both similar and dissimilar to that of ethics?

- What do we know about gender as a variable regarding human rights conditions?

I n our earlier dip into the pool of human subjective experience, we swam in and around the fringes of the discipline of psychology. This time we stroke further out into the waters inhabited by philosophy, psychology, political science, and sociology, because no discipline holds a monopoly on issues of right and wrong. Our goal in doing so is to measure the depth of **ethical** and **humanitarian** influences on human behavior. This effort to unravel the impact of morality breaks down into two categories: (1) ethics and (2) human rights.

An examination of moral considerations in this chapter affords the idealist school a rare opportunity to bask in the sunlight, relegating the realist school to an unusually defensive posture in the shadows. This is an area of human endeavor in which all sorts of intriguing questions come to mind, although finding definitive answers to those questions is as complex as it is rare. One of the greatest twentieth-century role models for morality was the Indian social reformer M. K. Gandhi (1869–1948), called "Mahatma" (Hindi for "great soul"). His **pacifist civil disobedience** in behalf of Indian liberation from British rule influenced most of the idealist thinkers of the century. His loving acceptance of Indian Muslims and Sikhs enraged some Hindu fundamentalists, who assassinated him in 1948. Richard Attenborough's film *Gandhi* (1982), featuring British actor Ben Kingsley in the title role, won an Oscar for best picture and is in fact one of the greatest film biographies ever made.

ETHICS

On the kind of world stage described in most of this book, where deceit and violence appear so frequently in the script, what role exists for the voice of ethics? Is it nothing more than a faint cry in the wilderness; something to pay lip service to but then ignore when put to the test of real world conflicts? Do the principles and values that quietly guide the lives of individuals disappear in the face of competition for huge stakes such as billion-dollar profits, cultural survival, or national power?

Ethical Resurgence

Ethical considerations have only rarely directed the behavior of nation–states. However, signs of their increased importance in the rapidly changing post-Cold War world do exist. Various political scientists have written books recently chronicling the importance of ethics. Felix Oppenheim says that while progress remains slow, ethical factors do permeate day-to-day relations between states.[1] William Korey's study of U.S. foreign policy concludes that ethical considerations have played a meaningful role in America, especially during the last decade, although more indirectly than directly.[2] Cathal Nolan examines the historical importance of ethics to key decisions

Indian holy-man Mahatma Gandhi in his modest attire.

reached by the following leaders: Otto von Bismarck of Germany, Winston Churchill of Britain, Franklin Roosevelt of the United States, Soviet Foreign Minister Eduard Shevardnadze, and United Nations General Secretary Dag Hammarskjold.[3] In a similar vein, George Lopez and Drew Christiansen find ethical concepts crucial to the modern era, particularly in the areas of north–south relations, the legitimization of force, and expanding human rights.[4]

Avenues of Ethical Influence

Ethical influences on the behavior of nation–states seem to manifest themselves in any of several ways. First, in democracies, society's moral values come through in the form of public-opinion polls, to which decision makers pay close attention. These general values help to set the parameters of the acceptable in a given society, establishing limitations for specific policies.

Just as domestic public opinion exerts influence, global public opinion represents a second ethical voice. On a day-to-day basis, leaders go to great pains to conform to international sensibilities and to convince the world that they are good global citizens. This fact is sometimes missed because the mass media sensationalize the few cases of defiance against the world community; behavior that is consistent with global norms is considered unnewsworthy and is downplayed by these same media.

Finally, and most directly, ethics enter the political picture via the personal values of key decision makers, who are human beings first and national leaders second. When Franklin Roosevelt decided against using gas warfare during World War II, his individual ethics played a key role—raising the intriguing question that if he had lived longer, would he have acted differently than did Harry S Truman in using the atomic bomb? Swedish diplomat Raoul Wallenberg was ethically motivated when he risked his life during the same war to save many thousands of European Jews scheduled for the Nazi gas chambers. Similarly, Robert F. Kennedy's account of the Cuban missile crisis, *Thirteen Days*, claims that President John F. Kennedy found morally abhorrent the military's advice to bomb Cuba as a means of getting rid of the Russian missiles placed there.

In an unusual wartime situation, neither American nor world public opinion had any chance to express themselves in regard to the question facing President Harry S Truman in 1945: how to end the Pacific War with Japan? Only the president and a small group of advisors even knew about America's possession of a new atomic bomb. A smaller circle still had any influence over what the president might choose to do with the super-weapon. It is difficult to imagine too many situations with larger ethical implications than this case study.

HIGH DRAMA ON THE WORLD STAGE:
Truman's Decision to Drop the Bomb on Hiroshima

Protagonists

President Harry S Truman—sworn in after death of President Roosevelt in April 1945

Henry L. Stimson—powerful secretary of war and general "overseer" of the Manhattan Project

James F. Byrnes—secretary of state

General Leslie Groves—army general heading the logistical side of the Manhattan Project

Robert L. Oppenheimer—Berkeley physicist heading the scientific side of the Manhattan Project

Otto Franck and Leo Szilard—physicists at the University of Chicago who sent a report to the president urging that the bomb *not* be used for military purposes against Japan

Emperor Hirohito—emperor of Japan with traditional status of divinity; his reign featured savage aggression against Manchuria and China, alliance with the Axis, and the 1941 attack on Pearl Harbor

Prologue

U.S. entrance into World War II occurred suddenly with Japan's sneak attack at Pearl Harbor on December 7, 1941, a date President Roosevelt predicted would "live in infamy." American resentment against anything Japanese ran very high, a feeling attested to by the relocation of one quarter million Japanese-American citizens into remote camps. Many lost their property as well as their freedom. This relocation was taken even though no Japanese-American citizen was ever convicted of espionage or sabotage. In fact, the most highly decorated unit among American forces was the "fighting 442nd"—made up of Japanese-Americans fighting in Europe. Interestingly, no similar denial of civil rights was even considered against German-Americans or Italian-Americans.

Victory in Europe was finally achieved in May 1945. The war with Japan, however, dragged on, with bloody battles over every Pacific island. Japanese atrocities against Allied forces were widely reported. The American people, ecstatic over the defeat of Hitler, wanted the "other" war to end as well. Throughout the summer of 1945 U.S. fire-bombings of Japanese cities were killing 100,000 people per day. The tenacious Japanese, however, remained un-

Destroyer USS Shaw explodes during the Japanese invasion of Pear Harbor, home of the American Pacific Fleet, on December 7, 1941.

willing to accept the only terms that America would offer: total unconditional surrender. A land invasion of Japan stayed on the back burner, because military estimates had projected that U.S. casualties in such a scenario could exceed 250,000 G.I.s.

Dramatic Plot

Into this frustrating milieu, a seeming miracle of science and technology stepped center stage. On July 16, 1945, the top-secret $4 billion Manhattan Project paid dividends as the United States successfully exploded the world's first atomic bomb in New Mexico. The huge project, headed by physicist Robert Oppenheimer on the scientific side and General Leslie Groves on the logistical side, created a super-weapon of twenty **kilotons**. With this new weapon, American leaders felt a sense of confidence about concluding the war on their terms.

A very difficult decision, however, confronted the inexperienced President Harry S Truman and his top advisors: Secretary of War Henry Stimson, and Secretary of State James Byrnes. Namely, how best to use this awesome weapon which only a few people really understood? Before Truman ascended to the presidency, the Manhattan Project was one of many items that Roosevelt had kept from him. Truman knew that *his* goal was to end the war as quickly as possible—on terms of unconditional surrender—and with a minimum loss of American lives. The vexing question that remained, however, was how best to do this? Seven different suggestions emanated from both the military Joint Chiefs of Staff and a special Interim Committee of advisors appointed by Truman:

1. The navy recommended a naval blockade of Japan to gradually starve out the Japanese.

2. A land invasion along the southern Kyushu region was favored by the army as the only certain guarantee of victory.

3. Continued daily fire-bombings of Japanese cities was favored by the air force as costing fewer American lives.

4. The majority of the Interim Committee advised Truman to use the A-bomb militarily by dropping it on a city with some military significance.

5. A minority on the Interim Committee preferred that the A-bomb be used in a harmless demonstration on Japanese soil—to inform the Japanese of what they were up against, and why they should surrender.

6. General McCloy of the Joint Chiefs alone suggested that an explicit verbal warning about the A-bomb be given to Japan in an effort to induce surrender.

7. A final option considered was to wait the Japanese out, since Allied victory was inevitable.

Each alternative had certain advantages and disadvantages. A blockade would lose few lives but would be time-consuming; loss of lives from a land invasion would be great but would ensure favorable settlement terms and be relatively fast; continued fire-bombings would cost time and great losses in Japanese civilian lives and property, but few U.S. soldiers would die; dropping the A-bomb on a city would be swift and devastating but might raise ethical questions and include environmental or health effects; a harmless demonstration of the A-bomb would not destroy property or lives but might fail to scare the Japanese into surrendering (and the United States had only two operational bombs); issuing a verbal warning could possibly save lives and induce surrender but might not be taken seriously by the intransigent Japanese government; waiting the Japanese out could save lives but would not be politically popular in a country that wanted the war to end quickly.

Adding to the complexity of Truman's decision was an eleventh-hour crisis of conscience for many scientists who had worked on the Manhattan Project. The program had been initiated at the suggestion of physicist Albert Einstein in order to beat Hitler to the atomic punch. Many of the scientists, so caught up in the technical challenge of creating this miracle weapon, didn't really think about the ethical dilemmas it created until faced with its possible use against Japan, which was not the original motivation for its production. Scientists such as Leo Szilard and Otto Franck could not accept its use against Japanese cities as ethically defensible, and advised against this option.

President Truman decided to use the bomb militarily against a Japanese city, without warning, while continuing to demand unconditional surrender. On August 6, 1945, the first A-bomb was dropped on the city of Hiroshima, resulting in 80,000 immediate deaths and about 40,000 long-term casualties from radiation poisoning. When the Japanese still failed to accept unconditional surrender, Truman ordered a second bomb dropped on Nagasaki on August 9, 1945. Four days later the Japanese government surrendered, ending World War II.[5]

Critical Analysis

President Truman faced a very complex decision, one that was still being debated on the fiftieth anniversary of Hiroshima—August 6, 1995—when a display at the Smithsonian Museum in Washington created a firestorm of controversy. Given the context of the times, the central goal, and the alternatives available, which path would you have chosen? Where specifically do you agree or disagree with Truman's decision?

When Truman made his decision, the Manhattan Project was top secret and the public completely unaware of it, so there was no public opinion to consider. However, he would be facing election in 1948, and how the various options would play in Peoria must have sat in the back of his mind. General Leslie Groves later argued that Truman had no real choice other than military use of the A-bomb, because if he had failed to use it, the mothers of all those soldiers who died invading Japan would have blamed Truman.

Where Truman may have been most susceptible to criticism was in clinging to total unconditional surrender from a Japanese martial culture in which losing face has traditionally been looked down on as worse than death. Truman also made no effort to communicate explicitly to Japan that it was up against a devastating new super-weapon—or to pursue secret feelers from the Japanese military asking for the Soviet Union to mediate an end to a war that Japan could not win. Truman adamantly stuck to unconditional surrender without diplomacy.

All such discussion is inherently speculative. Your opinion on this question derives as much from your values as from the facts of the case. Examining our own views on Truman's decision helps us to comprehend our fundamental beliefs—the ethical mind-set through which we view affairs on the world stage. For example, would you expect most realists to judge Truman's decision kindly or harshly? And would you expect most idealists to judge Truman's decision well or poorly?

• • • • • • •

Problems in Putting Ethics into Action

Applying ethical principles to world affairs almost invariably presents serious challenges. One problem is that two or more attractive moral ideals can conflict in the real world. The very soul of the discipline of anthropology conveys the value judgment that cultural differences should be respected. But Chapter 8 of this book discussed some of the complexities arising when the goal of cultural relativism brings us face to face with cultures practicing activities we consider immoral.

Second, there is the **level-of-analysis** problem. Ethicists have long argued that in addition to the motivation of the actor, we must take into account the context when assessing the morality of decisions. The operational milieu facing people like you and me is sufficiently different from that of the president of the United States, the head of General Motors, or the secretary general of the United Nations as to raise questions about the interchangeability of ethical principles from one level to the other. President Truman's milieu in the Hiroshima case is something we can only think about—we cannot recreate it.

Third, the history of the nation–state is replete with examples of powerful countries imposing their definition of morality on simpler societies. At times, ethics have seemed nothing more than footnotes to national power considerations, seemingly validating what ethicist Joel Rosenthal calls the realist's aphorism, "that the strong do what they will, and the weak do what they must."[6] When the strong throw their weight around today, they are often accused of **cultural imperialism**, violating a weaker culture's right to exist on its own terms. The image of the bully is neither attractive nor amicable, and powerful Western societies like the United States do what they can to elude such an unflattering image. But the influences that complex societies exert over simple ones remain pervasive and potent. They reach into every area of life, even into medical research projects such as the Human Genome Diversity Project headed by Professor Kenneth Kidd (Mini-case 10.1).

MINI-CASE 10.1
The Ethics of Gene Hunting

If you were a researcher working for the Human Genome Diversity Project, you would find yourself traversing the globe to take blood samples from isolated indigenous peoples. Far from your Yale University laboratory, you would be tracking down the 700 groups targeted by the Genome Project. This research fits under the umbrella of studying human evolution and diversity. Its more specific medical mission is to search for factors causing genetic (inherited) diseases to occur in different parts of the world.

Blood samples containing the genetic DNA footprints of 700 indigenous societies constitute the critical raw materials for this research. Since these nonliterate peoples are among the world's most remote, how do you go about extracting blood samples from them? Can you imagine trying to explain the intricacies of genetic research to people who are not even accustomed to seeing flashlights? If you work for Yale Professor Kenneth Kidd's Genome Project, you do not fully inform the subjects of what is happening to them or the purposes for which their blood will be used. You tell them the least amount possible that enables you to get their blood samples, and you mislead them a little if necessary. The methods used are a matter of some controversy.

To Professor Kidd, the Genome Project's motives bear the purity of scientific inquiry aimed at benefiting humanity's medical future. Genetic research represents the cutting edge of modern medicine, making great breakthroughs in pure science and applied science. With isolated indigenous cultures disappearing every day, this research needs to be conducted quickly and thoroughly. The unusual conditions of such remote research include the unfortunate need to mislead the indigenous subjects slightly. However, these people show no ill effects from contributing to this project, which is enabling them to be part of an altruistic endeavor in behalf of humans in the future.

Critics like Boston University professor of health law George Annas consider the project ethically flawed as a deceitful exploitation of unsuspecting subjects. They want to place this episode in the context of history's long list of whites exploiting indigenous peoples for their own purposes. Professor Annas views the Genome Project as tantamount to genetic imperialism: The subjects are being deceived into compliance, and deception is an unworthy midwife of scientific exploration. The price paid is too high for any knowledge gained; the project has allowed itself the unwarranted luxury of believing that its scientific ends justify untoward means.[7]

Do you see questions of right or wrong in the case of the Genome Project as cut and dried, or as fuzzy around the edges? Do you prefer Professor Kidd's view that the project is in the noblest scientific tradition of free inquiry? Or do you identify with Professor Annas's attack on the project as the unwarranted deception of naive and trusting peoples? Do the philosophies of scientistic versus humanistic social science perspectives come in handy for analytical purposes in this case?

Listen to What I Say? Or Watch What I Do?

Veteran American diplomat George Kennan recognizes some of the difficulties inherent in trying to pass moral judgment on other people or other countries. He suggests that on the world stage we are better off leading by example and setting a moral tone via behavior more than by words.[8] Or, as was expressed by another scholar, as an exemplar, America should strive to represent the "shining city on a hill," which others will want to emulate.[9] In some complicated situations, however, exemplary behavior is as elusive as a hard rain in the desert. The Vietnam War was fraught with moral dilemmas for the nation as a whole, for its top decision makers, and for its individual citizens. Among those struggling with the ethics of various paths of action were America's military draftees (see Mini-case 10.2).

MINI-CASE 10.2
The Moral Dilemma of Vietnam War Draftees

The U.S. has been fortunate among democracies by often enjoying a basic consensus on important foreign policy questions. American domestic politics have generally been partisan and highly charged, but considerably less so concerning world affairs. It took the Vietnam War to tear apart this normal foreign policy consensus. This controversy occurred partly because no explicit public decision to "Americanize" the war was ever made.

Prior to his assassination, President John F. Kennedy's policy was "limited partnership," excluding American forces from combat roles in Vietnam. In his 1964 campaign Lyndon B. Johnson portrayed Republican challenger Barry Goldwater as a warmonger capable of pushing the nuclear button in Vietnam, while depicting himself as the peace candidate. Johnson's highest priority was his domestic **Great Society program**, which he was unwilling to sacrifice at the altar of the Vietnam War.

However, the always shaky South Vietnamese government, supported for a decade by the United States, found itself on the verge of collapse in July 1965. Johnson's secretary of defense, Robert McNamara, returned from a tour of Vietnam concluding that the moment of decision had arrived for the United States: either abandon the South to the communists—admitting failure but cutting U.S. losses—or greatly expand its role, hoping for the best from an uncertain roll of the military dice.

During the month of July, Johnson made the critical decision. He effectively "Americanized" the war; most notably by sending more than 200,000 combat forces to replace South Vietnamese soldiers. Incredibly, these decisions were made without consultation with Congress or the public. They were, in fact, concealed and distorted. This action resulted in a "credibility gap" which ultimately proved to be Johnson's political undoing. Johnson also failed to finance his war honestly. Again hoping to protect his domestic Great Society, he refused to increase taxes or reduce government spending, choosing instead to print new money, causing rampant double-digit inflation in the 1970s.[10]

The Vietnam War was not only undeclared, it soon became very unpopular. By the late 1960s America was split, either for the war or against it; no middle ground existed. Strife-ridden college campuses imploded on themselves, going beyond debate by descending into recrimination and violence.

In this volatile political milieu, young men faced a question unusual for Americans: what to do about the military draft? U.S. ground forces in Vietnam had grown to more than 500,000, and relatively few volunteers came forward. Roughly half of college-aged males opposed the war for a combination of legal, religious, and political reasons. Five possible choices existed for those in opposition: (1) refuse induction and risk getting a prison sentence; (2) obtain landed immigrant status in Canada or another country that welcomed American draft dodgers; (3) if opposition was religiously based and applied to all wars, not just this one, apply for exemption as a conscientious objector; (4) swallow one's opposition to the war, accepting induction and likely Vietnam service; or (5) find a way around the draft by using one of the legal exemptions for things like higher education, child dependency, sole surviving son, or alternative service in the National Guard.

Doing the right thing, or exercising what political scientist Paul Kael calls "good international citizenship," wasn't a simple matter for young men opposed to the war in the 1960s.[11] They faced an ethical dilemma: most had been socialized to believe that they had a duty to obey the law of the land. However, having lost faith in a government that had deceived them on the issue of Vietnam, the legal duty argument crumbled for many young men. Yet only a few would seriously consider going to prison when they did not believe they had done anything wrong.

For the better educated, moving to Canada represented a viable, albeit disruptive, alternative. The most common means of avoidance for well-educated or well-connected young men was to obtain legal deferment status. An indisputable fact still rankles many people: it was mostly poor, uneducated, minority urbanites who fought the Vietnam War for the United States. The higher one's socioeconomic status, the less likely he would be snagged by the Selective Service system. Not surprisingly, a deep sense of bitterness was shared by the families of more than 45,000 war dead and 200,000-plus wounded. Ethical behavior becomes hard to define in such complicated situations, encouraging us to settle for what Kenneth Thompson calls "practical morality," or the idea that ethics can continue to function as a meaningful part of our decision making without its being the only consideration.[12]

Some of the 100,000 demonstrators who gathered at a rally in New York City to protest against the Vietnam War.

The place where people often feel safest confronting such complex questions as military duty in a controversial war is within the bosom of their religious beliefs. Not only does religion operate as a domestic agent of socialization as is discussed in Chapter 6, and as a basis for just war doctrine as is covered in Chapter 4, but it also works as part of the web of subjective forces weaving a tapestry of ethical values impinging on human behavior.

Religion and World Affairs

The social role of religion varies greatly around the world. The world's three largest religions differ in their involvement with public affairs. The largest religious group, 2 billion **Christians**, tend to fall in the middle of the spectrum, combining religion with politics

A ceremony of the Russian Orthodox Church inside St. Nicholas Cathedral, St. Petersburg.

less than do the world's one billion **Muslims**, but much more than do the 700 million **Hindus**, whose approach to public life might be described as one transcending politics. Historically, Roman Catholics and Muslims have confronted each other most dramatically—witness the eight Crusades from 1095 to 1291.

Only a few countries, such as Iran, operate as modern-day **theocracies**. The opposite extreme—officially **atheistic** countries treating religions with hostility—exists today only in the four remaining communist states: China, Vietnam, North Korea, and Cuba. In Spain, Russia, and the United Kingdom, among other countries, an official Christian religion exists but other religions are tolerated, as is the right not to practice religion. The U.S. Constitution contains two notions on religion: the "establishment clause," forbidding the state from creating an official religion; and the "free exercise clause," guaranteeing the right of individuals to practice their religious beliefs.

Regardless of their unique characteristics, however, all societies evolved with religions operating at their very foundations. Almost all religions share a few basic values, such as the encouragement of compassion, generosity, and honesty; and the discouragement of deception, murder, torture, and selfishness. Some variation on the theme of the **Golden Rule** is also common among world religions.

Religion's Dual Role

As John Rourke puts it, "Religion has played a dual role in world politics." Possessing a dark side as well as a bright side, religion has at times fueled militant fanaticism, but at other times fostered pacifism and humanitarian understanding.[13] Since the end of the Cold War, many religions have enjoyed something of a renaissance, most notably in the former Soviet Union and its satellite countries in Eastern Europe. In addition, world affairs scholarship, such as that of Douglas Johnston, has increasingly focused on the role of religious groups engaged in "peacemaking."[14] The Catholic Church played an important part in legitimizing the independent political role of the Solidarity Labor Union in Poland during the 1980s. In no other East European country was a religious institution so crucial to the gradual dismantling of communism.

Scores of religiously driven, local development initiatives in the Third World are chronicled by Mary Lean in her *Bread, Bricks and Belief: Communities in Charge of Their Future*. Tracing cases involving local Christian, Sikh, Hindu, Muslim, and Buddhist spiritual leaders, she draws optimistic conclusions about the impact of creative grass-roots solutions inspired by workers trusting in a higher power.[15] Praise has been accorded to such examples of religious inspiration contributing to grass-roots solutions to global problems. However, the darker face of religious intolerance must also be recognized.

Among international conflicts in recent decades, many have been worsened by religious tension. The Orthodox Christians of Greece and the Muslims of Turkey have conducted a long-standing battle over the disputed Mediterranean island of Cyprus, located between them. A U.N. peacekeeping force has been located there since 1964 in an effort to keep the combatants separated. India, while technically a secular state, has been experiencing a revival of Hindu fundamentalism, leading to many clashes with Pakistan, its largest Islamic neighbor. In March of 1993, Hindus destroyed a mosque reportedly built on the site of an ancient Hindu temple, an act that led to religious rioting and conflict with Pakistan. India and Pakistan have fought wars in 1947, 1965, and 1971.

Few international conflicts have been fueled more by religious fervor than the Jewish state of Israel's face-off with its Islamic-Arab neighbors. Major wars in 1948, 1956, 1967, and 1973 all involved religion in their incendiary mix. Adding to the intransigence of this religious conflict are its historical roots, traced back not centuries, but millennia.

Almost everyone feels some sympathy for the tiny Himalayan nation of Tibet, which has been in and out of Chinese control over the centuries. Under their spiritual leader, the Dalai Lama, Tibet's Buddhists have often fought to establish independence from the powerful Chinese. In 1950, shortly after the communist victory in China's civil war, Tibet was reincorporated into China. In 1959 the Tibetans rose up in defiance, only to be brutally defeated by China. The Dalai Lama remains in exile today, while Tibetans have become a minority to Han Chinese in their native land.

When religion contributes to existing international tensions and fighting breaks out between two countries—such situations jump out at us—demanding attention. In the modern world, however, religiously fueled international problems also arise in subtle, unexpected ways. The United States, United Kingdom, European Union, India, Iran, and scores of human rights NGOs have all become embroiled in a bizarre situation anticipated by none of them: the Salman Rushdie affair (see Mini-case 10.3).

MINI-CASE 10.3
Religious Freedom, Blasphemy, and Salman Rushdie

*S*alman Rushdie was born in India at about the time the United Kingdom was granting independence to its south Asian colony. Rushdie later immigrated to the United Kingdom, took up British citizenship, and embarked on a career as a novelist. Like many others in today's world, the bicultural Rushdie moved freely between the Islamic culture of his native India and the British culture of his new home. In some ways he felt part of both, in other ways part of neither. The author's fiction reflects this ambiguous mixing of east and west. But the cruel fate ready to befall him remained well hidden, especially from Rushdie himself.

In 1988 life was good for novelist Rushdie. He had recently won the coveted British Whitbread Prize for fiction, and he was in demand on the lecture circuit. The Whitbread

Figure 10.1

Prize and other accolades stemmed from his novel *The Satanic Verses*, an allegorical fantasy steeped in eternal issues of good versus evil. In it he questions some of the tenets of the Islamic faith under which he was raised in India.

Enter Ayatollah Khomeini, religious **imam** and father of the Iranian 1979 Islamic revolution. On February 14, 1989, Ayatollah Khomeini issued a *fatwa*, or death edict, against Salman Rushdie. His crime? Blasphemy against the Islamic religion in *The Satanic Verses*. The world's one billion Muslims were called on to implement the *fatwa*, with a $1 million reward for the holy warrior who succeeded. Ayatollah Khomeini's death later that year changed nothing. The Iranian Parliament, or Majlis, reconsidered the issue and reiterated its commitment to the death sentence by doubling the reward money.

Since that fateful day in February 1989 writer Salman Rushdie has been in hiding, under the protective custody of his British government—just where, nobody knows. He has probably been moving around quite frequently. No shortage of supporters have spoken out in Rushdie's behalf: human rights NGOs like The International Federation of Human Rights and Amnesty International, IGOs like the eighteen-member European Union, governments like the United States and Canada. Since 1993 he has been making surprise appearances to symbolize a modicum of control over his life: a writer's conference in New York, a U-2 concert—but all very guarded.

Much more is at stake here than the mobility of one writer. Most Western governments have interpreted this situation as an issue of freedom of expression, probably the most fundamental of all the liberties on which modern democracy rests. President Bill Clinton invited

Rushdie to the White House, in support of Rushdie's cause, a gesture that must have struck a sensitive nerve in Tehran, where an official newspaper responded that "Clinton's action was a mere political one intended to undermine Islam and to support the insulting words of Rushdie, as well as to combat the Islamic renaissance movement in the world."

Rushdie has not been the only target of ire. Iran severed diplomatic ties with Britain for one year as a protest against its support of Rushdie. U.S.–Iranian relations, which had been on a slow upswing in the late 1980s, plummeted over the Rushdie affair. A Norwegian publisher of Rushdie's book was assassinated for his efforts; forty people died in Turkey during an anti-Rushdie demonstration; a Japanese translator of the book was stabbed to death. This volatile issue will not go away as it involves individuals, nation–states, NGOs, IGOs, and even MNCs (many large chain bookstores dare not carry the book). An official Iranian journal says that "Rushdie can never save himself from the effects of his treason against the Islamic beliefs of one billion Muslims. Eventually, he will be consumed by the flames of the fire that he stoked with his treacherous efforts."[16]

Figure 10.2

Even more common in recent years has been the role of religion in igniting civil war within nation–states. Recent examples jump off the page: Catholics against Protestants in Northern Ireland; Hindus versus Muslims and Sikhs in India; Sunni and Shiite Muslims in Iraq; Druse and Maronite Christians in Lebanon; Muslims and Orthodox Christians in the Chechen part of Russia; Muslims and Christians in Soviet Georgia; Buddhists and Hindu Tamils in Sri Lanka; Christians and Muslims in Algeria; Orthodox Christians, Catholics, and Muslims in Bosnia.

The greatest risk of escalation in religious conflict exists in the former Soviet Union. The worst case scenario consists of repeating the Yugoslavian (especially Bosnian) debacle in the context of the former Soviet Union. Among the most frightening is a conflict that began in the late 1980s as a domestic (Soviet) clash, graduating to the international level with the collapse of the Soviet Union in 1991 (see Mini-case 10.4).

MINI-CASE 10.4
Rumble in the Caucasus: Armenia and Azerbaijan:

The people of the Caucasus mountain region of the former Soviet Union find themselves sandwiched between three larger religious and cultural traditions: the Orthodox Slavic world of Russia and Ukraine, the Islamic world of Turkey and Iran, and the Christian world of the Mediterranean countries. Armenia's 1.5 million people, now a separate nation–state, have a long and proud history, boasting their own language, writing, and religious tradition since the fourth century A.D.

Their fiercely independent brand of Christianity, the Armenian Apostolic Church, symbolizes the stability of traditional Armenian culture. Yet, as a very small nation, the Armenians have often fallen under the control of either the Russians, Turks, or Persians (modern Iran). From the time of Peter the Great 300 years ago, the Russians have been the dominant neighbor. The Azerbaijani nation of the Caucasus differs in many respects from that of the Armenians. Its 5.5 million citizens are a traditional Muslim people influenced mostly by Turkey and Iran, fellow Islamic countries. Although the land is mostly rural, the discovery of oil in the city of Baku during the nineteenth century resulted in urban development, with Turkey's brand of Sunni Islam becoming prevalent.

The problem that erupted between these peoples of the Caucasus in 1988 dealt with the area known as Nagorno-Karabakh, an Armenian region located in the Republic of Azerbaijan. Nagorno-Karabakh is an anomaly, owing its existence to the bizarre decisions made by Joseph Stalin when he was Soviet commissar of nationalities in the 1920s. Stalin had a penchant for moving whole nations around the map as if they were pieces on a game board. The Armenians of Nagorno-Karabakh were one of the unfortunate pawns in Stalin's game of ethnic chess.

Long-standing Armenian resentment over Nagorno-Karabakh's location within Azerbaijan was finally expressed to Kremlin leaders when Nikita Khrushchev loosened the grip of Soviet power in 1955. Armenian leaders asked to annex Nagorno-Karabakh back into Armenia, ending Azeri administration of the region. That request was tabled by Moscow; ten years later 100,000 Armenians demonstrated in favor of annexation. After their failure, no new initiatives occurred until the liberalization of Mikhail Gorbachev's *glasnost* policies, when Armenia sent a delegation to meet with him in 1987. Gorbachev raised false hopes by sending mixed signals

Figure 10.3

about Nagorno-Karabakh, the Soviets dashed these hopes in July 1988 by the ruling to continue Azeri control of the region. A Soviet declaration of martial law in 1991 temporarily halted protests by Armenians. Then a larger wave of violence struck in April 1992, when the Armenians established a corridor linking Nagorno-Karabakh with Armenia proper. With more than 3,000 people already killed and one-third of a million refugees, the situation got even tenser in June 1992 when Turkey threatened to intervene in behalf of its Azerbaijani allies.

The United Nations sent an observer mission in May 1993, when a tentative treaty halted bloodshed. It failed, however, to resolve the issue of Nagorno-Karabakh, which shows no signs of fading away. In 1994 fighting again broke out between Christian Armenia and Islamic Azerbaijan. Nagorno-Karabakh is partly a territorial dispute, but religious and cultural differences historically have complicated every proposed solution to the problem.[17]

HUMAN RIGHTS

Human rights can be viewed as a subset of the more general set of ethics in action. Since there are so many kinds of rights that people have by virtue of their humanness, the term *human rights* is reserved for those rights that spring from the relationship between citizens and their government. We can return once again to the ancient Greeks for inspiration, Aristotle said that "the basis of a democratic state is liberty." Traditionally, government has held most of the power,

Table 10.1 Internationally Recognized Human Rights

The International Bill of Human Rights recognizes the rights to:

Equality of rights without discrimination (D1, D2, E2, C2, C3)

Life (D3, C6)

Liberty and security of person (D3, C9)

Protection against slavery (D4, C8)

Protection against torture and cruel and inhuman punishment (D5, C7)

Recognition as a person before the law (D6, C16)

Equal protection of the law (D7, C14, C26)

Access to legal remedies for rights violations (D8, C2)

Protection against arbitrary arrest or detention (D9, C9)

A hearing before an independent and impartial judiciary (D10, C14)

Presumption of innocence (D11, C14)

Protection against ex post facto laws (D11, C15)

Protection of privacy, family, and home (D12, C17)

Freedom of movement and residence (D13, C12)

Seeking of asylum from persecution (D14)

Nationality (D15)

Marriage and the founding of a family (D16, E10, C23)

Ownership of property (D17)

Freedom of thought, conscience, and religion (D18, C18)

Freedom of opinion, expression, and the press (D19, C19)

Freedom of assembly and association (D20, C21, C22)

Political participation (D21, C25)

Social Security (D22, E9)

Work, under favorable conditions (D23, E6, E7)

Free trade unions (D23, E8, C22)

Rest and leisure (D24, E7)

Food, clothing, and housing (D25, E11)

Health care and social services (D25, E12)

Special protections for children (D25, E10, C24)

Education (D26, E13, E14)

Participation in cultural life (D27, E15)

A social and international order needed to realize rights (D28)

Self-determination (E1, C1)

Humane treatment when detained or imprisoned (C10)

Protection against debtor's prison (C11)

Protection against arbitrary expulsion of aliens (C13)

Protection against advocacy of racial or religious hatred (C20)

Protection of minority culture (C27)

NOTE: This list includes all rights that are enumerated in two of the three documents os the International Bill of Human Rights or that have a full article in one document. The source of each right is indicated in parentheses, by document and article number. D = Universal Declaration of Human Rights, E = International Covenant on Economic, Social, and Cultural Rights; C = International Covenant on Civil and Political Rights.

Source: Jack Donnelly, *International Human Rights* (Westview, 1993), p. 9

with citizens left in a rather tenuous position. As Table 10.1 shows, the concept of human rights serves to provide individuals with some specific ethical and legal tools to protect themselves.

An International Bill of Rights

The idea that every living person shares certain basic rights which governments cannot deny is a rather new one. Throughout most of the nation–state's history, the key concept of sovereignty has meant that other governments, IGOs, and NGOs were supposed to abide by the corollary principle of **nonintervention**: keep your nose out of the internal affairs of sovereign nation–states. Period.

The benchmark event that began to chip away at the old idea of nonintervention was the cataclysm known as World War II. Specifically, the Holocaust—Nazi Germany's obliteration of 6 million innocent Jews—shocked the world's collective conscience into *belated* action. Why emphasize the word *belated* here? Because, in truth, the rest of the world was not unaware in the 1930s what Hitler meant by his "final solution" for European Jewry; nor did the world lack evidence of his death camps from 1941 to 1945. But governments, religious leaders, and common citizens looked the other way.

Between 1933 and 1945, millions of European Jews tried desperately to flee. The overwhelming majority were refused entry to other countries, and in the end relatively few were saved. During this twelve-year period Britain took in 70,000, Argentina opened its doors to 50,000, 27,000 entered Brazil, and Australia admitted 15,000 Jews. The world's democracies opened their doors no wider than did hard-boiled dictatorships. The United States and Canada, whose national identities thrive on the idea of opportunity for the oppressed, for the most part turned a blind eye. Canada accepted but 5,000 and the much larger United States a total of only 200,000 from 1933 to 1945—a mere fraction of those seeking a safe haven. In *None Is Too Many*, Canadian historian Harold Troper points out that "With no states prepared to take Jews, the Nazis could only conclude that none cared." It is myopic to blame only the Nazis for the Holocaust, suggests Troper, because "the Jews of Europe were not so much trapped in a whirlwind of systematic mass murder as they were abandoned to it."[18]

The Diary of Anne Frank, The gripping story of a young girl's final days in hiding from the Nazis in an attic, conveys some of the terror felt by European Jews during World War II. The diary was turned into a Broadway play and then a fine film directed by George Stevens (1959). For anyone who goes to Amsterdam, a visit to the Anne Frank house, now a museum, is imperative. The old League of Nations, set up after World War I, had no legal provisions for human rights. However, the 1945 Covenant of the new United Nations would.

Another important precedent was provided by the 1946 Nuremberg War Crimes Tribunal, which introduced the idea of "crimes against humanity" as a basis for trying and executing some captured Nazi leaders. Equally crucial was the 1948 creation of the **Universal Declaration of Human Rights** as the cornerstone of specific rights accruing to all persons. The emphasis of the human rights movement concentrated on spelling out this quite new category of rights up through the 1960s, with the adoption of what are known as the two Human Rights Covenants: (1) the **International Covenant on Economic, Social, and Cultural Rights** and (2) the **International Covenant on Civil and Political Rights**. These two new definitions of types of human rights, when combined with the 1948 Universal Declaration, are called the **International Bill of Human Rights**.

Children behind a barbed wire fence at the Nazi concentration camp at Auschwitz, Poland, near the end of World War II.

Monitoring

By the 1970s the initial phase of spelling out specific categories of human rights gave way to efforts to check up on governments to see which were complying with human rights principles and which were not. Called **monitoring**, this activity required extensive field research. Some research was conducted by IGOs set up for this purpose; however, the crucial role of monitoring was assumed mostly by the growing number of NGOs, such as the Ecumenical Movement for Human Rights, Human Rights Watch, and the International Commission of Jurists—all unfettered by government controls.

When the London-based NGO Amnesty International won the Nobel Peace Prize in 1977, the status of all human rights NGOs received a major boost. Also the 1970s witnessed several nation–states beginning to incorporate human rights ideas into their operations. The U.S. Congress served notice in 1975 that it took human rights seriously when it formally linked U.S. foreign aid to the human rights record of recipient countries. A year later the American public elected Jimmy Carter as the first American president for whom the moral imperatives of human rights formed a foreign policy cornerstone.

Single-Issue Human Rights Movements

In the 1980s the human rights activities of NGOs and IGOs (both at global and regional levels) became well established and dependable. In addition to these general human rights efforts, considerable progress was made in developing institutions in five specific single-issue areas of concern: (1) workers' rights, (2) racial discrimination, (3) apartheid, (4) women's rights, and (5) torture.[19] The story of nonviolent black leader Steven Biko's (Denzel Washington) struggle against apartheid in South Africa is well chronicled in another Richard Attenborough-directed film, *Cry Freedom* (1987). The young and charismatic Steven Biko was murdered by South African security forces, and the truth emerged only because of the efforts of Biko's white friend, journalist Donald Woods, played in the movie by Kevin Kline.

While human rights issues took a back seat in President Ronald Reagan's foreign policy, other smaller Western countries stepped forward during the decade. Known collectively as the **like-minded countries**, these middle-level powers offered the world a visible profile as they integrated the values of human rights into the essence of their foreign policies. The Netherlands, Sweden, Canada, Finland, and Denmark led a half dozen other countries who gave the highest levels of foreign aid in the world, vocally criticized human rights abuses *wherever* they saw them, and deviated from the U.S. tendency to see human rights issues through the ideological lenses of Cold War conflict.

Considerable progress toward the protection of human rights has occurred since 1945. An International Bill of Rights now exists, and hundreds of NGOs like Amnesty International perform the daily work needed to monitor and publicize human rights abuses. Global IGOs, like the **U.N. Commission on Human Rights**, and regional ones, such as the **European Commission on Human Rights**, investigate thousands of cases of abuses reported to them. Treaties have been enacted and organizations set up to protect the five main single-issue areas of concern listed above. In addition, a global town meeting on the Protection of Human Rights was held in Vienna, Austria, in 1993 to mobilize world opinion in support of human rights.

Human Rights Report Card

Tremendous gains have been achieved in human rights since the end of World War II. However, if you look at the global report card published annually by the NGO, Human Rights Watch, the picture is grim. And it is grim in nearly every region of the world. Human Rights Watch opened its 1995 report with these ominous words:

> The will to uphold human rights failed dismally in 1994. Having bound and shelved the volume of high-sounding pronouncements made the year before at the World Conference on Human Rights, the major powers led a wholesale retreat from their implementation.[20]

If specific human rights have been identified and agreed to, then what's the problem? The problem comes dressed in a few different garments, but it can be traced back to the concept of sovereignty. Ultimately, whether or not states violate their citizens' rights rests in the hands of those decision makers running their governments. Other nation–states, IGOs, and NGOs can complain and criticize, but they can't compel abusive states to clean up their acts. Political scientist Jack Donnelly recommends that we hold limited expectations of human rights protection, warning that "when human rights conflict with even minor security, political, economic, or ideological objectives, human rights usually lose out."[21]

Theoretical Challenges to Human Rights

In addition to the sovereign ability of national leaders to define their national interest in ways inimical to human rights, Donnelly identifies two more theoretical challenges to the interests of human rights. First is *realpolitik*, or the prevalence of the realist view of foreign policy. In seeing the essence of foreign policy as consisting of the accumulation and use of power, the realist challenge to human rights is that it ignores human rights, simply thinking of the topic as irrelevant. Human rights advocates find this response frustrating, for it fails to take their cause seriously.

The other challenge is that of cultural relativism, especially the Oriental brand, which emphasizes collective, societal rights over the individual rights at the core of the international human rights movement. Cultural relativism takes the claim of universal human rights very seriously—so much so that it views efforts to impose Western notions of individual human rights as modern cultural imperialism no better than the economic and political exploitation of the rich over the poor in past centuries.[22]

Positivists and Naturalists

The argument of what is sometimes called the **Positivist School** of human rights is that while human rights should be respected, the communitarian (collective) rights of the society to protect itself must take precedence over the rights of the individual. The opposing school of ethically minded human rights advocates, usually from the West, is the **Naturalist School**. Basing their outlook on the concept of **natural rights**, the Naturalist School of human rights argues that before any social contracts were constructed, all people—simply as human beings in a state of nature—possessed certain inviolate natural rights such as the right to life.

The Naturalist School believes that when the Positivist School talks about cultural relativism, it is simply dodging the issue and covering up for human rights abuses. Individual rights, such as freedom from cruel and arbitrary punishment, lie at the core of human dignity, transcending cultural differences around the world.[23]

Almost no country escapes the fray concerning human rights abuses, a fact evidenced by the inclusion of the United States on Amnesty International's list of 110 countries guilty of significant human rights abuses in 1994. More often than not, however, this unpleasant glare of public disfavor is borne by Asian countries. Given its repressive communist political system, China has become accustomed to fending off charges of human rights violations. One such case dealt with American efforts to link the question of human rights with the issue of bilateral trade (Mini-case 10.5).

MINI-CASE 10.5
Sino-American Trade and Human Rights: Linkage?

In his 1992 presidential campaign, Bill Clinton had few foreign policy issues on which to distinguish himself from the incumbent, given George Bush's success in this area. Consequently Clinton used every opportunity to attack President Bush's reticence—as depicted in Figure 10.4— to take the ethical initiative on China's poor human rights record.

China's humans right record was very bad; some of the issues were prisoners producing exported goods, arresting political prisoners of conscience, denial of free speech, arbi-

Figure 10.4

Source: The Miami Herald (1992)

Figure 10.5

Source: Horsey, *Seattle Post-Intelligencer* (4 May, 1996)

trary arrests, use of child labor, and the brutality of the Tienanmen Square massacre. The skeletons in China's closet seemed overwhelming, as Figure 10.5 suggests. But there was one specific thing Clinton said he would do if elected: link the human rights issue to China's annual request for **Most-Favored-Nation (MFN) trade status** with the United States.

The new Clinton administration did in fact ratchet up the verbal pressure on China's human rights record; it also threatened to end MFN trade status if China did not improve on human rights. After much publicity linking these issues, President Clinton had his chance to act in 1994. Coincidentally, the decision on MFN trade status for China fell on June 4, 1994, exactly five years after China's bloody termination of the Student Democracy Movement in the streets of Beijing. For the most part, China had not made much effort even to create the appearance of cleaning up its human rights record. Its argument took two main forms: (1) that domestic human rights fall under the sovereignty of the ruling government: other nations should not interfere; (2) that the U.S. position was culturally biased and self-serving in its failure to comprehend and respect the nature of Oriental collectivist societies.

Clinton's predecessors, Ronald Reagan and George Bush, had chosen the path of **quiet diplomacy** concerning China's human rights record, hoping to influence Chinese leaders via behind-the-scenes talks while maintaining an amicable public posture. President Clinton,

Secretary of State Warren Christopher, and Trade Representative Mickey Kantor all embarked on a different path. They recited, vociferously and publicly, the litany of Beijing's violations. Neither strategy, quiet diplomacy nor confrontation, seemed to have much impact on the taciturn Chinese leadership, but human rights NGOs like Amnesty International hoped Clinton would play his ace in the hole by revoking China's MFN trade status.

Some critics claimed that President Clinton's tough talk about a link between trade with China and its human rights practices amounted to mere campaign rhetoric. Clinton's defenders countered that these issues are complicated and that what human rights advocates wanted him to do—revoke China's MFN trade status—came into direct conflict with one of Bill Clinton's central objectives: expanding the U.S. economy. Clinton and his economic advisors believed that the greatest potential for American economic growth was to be found in international trade. China, with one-fifth of the world's people and a rapidly growing economy under reform, represented the largest potential trading target. Powerful U.S.-based corporations were leaning heavily on Clinton to settle for merely verbal criticism of Chinese human rights and to leave China's MFN status intact.

Ethical considerations clearly lost out to commercial factors in this case. But it should be noted that they encountered the most vital commercial interests right at the top of Clinton's priority list. Furthermore, it was at least heartening to human rights activists that a genuine MFN debate took place in the United States, with ethical arguments vigorously advanced and taken quite seriously. That the ethically based position did not win the day in this controversial policy decision does not preclude it from doing so in other cases, however unrealistic may be the expectation that it will happen with regularity.

Women's Rights

While Asia is one region of the world that has taken a verbal beating over violations of citizens' political rights, like freedom of speech, assembly, and religion, all regions have been criticized for the pervasive violation of women's rights to equal treatment. Despite constituting a majority of the world population, most women experience unequal **life chances** and, according to sociologists, they warrant being described as a **minority group**. The 1995 U.N. *Human Development Report* concludes that "In no society do women enjoy the same opportunities as men."[24] Why should this be the case, and from what does this inequality spring? Why should a special treaty specifying rights of women, the 1979 Convention on the Elimination of Discrimination Against Women, be necessary?

Sex and Gender   One place to begin to look for an answer is in the definitions of some often misused words: **sex** and **gender**. Sex refers to biological differences and gender to differences between males and females resulting from socialization. The complex mix between nature and nurture in shaping human behavior makes it easy to confuse the roles of sex and gender. There are biological sexual differences that distinguish males from females. These include, for example, the following: males have greater grip strength, have more body weight in muscle, possess larger hearts and lungs, and are taller and heavier skeletened; females have larger pelvic areas, have more body weight in fat, and are less affected by nutritional shortages.[25]

However, when the impact of genetic, biological, and sexual differences are exaggerated and spill over into the area known as gender, confusion usually follows. Gender, rather than being biologically based, refers to those behavioral and attitudinal characteristics that are learned from society. Part of what we learn as gender roles derives from what is considered typical in our culture. The concepts of **masculinity** and **femininity** enable society to define what it expects both attitudinally and behaviorally from each sex.

Cultural Variation in Gender Roles   Cross-cultural studies from anthropology assist in efforts to sort out nature versus nurture. It is significant that the characteristics of sex roles vary greatly from culture to culture. Which sex is stronger, which weaker; which rational, which intuitive; who is more aggressive, who more passive? As early as the 1920s Margaret Mead's field research in New Guinea disclosed some tribes in which gender roles were dramatically different from those in the West.

For example, Mead described polar opposite sex roles in the Arapesh versus the Mundugumor groups, although neither had the sharp gender separations common to Western cultures. Among the Arapesh, "both men and women behaved in ways we would consider 'feminine': cooperative, un-aggressive, and responsive to the needs of others." Both Arapesh mothers and fathers engaged extensively in parenting activities. However, when Mead studied the Mundugumor, she found males and females sharing nearly the exact opposite sex roles. In this tribe of headhunters, both men and women had been socialized into roles we would typically consider "actively masculine: ruthless, aggressive, and positively sexed." Studies by other anthropologists also emphasize how differently sex roles can be assigned in different societies.[26]

In the same part of the world where Margaret Mead conducted her field research, the French painter Paul Gauguin recorded his impressions of the Tahitian people in the 1890s. Much of the same sense of **androgyny** described by Margaret Mead was also seen through Gauguin's more artistic, less scientific, eyes. Of the similarities between the Tahitian sexes Gauguin had this to say:

> Neither men nor women are sheltered from the rays of the sun nor the pebbles of the seashore. Together they engage in the same tasks with the same activity. . . . There is something virile in the women and something feminine in the men.[27]

The Women's Rights Movement   A body of literature establishing that women experience discrimination reaches back nearly 200 years. Louisa May Alcott's nineteenth-century novel *Little Women* chronicles the life of an intellectual woman forced to swim upstream against a strong male-dominated current throughout her life. In 1995 the fifth film version retold this story with a sense of how an intellectually gifted woman was made to feel like a square peg trying to fit into a round hole. In 1848 Seneca Falls, New York, hosted the initial women's rights convention in the United States, which was organized by Lucretia Mott and Elizabeth Cady Stanton, two pioneering women whose spirit parallels that of the fictional heroine in *Little Women.*

The 19th Amendment meant the right to vote for American women. Here Suffragettes protest in favor of its ratification at the Republican National Convention in June, 1920.

At the turn of the twentieth century the energies of American feminists were devoted to the cause of **suffrage**. Women recognized that without the right to vote they would not be taken seriously as players in the public arena. It was not until the dislocations of World War I reshuffled the deck of gender cards that the suffragette movement realized its goal: passage of the Nineteenth Amendment to the constitution in 1920.

If World War I was the first great cataclysm of world affairs in the twentieth century, World War II was the second, even greater one. Whereas women in the first great war had proven themselves by replacing men in demanding jobs on the shop floor of the civilian economy, in World War II they went a giant step further toward equity by donning the nation's military uniforms and getting into harm's way around the periphery of the battlefield.

With sustained economic growth in America during the postwar decades, the conditions were ripe for a more assertive women's rights movement to evolve. It was out of the volatile social milieu of the late 1960s and early 1970s that names and faces emerged as cultural icons of feminism. Many point to the publication of Betty Friedan's *The Feminine Mystique* (1963) as the symbolic beginning of the movement. Ms. Friedan delved into the subtler forms of sexist attitudes preventing women from reaching their potential, a theme that dovetailed nicely with the early stages of the human potential movement as a component of humanistic psychology in America. Others, like *Ms.* magazine editor Gloria Steinem, helped to move feminism closer to the mainstream of American consciousness.

In 1966 Betty Friedan helped found the National Organization for Women (NOW), a multifaceted lobbying group for women's rights. NOW has generally favored abortion rights and equitable pay for women, and in the 1970s it was instrumental in expanding the number of day-care centers in the United States. In the 1980s NOW led an unsuccessful effort to pass a proposed Twenty-seventh Amendment—the Equal Rights Amendment (ERA). The agenda of women's rights generated its broadest global attention during the 1995 World Conference on Women's Rights held in Beijing.

As the women's movement grew larger, it became more fragmented over both philosophy and methods. But as internationalist Betty Reardon notes, all agree on the basic premise that "women throughout the world suffer sex-based discrimination."[28] While many of the most creative salvos in the feminist war were fired from behind American barricades, the European countries proved somewhat more adept at institutionalizing the values of women's rights. European countries are smaller and more homogeneous than the United States, as well as more committed to equal distribution of human rights, so it is easier for them to put into practice many of the egalitarian ideals of women's rights. Figure 10.6 depicts some of the progress that has been made globally in advancing women's rights, but it also shows that much remains to be done, as does the compendium of factoids that follows Figure 10.6.

Factoids Depicting Sex-Based Inequality

- of 1.3 billion people in poverty, 70% are women
- women carry 53% of the burden of work in developing countries and 51% in industrial countries
- two-thirds of the world's illiterates are women
- women hold only 14% of managerial jobs worldwide
- only 10% of seats in world's parliaments are held by women
- in 55 countries there are either no women in parliament or fewer than 5% women
- only 6% of government cabinet positions are held by women
- global female wage is only 75% of average male wage
- all regions have higher female than male unemployment
- one-third of women in countries studied report sexual abuse

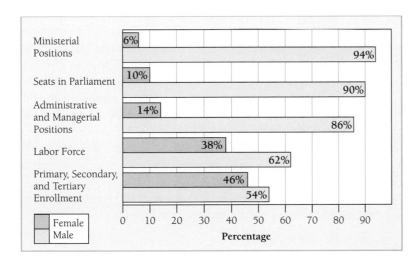

Figure 10.6 Progress in Gender Equality

Source: Human Development Report (Oxford University Press, 1995), p.48.

- one million Asian female children are forced into prostitution
- 100 million women undergo genital mutilation
- countries studied show one in six women was raped in her lifetime
- marital violence is a cause of female suicide
- a low rate of females in some south Asian countries is due to female infanticide
- the rate of depression for women is twice the male rate
- less than 20% of U.S. state legislators are women

Sexist Ideology   Part of the inequality problem stems from sexist ideology, or unsubstantiated beliefs that affect our thinking and behavior if left unchallenged. Many of these stereotypical beliefs consist of half-truths and faulty assumptions. Sexist ideologies usually stipulate rigid gender expectations, which make it difficult for people holding them to accept such realities as emotionally sensitive males, homosexual football players, female athletes, or aggressive women. These sexist ideologies not only are held by individuals but can also pervade social institutions like churches, schools, or political parties.

Sociologist Joan Ferrante cites an example of the U.S. Pentagon's military brass rejecting the results of a study they had commissioned because it concluded that "sexual orientation is unrelated to military performance." Gay men and women were shown to have served as well or better than heterosexuals, but that conclusion did not fit the prevailing ideology of those who decided to bury this particular report.[29] Ideologies do not materialize from thin air. Rather, they reflect the values of the society that produces them. In the case of sexism, much of it can be traced back millennia to the origins of the world's great religions—all of which blithely assume males to be the leaders, prophets, and generally superior half of the species. Many other social institutions have revised sexist attitudes much faster than have religions. The idea of the sexual **double standard** (affording more sexual liberty to males), which appears throughout recorded human history, has proven particularly resilient.

The Gender Development Index   In 1995 the first Gender Development Index (GDI) Report was released by the United Nations Development Programme. It ranks 130 countries on a global scale measuring gender equity and the overall condition of women. The countries faring best in the study were the Scandinavian countries of Sweden, Finland, Norway, and Denmark. Mostly African nations were at the bottom of the gender equity scale.

In general, it was found that during the last twenty years women's conditions in education and health have improved considerably. Unfortunately, the same cannot be said for economic and political conditions, neither of which has advanced measurably. By region, European and North American rankings were by far the highest. Sub-Saharan Africa did worst on the GDI, with Asia, the Arab states, and Latin America appearing in that order as we move up the scale toward the developed countries.

The Gender Development Index Report concludes with a five-point plan for accelerating progress on gender equity. In essence, the strategy calls for the following:

1. Efforts to win legal equality within the next ten years, which includes (a) ratification of the women's rights monitoring organization (CEDAW) by the ninety governments

that have yet to sign on, and (b) creation of an NGO—World Women's Watch—to prepare country-by-country reports.

2. Revamping of economic and institutional arrangements to extend the female workplace, especially (a) flexible work schedules, (b) tax incentives for women, and (c) changing laws on property, inheritance, and divorce.

3. A 30 percent target for female national-level decision makers, with firm timetables for achievement.

4. Government programs targeted to aid female education, reproductive health, and access to credit as three crucial areas for attention.

5. Both national and international efforts to create greater access for women to economic and political opportunities.

In addition to surveying gender equity by country, the GDI also analyzes women's rights data by region. The Arab Middle East is one region where serious discrimination against women is undeniable (see Mini-case 10.6).

MINI-CASE 10.6
Women in the Middle East

The 1995 Gender Development Index (GDI) reveals that on many dimensions of equity measurement, the Arab Middle East ranks low even when compared with developing countries in general. Concerning adult female literacy, the Arab Middle East is the second lowest region, falling a full 10 percent below all developing countries. Even worse, on the measure of female economic activity, the Arab region is by far the lowest ranked, falling well below one-half the average level for all developing countries. Likewise for the dimension of parliamentary seats held by women, where the Arab states' 4 percent is less than half the average of 10 percent for developing countries overall. One area in which the Arab states look better is in female school enrollment at all levels. Considerable progress in female education has occurred since the 1970s. Finally, on female life expectancy, these countries are average for developing countries.[30]

The NGO Human Rights Watch monitors the human rights situation in all regions of the world and publishes annual evaluations by region and by country. If anything, the 1995 assessment of women's rights in the Arab Middle East conducted by Human Rights Watch is more negative than that of the GDI. Human Rights Watch emphasizes that in most Arab countries secular governments are being directly challenged by militant Islamic fundamentalist groups who are determined to assume power. With plenty of human rights abuses perpetrated by both sides, women have often been the victims of overzealousness. The bottom line, according to the Human Rights Watch report, is that "governments in the region took few steps to end violations of women's human rights." They note that women still cannot vote or run for office in Kuwait, enjoy freedom of movement in Saudi Arabia, or dress as they wish in Algeria. Two women in Iran were stoned to death as punishment for adultery.[31]

The most comprehensive report on women's rights in the Middle East comes from Amnesty International, an NGO boasting membership of over one million which opposes torture, incarceration of prisoners of conscience, and capital punishment. AI operates openly and within the laws of the countries it visits, but it has nevertheless been kept out of some Arab Middle Eastern countries and been harassed in others. Arab countries are particularly sensitive about the category of women's rights. The AI report finds heartening evidence of new activism on the parts of some brave women in the region. For example, the first shelter for battered women in the region was set up in the Palestinian village of Kfar; in Bahrain, Sudan, and Algeria women have taken to the streets for peaceful demonstrations in favor of women's rights; a group of women in Tunisia signed a petition calling for respect for freedom of expression.

On balance, these favorable developments wilt in comparison to the hundreds of cases of inhumane treatment confirmed by Amnesty International. Women are caught in a relentless double bind: "In wartime, they are killed, taken hostage, raped, and driven from their homes. In peace, they are imprisoned and tortured for opposing the government, or simply for being related to political activists."[32] Often violations of women's rights occur with the blessing of discriminatory domestic laws in Arab countries. A small sampling of examples from the AI report conveys the dimensions of the problems:

- In Syria a senior dentistry student was abducted by the government in 1986 solely because of her brother's political activity; she has never been seen since.

- In Algeria a journalist named Rachida Hammadi and her sister were shot dead by Islamic fundamentalists who also killed 40 other journalists among 300 civilian women considered anti-religious.

- In Algeria seventeen-year-old student Katia Bengana was shot dead for not wearing the *hijab* (Islamic veil).

- In Israeli-occupied West Bank, eleven-year old Rana Abu Tuyur, on an errand of buying milk for her mother, was shot dead by Israeli soldiers, with no public disclosure of results of an official inquiry.

- In Iraq rape and sexual abuse have been used as weapons of terror in operations against Kurdish minorities in northern Iraq.

- In Sudan's civil war thousands of women have been imprisoned, raped, tortured, and executed.

- In Morocco several hundred women associated with supporters of a political group have disappeared.

- In Bahrain twelve women were killed by security forces while demonstrating for a reopening of the National Parliament (closed since 1975).

- In Egypt women students at the University of Cairo were held for two weeks without charges for peaceful protesting.

- In Morocco Khadija Benameur received a year in prison for joining a peaceful sit-in at her workplace.
- In Saudi Arabia 49 women were detained for violating the ban against women drivers.
- In Yemen women imprisoned for sexual offenses can be kept in jail indefinitely.
- In Iran women violating the dress laws receive 74 lashes via flogging, but adulterers receive death by stoning (while buried to their chest).

Chapter Synopsis

The new wave of idealism in the post-Cold War has activated renewed emphasis on ethical issues. While it can prove frustrating to try to pinpoint the relevance of ethics to real-world human behavior in its political, economic, or social manifestations, a growing body of social science literature suggests that—indirect as it may be—ethics plays a meaningful role as an influence on the behavior of actors on today's world stage. Although history is replete with examples of both ethical and unethical uses of the mixed blessing we refer to as organized religion, ethics and religion spill over to affect the collective mind-set in nearly all cultures. Therefore, the ethical component of human subjective experience cannot be studied without attention paid to the role of religion.

Human rights constitutes a subset of the larger set of ethics in action, and a decidedly recent one at that. In fact, the idea that every living and breathing person possesses certain rights protected from governmental infringement has become codified as a global principle only since the unspeakable crimes of the Nazi Holocaust pricked the human conscience. Under traditional international law, the principle of state sovereignty made it very difficult for concerned countries or the international community to intercede in the domestic affairs on behalf of aggrieved individuals. During the last half-century an impressive array of protections—sometimes called the International Bill of Rights—has emerged to assert fundamental rights. Of course, enforcing such rights is no mean assignment; however, an array of new IGOs and NGOs is busy attempting to do just that.

Since 1995 an annual report released by a United Nations agency ranks all countries in the world according to a Gender Development Index (GDI), intended to measure the relative equality or inequality of women in the world's countries. Overall, the condition of the world's women cannot be described as good; for example: 70 percent of those living in poverty are women, two-thirds of illiterates are women, only 14 percent of managerial jobs are held by women, depression among women is twice as bad as among men, and one in six women gets raped in her lifetime. The GDI reveals that women in Scandinavian countries of Northern Europe fare best, followed by the rest of Europe and North America. Sub-Saharan Africa, South Asia, and the Arab Middle East ranked as the most discriminatory regions by gender. As with the question of human rights generally, some encouraging improvements in women's conditions can be cited, but the big picture reveals that many grave problems continue as uniquely burdensome to women.

For Digging Deeper

Appleby, R. Scott. *The Ambivalence of the Sacred: Religion, Violence, and Reconciliation.* Rowman & Littlefield, 1997.

Donnelly, Jack. *International Human Rights.* Westview Press, 1993.

Esposito, John L., Ed. *The Oxford Encyclopedia of the Modern Islamic World.* Oxford University Press, 1995.

Hartsock, Nancy. *The Feminist Standpoint Revisited and Other Essays.* Westview Press 1997.

Hogan, Michael J. *Hiroshima in History and Memory.* Cambridge University Press, 1996.

Human Rights Watch World Report 1995. Human Rights Watch, 1995.

Juviler, Peter. *Human Rights for the 21st Century.* Sharpe, 1993.

Kael, Paul, Ed. *Ethics and Foreign Policy.* Paul and Company, 1995.

Korey, William. *The Promises We Keep: Human Rights, the Helsinki Process, and American Foreign Policy.* St. Martin's Press, 1993.

Lopez, George A. and Drew Christiansen, Eds. *Morals and Might: Ethics and the Use of Force in Modern International Affairs.* Westview Press, 1996.

Lukes, Steven. *Moral Conflicts and Politics.* Oxford University Press 1991.

Nolan, Cathal J., Ed. *Ethics and Statecraft: The Moral Dimension of International Affairs.* Praeger Publishers, 1995.

Oppenheim, Felix. *The Place of Morality in Foreign Policy.* Lexington Books, 1991.

Pettman, Jan Jindy. *Worlding Women: A Feminist International Politics.* Routledge, 1996.

"Women in the Middle East: Human Rights Under Attack," Amnesty International, 1995.

Key Glossary Terms

androgyny
atheism
Christians
cultural imperialism
ethical
European Commission on Human Rights
femininity
gender role
Golden Rule
Great Society program
Hindus
humanitarian
imam
International Bill of Human Rights

International Covenant on Civil and Political Rights
International Covenant on Economic, Social, and Cultural Rights
kiloton
level of analysis
life chances
like-minded countries
masculinity
minority group
Monitoring
Most-Favored-Nation (MFN) Trade Status

Muslims
Naturalist School
nonintervention
pacifist civil disobedience
Positivist School
quiet diplomacy
sex
sexual double standard
socialization
suffrage
theocracy
U.N. Commission on Human Rights
Universal Declaration of Human Rights

CHAPTER **11**

Macroeconomics and the Role of the United States

Thematic Questions

- How have humans historically organized efforts to produce, distribute, and consume goods and services?

- In what fundamental ways is the discipline of economics different from other social sciences?

- Which models of economic organization competed for approval during the twentieth century?

- What special role has the United States played in the world economy since World War II?

CORE OBJECTIVE

To analyze the means of subsistence devised by societies to produce, distribute, and consume goods and services.

The scientific viewpoint has pretty well defeated any remaining vestiges of humanism or historicism in modern economics—the most quantitative and empirical of the social sciences. There was a time when many social scientists derided economics as the "dismal discipline," because of its many abstract mathematical formulas. Those days have passed. A new drama unfolding on the world stage has caused economics to blossom faster than any other social science. Methodologically, economics borrows heavily from its cousins in the natural sciences but has little in common with the humanities. At some academic institutions, economics makes its home in the division of social sciences; in many others it resides in the division of business. The content of economics naturally overlaps both business and the social sciences.

THE AMERICANIZATION OF SCIENTIFIC ECONOMICS

Intellectual historian Dorothy Ross considers economics, political science, and sociology as the three pivotal social sciences in the "Americanization" of the social sciences during the latter nineteenth and early twentieth centuries. Her analysis in no way demeans the modern contributions of the other three social sciences (anthropology, psychology, geography), but she does think that the historical role of the three "core" disciplines sets them apart as shapers of the features of "Americanized" social sciences: quantitative, rigorous, empirical.[1]

In the American Gilded Age, after the Civil War and prior to World War I, an intellectual battle was waged concerning the proper scope and methods of the social sciences. Those adhering to French and German academic traditions (humanists) favored broad philosophical and historical analysis inseparable from ethical and moral considerations. Their academic homes were in the small, church-supported, private colleges which had typified American higher education since the late eighteenth century.

Their rivals had just begun creating "professional" graduate departments in America's new universities. These scientific critics of the humanists traced their intellectual lineage more to Britain than to the European continent. Their quest for natural science-like methods of social research went furthest and fastest in the discipline of economics, where measurement was most compatible with the subject matter. These social scientists wanted diversification in the form of an academic division of labor as the hallmark of professional disciplines applicable to the real world as agents of improvement; no other social science fit this ambitious bill as well as did economics.

One of the last generation of humanist-economists was Professor Edwin Seligman. Seligman's German-Jewish background was unusual, for few Jews held academic positions during the Gilded Age in America. His roots, however, were in the wealthy and influential New York City community, and his voice in the economics debate was clear and distinctive. But before long it became a voice of the minority. Seligman criticized new quantitative approaches and published economic treatises steeped in ethical and historical arguments.

Gradually his optimism and ethical idealism ran headlong into the chaotic world conditions leading to World War I, and the more detached, scientific, and professional voices of scholars like Francis Walker took over the discipline of economics. Francis Walker's graduate courses in economics at Yale University taught that moral philosophy was anachronistic in light of more powerful scientific tools of investigation, which he began describing as early as the 1880s in his *Political Economy* (1884). In retrospect, economics had less difficulty shedding its philosophical and historical identity and adopting the mantle of empirical science than did political science or sociology.

One century ago, then, these issues competed at the cutting edge of economics as a discipline: (1) whether its content would continue the tradition of philosophical and historical analysis of political economy, or would shift to narrower questions of human economic behavior; and (2) whether its methods would continue their humanistic orientation, or would change to quantitative and empirical techniques of science. Such was the changing face of economics in the 1890s. Today, at the millennium, the discipline is again affected by great changes. The modern variant, however, consists of the globalization of economics: the emergence of a seamless economy melding the micro (individual), macro (national), and mega (global) levels into a web of interacting components. Regardless of level of analysis, the key principles of economics continue to exert their influence on human beings.

BASIC CONCEPTS OF ECONOMICS

The existence of universal human needs necessitates the creation of **institutions** to meet those needs. Among such needs is a material means of subsistence—what in complex societies we call making a living. The result is an institution that produces, distributes, and consumes goods and services. It is called the economy. At the hub of **economics** is the question of how people go about coping with the central problem of economic life: scarcity. This scarcity stems from the juxtaposition of two realities: (1) the infinite range of goods that humans desire, and (2) the finite resources available to obtain those goods.

Economics involves humans interacting to translate resources into goods and services aimed at meeting our **economic wants** as well as our needs, then distributing goods and services to those who will consume them. The scarcity of goods and services forces us to make difficult choices, or to prioritize our desires from most pressing to least important. The difficult economic choices as to what will be produced, in what manner, and for whom can be left up to private individuals to decide for themselves, or the decisions can be made collectively through some public form of group process, or combined individual and group means may be used.

Factors of Production

To satisfy human economic wants, resources are committed to the production of goods and services. These **factors of production** consist of two types of human resources and two forms of nonhuman resources. **Labor** refers to the physical and mental effort that workers bring to the production process. Labor sells its skills as resources to the owners of the means of production, who are usually represented by paid managers specializing in the day-to-day operation of business and industry. In addition to the labor provided by workers, owners and their managers bring the second human resource to the production process—**entrepreneurship**, which entails the ability to conceptualize a business enterprise and the willingness to take personal financial risks in the competitive marketplace. The two nonhuman factors of production are more tangible. **Land** includes natural resources like water, forests, minerals, and property—all provided by nature. The other, **capital,** covers the gamut of equipment used in

A market involves people buying and selling goods and services. This open-air summer market in Boston, Massachusetts captures the interpersonal hustle and bustle associated with the market concept.

the process of production. It consists of material objects like buildings, tools, and machines. As nonhuman resources, land and capital add a great deal to the production process.

Markets—Supply, Demand, and Price

With scarcity as the basic economic problem, coupled with finite resources and expanding human wants, it is no wonder that these forces play themselves out as exchanges in a highly competitive forum known as the **market.** In simpler societies, economic transactions took place literally in centrally located marketplaces. While many simple societies have given way to more complex ones, we retain the label "market" to symbolize economic arrangements whereby people conduct exchanges for goods or services.

Critical to the operation of a market is the role of pricing, since it is the price system that determines who gets what, when, and how in a market arrangement. Goods and services are **supplied** on the belief that people will want to buy them—in other words, that there will be a **demand** for them. Demand for a good consists of the willingness on the part of people to buy a given quantity at a specific price. The market price for a given item is dictated in part by the relation between supply and demand. When the quantity demanded equals the quantity supplied, the market price is said to be the **equilibrium price,** since supply and demand balance each other at this price. Willingness and ability to pay both contribute to the prices set by the market, with demand, supply, and competition acting together to identify the market price of goods or services.

However, powerful forces can sometimes intercede to distort or negate the role of supply and demand in the pricing of goods. Occasionally the competitive nature of the market may be removed altogether by the existence of a **monopoly** over one or more commodities. For example, supply and demand have not been allowed to exercise their natural influence in the pricing of diamonds for a long time because of the international diamond monopoly known as De Beers (see Mini-case 11.1). Fortunately, the pricing of very few other commodities has been subverted as boldly as diamonds.

MINI-CASE 11.1
The De Beers Diamond Empire

Diamonds—in all their radiant (albeit hyper-marketed) glory.

People believe diamonds are very rare. They are not. Only an incredibly successful 100-year monopoly and marketing campaign have created this great self-fulfilling deception: the illusion that diamonds are extremely valuable has served to create its own reality. The marketing slogan that "diamonds are forever" has manufactured a powerful cultural imperative to buy them both as a good investment and as gifts symbolic of profound love. But who has the power, wealth, and skill to create such a potent illusion?

In the diamond industry, it is not a nation–state or an IGO. Rather it is the Oppenheimer family of South Africa, and its De Beers corporation, one of the most successful global **cartels** in history. By controlling the production, pricing, and marketing of diamonds, De Beers has managed to manipulate the entire industry. Its most important achievement has been to co-opt potential rivals into joining the cartel, in a conspiracy of sorts, rather than competing with it. By artificially limiting the supply of diamonds, the cartel stimulates demand that exceeds supply, thereby causing high prices for the diamonds available on the market. Diamonds are found where carbon is found; they are less rare than most people believe. Vast deposits of diamonds have been mined in other parts of Africa, Russia, Australia, and Canada. Thus far De Beers has been able to entice these diamond suppliers to join the cartel rather than compete against it.

In the United States such monopolistic practices as that of De Beers are regarded as economically unnatural and unhealthy. They are also illegal under U.S. antitrust laws. However, De Beers has long been able to get around this restriction by working through intermediaries in American markets. This practice makes diamonds more expensive in the United States than they ought to be, and in 1992 presidential candidate Bill Clinton vowed to do something about it. However, it is difficult to prove in court exactly what De Beers is doing, and his administration has been frustrated thus far in its efforts to prosecute De Beers, as well as other monopolistic enterprises that subvert the normal workings of supply and demand. The Clinton administration scored its first big victory in 1996 when the mammoth agribusiness Archer Daniels Midland lost an antitrust case and paid out $100 million in fines.

In ancient times the exchanges in marketplaces often consisted of direct item-for-item transactions known as **bartering.** Exchange through barter had the advantages of simplicity, directness, and immediacy. For example, if you were proficient at making hunting knives, you might directly exchange them for meat or blankets. However, for bartering to work well, a double coincidence of economic wants must occur: I must want your knife and you must want my blankets for us to satisfy our wants. Once the number of bartering participants increases, problems arise in the system. In many societies, one of the goods was then selected as a standard medium of exchange. In the Pacific island of Yap large stone wheels were chosen, the ancient Greeks used cattle, and indigenous Americans relied on strings of beads called wampum. **Money** as a measurement of exchange proved more durable, portable, and replicable, thus greatly facilitating commerce.[2]

National Economic Models

The key level of economic activity for more than three centuries has been the macro level, or the nation–state. Three common models of national economic organization have been provided by the **command** (government-directed) model, the **capitalist** (free-market) model, and the **traditional** (preindustrial) model. We said earlier that scarcity dictates that tough choices need to be made in answering the question of who gets, what, when, and how?

In societies that prefer collectivist forms of group decision making, the command model of central planning by an authoritative government has developed. When the Soviet Union led the world's thirteen communist countries, it was easy to place the command face with the communist name, as the archetype of collectivism at work. The four remaining communist countries—North Korea, Vietnam, China, and Cuba—continue to exemplify the undemocratic, bureaucratic, centralized, and authoritarian nature of the command economy.

The capitalist, free-market model has evolved in societies that are suspicious of extensive reliance on governmental authority. Capitalist economies give considerable latitude to the individual and rely on the forces of the marketplace (not governmental planners) to determine, through supply, demand, and pricing, who gets what, when, and how. Figure 11.1 illustrates the distinction often made today between the more **individualistic capitalism** based on the pursuit of self-interest, as found in the United States, the Netherlands, and United Kingdom, as opposed to the more **communitarian capitalism** based on serving the interests of customers and society, as found in Japan and Germany.[3]

The traditional, or preindustrial economy, which relies on hunting and gathering, horticulture, or pastoral means of subsistence still exists in many simple societies. However, the economic and political significance of these traditional societies is miniscule in the modern world, and economists and political scientists have in large measure left the study of preindustrialism to anthropologists and sociologists.

In reality, most twentieth century national economies have combined the command and capitalist models, with some leaning toward public control and others leaning toward private market forces. The ownership of property in mostly capitalist economies like the

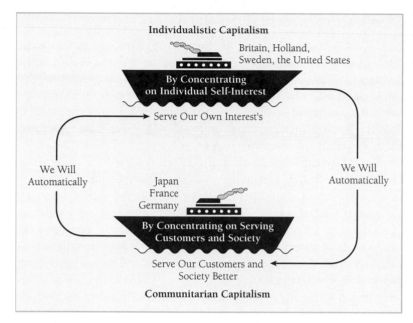

Figure 11.1 Individualistic and Communitarian Capitalism

Source: The Seven Cultures of Capitalism by Charles Hampden-Turner and Alfons Trompenaars. Copyright © 1993 by Charles Hampden-Turner. Used by permission of Doubleday, a division of Bantam Dell Publishing Group.

United States is primarily private, but with some public (governmental) ownership of property and a minimal amount of communal (private-group-owned) property. The global trend from the 1940s to the 1960s was toward a greater governmental role in the economy and governmental ownership of many industries, while the 1980s and 1990s has witnessed more reliance on private avenues of economic growth, resulting in the privatization of many government-owned industries.

Primary, Secondary, Tertiary Economies

Economists delineate other contrasting types of national economies besides the command versus capitalist models. One type is a trichotomy that related to the economy's level of sophistication in production, distribution, and consumption of goods and services. Most of the southern hemisphere LDCs remain mired in the **primary economy's** production of goods extracted from the earth—agricultural products such as bananas or cocoa, and raw materials like bauxite or tin. These undiversified economies share a colonial heritage and relatively low demand for their primary products, creating a **terms-of-trade** problem for countries like Nigeria, Bolivia, and Sri Lanka.

The **secondary** (industrialized) **economy** relies mostly on manufactured goods such as refrigerators, golf clubs, or furniture. Greece, Indonesia, and Hungary are examples of countries that are much more productive than the LDCs but still lagging well behind the world's upper-tier economies. In places like Canada, Germany, Japan, and the United States, national economies have evolved well beyond the industrial manufacturing of four decades ago. Today they inhabit the high-tech information age of complex services like bioengineering, computerization, and instantaneous global communication. In such **tertiary** economies information has become a critical link to power and wealth.

How Much Is Enough Governmental Involvement?

Economists are also fond of distinguishing between the **household, firm,** and **government** as the principal participants in the national economy. Most governments, that of the United States included, enjoyed their greatest level of economic intervention in the decades following World War II. The classical school of laissez-faire capitalism, traceable to Scottish philosopher Adam Smith, criticized government involvement in the economy as dysfunctional. It argued instead for faith in the guiding "invisible hand" of free-market forces. This view dominated the economic vision for nearly two centuries.

However, the shock of the **Great Depression** in the 1930s rendered the laissez-faire mantra of competitive self-interest vulnerable on numerous fronts. Unemployment climbed as high as one in four Americans, wages were 60 percent lower than in the previous decade, one-third of banks and businesses failed, while GNP dropped by one half. Massive suffering engulfed a nation without safety nets. Social services that are today taken for granted—like social security, Medicare, unemployment benefits, food stamps, and a sizable welfare program—simply did not exist when the Great Depression dislocated lives and spread havoc from Connecticut to California and everywhere in between.

The agent of change in combating the American Depression was President Franklin D. Roosevelt. His aggressive New Deal policies applied the theories of British economist John Maynard Keynes, who advocated increased governmental spending to prime the economic pump by creating jobs, thus starting the economy moving once again. Roosevelt created many new governmental programs and agencies, and once governmental expansion began, it continued unabated up through the 1960s. Challenges to "big government" have gained momentum ever since Ronald Reagan's electoral victory in 1980, but many features of governmental economic involvement seem unlikely to be removed any time soon.

Citizens wait in a 1932 bread line in New York City during the Great Depression.

Economic Dysfunctions and Keynesian Prescriptions

Governments are generally called upon to intervene when the national economy is malfunctioning. Fortunately, most economic dysfunctions do not rival the Great Depression of the 1930s in scope or depth. Lesser declines, when the economy fails to grow for three more consecutive quarters, are called **recessions.**

The inevitable ups and downs of the economy result in fluctuations known as the **business cycle.** Americans have been relatively well off in this respect, since recessions have been recorded during only 20 percent of U.S. history. One of the tools available to government in fighting a recession is **fiscal policy,** which aims to control taxing and spending revenues. Just as during the Great Depression, Keynesian theory calls for action to increase consumer demand during a recession. The prescription calls for government to add to the total demand by increasing its spending. It can also cut taxes to give consumers more money to spend. Keynesian theory also calls for government to run a deficit, or take on debt, to prime the economic pump.

Inflation Another form of economic malfunction, one that places a disproportionate burden on the poor (especially pensioners on fixed incomes) is **inflation,** characterized by rapidly rising prices and eroded purchasing power of consumer's money. Inflation is often caused by demand growing faster than production of goods and services. There are two main variants of inflation. The first is **demand-pull inflation,** caused by an increase in aggregate demand. When President Lyndon Johnson increased spending on the Vietnam War in the 1960s from $100 billion to $144 billion in three short years, without raising taxes or cutting governmental spending, he was condemning the nation to double-digit demand-pull inflation in the 1970s. High demand for military goods pulled the inflation rate up.

In the other form of inflation, **cost-push inflation,** increased cost of a critical good pushes up the rate of inflation. A prime example of cost-push inflation grew out of the two oil shocks of 1973 and 1979 caused by the Organization of Petroleum Exporting Countries (OPEC). When the thirteen OPEC countries agreed to cut their production of oil supplies to the world, they pushed the price of crude oil from under $3 per barrel in 1973 to over $38 in 1979.

Russia's current effort to move from a planned central economy to a more capitalistic economy has triggered annual inflationary rates of more than 100 percent. Brazil and Argentina in Latin America, and Israel in the Middle East, are other countries that have experienced triple-digit inflation in recent decades. The classic worst-case scenario, however, was Germany's skyrocketing inflation after World War I, which made the deutsche mark virtually worthless as a medium of exchange, forcing bewildered citizens to push wheelbarrows full of currency to purchase routine goods and services. America's double-digit inflation in the 1970s pales in comparison.

The Keynesian prescription for inflation is the opposite that for recession: cut government spending and increase taxes. The reduction of government expenditures will lessen total demand and equilibrate it with supply once again.

In addition to fiscal (tax) policy, government can also apply **monetary policy** in fighting recession and inflation. Monetary policy controls the flow of money and credit to influence economic performance. During recession, government can relax controls on the flow of money, thereby encouraging banks to lend more money at lower interest rates. Conversely, during inflation, government can restrict the flow of money, thereby discouraging banks from lending money and causing them to lend it at higher rates of interest when they do lend it.

ASSESSING ECONOMIC PERFORMANCE

As global competition has forced national economies into higher levels of competitiveness, methods for evaluating economic performance have taken on added significance. The most common traditional measure was **gross national product** (GNP), the total goods and services produced by citizens of a country, either at home or abroad. Since 1992 the United States has shifted to **gross domestic product** (GDP)—goods and services produced within the borders

A scene from the popular documentary film, Hoop Dreams *(1994).*

of a country—as its main evaluative tool. However, the differences between GNP and GDP are generally too minor to concern us here. **Per capita** (per person) measures of GNP and GDP also represent useful gross comparative data between countries, as do the rate of economic growth, level of price stability, level of consumer satisfaction, equitable wealth distribution, economic productivity (units of worker output), and net **national product** (**NNP**), the cost of machine depreciation subtracted from GNP.

My scientific colleagues find these measures crucial to understanding complex modern economies like that of the United States, where a mix of contrasting elements can exist side by side. For example, GDP and price stability in America remain excellent, but the trade deficit and federal debt are massive, growing, and troublesome to many economists. Scientific scholars believe that without sophisticated statistics, one is left with little more than impressionism: judgments lacking standards of evaluation. In contrast, humanistic social scientists consider many of the numbers used by economists as sterile **hyperfactualism**, quoting a famous observation that, in order of heinousness, there are lies, damned lies, and then statistics!

Hoop Dreams

To illustrate the point that the sterile recitation of numbers lacks insight, depth, and emotional meaning, a humanist scholar might cite this fact: of more than 100,000 boys who play high school basketball, most dream of playing some day in the National Basketball Association, but only a tiny handful will ever make it. You can repeat the statistical futility inherent in the infinitesimal odds of a high school basketball player's ever getting to the NBA until you are blue in the face, but none of this is internalized as meaningful by the boys playing basketball. However, sit them down in front of the riveting documentary film *Hoop Dreams* (1994), by Steve James, Fred Marx, and Peter Gilbert—and suddenly many of them get it. They can relate to the same message in a more humanly complex way when it is conveyed as real-life experience rather than abstract statistics. All of a sudden they realize that their chances are better (though still paltry) to win the state lottery than to play in the NBA.

A Yardstick for Quality of Life

Humanistic social scientists have welcomed a new measuring stick which economists bring to the task of assessment these days; it is the Human Development Index (HDI), which has been made available to the global community by the U.N. Development Programme annually since 1991. In addition to including the traditional economic performance numbers, the HDI delves into the more subjective realm of assessing quality-of-life issues, imparting a sense of contemporary relevance to the normal number crunching involved in assessing economies. But how did we get to a world dominated by so many complex and competitive national economies?

THE EVOLUTION OF WESTERN ECONOMIES

Humans have spent much more time under the conditions of hunting and gathering societies than any other means of subsistence. Neither these foraging societies nor later pastoral (herding) societies engaged in meaningful economic exchanges as defined above. It was not until the advent of the agricultural revolution around 10,000 years ago that transactions of goods and services began to typify human existence. As ancient civilizations like those in Egypt, Persia, and China blossomed, new institutions took on the task of meeting basic social, political, and economic needs.

The Middle Ages

The revolutionary developments in producing, distributing, and consuming goods beyond the limited capabilities of agricultural societies occurred mostly in Europe. The ancient civilizations faded away with the fall of the Roman Empire in 476 A.D. During the **Middle Ages,** or the next 1,000 years prior to modernity, the rural economies of Europe featured labor-intensive agriculture in the guise of **feudalism.** Peasants were little more than slave labor, legally bound to the land which they worked for their wealthy and powerful feudal lords. Agricultural surpluses produced wealth for the landowning class which prospered at the expense of the vast peasant class.

Mercantilism Replaces Feudalism

As political power in the seventeenth century rode the back of the rising nation–state from the local to the national level, so did economic power. This economic metamorphosis was known as **mercantilism.** It sought to use manufacturing-based trade as a vehicle for accumulating wealth for the state; Britain, Holland, and France were exemplars of the strategy. Under the **Industrial Revolution** which mercantilism encouraged, the merchant class of industrial owners replaced the feudal landed aristocracy as Europe's dominant class.

Modern sociologist Max Weber's 1930 treatise, *The Protestant Ethic and the Spirit of Capitalism,* traces the role of the Protestant Reformation in spiritualizing a set of values (thrift, savings, hard work) which facilitated the rise of an entrepreneurial class during the Industrial Revolution. Mercantilism thrived well into the nineteenth century but began to unravel as early as the American rebellion against this system's inherent unfairness to colonies. Mercantilism required **protectionist** trade policies to stuff the coffers of the state, and its death knell was sounded when the nineteenth century's most powerful country, Britain, staunchly advocated the opposite policy: **free trade.**[4]

Market Economy Replaces Mercantilism

Mercantilism had other problems as well. It fostered extensive governmental control of the economy and viewed the national economy as a mere vehicle for creating a powerful nation-state. It wasn't much concerned about what might benefit individual citizens or the private sector of the economy in general. Its narrow fixation on what was good for the state blinded it to the forces that make economies grow. The most deft autopsy on the corpus of mercantilist economics was performed by Adam Smith in his seminal work, *The Wealth of Nations* (1776). Most of what is now called classical economic theory derives from the brilliant analysis of Adam Smith. His laissez-faire injunction against governmental direction of the economy, the democratically based notion that individuals should be free to act in their best (and society's) interests, his description of the market being guided by an "invisible hand," and his insistence on free trade over protectionism all establish him as an intellectual giant.

Nothing less than "the greatest good for the greatest number of people" was what Smith's concept of the free market was believed capable of delivering. The true believers who witnessed that industrialization and market forces created unprecedented economic growth among Europe's heavyweight nations required no convincing. The accumulation of wealth was, nevertheless, very unevenly distributed, a situation leading to a nineteenth-century cottage industry in the chiding of market forces for their cold, dispassionate failure to offer a helping hand to the masses of poor, uneducated, and oppressed souls. Many critics of the market economy's blind eye to human suffering fell under the general rubric of **socialism,** a broad-based philosophy with a penchant for public rather than private ownership of property, a classless society, and a more equitable distribution of wealth.

Socialist Indictment of the Market Economy

The most comprehensive expression of socialist principles flowed from the prolific pen of exiled German philosopher Karl Marx (1818–1883). Marx created a complex theory of historical evolution, progressing through a series of stages and culminating in a final perfect stage of economic abundance and classless equality. Writing in the mid-1800s, Marx claimed that the transition from one stage to the next derived from the clash of competing classes, which in the case of the capitalist stage of history meant the privileged *bourgeoisie* (owners) pitted against the impoverished *proletariat* (workers). Marxism envisioned violent revolt by the proletariat as the inexorable midwife of the birth of socialism over the decaying corpse of capitalism. Like other philosophers of the 1800s, Marx was profoundly influenced by Charles Darwin's contributions to scientific explanations of natural phenomena, and he set out to discover parallel laws governing *social* phenomena. Hence his appealing claim that his theories bore the imprimatur of science and were rooted in "the iron laws of history."

Mixed-Market Replaces Market Economy

Socialist challenges to market capitalism were substantial. Nevertheless, the market economy, which had brushed aside mercantilism and unleashed the resilient forces of supply and demand, thus expanding the economic pie for those who succeeded, remained largely intact until the 1930s. It continues to exist today, although in a form greatly altered by twentieth-century cataclysms like World War I, the Great Depression, World War II, and the end of the Cold War. The transition has been from a market economy to a **mixed-market economy.**

All the largest economies in the world today fall into this category of mixed-market economy: they include *both* market forces and governmental institutions in the potpouri determining how goods and services get produced, distributed, and consumed. Mixed-market economies can be visualized along a continuum ranging from high market/low government, to low market/high government, including these countries: U.S.—Spain—Canada—United Kingdom—France—Germany—Finland—Japan.

Since the 1930s, Keynesian economics had concentrated on the *demand side* of the economy: decrease government spending and restrict the money supply during inflation, and do just the opposite when fighting a recession. It was in the demand for goods and services that Keynes called on the government to intervene. Since the 1970s, American economic thought has been influenced by a **neoclassical school** developed substantially at the University of Chicago. Neoclassicists, also known as **supply-side** economists because of their focus on that long-ignored supply end of the equation, have become much better known in the last two decades.

They want to turn more in the direction of a laissez-faire market; they counsel the government to reduce high taxes, which serve only as a disincentive for citizens to work hard. Supply-siders argue that lower tax rates will paradoxically bring in larger governmental revenues, because people will spend and invest the money not taken in taxes, with a resultant boost for the economy. When Ronald Reagan took office in 1981, most of his advisors were supply-siders. He soon reduced taxes, which spurred economic growth and created jobs—but also led to the record federal deficits which continue to pile up on the debit side of the ledger. It also caused the rich to get richer and the poor to get poorer during the 1980s, as the top 5 percent of the society saw its share of the economic pie increase by 14 percent while the lowest 20 percent simultaneously experienced a 12 percent decrease.[5]

Communist Competitors: There They Were...Gone

The only genuine threat to the very existence of Western-oriented, mixed-market economies in the 1900s came from the Eastern-oriented **communist economies,** which traced their philosophical roots back to the previous century's socialist tradition of criticizing capitalist economies for heartlessness. But the diverse paths to collectivism and equality advocated by socialist thinkers of the 1800s differed fundamentally from the monolithic systems which emerged in the 1900s under the label of communism. Socialism historically meant a key role for government in the economy, but socialism could be found coexisting with many different forms of political arrangements, from democratic to authoritarian. Communism, however, became synonymous with the fusion of **state economic monopoly** and political **totalitarianism** in one package, all under the dictatorial control of the Communist Party.

During the Cold War the Soviet Union and communist China led a total of thirteen communist countries in an internecine struggle against the enemy: Western democratic capitalism, epitomized by the United States. With 20/20 hindsight, it is tempting today to take for granted the collapse of communism and Western capitalism's victory in the Cold War. Since we know that to be what happened, it is tempting to believe that was the *only* way the situation could have turned out. But back in the days when I first darkened the doorstep of a college classroom, many of my professors and fellow students believed that the communist countries were running ahead in the race, and furthermore, that their undemocratic ways gave them built-in advantages over the more cumbersome Western way of catering to the individual at the expense of society's goals.

Of the thirteen communist countries which seemed so invincible a generation ago, only four remain intact in 1998: China, Vietnam, North Korea, and Cuba. Of these extant pillars of communism, only China can boast of an economy exhibiting impressive growth in recent decades, something it has achieved by abandoning many aspects of socialist economics while embracing basic principles of free-market competition. The obvious question begging for an answer is: what happened?

The Red Empire Awash in Red Ink   The short and bitter reply is that the communist countries derived their economic theories from Karl Marx, and Marx's analysis was dead wrong in many respects. The elites in communist countries used the mantle of Marxian scientific infallibility to legitimize the power that they exercised without democratic niceties—like competitive elections. Marx failed to anticipate the emergence of trade unions, which were to improve vastly the lot of workers in capitalist countries. He was wrong in his belief that selfish incentives were unnecessary to motivate people to be productive and that they would sacrifice for the general good of society. Marx's ideas, expressed 150 years ago, were impressive in their creative range and in their humanistic intent, but as supposedly infallible scientific laws and predictions they failed abjectly.

Each of the thirteen countries that adopted communism imparted something of a unique national twist to the raw materials of Marxism. Therefore, we cannot simply blame Marx's naivete for communism's failing when so many people of my generation feared, that it would succeed. Marx expected violent revolution to wipe away capitalism in the most *advanced* Western economies, like Britain, France, Germany, or the United States. In fact, revolution in communism's name occurred only in feudalistic, preindustrial economies. In other words, conditions were already so poor in places like Russia, China, and Vietnam that the communist systems set up there really had their work cut out for them.

By dragging their citizens through a wringer of oppression and sacrifice, some countries were able to achieve advances in production straight out of human hides. The Soviet Union proved particularly good at undertaking gargantuan public works projects such as electrification dams and canals for shipping, and, back when heavy industry was equated with economic vitality, they fared reasonably well. However, when the West took a quantum leap into the brave new world of high-tech computerization in the 1970s, the ossified communist systems were incapable of stimulating the creative juices required to graduate from industrialism to postindustrialism. People in communist countries had become good at taking orders but bad at taking either initiative or, worse yet, personal risks.

The system of central governmental control, with its Five Year Production Plans, ingrained quotas into the popular consciousness; it enshrined the value of quantity but ignored product quality. The absence of competition over goods and services, little by little, contributed to a deterioration in manufactured goods made in communist countries. The lack of competition within each communist economy was then mirrored by a parallel lack of international competition, since the unlucky thirteen avoided the global economy like poison ivy, opting to stay within the confines of their own economically incestuous trading network.

Communist countries were supposed to be more egalitarian than the money-grubbing capitalist alternative. But while these were relatively poor countries, poverty was not shared by all. What some referred to as a "new class" of Communist Party officials enjoyed the luxuries of life that their fellow citizens could only dream about. Many factors led to the demise of Communism as a global competitor, but the crucial ones were economic in nature.

The Shadow Economy

One unscientific warning signal that an economy is in trouble is the extent of its **underground economy,** which in communist countries was pervasive. Also known as the *shadow economy* or the *black market,* the underground economy is an unofficial, off-the-books network supplying goods and services that the official economy is unable or unwilling to provide. Tax avoidance serves as a potent incentive in many activities that are technically legal but capable of being hidden or falsified. Baby-sitters, self-employed plumbers, domestics, consultants, and moonlighting lawyers may find it easy to underreport or not report income bearing no paper trail. Rather different are the many economic wants that are met by goods and services hidden from public view for another reason: they are illegal. Prostitution, illegal gambling, child labor, bribery, and trafficking in drugs are often as lucrative as they are unsavory.

The size of the underground economy varies from country to country, and its exact dimensions are difficult to measure for obvious reasons. Economist Peter Gutmann puts the American shadow economy at about $840 billion ($200 billion illegal, $640 billion legal), or 13 percent of gross domestic product, and slightly higher than the ballpark figure of 10 percent often estimated by researchers.[6] The percentage is much higher in most European countries. It hovered around 50 percent in communist countries, where the official economy simply was not supplying the goods and services that consumers wanted. The transitional postcommunist Russian black market has been described as continuing to rival the above-ground economy.[7]

Economic Interdependence

The most recent economic wave to wash ashore has been the globalization of all economies. Irrespective of level (local, state, national) or direction (east, west, south, north), the global pull is ubiquitous. Figure 11.2 suggests that a virtual tidal wave of global trade has jacked up the volume of world trade, with a Pacific monsoon led by Japan, China, and the NICs as the vanguard of the storm.[8]

Institutions at the global level and the regional level have sprouted up and expanded to guide the trade parade. The eight leading economic powers (referred to as G-8) hold annual summit meetings to coordinate their economic strategies. They are the U.S., Canada, Japan, Germany, France United Kingdom, Italy, and Russia. Record-level investments in the American economy began in the 1980s and have yet to abate. Many thousands of multinational corporations (MNCs) spread their broad wings over every corner of the globe in search of cheap labor, ways to diversify their operations, and new customers. More than $1 trillion crosses

Figure 11.2   U.S. and World Trade, 1949-1973

Source: Steven Spiegel, *World Politics in a New Era* (Harcourt, Brace, 1995), p. 315. Data from International Monetary Fund, *International Financial Statistics Yearbook, 1979,* pp. 62-67.

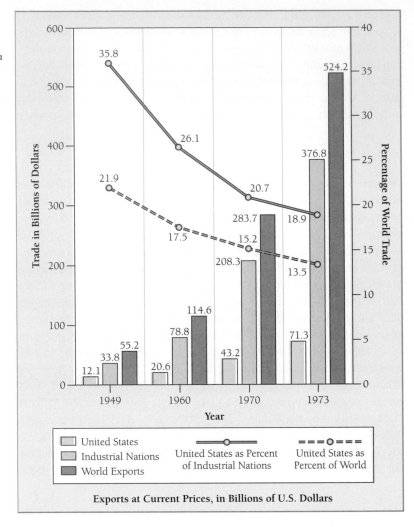

Exports at Current Prices, in Billions of U.S. Dollars

borders daily in the form of foreign currency purchases. The buzzword for the economic evolution that has dominated the last three decades can be one thing only: global interdependence.[9]

AMERICA'S TRANSITION TO THE GLOBAL MARKET
Global Hegemon No More

With a GDP exceeding $5 trillion, the United States still has the world's largest economy. However, America simply cannot control economic events in the world as it did during the past half-century. During the Cold War the United States enjoyed the status of an **economic hegemon,** similar to the preeminent British role during the latter half of the nineteenth century. Once the world's largest creditor, the United States since 1985 has been its greatest debtor. It found itself with a federal **budget deficit** of nearly $200 billion in 1996, totaling over $4 trillion. Until 1971 America had enjoyed **trade surpluses** throughout the twentieth century; however, by 1986 its **trade deficit** had ballooned to $170 billion, where it hovered for a decade, as is described in Figure 11.3.

In 1960 the U.S. share of world exports was 18 percent; by 1990 its share had declined to 12 percent. When the New York Stock Market crashed in 1987, *The Wall Street Journal* blamed the fall on the "cataclysmic power of the new global market."[10] Economics at all levels of analysis has evolved into a seamless global web more complex than anything before.

With all other major countries decimated by World War II, the United States emerged as unrivaled director of the 1945 capitalist drama playing on the world stage. An entire system of global institutions was created at the **Bretton Woods Conference** in 1944 to facilitate the open international economy then advantageous to American businesses. The deck was stacked with so many American aces that its citizens may have become accustomed to unreasonable expectations of perpetual affluence.

It was not until the 1970s that America encountered viable economic competition. This hiatus allowed its production facilities, work ethic, and managerial style to ossify somewhat. After at first ignoring their economic problems, many Americans sought to blame others for U.S. problems before finally getting down to the difficult task of improving competitiveness, beginning in the 1980s, and succeeding within a decade.

Fordism and Economies of Scale

American corporations had succeeded earlier under the model of **Fordism**—assembly-line **economies of scale** based on size as the competitive advantage. For many years, bigger was seen as better, and the corporations became slow, rigid, complacent, and bureaucratized. IBM, with its "Big Blue" image, seemingly unassailable for decades, served as a metaphor for U.S. business woes in general. Throughout the 1980s IBM clung tenaciously to its commitment to large mainframe computers, failing to react to a growing demand for small personal computers—which adaptable foreign firms proved creative enough to capture with cheaper

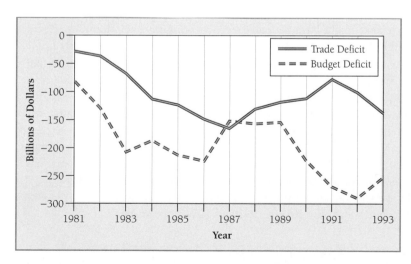

Figure 11.3 The Twin Deficits in the United States, 1981–1993, in Current Dollars

Source: Joan Spero and Jeffrey Hart, *The Politics of International Economic Relations* (St. Martin's, 1997), p. 29. Data from *Economic Report of the President* (Washington: Government Printing Office, 1995), 365, 394.

Figure 11.4

Source: Mac Nelly, *The Chicago Tribune* (1996).

IBM clones. During a two-year stretch, IBM lost over $13 billion! Top-heavy with upper management, Big Blue proved very resistant to change.

Transplant Needed: A New Corporate Culture

Widespread **downsizing** of personnel by giants like IBM, Kodak, Xerox, and Texas Instruments has human costs, a situation lampooned in Figure 11.4. Corporate downsizing has enhanced the immediate competitiveness of these companies, yet by itself it seems inadequate. What else must happen? The answer is a change in **corporate culture**; namely, long-term vision, flexibility, risk taking, labor–management cooperation, investment in Research and Development—every one of which initially proved difficult for U.S. managers to embrace.

When a Japanese wake-up call blasted the big-three automakers out of bed in the early 1980s, management instinctively sought a quick, high-tech fix in the form of robotics. Personified by General Motors Chief Executive Officer (CEO) Roger Smith, who refused to heed the 1970s Japanese lesson that fuel efficiency sells, Detroit's managerial elite still didn't get it. The Japanese were making better-quality cars at the time because of employee communications, worker initiative, corporate loyalty, and production flexibility—not, as Roger Smith thought, because they used robots.[11]

MINI-CASE 11.2
GM's Roger Smith Missed the Point

Corporate management might have benefited from viewing Michael Moore's sarcastic documentary film, *Roger and Me* (1986), which portrayed managers as badly in need of a reality check. Presented through the eyes of a laid-off Flint, Michigan, autoworker, GM's Roger Smith comes off as aloof, inarticulate, and grossly overpaid. *Roger and Me,* the most popular documentary of all time, tapped into a deep pool of frustration and resentment felt by American laborers as they struggled to cope with the economic dislocation caused by intensified global competition in the 1980s.

One decade later Moore followed Roger and Me with an angry book blasting corporate management, *Downsize This!* (1996). The U.S. loss of international economic hegemony has frustrated all Americans, but none so profoundly as its blue-collar class. Labor backlash proved problematic for the Clinton administration as it proposed the **NAFTA** and **GATT** treaties for congressional approval in 1993 and 1994 respectively.

Economic Nationalism

Many Americans are tempted to react to the suddenly more competitive international economy with economic nationalism, or what two economists call "aggressive unilateralism."[12] Political pressures will always exist for protectionism to provide short-term solutions to long-term economic dislocations, but classical economists warn that a nation embarks on that path at its own peril. As a long-time champion of free trade, and one that Figure 11.5 shows has cut tariffs in the postwar era, the United States would seem the likeliest country to resist any trend toward protectionist trade measures.

However, all countries engage in some form of protectionism. Despite its free-trade advocacy, the United States has "engineered import restrictions on an array of important products including textiles, apparel, shoes, cars, carbon and specialty steel, machine tools, motorcycles, and semiconductors."[13]

One study concludes that the United States has increasingly used **nontariff barriers** to imports, with 29 percent of its goods now protected.[14] Another finds that protective trade measures added an average of 35 percent to the price of the affected products and that every job saved through protectionism cost the U.S. taxpayer an average of $170,000.[15] Many economists counsel against protectionism, not only because it raises the price paid by consumers, but because it often results in deteriorating product quality by removing market competition.

Legitimate Protectionism

Under special circumstances, however, limited protectionism may be called for. For example, if it can be clearly demonstrated that a particular country is engaging in unfair trading practices, then some form of protectionism may be warranted to level the playing field. Also economists make an exception to the rule for **strategic industries** that make items vital to national defense, for cutting-edge **infant industries** requiring help to get off the ground, and for **Third World diversification** intended to help poor countries move beyond their sole reliance on primary products.

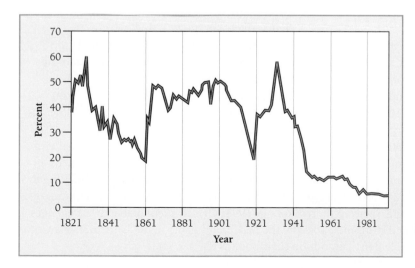

Figure 11.5 Average U.S. Tariff Rates on Dutiable Imports, in Percentages, 1821–1993

Source: Joan Spero and Jeffrey Hart, *The Politics of International Economic Relations* (St. Martin's, 1997), p. 56. Data from U.S. Department of Commerce, Bureau of the Census, *Historical Statistics of the United States;* and *Statistical Abstract of the United States* (Washington: Government Printing Office, various years).

Beleaguered by foreign motorcycle competition in the 1980s, the Harley-Davidson Company fought for and received Congressional protectionism. A decade later, this well-managed corporation was doing all the right things to compete internationally and no longer needed governmental assistance.

However, once the protectionist door is opened, it is often difficult to close it when it is no longer needed. It is also very difficult to draw the line separating valid from invalid claims for protection in what is a highly political process. The case of Harley-Davidson (Mini-case 11.3) is a refreshing one because here a brief protectionist boost helped innovative owners and managers to change their corporate culture in ways eluding many of the larger corporations. Harley-Davidson's enlightened policies brought it added efficiency and global competitiveness.

MINI-CASE 11.3
Harley-Davidson—
Hog Wild in the 1990s

B eginning in the late 1970s, the American motorcycle company Harley-Davidson wilted for a decade under a Japanese onslaught which annually grabbed more and more market share. Then, under the astute direction of Board Chairman Vaughan Beals and Company President Richard Teerlink, all that changed. By the mid-1990s it became nearly impossible to find anyone saying anything bad in print about Harley-Davidson. What happened in the interim?

On the verge of extinction in the early 1980s, Harley-Davidson boasts a success story that resulted from a variety of factors. But the one that enabled the rest to follow was the protectionist legislation passed by the U.S. Congress in 1983, when it slapped a hefty **tariff** on Japanese bikes imported into the United .States. As the only U.S. motorcycle company, Milwaukee-based Harley was given some unusual breaks. Rather than becoming lazy and complacent, however, Harley did the things a competitive firm needs to do: cut 40 percent of its workforce in 1982, modernized management techniques, pared down its oversized bikes, emphasized quality control, and devised more sophisticated marketing strategies.

As Harley celebrated its ninetieth anniversary in 1992, it produced the world's most sought-after motorcycle. Unable to keep up with demand, in 1993 management decided not to risk loss of quality by overproducing; the company began more creative marketing of Harley accessories rather than building too many bikes. Management has also ingrained a spirit of social responsibility into the corporate culture. Harley stock responded by returning 27 percent to investors in 1994. One marketing analyst exaggerates only slightly in claiming that "Harley-Davidson is possibly the best brand name in the United States. Coca Cola is a good brand name, but people don't tattoo it on their bodies."[16]

In the late 1980s Harley took another unusual step: it went to the U.S. Congress and asked for the removal of its protective tariff! A dozen years after protectionist legislation, Harley was clobbering the Japanese competition with a high-quality product at a competitive price—not to mention successfully capturing the image of freedom, independence, and defiance so well ingrained into the American national identity.

MINI-CASE 11.4
U.S. Ratification of the WTO

Three American presidents—Ronald Reagan, George Bush, and Bill Clinton—pushed for completion of the seven-year global trade negotiations known as the **Uruguay Round** of the GATT arrangement, predicting that it would be beneficial to America. Since the United States was the world's largest trader, one considered to have an open policy since World War II, it seemed obvious to these presidents that getting more restrictive traders to open up their markets was advantageous. Why, then, did President Clinton have such difficulty gaining congressional approval for the new GATT treaty in December 1994?

Tentatively approved by 124 nations, formally endorsed by the G-8 economic powers as "fostering growth, generating employment, and increasing prosperity," the agreement needed congressional approval to validate Clinton's signature on the document. There it encountered the same maelstrom of blue-collar backlash that had frustrated the NAFTA debate one year earlier. Like NAFTA, the GATT treaty had the procedural advantage of congressional "fast-track" status: it had to be voted either up or down, without amendments.

Laborers worrying about losing their jobs to cheap foreign wages were not the only opponents of the GATT. Isolationists like Pat Buchanan claimed U.S. sovereignty would be infringed on by the creation of a new trade bureaucracy (WTO) in Geneva. Some environmental NGOs, Greenpeace included, suggested that hard-fought ecological standards might be weakened by development-obsessed poor countries who would have a majority in the WTO. Protectionists like Emil Innocenti, owner of a small textile-dyeing business in New Jersey, feared being put out of business by unnecessary regulations.

Senator Ernest Hollings (D-SC) wanted to save the jobs of hundreds of thousands of textile workers in his home state. Radical right militia members predicted the WTO would help the "one-world conspiracy," but presented no evidence for their theory. Consumer activist Ralph Nader claimed that U.S. consumer rights could be endangered by the new WTO. Some local government officials pointed to the U.S.–Canadian trade pact, which had already challenged a Minnesota tax exemption for micro-breweries, as being unfair to big Canadian beer makers. Lane Kirkland of the AFL-CIO also demanded stronger labor regulations in the global treaty. Surely it was not a traditional liberal/conservative lineup that characterized the bloody fight over GATT approval.

Almost all economists and consumer groups favored the GATT. Among the prominent economists, Michael Boskin, former chief economic advisor to President Bush, argued that trade is "Not a zero-sum game where one side must lose what the other gains. Expanded trade is a positive-sum game, a potential win–win for all sides." He also noted that failure to approve the GATT would be disastrous to the world economy; he used the early 1930s—when protectionist tariffs reduced global trade by 75 percent, dooming the world to the Great Depression—as the worst-case scenario. A single-issue NGO, Alliance for GATT Now, calculated that GATT would add between $100 and $200 billion to the U.S. economy and create 1.4 million new jobs, while cutting tariffs by $744 billion worldwide. Alliance for GATT Now also said that the revised treaty would introduce new protection of **intellectual property** from piracy, an area of trade in which the United States had been burned badly by Chinese black market piracy of movies and popular music.

The Enterprise Institute and the Heritage Foundation, conservative Washington think tanks, applauded the agreement for "bringing the rule of law to international trade." Concerning the opponents' fear of an arbitrary WTO bureaucracy's stealing American sovereignty, Jeremy Rabkin pointed out that the WTO would have no army with which to enforce any decision that the United States might dislike, and that any member can withdraw from the WTO on six months' notice. The WTO would have no direct power over a huge trading country like the United States, although it might have a greater impact on smaller states. At the end of the struggle, President Clinton won congressional approval, and the new GATT treaty, creating the WTO, went into effect on January 1, 1995. But the depth of opposition to what economists almost universally considered beneficial to the United States reflected the anger felt by Americans forced to adjust to the vagaries of the new global economic order—an order evolving without American hegemony.[17]

U.S. Trade Frustration

During the heyday of the Cold War in the 1950s, President Dwight Eisenhower and his dour secretary of state, John Foster Dulles, made famous the policy of nuclear **brinkmanship.** In at least six instances, the United States used its nuclear advantage to seek diplomatic concessions from communist rivals by intimidation—a form of **compellance,** departing from the standard Cold War policy of nuclear **deterrence.** In the economy-driven 1990s, President Clinton engaged in a similar strategy that could be called **trade brinkmanship.** That is, using the huge U.S. trade volume to try to intimidate problematic trade partners with the threat of trade sanctions.

What basic problem was the U.S. trying to rectify through trade brinkmanship? Its massive trade deficit, averaging $170 billion annually since the mid-1980s. When the value of a country's imports exceeds the value of its exports, it must pay for the difference in some **convertible currency.** If it becomes large and chronic, a trade deficit constitutes a drain on the rest of the economy, inhibiting growth, savings, confidence, and investment.

Trade: Once a Means, Now an End in Itself

Having exceeded $4 trillion annually, world trade has become essential to economic growth. Once used largely as a means toward political or military ends, trade is now a coveted end in itself. Examples of past presidents using trade as a political club arise easily: President John Kennedy imposing Cuban trade sanctions to protest the communist Castro regime; most-favored-nation trade status denied to North Korea and Vietnam because they were communist countries; President Jimmy Carter levying trade sanctions against the Soviet Union after its 1979 invasion of Afghanistan; President Ronald Reagan's 1982 ban on trade with Libya because of state-sponsored terrorism; President George Bush's continuation of trade sanctions against South Africa for its apartheid policies. However, when President Bill Clinton uncoupled human rights concerns from the issue of MFN status for China in June 1994, he highlighted a shift already underway: playing political football with trade no longer makes good economic sense.

Pacific U.S. Trade Headaches

Contemporary U.S. trade with Europe, the Americas, and the former Soviet Union proceeds fairly smoothly. The largest trade relationship in the world, that between the United States and Canada, is a model of comity and mutual benefit. Canada runs a $12 billion surplus in merchandise goods, balancing out an almost equal U.S. surplus in services. In 1995 the two-way North American trade in merchandise goods alone was growing by $900 million per week.[18]

America's trading headaches originate mostly in Asia, home to nearly half the world's population and most of its hottest economies. Asia's economic giant, Japan, producing two-thirds the American GDP with only half the population, has long sent U.S. presidents in search of an economy-sized bottle of aspirin. The United States trades with over 170 countries, yet fully one-third of its annual trade deficit derives from trade with Japan. Presidents Nixon, Ford,

Figure 11.6

Source: H Payne, *Scripps-Howard* (April 1994).

Carter, Reagan, and Bush all used quiet diplomacy behind the scenes to address the problem. The results were mostly vague Japanese promises to open their markets wider to American products in the future. The situation created the kind of frustration captured in Figure 11.6.

Shaken by a record deficit with Japan of $60 billion in 1993, President Bill Clinton decided to follow a more public, assertive, and quantitative path. He and his U.S. trade representative, Mickey Kantor, began following a "results-oriented" policy: requiring measurable progress in market access for American goods, sector by Japanese sector. Demanding quantitative progress in thirty-one areas, such as insurance services, medical equipment, telecommunications, and auto parts, they promised to invoke punitive tariffs on specified Japanese goods if results were not forthcoming.

To everyone's relief, the United States did not invoke sanctions, which could have led to a disastrous trade war. But no sooner had Japan met one quota than the Clinton administration imposed another deadline for avoiding sanctions. Trade brinkmanship's tough line seemed popular with an American public generally unimpressed by Clinton's foreign policy record. Still, trade brinkmanship involves risks reminiscent of those run by Eisenhower's nuclear brinkmanship forty years earlier—although in this case the threat was a trade war rather than a nuclear war.

Gung Ho (1987) Reflects the Cultural Chasm

Ron Howard's humorous film *Gung Ho* (1986), starring Michael Keaton, measures the cultural chasm separating the American and Japanese in their economic relations, and finds it to be extra large. Filmed in eastern-Ohio rust-belt towns, *Gung Ho* amplifies the dissonant noise stemming from the resurrection of an auto plant by Japanese investors. The film's motif begins and ends with clashing cultures. In between, American workers find themselves in a purgatory of futile resistance to the inscrutable ways of Japanese management.

American individualism versus Japanese communitarianism—therein lies the rub of both the general cultural impasse and the palpable tension in *Gung Ho*. Many of the same disconcerting points about Japanese transplants in America are made in a book of interviews by Laurie Graham, *On the Line at Subaru-Isuzu: The Japanese Model and the American Worker* (1996).

MINI-CASE 11.5
Motorola and the Japanese Market

Motorola represents the quintessential American success story on the global economic stage. Its 1980s management did all the right things that eluded corporate giants like IBM, Kodak, and Xerox. Motorola not only took the obvious steps of streamlining its workforce and reorganizing its management structure, it also opened communications between management and labor, invested aggressively in research and development, engaged in long-range planning, internationalized its operations, and took risks on new products. The payoffs were immense, with Motorola holding 40 percent of the world's booming cellular phone business by the early 1990s. But in Japan a different story played itself out.

In 1987 the Japanese government divided Japan into two cellular phone regions. In the more profitable Tokyo region, Motorola phones were incompatible with the transmitting systems set up by their Japanese competitor. Motorola protested to the U.S. government, which achieved a 1989 agreement promising Motorola "comparable market access" in Tokyo. In 1992 and 1994 Motorola lodged complaints about a lack of results. In 1995 President Clinton and Mickey Kantor went public, boldly criticizing Japan of "a clear-cut and serious case of failing to live up to its commitments" and threatening sanctions if progress failed to materialize. As usual, shortly before the deadline, enough progress was reported to avoid the imposition of trade sanctions.[19]

Intellectual Property in China

Another vexing problem the United States faces is policing its heavy **services trade** exports, such as films, insurance, banking, computer software, and music. This service export emphasis contrasts sharply with the **merchandise trade** that characterizes most American imports. In the 1990s conflicts over copyright piracy occurred mainly with the source of America's second-highest trade deficit ($39 billion in 1996)—China.

With its more than one billion people and annual economic growth exceeding 10 percent, communist China has become the "mother of all emerging markets," currently ranking second only to the United States in attracting **direct foreign investment** ($31 billion in 1994). But, while U.S. corporations like Gillette razors, Polaroid cameras, Lotus software, Lehman Brothers investors, and McDonald's hamburgers are all eagerly mining the Chinese gold rush, piracy has devastated the profits of some corporations.

Clinton's trade representative, Mickey Kantor, claimed that U.S. companies lost $1 billion in 1994 to copyright theft, with nearly 100 percent of videotapes and 94 percent of computer programs sold in China illegally. More than twenty factories in southern China produced over 75 million pirated compact discs per year, mostly for the export market. The United States had been negotiating with China since 1992 to tighten its intellectual property rights laws, but enforcement continued to be very lax.

In a carbon copy of Clinton's trade policy toward Japan, the strategy with China consisted of (1) threatening trade sanctions if progress was not made in certain sectors (2) negotiating to achieve specified standards by a certain date, and (3) reaching an eleventh-hour agreement, narrowly staving off sanctions and a possible trade war. With China, the demands included removing trade barriers to legal American films, music, and computer products so as to lower demand for pirated products; cracking down on illegal production (mostly in the form of compact discs); and dropping barriers to agricultural products like wheat and citrus fruits.

A February 28, 1995, deadline was set. Pending improvements, the United States pledged to impose punitive 100 percent tariffs on twenty-three categories of Chinese products, ranging from toys to watches to athletic shoes. Chinese officials promised to retaliate against American cigarettes, alcohol, and cosmetics, if necessary. Can a viable long-term trade policy operate on the basis of threats, negotiations, and last-minute agreements?[20] What do you think?

Normalizing Trade with Vietnam

President Clinton was also studying U.S. trade deficits with other Asian countries, such as Taiwan. Despite having only 20 million people, Taiwan has a vibrant economy that exports $26 billion in goods, for a trade surplus of about $9 billion with America. In addition to playing trade brinkmanship with old partners, the Clinton administration also looked to open new Asian markets for U.S. goods, especially in Vietnam. Under the name of *doi moi,* Vietnam has been conducting its own Chinese-style market reforms, including opening the country to Western investment. Communist Prime Minister Vo Van Kiet expressed a most un-communist-sounding goal: "To make our people rich." Starting from a paltry base ($200 GNP per capita), Vietnam has a long way to go before rivaling the Asian miracles of South Korea, Taiwan, or Malaysia. However, it has a literate population of 60 million as well as assets such as oil and timber, and many MNCs are looking to expand there, including Mobil Oil, Coca Cola, American Express, and United Airlines.

A major step toward Vietnam's economic renaissance was taken in 1994, when President Clinton lifted a thirty-year-old U.S. trade embargo. Only because of Vietnam's trading potential was Clinton willing to take the flak he received from veterans' groups for lifting the embargo. There are seventy listed cases of American soldiers who are missing in action and may have been captured alive, but veterans' groups claim the real number is actually much higher. As an active protestor against America's Vietnam War in the 1960s, President Clinton found himself vulnerable to criticism from military groups uncomfortable with his seemingly incompatible role as armed forces commander-in-chief. Until the Vietnamese government provides more help accounting for MIAs, veterans' groups will remain critical of Clinton's opening trade ties with Vietnam.[21]

Trade may represent the most frustrating area for the United States in the post-Cold War era, but it is not the only one. In many areas the once-dominant economic hegemon seems to be tiring on the world stage while other aggressive and talented players take over the spotlight from time to time. In addition to trade deficits and federal budget deficits, the U.S. economy in the early 1990's suffered from low national savings rates, excessive consumption based on credit, as well as decreasing worker productivity. Although no longer the global hegemon, however, America still boasts the largest economy as well as the potential to rebound from some economic hard knocks. What specific kinds of economic institutions, human and nonhuman resources, and economic climate does the United States have at its disposal to revitalize its global role?

U.S. ECONOMIC CLIMATE AND INSTITUTIONS

In both human and nonhuman resources, America's raw materials for economic regeneration are immense and unrivaled. The United States is blessed with one-third of the world's coal reserves, even more of the world's natural gas, massive fresh water supplies, extensive forests, metals and ores in abundance, fertile farmland, and favorable weather conditions. Human resources among its 250 million citizens are no less impressive, including cutting-edge high technology skills, a rich entrepreneurial tradition, a ranking of second on the Human Development Index, per capita GNP of about $24,000, life expectancy of 76 years, an abundant immigration-fueled labor pool, and the most accessible higher education system in the world.

America's business climate is similarly conducive to economic success. Social values inherent in educational and other kinds of institutions favor a business orientation. The pervasive Protestant work ethic virtually equates business success with divine approval. The political system is stable enough to encourage foreign investment in American enterprises. Private ownership of the means of production is higher than in other advanced economies, like Japan or the European countries. Even many utilities, such as power companies, are extraordinary in their level of private ownership in the United States. When inevitable dips occur in the business cycle, U.S. governmental fiscal and monetary actions have become increasingly adept at softening hardships. American values include strong backing for the economic system and confidence in its inherent capabilities.

Regulated Capitalism in America

The modern U.S. economy provides a relatively free market. It leans toward capitalism more than most other mixed-market developed countries. Its system might be most aptly described as **regulated capitalism.** Three forms of business organization characterize the American experience. The most important in the earlier stages of U.S. economic history was the **individual proprietorship,** which still ranks as the most common form, although its share of the market has waned. Often people pool their resources and skills when establishing a business or when expanding or merging existing businesses, and the result is the **partnership.** Individual proprietorships and partnerships are more vital to the economies of Japan, France, and Italy, where small businesses play a big role, than in the United States, where large **corporations** rule the roost.

Corporate America

The legal status of a corporation is established by its receipt of a charter from the government, giving the corporate business a personal identity of sorts, with certain rights and duties. Like you and me, a corporation pays taxes and can be summoned into court for a lawsuit. Managerial expertise is the backbone of corporate structure, which in America tends to be quite large. At the apex of the corporation are the chief executive officer (CEO), chairman of the board of directors, and senior vice-presidents. A power elite of relatively few people run America's corporations, in a manner described by corporate lawyer A. A. Berle, Jr., as a "self-perpetuating oligarchy."[22] America's corporate elites are also paid much better than their counterparts in other industrialized countries: annual salaries and benefits of several million dollars are typical for CEO's in the 500 largest corporations.

Economic Sectors Ready for Globalism

At least part of the U.S. economy must be doing something right: the 1996 figures based on 230 criteria analyzed in the World Competitiveness Yearbook ranked America number one after a hiatus of a few years dominated by Japan.[23] An economy as large as America's consists of various segments known as economic **sectors.** What are the prospects for the major sectors of the U.S. economy in a globally competitive age? Services, finance, and agriculture have all the tools to continue doing well globally. The other two major sectors, however, manufacturing and labor, seem to be in trouble.

To call the United States a tertiary economy these days is not an exaggeration, since over half of GDP now derives from service sector activities like medical services, legal services, education, and popular entertainment. No tangible goods are produced in the service sector. While we have traditionally been accustomed to thinking of productivity in concrete terms of physical goods, we must adapt to the fact that high value is placed on the intangibles provided by modern service economies.

The financial sector features institutions set up to transfer money between borrowers and savers. The world of finance is undergoing dramatic electronic innovations, speeding up every form of financial transaction and weakening borders as barriers to global finance. Americans have created much of the software that drives today's automatic teller machines (ATMs), enabling us to bank at all hours without interacting with a human employee of the bank, and we are well positioned to capitalize on the new world order in banking. The bankers' bank in the U.S. economy is the Federal Reserve System, better known as the Fed, where banks can deposit money and borrow, just as we do at our banks. The Fed, founded in 1914 to regulate money and banking, was one of the earliest governmental regulatory institutions.

The third sector positioned to do well globally is the agricultural sector. One of the most fundamental changes in American history has been the urbanization of its population. Now three-quarters urban, a century ago it was three-quarters rural, with the family farm as the basic socioeconomic unit. A clear majority of Americans labored on farms in those days; today a mere 3 percent work in agriculture. Yet the seeming anomaly is that relatively few Americans produce enough food to feed not only other Americans, but a significant chunk of the world as well. The answer, of course, lies in the massive size of today's **agribusiness.** The family farm is obsolete; huge corporations using chemical-intensive methods, irrigation, and even genetic engineering of plants, are in. The ecological costs of American agribusiness are sizable and will be addressed in chapter 14. However, if viewed only from the perspective of economic productivity and competitiveness, the output of the American agricultural sector is unprecedented.

Sectors Overwhelmed by the Global Market

The prospects for the manufacturing and labor sectors of the economy seem unlikely to rival those of the service, financial, and agricultural sectors any time soon. If you travel anywhere on the northern tier along U.S. Interstate 90 between Buffalo and Chicago, you will get a sense of the massive hollowing out of America's rust belt that has occurred since the 1970s. Here the plight of the manufacturing and labor sectors come together in vivid relief. Where once stood robust factories working three shifts daily to meet back orders of steel, aluminum, and automobiles, you would now witness many empty, run-down shells with broken windows to match the broken hearts of laid-off union laborers and their families. Such are the dislocations caused by a global economy in which manufactured goods are produced more cheaply in Tunisia or Taiwan or Turkey.

The U.S. manufacturing sector has slipped to a mere 20 percent of GDP, and with aging factories, high labor costs, adversarial management-labor relations, and many new global competitors, it is hard to imagine the sector that produces tangible goods doing well.

When times are difficult in the manufacturing sector, the profile of the labor sector will also look unappealing. The labor sector provides the workers required by enterprises to produce whatever kind of output they seek to distribute. Only 15 percent of U.S. workers today work in the labor sector.

In general, American labor had it much better over the last fifty years. The growth in size and influence of labor unions in the 1930s was facilitated by popular sympathy for workers during the Great Depression, leading to the passage of the National Labor Relations Act of 1935, a law favorable to organized labor. In most states, the unions have enjoyed the right to **collective bargaining,** which has provided some leverage in negotiations with management. The United Auto Workers (UAW), United Mine Workers (UMW), and the Teamsters (truckers) epitomized labor's higher profile days.

The arrival of labor as a major player on the American political scene did not occur without courageous organizers taking great risks. John Sayles's gripping film, *Matewan* (1987), uses a real-life company-directed massacre of striking West Virginia coal miners to illustrate the violent nature of unionism's baptism by fire in America. These same unions played a key role in converting the market economy from the brutal and impersonal enrichment of the few at the expense of the many, a situation condemned by Karl Marx, into the safety net featuring unemployment insurance, social security, Medicare, food stamps, and welfare benefits for our less fortunate citizens.

Chapter Synopsis

The quantitative nature of economics has facilitated the rigorous application of scientific methods as has no other social science. But since economic institutions are human institutions, the unpredictability of the human element also bleeds through the elegant mathematical models devised by economists. How humans deal with the scarcity of goods and services derives from both objective and subjective factors. In the twentieth century, command, capitalist, and traditional models have dominated the competitive discourse concerning economic form and structure. In the longer historical evolution traceable to the early Middle Ages, feudalism eventually gave way to mercantilism, which in turn gave way to the market economy. In the wake of Marxian socialism's demise, the principal intellectual battle in the 1990s is between two variants of the market economy: individualistic capitalism and communitarian capitalism.Macro-level economics has generally dominated the scene during the heyday of the nation–state for the last 350 years. Many objective measures of pro-

ductivity have been devised to assess the performance of macro-level economies. Among them, GNP, GNP per capita, NNP, HDI, growth rate, balance of payments, and trade balance have been emphasized as important. The most important new reality in recent decades, however, has been the globalization of economics and the blending together of micro, macro, and mega levels of analysis as interdependent. In this context, international trade has assumed a vital role and heated battles have been fought between the forces of free trade and protectionism. The domestic struggle in the United States over the NAFTA and WTO treaties typified this toe-to-toe shouting match profoundly affecting economic winners and losers in the global economy.

After World War II the United States assumed the role that Britain had filled during the previous century: global economic hegemon. Forced to take on many new responsibilities, the United States created the Bretton Woods system of institutions intended to rebuild the world economy under the banner of free and open trade, with the United States poised to benefit from the highly competitive quality of its postwar goods and services. However, by the 1970s and 1980s the hegemonic U.S. posture was being challenged by competitors from Europe and Asia. By the 1990s, true hegemony was a luxury of the past for the United States, yet as the world's largest, most diverse, and (once again) most productive economy, it remains the single most important national player, albeit a less dominant one. Expanding exports has been a major objective of recent U.S. administrations, and trade deficits with Asian competitors has become a serious political issue worrying recent U.S. presidents.

For Digging Deeper

Bleaney, Michael. *The Rise and Fall of Keynesian Economics*. St. Martin's Press, 1984.

Byrns, Ralph T., and Gerald W. Stone. *Economics*. HarperCollins, 1993.

De Borchgrave, Arnaud. *Russian Organized Crime*. CSIS Books, 1996.

Galbraith, John K. *The Culture of Contentment*. Houghton Mifflin, 1992.

Gottheil, Fred. *Principles of Macroeconomics*. South-Western, 1996.

Heilbroner, Robert L., and Lester C. Thurow. *Economics Explained*. Simon & Schuster, 1982.

Horvat, Branko. *The Political Economy of Socialism: A Marxist Social Theory*. M.E. Sharpe, 1982.

Kent, Calvin A., Ed. *Entrepreneurship and the Privatizing of Government*. Greenwood, 1987.

Lazonick, William. *Business Organization and the Myth of the Market Economy*. Cambridge University, 1991.

Malkin, Lawrence. *The National Debt*. Mentor, 1988.

Reich, Robert B. *The Work of Nations*. Knopf, 1991.

Temin, Peter. *Lessons from the Great Depression*. MIT Press, 1989.

Thurow, Lester C. *Head to Head: The Coming Economic Battle among Japan, Europe, and America*. Morrow, 1992.

Weber, Max. *The Protestant Ethic and the Spirit of Capitalism*. Scribner, 1958.

Weintraub, Sidney. *NAFTA at Three: A Progress Report*. CSIS Books, 1997.

Internet

Data Map of U.S. http://www.census.gov/datamap/index.html
National Technical Information Service (NTIS) http://wnc.fedwork.gov
Statistical Abstract of the U.S]http://www.census.gov:80/stat_abstract/

Key Glossary Terms

agribusiness	budget deficit	cartel
bartering	business cycle	collective bargaining
Bretton Woods Conference	capital	command model
brinkmanship	capitalist model	communist economies

communitarian capitalism
compellence
convertible currency
corporate culture
corporation
cost-push inflation
demand
demand-pull inflation
deterrence
direct foreign investment
downsizing
economic hegemon
economic sectors
economic wants
economics
economies of scale
entrepreneurship
equilibrium price
factors of production
feudalism
firm
fiscal policy
Fordism
free trade
General Agreement on Tariffs
and Trade (GATT)

government
Great Depression
gross domestic product (GDP)
gross national product (GNP)
household
hyperfactualism
individual proprietorship
individualistic capitalism
Industrial Revolution
infant industries
inflation
institution
intellectual property
labor
land
market
mercantilism
merchandise trade
Middle Ages
mixed-market economy
monetary policy
money
monopoly
neo-classical school
net national product (NNP)
nontariff barriers

North American Free Trade
Agreement (NAFTA)
partnership
Per capita GDP
Per capita GNP
primary economy
protectionism
recession
regulated capitalism
secondary economy
services trade
socialism
state economic monopoly
strategic industries
supply
tariff
terms of trade
tertiary economy
Third World diversification
totalitarianism
trade brinkmanship
trade deficit
trade surplus
traditional model
underground economy
Uruguay Round

CHAPTER 12

International Economics

CORE OBJECTIVE

To outline the changing nature of the international economic system and some of the major theoretical interpretations of its behavior.

Thematic Questions

- Where and how does interdependence manifest itself in the international economy?

- What considerations account for the transition from mercantilist to free-trade philosophies?

- What are the causes and possible cures for southern hemisphere poverty?

- In what ways has the end of the Cold War affected the substance and process of international economics?

The theme of **interdependence** bubbles up through the pages of this book as regularly as the geyser known as Old Faithful at Yellowstone Park. One of the most important examples of interdependence is in the emerging seamless economic web tying humans together at every level of organization, as well as between levels. Whether the level is micro (local), macro (national), or mega (global), dynamic forces of market economics serve to link people together, significantly reducing isolation in the process. The old line dividing the domestic economy from the international economy has blurred almost to the point of irrelevance. All these trends mean that your existence and mine are more immediately and deeply affected by economic happenings in faraway places.

Since we no longer have the option of considering events in distant places merely as "their problem," let's examine some of the forces of economic interdependence tugging at our consciousness. We will look at what has traditionally been called international economics—what in reality consists of mostly orderly interactions between affluent northerners. Next we will examine the more contentious economic agenda of poor South against rich North, which generates considerably more sparks. But we will trace briefly the historical evolution of the modern international economy.

INTERNATIONAL ECONOMIC CHRONOLOGY

- **1500–1920:** European powers colonize much of world
- **1750–1825:** English Industrial Revolution results in accumulation of great wealth in Britain
- **1839–1842:** Opium War—Chinese attempts to halt English sale of opium in China fail; British power increases
- **1848:** Karl Marx's *Communist Manifesto* advocates proletarian revolution against oppressive bourgeoisie
- **1850–1900:** growth in trade accompanies spread of Industrial Revolution to America and Europe
- **1860:** Chevalier Treaty—MFN trade status created in Franco-British agreement
- **1870s:** U.S. railroads transport American grain for sale in Europe, reducing prices and causing protectionist backlash
- **1870–1914:** gold standard of fixed exchange rates
- **1914–1918:** World War I—system of international trade crumbles; France and Britain much in debt to the United States
- **1924:** Dawes Plan—monetary plan for U.S. loans to Germany to pay reparations to France and Britain, who then pay the United States
- **1928:** Fed—jacked-up interest rates break the monetary cycle of the Dawes Plan, creating a crisis in the German economy
- **1929:** Crash—U.S. stock market in October collapse
- **1930:** Smoot-Hawley—high U.S. tariff leads to trade war and exacerbates economic failure

- **1939–1945:** World War II—only the United States emerges from the ashes of war as economic hegemon
- **1945–1973:** Bretton Woods system—fixed-rate gold/dollar exchange system bolsters U.S. role as leader of free trade
- **1946:** World Bank—global lending role
- **1947:** IMF—currency exchange rate stabilization
- **1947:** GATT—global trade expansion via tariff reductions
- **1947–1991:** Cold War aid—United States and USSR use economic aid as a tool to fight the Cold War
- **1960:** OPEC—thirteen nations join oil cartel aiming to control world production (supply)
- **1960s–1970s:** nationalization—many poor countries take over MNC operations in their countries, increasing the trend toward government ownership
- **1971:** the Nixon shocks—the United States withdraws from fixed conversion exchange system based on the dollar; slaps on wage and price controls and protectionist trade measures
- **1973:** free floating currency—U.S. unilateralism leads to the collapse of the Bretton Woods system
- **1973 and 1979:** oil shocks—OPEC production quotas lead to lower supply and great demand and price increases for "black gold"
- **1974:** NIEO—poor countries organize their bargaining position with an explicit agenda of complaints
- **1979–1983:** global recession—growing debt of Third World countries worsened by deep recession
- **1980s–1990s:** privatization—global trend shifts toward reduced governmental ownership and return of industries to the private sector
- **1991:** Gulf War—the United States leads military action to protect oil supplies and allies pay much of the bill
- **1994:** The United States continues MFN trade status for China; NAFTA takes effect; the United States lifts trade embargo against Vietnam
- **1995:** WTO—Uruguay Round of GATT succeeds in expanding GATT into the Geneva-based trade organization, the WTO, with provisions for further reduction of trade barriers[1]

EVOLUTION OF THE INTERNATIONAL ECONOMY

In *A Concise Economic History of the World from Paleolithic Times to the Present*, Rondo Cameron chronicles the long and winding commercial road followed by the traders who have linked together all types of societies, from simple to complex, and from near to far, since ancient times. Trade and exchange—whether by barter or monetary means—have always played

Table 12.1 British Industrial Dominance, 1800, 1860, and 1913 per capita level of industrialization; (Britain in 1900 = 100)

1800		1860		1913	
Britain	16	Britain	64	United States	126
Belgium	10	Belgium	28	Britain	115
Switzerland	10	Switzerland	26	Belgium	88
France	9	United States	21	Switzerland	87
Netherlands	9	France	20	Germany	85
Norway	9	Germany	15	Sweden	67
United States	9	Sweden	15	France	59
Germany	8	Norway	11	Canada	46
Sweden	8	Netherlands	11	Denmark	33
Denmark	8	Austria-Hungary	11	Austria-Hungary	32
Austria-Hungary	7	Denmark	10	Norway	31
Japan	(7)	Japan	(7)	Japan	20

Numbers in parentheses are best-guess estimates.
Source: Herman Schwartz, States Versus Markets (St. Martin's, 1994), P. 89. Data from Paul Bairoch, "International Industrialization Levels from 1750–1980," *Journal of European Economic History, 11*, no. 2 (Fall 1982), 281, 286, 330.

a vital role in the global human drama.[2] With the Industrial Revolution, however, an exponential increase in trade and financial flow rippled from the shores of the British Isles during the eighteenth century. High agricultural productivity, a mobile labor market, and available capital allowed Britain to ride the engine of the Industrial Revolution all the way to global hegemonic status as the greatest naval and commercial power in the 1800s, as is shown in Table 12.1.England's landed gentry class had enjoyed the benefit of protectionist trade measures enacted in its behalf by the British Parliament. These tariffs, quotas, and other limitations on imported goods made such purchases more expensive for the British public in general but benefited the class of landowners. Britain's mercantilist trade policy had been well established for quite some time, and its rural elite must have been distraught and perplexed when Parliament repealed its protectionist barriers, known collectively as the **British Corn Laws**, in 1846.

Political scientist Robert Gilpin emphasizes the significance of England's moving in mid-century to a new economic policy based on the classical economic formulations of Adam Smith and David Ricardo, both of whom considered a free and open trading system as the golden route to both economic gain and cooperative ventures in related areas.[3]

Britain and Free Trade

Given Britain's international clout at the time, when it talked a new game of free trade, other countries listened. They also took similar actions to ease existing trade limitations. As early as 1860 an important precedent was set with the Franco-British Chevalier Treaty, establishing **most-**

favored-nation (MFN) trade status, making British textiles and stoneware cheaper in France, and French wine and cheese less dear in Britain. According to Rondo Cameron, the next couple of decades witnessed the freest trade in Europe of any time prior to World War II.[4]

Greater economic interdependence was a by-product of the trade explosion of the nineteenth century. So was the rapid growth of the United States, France, and Germany as viable competitors hoping to catch up with British power and wealth. Technological innovations added to the expansion mania of the latter 1800s. America's railroads enabled it to transport grain and manufactured goods for export to the European market during the heady days of the U.S. post-Civil War Gilded Age.

While the international economy continued to grow until the outbreak of World War I in 1914, familiarity seems to have bred discontent among the countries now linked together by trade. Political scientist Steven Spiegel says that two main factors contributed to strife and a return to more protectionist trade policies among the great powers: (1) competition for international markets had become intense, since politically sensitive governments sought to shelter their at-risk industries; and (2) there was a resurgence of nationalistic pride in many countries, particularly Germany and Italy. With the new nationalism came increased expenditures for national defense; tariffs helped raise funds for the military. Amid increasing disarray, the fixed exchange system known as the **gold standard** stood solid as Gibraltar, and all nations continued to set the value of their currencies to gold until 1914.[5]

World War I's Unfinished Economic Business

The great toll of World War I was measured not only in war dead and in reduced political power for many nations, but also in economic costs, which were staggering. The United States, serving as the "arsenal for democracy," was the only major economic winner. As fighting drew to a close, America's industrial muscles were both flexed and bulging. The major defeated nation, Germany, faced crippling **reparations** payments to the two victors who demanded them: Britain and France. In turn, these two victors owed the United States more than $10 billion each in war debts.

An ingenious solution to this seeming dilemma was created in 1924 in the form of the **Dawes Plan**, essentially a win–win–win resolution of the impasse over postwar payments. U.S. sources lent money to Germany, who used it to pay its reparations to France and Britain, who then were able to pay their war debts to the United States. The cyclical monetary solution of the Dawes Plan worked until 1928. In that year the American stock market was booming out of sight as a result of highly speculative investments.

In response, the American institution responsible for monetary policy, the Fed, was nervous over market speculation and decided to raise interest rates to slow down the market as well as the economy in general. However, inadvertently the Fed's move also frightened international investors, and the cycle of the Dawes Plan was broken, replaced by economic nationalism, which made things even worse. The German economy collapsed altogether amid unbelievable levels of **hyperinflation** and political instability. The stock market crashed in 1929, the *Smoot-Hawley tariff* passed Congress in 1930, and the gold standard was a relic of the past by the time the Great Depression settled in for a decade-long disaster.

The leaders of the seven leading economic powers (G-7) prepare to give the final report after their summit meeting held in Miami, Florida in 1975.

American Hegemony and the Bretton Woods System

The mammoth dislocations of World War II finally ended the Depression and created a new global economic hegemon in the United States. The Bretton Woods system, which came out of the 1944 Bretton Woods Conference, beautifully served America's goals. It regulated trade under U.S. leadership and pushed the world toward freer trade, especially with the biggest market: America. A fixed exchange rate based on the dollar's value in gold at $35 per ounce stabilized financial exchanges. Global lending institutions helped to funnel U.S. economic aid to finance reconstruction of allies and enemies alike.

The late 1940s and 1950s could hardly have unfolded more favorably for U.S. global economic policy. By 1971, however, the United States had to give up its ephemeral run as global hegemon; it looked to multilateral help from its allies, largely through the annual summits of the **Group of Seven (G-7)** leading industrial powers. The G-7 became the G-8 with the admission of Russia in 1994. The United States withdrew its support for the fixed-dollar exchange rate system, which was soon replaced by a free-floating (supply-and-demand) currency exchange rate that changed from day to day. By the time of the two oil shocks of the 1970s, the Third World countries served notice through the OPEC cartel that business as usual had ceased.

In 1974 the formalization of the New International Economic Order (NIEO) gave flesh and blood to poor countries' demands to assist them in competing globally. By the 1980s and 1990s a wave a privatization accompanied a global trend toward democratization and contributed to many governments' divesting themselves of industries seized during a rash of nationalization during the 1950s and 1960s. Principles of free market economics have clearly enjoyed a renaissance in recent years, reversing much of the earlier momentum toward government ownership in many parts of the world.

The economic distance between different peoples has shrunk; even the remotest so-cieties are becoming aware of how the shrinking world affects them. Global wealth has been fed largely by huge increases in trade volume, and nothing symbolizes interdepen-dence more than trade. MNCs have also gotten bigger and more ubiquitous as their eco-nomic tentacles reach out to every part of the globe. The collapse of communism and the victory of the idea of democratic capitalism have hastened some of these changes. Yet many of them were well underway decades ago and developed rather independently of the Cold War and its demise.

THEORY OF INTERNATIONAL TRADE AND FINANCE
Trade

A century or two ago it was conceivable for a country to seek what economists call **autarky**, or economic self-sufficiency. Autarky is no longer a realistic goal. Since valued natural resources like oil, gold, coal, forests, and water, as well as human resources such as education, techno-logical skill, entrepreneurship, and cultural homogeneity, are found sporadically around the world, societies find it mutually beneficial to trade for what they lack. It is not even necessary for a society to have an **absolute advantage** in producing a good—say, sombreros in Mexi-co—in order to trade that item. All that is required for trade is that it have a **comparative ad-vantage** in sombrero production.

The British economic philosopher David Ricardo (1772–1823) was the first to illus-trate the mathematical justifications for comparative advantage and thus free trade, cap-sulized in Table 12.2. Every country benefits from exporting those goods in which it has a comparative advantage. Mexico may not be number one in their production, but if churning out sombreros is what it does relatively well, then it should trade them for goods in which it has a comparative disadvantage, say, ice skates from Canada. "Mutual gains will lead to spe-cialization in each country, making goods less expensive and production more efficient for both."[6] The idea of comparative advantage has become so well ingrained into classical eco-nomic theory that many economists now consider it to be a **scientific law** rather than mere-ly a theory; it is one of the most potent arguments in favor of free trade.

Not everyone is convinced by the smooth logic of comparative advantage and free trade. Its very antithesis, protectionism, often arises when great pressure is placed on legislatures to enact laws shielding faltering domestic industries from foreign competition. Protectionism is a short-term political expedient often criticized by economists but tolerated as an inevitable part of the human drama by political scientists. On this issue, economists tend to embrace the spirit of what we have been referring to as idealism, whereas political scientists often view protectionism from a realist perspective.

Tariffs used to be the most common form of protectionism, until the disastrous Smoot-Hawley tariff of 1930 gave all direct taxes on imports a bad name when it raised them to record levels of 60 percent. In 1933 retaliatory tariffs had cut world trade to a mere one-third of its 1929 level.[7] A half-century of U.S. cheerleading for the GATT treaty also encouraged tariff re-ductions, which have accompanied each successive negotiated round of the GATT.[8] Newer

Table 12.2 Comparative Advantage and the Gains from Trade

Start with two countries, such as Japan and the United States. Each produces cameras and computers. Assume that the hypothetical figures below show output per hour for workers in each country.

	Worker Productivity	
	Japan	*United States*
Units of camera output per hour	9	4
Units of computer output per hour	3	2

Clearly Japan has an absolute advantage in both products, as Japanese workers are more productive in turning out cameras and computers than the American workers. Does this mean the two countries cannot benefit by trading with one another? If trade does occur, should each country continue to allocate its resources as in the past? The answer to both questions is no.

Each country should specialize in that item in which it has the greatest comparative cost advantage or least comparative cost disadvantage, and trade with others. Because Japan is three times more productive in cameras than computers, it should direct more of its resources into the photographic industry. One cost of doing so is lost computer output, but Japan can turn out three additional camera units for every computer unit given up. The United States, on the other hand, can obtain only two computer units.

Like their Japanese counterparts, American workers are also more productive in making cameras than computers. Still, U.S. resources should be directed to computers because the United States is at a smaller disadvantage compared with Japan in this area. If the United States specialized in computers and Japan in cameras and they trade with one another, each will benefit. The following scenario shows why.

Begin with 100 workers in each industry before specialization:

Japanese Output
Cameras: 900
Computers: 300

United States' Output
Cameras: 400
Computers: 200

Shift 10 Japanese workers from computer to camera production; Shift 20 American workers from camera production to computers:

Japanese Output
Cameras: 990
Computers: 270

United States' Output
Cameras: 320
Computers: 240

Trade 80 Japanese cameras to the United States ; Trade 30 American computers to Japan

Japanese Benefits from Trade
Cameras: 910
Computers: 300

United States' Benefits from Trade
Cameras: 400
Computers: 210

By shifting Japanese resources into the production of cameras and U.S. resources into computers, the same total inputs will cause camera and computer output to rise 10 units each. The reason is that resources are now being used more efficiently. Benefits to both countries can be realized when each trades some of its additional output for the other's. Japan ends up with more cameras than before specialization and trade and with the same quantity of computers, while the United States finds itself with more computers and the same number of cameras. More output in both countries means higher living standards.

The message derived from the logic of comparative advantage is clear. If all countries were to concentrate on those products they can produce most efficiently, the world's output and income would increase, and everyone's standard of living would rise.

Source: Charles Kegley and Eugen Wittkopf, *World Politics: Trend and Transformation,* (St. Martin's , 1997), p. 208.

Imported Japanese cars being un-loaded on a New Jersey dock.

nontariff barriers (NTBs) are more subtle in creating an obstacle course for free trade. Restriction through product **quality standards** has become common. For example, when California placed rigorous emission controls on all cars sold there, it became impossible for autos from certain countries to meet its tough clean air standards.

Limits on the number of units for a given commodity can also cut down on imports. These **import quotas** may directly restrict the number of items which a foreign company can sell in the United States, or they may more informally negotiate for limits. An example of the latter case occurred in 1980. With Detroit's Big Three lagging behind the fuel-efficient imports, the U.S. government placed pressure on the Japanese to accept so-called **voluntary export restraints (VERs)**, which continue today to limit the number of Japanese cars unloaded onto American docks.

MINI-CASE 12.1
VERs and Japanese Autos

Japanese automobiles were not the first goods from that country to be subject to protectionist quotas by the United States. In the 1950s Japanese textiles were also limited by a seemingly voluntary arrangement actually bordering on threat.[9] The term "voluntary export restraints" is a misnomer, for it usually implies retaliation if a bilateral trading partner fails to limit the number of units imported into our domestic market. In other words, it is a form of "voluntary coercion" allowing us to restrict imports while continuing to pay lip service to the abstract concept of free trade. VERs are informal bilateral arrangements which are not supposed to supersede principles, procedures, or commitments called for under global treaties such as the GATT. In reality, they often violate at least the spirit of the GATT, yet they manage to fall through the legal cracks because of their nonbinding and unofficial nature.[10]

In 1980 the world had just endured a decade of oil shocks and tenfold increases in crude oil prices. American automakers, failing to heed the Japanese subcompact lesson, continued building large gas-guzzlers. Protectionist political pressure was building up to shield America's largest manufacturing industry, and the Japanese leaders knew it. Fearing U.S. retaliatory action, Japan accepted a U.S. proposal to limit Japanese imports to 1.62 million units in 1981, down from 1.8 million in the last year before the VER. The agreement was renewed for a second year at 1.62 million, before easing up slightly in future years. "The imposition of the VER has had a profound influence on the U.S. market," according to international economists Steven Husted and Michael Melvin.[11]

Economist Robert Crandell predicted in 1980 that the sticker price on American cars would jump $2,000 after the VER. While Crandell overshot the mark slightly, he didn't miss by much. Detroit slapped on average increases of 14 percent while its sales fell by 10 percent between 1980 and 1981. Likewise, the cost of Japanese cars in America rose by 20 percent as its imports declined by 3.3 percent under the first year of the VER.[12] The VER also spurred increased imported cars from South Korea, Germany, and Sweden.

But the trading game of cat and mouse can be played in both directions across the Pacific, and Japanese corporations such as Honda and Toyota have countered the VERs by building **transplants** in Marysville (Ohio), Georgetown (Kentucky) and elsewhere. They also now engage in **upscaling**, making pricey numbers like the Lexus, Acura, and Infiniti, which turn a greater profit per unit sold. Whoever has benefited most from the VER on Japanese autos, it does not seem to be the American consumer, for whom the cost of both imports and domestics increased.[13]

We again turn to the Japanese government for an example of another form of NTB: **subsidies**. These may be direct payments to domestic companies, or tax breaks, or price supports which help a local firm to cope with foreign competition. If subsidies are substantial, they may even allow a company to sell its products abroad well below the actual cost of production, a practice known derisively as **dumping**. When Japanese semiconductors were being sold very cheaply in the United States in 1988, American competitors complained loudly to President Ronald Reagan, who then accused Japan of dumping semiconductors on the U.S. market. The American companies claimed that the Japanese goal was to drive American producers out of business, then raise prices sharply in a field with few competitors. Reagan succeeded in forcing Japanese price adjustments on semiconductors.

Finally, we all know how effective marketing is in getting people to confuse wants with needs. Corporations wouldn't spend billions to advertise their products if the strategy were not successful. **Advertising limits**, restricting the amount a foreign company can spend on marketing in the United States, can help to contain the sales of foreign competitors like Fuji film or Lowenbrau beer, thus extending a helping hand to U.S. companies like Kodak or Samuel Adams.

Finance

Interdependence is fostered by the globalization of money just as surely as by the trade explosion. Daily international currency exchanges alone total $1 trillion, and electronic fund transfers average a mind-boggling $3 trillion a day. Since countries almost never trade by barter, money greases the skids for international exchanges of goods and services. The sheer volume of money flowing from country to country means that central banks, like the German Bundesbank, or the Fed in the United States, have lost much of their ability to affect the relative value of currencies through large-scale buying and selling. They simply find it harder today to use their monetary reserves to manipulate a meaningful percentage of the currency in circulation.

Each nation–state has its own currency. In order for international business to operate smoothly, the relative value of the Spanish peseta, Mexican peso, Australian dollar, British pound, Dutch gilder, and Japanese yen must be readily calculable. There are two principal ways of determining currency values. Under the **fixed exchange-rate system**, currencies are set at specific rates vis-à-vis one another. The fixed-rate system has the advantages of simplicity and predictability.

From 1870 until World War I the fixed-rate system was called the **gold standard**, since in theory each currency was convertible to gold. The idea of using gold as the basis for currency exchange was first broached by England as early as 1821. From 1945 to 1973 another fixed-rate method, the **Bretton Woods system**, was based on confidence in the U.S. dollar rather than gold. Since 1973 more of a purely market-driven solution has existed: the **floating exchange-rate system**, in which prices fluctuate daily according to supply and demand. The actual rate of a nation's currency is more naturally attuned to the overall strength of its economy in a floating-rate system than in the more arbitrary fixed-rate mechanism.

With globalized trade and finance, can global banking be far behind? International lending by private banks totals about $10 trillion annually. British banks lead the international lending parade, with $1 trillion going out to foreign borrowers each year. However, one particular British bank, Barings, may wish it had internationalized its operations somewhat more cautiously (see Mini-case 12.2).

MINI-CASE 12.2
Nick Leeson Bankrupts Barings

*L*ike any other major change, global interdependence has produced both good and bad, exhibiting a downside as well as an upside. For Britain's oldest merchant bank, the venerable Barings, the downside degenerated into a nightmare. As one of the leading banks in the most aggressive country pursuing global lending and investment, Barings may have spread its international presence too thinly too quickly. What brought down the 232-year-old Barings bank were the irresponsible actions of a 28-year-old financial trader who was left largely unsupervised in Barings's far-off Singapore office.

Nick Leeson had been investing large sums of Barings money on the direction of the Japanese stock market, which he believed was going to go up in 1994 and 1995. But it went down, and down, and down. In the end, young Leeson had invested $1.38 billion in unauthorized Barings money on his horrible hunch. He then spent frantic months forging documents, lying to superiors, and deceiving auditors in a futile effort to conceal his world-class theft. In the process, he tricked the Singapore exchange, known as SIMEX, into releasing $115 million in bogus earnings to his Barings account. Like a compulsive gambler loose at the racetrack, Leeson's bets became bigger and bigger in an attempt to win back quickly what he had lost more slowly.

The damage to Barings's bottom line added up to a death sentence: losses of $1.38 billion—even a two-century-old institution could not recover from that. In 1995 Leeson pleaded guilty to two of eleven charges against him and received a sentence of six and a half years in prison.

How could such a thing happen? First, Barings had grown internationally, apparently without holding its overseas employees accountable. Too much authority was accorded an inexperienced trader in stock futures, and too little attention was paid to clues of impropriety that popped up periodically. Second, we are not talking about hard cash transferred in hands-on meetings between real people. Rather, in this age of electronic finance, massive monetary transfers occur silently in nanoseconds from computer terminal to computer terminal, with no paper trail or verbal conversation.

But while Barings bears some of the blame, and the technetronic age bears some of the blame, most of the blame falls on Nick Leeson. He bears individual responsibility for his illegal and unethical behavior. We can only hope that the ethics of others in similar circumstances will prove more substantial. What is your opinion of the sentence Leeson received? Is six years and six months too little, too much, or about right for his crime?

In roughly one hundred of the thousands of international banks operating today, moral issues, uncharacteristically, *do* play a prominent role in their operations. For example, these banks do not charge interest on loans to borrowers. Yes, these banks charge customers no interest. The reason is a religious one deriving from the holy book of Islam, the Koran, which forbids making profits by charging interest.

These Islamic banks, mostly in the Arab world, still manage to link borrowers and lenders interested in doing business. They also offer checking services and trade-related services on a fixed-fee basis. The funds handled by Islamic banks cannot be invested in companies that produce armaments, alcohol, pork, or gambling—which are also forbidden.[14]

Competing Theories of International Political Economy

Three broad theories dominate the landscape of the international political economy. We have encountered parts of each in earlier discussions. The three theories are **economic idealism, economic realism,** and **economic Marxism**. Politics and economics overlap in a major way at the global level, and each modern theory is grounded in that realization.

Economic idealism, sometimes called economic liberalism, owes its intellectual underpinnings to the eighteenth-century classical writings of David Ricardo and Adam Smith. Economic idealism considers trade barriers as debilitating obstacles to economic growth and advocates free trade instead. The arguments of comparative advantage and laissez-faire both constitute genuine articles of faith for economic idealism. Since the pure market operates as efficiently as any human endeavor can aspire to, governments need to intervene only rarely.

A belief in the individual's capability to recognize and act rationally upon his or her best interests also lies close to the heart of idealists. Nations are considered little more than collections of such rational, wealth-seeking individual actors. It is people that create wealth, say the economic idealists.

Economic realism views the role of the national government as vastly more active and vital than does idealism. Economic realism looks first to the power relations of states for clues as to appropriate economic policy for a given nation-state at a given time. The relative power of states dictates what they can and cannot do in specific economic areas, like trade. It is the nation-state, not the individual, that economic realism sees as consistently acting rationally on the world stage; such rationality leads states to subsume economic policies to the quest for power, most often defined in military terms.

Prior to the nineteenth century, economic realism shaped the mercantilist belief that trade interests must serve the higher master of power politics. Economic realists feel comfortable with protectionism designed to promote the power status of the state in what is perceived as a hostile sea of sharks. The idea is that, without a strong defense, the very existence of the state is naively left in jeopardy.

Just as strongly as economic realists are committed to the primacy of politics over economics, *economic Marxists* believe the exact opposite: economics shapes and directs all aspects of social existence, including politics. Specifically, it is the economic interests of competing **classes** that economic Marxists consider vital. Both the individual (idealism) and the nation–state (realism) are viewed as minor actors when compared with the battle raging between the dominant and oppressed classes in each society.

In capitalist countries the revolutionary working class, or proletariat, must rise up to overthrow the owners of the means of production, the bourgeoisie. The domestic working-class struggle for liberation gets transferred to the international level, where capitalistic nations have joined together to extend their subjugation of the poor to the global level. As a result of global oppression, the world has divided into two broad categories: the core (rich North) and the periphery (poor South). Workers of the world should, and will, unite to overthrow their insensitive oppressors.[15]

Although no longer the global economic hegemon, the U.S. $5.3 trillion economy still serves as the symbolic target for attacks by economic Marxists. Proponents of this economic theory suffered a severe blow when communist systems in the Soviet Union and eight Eastern European countries crumbled from 1989 to 1991, but they are by no means finished. Some still cling to Marxist ideals, pointing a finger of blame at the clumsy application of Marxism—not Marx' theories themselves.

Since the United States is still a global economic and military superpower, let's look at some of the challenges it faces in this post-Cold War transitional era.

NATION-STATE ECONOMIES CHALLENGING AMERICA

The Soviet Union acted as the rival military superpower during the Cold War, a time when America was the planet's only economic hegemon. Today there is no economic hegemon. However, Japan and Germany have risen to the top of the heap to challenge America as economic superpowers.

Economic Superpowers

Many aspects of the modern stories of Japan and Germany seem strikingly similar. Both witnessed martial traditions gone haywire in the 1930s, culminating in aggressive state socialism, or **fascism**. Not merely defeated in World War II, they were humiliated into accepting unconditional surrender at the hands of the Allies. U.S.-germinated seeds—in the form of alien democratic principles—were planted, quickly took root, and developed stable institutional vines. The fertilizer that nourished this remarkable growth was in each case unmistakable: an economic miracle legitimizing the postwar systems created in Japan and Germany.

Fearing that militarism was buried deep down in the soil of these cultures, the United States imposed pacifistic constitutions on its ex-enemies. Military maneuvers were limited to defensive operations on their own soil, nuclear weapons were prohibited, they were kept off the U.N. Security Council, both countries were tied to U.S. Cold War alliances against the Soviet Union, and their military budgets were limited. These restrictions allowed Japan and Germany to focus on economic rather than military competition while resting under the U.S. nuclear umbrella.

Forty years went by before Japan spent even one percent of GNP on defense, while America was spending 7 percent and the Soviet Union about 20 percent on military matters. Whereas the Americans and Soviets put their best and brightest young minds in quest of ever more sophisticated weaponry, their Japanese and German counterparts put resources into **neo mercantilism**—especially the research and development of manufactured goods for export. Before too many decades passed, World War II's vanquished had grown into economic giants.

World Bank figures reveal that in 1994 Japan and Germany ranked second and third to the United States, with GNPs of $2.9 and $1.4 trillion, and GNP per capita of $23,700 and $21,000, respectively. Japan ranked either first or second in the U.N.'s human development index (HDI) for quality of life, and Germany ranked in the top dozen, behind eight of its Northern European neighbors. West Germany had been higher before it absorbed the former communist East Germany in 1990. Japan has supplanted the United States as the world's largest foreign aid donor, while Germany's status has been enhanced by its leadership in the burgeoning European Union. In the 1990s these two are the only national economies that contend with the United States for superpower status.

Both cultures, however, remain divided over the same question: should they become more assertive players on the world stage? In some ways, making money behind the scenes, while the United States led the charge during the Cold War, felt comfortable to the Japanese and Germans. Acutely aware of nationalistic excesses in their recent past, they seem not to trust themselves with too much power. When the United States led the 1991 coaliton in the Persian Gulf War against Iraq, America wanted Japan and Germany to send military-support personnel. They balked, choosing instead to open their wallets wider as compensation. Further, both powers warrant a position as permanent U.N. Security Council members but neither has pushed very aggressively for such a role.

Finally, each nation worries that its economic miracle consists of ephemeral smoke and mirrors, and thus it follows cautious policies while searching for a middle-ground identity between the extremes of militarism and pacifism. Germany wonders about its ability to cope with the effects of reunification: unemployment, inflation, a $100 billion price tag, and problems supporting its many immigrants. While the international community sees Japan and Germany as poised for stardom, the protagonists themselves seem ambivalent about accepting marquis billing.

Major Economic Powers

Beneath this top tier of economic superpowers are the other four members of the **Group of Seven (G-7)** industrial powers: France, Italy, the United Kingdom, and Canada—all in the $500 billion to $1 trillion GNP range. These major economic powers regularly consult with the superpowers in organizations like the G-7, OECD, World Bank, and IMF but do not have the same clout as the United States, Japan, or Germany. France leads the group with a $1 trillion GNP, which breaks down to $17,800 per capita. Then come Italy and the United Kingdom, in close proximity, at $872 billion and $834 billion GNP, with per capita figures of $15,200 and $14,600, respectively. Rounding out the bottom of the major economic powers is Canada, at $500 billion GNP and $19,000 per capita.

Moderate Economic Powers

Below the major powers is a category of moderate economic powers, with GNP in the $150–500 billion range. In descending order, by GNP in billions of dollars, are China ($393), Brazil ($375), Spain ($358), India ($287), Australia ($242), Netherlands ($237), Switzerland ($197), Sweden ($184), Mexico ($170), Belgium ($162), and Russia (current data uncertain). Among these moderate powers, three paradoxical high-potential, underachievers stand out as potential major economic powers in the twenty-first century: China, Brazil, and Russia.[16] All have large, diverse, and relatively well-educated populations, impressive natural resources, and pivotal roles in at least one global issue area—population for China, environment for Brazil, and nuclear armaments for Russia—ensuring that their voices will be heard.

A final category, one defying easy numerical classification, consists of the NICs of east Asia. These former colonial possessions, sharing the legacy of poverty common to Third World countries, have risen above the crowd in the last decade or two. Following the Japanese model of neomercantilism, they have achieved flexible production through hard work, managed economies, American support, and a cultural emphasis on education. The result has been impressive economic growth in South Korea, Singapore, Taiwan, Hong Kong, and Malaysia. South Korea leads the group in total GNP at $186 billion, while Singapore leads in GNP per capita with $10,450.[17]

The rapid pace of modern technological change has also produced economic winners and losers. One such technological innovation contributed to the rise of east Asia as a region to be reckoned with. This innovation is not all that glamorous; it has largely been ignored by the news media; yet international economists well understand its significance. I am referring to the story of **containerization** (Mini-case 12.3).

MINI-CASE 12.3
Containerization: The Quiet Revolution

B ack in the seventeenth and eighteenth centuries tiny Holland was the strongest trading country in the world. Part of Dutch riches derived from long domination of the Asian trade. Dutch vessels represented what amounted to state-of-the-art container ships of the time. Brisk East–West trade began mostly with Chinese tea, purchased by the ton for tea-loving Britons by the British East India Company. Other exotic spices of the Orient were soon in demand by the growing rich merchant class in the Occident.

But the determined Chinese were obsessed with British silver and would settle for nothing less. Not until England artificially created demand for a new commodity in China—opium—producing more than 12,000 Chinese addicts by 1836, did the British have a saleable commodity to leverage Chinese tea. Henceforth, tea and opium embraced one another in a devil's dance.

In our day, profits from East–West trade have shifted decidedly toward the Orient, with Japan, Hong Kong, Taiwan, and South Korea leading the way. Cheap containers and cheap labor costs have boosted east Asian economies with a vengeance. This trade has been profitable for the east Asian NICs. It has also been a boon for the 250 million American consumers. It has been disastrous for several hundred thousand U.S. laborers working in industries like textiles, televisions, steel, toys, and shoes.

World trade has been revolutionized through efficiency based on standardized container ships. Uniformity is the name of the transportation game today, as everything from computers to fish to toys traverse the seven seas in steel containers. The heaviest traffic steams nonstop across the Pacific Ocean between Seattle and Hong Kong, or Kobe and Vancouver, or San Francisco and Taipei. Eight million containers pass through Hong Kong's busy harbor each year.

Physically these containers look just like the beds of the tractor-trailer trucks seen along U.S. interstate highways. In fact, many of them, unloaded directly from ships, are rolling across interstate 70 to St. Louis, or interstate 90 to Chicago, in less than two hours. Hong Kong's Oriental Container Lines (OOCL) now leads all shippers; their gold-colored OOCL logo on containers traveling all across America.

What are the benefits of shipping via standardized metal containers? They are secure from physical damage, completely sealable to foil thieves, interchangeable anywhere in the world, less expensive than other forms of transport, and uncommonly reliable. Containers make goods so maintenance free that crews aboard commercial liners have been reduced in number to cut expenses in what is now a highly competitive shipping business. Just a few years ago there were over 100 shipping companies, but today a select few rule the waves. This relatively simple-looking new technology has transformed global shipping and created big winners and losers in its wake.[18]

In effect, all of the groups of successful nations we have discussed challenge the United States in ways unimaginable only a few decades ago. America holds a paradoxical position in the post-Cold War: since it bested its Soviet nemesis, no other military power can match its global reach; yet, despite maintaining the world's largest economy, it finds itself hobbled by a massive budget debt, record trade deficits, a growing chasm between rich and poor, and a falling standard of living for a majority of its citizens. Furthermore, other countries don't listen to the United States quite the way they used to. Just a century ago Great Britain faced a near-identical erosion of economic hegemony, at the hands, ironically, of America.

Non State Threats to U.S. Economic Status

Besides nation–state competitors, America's fifty-year economic hegemony faces a wave of problems from nonstate actors and changing global forces. They all contribute to a burden of frustration carried on America's shoulders as it approaches the new millennium. When we look back at the economic stability of the Cold War era through the lens of the early post-Cold War, it almost seems as though economic heaven and hell have suddenly broken loose from their moorings. Everything is not only drastically different, but also very much in flux. The United States certainly has further to fall from its fifty-year pinnacle of economic power than do rival nation–states, but they too feel a loss of control or efficacy.

Back to the Future: Markets Overwhelming State Policies

Economist Herman Schwartz's incisive *States Versus Markets* provides a broad historical understanding of trends in the global economy. Today we witness market pressures overwhelming and frustrating state policies in many different contexts. For Americans whose historical memory is limited to about fifty years, since the end of World War II, this phenomenon of markets overwhelming nation–state policies seems bizarre. Professor Schwartz argues that it is not so novel after all, but constitutes a shift, in effect, *back to the future:*

> Markets constantly, impartially, and unconsciously change the distribution of production in geographic space. States intervene to help or hinder this market-driven redistribution, but on an intermittent and self-interested basis, often with unintended results. States experienced their greatest success in controlling international and domestic markets during the post-World War II era. Far from being typical, the stability and successful state intervention of the postwar period represented a dramatic departure from the typical processes of the global economy. The global economy is in fact moving *back to the future*, resembling more and more the global economy of the nineteenth century.[19]

For those born during the Cold War period, the prevailing world economy seems like the natural state of affairs. Herman Schwartz argues convincingly that such a perception is illusory, but easily correctable by an examination of global economics over a longer time. He makes another powerful point: this new development is not good news for nation–states in general, and for the United States particularly, which he describes as "economically in decline from the top down, as well as from below."

Professor Schwartz's analysis points to the private sector, especially MNCs, as profoundly affecting the global economy. Many economists consider the weakening of the nation–state as inexorable, maybe even desirable. A different opinion, however, comes from activists Jeremy Brecher and Tim Costello, who believe stirrings exist for a grass-roots movement against the consequences of the deregulated global market, wherein nation–states look more and more like spectators rather than movers and shakers.

MNCs' Critics

Brecher and Costello contend that MNCs care not one whit about environment, human rights, or labor conditions; yet by competing to attract these "footloose corporations," unwitting communities encourage a disastrous "race to the bottom." The end result, according to these pessimistic authors, is that "The New World Economy is a disaster that has already happened." They see hope only in radical people's movements bubbling up simultaneously around the earth to challenge the reigning corporate powers that be.[20]

What is it about MNCs that impels southern national leaders and northern hemisphere activists like Brecher and Costello to shower MNCs with a chorus of jeers? In an earlier chapter we talked about how, fairly or unfairly, unfavorable movie images have contributed to negative perceptions of top corporate executives. The fact is, however, there are real-life CEOs who need no Hollywood-style embellishment to portray them as nasty characters.

One would be hard-pressed to find a more self-congratulatory autobiography than corporate mogul Albert J. Dunlap's *Mean Business: How I Save Bad Companies and Make Good Companies Better* (1996). Dunlap's specialty is taking over faltering corporations, "downsizing" (firing people) extensively to reduce costs, turning a quick profit for shareholders, and then moving on to another troubled corporate giant. In 1993 he took over the Scott Paper Company, eliminated 70 percent of upper management, and fired 11,200 employees, or 35 percent of Scott's payroll. By 1995 Scott was debtfree and its shareholder stock had increased from $2.5 billion to $9 billion. The personal payoff for Albert Dunlap? In his own words, "After twenty months of intense work I left Scott $100 million richer than when I arrived." Sunbeam hired him to do the same shortly thereafter.

For his slash-and-burn tactics, Dunlap has earned two nicknames: "Chainsaw Dunlap" and "Rambo in Pinstripes." Dunlap argues unapologetically that it is a CEO's job to put shareholders first, not employees. His many critics disagree that the issue is really that simple. Joseph McCann, dean of the Business School at Pacific Lutheran University, says, "This scorched earth policy benefits no one but Al Dunlap and a handful of shareholders." Management consultant Tom Peters, author of *In Search of Excellence* (1991), believes that while corporate re-

Al "Chainsaw" Dunlap, master of the quick-fix through corporate downsizing, found various ways to show disdain for his critics at the news conference after his corporation du jour (Sunbeam), bought out Coleman camping gear, Mr. Coffee machines, and First Alert smoke alarms on March 2, 1998.

structuring is necessary, Dunlap's quick-fix "chainsaw" approach fails to address underlying long-term problems and suffers from superficiality.[21] As if corporate elites needed another black eye, read what laborer Mario Brito Dumas has to say (Mini-case 12.4).

MINI-CASE 12.4
Mario Brito Dumas: Suing over Sterility

L ike all other private enterprises, MNCs are in business to make a profit, and few scholars would question their right to do so. But when efforts to make money blind them to the human rights of others, the profit motive takes on a sleazy demeanor. Consider the case of Mario Brito Dumas, banana plantation worker in Naranjal, Bolivia. In 1972 Mario and his wife experienced the birth of their first child. To their chagrin, this event was not to be repeated in their household.

Why? Because from 1975 to 1980 Mario Brito spent his long workdays filling large injectors with a bug-killing pesticide that was to be infused into the roots of banana plants. Mr. Brito recalls that "Everything I ate tasted bitter and gave me stomachaches." What he was exposed to for at least five years was a chemical called dibromochloropropane, or DBCP. In 1977 DBCP was found to cause sterility in men working at a California chemical plant; use of the pesticide became highly restricted in the United States, but not in developing countries. Like the plant workers in California, Mario Brito became sterile.

Chemical companies such as Dow Chemical had large stocks of the chemical and continued shipping it to fruit companies in other countries for a decade after the 1977 finding that it caused sterility. One of the largest fruit producers, Standard Fruit, warned Dow Chemical that if it stopped shipments of DBCP, Standard Fruit would consider that a "breach of contract." Dow continued sending the DBCP with the knowledge that no U.S. law prohibits the export of chemicals banned for use on American soil.

Mario Brito has joined with 20,000 other plantation workers from twelve poor countries to file lawsuits against Dow Chemical, Shell Oil, Standard Fruit, and Del Monte Fruit. Considerable scientific evidence links DBCP with not only sterility, but perhaps also birth defects and cancer, and the workers argue that they were exposed to a known hazard with no warning from companies who cared more about profits than workers' health.

The issue of U.S.-barred pesticides being exported for profit first gained notoriety with the 1981 publication of *Circle of Poison*, by David Weir and Mark Schapiro, which traced pesticides exported to poor countries, used on products, and then unwittingly imported by Americans—including coffee, cotton, and bananas. An even more poignant warning of this danger appeared in the award-winning documentary film *Pesticides: For Export Only*, produced by Robert Richter, which examines pesticide use in a tiny fishing village in Ghana.[22]

Just when we seem ready to paint the scarlet "V" for villain on the chest of CEOs, however, along comes Aaron Feurstein to complicate the corporate portrait (see Mini-case 12.5).

MINI-CASE 12.5
Humanist in Pinstripes: Aaron Feurstein

A few decades ago, thriving textile factories provided good jobs for many workers in New England. Most of these plants have long since disappeared, as the American market has been flooded with imported clothes from countries with much lower labor costs than the United States. In 1981 it seemed certain that Malden Mills in Lawrence, Massachusetts, would be chalked up as another textile mill down the tubes. When Malden Mills CEO Aaron Feurstein was forced to file for bankruptcy protection, few experts expected his company to survive.

However, Feurstein's approach to Malden Mills's faltering status was a creative one: he invested heavily in research and development. The result? Patents on two synthetic fabrics called Polartec and Polarfleece, designed for use in outdoor wear by pricey manufacturers like L.L. Bean and Patagonia. These patented fabrics became much in demand, and Malden Mills seemed to have beaten the odds by doing well in a tough international clothing market.

Then, on December 11, 1995, a disastrous fire leveled the factory, putting Malden's 3,000 employees out of work just before Christmas. What was CEO Feurstein to do? The factory's security director, Bob Fawcett, said: "Another person would have taken the insurance money and walked away. I might have done that. But he's [Feurstein] not that kind of person." After the December fire, Feurstein surprised many people by announcing he would pay all employees for a month—which at least got them through the holiday season. Then, mouths dropped when he did it for a second month. By the time Feurstein forked out a third month's salaries to

Malden Mills President Aaron Feurstein, right, receives a warm welcome from his employees as he arrives on December 14, 1995, to announce that he will continue paying them while their burned-out factory can be rebuilt.

all his workers, he had spent several million dollars covering the payroll of a company with an uncertain future. To say that his employees regarded him as a saint would not be hyperbole.

But it seems that CEO Feurstein was more than a humanist with a checkbook, he was an excellent businessman as well. Before the fire, Malden Mills turned out 130,000 yards of fabric a week. A few weeks after the fire: 230,000 yards. Why did he do what he did? "I have a responsibility to the workers, both blue-collar and white-collar," said Feurstein. "I have an equal responsibility to the community. It would have been unconscionable to deliver a death blow to the cities of Lawrence and Methuen." When asked how most other CEOs' approach differ from his, he replied, "I consider our workers as an asset, not an expense." His religious beliefs come through when he quotes the ancient Hebrew scholar Hillel, who said, "In a situation where there is no righteous person, try to be a righteous person." You would have to read no further than the jacket cover of Al Dunlap's *Mean Business* to realize that a Grand Canyon of philosophical differences separate Aaron Feurstein and Al Dunlap as corporate CEOs. That philosophical Grand Canyon might even rival the rich/poor global chasm which is the essence of the remainder of this chapter.[23]

POLARIZATION OF NORTH AND SOUTH
Further Complications for America

Other changes also present problems for the United States. The 75 percent of the world's people living in the South produce only 20 percent of global GDP. The wealthiest 20 percent of the world's people earn $61 for every $1 earned by the poorest 20 percent. In the decade between 1985 and 1995 the gap between rich and poor countries grew by 16 percent.[24] The undeniability that the rich are getting richer while the poor are getting poorer has led many

Poor women washing clothes in the stream running through a shanty-town in Teheran, Iran.

scholars to warn of global dangers around the corner. For example, international legal scholar Richard Falk writes, "Ultimately, unmet economic problems may lead the poor to desperate politics versus the rich."[25]

The Third World countries, or LDCs, taken collectively, total nearly 130 nation–states. Also called the **Group of 77 (G- 77),** this bloc has pushed a distinct agenda at various international conferences. Its **New International Economic Order (NIEO)** calls for changing the rules of the international economic game in order to find new ways for poor countries to develop—essentially an international version of an "affirmative action" program.

Ironically, in responding to domestic austerity pressures, especially after the Republican Congressional victory in 1994, the United States has been slicing its foreign aid budget, not expanding it. The Clinton administration cut the $13.7 billion aid budget by 15 percent during his first two years in office. The United Nations asks rich countries to give .6 percent of GDP to foreign aid, but only a few actually do so. In 1946 America was giving 1.75 percent, but by 1995 the figure had slipped to 0.117 percent of GDP.[26]

The first international conference devoted exclusively to North–South issues was the 1964 U.N. Conference on Trade and Development (UNCTAD I). Political scientist Richard Mansbach summarizes six demands which germinated at UNCTAD I and became codified ten years later at a special session of the U.N. They represent the crux of the G-77's agenda for reform:

1. Increasing nation–state and IGO regulation of the activities of multinational corporations (MNCs), by which people in poor countries feel overwhelmed and abused. Codes of conduct for MNCs would be a step in the right direction.

2. Transferring technological hardware and know-how from the computer-literate North to the computer-ignorant South.

3. Reforming the trading order to aid the development of poor countries, including controversial preferential pricing for primary products exported by the South.

4. Providing special aid for developing countries with debt problems, since the debt crisis is a global issue affecting everyone. The debt burden of poor countries reached $1 trillion by the late 1980s.

5. Increasing economic aid (bilateral and multilateral) from rich to poor countries to meet the U.N.-designated level of .7 percent of GDP.

6. Revising voting procedures in IFIs like the World Bank and IMF to give poor countries more influence over decision making.[27]

Let's examine the role played by the United States at the initial UNCTAD I meeting, which the poor countries considered as the crucial take-off point for the evolution of the NIEO.

MINI-CASE 12.6
UNCTAD I and America

The United States had long resisted earlier efforts by the less-developed countries **(LDCs)** to convene a global session for airing development concerns, and had been successful in preventing one. President John F. Kennedy, however, was concerned in the early 1960s with Latin American development as a counterweight to communism's entrenchment in Castro's Cuba. America's allies in Latin America were vocal proponents of a development meeting, and Kennedy's ambassador to the U.N., Adlai Stevenson, convinced the president to reverse the old U.S. position opposing such a conference.

While the United States went through the diplomatic motions at UNCTAD I, its hidden agenda consisted of placating the LDCs without agreeing to do anything. For the LDCs, by contrast, "this was considered the most important event since the founding of the United Nations." The LDCs particularly disliked one of America's pet institutions, the GATT, which poor countries saw as a "rich man's club" where they had minimal influence over trade decisions.[28]

The intellectual underpinnings of the LDC position at UNCTAD I were explicated by Dr. Raul Prebisch, executive secretary of the U.N. Economic Commission for Latin America. His description of the **terms-of-trade problem** (LDCs relying on the exportation of stagnant primary products in a futile attempt to purchase appreciating manufactured goods from the MDCs) confronting LDCs convinced them that they could never become competitive without big changes in the international economy. The remedies that he favored were all opposed by the United States, especially price-setting for primary products, expanded foreign assistance, and reduction of agricultural import barriers put up by wealthy countries like the United States, Japan, or France.

The LDCs attempted to unite prior to the conference. However, they were so badly divided on many issues that they had to work out compromises to their proposed resolutions prior to presentation at the meeting. They were not able to negotiate freely or effectively at the conference, since their rigid positions had been so difficult to work out among themselves.

On the other side, the powerful United States (unlike the Soviet Union, United Kingdom, Japan, and France) was as rigid as the LDCs and proved uninterested in arriving at any compromise agreement. "The U.S. came with little to offer the G-77, and little is what they offered. Without active U.S. engagement in negotiating, few meaningful compromises were possible."[29]

The Cancun Conference

Although the United States has long resisted starting down the slippery slope of legitimizing the G-77's agenda of **distributive justice** included in the NIEO; in 1983 a watershed event occurred regarding America's role in the North–South dialogue. Under President Ronald Reagan—no fan of arguments that the North owes poor countries a new start—the United States found itself pressured from all corners (allies included) to participate in the 1983 Global Conference on Poverty in Cancun, Mexico.

Rather than isolate itself by skipping the meeting, the United States participated in the process, but without conceding substantive validity to the idea that it owes anybody distributive justice. However, by its very presence, the United States made it more difficult simply to ignore the shrill voice of the South, as it had previously done. The LDCs are better organized and more numerous than ever. They also hold new issues over the heads of the more-developed countries (MDCs)—like the ecological importance of the vast rain forests in their possession.

U.S. participation under President George Bush in the 1992 Earth Summit in Rio de Janeiro again resulted in near isolation on some vital environmental issues. As in Cancun, by virtue of its being there, America legitimized the open-ended North–South dialogue, which it generally prefers to ignore. Since the poverty gap has widened in recent years, it appears unlikely that the LDCs and their demands for distributive justice will disappear. Some philanthropic NGOs, like the Panos Institute, seek to amplify the voice of LDCs loudly enough for their developmental concerns to be heard by northern MDCs, with rational dialogue as the goal.[30]

On occasion, international **cartels** have also troubled the United States, although only rarely have they prevented America from doing what it wanted to do. These producers' organizations try to control the supply and price of primary products by limiting competition. Their ultimate dream features a monopoly of global control over a given commodity. However, cartels are inherently unstable: they seek unity among diverse countries, which is difficult to maintain for long. The temptation for a maverick country to break from the agreed-upon quota system and benefit from higher prices will always threaten cartels. The modern prototype for southern hemisphere cartels has risen around the global supply and demand of oil, as is described in Mini-case 12.7.

MINI-CASE 12.7
OPEC—Rise, Demise, Limbo

The Organization of Petroleum Exporting Countries (OPEC), founded in 1960 at the behest of Venezuela, hoped to increase oil prices by limiting supply, thus creating higher demand for their commodity. OPEC eventually grew to thirteen countries, mostly from the Middle East. From 1960 to 1973 OPEC's presence on the world stage was barely noticed by most countries. In 1970 a barrel of oil cost only $1.35. But not for long.

When the October 1973 **Yom Kippur War** broke out between Israel and its neighbors, OPEC's Arab majority convinced the other members to impose an oil **embargo** against Western states that supported Israel. As world oil supplies dwindled, prices skyrocketed, as is traced in Figure 12.1. Some countries that had supported Israel, such as Japan, changed their policies. OPEC countries were producing two-thirds of global oil output in the 1970s, and so prices jumped to an unprecedented $38 per barrel by the end of the decade. OPEC felt supremely confident as its coffers bulged with more than $1 trillion in 1970s **petrodollars**. As hard as the "oil shocks" of the 1970s hit the wealthy countries, in the long run they hurt the LDCs much worse, contributing to their severe debt crisis in the 1980s.

If the story ended there, the OPEC saga would read as one of the great success tales in the history of cartels. Things were to change, however, in the 1980s. The eight-year Iran–Iraq War divided the OPEC countries, as did the 1991 Persian Gulf coalition against Iraq. Also, Western countries undertook serious conservation efforts, like building fuel-efficient cars, thus reducing demand for OPEC oil. The inflated price of oil also spurred new players: Britain, Mexico, and China all drilled for black gold, contributing to an eventual oversupply. By the 1980s, oil prices settled at a more modest price, in the midteens per barrel, where they have for the most part remained. Accordingly, OPEC's political role in world affairs has been limited since the heady days of its 1970s revival.

Figure 12.1 Real Price of Oil, 1950–1993, in Constant 1993 Dollars per Barrel

Source: Joan Spero and Jeffrey Hart, *The Politics of International Economic Relations* (St. Martin's, 1997), p. 286. Data from British Petroleum, *BP Statistical Review of World Energy* (London: 1993) and electronic database (London: 1992); Worldwatch estimates based on ibid., and on Department of Energy Information Administration, *Monthly Energy Review February 1994* (Washington, D.C.: Government Printing Office, 1994).

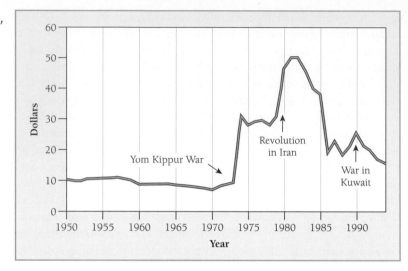

OPEC will not soon sneak up on the rest of the world as it did in 1973, nor will it match its former political influence. Yet when fortuitous circumstances arise, OPEC should be able to make life uncomfortable for its adversaries, at least temporarily. Although the United States is not as dependent on Persian Gulf oil as the Japanese or Europeans, it remains vulnerable since it imports about half its petroleum needs; and OPEC may again unify sufficiently to produce difficulties in the MDCs.

OPEC's relative success has encouraged new cartels to spring up in uranium, gold, silver, diamonds, and fourteen other primary products. Growing in number, sophistication, and profit potential, cartels are likely, though sporadically, to produce the kinds of problems that the De Beers corporation (Mini-case 11.1) has recently caused the U.S. Justice Department's antitrust division. In December 1994 President Clinton's head of antitrust activities, Anne Bingaman, "suffered a humiliating defeat after suing General Electric on charges it conspired with De Beers of South Africa to fix industrial diamond prices." Clinton's presidential campaign had pledged to break up powerful monopolies, which its Republican predecessors had ignored, De Beers included.[31]

Economic Multilateralism: A Hard Nut for American Culture to Crack

Historically, America's behavior on the world economic stage can be characterized as **unilateralist**, or preferring to function alone. The image of the strong loner is deeply embedded in American culture. The maverick sheriff, boldly calling the shots to protect freedom and security has been the staple of America's most indigenous movie genre—the western. Director Stanley Kramer's classic, *High Noon* (1952), is a thinly veiled defense of self-reliant individualism, filmed during the heyday of Wisconsin Senator Joseph McCarthy's anticommunist witch hunts. In it, Hollywood icon Gary Cooper plays the resilient marshal saving his frontier community from the bad guys—not with a posse, but on his own. America's economic role on the world stage has been comparably independent and stubborn as Gary Cooper in his starring role in *High Noon*.

In the real economic world of the 1990s, however, America finds itself enmeshed in a global web sharing a quite different ethos of **multilateralism**. This global penchant for collective responsibility manifests itself most directly in the intergovernmental organizations (IGOs) that are developing at both the regional and global levels. Of the regional economic IGOs, the European Union (EU) serves as the prototype emulated by others. As such, the EU constitutes a problem for the United States both practically and symbolically. Why?

Practically, this is so because the unified EU boasts GNP of more than $6 trillion (20 percent higher than United States) and has succeeded in cutting into more and more of America's long-running leadership of world trade. Symbolically, the EU is a problem because it places competitive pressure on other regional IGOs (like the Andean Pact, NAFTA, APEC, Gulf Cooperation Council, Black Sea Economic Cooperation Zone, and Southern Africa Customs Union) to match Europe's integrative activities. Obvious difficulties thus arise for an American culture attuned not to notions of cooperative, multilateral endeavor, but rather to self-reliant unilateralism. At the very least, the traditional American mind-set is being called upon to adapt and change its national self-concept. Much of this pressure will continue to originate in the impatient southern hemisphere.

GENERAL THEORIES OF ECONOMIC DEVELOPMENT

The **conventional theory** and the **radical theory** provide sharply contrasting explanations which dominate the debate over the causes and cures of economic underdevelopment in the South. Each of these theories essentially stands the assumptions and the logic of the other on its head in arriving at its own conclusions about the correct path to economic development. The conventional theory has been generally more accepted over a longer historical and broader geographic span, but the radical theory's minority status has not detracted from the ferocity of many of its committed proponents.

The conventional theory lays the blame for lack of economic development squarely at the feet of the internal conditions of poor countries. The continuous cycle of poverty is attributed to the cultural, political, and economic weaknesses inherent in these countries. Corrupt political leadership, illiteracy, inefficiency, waste, a peasant culture, overpopulation, high crime rates, and low worker productivity all contribute to most traditional societies remaining mired in the mud of economic underdevelopment. According to the conventional theory, one need look no further than this dysfunctional societal milieu to find the culprit for poverty in the South. If the problem is seen as indigenous, then the conventional solution is decidedly external.

In order to offset all these negative internal conditions, the conventional idea is for international aid, low-interest loans, and technical training to arrive from the rich countries. The cycle of poverty can be broken by means of modernizing changes based on the Western model of economic growth, especially by increased trade. If economic salvation exists for the poor, it must come through greater exposure to the northern hemisphere's more advanced ways. Traditionalism must give way to modernity. This generally means achieved rather than ascribed status in social relations, democratic political values, tolerance of cultural diversity, and a market-based economy as the multiple engines of development.

According to the radical theory, in contrast, the above analysis is akin to a case of economic dyslexia. Radical theorists view the causes of underdevelopment as deriving from an inherently inequitable international system. A form of global exploitation whereby the rich blithely continue to take advantage of the poor causes the imposition of the cycle of poverty on people in poor countries. Greed, insensitivity, rampant materialism, and ethical myopia characterize the world's rich, who have set up seemingly innocuous world institutions to perpetuate their exploitation-based affluence. Dealing with these institutions, says the radical theory, will only solidify the subservient position of the global poor.

The solution to the dependency dilemma, according to the radical theory, is for the poor to sever their present economic ties with the rich. They are advised to become more self-reliant by forming coalitions with other poor countries to renegotiate fairer economic relations with the MDCs. Radical theorists criticize MNCs as the arms of oppression and call for regulation of their behavior. They must also diversify their economies to reduce the insidious effects of the terms-of-trade problems facing them. Above all, the radical theory assumes that while solutions to such complex problems may be elusive, more assertive, creative, and nontraditional solutions must be tried.[32]

One small example of creative problem solving is offered by the BancoSol in Bolivia, Latin America's first private commercial bank for the poor. If the one hundred Islamic banks discussed earlier seemed unusual, then BancoSol ought to appear Martian-like. Its sole owner, Bernardo Santa Maria, makes small loans of $25 to $300 to micro-entrepreneurs (such as street vendors or Indian artisans) who may want to hire short-term employees or buy materials for their shantytown small businesses. Mainstream banks cannot be bothered with such a motley clientele. BancoSol differs from most other programs intended for the poor in that it is a profit-making business, not a charity or a governmental grant program. Señor Santa Maria's clients make weekly payments, and his fledgling bank boasts a repayment rate of 99 percent over five years of operation—a record Chase Manhattan might well envy. BancoSol may not save the world, but it is one soul's creative response to the needs of the poor.[33]

SPECIFIC DEVELOPMENT STRATEGIES

The conventional and radical theories illustrate how economists conceptualize the daunting task of economic development. But how have poor countries actually gone about trying to develop their economies? What policies have they followed in hopes of leaving the ranks of the LDCs?

Import Substitution

The strategy most compatible with the radical theory of development is **import substitution**. This has been followed by some African countries such as Tanzania and Kenya, Latin American states such as Brazil, Argentina, and Chile, as well as India, Mexico, and China (up to the death of Mao Zedong in 1976).

Import substitution parallels the radical theory by making economic self-sufficiency its highest priority. The government plays a key role in manipulating domestic economic forces to facilitate the development of domestic industries and thereby reduce imports from the North. Competition in the global market can be fierce, and we discussed earlier some of the legitimate reasons for limited protectionism under special circumstances for a limited time. However, import substitution goes much further toward making protectionism the cornerstone of its economic development policy.

High tariff barriers are erected on some goods to reduce foreign competition. The exchange rate of the domestic currency is overvalued to make imported goods cheaper and exported goods more costly. The government also provides subsidies and other forms of assistance to get infant manufacturing industries on their feet, thus diversifying the economic base. Finally, the production of more sophisticated capital goods for export is called for. However, this latter phase is difficult to achieve, since it depends largely on high levels of foreign investment, which has by now been scared off through **autarkical** (self-sufficiency) policies.

In theory, many aspects of import substitution appeal to poor countries seeking to break free from a legacy of domination by wealthy countries. In practice, though, despite some short-term initial successes, import substitution policies have not fared well: in no country has it served over the long term to liberate a poor southern country from economic dependence or to create sustained economic development. In fact, economist Robert Alexander's analysis concludes that import substitution has usually resulted, ironically, in an increased dependence on capital and imports from northern industrial states.[34]

Import substitution represents extensive governmental interference in economic affairs, creating artificial domestic conditions, such as an overvalued currency, high tariff barriers scaring off imported goods and denying them to domestic citizens, a balance- of- payments deficit, and a growing debt burden. In short, import substitution has turned out to be more of a dead end than a royal road to independence.

Export-Led Industrialization

The development strategy closest to the conventional theory is **export-led industrialization**; its best-known practitioners have been the NICs of east Asia. As Steven Spiegel points out, "Export-led industrialization seeks to promote development by working within, rather than against, the global economic system."[35] Singapore, Taiwan, Hong Kong, South Korea, and other governments have intervened in their economies for the opposite purpose than did, for example, Tanzania and Argentina, who have followed import substitution strategies.

The east Asian NICs have undervalued their currencies (rather than overvaluing them) to encourage exports, thereby making their exported goods cheaper and imported goods more expensive. The results have been quite favorable over three decades of growth. While other factors also help to account for the success of the NICs, the export-led growth strategy is considered by many economists as the key ingredient in the mix.

Collective Bargaining

A tongue-in-cheek slogan summing up import substitution might be, "Pull the curtains and bar the door, Katie," and for export-led industrialization, "If you can't beat em, join em." A third strategy, flexibly attuned to either the conventional or the radical theory, is called **col-**

lective bargaining. It grew out of some of the global conditions coalescing in the 1970s. Its sharply contrasting slogan might be, "One for all, and all for one." Just as the term "collective bargaining" has applied in American society to efforts by laborers to improve their circumstances by organizing for effective negotiation, it also fits the international scene where poor countries hope to redefine the rules of the international economic game.

Membership in the G-77 is bulging at the seams. The logic here is that a unified voice representing a majority of humanity cannot easily be ignored. Therefore, the advice to poor countries is simple: pool your resources to fight for reforms in your collective best interests. The NIEO, discussed above, shapes the contours of the message. However, collective bargaining is a development strategy long on process but short on content. While many poor countries still have faith in southern solidarity as a potent force, much of the 1970s euphoria over the demands of the NIEO and the success of the OPEC cartel in that decade has since waxed and waned. Collective bargaining for the G-77 in the 1990s looks a lot like a medium in search of a message. This vast pool of nations clearly shares poverty and a legacy of dependency, but that fact in no way guarantees their seeing eye to eye on complex priorities in quest of economic development.[36]

WINNERS AND LOSERS IN ECONOMIC DEVELOPMENT

Yale historian Paul Kennedy's cogent analysis of winners and losers in the economic development game during the last three decades of the twentieth century provides some intriguing insights. Most striking among the regional patterns he discerns is the fact that from the 1960s to the 1990s East Asia and Sub-Saharan Africa have headed in completely different directions. East Asian economies have grown at a rapid pace, while some African economies are worse off than thirty years ago. It is no coincidence that the east Asian countries have followed export-led industrialization strategies while the African states have preferred import substitution policies.[37]

South Korea and Ghana

Kennedy focuses on South Korea versus Ghana—two countries with identical GDP per capita of $230 in the mid–1960s—as symptomatic of huge regional disparities. Both were agricultural societies which had suffered through long colonial domination. Extensive natural resources seemed to augur well for Ghana when it gained independence in 1957; so did its status as a major exporter of cocoa. But after independence it initiated import substitution policies, which resulted in precipitous declines in cocoa exports. Ghana's policies were intended to replace reliance on agriculture with development of manufactured products, but that plan did not work. Ghana's GDP per capita fell from $500 in 1957 to $310 in 1983.[38] In 1995 it ranked 129 of 174 countries on the HDI quality of life index, with average life expectancy of 56 years and literacy rate of 61 percent.[39]

South Korea, by contrast, has followed a policy of export-led industrialization. Its exports increased at a rate of 24 percent per year over the same three decades. By the 1990s South Korea had become ten times as prosperous as Ghana, and the world's thirteenth largest trading nation. It ranks 31 among the world's nations on the HDI quality of life index; its people have a life expectancy of 71 years, a literacy rate of 97 percent, and GDP per capita of more than $10,000 annually.

Import substitution in Ghana versus export-led industrialization in South Korea offers a potent contrast in strategies. However, Paul Kennedy recognizes a number of other considerations at work in these two countries as they careened in opposite directions from the 1960s to the 1990s. In Ghana, as in most of Africa, population has exploded, urbanization has produced gross overcrowding, women have been denied equitable life chances, national debt has piled up, traditional beliefs have remained unchallenged, and either war or political instability has made havoc commonplace.

In marked contrast, most of east Asia, including South Korea, has valued education very highly, engaged in high national savings and low credit rates, fostered a strong political system, followed flexible mixed-economic strategies, and followed Japan as a regional role model.[40] Important lessons for the other LDCs lie in the different paths taken by South Korea and Ghana. It may be in the interests of people everywhere for the LDCs to emulate the South Korean model rather than the Ghanaian one.

Chapter Synopsis

Between the system of colonial exploitation and the Industrial Revolution, the European countries established massive wealth between the seventeenth and twentieth centuries. Much of the history of the international economy in recent decades has revolved around efforts to either dislodge or protect the legacy of highly concentrated wealth. Anti-capitalist forces first coalesced around Marxism, yet its global demise has not weakened the resolve of poor southern hemisphere countries to alter the maldistribution of wealth through vehicles like the NIEO. But the action on the international economic stage is not restricted to rich nations versus poor nations. Many new non-state actors have emerged as players of consequence, and the hegemonic status of the nation–state no longer can be taken for granted. International conflict over scarce goods and services, however, should not obscure the fact that the great majority of international economic exchanges occur on a daily basis and in an orderly manner. Deep and serious conflicts are genuine, but pacific economic and financial transactions remain the rule rather than the exception.

Various theories compete for dominance in the global milieu. Economic idealism, economic realism, and economic Marxism purport to describe and an-

alyze the broad spectrum of international economics. Similarly catholic in scope, the conventional and radical theories of poverty offer sharply contrasting views on the causes and potential cures of hemispheric poverty. The mammoth volume of the international economy today raises the ante concerning monetary exchange rates, with winners and losers deriving from how the world community decides to go about exchanging one currency for another. Variations on fixed and floating exchange rates have been used during different historical periods. One of the reasons exchange rates are so important is that trade has exploded to exceed $4 trillion annually. The success story of the east Asian NICs has followed a script of neomercantilist trade emulating the Japanese model. While David Ricardo's time-tested theory of comparative advantage remains an unassailable article of faith among most economists, political pressures for protectionism invariably arise, and the contest between free trade and protectionism will continue to be our constant companion.

No other international economic issue rivals the widening North–South chasm for staying power. For the South, nothing less than distributive justice is acceptable. In sharp contrast, the North wishes to maintain the status quo as long as possible. The two sides are far apart and the passage of time has done nothing to resolve their fundamental differences. Even among the poor countries, unity is elusive. Should they pursue policies of import substitution, export-

led growth, or collective bargaining? Paul Kennedy's intriguing comparison of two countries typifying two regions heading in different directions (Ghana/Africa, South Korea/east Asia) at least provides grist for the analytical mill concerning this vexing dilemma.

For Digging Deeper

Brecher, Jeremy, and Tim Costello. *Global Village or Global Pillage: Economic Reconstruction from the Bottom Up*. South End Press, 1994.

Davidian, Zaven N. *Economic Disparities Among Nations: A Threat to Survival in a Globalized World*. SIPRI Publications, 1994.

Ensign, Margee. *Doing Good or Doing Well? Japan's Foreign Aid Program*. Columbia University Press, 1993.

Fay, Stephen. *The Collapse of Barings*. W.W. Norton & Company, 1996.

Husted, Steven, and Michael Melvin. *International Economics*. University of Pittsburgh Press, 1995.

Kanter, Rosabeth. *World Class: Thriving Locally in the Global Economy*. Kumarian Press, 1994.

Kennedy, Paul. *Preparing for the 21st Century*. Random House, 1993.

Krasner, Steven D. *Structural Conflict: The Third World Against Global Liberalism*. University of California Press, 1985.

Mortimer, Robert. *The Third World Coalition in International Politics*. Westview Press, 1984.

Murray, Geoffrey, and Audrey Perrera. *Singapore: The City State*. St. Martin's Press, 1995.

Obstfeld, Maurice, and Kenneth Rogoff. *Foundations of International Macroeconomics*. MIT Press, 1996.

Otero, Maria, and Elisabeth Rhyne, Eds. *The New World of Microenterprise Finance*. Kumarian Press, 1994.

Robison, Richard, and David Goodman. *The New Rich in Asia: Mobile Phones, McDonald's, and Middle Class*. Routledge, 1996.

Spero, Joan, and Jeffrey A. Hart. *The Politics of International Economic Relations*. St. Martin's Press, 1996.

Thomas, Darryl C., *The Theory and Practice of Third World Solidarity*. Greenwood, 1995.

Internet

The International Monetary Fund http://www.imf.org
Microcredit Summit Secretariat http://www.igc.org/results
United Nations Research Institute for Social Development http://www.unrisd.org
U.S. Trade and Development Agency http://www.tda.gov/
World Trade Organization http://www.unicc.org/wto/Welcome.html

Key Glossary Terms

absolute advantage
advertising limits
autarkical
autarky
Bretton Woods system
British Corn Laws
cartel
class
comparative advantage
containerization
conventional theory
Dawes Plan
distributive justice
dumping
economic idealism
economic Marxism
economic realism

embargo
export-led industrialization
fascism
fixed exchange-rate system
floating exchange-rate system
gold standard
Group of Seven (G-7)
Group of 77 (G-77)
hyperinflation
import quota
import substitution
interdependence
most-favored nation status
  (MFN)
multilateralist
neomercantilism
New International Economic

  Order (NIEO)
non-tariff barriers (NTBs)
petrodollars
quality standards
radical theory
reparations
scientific law
subsidies
terms-of-trade problem
transplants
unilateralist
upscaling
voluntary export restraints
  (VERs)
Yom Kippur War

CHAPTER **13**

The Physical Backdrop to the Human Drama

CORE OBJECTIVE

To use spatial and geographical concepts in explaining both the historical behavior of nation–states and the confluence of the great global problems of the day.

Thematic Questions

- How well or poorly has our species managed nature?

- Which geographic considerations relate to the relative power of nation–states?

- In what ways does the history of geography illustrate both the uses and abuses of social science disciplines in human affairs?

- Which key concepts vital to addressing modern global issues were derived from the discipline of geography?

More than 2,000 years ago Aristotle observed that "In all things of nature, there is something of the marvelous."[1] Studying the Earth as the natural home of humankind is one of geography's major tasks. Approximately 5.7 billion humans live on the face of our planet, interacting with a physical environment that affects the way we live. Although humans have been around for less than one percent of the Earth's history, Homo sapiens have managed, for better or worse, to exert a disproportionate influence on the surrounding environment. It is not difficult to find examples of poor human management's leading to disastrous consequences for land, agriculture, and society. For example, it must not have taken long for the nineteenth-century Australians who brought jack rabbits into that country to regret unleashing these predatorless procreators down under.

In late 1997 hundreds of forest fires in the southeast Asian country of Indonesia were burning more than 750,000 acres of rain forest at one time. A huge haze covered an area one-third the size of the continental United States; a single day's exposure equaled that of smoking forty cigarettes. More than 35,000 people contracted respiratory disease from the thick smoke in the first two weeks. What caused such a mess? One factor contributing to this ecological disaster was the existence of unusually dry conditions in the region. But this was not the real culprit. The practice of poor peasants' setting fires as a cheap way to clear land for subsistence farming was chiefly to blame.[2]

In the same general Pacific region of the world the disastrous saga of the microstate called Nauru is hard to top for human mismanagement. A unique raised atoll, or tall coral reef, tiny Nauru was blessed by nature—more specifically by birds—with the richest phosphate reserves on the planet. This isolated island was for countless centuries the prime breeding destination for birds in the Pacific Ocean, and thus the recipient of massive amounts of bird guano. Wall-to-wall guano led directly to world-class phosphate deposits.

In 1968 Nauru's native inhabitants gained political independence from their Australian overseers. And what did they do with this newfound control of their destiny? They proceeded to overmine phosphate frenetically enough to provide the 10,000 residents with the highest per capita income in the world! But the plight of the Nauruans gyrated from boom to bust as their phosphate reserves disappeared. One outside observer calls Naura "a deforested lunar landscape spiked with hundreds of tall coral pinnacles up to eighty feet tall. Only the rim of the island is still habitable."[3] Consequences even more tragic than those confronting the Nauruans flowed from the nineteenth-century Irish potato famine (see Mini-case 13.1), a historical case study rife with many important issues, including land management ones.

MINI-CASE 13.1
The Irish Potato Famine

The potato was transported from South America to Europe by Sir Walter Raleigh in 1570 and was introduced into Ireland in the 1580s. Ireland was a small, poor country and by 1650 the potato had taken over as its chief food source.

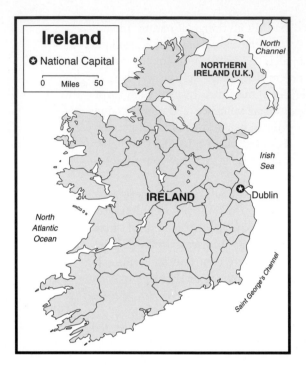

Ireland

⊗ National Capital

0   Miles   50

North
Channel

NORTHERN
IRELAND (U.K.)

Irish
Sea

IRELAND

⊗ Dublin

North
Atlantic
Ocean

Saint George's Channel

Figure 13.1

A potato famine caused by a fungus deadly to the plant hit Ireland hard in the 1840s. With one-fourth of the nation's farmland planted in potatoes, the effects proved devastating. But the bad news of a severe blight in 1845 proved a mere warm-up for the total destruction of the 1846 crop. In the century leading up to the potato famine, Ireland's population had experienced the highest increase in Europe: from 1.5 million in 1750 to 8.5 million in 1850. Large Irish families had become accustomed to feeding themselves with the inexpensive, ubiquitous, and nutritional potato. Thus just as the Irish population was shooting through the roof, its main agricultural staple was yanked from the table.

Exacerbating the problem even further was Ireland's system of land rental, as opposed to land ownership. Most farmland was subdivided into tiny holdings. The tenants rented small parcels of this land through contracts purchased from absentee (often English) landlords. When things got very bad for potato-growing tenants in the 1840s, about 70,000 of them lost their ability to pay the rent, so they were left homeless as well as destitute.

After 1846, 3 million people went on the government's welfare rolls, but many others did not qualify for the dole. Nearly one million of Ireland's 8.5 million people died as a result of the potato famine. Ireland was not to gain political independence until 1921; during the potato famine it was part of Great Britain. Some of the blame for this tragedy is attributable to the British government in London, which took a hands-off approach to the crisis, justifying its laissez-faire attitude as a philosophical commitment to governmental noninterference in economic matters.

A variety of agricultural, economic, political, and cultural factors contributed to the disastrous Irish potato famine. However, each component in the puzzle reveals aspects of poor human management of the Earth's inherited resources.[4] Humanities-oriented social scientists would likely point to the Irish famine as a situation in which influential decision makers, in both the public and private sectors, lacked simple humanitarian compassion. Numerous persons, groups, and countries could have helped—but didn't. Many historical accounts of the famine have judged the seeming callousness of various community and national leaders very harshly indeed.

An incredible 2 million Irish people left the country between 1840 and 1850. The current population of Ireland is only 3 million, one-third of the peak it reached in 1840. The United States, Canada, and Australia became the main destinations of Irish immigrants. Today the Irish diaspora is made up of an even more amazing 70 million descendants of those who left the Emerald Isle. In 1995 Ireland's first female president, Mary Robinson, expressed a global perspective befitting such a scattered nation when she said, "Irishness is not simply territorial." She went on to encourage Irish people from around the globe to keep in touch via the miracle of the Internet, adding further that "Emigration is no longer something with a finality that is sad."[5]

One of the elements that binds a dispersed nation of people like the Irish is ethnic pride. Historian Thomas Cahill's book, How the Irish Saved Civilization (1995), tells the untold story of Ireland's heroic role from the fall of the Roman Empire in 471 A.D. to the rise of medieval Europe. In Ireland's first century of literacy, its monasteries protected monks who transcribed the ancient wisdom of the Greeks and Romans. It was Ireland that cultivated these vital pillars of Western civilization until Europe, then in disarray and decline, could gradually stabilize itself. Cahill's account of the contributions of these unsung heroes unearths numerous intellectual gems warranting pride in Irishness.

GEOGRAPHY AND GEOLOGY

Academic courses exploring the human–Earth relationship are not a new phenomenon. In fact, the subject was being taught in departments of geology (earth science) in American universities more than a hundred years ago. William Morris Davis, who taught in the geology department at Harvard around the turn of the century, is credited with starting modern geography in America. By mid-twentieth century, geographers had begun specializing in subfields related to other social sciences, such as cultural geography, political geography, and economic geography. The content of geography still represents the closest social science link to the natural sciences.

Although a distinct discipline of geography has occurred fairly recently, the serious study of the location of things can be traced back to ancient Greece. The Greek scholar Eratosthenes coined the term "geography," meaning "the description of the earth," as early as the third century B.C. In the second century A.D. Claudius Ptolemy compiled his impressive Geographia, which contained information about sailing distances, key physical landmarks, and drawings of coastlines.

Geography involves an interest in land, space, and the interaction between people and the Earth. A simple shorthand used by some suggests that "if you can map it, it must be geography."

Ancient Greek scholar, Claudius Ptolemy, one of the pioneers who paved the way for the modern social science discipline of geography.

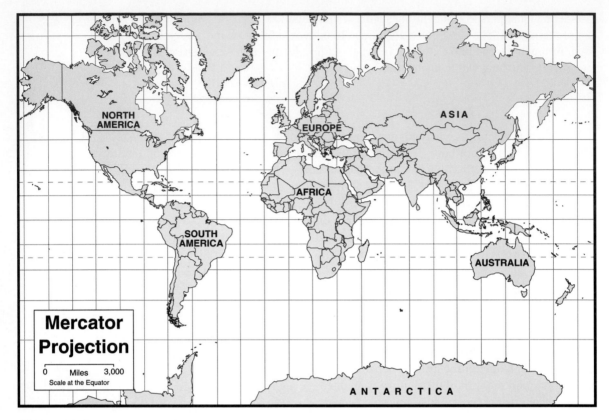

Figure 13.2

MERCATOR PROJECTION MAPS

Maps turned out to be very helpful for London officials one century ago, when they were used to track the spread of a cholera epidemic to the city's water system. Since they aim to simulate reality, the drawing of maps may seem simple and straightforward. The process, however, is anything but simple. All maps distort reality in some way, shape, or form.

Consider, for example, the 400-year-old Mercator projection map which has dominated English-language textbooks for generations. Originally intended as a navigational tool, it served that purpose admirably. However, on the Mercator map the relative size of land masses is all wrong: Europe and Russia appear much larger than reality, while Africa and South America seem much smaller than reality.

The new GeoSphere Project, headed by Thomas Van Sant, seeks to resolve some of these problems by linking together satellite photos, for both greater accuracy and more visually inspiring maps.[6] The geographer's spatial perspective provides insight into humanity's organization of physical and social space, yet it sometimes receives scant attention in social science texts that treat it solely as a natural science.[7]

GEOGRAPHY AND OUR COMPREHENSION OF WORLD AFFAIRS

Geography resides near the natural sciences and deals with the planet's complex relationship to society. Geography's contribution to our understanding of world affairs has varied according to time and circumstance. At times, social scientists have overemphasized geography's role in explaining the behavior of nations in international affairs. This approach led to ambitious causal **models** spouting laws of national behavior strictly on the basis of geographic factors. The abuse of all-explanatory models peaked earlier in this century in the hands of aggressive dictators seeking to rationalize imperialistic policies.

Contemporary scholars carefully avoid exaggerated claims about the power of geographic explanations. But if kept in proper perspective, geographic concepts can help account for many aspects of world affairs. Let's break down geographic contributions into two categories: (1) those relating to the traditional emphasis on nation–states as key actors, and (2) those oriented toward a newer world of global interdependence, especially as related to global issues.

GEOGRAPHY AND THE TRADITIONAL NATION–STATE

Looking back over the last 4,000 years, we can map a rough geographic progression of power. Starting from Egypt in the Middle East, moving to Greece and Rome in Southern Europe, then settling in Western Europe over the last 500 years, centers of power have followed a spatial migration. For about the last 350 years of European-centered power, the nation–state has been the dominant actor on the world stage, some having clearly been more dominant than others. Among the range of factors contributing to national power we find varied geographic conditions at the foundation. Climate, location, natural resources, size, and topography all figure into the power equation.

Climate—in the form of weather, precipitation, and wind—provides definite advantages or disadvantages for a country. The earth is comprised of climatic zones: equatorial, arid, temperate, and polar. The ability to grow food and perform work in the temperate zones (40 to 60 degrees north and south of equator) exceeds that of the equatorial, arid, and polar zones.

Somewhere between 20 and 90 inches of annual rainfall is generally needed for agricultural purposes. The United States, Canada, France, and Ukraine, among other countries, reside in such temperate climates, which facilitate both agriculture and work. In contrast, countries such as Ecuador, Burundi, Yemen, and India suffer from various climatic handicaps. Nevertheless, exceptional countries defying climatic liabilities to prosper, such as Israel and Singapore, can easily be cited.

Roughly 1,000 years ago a thriving ancient civilization, the Mecho Indians of northern Peru, was wiped out with a single stroke of nature's climatic brush in the form of El Niño, an unpredictable climatological and oceanic event occurring sporadically off the west coast of South America. It starts with a weakening of the east-west trade winds,which causes the waters of the Eastern Pacific to warm and tropical rainfall to shift from Indonesia to South America. This results in severe weather patterns in many parts of the world.

Nature's fury was the real star in the Warner Brothers action movie, Twister *(1996). Here, meteorologists played by Bill Paxton and Helen Hunt are supposed to be tracking storms to study them, but find themselves scrambling to escape an oncoming tornado.*

When El Niño came to call in 1982–1983 it left in its wake droughts in Brazil, flooding in Chile and California, and heavy snowfall in central North America. The next El Niño, in 1997–1998, was causing dry conditions in the Amazon rain forest as this text was going to press. The Brazilian city of Manaus recorded its worst smoke readings on record (and a 40 percent rise in respiratory disease) because of burning forests.[8] The term comes from the Spanish reference to the Christ Child, since El Niño generally arrives in Latin America during the Christmas season.[9]

The vagaries of weather were graphically portrayed in filmmaker Jan De Bont's hit adventure movie, Twister (1996). The film traces two young tornado-tracking scientists in their quest to learn more about twisters. Sophisticated special effects must have left many theater-goers with a sense of whiplash after being repeatedly jolted by the picture's frequent close calls with windblown disaster on the Oklahoma plains. In a country besieged by about 1,000 tornadoes annually, U.S. audiences proved a real pushover for Twister's action-packed high anxiety.

Modern humans in truth ought to feel grateful for the relatively stable and benign climate which has existed on Earth during the 10,000 years since the last Ice Age. Recent evidence from a scientific study conducted in Greenland's ice sheet shows how relatively unusual this interglacial period has been. The study also shows that rapid climatic change can occur not only over centuries, as was previously known, but over periods as short as a decade. The evidence suggests climatic instability as the long-term norm; the stability witnessed over the last ten millennia is more of an exception.[10]

Location can affect national power in strictly geographic terms, such as access to the sea, control of transportation routes, and availability of natural resources. Kuwait, Malta, and the United Arab Emirates, respectively, illustrate these considerations. Location can also influence national power in strategic terms. One's neighbors can affect one's national health—or even existence. Certainly Canada and Mexico have benefitted more from location than Tibet, Poland, or Korea. Switzerland's locus at the center of Europe surrounded by large countries has influenced its age-old neutrality; a classic case of location shaping foreign policy. The small city of Adrianople, located near modern Constantinople, has witnessed more great military battles (thirteen) than any other city in the world. Adrianople's unique status in military history stems directly from its precarious location where Asia and Europe meet and where the Bosporus serves as a narrow neck connecting the Atlantic Ocean and the Black Sea. In sharp contrast, the United States has always felt comforted by the Atlantic and Pacific Oceans when war has broken out in Europe or Asia.

In an age when humanity begins to bump its head on the global ceiling by depleting nonrenewable resources, the significance of raw materials like oil, water, soil, iron, uranium, titanium, rain forests, and clean air becomes magnified. Saudi Arabia's oil clearly enhances its power in the world. Canada's water resources make it the envy of water-poor countries like Israel and Kazakhstan. Ukraine's dark, rich soil allows it to blossom in ways that neighbors in Turkey and Azerbaijan can only dream about. South Africa possesses uranium, a rare ore coveted by nuclear hopefuls such as North Korea, Iran, and Iraq. The earth's natural lungs, its rain forests, which are suffering from something akin to global emphysema, have increasingly become recognized as vital to survival of the planet. Yet resource-poor Japan, seemingly always the exception, has managed to grow the world's second largest economy without domestic energy sources or much arable land.

The sheer size of a country does not directly produce power, but it does have numerous indirect influences. It is a latent factor augmenting such things as capacity for population growth, natural resources, defensibility, and both human and ecological diversity. Russia, Canada, China, the United States, and Brazil, the world's five largest countries, seem blessed when compared with most of the other 190-some countries in the world.

MINI-CASE 13.2
Land, Location, and the Netherlands

N ation–states come in all shapes and sizes. The Netherlands is notable for the amount of dry land which it has created by human intervention. Fifteen million people live in the Netherlands (Holland) on a land area of roughly 12,500 square miles, making it continental Europe's most densely populated society (90 percent urban). Sixty percent of both its land and its people lie below sea level. An ingenious and laborious system of dikes has been constructed to liberate the former sea bottom. As early as the seventeenth century, Dutch windmills were being well used to keep lowlands drained of seawater.

The Dutch war to maintain the integrity of its dikes has been a constant one, and battles have been both won and lost over the centuries. A severe storm in 1953 caused many seaward dikes to give way, drowning 1,800 unlucky victims. Property damage ran into billions of dollars. To prevent a recurrence, a massive and complex effort was undertaken: enclosing the estuaries of the Rhine River at their mouths, thus reducing the amount of coastline. The Rhine now gets channeled through a series of sluices which remove salt and polluted freshwater; the dam stays closed most of the time to hold out the seawater.

While efforts in the Netherlands have been sophisticated and determined, the Dutch find themselves in a never-ending struggle with the natural consequences of living in an unnatural environment, namely, below sea level. Located otherwise favorably in the heart of Western Europe, next to Belgium and Germany, the Dutch have made the most of their seaward vulnerability and enjoy a world-class standard of living. Their in-

North
Sea

Amsterdam

NETHERLANDS

GERMANY

BELGIUM

Netherlands

⊙ National Capital

0   Miles   50

Figure 13.3

come ranks sixteenth globally; even more impressively, the Human Development Index rates the Netherlands fourth in the world in quality of life.[11] Humanistic social scientists have welcomed the United Nations' use of the HDI since 1990 to provide texture to the standard economic measurements such as GNP.

Historically a small but great sea power, the Netherlands has been a leader among global traders for centuries; when Russia's Peter the Great traveled incognito to Europe to learn shipbuilding in the late 1600s, he went straight to Holland. This small country teetering on fragile stilts also became a colonial power in the eighteenth and nineteenth centuries. While many countries have overcome geographic liabilities to prosper, the Netherlands, by creating the very soil on which to build its nation–state, is a hard act to follow.[12]

The proliferation of nation–states, caused at one time by **decolonization** but more recently by disintegration such as in the Soviet Empire, creates small countries of questionable economic and military viability. Armenia and Kirghizia from the former Soviet Union seem small with populations of about 3 million. Yet size is a relative concept. Thirty-eight microstates have fewer than one million people; some are as small as Kiribati (76,000) and Nauru (10,000). The Maldive Islands and Andorra are nearly as tiny.

Finally, topography also affects national power. Physical features such as altitude, mountains, plains, marshes, and rivers can influence concentrations of population, agriculture, defensibility, communications, or industrial capacity—each relevant to a country's power. As a strategic factor, topography has historically made it easy for Germans to invade Poles, Russians to invade Ukrainians, Mongols to invade Russians, Arabs to invade Persians, and Hutus to invade Tutsis. More fortunate have been the Swiss, Georgians, Chileans, and Tibetans, who have all been sheltered by impressive mountain ranges.

RUSSIA AND AMERICA COMPARED

What better countries to compare for geographic influences on historical development than the two great rivals of the second half of the twentieth century—the former Soviet Union and the United States—particularly since geography seems so fickle, often deciding to be kind to one while cruel to another. Also, the fact that North Americans take for granted their blessed natural bounty warrants this comparison of cards drawn by the United States and Russia.

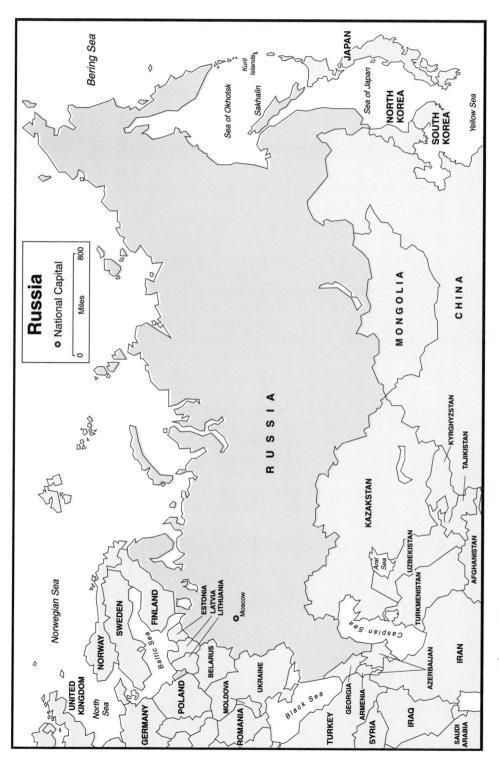

Figure 13.4

Historically less modern than Western countries, Russia has been subject to the vagaries of geography. A book by historian John LeDonne makes the case that the physical environment has consistently influenced Russia's past.[13] In general, Russia has been treated about on a par with America in size and natural resources, but much more shabbily in terms of location, terrain, borders, climate, and **arability**. In no major respect does Russia enjoy a significant natural advantage over North America.

In size, the former Soviet Union (FSU) took up one-sixth of the world's land mass, 8.6 million square miles, compared with 3.6 million square miles for the world's fourth largest country, the United States. Even Russia now by itself remains the world's biggest country, spanning eleven time zones; it takes ten days to travel from St. Petersburg to Vladivostok by train. A road sign in Vladivostok identifies the motoring distance to St. Petersburg as 9,329 kilometers. The sun truly never sets on Russia.

Such massiveness contributes indirectly to such benefits as diversity, natural resources, national defense, varied energy sources, ecological **carrying capacity**, and potential population expansion. Russia stacks up well against the United States on size. Such vastness, however, also involves liabilities, most notably transportation. Important resources like oil, coal, uranium, and bauxite, located on the other side of the Ural Mountains in Siberian Russia, are not easily moved to European Russia, where the people and industries reside.

Like America, Russia's continental vastness contributed historically to an expansionist, frontier mentality. By the middle of the seventeenth century Russia had expanded eastward to Siberia and the Pacific. Continental vastness also figures into what is often referred to as the depth of the Russian soul: confronted with a daunting horizon of seemingly endless plains, Russians have tended to retreat within themselves. Unfortunately, as in the United States, continental vastness has encouraged environmental **profligacy**. Ascribing an infinite carrying capacity to their country, Russians and North Americans have proven much more wasteful than Western Europeans or east Asians—despoiling the environment and piling up garbage, including nuclear waste and other hazardous materials. Size, nevertheless, remains the area where Russia compares geographically best to America.

Related to size, Russia and America both benefit more than most countries when it comes to natural resources. The twentieth century has been the oil century, and Russia ranks as the top producer of crude, possessing 10 percent of world reserves. Equally astonishing, Russia owns fully one-half of known iron deposits, one-fifth of hard-coal deposits, one-third of the world's water power, and one-quarter of the world's forests.

Rivers in particular have played a vital role in Russia's development. Its 180,000 miles of rivers—long, swift, and navigable—have provided conduits of communication as well as transportation; boats in summer, skis and sleds in winter. Its lakes are unbelievable: Lake Baikal contains 20 percent of the world's fresh water; Lake Ladoga ranks as the largest European lake. If nations competed over natural resources, Russia would make it to the World Cup every time, slightly ahead of the United States.

Russia being a land of many paradoxes, its outsized resource advantages are overwhelmed by numerous naturally induced problems. First and foremost is climate. Stereotypes about frigid Russian winters are not far off the mark. Three-quarters of Russia experiences extremely cold winters, with average January temperature below zero (Fahrenheit). One-third of the country experiences **permafrost**—perpetually frozen ground. On occasion the harsh Russian winter has proven beneficial, as when it sent the invading armies of Napoleon in 1812 and Hitler in 1944 scurrying for the border.

Many of Russia's natural resources lie under the permafrost, difficult, but not impossible, to retrieve. Ironically, while surrounded by many seas (35,000 miles of coastline), most are ice-bound, leaving Russia the most landlocked nation in the world. These facts help explain Tsar Peter the Great's insatiable quest for warm-water ports. He literally carved one out of swampland on the Baltic Sea in 1703: the city of Saint Petersburg. For most westerners, the snowy, frozen expanse captured in David Lean's 1965 film, Dr. Zhivago, represents their dominant image of the Russian physical milieu. They could do much worse in comprehending reality.

Former KGB Colonel Mikhail Lyubimov, now a popular Russian novelist, wrote a doctoral dissertation on the subject of the Russian national character. Lyubimov believes:

> Climate is a major factor in forming the Russian national character; we live under very hard conditions. These conditions make Russians very adaptable and patient. We are not systematic workers. We swing back and forth between frenzy and lethargy—according to the seasons. The Russians have very little sense of balance.[14]

Closely related to climate, agricultural problems have haunted Russians for nearly a millennium. Soil is generally poor, as Russia has the highest percentage of marshland (20%) of any country in the world. More troublesome, however, is rainfall: there is not enough of it and it comes at the wrong times (summer rather than spring). These factors make for short growing seasons and low productivity. A mere 11 percent of Russian soil is arable, that is, suitable for cultivation.[15]

Topography also plays some funny tricks on the Russians. An amazingly flat country, its only impressive mountain ranges lie to the south, separating it from neighbors in the Caucasus (Armenia, Georgia, Azerbaijan) and Central Asia (Kazakhstan, Uzbekistan, Kirghizia, Tadzhikistan, and Turkestan). The only north–south chain, the Ural Mountains, separates European from Siberian Russia but look like mere hills to Europeans and North Americans.

This flat Eurasian plain has contributed to trepidation among Russians whenever they have been weak during their 1,000-year history. Attacked over the centuries by Varangians, Turks, Mongols, Poles, Swedes, Teutonic Knights, Japanese, Chinese, French, and Germans, Russians tend to be **xenophobic**. In World War II alone they lost 26 million people. The brief 200-year history of the United States includes no remotely comparable experience, and geography helps to explain why.

Finally, location has also haunted the Russians. The most obvious problem is Russia's northern latitude. Moscow's latitude equals that of Edmonton, Alberta, while Saint Petersburg's rivals that of Anchorage, Alaska. This latitude contributes to many of the climatic and agricultural dilemmas cited above.

The gods of location have also smiled upon the United States by providing Canada and Mexico as neighbors. Russia has been less fortunate. It borders on thirteen other countries, all of which have been hostile to Russia at one time or another. Some, like China, even possess nuclear weapons—and long-standing **irredentist** claims against chunks of Russian territory. In 1969 China and the Soviet Union came to blows, with hundreds of soldiers killed in battles along the Ussuri River basin and in the Dzungarian Gates region between Kazakhstan and Sinkiang Province.

The vast loneliness of Siberia's wilderness seems palpable in this portrait of a reindeer herder in eastern Russia.

Of all the paradoxes that could be endemic to as large and heterogeneous a society as Russia, none likely exceeds that of size and natural resources being overwhelmed by devastating climatic, agricultural, topographical, and locational problems. Over their 1,000-year history, Russians have often been on intimate terms with invasion, starvation, and isolation. Some of these problems are attributable to Russia's traditional authoritarian political and social systems: tsarism and communism. However, these political and social systems have always been influenced by the harsh realities of human existence in the forbidding geographic space known as Russia. By comparison, North Americans have been guests at a cakewalk.

Scientifically oriented scholars might scoff at attributing aspects of social reality to Russian geography, arguing that alleged links between Russia's physical environment and its society cannot be verified and so can be no more than curiosities. Besides, the Swedes and Finns experience similar physical realities yet enjoy higher-quality lifestyles than the Russians.

Conversely, we can imagine humanistic social scientists shaking their heads over what they see as narrowly focused scientism. Humanists might harken back to winter visits to Russia—subzero temperatures, long spells of darkness, streets nearly devoid of human life, introspective faces on the few people in public view, and the ground so hard that a shovel struck against it produces only sparks—causing these humanists to shudder when recalling the harshness of January in Moscow. They would probably feel at a loss to translate such subjective experiences into language palatable to scientifically oriented colleagues.

Geography and National Power

Geographic considerations form a vital base for national power. Ultimately, however, it is people that shape political events. Geography plays a supporting role in the drama taking place on the world stage; a starring role is more than it ought currently aspire to.[16] Power is a complex and multifaceted concept and also a relative concept. It consists mainly of a country's ability to get its way in a competitive world. Tangible attributes like natural resources play a role, but so do intangible factors such as quality of leadership, strong national will, and unifying belief systems.

In addition to looking at how factors like climate, natural resources, location, size, and topography affect the power status of individual nation states, geographers also examine the bigger picture: what forces shape the distribution of power in the overall global system? What macro-level considerations are at work at this level?

Historically, the attempt to explain world politics through geography—**geopolitics**—had its heyday during the nineteenth century's infatuation with **social Darwinism**. American naval Admiral Alfred T. Mahan (1840–1914) looked to the seas, arguing in his twenty books that the nation that held naval power controlled world power. His The Influence of Sea Power upon History, 1660–1783 (1890) warmed the hearts of neophyte expansionists and imperialists at the end of the nineteenth century.

The most quoted of the geopoliticians, Sir Halford J. MacKinder (1869–1947), posited that Who controls the Heartland [Eastern Europe] controls the world island; who controls the world island controls the world. Neat, concise, and powerful, his Heartland analysis provided the terra firma counterpart to Mahan's oceanic vision of greatness. MacKinder's ideas proved magnetic to others, like Yale professor Nicholas J. Spykman (1893–1943), who developed the rimland (coastlands) dictum: Who controls the Rimland rules Eurasia; who rules Eurasia controls the destinies of the world.

Sir Halford J. MacKinder (1869–1947), whose Heartland Thesis was one of the most famous geo-political theories during geography's infancy as a social science discipline.

All these grand geopolitical theories suffered from some basic flaws. For one thing, they engaged in **reductionism** by grossly oversimplifying history. Second, they claimed a level of **determinism** plausible only in the natural sciences; neither humans nor their institutions can be accounted for with such facile certainty. Although guilty of an overzealous quest for objective laws governing human behavior on the world stage, the geopolitics of Mahan, Mackinder, and Spykman did relatively little direct or tangible harm to human beings.

Not so with the German **pseudoscience** known as Geopolitik, which featured some dangerous characters. Consider Frederick Ratzel (1844–1904), who viewed nation–states as organic entities needing to expand or die. Ratzel was trained originally as a biologist, and organic metaphors flowed easily from his pen. One of this Leipzig University professor's most famous dictums held that states need food in the form of Lebensraum [living space].

Ratzel's disciple, the Germanophile Swedish professor Rudolf Kjellen (1864–1922), took many of the same ideas even further in his book The State as a Form of Life (1916). Whereas Ratzel had argued that the state was *like* a living organism, Kjellen said that it in fact was one. Kjellen's book was used by many Germans after their country's defeat in World War I to justify the idea of a revenge-minded German superstate rising from the ashes of degradation.

The subsequent writings of a career army officer, Karl Haushofer (1869–1946), illustrate the dangers of pseudoscience presented in the guise of genuine science. He believed Germany should have won World War I and he sought to avenge its unjust defeat. Haushofer distorted the ideas of Ratzel, MacKinder, and others, bending them to a specific political agenda: to rationalize German defeat in World War I, to support the Nazi Party, and to create a case for German territorial expansion. Haushofer became a professor at the University of Mu-

The sad story of Nazi apologist Karl Haushofer (1869-1946) illustrates how pseudoscientific theories of national destiny were abused by some scholars to justify the aggressive ambitions of German dictator Adolf Hitler.

nich when the Nazis came to power in 1933, and he organized of group of disciples around him to propagate their so-called science of Geopolitik.

To many Germans, disheartened by their country's malaise after World War I, Haushofer's half-baked theories of a German heartland, living space, racial superiority, and economic autarky represented food for the national spirit. Later falling out of favor with dictator Adolf Hitler near the end of World War II, Haushofer was banished to the Dachau concentration camp, where he committed suicide shortly after the war. All other theories of geopolitics suffer at the hands of Haushofer's abuse of the scientific imprimatur. The warning? Beware of **pseudoscience** and simplistic **fallacies** of single cause. Few more telling examples of overzealous scientism exist in the humanist's arsenal of criticisms against science run amok.

GEOGRAPHY AND THE NEW GLOBAL INTERDEPENDENCE

Somewhat bruised by its historical maltreatment at the hands of German Realpolitik, contemporary geography brings entirely new data, concepts, and theories to the modern world. Rather than focusing only on the nation–state and questions of national power, modern social scientists increasingly look to the web of interdependence and its global issues. In this endeavor, geography plays a critical role.

The key insight to dealing with the great global issues lies in their interrelatedness. Twenty or thirty years ago initial efforts to attack these problems concentrated on one at a time. Today we better understand them as a system: what happens to one affects the others as well. No other social science discipline has proven as instrumental as geography in comprehending the links between global issues.

Geography also forces social scientists to look at connections that have long been ignored: society and culture with environment, environment with population, population with food, food with energy, ad infinitum. Whereas political geography overextended itself in its earlier life (geopolitics), today cultural (see Mini-case 13.3), ecological, and economic geography all contribute greatly to the newer effort to deal with global crises.

MINI-CASE 13.3
The Spread of English

C ultural geography looks at the link between location and human lifestyles, and the spatial distribution of languages is a topic that interests such geographers. More than 3,000 languages are in use around the world, although only about 200 are internationally significant, with 95 percent of humanity speaking fewer than 100 of these. Among the identifiable families of languages, the **Indo-European** is the largest group, and English is the most widely spoken Indo-European language.

The English language was brought to Britain by the Angles, Saxons, and Jutes—three Germanic tribes from whose languages English was synthesized. When Britain was converted to Christianity in the seventh century, elements of the Greek and Latin languages also drifted into the evolving English language. The French-speaking Normans conquered England in 1066, an event that resulted in a strange split: the upper classes speaking French, the lower classes English, until English became universal around 1200.

From these humble origins has blossomed an extraordinarily successful story. If for centuries the sun never set on the British Empire, then the sun also never set on the English language. Seeds were sown on every continent for English to help cultivate a variety of newly emerging cultures.

Today 350 million people speak English as their native tongue, while about 400 million others speak it as a second language. Perhaps more important, English has become the acknowledged language of international business, politics, and entertainment. English's unique international status is fortunate for North Americans, whose second-language skills pale in comparison to those of people in most other parts of the world.[17]

Geography's penchant for the big picture as well as the connections between seemingly disparate elements is useful and instructive. Our comprehension of the globe as an **ecosystem** with regional and local subsystems stems from what geographers have taught us about ecological unity. Where would human global consciousness be without the array of climatic, oceanic, topographical, and planetary maps and photographs that enable us to see beyond the parochialism of our national experiences? A timely new application by George Demko and William Wood represents the thin edge of this intellectual wedge. In an integrative approach, they creatively apply geographic principles to examine wide-ranging global issues in their Reordering the World: Geopolitical Perspectives on the Twenty-first Century.[18]

The agenda of global problems confronting humanity can be overwhelming. Viewed alone, each seems daunting. Taken together, they have been known to induce panic. Who can even identify them all? Ozone depletion, terrorism, mega-cities, deforestation, nuclear accident, petroleum depletion, AIDS, water scarcity, genocide, refugees, pollution, hazardous waste disposal, desertification, global warming, malnutrition, illiteracy, species extinction, starvation, poverty, unemployment, rich–poor gap, discrimination, overpopulation, greenhouse effect, nuclear proliferation, and war do not even exhaust the set of global problems. Geography helps us keep our feet firmly planted in the concrete physical realities of planet Earth while contemplating this rapidly changing landscape of global issues.

Chapter Synopsis

While humans have been present for less than one percent of the Earth's history, we have exercised an outsized influence over the natural world. Unfortunately, relatively short-sighted exploitative values have shaped human management of this planet. Numerous examples can be cited which add to up to an unnerving conclusion: if we continue on our current trajectory of resource depletion and pollution, a habitable planet may no longer exist either for us or for other current species. Spatial and ecological concepts reside not only at the heart of comprehending the mess we have created, but also at the soul of efforts to clean it up and avoid a reprise.

Since the possession and exercise of power affects how humans exercise free will, and since nation–states have been the key actors exercising power on the world stage in recent centuries, social scientists have often puzzled over just what it is that makes some states more powerful than others and thus able to get their way. Toward that end, the past century has witnessed many mechanistic, purportedly scientific, geographic theories. Most were reductionist in nature; some were abused by academic apologists for dictators looking to justify expanding their borders. All bit off more intellectually than they could chew, thus giving geographic theories of national power a bad name. By falling prey to the fallacy of single cause, these ambitious accounts of national power eventually were relegated to the academic dustbin of intellectual excesses, not to be repeated.

But as the star quality of the nation–state has begun to wane, and as human consciousness has shifted more toward pressing global problems that do not respect national boundaries, geography's intellectual balloon can once again be seen riding high on the social science horizon. No other discipline provides such a rich vein of data, concepts, and theories to comprehend the linkages between issues like population, environment, food, energy, and development. Ironically, the technologically most advanced civilization in the world (Western) has been least able to understand a simple reality: Homo sapiens does not reside at the apex of a natural world created for its exploitation. To the contrary, we are a part of an ecology rather than above it. Geography provides us with myriad intellectual tools to understand this simple but critical truth.

For Digging Deeper

Boyd, Andrew, An Atlas of World Affairs. Routledge, 1992.

Cahill, Thomas. How the Irish Saved Civilization. Bantam Doubleday Dell, 1995.

Chaliand, Gerard, and Jean-Pierre Rageau. Strategic Atlas: A Comparative Geopolitics of the World's Powers. Viking Penguin, 1995.

DeBlij, H. J., and Peter O. Muller. Geography: Realms, Regions, and Concepts. John Wiley and Sons, 1994.

Demko, George J., and William B. Wood. Reordering the World: Geopolitical Perspectives on the Twenty-First Century. Westview Press, 1994.

Geography for Life: What Every American Should Know and Be Able to Do in Geography. National Geographic Society, 1994.

Glassner, Martin Ira. Political Geography. John Wiley and Sons, 1993.

Hardwick, Susan, and Donald Holtgrieve. Patterns on Our Planet: Concepts and Themes in Geography. Macmillan, 1990.

LeDonne, John P. The Russian Empire and the World, 1700–1917: The Geopolitics of Expansion. Oxford University Press, 1997.

Monmonier, Mark. How to Lie with Maps. University Chicago Press, 1996.

Nolan, Cathal J. The Longman Guide to World Affairs. Longman, 1995.

Rheingold, Howard. The Virtual Community: Homesteading on the Electronic Frontier. Addison-Wesley, 1993.

Rubenstein, James M. The Cultural Landscape: An Introduction to Human Geography. Merrill Publishing, 1989.

Internet

Geographic Names Information System   http://www-nmd.usgs.gov/www/gnis/gnisform.html

MapQuest   http://www.mapquest.com

National Spatial Data Clearinghouse   http://nsdi.epa.gov/nsdi/

Key Glossary Terms

arable	fallacy	pseudoscience
carrying capacity	geopolitics	reductionism
decolonization	Indo-European	social Darwinism
determinism	irredentism	xenophobic
ecosystem	model	
environmental profligacy	permafrost	

CHAPTER **14**

Global Ecological Problems

Thematic Questions

- Which core elements characterize the globalist outlook?

- Where does the expansion model of human progress fit into this big global picture?

- In what basic ways do the ecological optimists and pessimists differ?

- How is the concept of carrying capacity revolutionary when applied to the way humanity has chosen to live in societies for 10,000 years?

- How do all the ecological issues have a North versus South tension lurking beneath the surface?

CORE OBJECTIVE

To show how ecological issues like environment, population, food, and energy provide flesh and bones to the intellectual paradigm shift from internationalism to globalism.

T he key concept of interdependence also applies to four great global issues: environment, population, food, and energy. What happens to one area affects the others, often profoundly, in ways that were not appreciated mere decades ago. It no longer makes sense to approach these worldwide problems as separate phenomena; an integrated, **ecological approach** is needed, one that ties together these four issues. While all social sciences contribute to this effort, geography bears the lion's share of the burden. But what explains the ascendancy of the ecological approach?

A GLOBAL ISSUES PARADIGM SHIFT

Only during the latter half of the twentieth century have we begun thinking in complex ways about such issues as environment, population, food, and energy. Only during these last fifty years have such issues been understood as global rather than national problems. Despite their newness, a sea change—a genuine **paradigm** shift—has washed over the intellectual turf inhabited by these global issues. This new thinking has been carried ashore by the momentum of three potent conceptual waves: **finiteness** in the late 1960s to early 1970s, **interdependence** in the 1980s, and **sustainable development** in the 1990s.

Finiteness

Biologists, ecologists, and anthropologists were among the first scholars to see beyond the national implications of environment, population, food, and energy to the bigger picture of global connections. In the late 1960s and early 1970s the first wave of ideas featured the revolutionary notion of limits, or finiteness. Just maybe, suggested scientists, the earth on which we live cannot absorb all the damage that our species inflicts upon it. Could it be that we are running out of rain forests, oil, drinkable water, and arable land?

What made the idea of limits revolutionary was that it challenged one of humankind's cherished equations: expansion equals progress. This **expansion model** had served our species pretty well during thousands of years of civilization. In the process of relying on technological fixes to new problems we came to assume that bigger was always better and that our resources and potential growth were both limitless. However, problems like hunger, air pollution, dwindling petroleum reserves, and skyrocketing population growth forced a reappraisal of the expansion model of progress. We seemed poised to begin bumping our heads against a finite global ceiling.

In those early days of ecological awareness, the unsettling idea of global limits was a lot for humanity to ponder. Coping with such a revolutionary concept seemed manageable only within the comfortable confines of academia's social science disciplines. For the most part, geographers studied the environment, sociologists examined population questions, economists and political scientists looked closely at energy policy, and food problems were left primarily to the biologists. Each global issue area was treated as a distinct bailiwick separate from the others. The identification of problems and solutions was conducted with minimal communication between scholars researching different global issues. Rather than functioning as loose membranes, the walls between different academic disciplines had hardened into formidable barriers. In this atmosphere, the notion of interdisciplinary sharing disappeared between wide cracks in academia's hallowed halls.

Interdependence

By the 1980s a second conceptual wave materialized: interdependence. As if woven by a gigantic intellectual spider, a global web of inextricable links gradually came into sharper focus. Awareness of global interdependence developed in two categories: (1) economic connections through trade, international investment, and expanding corporations; (2) clearer understanding of the links between the global issues: what happens in the areas of environment, population, food, and energy invariably affects the others as well.

Since the concept of interdependence is an abstract one, scholars resorted to metaphors by painting pictures with words in hopes of illustrating the global web. These images included those of the global village, spaceship earth, and a shrinking world. But many national governments didn't seem to get it: they continued to operate on a business-as-usual basis, ignoring the extent to which everybody's fate was now linked to everyone else's. As a result, new actors began challenging the long-dominant nation–state in a contest for the hearts and minds of humanity. To the chagrin of national leaders, many citizens were now extending loyalties to other creative entities springing up to steal the state's ecological thunder.

Sustainable Development

The 1990s offered the chance to break away from Cold War thinking, a mentality that had been characterized by simplistic world-views and rigid alliances. The obsession of the Cold War was with a bipolar (U.S. vs. USSR) world locked into a **zero-sum** game: whatever was good for the Soviets was bad for us, and vice versa. The titanic East–West struggle dominated human consciousness for four decades, leaving precious few resources to deal with new global issues. In the 1990s, however, thinking became more creative as the potential for a peace dividend that would provide more resources to environment, population, food, and energy became apparent.

The most creative crest of this third wave consisted of a new sort of fusion. In the 1980s interdependence had led to a fuller appreciation of the links between the ecological global issues. In the 1990s this notion broadened to include a concept long viewed as conflicting with the ecological global issues: **development**. The majority of the world's countries are poor, and they want to increase their economic output in order to improve their standard of living. Traditionally, scholars thought that development and the ecological global issues were inimical to one another: whatever the poor countries did to chase after the holy grail of development, ecological problems would follow in their wake.

But now some scholars argued that development and ecological concerns were not necessarily hostile to each other. The revolutionary concept of the 1990s was sustainable development. The poor countries had to be allowed to develop, but they had to do so responsibly, in a way that respected the right of future generations to inherit a habitable earth. Sustainable development said that human ingenuity must find paths to development that do

Small solar energy panels put to good use in rural India.

not deplete the earth's resources; it must find paths that allow us to live off the interest without disturbing the principal of our investment in this planet; it must find paths that respect the sanctity of the natural environment. In the words of environmental policy analyst Donald Wells, "Environmental protection is not a choice; it is a necessity."[1]

An Interdisciplinary Trend

Each step in this evolving process has broadened the scope of our vision. Each step has emphasized the connections between phenomena previously seen as separate. Each step has created a bigger picture in defining the problem before us, as well as possible solutions to it. The evolutionary flow has also emphasized interdisciplinary sharing among the social sciences. Along the way, academic analysis has jettisoned parochialism and embraced universalism, making this quest less segmented and more unified.

Nothing less than a paradigm shift has occurred since the 1960s were turned on their head to reveal the 1990s. Our definition of the scope of global issues has expanded, and so has the complexity of tasks demanding action. No one says that coping with such an ambitious agenda will be easy, but at least a consensus has been forged. Most of us are on the same page of the script today in addressing the great global issues—a script making its way toward sustainable development.

CONCEPTUALIZATION
Optimists and Pessimists

The ecological problems confronting humanity are numerous and serious. Exactly how urgent, however, remains a matter of contention. Optimists like business professor Julian Simon believe that the historical record demonstrates continuous human progress and that ingenious technological solutions will defeat our problems. These optimists see much of contemporary ecological "gloom and doom" over global issues as hysterically exaggerated.[2]

More pessimistic observers, such as Worldwatch Institute researcher Hilary French, warn that nations cannot continue stripping the earth's resources and polluting its environment without disastrous consequences. The pessimists believe that humanity must make drastic changes to avoid pending catastrophe.[3] The Worldwatch Institute's Lester Brown releases an annual edition, entitled *The State of the World*. In the 1995 issue he concluded: "Though the threat of nuclear destruction has lifted, the planet is no less at risk. While there has been some environmental progress in the individual countries, the state of the world has mostly gone downhill."[4]

Garrett Hardin's Tragedy of the Commons

In addition to ecological global issues' being abstract, they also seem rather distant from us. Therefore scholars have created ingenious metaphors to illustrate their features. In order to convey the concept of finiteness (global limits), biologist Garrett Hardin developed the **Tragedy of the Commons**, which asks us to imagine a medieval pasture open to herders for grazing cattle.[5] The grazing commons works well as long as the number of cattle remains in balance with the ability of the pasture to support enough grass to feed the cattle. If no legal limits are placed on the number of cattle a herder may graze, each herder is motivated by profit to expand his or her herd. Consequently, the individual herder reaps all the benefits of expansion, while the ecological costs of expansion are divided among all herders.

Expansion by many herders, however, conceals an ecological trap. Tragedy looms when herders—acting in seeming self-interest but to their ultimate detriment—overshoot the **carrying capacity** of the commons. Theoretically, herders are able to limit their cattle, allowing each other to survive while preserving the ecosystem; but if self-interest prevails, all herders will eventually lose out. Forging an agreement to restrain herd size will work only if it is adhered to by all. However, agreements often break down, since the system encourages **free riders** to take advantage of others' restraint to expand both their herd and their profit. The psychology of competition for finite resources illustrated in the Tragedy of the Commons bodes ill for the sovereign, competitive approach to global issues characteristic of nation–states.

Shortening Doubling Time: A Lily Pond Metaphor

Dennis Meadows's simile of a lily pond also provides a conceptual tool to grasp the dynamics of global limits, especially concerning **exponential growth** problems such as population. Unlike the case with arithmetic progressions (e.g., 2, 4, 6, 8, 10), with geometric progressions (e.g., 2, 4, 8, 16, 32, 64, 128) subsequent doubling times become shorter and shorter. The setting for this parable is a pond which we want to use for various recreational purposes.

If on the first day of the month there is one lily pad on the pond, no problem arises in the pond's use. If the lily pads double each day, we then have two on the second day, four on the third day, eight on the fourth day, and so on. On the twenty-ninth day we find ourselves with half the pond covered. At this point there are two ways we can view the situation, each with vastly differing implications: (1) since half the pond remains empty, there seems to be plenty of space for our other purposes, and we have nothing to worry about; or (2) while there may momentarily be considerable open space on the pond, since the lilies are reproducing geometrically (not arithmetically), we must act immediately if we are to prevent the entire pond from being covered.[6]

Deep Ecology

A concept emerging in recent years challenged Westerners to change how we conceive of the human relationship with the environment. Instead of thinking of nature as a resource to be used for human needs, **deep ecology** argues that the true value of nature is intrinsic.[7] Species of flora and fauna have their own right to compete for existence, independent of what they can do for humanity.

Deep ecology is philosophically closer to many traditional cultures (which see humans as merely part of the cycle of life) than it is to modern Western civilization (which views humanity as superior to the rest of nature).[8] By considering itself to have gained mastery over nature, humanity has gotten itself into hot water more than once. Occasionally such thinking has deposited us in cold water, which, as Mini-case 14.1 suggests, can be equally bad.

MINI-CASE 14.1
Lessons of the Titanic Disaster

Prior to the outbreak of World War I, human consciousness in the early 1900s glistened with confidence over the explosion of technological innovations which seemed to provide dominion over nature. Our arrogance reached a peak when U.S.-based White Star Lines, backed by financier J. P. Morgan, built the world's largest ocean vessel, the *Titanic*. Its designer, Thomas Andrews, boldly claimed that this monument to technological sophistication was unsinkable. White Star Lines built the *Titanic* and its double, the *Olympic*, to gain a competitive advantage over the Cunard Line's sleek new passenger vessels, the *Lusitania* and the *Mauritania*.

When initial radio reports claimed that the *Titanic* had struck an iceberg in the North Atlantic four days into its maiden voyage, White Star Lines vice-president Philip Franklin's initial statement on the morning of April 15, 1912, confidently assured the world: "The *Titanic* is unsinkable. The passengers will experience nothing worse than inconvenience." Before midnight of the same date, a shaken Philip Franklin mumbled to reporters: "I thought the *Titanic* unsinkable. I based my opinion on the best expert advice. I do not understand it."

Within hours of striking an iceberg, the supposedly invulnerable 46,000–ton *Titanic* lay broken in two, more than two miles beneath the icy Atlantic surface. Although 675 lucky survivors were rescued, 1,522 people died a cold and frightening death. Many critics consider it the pinnacle of folly for nearly everyone to have believed any ship unsinkable.

Smugness contributed to a variety of inadequate safety precautions. Lifeboats existed for only one-third of those aboard. Eight telegrams warning of ice fields that fateful night were not viewed as important aboard the *Titanic*, even though other ships, such as the *Californian*, had stopped for the night while the *Titanic* steamed along at 22 knots. An unusually warm winter had loosened much ice in the North Atlantic that year. There was no public address or alarm system aboard ship, and the two lookouts on duty in the crow's nest did not have binoculars. Author Walter Lord concludes: "Complacency is written all over this story. Everyone believed that nothing bad could happen."

One manifestation of complacency consisted of the *Titanic's* lax safety measures, which stood in sharp contrast to the unprecedented shipboard luxury. It boasted the first shipboard swimming pools, Turkish baths, gymnasiums, squash courts, ballrooms, libraries, lounges with fireplaces, and world-class service—matching the world-class distortion of priorities oozing from this case. James Cameron's blockbuster movie, *The Titanic* (1997) set all kinds of box office records en route to immortalizing this dramatic tale on film.

The concept of deep ecology may have come in handy, had it been rattling around in the Western psyche in 1912. Confidence in the human condition had been steadily rising since the advent of the Industrial Revolution around 1750, but confidence showed signs of eroding. The dark cloud hovering over the *Titanic* disaster turned out to be a harbinger of worse things to come, as the sky caved in two years later with the start of World War I.[9]

Cooperation and Intergenerational Equity

Traditionally it has been believed that, in world affairs, competition typifies behavior on the truly crucial questions, and cooperation is reserved for smaller matters peripheral to national interests. However, in the 1990s many scholars began to report on cooperative efforts aimed at solving the vexing set of global ecological issues. Environmental think-tank analysts Gareth Porter and Janet Brown emphasize in *Global Environmental Politics* (1996), as one of their recurrent themes, that nation–states with divergent interests are increasingly acting collectively and cooperatively in behalf of environmental protection.[10]

Developing alongside deep ecology and ecological cooperation has been the concept of **intergenerational equity**. This concept asks us to look ahead in time to the kind of future we will bestow on posterity. Humanity's ascent has generally followed an upward trajectory during most of our long history. Intergenerational equity argues that we owe future generations nothing less than what we inherited from our forebears. This sense of "planetary trust," says Edith Brown Weiss, means that "each generation holds the earth as a steward in trust for its descendants, which strikes a deep chord with men and women of all cultures, religions, and nationalities."[11]

The challenge laid at our feet by intergenerational equity is nothing less than this: take care of today's needs without destroying the world that our grandchildren will inhabit. Intergenerational equity leads us to think mostly about reducing our consumption of nonrenewable resources, such as oil. However, it can also relate to our penchant for ill-advised interventions into the natural order of things, as the case of *Bufo marinus* (Mini-case 14.2) illustrates.

MINI-CASE 14.2
Bufo Marinus

I n the 1940s Florida had not yet become the crowded and bustling state that it is today. Farming was crucial to its economy, and sugar cane was a natural winner in Florida's warm, wet environment. But widespread use of pesticides was still in the future, and sugar cane farmers were always looking for ways to defeat the beetle which was having a heyday with their crops. Desperate farmers tried some rather bizarre solutions, but probably none as strange as the story of *Bufo marinus*.

The scientific (Latin-derived) name *Bufo marinus* refers to a large South American marine toad which happens to be fond of pests like the beetle that was infesting Florida's sugar cane fields in the 1940s. Consequently, some farmers, apparently tunnel-visioned, decided to roll nature's dice, hoping for a solution to their pest problem. They brought quantities of *Bufo marinus* north to Florida and pointed them in the general direction of the hated sugar cane beetles. *Bufo marinus* never did multiply sufficiently to increase the sugar cane harvest. But they certainly have become numerous enough, and nasty enough, to rank as pests themselves.

These hefty toads weigh about three pounds and measure around seven inches from stem to stern. They have been described as resembling Jabba the Hutt of *Star Wars* movie fame. *Bufo marinus* possesses large glands behind each eye which extend down its back. These glands hold a white, milky toxin which the toad can excrete when it feels threatened. Every year a few dogs are killed in Florida by a dose of this toxin. Curator of the Everglades National Museum Dr. Walter Mischaka likens the noise made by *Bufo marinus* to the sound of a distant tractor. His description of the toad's appearance is even less flattering: "It looks like a large cow-pie."

Humans are not immune to the toxin and can become quite ill from exposure. Dr. Roseanne Philen, of the Center for Disease Control in Atlanta, reports that four men in New York died in 1995 from ingesting it. They misunderstood its intended use, thinking it an oral aphrodisiac. They were supposed to rub it into the genital area, not swallow it. Its sale in the United States is now illegal. It's hoped that its users were more prudent in Mesoamerica's ancient Mayan civilization, where the toxin was taken for religious purposes as a hallucinogen.[12]

Sustainability

Of all the new ecological concepts, none rivals sustainability in setting the global agenda for the twenty-first century. This relates to managing and protecting the global environment while seeking to provide quality of life for all. Sustainable development encompasses moderation of consumption in the MDCs, use of technologies tailored to the needs of local conditions, and new attitudes on the part of everyone. Both of the term's components are vital: the "sustainable" part means renewability, while "development" speaks to the right of LDCs to grow economically to a higher standard of living.

Sustainable development represents the crux of *Agenda 21*, the program of action agreed upon at the 1992 Earth Summit in Brazil. Canadian diplomat and secretary-general of the Rio Summit, Maurice Strong, candidly called it a "Herculean task" in his opening speech. International lawyer and environmental activist Daniel Sitarz argues that the "system of incentives and penalties which motivates economic behavior must be re-oriented to support sustainability."[13] Obviously, much needs to happen before the international community demonstrates the ability to accomplish such a lofty goal.

SCOPE OF THE PROBLEM

Humanity has left a deep and dark collective footprint in the ecological sand. William Stevens teases that "*Homo sapiens* rivals grand forces like the movement of continents, volcanic eruptions, asteroid impacts, and ice ages as an agent of global change."[14] As is stated above, the current conceptualization of global issues requires us to understand them as interacting parts of a finite system. Still, to appreciate the complexity of these global problems, we must examine bits and pieces of the global mosaic as discrete entities. Such atomization aids comprehension of the dimensions of the problem, without negating the countless linkages between the ecological issues.

During four decades of Cold War military tension between the United States and the Soviets, the world pushed environmental, population, food, and energy issues to the back burner. With human consciousness and resources now largely freed from the threat of nuclear Armageddon, paying serious attention to the ecological global issues becomes imperative. That's easier said than done, however, since human nature at times tends to avoid anything that looks very threatening. It took the Cuban missile crisis of 1962 to shake our psychological denial of the nuclear dilemma. Hopefully, a comparable ecological brush with disaster is not required to awaken humans to the palpability of these ecological problems.

Since each global issue represents a complicated labyrinth, let us examine their factual and analytical profiles individually.

ENVIRONMENT

Consider the following factoids:[15]

1. Deforestation:

   - At midcentury, 12% of the globe was covered with tropical forest; today only 6%.
   - Fifty million acres (78,750 sqare miles) of forest are lost annually, and reforestation replaces only 10%.
   - Tropical rain forests occupy only 6% of the world's surface, but they nourish over 50% of all species.
   - One billion people depend on wood for energy, sacrificing many forests to domestic needs like cooking.
   - Poor countries cut their trees for export to earn capital to pay large international debts. Brazil earns $6 billion annually from such sales.

- Deforestation leads to increased wood prices, loss of biodiversity, soil erosion, and global warming.

- Deforestation results in an additional annual 1.9 billion tons of carbon dioxide, which would have been otherwise absorbed.

- Half the forest reserves of the Himalayas were lost between 1950 and 1980, contributing to massive soil erosion.

- Latin America contains 60% of the world's tropical forests and its greatest biodiversity. Tiny Panama has as many plant species as all of Europe.

- From 1980 to 1985, West Africa led all regions with an annual deforestation rate of 2.2%, followed by Central America (1.5%) and Insular Africa (1.2%).

- The world's highest deforestation rate is in Ivory Coast, which has destroyed half its forest cover in two decades.

2. Air pollution and emissions:

- Worldwide, 6 billion tons of carbon are being poured into the atmosphere annually.

- The scientific consensus is that average global temperatures are between 0.3 and 0.7 degrees C. warmer than a century ago.

- Global carbon dioxide emissions have grown by 278% in four decades; 26 billion tons of carbon dioxide are discharged annually.

- Global emissions of CFCs (chlorofluorocarbons) amount to 400,000 tons.

- In addition to causing skin cancer, emissions of CFCs (which deplete the ozone layer) also contribute to the greenhouse effect.

- The World Meteorological Organization reports that in 1994 depletion of ozone above Europe, Siberia, and polar areas exceeded 10%.

- China increased its coal output more than twentyfold between 1949 and 1982, while in India emissions of sulfur dioxide from coal and oil have nearly tripled since the early 1960s.

- In 14,000 eastern Canadian lakes most fish have been killed by acid rain.

- Germany's atmosphere absorbs 2.8 million metric tons of sulfur dioxide each year.

- Burning of 30,000 sqare miles of Brazilian forests in 1988 accounted for 10% of the global production of carbon dioxide for that year.

- Mexico City is providing coin-operated oxygen stations to enable people to cope with severe air pollution.

- In Mexico City seven out of ten newborns have excessively high lead levels in their blood.

- Over 2.5 billion tons of pollutants were released into America's air in 1988.

- More than 44% of air pollution and 85% of urban smog in America stem from its motor vehicles.

- In 1980 New York City led the U.S. with 273 unhealthful air pollution days, followed by Los Angeles (264) and Cleveland (225).

3. Abuses of the land:

- Since midcentury 4.6 million square miles of land have been degraded. Land desertification increases at a rate of 30,600 million square miles annually.

- Annual economic losses due to desertification are $42 billion.

- The search for more food production contributes to deforestation, overgrazing, overcropping, and overfertilization.

- Global topsoil losses are 24 billion tons annually.

- Since midcentury the world has lost one-fifth of the topsoil from its cropland.

- Lands now coming under cultivation are mostly of marginal utility, so what is gained from burning forests is ephemeral while the damage wrought is permanent.

- Land under irrigation doubled between 1900 and 1950 and increased more than two and a half times since then, to a global level of 250 million hectares. China, Egypt, India, Indonesia, and Peru now rely upon irrigated land for more than half their food production. The result is salted lands, declining aquifers, shrinking lakes and seas, and destruction of wildlife habitats.

- To irrigate Soviet cotton, the Aral Sea has dropped 14 meters, shrinking from 67,000 to 40,000 square kilometers, losing 40% of its area and 60% of its volume. Mineral concentrations, like salt, have tripled, killing all marine life.

- In less than a decade Saudi Arabia's water reserve has dropped by one-fifth because of irrigation of crops, and one study estimates it will disappear by 2007.

- In West Africa eroded topsoil has reduced land productivity by 50%.

4. Fresh water and oceans:

- Although 71% of the globe is water, 96.5% of that is salt water and 2.4% is ice or snow, leaving only 1.1% available to humans.

- Almost 40% of the world's people rely on water from rivers shared by other countries.

- Demand for fresh water doubled between 1940 and 1980 and will do so again by year 2000.

- Of the globe's fresh water, 92% gets used for agricultural or industrial purposes.

- New fishing technologies have caused dramatic reductions in many oceanic fish species.

- Global per capita water consumption has increased by 50% since midcentury.

- Engineers have built 36,000 large dams for power and irrigation, and rare is the river that continues to flow freely to the sea.

- Almost one half billion people are classified as living in "water-scarce" areas (less than 725 gallons per person a day).

- Nine of fourteen Mideast countries face water-scarce conditions.

- Only 15% of Ugandans have safe drinking water, and their supply per capita equals only 8% of American supply.

- The global fish catch now exceeds the maximum sustainable yield of 100 million tons annually.

- One-quarter of oceanic pollution comes from oil and gas spillage, while nearly half emanates from the wastes dumped into the oceans by the world's rivers.

- Fifty-six million Egyptians depend on water from the Nile River, all of which originates in other countries.

5. Waste and toxicity:

- A plastic holder for beer or soft drinks does not degrade for 450 years. Each year 100 million pounds of plastics are dumped into the sea, and many animals try to ingest them.

- The Japanese use 30 million disposable cameras every year.

- Hong Kong's 8 million people dump 1,000 tons of plastic into its harbor daily.

- Chemicals like PCBs and DDT are being found in the tissue of Arctic penguins and seals which have never been near humans.

- One-sixth of Great Lakes inhabitants have been exposed to the highly toxic substance dioxin.

- In January 1993 the oil tanker *Braer* split apart off the coast of Scotland in the ecologically fragile North Sea, spilling 26 million gallons of light crude oil.

- Over 125,000 tons of toxic waste are sent by Europe to the Third World annually.

6. United States and the ecosphere:

- The average American uses about 60 gallons of water daily at home, but only two quarts are ingested bodily.

- In 1990, 405 billion gallons of water were taken for use in the U.S.: 192 billion for electricity, 137 billion to irrigate crops, 35 billion for industrial purposes, and 41 billion toward the public water supply.

- The U.S., with 5% of world population, uses one-quarter of total fuel, ranking first in greenhouse gas emissions.

- Per capita fossil fuel consumption in the U.S. is fifty times greater than that in India.

- The average American consumes four times more steel and 23 times more aluminum than the average Mexican.

- One metric ton per capita of toxic waste is produced in the U.S. every year.

- The U.S. produces one quarter of the world's pollution; daily per capita consumption of goods exceeds the average person's weight. The average American in the year 1988 threw out 1,460 pounds of garbage.

- Americans go through 150 times more trees than Indians per capita, and recycle less.

Background to the Issue

Social scientists owe a debt to geography for pioneering the ecological, integrative approach to studying global issues. For too long, social sciences discounted the role of the physical environment as the backdrop for human behavior. Of the global issues we are examining here, the environment generates the greatest concern today, especially among youth. As the popular expression reminds us, "We all live downwind." Emotional attachment to the well-being of whales and other animals that are symbolic of environmental integrity can run very deep. The environmentally conscious film *Free Willy* (1993) extols the virtue of young people coming to the aid of a whale in distress. The credits at the end of *Free Willy* listed a phone number for information on ways to "save the whales." The weekend of the film's debut, 40,000 calls flooded into the understaffed office.

In Germany the environmental movement called the **Greens** has grown large enough to overcome the 5 percent **exclusion rule** (the percentage of the vote normally required for official status) to become one of only a few bona fide parliamentary political parties. In many affluent countries environmentalism has assumed the aura of a secular religion, attracting legions of devoted true-believers. Environmental consciousness on the planet in the last quarter-century has bloomed to an extent unimaginable at the first Earth Day celebration in 1970. Nevertheless, paradox—often the bed fellow of complex global issues—is rife concerning the environment. As Lester Brown pointed out above, attitudes have changed, specific improvements have occurred in many countries, but in many ways the big picture continues to look grim.

Generalizing about the environmental issue presents a huge task encompassing many components. Perhaps the simplest way to view the question is to consider it as a problem of **pollution**, that is, the inability of ecological systems to cleanse themselves of irritants introduced by humans. Pollution threatens the viability of three interrelated physical systems: air, land, and water.

Air Pollution

What could rival the purity of the air we breathe as a vital issue? Yet the myriad forms of air pollution that threaten our health derive almost wholly from forces unleashed by humans. Some forms of air pollution are invisible to our five senses: therefore we depend on scientists for more esoteric data. Much air pollution, however, is only too visible to even the most causal observer. Global warming, ozone depletion, acid rain, and smog raise critical concerns about humanity's ability to live an eco-friendly lifestyle.

Global Warming

The LDCs criticize the MDCs, particularly the United States, for burning massive amounts of fossil fuels (wood, coal, oil, gas). North Americans' love affair with the private car is responsible for more than half of the **greenhouse gases** released in America by the burning of fossil fuels. Greenhouse gases such as carbon dioxide, methane, and nitrous oxide soak up the earth's infrared radiation, trapping it close to the surface, thus contributing to warming global temperatures.

Gareth Porter and Janet Brown claim that most experts fear that the greenhouse effect, and resultant global warming, will lead to (1) rises in sea level by five feet before the year 2050; (2) a decline of nontropical forests; (3) increased air pollution, tropical diseases, and species extinction; and (4) a northward shift of arable farmland.[16] Most studies predicting future problems from global warming involve computer simulations of very complex phenomena. However, Donald Wells refers to additional meteorological evidence, such as snow melting from the high Arctic a little earlier each year, annual thinning of Arctic ice caps, and the U.S. experiencing five of the hottest years on record during the 1980s. The severe drought of the summer of 1988 alarmed many previously unconcerned Americans about global warming.[17] But it is mostly small, low-lying island nations that have expressed the greatest concern about global warming. Why? Because they fear global warming will lead to melting of polar ice caps and flooding of their vulnerable coasts. The popular image of flooding from global warming comes through in an expensive 1995 Hollywood movie.

A worst-case nightmare of the melting polar ice caps scenario is portrayed in Kevin Costner's *Waterworld* (1995), the costliest feature film up to 1995 ($200 million). As depicted in *Waterworld*, it is not only small island-nations that find themselves under water, but absolutely *everyone* on earth, or, more properly, on the planet, because no earth remains above water in this depressing film.

Although the film was both critically and commercially a failure, the good thing about it was that this ugly glimpse at the results of melting polar ice caps could help convince us to burn less fossil fuels. Air quality is the most immediate casualty of humanity's fossil fuel fixation, but in the long term we also face the eventual depletion of these energy sources.

Ozone Depletion

Although some differences of opinion exist over the urgency of the fossil fuel-induced greenhouse effect, consensus does reign concerning the depletion of the earth's protective **ozone layer**. Ironically, while ozone (a molecule with three oxygen atoms) is one of the most noxious elements contributing to urban smog, it works to our advantage in the earth's stratosphere (10–15 miles up). As chlorofluorocarbons (CFCs)—found in the freon gas in older air conditioners, aerosol spray cans, Styrofoam, and some solvents—eat away at the atmosphere's protective ozone layer, humans become exposed to harmful ultraviolet (UV) radiation from the sun.

The use of CFCs is associated with the lifestyle of the rich countries. They are also *causing* lifestyle changes these days. For generations the prescription for healthy children included lots of fresh air and sunshine. However, children are particularly susceptible to skin damage from UV radiation, and alarming increases of skin cancer among young people are being reported around the world—especially in Australia, where the ozone layer is being eaten away very rapidly. Modern medical experts are warning parents to have their children use protective sunscreen with a blocking factor of at least fifteen to protect their children from overexposure. Putting on hats, wearing long-sleeved shirts, and avoiding the midday sun are also now recommended by most dermatologists.[18]

Aerosol spray cans among modern industrial garbage.

Unfortunately, the hazards of UV radiation exposure do not end with skin cancer. Exposure also weakens the immune system and is damaging to certain crops, like beans, peas, and cotton.[19] A major 1988 research project mobilized the world community to action: it found that the northern hemisphere's ozone layer had been reduced by 3 percent between 1969 and 1986.

Acid Rain

To what extent **acid rain** is seen as a serious problem depends to some extent on where you live. Burning fossil fuels spews nitric acid and sulfuric acid into the atmosphere. Increased acidity in the air can damage plant life, especially trees, and kill fish living in streams and lakes. Beginning in the 1960s, taller industrial chimneys were introduced to disperse pollutants. Because of this dispersion, as well as the prevailing westerly winds, much of the pollution from industry and coal-fired electric power plants in the Ohio valley, for example, finally comes to rest in upstate New York and Canada.

More than 10,000 Canadian lakes are reportedly devoid of fishing because of acid rain. Canadians generally become much more exercised over this issue than do U.S. residents. The problem is also viewed with alarm in much of Northern Europe, especially in Germany, where the term *Waldsterben* (forest death) is often heard.

Smog

We all have an ugly image in our heads as to what the rather unscientific term "smog" refers to. If you live in one of North America's largest cities, you can see it, smell it, and sometimes even feel it. Some have derisively called it "air apparent." It corrodes our buildings and brings spasms of grief to our respiratory systems; if such an aesthetic nightmare did not exist, horror novelist Steven King surely would have invented it.

Smog results when pollutants released exceed the air's carrying capacity, that is, its ability to cleanse itself. More specifically, it is both particulate matter (like dust) and gaseous substances (like carbon monoxide) that create smog. Los Angeles, New York, Chicago, Denver, Saint Louis, and Cleveland, among other cities, often head the annual list of places with the most days of "unhealthful air quality." America's nearly 200 million motor vehicles, concentrated in and around cities, cause well over three-fourths of urban smog.

Land Pollution

Human abuse of the land on which we live takes myriad forms. One scholar refers to land as a "thin veneer of life being placed under increasing stress."[20] With a billion more mouths to feed every thirteen years, humanity needs to find ways to expand agricultural productivity. Yet nearly all such methods tend to degrade the soil. Irrigation lowers water tables, causes soil erosion, destroys wildlife habitat, salts the land, creates waterlogging, and increases the likelihood of conflict over scarce fresh water. You need only look in the direction of the Aral Sea area of the former Soviet Union to see the human suffering wrought by desert expansion at the expense of overgrazed or overfarmed land.

Deforestation

The causes of deforestation are multiple, but they all exert stress on available land resources. They include (1) commercial logging; (2) clearing of forests for human settlements; (3) slash-and-burn techniques to clear land for crop rotation; (4) large-scale, chemical-intensive export agribusiness; and (5) overpopulation. Forests are disappearing at a rate of about 6.8 million acres each year—equivalent in size to the state of Washington.[21]

The most extensive destruction of tropical rain forests has occurred in Brazil's massive Amazon basin. The Brazilian government exacerbated the problem in 1970 when it created land incentives for farmers to colonize the basin: 100 free acres were given to anyone willing to clear the jungle to grow crops. Until 1988 it was almost exclusively northern hemisphere ecologists who complained about the global consequences of Brazil's blind eye toward deforestation. Then a popular activist called Chico Mendes, who was working in behalf of poor rubber tappers and agitating for rain forest protection, was killed so his voice of protest would be silenced. The martyrdom of Chico Mendes became an international cause, publicizing the plight of the rain forest and helping turn the tide of public opinion in Brazil against business interests exploiting the Amazon's resources.

The negative consequences of deforestation include much more than merely the loss of trees. The number of species in the world is unknown but estimated to be more than 10 million. Most consist of yet-to-be identified insects in tropical forests. Biologist Edward Wilson calculates the annual species loss at between 4,000 and 6,000 species (plant and animal) that become extinct each year as a result of deforestation. This loss reduces biological diversity and impedes nature's ability to adapt to change.[22]

Biodiversity is the term given to this double hit: losing thousands of species in addition to the range of genetic diversity within species. Aspirin was derived from the willow tree in 1897 by the German Bayer company and today 29 million are taken annually by people. The

The kind of rain forest burned down for subsistence agriculture in tropical Brazil.

rosy periwinkle plant found in tropical forests provides the drug for leukemia. Medical science's continuing discovery of wonder drugs, which depends on newfound chemicals from unexplored species, is threatened by loss of biodiversity. So is our ability to protect the world's food supply from the numerous pests eager to adapt in order to defeat current pesticides.

Water Pollution

American philosopher and statesman Benjamin Franklin once quipped that you discover the true value of water at the moment your well runs dry. Global demand for fresh water now doubles every twenty years while in many areas of the globe the available supply dwindles to a mere trickle. Fresh water may indeed replace oil as the liquid gold of the twenty-first century. Particularly likely is increased political and military conflict over water sources shared by more than one country—affecting nearly half of humanity. Human activity has managed to pollute not only sources of fresh water, but the massive salt water of the planet's oceans as well. Although we make conceptual distinctions between fresh water and salt water, ultimately "The world's water system, like its air, is one great interrelated system."[23]

Issues of quantity as well as quality pervade our water-related concerns, although poor water quality (pollution) seems a more immediate problem than quantity (volume available). Only 3 percent of the earth's water is fresh, yet that 3 percent is vital to human existence. Two-thirds of fresh water goes to agricultural irrigation, one-quarter goes to industrial use, and less than 10 percent goes to direct human consumption. Exacerbating the problem is that fresh water is very localized. For example, Lake Baikal in Russia holds 20 percent of the world's fresh water, as do North America's five Great Lakes. Taken together they comprise nearly half of global fresh water.

When such abundance is contrasted with arid countries like Kenya and Ethiopia in Africa, it is not hard to see why some observers predict that water wars may loom ominously on the horizon. In the Middle East, Israel, Jordan, Syria, and Lebanon all draw groundwater from common underground aquifers which are being overpumped. The Nile River runs through nine countries while the Zambesi River traverses eight nations, providing many flashpoints for plausible conflicts over water rights. Egypt, for example, is completely dependent on sources of water beyond its boundaries. Battles in the 1930s over California's water rights were poignantly captured in Roman Polanski's slick film *Chinatown* (1977), starring Jack Nicholson as a private investigator who stumbles into power games way out of his league. International life-and-death water-use conflicts could make *Chinatown*'s water wars seem sedate in comparison.

Humans have no shortage of ways to pollute water supplies: sediment (soil and minerals), sewerage, infectious organisms, fertilizer by-products (nitrogen and phosphorous), synthetic organic chemicals, inorganic chemicals, radioactivity, and thermal (heat) pollution. About three-fourths of oceanic pollution derives from land-based sources like industrial waste, sewerage, synthetic organic compounds, and agricultural runoff. Marine pollution is also aggravated by 3 to 4 million tons of oil discharged into the sea every year, with various aspects of marine transportation accounting for one-third of oil entering the ocean. More oil actually enters oceans through routine bilge-cleaning by ships than through accidental oil spills, but spills have an enormous psychological impact on the general public.

The first major spill billed by the mass media as an eco-catastrophe was the 1969 blowout of the Union Oil Company's drilling rig near Santa Barbara, California, when 3 million gallons of oil left a 200-mile oil slick which stained southern California's white beaches. One of the worst oil disasters was man-made: Saddam Hussein's 1991 act of wartime eco-terrorism when he discharged enough oil into the Persian Gulf to cover 350 miles of coastline and kill about 25,000 seabirds. The most widely studied accident, however, was the worst spill on American territory, the 1989 *Exxon Valdez* disaster in Alaska's Prince Edward Sound (Mini-case 14.3).

MINI-CASE 14.3
Exxon Valdez

Despite fresh memories of the 1969 Santa Barbara oil spill, the reduced petroleum supplies and sharp price increases that accompanied the 1973 oil shock raised popular fears of long-term oil shortages. Therefore in November 1973 U.S. President Richard Nixon approved construction of an 800–mile pipeline to connect the North slope of Alaska, with its 30 billion barrels of untapped oil, to the southern Alaska port city of Valdez. Built across inhospitable terrain, the Alaska pipeline began carrying oil in 1977 and soon lived up to its billing as a relatively safe and efficient means of transporting oil from the remote Alaskan northern slope. But once oil reaches the southern port of Valdez, it must be shipped to its destination by commercial supertanker, a task that is a higher-risk proposition.

Despite calm seas and good visibility, disaster struck Prince William Sound on the night of March 24, 1989. After being at sea for only three hours, the *Exxon Valdez* struck the well-known Bligh reef, a mere 22 miles from its point of departure. Captain Joseph Hazlewood radioed in the leak, which eventually resulted in 20 percent of the tanker's 1.3 million barrels of oil coating the Sound and choking the life out of it. One official described it as "a fish and wildlife holocaust," in which 1.5 million birds died, including 150 bald eagles. Captain Hazlewood ultimately faced criminal charges for drunkenness and negligent recklessness, his bail set at $1 million.

The cleanup operation in landlocked Prince William Sound seemed almost as pathetic as the spill itself. Exxon did not have the required equipment on hand to respond to the disaster. Furthermore, it took Exxon fourteen hours for its first containment team to arrive on the scene. In the meantime, Exxon refused offers by local fishermen to assist in the cleanup; they sat by in frustration as they witnessed their livelihood turn belly-up in the 40–mile slick resulting from high winds and a perfunctory cleanup.

When Exxon officials did appear, they seemed concerned more with controlling their damaged public image than with tangible responses to the environmental disaster. Eventually $125 million in government fines were levied against Exxon, and $109 million in civil penalties were also paid out by Exxon.[24] Scientist Garry Brewer argues that the bad news of the Prince William Sound debacle does not end with environmental destruction and corporate irresponsibility. Since it was immediately clear that Exxon would be fending off lawsuits over the *Valdez* spill for years, secrecy became the norm. The Alaskan attorney general went so far as to order scientists to "keep their data on the spill under wraps," in order not to weaken legal cases against Exxon. University of Michigan ecologist Brewer considers free scientific inquiry as the unsung loser in this case: here was an unprecedented pristine natural laboratory under stress from a massive oil spill, and science's greatest enemy—secrecy—ruled the day, impoverishing the free flow of information and reducing our ability to respond to the next comparable situation.[25]

North–South Environmental Issues

Deforestation is symbolic of the deep perceptual divisions between North and South. Deforestation is seen by many Third Worlders as necessary to their economic development, much as it was during the nineteenth century for the United States. Claiming that wealthy nations have failed to meet LDC demands under the banner of the **New International Economic Order (NIEO)**, poor countries blame the MDCs for allowing poverty to remain the norm in the South, forcing LDCs to engage in destructive practices such as deforestation. The North–South battle over rain forests boils down to the northern contention that these are resources of the global commons versus the southern retort that they are resources of sovereign discretion.

The LDCs tend to see the following as issues on the northern agenda: biodiversity, global warming, ozone depletion, and conservation. The real burning environmental questions for poor countries, however, are urban air and water pollution, erosion and salinization of farmland, and containment of toxic chemicals.[26] From the southern perspective, wasteful northern lifestyles have caused most pollution, and therefore it is the MDCs who should pay the cleanup costs. The contemporary buzzword among the LDCs is **environmental space**: they demand that less environmental space be consumed by the north and more be provided for them. Historian Paul Kennedy warns that the environmental issue is the first in which "what the South does can hurt the North."[27]

When it comes to waste and toxicity, the battle lines again assume a decidedly North versus South posture. Solid waste is accumulated in astonishing volume in wealthy "throwaway" cultures. Toxic wastes, nuclear waste, and industrial by-products (e.g., PCBs, asbestos,

Garbage barge being loaded in New York City for transport to a destination as far away from the Big Apple as its residents can send it.

and lead) are self-evidently dangerous; therefore the dilemma posed by disposing of them should come as a shock to no one. Conversely, many seemingly innocuous forms of waste, such as plastics, constitute problems mostly by their huge volume of nondegradable material. The North–South confrontation heats up when wealthy countries try to unload their refuse onto poorer countries often desperate enough to take it when the price is right.

In the North–South environmental drama, the spotlight shines most intently on the United States. In some respects this pivotal country epitomizes the global paradox. No other country has passed as much legislation or put as many resources into environmental protection. But no other country has consumed or despoiled as much. The numbers are amazing: with 5 percent of world population, the United States uses one-quarter of the earth's fuel and produces one-quarter of global pollution, ranking first in greenhouse gas emissions.

The issue, however, goes beyond statistics. America acts as the leader of the democracies and prides itself on foreign policies born of idealism as well as *realpolitik*; we like to think we try to do the right thing. But on environmental questions the United States has often been accused of failing to do the right thing, even sometimes by our closest allies: the Europeans, Canadians, and Japanese. In the case of the 1992 Rio de Janeiro Earth Summit, the United States was isolated on some major subjects of controversy—as when it refused to sign the biodiversity agreement—and was considered an ecological malingerer by most of the world.

POPULATION

Consider these population factoids:[28]

- People alive on the earth today constitute about one-quarter of all those who have ever lived. More people have been added to global population in the final fifth of the twentieth century than at any other time in history.

- It required 14 million years for *homo sapiens* to reach one billion in 1800; 130 years went by before humans hit the 2 billion mark in 1930; then 30 years passed for population to get to 3 billion in 1960; then only 15 years were needed to arrive at 4 billion people in 1975; 12 years later the figure of 5 billion was reached in 1987.

- Three people are born per second, one-quarter million per day on earth, and nearly 100 million per year.

- India has one million new people each month.

- It took two centuries (1650–1850) for world population to double from 550 million to 1.18 billion; the next doubling took only 100 years (1850–1950) to go from 1.18 to 2.56 billion; a third doubling took only 41 years (1950–1991), from 2.56 to 5.42 billion.

- The MDCs will double their population in 138 years, the LDCs in 33 years, Africa in 24 years.

- Third World health advances have added to population growth as global infant mortality rates dropped 38% between 1970 and 1992 (from 97 to 60 per 1,000 births).

- One of every three inhabitants of earth is a child, who, before long, will mature and desire to raise a family.

- Only one working-age adult exists to support a child under 15 in the LDCs; whereas three working-age adults exist to support every child in the MDCs.

- The U.N. Population Fund estimates global population growth to reach 10.6 billion by 2050 and 11.6 billion by 2150.

- Between now and 2025, 95% of world population growth will occur in the LDCs.

- The 3.7 billion Third World people of 1985 will grow to 4.8 billion in year 2000. However, among developed countries the increase will be only from 1.2 to 1.3 billion people.

- In 1950 fewer than one-third of the world's people inhabited cities; by 1990 the total had risen to more than 40%; by year 2020, 60% will be urban dwellers.

- By the turn of the century Mexico City is predicted to have 26 million, Calcutta 17 million, and Bombay 16 million residents. Already by 1995 more than 3 million people in Mexico City were without access to the sewage system.

- By year 2000, 21 "megacities" of 10 million or more will exist—eighteen will be in the Third World.

- Because of the "momentum factor," population growth will continue for fifty to seventy years after replacement-level fertility is reached. It takes a long time to slow down, and even longer to come to a halt.

- Because of the momentum factor, annual growth rates have dropped from 2% in 1970 to 1.7% percent in 1995. Yet nearly 100 million people are still born per year.

- When populations get basic sanitation and medical service, fertility rates (births) overtake mortality rates (deaths): more people live longer and population swells.

- The current fertility rate for women (average number of children in a lifetime) is 2.1 in the U.S. and Sweden, 8.5 in Rwanda, 6.4 in Saudi Arabia, 4.6 in Mongolia and Bolivia, 1.5 in Germany, and 1.3 in Italy.

- In 1955 the annual growth of world population was less than 50 million; today it is almost 100 million.

- Whereas LDCs must support many millions of young people, the developed nations have to care for rapidly aging populations.

- Nine of ten babies born are in the developing world.

- The U.S., long the major supporter of Third World family planning programs, reversed its previous position under President Ronald Reagan in 1985, by abruptly withdrawing aid from those clinics that also provided abortion counseling or services.

- J. Brian Atwood, head of America's Agency for International Development, says that "excessive population aggravates poor health conditions, perpetuates poverty, and inhibits saving and investment."

- Lagos, Nigeria, is thirteen times as densely populated as New York City.

- Nigeria's population is predicted to rise from 90 million in 1980 and 119 million in 1990 to 161 million by the year 2000 and an incredible 471 million by 2050.

- Sub-Saharan Africa has the highest projected regional growth rate of 2.8% per annum; Muslim Middle Eastern countries have a 2.5% rate; the developed countries have only a 0.5% rate, with some, such as Germany and Italy, at 0% growth rate.

- Sub-Saharan Africa's growth rate is 82% higher than global averages.

- Between 1970 and 1992 life expectancy in Sub-Saharan Africa jumped from 42 to 52 years, while the death rate dropped 25% (from 20 to 15 per 1,000 population).

- Africa's population, half that of Europe in 1950, matched Europe's by 1985 and will triple Europe's within thirty years (1.58 billion to 512 million).

- China's 1.2 billion population is greater than that of the world 165 years ago.

Background to the Issue

Paradox also pervades analysis of population as a global issue. Some progress has been made, such as cutting the global population increase from 2 to 1.7 percent over the last twenty five years. One nagging question, however, is whether it is not a case of too little too late. The fertility rate constitutes only part of the population equation, however; the mortality rate is also vital in accounting for population trends, and advances in modern medicine have greatly reduced the mortality rate in most LDCs.

Because of the potency of the **momentum factor** in population growth, time lags also present problems. Charles Kegley and Eugene Wittkopf say that we will continue to see at least half a century of population growth, even after replacement-level fertility has been reached. The three main variables affecting population dynamics are fertility (birth rates), mortality (death rates), and migration (movement).[29] Paul Kennedy uses the analogy of a supertanker at sea to illustrate the momentum factor in population growth, which will require a long time to slow down, and an even longer time to stop.[30]

Regional Variation

While certain global demographic patterns are clear, paradox again appears when we examine the tremendous variation occurring by country and by region. The most stunning contrasts exist between the rich MDCs, whose populations are barely replacing themselves, and the LDCs, where fertility rates higher than five children remain common. In some oil-rich Arab states, governments have undertaken aggressive pro-natalist programs, resulting in some of the world's highest fertility rates in, for example, Libya (7.6), Iraq (7.1), Jordan (7.8), Kuwait (6.9), and Oman (7.2). In the crowded country of Bangladesh 768 people cram themselves into every square kilometer, whereas population density in the United States is only 27 people per square kilometer.

Humanity recently passed a dubious milestone: more people now live in cities than in the countryside. Most of the cities bursting at the seams are in the LDCs, many of them exceeding 10 million crowded inhabitants. Some observers consider Kinshasa, Zaire, as possibly the worst capital city in the world. Journalist Eugene Linden attributes the conditions there largely to the corrupt "kleptocracy" of President Mobutu Sese Seko. Kinshasa's 4 million residents struggle to cope with an 80 percent unemployment rate and hyperinflation in excess of 3,000 percent. For a country blessed with natural resources like gold, diamonds, and fresh water, the residents of Zaire's capital city remain dirt poor. In 1991 elite army troops went on a looting spree after receiving no pay for months. The economy collapsed, foreign businesses fled the country, but health epidemics and massive starvation did not disappear.[31]

Resharpening Malthusian Pencils

The **United Nations Population Fund** argued in a 1992 report that "Population is intensifying hunger and poverty and straining the earth's resources."[32] The idea that population must be tied to other global issues for anyone fully to comprehend its dynamics is not really new. Two centuries ago British mathematician and clergyman Thomas Malthus established an innovative model showing how world population was increasing exponentially while global food supplies grew only by arithmetic progression. His predicted dire food shortages were averted by technologically based agricultural expansion. Many scholars, however, are dusting off Malthus's *Essay on Population* (1798) and applying it to current conditions.

While conceptually linking population to other global issues is not novel, it has been largely ignored by the academic establishment studying population since the post-World War II baby boom. The most authoritative world meeting on population, the 1994 **Cairo Conference**, attempted to rectify this academic tendency to compartmentalize its analysis, calling on governments "not just to make family planning services available to all, but also to take measures to reduce illness and poverty, improve educational opportunity, and work toward environmentally sustainable economic development."[33]

A Holistic Approach

The need for a **holistic** approach—avoiding the tempting fallacy of single cause—finds a clear voice in Timothy Weiskel, director of Harvard's Seminar on Environmental Values. The first monocausal explanation of population growth to gain currency in the 1950s and 1960s pointed to the shortage of birth-control techniques as the culprit. This was followed in the 1970s and 1980s by the theory that poverty caused excessive population. It seems clear today that the search for a universal magic bullet theory is naive and doomed to failure.

These are complex problems which vary from place to place according to local cultural conditions. In many traditional cultures, aspects of male dominance often contribute to values favoring high fertility, large families, and public male roles versus private female roles. Governmental leaders in many traditional societies have also worsened the problem by so-called pro-natalist policies, creating incentives for having large families. Their mentality has been that large populations contribute to national power by providing the large armies and labor pools essential to fighting wars. While a global perspective reveals such thinking to be self-defeating and antiquated, it does not seem so to parochial political elites in poor countries. Yet even when the governments of LDCs have the right intentions, population problems seem to multiply. Take India's failed family planning program, for example (Mini-case 14.4).

MINI-CASE 14.4
ZPG as an Indian Policy Goal

As India's population pushes up toward one billion people, many experts have predicted that it will surpass China to become number one within two decades. An astonishing 36 percent of the Indian people are still in their prereproductive years, building a huge bubble of population momentum in the pipeline. What exactly does that mean? The situation can only get worse before it gets better. The great irony is that India was one of the leaders among LDCs in recognizing how runaway population growth hinders economic development: shortly after its 1947 independence it enacted policies aimed at eventual **zero population growth (ZPG)**.

India's family-planning program began operation in 1951, but it was underfunded and limited to promotion of the rhythm method (periodic abstinence) among urban residents. It failed. The 1961 census revealed a continued increase in population growth rate, shocking the government into spending more money on three new initiatives: (1) making available interuterine devices (IUDs) on a wide scale, (2) expanding services to rural areas, and (3) launching a mass media campaign pushing birth control.

When the 1971 census showed that rates of growth were still climbing, desperation seems to have squelched good judgment in India's family-planning program. Both questionable new policies and their overzealous application unleashed a backlash of grass-roots resistance in the 1970s. In this vein, prohibiting girls under eighteen from marrying caused some political conflict; so did the passage of a very liberal abortion law.

The real explosive issue, however, was male sterilization, which dominated family-planning efforts in the 1970s. Public health officials were given quotas for vasectomies in their districts, and various cash and other incentives were created, not only for public officials but for male recipients as well. Abusive application of male sterilization resulted in coercive measures convincing men to go under the knife. From 1976 to 1977 an incredible increase in vasectomies occurred: from 2.7 million to 8.3 million. The 1980s witnessed a shift from male to female sterilization, which proved less controversial. Nevertheless, Anne Nadakavukaren believes "Over-reliance on sterilization as the chief means of limiting fertility is the main reason for the program's negative public image." She also argues that inadequate availability of condoms and birth control pills have been major technical weaknesses, while poor public education efforts have plagued the nontechnical side of family planning.[34]

We now better understand how the population dynamics of local communities are affected by the workings of the global economy, especially the terms-of-trade problem facing LDCs as discussed in Chapter 12. Africa, where the population problem is most acute, finds itself locked into a massive feedback loop: "Having more children creates a vicious circle, the only perceived solution for which is to have even more children."[35] Any search for solutions must begin with the premise that excessive population is a very complex problem.

FOOD

Consider these food factoids:[36]

1. Global statistics:

    -   About 700 million people suffer from chronic malnutrition.
    -   Precise numbers for starvation are hard to come by, since people do not officially die of starvation. Other conditions, resulting from weakened bodies, are identified as causes of death.
    -   Almost 15 million children die annually of causes related to hunger, translating to 41,000 every day.
    -   Food production from 1950 to 1975 exceeded population increases. However, global grain production since 1984 has increased annually by less than 1%, thus producing an 11% actual decrease in per capita grain supplies.
    -   Price subsidies granted to growers in wealthy countries come to $250 billion per year.
    -   Ozone depletion reduces oceanic seafood production; this seafood provides one-third of animal protein consumed by humans.
    -   Annual increases of 28 tons of grain are required to match population increases, but recent annual gains have been only 15 million tons.
    -   World agriculture will be asked over the next three generations to produce an amount of food equal to that produced over humanity's 10,000 years of agriculture.

2. Logistics:

    - Present food production is generally adequate, but its distribution is not. Civil wars, natural disasters, and poverty prevent access to extant food supplies.

    - Debt-ridden LDCs, lacking export earnings needed to pay for importation of food, are encouraged by IFIs to increase their domestic food production, generally with severe environmental consequences.

    - Wealthy countries account for most production, distribution, and consumption of food. In the 1980s the bulk of commercially exported food went to relatively well-off countries like Japan, the Soviet Union, and oil-rich Arab countries.

    - While some countries have standing surpluses of grain, no automatic mechanism exists for committing such supplies to needy countries.

    - The "oligopolistic" grain trade is dominated by five companies. Two of these, Cargill and Continental, handle half the grain exported annually by the U.S., which amounts to 25% of all grain exported worldwide.

    - Wealthy countries pay farmers to keep land out of production.

3. Green Revolution:

    - The "Green Revolution" has entailed heavy irrigation and pesticide use, causing environmental degradation.

    - Uses of biotechnology in the Green Revolution contribute to lessening genetic diversity among key plants, which leaves them more vulnerable to diseases and pests.

    - In early days of the Green Revolution scientific discoveries were shared in the public academic domain. Today new biotech industries seeking huge profits increasingly deny knowledge to their rivals.

    - Modern agriculture is highly mechanized, thus dependent on petroleum, contributing to carbon dioxide emissions.

    - When the world's drylands (43% of total land) revert to desertification, hunger follows almost axiomatically.

4. LDC statistics:

    - During the 1980s average caloric intake in developed countries (3,404 calories) exceeded by one-quarter the world average (2,617 calories), and by more than one-third the LDC average (2,473 calories).

    - One-half of children under age five in LDCs are seriously undernourished.

    - The inability of LDCs to feed themselves stems largely from internal factors like population growth, soil erosion, civil wars, desertification, and poor leadership or corruption.

    - If the harvested area in the LDCs remains at 0.7 billion hectares, then each hectare must more than double its yield to maintain the present inadequate diet for future populations in the developing world.

- More grain is eaten by livestock in the U.S. and Russia than by humans in the LDCs.
- Poor agricultural productivity makes many LDCs dependent on imported food.

5. Countries and regions:
   - In the Sub-Saharan nation of Senegal more than half of the cropland is used for growing peanuts exported to Europe.
   - Per capita grain production (a key indicator of food supply) continues to fall in Latin America as well as in Africa.
   - In Sudan's civil war, warring sides used food as a weapon by blocking food shipments from their rivals' regions.
   - In Africa per capita food production has dropped 20% from its apex in 1967.
   - China boosted grain production by 50% from 1976 to 1984, but it has yet to duplicate 1984 levels.
   - India tripled wheat harvest between 1965 and 1983 but has stalled at 1983 levels while its population spirals out of control.
   - In 1992 civil war and drought led to 3.1 million people in Mozambique being in need of food aid.
   - Egypt (99%), Suriname (85%), Oman (85%), and Pakistan (75%) irrigate the highest percentages of their croplands of any nations on earth.

6. United States:
   - The average American consumes five times the agricultural resources of the average person in India.
   - A typical American consumes three times the protein that the human body can utilize.
   - U.S. food aid has always been subsumed under politico-military considerations.

Background to the Issue

In this era of instantaneous global communication, it is the sensational, immediate story told by television's roving eye that usually captures the human heart. In 1992 the U.S. military became directly involved in Somalia only after Americans were haunted by television images of rail-thin people starving to death amid civil war. Likewise, the time to exit Somalia came in March 1994, when poignant, but quite different, pictures inundated America's living rooms: the body of a U.S. pilot disrespectfully dragged through the streets of Somalia's capital city, Mogadishu.

When it comes to food issues, the pervasive, potent, and episodic nature of the communications media causes a short-term fixation on an immediate starvation crisis, as happened in the cases of Somalia, Sudan, and Ethiopia. Consciences are pricked, money is raised, food aid gets sent, and starvation again gets headed off at the pass. Then television's impatient eye seeks another equally sensational story. Americans have been led to focus on these short-term famines to the exclusion of equally important long-range problems where hunger interfaces with international economics, environmental degradation, and domestic political conflict. Famines used to be caused largely by natural disasters (droughts, floods), but most contemporary famines are attributable to human behavior.

Journalist Robin Wright points out that there are three distinct degrees of hunger. Most severe is **acute hunger**, situations in which death is imminent from an absolute lack of food. Next comes **chronic hunger**, referring to food inadequate for health and growth. Finally, those suffering from a diet deficient enough to result in a shortened life expectancy are said to be in a condition of **hidden hunger**.[37]

Same Old Story: Multiple Causation

The deceptive thing about hunger is that, contrary to what most Americans think, production of enough food is only a small part of it. It involves many more things only dimly understood by the public: (1) distribution problems, (2) inability of LDCs to pay for food imports, (3) structural trade disadvantages accruing to Third World countries, like the terms-of-trade problem, and (4) abuse of the land. It is also difficult for Americans to relate to hunger as a serious long-term problem when one-third of Americans are considered obese.

Although the **Green Revolution** produced marvelous increases in productivity for a couple of decades, particularly in Asia, its advances have large-

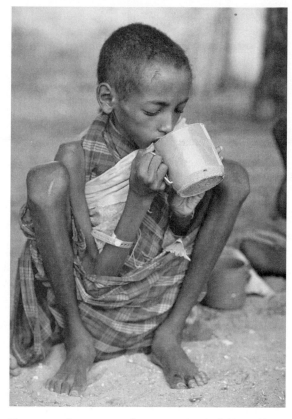

Heart-wrenching images of starving Somali children, like this one, played a key role in mobilizing the United States and the United Nations to intervene in Somalia's bloody civil war.

ly run their course, showing no significant gains over the last ten years. In addition, the Green Revolution leaves a host of environmental abuses in its wake. Mostafa K. Tolba, former executive director of the U.N. Environment Programme, accuses the Green Revolution of "making agro-ecosystems increasingly artificial, unstable, and prone to rapid degradation."[38] Current exploration of biotechnology could conceivably provide some future "miracles." But the far greater problem of getting food to poor people incapable of paying for it cannot be resolved by an eleventh-hour scientific discovery.

Like all the global issues, food is a multifaceted set of connected problems requiring attention to the big picture of how changes in one area affect another. It is too easy for humans to engage in tunnel vision, getting lost in the solution of a small part of the problem without seeing how other related factors are affected. As former U.S. Secretary of Agriculture Orville Freeman points out, it will do us no good to solve the food production problem by blithely destroying the environment, yet, dealing with both issues will require a "difficult balancing act."[39]

In addition to studying the link between food and environment, we must also examine the connection between food and population—an equally powerful relationship. Geometric increases in population coupled with declining food productivity add up to a dangerous future scenario. The concept of limited carrying capacity, so central to Garrett Hardin's Tragedy of the Commons, is critical to our understanding the dynamic interaction of the global-issues triangle discussed thus far: environment—population—food.

ENERGY

Consider these Energy Factoids:[40]

1. Global consumption:

   • As populations increase and economies industrialize, global nonrenewable energy supplies become increasingly scarce.

   • A close correlation exists between economic growth and energy consumption.

   • The world's 2.5 billion people in 1950 consumed 2.5 billion tons of coal-equivalent energy. While population increased rapidly, energy consumption grew twice as fast. By 1979 the world's 4.4 billion inhabitants used 8.7 billion tons of coal-equivalent energy.

   • Global commercial energy production increased by one-third from 1971 to 1991, with fossil fuels constituting 90% of 1991 output.

   • Energy is the "master resource," because the extraction of all other resources depends on availability and prices of energy.

2. Oil:

   • Abundant, cheap oil helped the post-World War II recovery of Germany and Japan and got consumers used to energy-intensive technologies, like the automobile, causing huge increases in demand for energy.

   • A century ago fuelwood was the main energy source. Early in the twentieth century, coal replaced fuelwood and by 1913 accounted for 75% of world energy consumption. The internal combustion engine triggered the shift to oil. In 1950 oil was only one-third of energy production, but by 1965 it had matched coal production and by 1975 was unmatched by any other source.

   • The Middle East holds 60% of known oil reserves. Saudi Arabia, Kuwait, Iran, and Iraq control over half of proven reserves.

   • Oil is the world's biggest and most pervasive business.

   • Of the top twenty companies in the Fortune 500 list, seven are oil companies.

   • Oil as a commodity is intertwined with national power and strategy.

   • Oil has created its own form of hydrocarbon society, a civilization structured around its production, distribution, and consumption.

   • Currently over half of every oil barrel becomes vehicle fuel.

- Rapid fluctuations of world oil prices constitute a major source of global financial and political disruption.

3. Other energy sources:

- In the late 1980s, 38% of world energy came from petroleum, 30% from coal, 20% from natural gas, 7% from hydroelectric, and 5% from nuclear power.

- In 1990 coal produced 40% of the electricity in developed countries, while nuclear power and oil contributed only 24% and 9%, respectively.

- The 1986 Chernobyl nuclear accident in Ukraine resulted in 32 instant fatalities and 500 hospitalizations, with 135,000 people evacuated. By 1994 Ukraine listed 8,000 deaths as attributable to the Chernobyl explosion and its radiation.

- Global nuclear power consumption increased 7% annually in the 1980s, despite the Chernobyl accident, providing 65% of the electricity in France, 52% in Taiwan, 42% in Sweden, and 25% in Japan. No new plants were built in the U.S. during the 1980s.

- In 1992 over 400 nuclear reactors were working in 27 countries with 72 new reactors under construction. The U.S. had 109 operating reactors, France had 56, and Japan, Russia, and the United Kingdom were other major users.

- The need to store radioactive wastes safely for 10,000 years presents a daunting logistical problem which works against expansion of nuclear power generation.

- Natural gas tends to be located near oil fields, and the Middle East and former Soviet Union account for two-thirds of all known reserves.

- Environmentally friendly energy makes up a small portion of global energy. In 1991 renewable energy sources contributed only 6% of total energy in the industrialized countries, hydroelectric accounting for 5.9% and other sources (wind, solar) accounting for only 0.1%.

4. LDC consumption:

- Half of world energy consumption now occurs in LDCs.

- From 1986 to 1992 the industrialized countries increased oil use by 10.2%; the LDCs consumed an average of 32.9% more oil, ranging from 78.9% in Asia to 19.1% in Latin America.

- From 1980 to 1992 total energy consumed by wealthy countries increased by 20%, but LDC energy consumption went up 101%.

- The greatest increases in energy use today are occurring in LDCs, but wide variations exist: Pakistan and Ghana had equal 1991 per capita incomes, but Pakistan consumed more than 50% more energy per capita than did Ghana.

- China, the world's sixth-largest producer of oil, became a net oil importer in 1993. Fuel for its new vehicles is scheduled to begin arriving from the Middle East.

- Energy consumption has more than tripled in India since 1970.

- Energy consumption has increased twenty-two-fold in China since 1952.

5. United States:

- The U.S.'s 5% of global population consume 30% of global energy.

- The peak year of world oil consumption, 1979, witnessed the use of more than 31,000 gallons of petroleum per second, with the U.S. consuming more than one-fourth of the total.

- The U.S. uses almost as much oil as it did in 1973 but imports a higher percentage (46.6% today as opposed to 37.2% in 1973).

- Japan and Europe have been more energy-efficient than the U.S.: in 1991 all had comparable per capita incomes but U.S. energy consumption was more than twice that of its counterparts.

- Energy has always been abundant and cheap in the U.S. In 1993, Americans drove their vehicles 2.2 trillion miles.

6. Projections:

- Third World energy consumption in 2020 is predicted to be three times higher than in 1985.

- Despite energy conservation efforts, some experts predict a 125% surge in global energy demand by 2025.

- At current production levels, proven oil reserves are estimated to disappear by 2025.

- By 2010 the MDCs are expected to account for 45% of global energy demand, the former Soviet bloc for 15%, and the LDCs for 40%.

Background to the Issue

If environmentalism seems much like a secular religion, and population leads to heated North–South battles over responsibility for straining global resources, and famines can be manipulated by the media for sensationalism, then energy might look like the forgotten stepchild of the global issues—forgotten, that is, until the next **oil shock** takes our breath away. With stable oil prices in the 1990s, it seems perfectly natural to take oil for granted. It wasn't so easy for President Jimmy Carter. Reeling from the impact of skyrocketing oil prices in the late 1970s, Carter declared the "moral equivalent of war" to combat the energy crisis. His critics were later to chide his hyperbole, making an acronym out of his famous call to arms over energy: MEOW.

Oil Shocks: The Prize Oozing Through Our Fingers

As Daniel Yergin suggests, "oil has meant mastery during the twentieth century."[41] Control of the "oil prize" has shifted hands from time to time, leaving political and economic turmoil in its wake. Three oil shocks have rocked the global economy in recent decades—brief reminders that the supply and price of industrial society's black gold are fragile. The first grew out of the 1973 Yom Kippur Arab-Israeli War. The newly united OPEC oil countries, having recently gained control of production and pricing from the big oil MNCs (like Shell, British Petroleum, and Exxon), used oil as a diplomatic weapon. As a result, oil prices quadrupled between October 1973 and January 1974. Shortages in the United States led to rationing and unprecedented lines at American gas stations, as panic gripped the national mood.

The second oil shock occurred in 1979, in association with the Iranian revolution. Iran, a close U.S. ally under the ruling Shah of Iran, changed political masks overnight. The Ayatollah Khomeini replaced the Shah with a fundamentalist Islamic theocracy, which branded America "the Great Satan." By the time the decade was over, world oil prices had increased by 1,000 percent, ushering in a brief flirtation with conservation of energy and minimalist thinking.

The final oil shock erupted out of the Iraqi invasion of oil-rich but weak Kuwait in August 1990. Three months before Saddam Hussein's aggressive attack on neighboring Kuwait, crude oil sold for about $15 per barrel; by September 1990 it had spiked at more than $40 per barrel. Given the centrality of oil to the global economy, no wonder global shock and panic ensued. What seems most intriguing is the human capacity to forget such experiences, generally failing to make adequate preparation for the next oil shock.

Alternative Energy Sources

Two hundred years ago wood provided the energy fueling the Industrial Revolution. A century after that coal had taken over as the fossil fuel of choice. During the twentieth century oil reigned supreme. With all of the environmental problems associated with the massive burning of these fossil fuels, alternative sources of sustainable energy are being sought as we slide into the twenty-first century. Some observers consider this conclusion to be an unassailable no-brainer. Yet the need for renewable energy sources has translated into precious little research and development (R&D).

One reason is political: some of the largest corporations (automakers, oil companies, shipping companies, tire makers) have vested interests in propping up petroleum as king of the energy hill. Their lobbying efforts work against the government's investing its resources in alternative energy sources like solar, wind, hydroelectric, or geothermal power. Part of the lethargy stems from economics; methods of sustainable energy production that we actually know how to create, especially solar power, has not been cost-competitive with the price of oil in today's market. A major part of the problem is also scientific and technological: scientific in that we simply do not know about the feasibility of certain forms of alternative energy (such as geothermal power), and technological because problems arise in the practical application of alternative energy that has already been proven scientifically feasible (like nuclear power).

In the 1950s and 1960s the public image of the atom as a panacea for both our military/defense problems and our future energy problems was excellent. Within a couple of decades that sense of confidence and trust in "our friend the atom" had largely disappeared. The single most important symbolic event tarnishing the image of peaceful atomic energy in the United States was the scenario played out at the Three Mile Island nuclear power plant in Pennsylvania. There a malfunctioning valve on March 28, 1979, led to the uncovering of the plant's nuclear core. Very little radioactivity escaped from the power plant, but it was enough to launch the news media on a feeding frenzy over the potential for a **nuclear meltdown**.

Coincidentally, a popular movie called *The China Syndrome* (1979), premiered a few weeks prior to the events at Three Mile Island. *The China Syndrome* explored the nuclear meltdown theme and fed public awareness of the dangers associated with nuclear energy production. Jane Fonda and Michael Douglas starred as a resourceful television reporter and her cameraman who uncover unsettling details about a cover-up of nuclear malfeasance. Both the Three Mile Island incident and *The China Syndrome* film magnified the effect of the other, alerting people to potential risks in the process. However, 7,000 miles from Pennsylvania, in a town called Chernobyl, potential risks turned into the real thing on April 26, 1986 (Mini-case 14.5). As quickly as the 1970s oil crises had generated R&D money for atomic energy, the Chernobyl disaster squelched enthusiasm over nuclear power as a relatively clean alternative to fossil fuels.

MINI-CASE 14.5
The Soviet Union's Radioactive Achilles Heel

Fifty miles north of the Ukrainian capital city of Kiev, plant technicians at the Chernobyl nuclear reactor were conducting a special test to see how long its turbines could generate power after the steam supply had been shut off. Later investigations were to reveal six violations of rules breached by the 1986 test. The result was a steam explosion which blew apart the 1,000–ton reactor as if it were made of papier-mâché. Thirty separate fires began around the power station, the worst of which was an uncontrollable blaze in the graphite core of reactor number four. Heroic firefighters became the first casualties of the disaster. Within a few days 135,000 people were evacuated from the area around Chernobyl. Still referred to derisively as the Dead Zone, this area within a 20-mile radius of the plant now serves as a scientific laboratory for studying long-term ecological effects. It may be 1,000 years before people can return to live here.

The Soviet government reported only thirty-two immediate deaths and about 500 hospitalizations around Chernobyl. But as the 1945 Hiroshima and Nagasaki experiences had previously demonstrated, the most insidious long-term problems derive not from the initial blast but from the effects of radioactivity: genetic diseases, chromosome aberration, and weakening of the human immune system. Dangerous levels of radiation were soon reported in twenty countries in Eastern and Northern Europe. Radioactive fallout in the Ukraine actually turned out to be less serious than in the Soviet Republic of Belarus, because of prevailing winds at the time. In a town of 45,000 called Krypiat, near Chernobyl, seven cases of childhood cancer had been reported in the decade before the 1986 disaster, whereas 424 occurred in the decade between 1986 and 1996. As of 1994, Ukrainian authorities listed 8,000 deaths as attributable to radiation from Chernobyl.

The number four reactor at Chernobyl lies under a hastily constructed cement sarcophagus today. Throughout the rest of the former Soviet Union, sixteen nuclear reactors with a design identical to Chernobyl's continue to churn out electricity. By the mid-1990s over 500 nuclear power plants existed in twenty-seven countries, including 119 in the United States. What is your opinion about nuclear power as an alternative to the burning of fossil fuels? Can nuclear power carry a larger share of the energy burden in the twenty-first century? Or did Three Mile Island and Chernobyl permanently halt chances for the atom to generate the majority of our electricity?[42]

Chapter Synopsis

Social scientists sometimes overuse the image of a paradigm shift. However, in this context the concept genuinely works. When we stopped seeing the highest expression of human endeavor as the nation–state and when we understood the bigger picture of human connections that ignore national borders, there was a revolutionary metamorphosis. Similarly, when the concepts of finiteness, interdependence, and sustainable development liberated our thinking from atomistic, discipline-bound tunnel vision, a qualitatively novel consciousness emerged to face the daunting challenges posed by global issues like environment, population, food, and energy. Such intellectual battles are not won without casualties. Among them is the expansion model of human progress which has served our species well throughout recorded human history. The beliefs that bigger always means better and that we can rely on technological fixes to rescue us from whatever dilemma confronts us lie torn and tattered on the battlefield of ideas. Whether we can find a sustainable alternative in our bag of tricks remains an open question—and a vital one.

The palpable stuff of the paradigm shift to globalism consists of thousands of factoids that beg for collection, organization, and analysis. Performing this scientific sorting process leaves us with one inescapable conclusion: We have problems here. The unsettling reality that "we all live downwind" has settled into even the sand surrounding the heads of the most determined ostriches among us. Problems like pollution, deforestation, ozone depletion, and global warming just won't go away. But environmentalism has assumed the face of a secular religion among young people in many rich countries and offers reasons for hope. The momentum factor makes the population issue look like a supertanker at sea desperately trying to turn around in order to avoid pending disaster. The 5.7 billion people now living on the face of the earth constitute 25 percent of all humans who have ever lived, and we are adding 100 million new people per year. Holistic approaches recognizing the multicausal nature of the population problem are needed. While televised images of rail-thin souls starving to death amid civil war are the catalysts that drive U.S. food policy today, we must also deal with the global food problem in a long-term manner based on the fact that the production of sufficient amounts of food does not lie at the heart of the food problem. If our consciousness regarding food issues seems driven by a fickle network television lenses, then our attention to global energy problems makes us look like sufferers of amnesia. Only when oil shocks (1973, 1979, 1990) paralyze us with fear do we engage the issue. Longer-term vision is necessary to deal with the global energy issue.

With the advent of the 1992 Earth Summit, a fragile global consensus has been articulated for the first time. That consensus rests on the untested shoulders of sustainable development. This most crucial ecological idea of the 1990s contains something for everyone: sustainability satisfies the North's desire for responsible stewardship of finite resources; development satiates the South's insistence on the right to increase standards of living in the manner of northern countries. Can these unlikely bedfellows produce new lifestyles that satisfy the divergent agendas of North and South? If this shotgun marriage can bear magical fruit, it will have to overcome wholly different philosophical outlooks epitomized by the current battle over rain forest suzerainty. To the South, rain forests are the sovereign property of Brazil, Indonesia, or Cameroon, leaving the North with little to say about their disposition. In sharp contrast, the North sees rain forests as shared resources affecting the global commons. We can only hope that human ingenuity can fit this round peg into the square hole.

For Digging Deeper

Art, Henry W. *The Dictionary of Ecology and Environmental Science*. Henry Holt, 1995.

Brown, Lester R. *The State of the World 1995*. W.W. Norton, 1995.

Choucri, Nazli, Ed. *Global Accord: Environmental Challenges and International Responses*. MIT Press, 1993.

Cunningham, William P. *Understanding Our Environment: An Introduction*. William C. Brown, 1996.

Fenton, Thomas P., and Mary J. Heffron, Eds. *Food, Hunger, Agribusiness: A Directory of Resources*. Orbis Books, 1987.

Hardin, Garrett. *Living Within Limits: Ecology, Economics, and Population Taboos*. Oxford University Press, 1993.

Hempel, Lamont C. *Environmental Governance: The Global Challenge*. Island Press, 1996.

Kennedy, Paul. *Preparing for the Twenty-First Century*. Random House, 1993.

Pirages, Dennis C. *Building Sustainable Societies: A Blueprint for a Post-Industrial World*. Mitchell E. Sharp, 1996.

Porter, Gareth, and Janet Welsh Brown. *Global Environmental Politics*. Westview Press, 1996.

Sale, Kirkpatrick. *The Green Revolution: The American Environmental Movement, 1962–1992*. Hill and Wang, 1995.

Sessions, George, Ed. *Deep Ecology for the Twenty-First Century*. Random House, 1995.

Swanson, Timothy, *The International Regulation of Extinction*. New York University Press, 1994.

Vandermeer, John, and Yvette Perfecto. *Breakfast of Biodiversity: The Truth about Rainforest Destruction*. Food First, 1995.

Wells, Donald T. *Environmental Policy: A Global Perspective for the Twenty-First Century*. Prentice Hall, 1996.

Yergin, Daniel. *The Prize: The Epic Quest for Oil, Money, and Power*. Simon & Schuster, 1991.

Internet

The Earth Times   http://www.earthtimes.org

Global Land Information System   http://edcwww.cr.usgs.gov/webglis

Planned Parenthood   http://www.igc.apc.org/ppfa/

Resources for Energy and the Environment   http://www.polisci.wvu.edu/nrcce/intguide.html

Key Glossary Terms

acid rain	chronic hunger	environmental space
acute hunger	deep ecology	exclusion rule
Cairo Conference	development	expansion model
carrying capacity	ecological approach	exponential growth

finiteness
free rider
greenhouse gases
Green Revolution
Greens
hidden hunger
holistic
interdependence

intergenerational equity
momentum factor in population
New International Economic
 Order (NIEO)
nuclear meltdown
oil shock
ozone layer
paradigm

pollution
positive-sum game
sustainable development
Tragedy of the Commons
United Nations Population Fund
zero population growth (ZPG)
zero-sum game

CHAPTER 15

Solving Ecological Problems

Thematic Questions

- What kinds of institution building has occurred in the issue areas of environment, population, food, and energy?

- How has the nation–state behaved in comparison to other actors in the process of building structures for discourse on these issues?

- Are there policy principles that can help guide all actors struggling with global issues on the world stage?

- Do any innovative approaches bode well for finding creative solutions that go beyond traditional strategies applied by nation–states?

CORE OBJECTIVE

To point
in the
direction of
solutions to
the vexing
array of
global problems
by identifying
infrastructures
for discourse
and policy
principles for
subsequent
action.

It will require a stretch for human ingenuity to solve the vexing array of global ecological problems. Many observers concerned about environment, population, food, and energy consider the nation–state to be, in a sense, on probation. Having proven unsuccessful in dealing with global issues, countries will need to demonstrate both commitment and creativity in order to regain the confidence of their citizenry. The strategies chosen by nation–states to cope with such pervasive dilemmas must spring from holistic understandings. Piecemeal actions based on a failure to comprehend the interrelatedness of global issues will not only be unsuccessful; they may even be dangerous. The traditional model of competitive nation–states must share time with modern **globalism**, which views all problems through the prism of interdependence.

The basic fact of life stemming from a globalist perspective is the widening chasm between North and South, rich versus poor, MDCs against LDCs. Viewing global issues like population or food as someone else's problem is shortsighted. The combination of global transportation, sophisticated weapons technology, and desperate Third Worlders makes the rich vulnerable to international terrorism, as the 1993 bombing of New York's World Trade Center so poignantly illustrated. Another necessary attitudinal shift consists of **anticipatory thinking**. Things change so rapidly today that humans have lost the luxury of waiting until a global problem becomes acute before dealing with it. The metaphor of a geometrically expanding lily pond discussed in Chapter 14 is instructive in this regard.

It seems almost axiomatic that people in most parts of the world seek **economic development** as a fundamental human right. However, if LDCs merely repeat the role that northern countries played on the world stage, catastrophe may be waiting in the wings. Quality of life should be sought for all humans, but the challenge is to pursue quality of life without despoiling the environment, consuming all the earth's resources, and exceeding global carrying capacity through an unbridled population explosion. The tug-of-war over global issues ought not pit economic development on one side of the drama against the ecological global issues on the other side. The trick will be for neither side either to win completely or lose completely.

A complex mix of strategies must be applied. No single panacea or magic bullet exists in the real world. Like research medicine's battle against cancer, the struggle can be won one small victory at a time, in the absence of a single miraculous discovery. Modern technology takes a polemical beating in much of the ecological literature, since it has often contributed to environmental degradation and resource consumption. But while technology represents part of the problem, it can also be part of the solution; it cannot simply be discarded, as some environmental purists would have it.

This brings us to the question of action. What should humans be doing about global issues? What is already being accomplished and what remains to be done? One way of dividing the action agenda is to look at: (1) the creation of institutions for global solutions and (2) the pursuit of policy principles to guide the various actors involved in global issues.

ACTION I: INSTITUTIONS FOR GLOBAL SOLUTIONS

The process of adapting to a changing world and adopting new attitudes and policies is an incremental one. Before consensus-based policies can be implemented, dialogue must become institutionalized. Structures and institutions are required to give organizational life to new ideas. For the last three decades a series of **global town meetings** have addressed

Delegates discussing issues at the grandest global meeting ever assembled—the 1992 Earth Summit held in Rio de Janeiro, Brazil.

problems of economic development, the environment, population, food, energy, and related issues.[1] In most cases they have grown out of special needs identified within the General Assembly of the United Nations. Some have produced important **treaties** and **conventions**. All have generated heated debate.

UNEP

The 1972 Stockholm Conference on the Human Environment energized global activity on the environmental front when it concluded that states have the responsibility to ensure that activities within their jurisdiction do not cause damage to the environment of other states. The Stockholm Conference produced what has become the leading global environmental agency, the **United Nations Environmental Programme (UNEP)**, which coordinates all matters related to the environment. It also runs the **Earthwatch** reporting system of global data and traces environmental changes. The UNEP has an annual budget of $40 million and is headquartered in Nairobi, Kenya. Negotiations leading to the 1989 **Montreal Protocol** on ozone layer protection were conducted under the auspices of the UNEP. The UNEP also served as a catalyst to agreements on transportation of hazardous wastes and trade in endangered species.

UNCED: The Earth Summit

The greatest of all global town meetings occurred in Rio de Janeiro, Brazil, in 1992. The **United Nations Conference on Environment and Development (UNCED)**, or the Earth Summit, brought together 178 countries and was covered by 8,000 journalists. Predictably, North–South disputes captured the headlines. The LDCs wanted an expression of their right to develop economically and a greater onus of responsibility for environmental decay placed on the rich countries, whom the LDCs claim caused most of the pollution. The MDCs, of course, opposed all such initiatives, killing most in early drafts of the conference document.

The North wanted clear restrictions on the use of forest resources, arguing that southern rain forests are first and foremost **global resources**, as the earth's lungs, and that therefore they require global regulation. The South continued to define forests as the **sovereign property** of each nation. Malaysia's head negotiator drew a line in the sand by claiming that "Forests are clearly a sovereign resource—not like atmosphere and oceans, which are a global commons."[2] The LDCs also wanted much greater financial aid for environmental cleanup, but in the end they received only a fraction of what they requested.

Despite the North–South schism, an 800-page document dealing with 120 topics finally emerged: Agenda 21. A U.N. Commission of Sustainable Development was formed to implement this ambitious program. According to environmental lawyer Daniel Sitarz:

> The bold goal of AGENDA 21 is to halt and reverse the environmental damage to our planet and to promote environmentally sound and sustainable development in all countries on earth. It is a blueprint for action in all areas relating to the sustainable development of our planet into the 21st century.[3]

The World Bank's Global Environment Facility (GEF)

The most contentious aspect of trying to solve any of the global issues can be summed up in one word: money. Large amounts of it will be distributed, making for financial winners and financial losers. In 1991 a new global institution was created to administer resources aimed at solving ecological problems. Called the **Global Environment Facility (GEF)**, it is a product of the **World Bank**, where the MDCs exercise control through procedures of **weighted voting**. Since the MDCs put up the money for the GEF's budget ($1.2 billion for 1991–1994, and $2 billion for 1994–1997), they want to influence the decisions on how it is spent. The LDCs, in sharp contrast, have argued unsuccessfully for a system of **one country, one vote**, since they have little voice in the GEF's current system of weighted voting.

Building Up to the Cairo Conference on Population

The population issue first exploded onto the global agenda at the 1974 **Bucharist World Population Conference** in Bucharest, Rumania, where LDC insistence on NIEO demands, such as for redistribution of wealth, prevented any major agreements. In 1984, however, at another U.N. conference, the **Mexico City World Population Conference**, North–South rancor abated considerably. The general statements emanating from both conferences reiterated the right of individual nation–states to deal with the population problem in ways consistent with their own social traditions.

The most influential session, however, was the 1994 **Cairo World Population Conference**, attended by more than 170 countries and thousands of NGOs. The delegates unanimously adopted a 113-page "Program of Action," which pledges spending $17 billion annually on family-planning programs. In addition, it reflects the conclusion of many recent studies that education among women leads to reduced fertility rates. Therefore, it calls for funding new female education programs. The major dissenters to early draft resolutions of the "Program of Action" were unlikely bedfellows: Muslim fundamentalists and the Catholic Church, who both believed that initial drafts on family planning encouraged abortion. Pope John Paul

II wrote well-publicized letters to President Bill Clinton and to Pakistani Dr. Nafis Sadik, Conference secretary general. Various compromises resolved most of the differences, and there was minimal dissent to the final document.

The Rome Conference and Creation of the FAO

The most important conference in the area of food was the 1974 **Rome World Food Conference**. The Rome Conference made a series of recommendations that were later endorsed by the U.N. General Assembly. Some established new institutions, such as the **World Food Council (WFC)**, which was created in 1975 to monitor and coordinate all aspects of the U.N. food security system. Also an **International Fund for Agricultural Development (IFAD)** was begun in 1977 to help the rural poor in LDCs to improve food production. These organizations supplement the activities of the world's most important and oldest (1945) food IGO—the **Food and Agricultural Organization (FAO)**, which supplies food aid and technical help to LDCs. Its members pledge to cooperate in order to raise levels of nutrition and to improve the production and distribution of food.

The Energy Issue: Less Institution Building

Far less institution building has coalesced around the energy issue. Although a **World Energy Conference** was held in 1981, the most important development was the U.S.-led construction of the **International Energy Agency (IEA)** in 1974, intended to oversee the sharing of oil by the industrialized countries. Having grown directly out of the first oil shock of 1973, the IEA seeks to create cooperation for (1) building and sharing stocks of oil, (2) promoting cost-sharing for conservation programs, and (3) facilitating the development of alternative sources of energy.[4]

In general, the current state of institution building and dialogue attendant to the global ecological issues has become fairly robust, especially when contrasted with what existed a mere three decades ago. While some observers think the pace of activity in these areas needs to be quickened, reasons for tempered optimism do exist. The most important catalysts for action have been NGOs like Oxfam, United Support of Artists for Africa, Live Aid, World Wildlife Fund, Greenpeace, World Conservation Union, American Forestry Association, and the Sierra Club. Many IGOs have also contributed to the process of institution building but have been hampered by states' unwilling to let them become too powerful.

ACTION II: GUIDING POLICY PRINCIPLES

Merely creating dialogue within institutional forums, by itself, solves no global problems. Enlightened policies need to be pursued by all actors who influence global issues: nation–states, NGOs, IGOs, MNCs, and IFIs. The scope of this chapter leans toward a broad-based perspective rather than toward the micro-management of specific solutions to precise ecological problems. Within that general framework, however, policy principles can be spelled out. Since nation–states still remain the most powerful actors, their behavior is critically important, and these general principles relate to all actors on the world stage, only more so to nations.

Multilateralism

National leaders tend to guard jealously national sovereignty and autonomy. They bristle at the suggestion that other entities (like IGOs, NGOs, or MNCs) have the authority to tell them what to do. Political machismo in a democracy, especially an individualistic one like the United States, has great popular appeal. On the international stage, politicians project such rugged individualism through tough rhetoric, defiance, and unilateral action. Unfortunately, going it alone runs against the grain of the interdependent world in which we now live. Solving global issues usually demands cooperative endeavor, which means multilateralism and compromise, not unilateral action. While applying most directly to the United States, this principle is relevant to other nation–states as well as to other actors who become overly star-struck.

Grass Roots Initiatives

A new respect for the significance of **grass roots** movements and the role of creative individuals is also a valid policy parameter. The computer revolution transforms information into power—which individuals wield as well as nation–states, and in some cases even better. As expressed by James Rosenau:

> At the micro-level, the analytic skills of individuals have increased to a point where they now play a different and significant role in world politics, a role which has intensified both the processes of structural bifurcation [between states and other actors] and the breakdown of authority relations.[5]

Female Empowerment

In poor southern countries, which comprise three-fourths of humanity, women perform 60 percent of the work for 10 percent of the income. **Female empowerment** is another impor-

Poor women tending fields in the western African country of Cameroon.

tant policy guideline. The inferior status experienced by most of the world's women is not only a human rights issue of justice, but also an economic development issue. A spate of recent studies suggest that unleashing the potential of the world's women represents a viable policy available for sustainable economic development. Expanded education for Third World women, for example, dampens population growth, since the evidence shows that educated women have fewer children, regardless of culture.

Ecological Policy Dialogue

We live in a world of dazzling scientific discovery: every five years the body of scientific knowledge doubles, and the information available in the computer age seems infinite. A predictable problem results when the **communications gap** between the scientific pioneer and the public policymaker becomes too great. Just as when Albert Einstein warned that the sudden creation of nuclear weapons had changed everything except the way our species thinks, today a yawning chasm separates what science knows about global problems like environment, population, food, and energy, from what policymakers believe to constitute reality.

In *The International Regulation of Extinction* (1994) Cambridge University ecologist Timothy Swanson stresses the need to build bridges between the scientific community and global policymakers in nation–states and other institutions.[6] Just as it probably was not prudent that President Franklin Roosevelt failed to provide any information about the atomic bomb project to Vice-President Harry Truman during World War II, so too ought we try to avoid ecological ignorance among contemporary policymakers.

Aid and Assistance

It is equally obvious that global issues cannot be seriously addressed without major increases in **technical aid** and **financial aid** from North to South. Again, however, multilateralism should pervade schemes for assistance. Too frequently during the Cold War, foreign aid from countries like the United States was driven by political objectives and added little to development of the South. In order to avoid the waste and inefficiency of general government-to-government foreign aid, assistance should be directed not only multilaterally but also **sectorally** and for specific purposes, applied more by IGOs and NGOs than by Third World national governments.

Democracy and Devolution

Many scholars have argued that **democratic** government acts as a check against the human and ecological abuses which have historically been associated with authoritarian regimes. Relating to the issue of hunger, journalist Sylvia Nasar writes, "Whether or not a country starves depends more on whether it has a free press and democratic government than whether it has enough grain."[7] It has also been said often that within democratic governments, both North and South, economic development activities should **devolve** to local initiative through a general decentralization process. Given the poor record of nation–states in these economic areas, NGOs and other pressure groups should also demand that many development activities be **privatized** out of the public domain in search of greater efficiency than has been the case with governmental programs.

Model: NICs as Trading States

While it surely is not possible for all LDCs to emulate the recent economic development of NICs like Taiwan and Singapore, something valuable has been learned from these east Asian success stories, as was chronicled in the comparison between South Korea and Ghana at the end of Chapter 12. Above all, the United States and other countries should encourage the emergence of trading states, since this path to growth currently seems to offer the best prospects. Although some serious economic problems exploded in the Asian NICs during 1998, these countries still represent the best-case-scenario for other Southern hemisphere states to copy. No other model seems as promising.

Aggressive Regulation

In his analysis of Garrett Hardin's Tragedy of the Commons, political scientist Marvin Soroos examines four general strategies for avoiding a collapse of the communal pasture. In numerous similar real-world situations, our policy choices boil down to (1) encouraging voluntary restraint through education and social pressure, (2) adopting regulations that limit pasture access and use, including stiff penalties for violations, (3) partitioning the pasture into fenced-in plots, or (4) abolishing private ownership in favor of communal ownership. Soroos's conclusion is that in the hypothetical "commons," and in the real world, only the regulation of access and use, backed by penalties with teeth, stands a chance of solving existing global problems.[8]

Marvin Soroos's emphasis on aggressive regulation of access and use for our global commons (such as the oceans or the atmosphere) dovetail with Donald Wells's advocacy of command-and-control ecological policies for a sustainable future. This strategy entails the construction of a "large body of rules and regulations enforced through complex institutional structures." This hard-nosed approach needs to be **intergovernmental**, that is, applied at all levels of government, from local to state to national to international.[9]

Environmental Accounting

Many ecological writers have also called for innovative methods of bookkeeping to reflect the realities of long-term environmental costs associated with many forms of economic expansion. Heading the list is **environmental accounting**, which uses resource depletion and pollution of the ecosystem in computing the bottom line of a nation's wealth. Since so much of the modern world is market driven, the more market-related policy principles that promote ecological awareness, the better off we will be.[10]

Green Consumerism

Another policy principle relates to private individuals and groups like NGOs rather than governmental entities. Recent examples of voluntary lifestyle changes toward a sustainable existence are impressive, especially in Northern Europe. The harmony of simplicity has led increasing numbers of citizens to engage in positive actions like recycling, as well as negative ones, like boycotting the products of polluting companies. These activities have been dubbed **green consumerism**.[11]

Germany's model recycling system includes separating recyclables into plastic and metal (left), paper (right), and all others (center). Stations like these are commonplace in every German neighborhood.

Public pressure for green consumerism in Germany resulted in a 1991 law which has made Germans the world's champion recyclers. This law creates market incentives for corporations to reduce the packaging around consumer products, which makes up half of all residential waste in Germany. Incentives have also been given to consumers to place packages with a green dot (for ecological responsibility) in collection bins placed in each neighborhood. "In Germany, the polluter pays!" This recycling law has been so successful that France and the Netherlands have recently copied it.[12]

Green Justice

A final policy principle for those of us in the MDCs to consider is that of **green justice**, or fairness in allocating responsibilities for the creation of pollution, as well as duties (especially financial) for cleaning it up, toward a sustainable future. The poor LDCs argue that the rich North must (1) reduce its occupation of **environmental space**, (2) lead the political and financial effort to reverse environmental decay, and (3) give LDCs equal representation in the institutions that distribute financial assistance for development.[13]

These are complex and controversial issues, and only the most naive among us would expect the North fully to accept these arguments made by the South. However, at the least, the MDCs have a responsibility to think through these arguments with an eye toward green justice whenever feasible. None of these changes can be expected to occur easily, since, as historian Paul Kennedy concludes, "The forces for change facing the world could be so far-reaching, complex, and interactive that they call for nothing less than the reeducation of humankind."[14]

WIN–WIN SCENARIOS: DEBT FOR NATURE SWAPS

One of the unfortunate legacies of the Cold War era stems from its simplistic view that foreign affairs consist of **zero-sum games**: whatever one side loses, an equal gain is assumed to accrue to the opposing side. Lingering zero-sum thinking makes it harder for us to believe that **positive-sum games**, or win–win scenarios, amount to anything more than a mirage. Expanded trade, as discussed in Chapter 12 of this text, represents one such example of a positive-sum game. Another is the range of creative solutions falling under the rubric of debt-for-nature swaps.

The metaphor of the Tragedy of the Commons discussed earlier can be applied to a wide range of dilemmas in which people consider some resource to be of global importance. Obvious examples include the Chernobyl nuclear accident, acid rain, ozone depletion, destruction of wetlands, coral reef pollution, species extinction, and burning rain forests. In such situations, people considering themselves global citizens may try to exert influence over events in far-off, sovereign countries.

In situations known as debt-for-nature swaps, efforts are made to influence the environmental policies of a Third World country in possession of a key resource. These efforts have revolved around the confluence of two global problems: environmental abuse—especially of rain forests in LDCs—and the intractable debt burden borne by many of these poor countries. Through classic bargaining, or negotiation, both of these frustrating problems are attacked simultaneously—thus the win–win nature of the endeavor. As the concept was initially proposed in 1984, by the World Wildlife Fund's Thomas Lovejoy, a debtor LDC pays off part of its debt by promising to preserve some environmental resource which it controls. "In a single transaction, the debt burden of the developing nation is reduced, and global environmental protection is enhanced."[15]

Three groups of players work together in debt-for-nature swaps: (1) the debtor nation (often its national government, local conservation NGOs, and the country's central bank); (2) donor or-

Figure 15.1

ganizations, known as debt purchasers (usually conservation NGOs or environmentally conscious nation–states); and (3) the creditor agency holding the LDC's debt (typically a commercial bank).

The debt-for-nature process boils down to these key steps. First, general terms of an agreement in concept between the debtor nation, external donor, and creditor financial institution are negotiated. Then the financial transaction, whereby the debt is purchased by the external donor and then traded to the debtor nation for environmental concessions, is carried out. Finally, implementation of the environmental agreement, which often involves long-term commitments to manage some environmental resource (usually with a local NGO as watchdog), takes place. Let's look at a few examples.

Bolivia

In 1987 the first debt-for-nature swap occurred between Bolivia and a U.S.-based NGO called Conservation International. The Bolivian government received a reduction of its debt with a commercial bank by $650,000, which Conservation International bought for the heavily discounted price of $100,000. Bolivia's global image was also enhanced as the country served as a pioneer in this creative new form of problem solving.

Conservation International in turn benefited from the swap. The Bolivian government agreed to expand its Beni Biosphere Reserve (a protected zone created in 1982 and managed by the National Academy of Sciences) by 3.7 million acres, promised maximum legal protection for the Reserve, and established a $250,000 endowment to fund long-term management of the protected area.

Ecuador

A few months after the Bolivian swap, a similar deal occurred in Ecuador. The World Wildlife Fund and the Nature Conservancy purchased $10 million of Ecuadorian debt at face value, then traded it for the acquisition and management of nature preserves, management of currently protected areas, and the training of environmental professionals. Implementation of the agreement was entrusted to Fundación Natura, an Ecuadorian environmental NGO.

Costa Rica

Costa Rica, one of the most environmentally aware Latin American countries and the only nation–state without a standing army, got into the act later in 1987. A collection of international and domestic conservation groups purchased $5.4 million in commercial debt from Fleet National Bank and Swiss Bank at a discount. In return, the Costa Rican government established the National Resources Conservation Fund (NRCF) to finance parkland acquisition and administration, as well as training for environmental professionals.

By 1996 Costa Rica was leading in the number of swaps arranged, with six transactions totaling $60 million of debt relief. While most swaps are financed by conservation NGOs, two of Costa Rica's have been funded by nation–states: the Dutch government's donation of $30 million for reforestation projects, and Sweden's gift of $25 million to create a new national park.

Philippines

In 1988 the World Wildlife Fund bought $2 million in Philippines debt, which it traded for protection of the Saint Paul Subterranean River National Park, El Nido National Marine Park, and for professional training programs. The deal was overseen by a Philippine NGO called the Haribon Foundation.

Madagascar

Madagascar became the first African country to engage in a debt-for-nature swap in 1991. The World Wildlife Fund acquired $3 million of Madagascar's debt in exchange for commitments to long-term parkland management and hiring of park rangers. An unusual feature of this deal was the involvement of the U.S. government's Agency for International Development, which contributed $1 million to the endeavor.

Conclusion

While chances for the expansion of debt-for-nature swaps appear promising, they do not represent the sole solution to either the LDC debt problem or the problem of environmental abuse. However, as creative responses to these global problems, they possess sym-

The lush, raw beauty of the Sarapiqui rain forest in Costa Rica is hard to surpass.

bolic value. Past failures suggest that radically different responses to global dilemmas must be explored, and such win–win scenarios can help expand the envelope of human imagination. These swaps also illustrate the key roles played not only by countries, but by conservation NGOs and MNCs as well.

Aggressive Criticism of Debt-for-Nature Swaps

Biologists John Vandermeer and Ivette Perfecto, however, sharply criticize what they call the Mainstream Environmental Movement, particularly its debt-for-nature swaps. In their 1995 book, *Breakfast of Biodiversity: The Truth About Rainforest Destruction*, they claim that debt-for-nature swaps typify the new thinking among environmental groups, which is content with "raising large sums of money to purchase and protect islands of rainforest with little concern for what happens between those islands, either to the natural world or to the social world of the people who live there."[16] They argue that it is self-delusion to believe these small islands of protected land really make much difference. What really counts, they suggest, is what happens to the land and the people *between* these islands.

Vandermeer and Perfecto claim that debt-for-nature swaps have failed in the place where they have their greatest chance for success: Costa Rica, which they examine closely. They train an idyllic spotlight on the rain forests of Sarapiqui county, along Costa Rica's beautiful east coast:

> Here you can experience that special feeling that inspires poets and explorers—from the myriad vegetative forms so evident even on first glance to the misty mornings that invoke mysterious feelings and bucolic images of paradise lost.[17]

The high temperatures and heavy rainfall of this equatorial climate create lush tropical vegetation, unbelievable numbers of plant and animal species, and some of the world's greatest natural beauty. But Vandermeer and Perfecto suggest that while God may be in her heaven and all may seem right with the world *within* the Sarapiqui protected forest, big problems loom as soon as we step *outside*.

The biggest problem, they say, is the banana, since five major MNCs are busy converting forest to plantation in order to sell this fruit abroad. The issue of bananas in Costa Rica could be rubber trees, oranges, or cattle in other Latin American countries. No matter; the pattern repeats itself as a six-stage progression: (1) MNCs identify opportunity for market expansion of an agricultural product (e.g., bananas); (2) they buy land and cut it down; (3) they bring in eager workers from around the country; (4) after a period of boom the product goes bust on the global market; (5) the unemployed workers cannot find other work and seek land on which to grow subsistence crops; (6) the only land available requires a slash-and-burn onslaught of the rain forest.

Vandermeer and Perfecto describe an unsettling irony: while Costa Rica is considered a "showcase of conservation," it is unwittingly contributing to destruction of the rain forest. But they don't blame the debt-ridden Costa Rican government for seeking cash by exporting bananas to raise much-needed currency. They blame wealthy landowners in Costa Rica, whose stranglehold over the land makes it impossible for the masses of poor people to seek food security on a small plot of their own. They blame the international economic system, which forces poor countries to exploit their resources in order to export crops for hard currency. They blame MNCs for luring workers to new plantations, then leaving them high and dry when the soil gives out or when they decide to move to another country.

Vandermeer and Perfecto call for a "radical rethinking"—the sort of radical rethinking that can land you in deep trouble in Latin American countries where freedom of speech rests on a shaky foundation. Above all, however, they wish to convey that rain forest problems are too complex to be solved through the Mainstream Environmental Movement approach, and that their Political Ecology Strategy, which looks at questions of political economy as well as biological matters, is more realistic as a long-term solution.

What do you think about these two conflicting visions of saving the rain forests? The Mainstream approach concentrates on protecting pristine islands of rain forests in poor countries, and one of its favorite projects today is the debt-for-nature swap pioneered by Thomas Lovejoy of the World Wildlife Fund. Conversely, Vandermeer and Perfecto's more radical Political Ecology Strategy wants to attack the political and economic injustices which they see at the heart of peasant food insecurity leading to deforestation pressures. Which do you find more convincing, and why?

Chapter Synopsis

The scope, depth, and urgency of the ecological global issues (environment, population, food, energy) chronicled in Chapter 14 have been known to induce either panic or despair. All responsible scholars acknowledge their seriousness and the need to address them in earnest. Easier said than done. Most disconcerting is the likelihood that business as usual—the expansion model of progress and the big techno-fix—seems likely to worsen matters in a world of multiple finite carrying capacities. But hope for human ingenuity to expand the imaginative envelope is grounded in a variety of extant creative responses. Innovative strategies like debt-for-nature swaps not only belie creativity, they also represent win–win scenarios (positive-sum games), which seem to be facilitated by the end of the Cold War. The post-Cold War era has liberated us from the internecine and costly East–West obsession and freed up time and resources to address global issues more diligently than in the past. This creative endeavor must begin with the new paradigms of globalist thought emphasized in the previous chapter.

Adapting to a changing world and adopting new attitudes and policies is an incremental process; dialogue must be institutionalized via new structures. The lifeblood of such institutions for global solutions has consisted of a series of global town meetings during the last three decades focusing attention on these global issues. Most have been sanctioned by the General Assembly of the United Nations, and all have generated heated debate. The Earth Summit of 1992 spawned a blueprint for action called Agenda 21 and gave new duties to existing institutions like the UNEP and the GEF. The Cairo Population Conference of 1994 similarly attracted thousands of NGOs and just about every nation on earth. Its Program of Action pledges $17 billion for family planning and encourages new funding of female education programs in poor countries. The biggest food conference occurred in Rome in 1974 and resulted in the creation of the WFC to monitor and coordinate all aspects of the U.N. food security system, and the IFAD to help rural poor people improve food production. The U.S.-led IEA was formed in 1974 for the rich nations to share oil reserves and cope with shortages by conservation. A World Energy Conference took place in 1981, but new organizations were not created as they were for the other three issue-areas discussed here. Agenda-setting forums now exist to address global issues in a systematic fashion.

But what are nation–states, IGOs, NGOs, IFIs, and MNCs supposed to do to cope with these global problems? What philosophies and priorities should direct their behavior? The articulation of principles that can encompass all these actors must necessarily tend toward the abstract and general. Furthermore, micromanaging specific aspects of these global issues is beyond the scope of this chapter. These policy principles relate to all the actors cited above, but even more so to the nation–state, which remains the single most vital participant in the global drama. Multilateralism, grass-roots initiatives, female empowerment, ecological policy dialogue, sectorally specific aid, democratic devolution, encouraging trading states, aggressive regulation of access and use, environmental accounting, green consumerism, and green justice all merit consideration as philosophically enlightened policy objectives for ecological players in this evolving drama.

For Digging Deeper

Choucri, Nazli, Ed. *Global Accord: Environmental Challenges and International Responses.* MIT Press, 1993.

Cohn, Steven M. *Too Cheap to Meter: Analysis of the Nuclear Dream.* SUNY Press, 1997.

Hardin, Garrett. *Living Within Limits: Ecology, Economics, and Population Taboos.* Oxford University Press, 1993.

Hempel, Lamont C. *Environmental Governance: The Global Challenge.* Island Press, 1996.

Pirages, Dennis C. *Building Sustainable Societies: A Blueprint for a Post-Industrial World.* Mitchell E. Sharp, 1996.

Porter, Gareth, and Janet Welsh Brown. *Global Environmental Politics.* Westview Press, 1996.

Sessions, George E. *Deep Ecology for the Twenty-First Century.* Random House, 1995.

Swanson, Timothy. *The International Regulation of Extinction.* New York University Press, 1994.

Vandermeer, John, and Ivette Perfecto. *Breakfast of Biodiversity: The Truth About Rainforest Destruction.* Food First, 1995.

Key Glossary Terms

anticipatory thinking
Bucharest World Population Conference
Cairo World Population Conference
communications gap
conventions
democratic
devolution
Earthwatch
economic development
environmental accounting
environmental space
female empowerment
financial aid
Food and Agricultural Organization (FAO)
Global Environment Facility

(GEF)
global resources
global town meetings
globalism
grass roots
green consumerism
green justice
intergovernmental
International Energy Agency (IEA)
International Fund for Agricultural Development (IFAD)
Mexico City World Population Conference
Montreal Protocol
one country, one vote
positive-sum game
privatization

Rome World Population Conference
sectoral
sovereign property
technical aid
treaties
United Nations Conference on Environment and Development (UNCED)
United Nations Environmental Programme (UNEP)
weighted voting
World Bank
World Energy Conference
World Food Council (WFC)
zero-sum game

CHAPTER **16**

Trends in Our World: What Social Scientists Can Tell Us

Thematic Questions

- Of what value is trend analysis?

- What is distinctive about Benjamin Barber's *Jihad vs. McWorld: How Globalism and Tribalism are Reshaping the World (1996)*?

- Is either Jihad or McWorld winning their titanic struggle?

CORE OBJECTIVE

To provide a comprehensive framework incorporating the disparate trends occurring in our rapidly changing world.

The case study on Tsar Nicholas and the Romanov family discussed in Chapter 3 showed how fundamental disagreements over historical *fact* can fester for many decades. Chapter 10, discussing the decision to drop the bomb on Hiroshima, described the bitter *interpretive* differences which were still raging on the fiftieth anniversary of Hiroshima in 1995. We learned from the Czechoslovakian and Dominican cases discussed in Chapter 9, both in the 1960s, how matters of historical fact and interpretation can long remain matters of controversy.

Given the differences that often divide scholars over facts and interpretations about the *past*, it should come as no surprise that social scientists have little interest in trying to predict the *future* course of human events, whether social, political, or economic in character. This reluctance is especially strong in the current world of change, uncertainty, and complexity. The relatively more stable and simplistic world of the Cold War era seemed more user friendly to prognosticators. Yogi Berra, inducted into the Baseball Hall of Fame for his skill as a catcher and not for his intellect, allegedly said that it is hard to make predictions—especially about the future.

However, in between writing and rewriting the script for the human drama's historical past, and bemoaning the futility of guessing about future twists and turns in such a complicated script, scholars have carved out a swath of interpretive ground by defining the scope of the *present* rather loosely. To social scientists, the scope of the present is not confined to the narrow strictures of the current moment, day, or month. By conceiving of the global present as stretching from the end of the Cold War until the first few years of the twenty-first century, social scientists are able to identify current **trends**.

While there is no guarantee that any current global trends will continue well into the next century, it seems reasonable to expect their influences still to be felt during the next decade. According to paleontologist Stephen Jay Gould, "We are fascinated by trends, in part because they tell stories by the basic device of imparting directionality to time, in part because they so often supply a moral dimension to a sequence of events: a cause to bewail as something goes to pot, or to highlight as a rare beacon of hope."[1]

It is to current trends, then, that we turn for clues about the shape of the unfolding human script. First we will look at the big picture by trying to isolate general trends discernible at the global level. For this purpose we rely on a theory recently advanced by Benjamin Barber of Rutgers University. In addition, we will isolate more specific trends, which cut across all aspects of human endeavor and rely on scholars from all six disciplines—sociologists, anthropologists, political scientists, economists, psychologists, and geographers—in measuring the current pulse of the human drama.

BENJAMIN BARBER: JIHAD VERSUS McWORLD

The great majority of scholars writing about present trends carefully limit their analysis to manageable topics that can be studied in depth. The bipolar Cold War, featuring military and ideological competition between the Americans and Soviets, dominated activity on the world stage for half a century. One decade after the historic demise of the Cold War, many current trends seem at the very least unrelated, and possibly even contradictory to one another. For most observers of these developments, the unsettled state of current affairs necessitates a strong *caveat* when they attempt to identify trends: look to the smaller (micro-level) segments of human affairs and avoid the bigger questions of what it all means.

In *Jihad Vs. McWorld: How Globalism and Tribalism Are Reshaping the World* (1996), Benjamin Barber exhibits the bold vision needed to address the vexing macro-level questions of the day. He is looking for a universal handle to explain the inexplicable to the general reader in a clear manner. He is looking for an overarching synthesis that ties together disparate and seemingly contradictory trends reported by his colleagues. He is looking for big answers to big questions at a time when most other scholars prefer to seek small answers to small questions. For all these reasons, Professor Barber's book is used here as the general framework for describing broad global trends emerging from the ashes of the Cold War.

Barber chooses the colorful and evocative terms *Jihad* and *McWorld* to symbolize two great opposing forces currently at war with each other. In addition to arguing that these forces are hostile to one another, he considers them to possess relatively equal strength, making the outcome of their struggle crucial to humanity's future. These are synonyms that might be used to juxtapose the essence of the forces of *Jihad* and *McWorld*:

Jihad:	McWorld:
tribal	universal
local	global
fragmentation	integration
centripetal	centrifugal
parochial	cosmopolitan
emotional	cool
identity driven	market driven
tradition	modernity
heterogeneity	homogeneity

Fleshing Out the Meaning of Jihad

While the term *Jihad* derives from Arabic and Islamic traditions, it has a variety of meanings, and Barber uses it in the sense of "dogmatic and violent particularism."[2] About thirty wars were raging in the world in 1996, and most of these were civil wars, not wars between countries. The quest for racial, ethnic, or religious identity at increasingly local levels is what drives the numerous civil wars that have made recent headlines. Rwanda, Bosnia, Chechniya, Georgia, Nigeria, Liberia, and Somalia are just a few recent flashpoints which happen coincidentally to end in the letter "a."

The end of the Cold War loosened the American and Soviet grip over the rest of the world, allowing pent-up group identities to assert their frustrated demands for recognition as independent players. When President Woodrow Wilson championed the principle of the self-determination of nations near the beginning of the twentieth century, he surely could not have envisioned the fragmented state of the world near the end of the same century.

Prior to the outbreak of World War I in 1914, only about 40 nation–states existed. In the post-Cold War era that number is approaching 200, with no signs of abating. Barber laments that, in its most virulent strain, Jihad is "a kind of animal fear propelled by anxiety in the face of uncertainty and relieved by self-sacrificing zealotry."[3]

Muslims, shown here worshipping in a mosque, represented one of the factions of the Bosnian civil war in the early 1990s.

Orthodox Serbs, shown worshipping their Christian God, represented one of the factions of the Bosnian civil war in the early 1990s.

McWorld: More Benign than Jihad?

Jihad's opposite, McWorld, results from the shrinking effect of MNCs' pursuing unfettered global markets for their ever-growing range of products. The general failure of global communism as an alternative to market capitalism has weakened the entire notion of governmental oversight and left corporations freer to seek profits than they have been in at least a century. **Deregulation** has led to merger mania, resulting in behemoth corporations in everything from computer software to book publishing to entertainment, looking suspiciously like monopolies—once a dirty word in the American lexicon.

Particularly unsettling to citizens of other countries is that McWorld's vanilla flavor seems distinctly North American, a perception leading to fears of a dominating commercial civilization that mistakes shopping malls for cathedrals of community. In his inimitable style, Barber goes after McWorld's jugular vein, claiming that it creates forces that:

> demand integration and uniformity and that mesmerize the world with fast music, fast computers, and fast food—with MTV, Macintosh, and McDonald's pressing nations into one commercially homogeneous global network: one McWorld tied together by technology, ecology, communications, and commerce.[4]

Jihad and McWorld Need Each Other

The fragmenting, hot tribal loyalties of Jihad function as the diametric opposite of McWorld's cool homogeneity. These two powerful forces detest each other. But, like many enemies, they also thrive on this relationship with their antithesis. Barber says, "Jihad needs McWorld as shadows do the sun."[5] Besides antipathy toward each other, they also share hostility toward the integrity of the nation–state system which has evolved during the last 350 years: Jihad—because it wishes to break free from the centralized nation–state's control over smaller units of ethnic, racial, and religious identity; McWorld—because the nation–state has been the sole public entity capable of threatening the global corporation's bottom line, which is so dear to its shareholders.

Thus rather than being only repelled by one another, Jihad and McWorld are locked in a bizarre embrace, a classic dance entailing push as well as pull. As individual citizens, this interaction leaves each of us susceptible to the influences of both forces. "Jihad pursues a bloody politics of identity, McWorld a bloodless economics of profit. Belonging by default to McWorld, everyone is a consumer; seeking a repository for identity, everyone belongs to some tribe."[6] But since the relationship of Jihad and McWorld in the social world is inimical, its hostility spills over into our individual psyches.

This split is so sharp that it forces us to choose sides in the fracas; neutrality is not a viable option. Barber sees the forces of Jihad enjoying many short-term advantages likely to keep its fragmenting tendencies in the news during the next decade or two. However, he considers the market-driven forces of McWorld as likely to win out in the long run, for better *and* for worse.

OTHER SPECIFIC TRENDS

While Barber's vision provides us with a huge canvas containing some broad, bold, black-or-white brush strokes, many other social scientists have provided smaller, yet thoughtful, sketches of trends using shades of gray to supplement Barber's starkly clashing images. Of the many trends that have been written about, we will examine eleven which have not been treated earlier in this book. They include five that feed the fires of Jihad (massive migration, loose nukes, bipolar to multipolar world, toward a North–South agenda, and zones of peace/zones of turmoil), five that are more congenial to the momentum of McWorld (merger mania, privatization, mobile microbes, videology, and from hard power to soft power), and one that is ambivalent about the Jihad versus McWorld clash: rapid change.

In *International Futures: Choices in the Creation of a New World Order* (1996), futurist Barry Hughes says that trend identification is one of the most important ways to study change. Trend projection requires a certain amount of faith in the validity of **extrapolation**, by which we assume that current conditions will continue into the future. While useful, studying trends has certain limitations. To illustrate, Hughes tells the story of a person falling from the top of the Empire State Building, who asked a friend while passing the fifty-first window, how he was doing. The technically correct, but very misleading, trend analysis was "so far so good."[7]

Stephen Jay Gould calls the classic case of coin tossing among gamblers as one ripe for misapplied trend analysis: the chances for flipping five consecutive heads is $1/2 \times 1/2 \times 1/2 \times 1/2 \times 1/2$, or a one in thirty-two chance—rare but far from impossible. Mistaking random chance for a nefarious trend, some gamblers have interpreted this event as evidence of cheating, leading to shootings in both real life and in Hollywood movies.[8] Imperfect as it is, trend analysis will have to suffice in our effort to steal a glimpse of the global future.

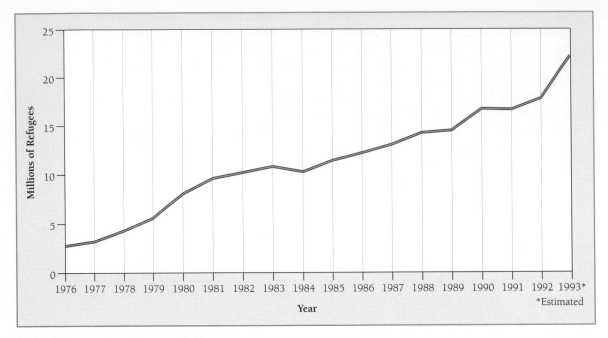

Figure 16.1   Tracking a Tidal Wave

The number of people driven from their homes has increased nearly tenfold since the mid-1970s.

Source: In Dick Kirschsten, "No Refuge," *National Journal,* September 10, 1994, pp. 2068–2073. © 1994 by National Journal, Inc. All rights reserved. Reprinted by permission.

TRENDS FEEDING JIHAD'S TRIBALISM

Massive Migration

During the Cold War era **refugees** claiming to flee from political persecution in communist countries served as useful pawns in the propaganda struggle conducted by the United States and its allies. It was easy for escapees from Cuba, the Soviet Union, China, or Czechoslovakia to receive political **asylum** in the West. However, those unfortunates fleeing from noncommunist African, Asian, or Latin American countries were labeled as economic (not political) migrants and were generally denied admission to the United States and allied countries.

The contrasting televised images from the Caribbean between easy admission for those displaced from Castro's Cuba and a closed door for thousands of desperate "boat people" from Haiti haunted Presidents Ronald Reagan, George Bush, and Bill Clinton. The U.S. certainly has not been stingy by refusing entry to all. It has in fact long received many more immigrants than any other country. Since U.S. immigrants include large numbers of both legal and illegal ones, exact figures remain elusive, but one million annually is often cited as an average number of new faces.

Since the end of the Cold War two developments have contributed to a growing global crisis: (1) the dislocation caused by many new civil wars has greatly increased the number of people fleeing from their native lands; (2) countries to which refugees have traditionally gravitated—like the United States, Canada, Germany, and Australia—have begun to pull up the drawbridges by tightening admission standards. One of these conditions alone (increased dislocation or closing borders) would be problematic for the global refugee situation; together they are catastrophic.

In the two decades between the mid-1970s and the mid-1990s the number of people fleeing has increased tenfold, as is graphically portrayed in Figure 16.1. A total of 23 million have left their home countries and twenty-six million have been dislocated within their own countries. According to the U.N. High Commission for Refugees, more than 80 percent of those fleeing are people of color from Africa, Asia, or the Middle East. This problem seems likely to worsen in the post-Cold War era and should exacerbate the fragmenting, divisive, and desperate characteristics of Jihad in the years to come.[9]

Loose Nukes

During the Cold War the Soviet Union gave headaches to American military planners because of its strength. Today the Russians continue to give American policymakers nightmares, but because of their military weakness, not their strength. In the late-1990s U.S.–Russian relations are cordial and few observers fear war between these two countries. If Americans do not fear nuclear war with Russia, then what is causing alarm concerning the Russians?

Put simply: loose nukes. The good news in 1991 and 1993 was that the Russo-American **START treaties** reduced these nations' massive nuclear weapons arsenals by about one-third. The bad news about sloppy Russian handling of nuclear materials, however, continues to pour in. As "live" weapons, Russia's nuclear warheads were kept under close scrutiny by its disciplined military. When "dismantled," however, 3,000 warheads annually are now turned over to the much less efficient and trustworthy Ministry of Atomic Energy (Minatom).

A total of 700 tons of weapons-grade plutonium are now housed in ninety facilities across Russia that have been deemed by America's CIA as having poor security. When you realize that as little as thirteen pounds of enriched plutonium can fuel a basic atomic bomb, you have to get a little nervous. Then factor in the depressed condition of Russia's transitional economy—with thousands of unemployed scientists—and you may begin to pine nostalgically for the good old days of the Cold War.

In August 1994 the first conviction of a Russian nuclear scientist for nuclear theft received global media attention. Leonid Smirnov, scientist at the Luch plutonium factory outside of Moscow, admitted stealing over 100 pounds of plutonium. Smirnov was caught not by Russian authorities, but rather by German police in Munich when the sale of the hot plutonium went bad. Since the Russians maintain no comprehensive inventories of nuclear materials, the director of the Luch factory was unable to verify the theft of plutonium. And making the story even more bizarre, Smirnov received only three years' probation for his crime—hardly the sturdy stuff of deterrence for would-be copycats.

The Clinton administration made passage of the 1995 **Nuclear Non-Proliferation Treaty (NNPT)**—a permanent extension of an earlier 1970 treaty—one of its foreign policy priorities. Most experts consider the NNPT a positive step in discouraging the spread of nuclear weapons. None believes that it guarantees success in this complex endeavor, however. Most nuclear hope-

Missile-laden trucks rolling past an impressive portrait of Vladimir Lenin on Moscow's Red Square, during the 70th Anniversary of the Soviet Revolution, celebrated near the end of the Cold War in 1987.

fuls are unlikely to be greatly influenced by the NNPT. The current roster of rogue states includes Iraq (which spent $10 billion in the 1980s trying to build one), Iran, North Korea, and Libya. But even more disconcerting than rogue states may be the kinds of desperate terrorist groups discussed in Chapter 9. What mayhem could be wrought should a group like Hamas in the Middle East, the Provisional Wing of the Irish Republican Army in Britain, or the Shining Path in Peru obtain a nuclear weapon?

Traditionally, two practical problems have deterred nuclear hopefuls: (1) the necessary scientific and technical know-how was limited to a few places in the world with impressive security measures; (2) the rare and expensive nuclear materials (plutonium or uranium) were extremely difficult to obtain. In the current age of instantaneous information and global interdependence, however, both of these barriers to spreading nuclear weapons have been seriously breached. If a rogue state or terrorist group can obtain a nuclear weapon through smuggling, it can sidestep the five- to ten-year period required to develop the bomb on its own. We almost surely will hear more about this dangerous subject in the future, and what we hear is likely to resonate most loudly in the raucous corridors of ethnic, racial, and religious Jihad.[10]

From a Bipolar to a Multipolar World

The historical record during more than three centuries of the nation–state system has taught us certain lessons about the tendencies of different power configurations between nations. For example, unipolar systems, which are systems dominated by one country, tend to be fairly stable while they last, but they usually run their course quickly and evolve into something different. Bipolar systems, controlled by two countries, are relatively stable, predictable, and secure, but they encourage escalation of tension through overzealous demonizing of the other side of the balance of power. The dynamics of tripolar configurations of power encourage gross imbalances leading to two forces' joining together against the third. Multipolar systems of power have maintained peace and security most effectively when a large number of fairly equal nations have been able to construct counterbalancing alliances strong enough to deter other alliances from acting aggressively. Multipolar systems with relatively small numbers of national powers have made cooperative activities more difficult than in larger multipolar systems, but all have eventually collapsed into violent struggles for supremacy.[11]

A five-decade standoff between the United States and Soviet alliances during the Cold War provided plenty of practice in coping with the escalatory temptations inherent in a bipolar power struggle between two true believers. While luxurious hindsight consoles us with the realization that the tense Cold War never resulted in a direct, hot shooting war, there was never any guarantee of how the situation would end. At the dying cusp of the Cold War, for what journalist Charles Krauthammer called a fleeting "unipolar moment," the United States stood alone as unchallenged global superpower when it led the 1991 allied liberation of Kuwait from Iraqi occupation. Whether America's reign as undisputed top dog continues to hold true is a matter of sharp controversy. The point on which most observers agree is this: even if the U.S.'s unipolar moment has not yet ended, it soon will.[12] The map in Figure 16.2 reveals the multipolarity of the post-Cold War era.

Students of world affairs, such as Henry Kissinger, expect the multipolar system to feature a pentagonal shape, with relative parity enjoyed by the United States, Japan, Germany, China, and Russia.[13] While the United States will probably maintain its military advantages over the rest of the field, military factors have been giving way to economic ones in assessments of national power. The rise of economic determinants of power also complicates differentiation between friend and foe. For example, Japan might be a natural U.S. ally militarily but a natural competitor economically. Similarly, China could develop into an American ally economically but a rival militarily. Whom do you trust in such a scenario—Japan, China, or neither one?

The subtle nuances of flexible and creative diplomacy which the emerging multipolar field demands may prove especially challenging for the United States. Traditionally the United States has gyrated wildly between the extremes of noninvolvement (isolationism) when possible, and all-or-nothing struggle (war or cold war) when necessary: "The United States will have to learn a role it has never played before; namely, to coexist and interact with other great powers."[14]

Toward a North–South Agenda

The kind of issues that the international community spends its time discussing—its agenda—goes a long way toward defining the scope of what is possible. The international agenda focuses global consciousness in certain directions at the expense of other directions. During the long Cold War epoch the focus was decidedly East–West, as U.S.–Soviet military and ideological tension permeated the very soul of global consciousness. With their vast nuclear arsenals rendering humanity's existence fragile, it was easy for the superpowers to dominate the global agenda, which they did with alacrity.

In the post-Cold War, however, the collective human mind has wandered in a very different direction: North–South. Whereas the earlier, politically conscious agenda revolved around superpower military competition, the current economically conscious agenda is shaped by the growing gap between rich and poor. Issues of economic development, cultural autonomy, and a psychological need for equality drive the dialogue of the North–South agenda—one just as contentious as the Cold War military agenda before it.

Naturally, most of the energy for the new agenda—rooted as it is in the growing gap between the rich North and the poor South—comes from the South. The perceived unfairness of the South's inherited colonial legacy, as discussed in Chapter 12, often leads to a sense

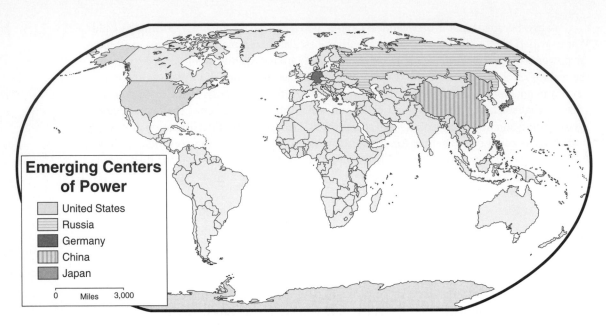

Figure 16.2   Emerging Centers of Power in a New Multipolar System

Source: Charles Kegley and Eugene Wittkopf, *World Politics* (St. Martin's, 1994), p. 101.

of righteous indignation in statements by leaders of poor nations. While the South currently lacks the collective power to bring about its desired economic and cultural changes, its sheer numbers have swollen to nearly 130, and this majority status allows the South to influence the content of the global agenda and to be heard in many international organizations.

The South's complaints are not limited to economic disparities. Just as economic demands have been issued in the New International Economic Order (NIEO), demands for greater influence in the global distribution of news and information have been advanced in the New World Information Order (NWIO). An already huge technological gap is becoming a chasm as the geographic distribution of computers and access to the Internet spreads like wildfire in the North, while barely a spark can be seen in the South. Historically, the South has been dependent on MNCs to transfer technical know-how, a system that hasn't worked for poor countries, since MNCs are motivated by profits, and these do not contribute to the development of the South.[15]

Little imagination is required to envision how 130 poor countries—very unhappy over the rich getting richer and the poor getting poorer, in a shrinking world filled with sophisticated weapons available to terrorists—adds fuel to the fires of Jihad. It is no wonder that the new agenda of North–South issues has captured the world's attention as poignantly as did the superpower standoff during the Cold War.

Zones of Peace—Zones of Turmoil

Commentators have disagreed vehemently in assessments of just how lucky, or unlucky, the world is in the post-Cold War era. Some describe a plethora of good things happening around us today, while others recite a litany of woe to fret about. Part of this divergence can be understood if one knows exactly where different observers are looking when they evaluate the new world order. Not surprisingly, the gaze of the optimists is decidedly northward, whereas a southward vector pervades the vision of the pessimists. The theme of this trend, zones of peace—zones of turmoil, is not only that the economic prospects for people in the North are superior to those living in the South, but also that other, more subtle quality-of-life differences are equally crucial.

Max Singer and Aaron Wildavsky have developed the most compelling argument for the existence of what has come to be called zones of peace—zones of turmoil. Their analysis is tied to studies describing the emergence of a democratic peace as discussed in Chapter 4: modern democracies do not go to war with one another. Singer and Wildavsky conclude that "wealth and democracy and peace go together."[16] They find it very encouraging that the top twenty-five wealthy countries today are all democracies and that, for the first time, democracies hold the bulk of world power. Human existence is arguably better than ever in much of the northern zone of peace.

Were it only so for the 85 percent of the globe's 5.2 billion people who live in undemocratic countries—the zones of turmoil making up the largest part of the southern hemisphere. The overwhelming majority of international and civil wars in recent decades have taken place in the undemocratic zones of turmoil. The trend of bifurcation into zones of peace and zones of turmoil can only worsen the explosive division of the world into rich versus poor hemispheres. Together they contribute mightily to the angry mood of injustice which underlies the emotional energy so apparent in Jihad's violent confrontations.

TRENDS CONGENIAL TO MCWORLD'S HOMOGENIZATION

Merger Mania

Wall Street loves corporate mergers. Why? Because every time a giant corporation buys another one, Wall Street lawyers and investors make millions of dollars: $1,432 million in fees relating to 1,400 mergers forged in 1996 alone. Although they don't usually participate directly in corporate mergers, whether hostile or friendly takeovers, these must seem like manna from heaven to Wall Street investment firms like Goldman Sachs and Solomon Brothers. And the momentum toward corporate consolidation begun in 1980 picks up steam every year, looking more now like an avalanche of "commercial totalism" than a mere trend.[17]

While the concentration of ever fewer major corporate players can be seen in all areas of commerce, nowhere is it more apparent than in the vital realm of global communications. The frenzy of media mergers includes both hardware and software, the medium and the message. Media analyst Ben Bagdikian describes the characteristics of this trend toward conglomeration; he also worries about the reduction of mass media corporations from forty-six in 1981 to twenty-three in 1991, and the number dwindling still further since then to about ten giants dominating the world's lifeblood of communication: radio and television outlets, newspapers, books, entertainment venues, and magazines.[18]

Can this trend auger well for commercial competition, which is the backbone of capitalism? What happens to the free flow of ideas when Viacom, Time Warner, Turner Broadcasting, and Capital Cities/ABC control the bulk of the infotainment industries? What are the implications for democratic government and civil society when media moguls like Robert Maxwell and Rupert Murdoch own not hundreds, but thousands of avenues to communicate their particular view of the world? Ben Bagdikian's opinion of the "media lords of the global village" sounds very much like Benjamin Barber's take on the ubiquitous qualities of McWorld:

> They exert a homogenizing power over ideas, culture and commerce that affects populations larger than any in history. Neither Caesar nor Hitler, Franklin Roosevelt nor any Pope, has commanded as much power to shape the information on which so many people depend to make decisions about everything from whom to vote for to what to eat.[19]

A case in point would be the coverage of the 1991 Persian Gulf War. The rapidly disappearing line between hard news, technological wizardry (both on the battlefield and in the newsroom), and flashy entertainment created something new. We saw behind-enemy-lines coverage by CNN's Peter Arnett and Bernard Shaw of live cruise missile attacks on Baghdad, which were thrilling. We saw U.S. pilots drop laser-guided smart bombs straight down the chimneys of Saddam Hussein's weapons facilities and power plants, which was equally thrilling. After hearing General Norman Schwarzkopf explain the game plan on the chalkboard, we witnessed an American-led coalition thoroughly rout Iraq's vaunted Republican Guards, which was even more thrilling.

Nearly all U.S. citizens must have felt a sense of pride. What could possibly be amiss in a success story worthy of Hollywood scriptwriters? No one wants to rain on a victory parade; yet there are some risky elements in both the transmission and content of this rosy story. Although the visual images of the Gulf War broadcast by CNN were stunning, they were the only images broadcast to all corners of the globe. These potent pictures affected the analysis of current events commentators everywhere, partly by making anyone who was less than enthusiastic about the Gulf War seem like a hopeless stick-in-the-mud. Also the U.S. military, having learned well its painful lessons in Vietnam, exercised tight control over reporters in the war zone, shuttling them around in "press pools" and spoon-feeding information when and where the government chose to do so.

Accounts of the war, then, were well orchestrated by the U.S. government, and Joint Chiefs chairman Colin Powell's crisp narration of videotaped military strikes left little incentive to question the official orthodoxy. While the world community's objectives were reasonably well achieved this time out in the sands of Kuwait, the information monopoly forged during the Gulf War reveals some possible dangers: it illustrates the potential to define great events with one account—an idea hostile to the core value of free expression which America espouses both at home and abroad.[20] Many media analysts called into question CNN's corporate judgment of newsworthiness a few years later when it engaged in excessive coverage of the O.J. Simpson murder trial. As the supposed bastion of hard news on a global basis, CNN catered to crass commercialism by devoting thousands of hours to covering this case rich in titillation but poor in newsworthiness. Some observers had hoped for more from a network that aspires to preeminence in the business of news reporting and analysis.

Privatization

One of the major dilemmas confronting every society over the centuries has been distinguishing **public** from **private**. Services that affect everyone in general—like education, health, sanitation, safety, welfare, environment, and justice—have usually been handled by government, which makes public decisions on behalf of the citizenry writ large. The special interests of individuals and groups are generally left to the private sector to sort out. The precise balance of public and private domains must be determined by each society. The biggest headache usually comes in defining areas of economic life that are sufficiently public in nature to warrant governmental control of economic activities, as distinct from those that are better left to the competitive processes of the market.

In Chapter 11 we examined various theories of political economy. Two centuries ago Adam Smith's classical economic theory of laissez faire argued that a beneficent "invisible hand" directs the market and should remain free from governmental interference. When the human condition in America and around the world deteriorated badly during the Great Depression of the 1930s, British economist John Maynard Keynes advocated that the government should "prime the economic pump" by investing large sums of money, thus creating jobs and spurring economic growth.

As implemented by President Franklin D. Roosevelt, this approach meant creating new governmental public works agencies as well as a safety net of social services for the poor and unemployed. By the 1970s, growing dissatisfaction with the inefficiencies of Keynesian-inspired governmental bureaucracies led to demands, by economists known as the Chicago school, for cutting back the size of the public sector. Ronald Reagan's presidency spearheaded a wave of "supply-side" economic theory favoring the cutting of taxes while reducing governmental spending. Supply-side economics also touted deregulation and privatization as ways to increase the scope of the private sector at the expense of the public sector.

Converting publically owned and operated companies into private enterprises (in the hope of enhancing efficiency and reducing taxes) is a major trend discernible worldwide during the last two decades. Pervasive privatization is yet another trend that was greatly influenced by the collapse of the Soviet Union and subsequent disappearance of global communism as an alternative to modern capitalism.

Scholars like Herbert Schiller accept the value of capitalist economies but worry that, without a sufficient public presence in the economy, only self-interest matters and the common voice of the public good withers away. Unchallenged and unfettered, the profit motive that drives capitalistic self-interest is pursued to the exclusion of commonweal issues (like justice, equality, and freedom) which lie at the core of the civil society. A healthy balance between public and private domains seems the best prescription for any society looking to foster both economic viability and the free discourse over public issues conducive to democracy. According to Schiller, the unhealthy reality is that "for the first time in almost a century, capitalism exists without powerful, organized opposition."[21]

Privatization and deregulation reduce governmental oversight of the economy in ways that foster the commercial imperative of Benjamin Barber's McWorld. It is meaningful that the nation–state is weakened by privatization and deregulation, because historically only the nation–state among actors on the world stage has been able to rein in the selfish tendencies of the MNC and integrate its special interests into a context of public interests—defining the greatest good for the greatest number. Barber emphasizes that the onslaught of McWorld is not a conscious conspiracy. There are no actual nefarious characters to blame for its excesses. McWorld operates on "automatic pilot," but not an inscrutable automatic pilot. Rather, it is an automatic pilot driven by commercial and consumer values, greed, monopolization, a weakened nation–state, and faith in deregulation and privatization.

Mobile Microbes

We have seen how many social scientists have called for expanding our notion of security beyond the Cold War fixation on military security. Post-Cold War scholars have written extensively about environmental security as the most urgent area requiring attention. Tangential to the ecological new thinking has been an awareness of an issue of micro-security: mobile microbes. If humans don't doom our species by nuclear weapons or environmental degradation, we just might do so through exposure to lethal bugs and/or viruses.

Infectious diseases kill more people than cancer and heart disease combined; in 1993 the global loss of life from infectious diseases amounted to 16.5 million deaths.[22] With the post-World War II discovery of antibiotics, it looked like such traditional scourges as tuberculosis, polio, diptheria, syphilis, and hepatitis had been vanquished forever. Not so. Compounding the return of these old nemeses is the appearance of frightening new threats like the AIDS virus, Ebola virus, and Hanta virus. At least six major bouts with lethal microbes have been reported in the United States during the mid-1990s.[23] Hollywood wasted no time in capitalizing on growing fears with its taut medical thriller, *Outbreak* (1995). Dustin Hoffman stars as a courageous American medical researcher who dives into an Ebola-infested village in Zaire to locate "ground zero," that is, to discover when and how the disease spread from primates to humans.

Viruses are the simplest of living organisms. In fact, they are only half alive at best, but that is no reason to underestimate them. According to Columbia University's Dr. Harold Neu, "bacteria are cleverer than men." They have begun adjusting to a "world laced with antibiotics" through changes in their genetic makeup. The AIDS virus in particular has been subject to rapid mutations.[24] AIDS has another advantage as a potential threat to our species: it remains dormant, hiding its presence and therefore spreading undetected. About 20 million cases of full-blown AIDS now exist globally (mostly in poor countries). Other highly sensational strains, like the Ebola virus, produce more bizarre and immediate symptoms, making them more susceptible to quarantine.

What accounts for this mounting world health crisis? In an era of astounding medical advances, how can we take viruses seriously as harbingers of human extinction? The answers are not simple, but they are discernible:

1. *Ecological trespassing*. As humans find new reasons to move into pristine rain forests and remote ecosystems, we encounter many of the thousands of novel microbes that are strangers to us. Some of them have to be lethal ones.

Portrait of a mother embracing her son, who is afflicted with the AIDS virus.

2. *The international mixing bowl.* Modern air travel affords ample opportunities for viral hitchhikers to spread around the globe. This is a real downside of the shrinking world.

3. *Overprescription of antibiotics.* Physicians unsure of how to treat some diseases write too many prescriptions for antibiotics, even though they are useless against viruses. Not only does this practice waste money, it also weakens the patient's immune system and helps the virus to adapt (mutate) to current antibiotics.

4. *Human-induced ecological disruption.* Stable ecosystems provide a set of checks and balances on the growth of microbes, but during periods of disruption the advantage is shifted toward mobile microbes.

5. *Social disruption.* Traumatic events like civil wars uproot millions of people and place them in overcrowded situations with poor sanitation and inadequate public health services.

6. *Poor countries.* The spread of infectious diseases is most acute in poor areas with bad sanitation and impure water.

Plague and pestilence are far from new problems, since more humans have fallen to these forces than to warfare. Dennis Pirages notes, "History is littered with the remains of societies that have succumbed to attacks from various small organisms."[25] The agricultural revolution 10,000 years ago—heralded often in this book for its contributions to human society—also contributed to the transfer of diseases from domesticated animals to humans. Overconfidence may have allowed us to ignore these realities in recent decades, but we would do well to engage in public education concerning the problem of deadly microbes. Post-Cold War policymakers should also reallocate resources to support woefully underfunded organizations like the World Health Organization and the Centers for Disease Control.

Videology

At the beginning of the 1900s the great Russian novelist Leo Tolstoy marveled at the potent resources available to the nascent film industry, predicting that it would become "the art form of the twentieth century." Near the century's end, film critic Roger Ebert concludes that Tolstoy's vision was prophetic.[26] It is largely for this reason that I have used feature and documentary films in this textbook to illustrate key concepts and events. Visual images seem to lodge themselves stubbornly in our consciousness. These images do more than merely entertain us: they convey a subtle form of **videology**. Benjamin Barber concurs:

> More than anything else this has been the Movie Century, an epoch in which film and video and the images they mediate have replaced print and books and the words they once brokered as the chief instrumentalities of human communication, persuasion, and entertainment.[27]

Like most other aspects of McWorld, the films, television sitcoms, MTV fare, news coverage, sports, and home shopping that collectively comprise videology bear a decidedly North American flavor. We have already noted that the ownership, organizational structure, and hardware of communications are dominated by the United States. Cars, television, and running shoes may not be made here as they used to be, but the bulk of the software (the content, the brains) of McWorld's age of videology is mostly produced in America. And the U.S. audiovisual industry is *very* big business—second only to the aerospace industry—$3.7 billion in exports to Europe alone in 1992.

Nowhere does this cultural product ooze Americana as in the movie business. The Hollywood look, sound, and feel are recognizable to nearly every high-school student in the world. Of the 222 most watched films around the world in 1991, 191 were made in Tinseltown, USA, even though scores of countries have domestic film industries.[28] Very fine films are produced in Australia, Canada, France, India, Japan, China, Germany, and elsewhere. They are, however, small enterprises lacking the economies of scale that provide Hollywood studios with massive marketing budgets. Some American films today cost nearly $200 million. In Europe, where many countries make excellent films, their combined output of pictures exceeds the 450 annually made by Tinseltown, yet an amazing 85 percent of film revenues in Europe come from American movies, whereas less than 2 percent of revenues in America derive from European pictures.

Of course American films are not surrogates for the devil incarnate. What critics of Hollyworld decry is the same risk cited earlier for CNN serving as the *only* source of visual data for the 1991 Persian Gulf War: it may be unhealthy and undemocratic to allow one vision of the world be the sole vision for everyone. While Hollywood movies can span both art form and business, a persistent tension stalks this schizoid enterprise; it is a tension typically resolved by sacrificing artistic expression to the imperative of the bottom line whenever art and business bang heads.

Not surprisingly, then, the governments of many countries, individually and collectively, have sought ways to loosen the grip of American popular culture over their domestic arts and entertainment. Former French Culture Minister Jack Lang led an effort to require at least 60 percent of video programming on French television and 40 percent of radio music to be French in origin. The European Union has acknowledged some of the French arguments and

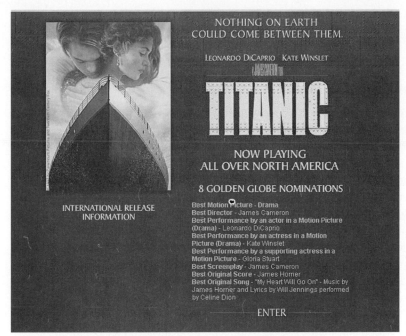

Audiences loved the melodramatic love story concocted by James Cameron in his feature film about the 1912 Titanic disaster. Titanic (1997) set records at both the box office and on Oscar night. However, Cameron's movie failed to convey the magnitude of human folly that led to the ship's sinking; the A&E network's documentary did it much better.

tried to set limits on American programming for Europe as a whole. While such efforts have garnered a lot of publicity, slowing videology is not such a simple matter.

Some observers have called for more co-productions between Hollywood and film studios from other countries, with the intention of increasing foreign input. Thus far, however, film writer Derek Elley thinks that the net result has been just the opposite, with co-productions being dominated by Hollywood's vast human and material resources.[29] Back in the 1970s Irish statesman Sean McBride served as a northern spokesman for the poor southern countries' proposed New World Information Order (NWIO). Nothing tangible resulted from the verbal sparring over the NWIO, partly because the United States remained vehemently opposed to efforts to democratize the global definition and distribution of news and other types of information. Many of the old principles behind the NWIO resurfaced in the 1990s, usually with the Hollywood film industry as the prime target.

Defenders of American cultural hegemony argue that it is not our fault if people in other countries choose to watch movies by Kevin Costner and Ron Howard rather than homegrown cinema. According to their view, this is a case study of freedom in operation. Competition, the natural capitalistic order of things, happens to have allowed Tinseltown's skillful image-making to become universally popular.

The opposing perspective argues that reality is not so simple. While global consumers may be theoretically free to choose their fare, in reality they are overwhelmed by an avalanche of videology. Slick, titillating, and hot, the American cultural product is marketed exactly like running shoes or sports vehicles. An irresistible psychological image is sold, and sold, and sold again, because of economies of scale, and this selling translates into piles of money to induce customers into believing the image being sold is not merely desirable but necessary. Which position do you agree with? Is pervasive American pop culture the benign result of market competition, or is it an unhealthy commercial sameness deadly to creativity and free discourse?

From Hard Power to Soft Power

The varied and potent forces that we have associated with McWorld's relentless push toward homogenization create a synergistic effect: by mingling freely, they compound the overall impact of each. That is why all of the McWorld-enhancing trends discussed earlier seem to blend together like so many food colorings added to a cake. You can't blame the cake for taking the shape of the pan it was baked in, and the shape of McWorld has been distinctively strong and consistent. The last trend covered here—from hard power to soft power—is one more of those bright food colors tamed by McWorld's alluring shape.

One of the liabilities of relying on hard power (military force) during the Cold War was that hard power often did not work—witness Vietnam for the United States and Afghanistan for the Soviet Union. Another shortcoming of hard power is that it is extremely expensive. Political scientist Richard Rosecrance traces the huge consequences of the United States spending 50 percent of its research and development budget on armaments during the Cold War while Japan was spending 99 percent of its R&D funds on civilian production.[30] Many other writers have identified good reasons for the post-Cold War trend of greater reliance on soft power.

Harvard University scholar Joseph Nye defines soft power as "the ability to achieve desired outcomes in international affairs through attraction rather than coercion." Traditional contributors to power, such as geography, raw materials, and population, are giving way to technology, education, and institutional flexibility as the foundation for soft power. In earlier chapters we discussed economics as a key part of today's subtler notions of power, but Nye insists that the basis of soft power is even broader than economics: "knowledge more than ever before is power."[31]

Westerners take for granted the free exchange of information in an open, civil society; therefore they underestimate its importance. The comparative information advantage of Western democracies is quieter and subtler than their advantage in nuclear weapons or in gross domestic product. But the ability to gather, process, distribute, and act upon information is today just as vital to national power. The Soviet Union did not collapse for lack of military assets or natural resources. Its repressive, bureaucratic, top-down system prevented the Soviets from sharing in the computer-generated explosion of information which began in the 1970s and has reshaped the world forever. Starved of the lifeblood of information, falling further behind the West, the Soviet people hungered for those freedoms that were systematically denied to them under the communist regime.

RAPID CHANGE

The wild card in this confusing deck of integrating versus disintegrating cards may be the pervasive but unpredictable impact of constant change. It has become a cliché to observe that never before has change occurred as rapidly to human society. Clichés may appear trite because of repetition, but that does not make them untrue.

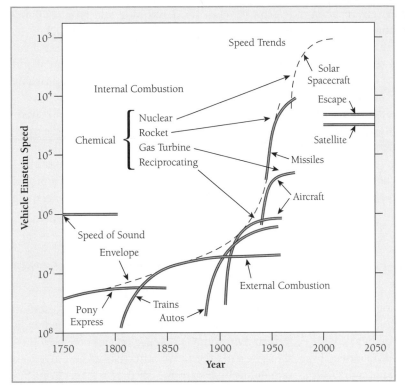

Figure 16.3
Trends in Transportation Speed

Source: Barry Hughes, *International Futures: Choices for a New World Order* (Westview Press, 1996), p. 31. Data from Robert U. Ayres, Hudson Institute, Indianapolis, Indiana. Reprinted by permission of Hudson Institute.

The speed at which our world changes today is easiest to comprehend in the realm of technological innovation. An example is the advances in the computing power of the machines used to perform calculations. Figure 16.3 covers a wide range of technological innovations related to means of transportation used to get from point A to point B. Finally, the hardware used for communicating with others almost instantaneously is another obvious illustration of technological innovation contributing to rapid change in our lives. Other forms of social, cultural, or political change may be equally important but less apparent.

Social scientists don't rely on crystal balls to predict the future, and there is no way for us to know which forces the revved-up engine of change will help more: the forces of Jihad or the forces of McWorld. The further we project the trends discussed in this chapter into an uncertain future, the riskier and more tenuous our extrapolations become. Like the tricky business of predicting the trajectory of the Wall Street stock market, assuming that current global trends will continue indefinitely is fraught with hidden traps.

About the best we can do confidently almost a decade into the post-Cold War era is to conclude that cataclysmic global changes are underway, changes that rival this century's two earlier transmutations—World War I and World War II—each of which profoundly altered the behavior of all actors on the world stage and even helped to create some new ones. Yet while we can contrast the Cold War and post-Cold War worlds in many specific ways, we don't possess enough data to define the essence of the present epoch.

Benjamin Barber's examination of tension between Jihad and McWorld gives us information, research findings, and insights to sort out the intellectual wheat from the chaff. Its counterintuitive view that the world can be, and in fact is, coming together and falling apart simultaneously helps us to get beyond superficial characterizations of the current world order. Like many useful conceptual tools provided by social scientists, his paradigm probably raises more questions than it answers.

While neat and simple answers to complicated social phenomena may exude some short-term appeal, their staying power often fizzles over time. Don't underestimate either the practical social value or the personal satisfaction derived from asking tough questions about the complex real world in which we live. When British writer Aldous Huxley defined an intellectual as "someone who has discovered something more interesting than sex," critics probably accused him of hyperbole. Nevertheless, Huxley's colorful phrase speaks volumes concerning the vitality of the life of the mind as central to human experience.

Chapter Synopsis

Trend analysis is risky business in our fast-paced world of constant change. An additional burden is borne by the social scientist brave enough to engage in prognostication: many current trends identified by researchers seem to contradict one another. While many researchers describe a world that is breaking apart, others see a world coming together. In the unsettled and complex post-Cold War, few have the courage and vision of Benjamin Barber in trying to fathom the unfolding picture of the human drama. Barber's overarching synthesis of push and pull is dichotomized into the images of Jihad versus McWorld. Jihad refers to the "dogmatic and violent particularism" endemic to racial, ethnic, or religious fragmentation. It is emotional, tribal, and local in character. In sharp contrast stand the forces of McWorld—centrifugal, market driven, and global. McWorld involves the shrinking effect wrought by MNCs pursuing unfettered global markets for their products. Counterintuitively, while Jihad and McWorld clearly detest one another, they also seem to thrive on their odd relationship. Do they need each other as a means of defining themselves by negation?

Five current trends which feed the fires of Jihad are described and analyzed. Massive migration covers the crises attendant to 23 million refugees forced by natural and human disasters to flee their homelands and 26 million dislocated within their own countries. Loose nukes show how Russia represents the tip of a nuclear iceberg ready to ram some unsuspecting ship of state as arms reduction agreements have ironically exacerbated the risk of nuclear materials and know-how falling into the hands of rogue states or terrorist groups. The shift from a bipolar to a multipolar configuration of power in the world in the post-Cold War era also creates a milieu of increased complexity, uncertainty, and shifting alliances. The move from an East–West to a North–South global agenda is based on the widening chasm between rich and poor countries—a chasm likely to cause desperate actions by the poor South. Finally, the emergence of zones of peace—zones of turmoil chronicles the rise of fragmentary and violent Jihad in the zones where the majority of humans reside.

Conversely, five trends congenial to McWorld's homogenization preen for recognition. Merger mania has been underway since 1980 and has reduced the number of competitive corporations in areas like communications, computer software, and banking (to cite but a few), resulting in "commercial totalism" looking much like monopoly. A massive move toward privatization and deregulation has increased the scope of the private sector of special interests at the expense of the public sector, diluting commonweal values like justice, equality, and freedom. Expanded notions of security in the post-Cold War include mobile microbes, new killer viruses like AIDS or Ebola as well as old nemeses such as tuberculosis and syphilis. The shrinking effect of interdependence and human carelessness raises the specter of threat to all humans. Videology refers to the homogenizing effect of visual imagery eclipsing the written word as the essence of human communication. Videology's global infotainment industry is North American in form and lowbrow in content. Finally, the shift from hard power to soft power homogenizes the information that makes the world go around, as knowledge supersedes force and attraction eclipses coercion.

For Digging Deeper

Bagdikian, Ben. *The Media Monopoly.* Beacon Press, 1994.

Barber, Benjamin R. *Jihad vs. McWorld: How Globalism and Tribalism Are Reshaping the World.* Ballantine Books, 1996.

Brown, Lester R. Christopher Flavin and Hal Kane. *Vital Signs 1996: Trends that Are Shaping Our Future.* Worldwatch Institute, 1996.

Crocker, Chester A., and Fen Osler Hampson. *Managing Global Chaos: Sources of and Responses to International Conflict.* U.S. Institute for Peace Press, 1996.

Doctors Without Borders. *World in Crisis: The Politics of Survival at the End of the 20th Century.* Routledge, 1996.

Garrett, Laurie. *The Coming Plague: Newly Emerging Diseases in a World Out of Balance.* Farrar, Strauss, and Giroux, 1994.

Hughes, Barry B. *International Futures: Choices in the Creation of a New World Order.* Westview Press, 1996.

Kellner, Douglas. *The Persian Gulf TV War.* Westview Press, 1992.

Klare, Michael T. *Rogue States and Nuclear Outlaws: America's Search for a New Foreign Policy.* Hill and Wang, 1996.

Moynihan, Daniel P. *Pandaemonium: Ethnicity in International Politics.* Ohio University Press, 1993.

Nye, Joseph S. *Bound to Lead: The Changing Nature of American Power.* Basic Books, 1990.

Powers, Stephen, David Rothman, and Stanley Rothman. *Hollywood's America: Social and Political Themes in Motion Pictures.* Westview Press, 1996.

Rosati, Jerel, Joe D. Hagan, and Martin Sampson III. *Foreign Policy Restructuring: How Governments Respond to Change.* University of South Carolina Press, 1995.

Sheffield, Charles, Marcelo Alonso, and Morton Kaplan, Eds. *The World of 2044: Technological Development and the Future of Society.* Professors World Peace Academy, 1994.

Singer, Max, and Aaron Wildavsky. *The Real World Order: Zones of Peace, Zones of Turmoil.* Chatham House, 1993.

Smith, Anthony. *The Age of Behemoths: The Globalization of Mass Media Firms.* Brookings Institution, 1991.

Weiner, Myron. *The Global Migration Crisis.* HarperCollins, 1995.

Zimmerman, Barry, and David Zimmerman. *Killer Germs: Microbes and Diseases that Threaten Humanity.* Contemporary Books, 1995.

Internet

The Internet Movie Database   *http://www.us.imdb.com*
The World Health Organization Reports   *http://www.who.ch*

Key Glossary Terms

asylum	(NNPT)	START treaties
deregulation	private	trend
extrapolation	public	videology
Nuclear Non-Proliferation Treaty	refugees	

APPENDIX: THE CONSTITUTION OF THE UNITED STATES

THE PREAMBLE

We the People of the United States, in Order to form a more perfect Union, establish Justice, insure domestic Tranquility, provide for the common defense, promote the general Welfare, and secure the Blessings of Liberty to ourselves and our Posterity, do ordain and establish this Constitution for the United States of America.

ARTICLE I—THE LEGISLATIVE ARTICLE

Legislative Power

Section 1 All legislative Powers herein granted shall be vested in a Congress of the United States, which shall consist of a Senate and House of Representatives.

House of Representatives: Composition; Qualifications; Apportionment; Impeachment Power

Section 2 The House of Representatives shall be composed of Members chosen every second Year by the People of the several States, and the Electors in each State shall have the Qualifications requisite for Electors of the most numerous Branch of the State Legislature.

No Person shall be a Representative who shall not have attained to the Age of twenty five Years, and been seven Years a Citizen of the United States, and who shall not, when elected, be an Inhabitant of that State in which he shall be chosen.

Representatives and direct Taxes[1] shall be apportioned among the several States which may be included within this Union, according to their respective Numbers, *which shall be determined by adding to the whole Number of free Persons, including those bound to Service for a Term of Years, and excluding Indians not taxed, three fifths of all other Persons.*[2] The actual Enumeration shall be made within three Years after the first Meeting of the Congress of the United States, and within every subsequent Term of ten Years, in such Manner as they shall by Law direct. The Number of Representatives shall not exceed one for every thirty Thousand, but each State shall have at least one Representative; and until each enumeration shall be made, the State of New Hampshire shall be entitled to chuse three, Massachusetts eight, Rhode-Island and Providence Plantations one, Connecticut five, New-York six, New Jersey four, Pennsylvania eight, Delaware one, Maryland six, Virginia ten, North Carolina five, South Carolina five, and Georgia three.

When vacancies happen in the Representation from any State, the Executive Authority thereof shall issue Writs of Election to fill such Vacancies.

The House of Representatives shall chuse their Speaker and other Officers; and shall have the sole Power of Impeachment.

Senate Composition: Qualifications, Impeachment Trials

Section 3 The Senate of the United States shall be composed of two Senators from each State, *chosen by the Legislature thereof,*[3] for six Years; and each Senator shall have one Vote.

Immediately after they shall be assembled in Consequence of the first Election, they shall be

---

[1] Modified by the 16th Amendment
[2] Replaced by Section 2, 14th Amendment

[3] Repealed by the 17th Amendment

divided as equally as may be into three Classes. The Seats of the Senators of the first Class shall be vacated at the Expiration of the second Year, of the second Class at the Expiration of the fourth Year, and of the third Class at the Expiration of the sixth Year, so that one third may be chosen every second Year; *and if Vacancies happen by Resignation, or otherwise, during the Recess of the Legislature of any State, the Executive thereof may make temporary Appointments until the next Meeting of the Legislature, which shall then fill such Vacancies.*[4]

No person shall be a Senator who shall not have attained to the Age of thirty Years, and been nine Years a Citizen of the United States, and who shall not, when elected, be an inhabitant of that State for which he shall be chosen.

The Vice President of the United States shall be President of the Senate, but shall have no Vote, unless they be equally divided.

The Senate shall chuse their other Officers, and also a President pro tempore, in the Absence of the Vice President, or when he shall exercise the Office of President of the United States.

The Senate shall have the sole Power to try all Impeachments. When sitting for that Purpose, they shall be on Oath or Affirmation. When the President of the United States is tried, the Chief Justice shall preside: And no Person shall be convicted without the Concurrence of two thirds of the Members present.

Judgment in Cases of Impeachment shall not extend further than to removal from Office, and disqualification to hold and enjoy any Office of honor, Trust or Profit under the United States; but the Party convicted shall nevertheless be liable and subject to Indictment, Trial, Judgment and Punishment, according to law.

Congressional Elections: Times, Places, Manner

Section 4   The Times, Places and Manner of holding Elections for Senators and Representatives, shall be prescribed in each State by the Legislature thereof; but the Congress may at any time by Law make or alter such Regulations, except as to the Places of chusing Senators.

The Congress shall assemble at least once in every Year, *and such Meeting shall be on the first Monday in December, unless they shall by Law appoint a different Day.*[5]

Powers and Duties of the Houses

Section 5   Each House shall be the Judge of the Elections, Returns and Qualifications of its own Members, and a Majority of each shall constitute a Quorum to do Business; but a smaller Number may adjourn from day to day, and may be authorized to compel the Attendance of absent Members, in such Manner, and under the Penalties as each House may provide.

Each House may determine the Rules of its Proceedings, punish its Members for disorderly Behaviour, and, with the Concurrence of two thirds, expel a Member.

Each House shall keep a Journal of its Proceedings, and from time to time publish the same, excepting such Parts as may in their Judgment require Secrecy; and the Yeas and Nays of the Members of either House on any question shall, at the Desire of one fifth of those Present, be entered on the Journal.

Neither House, during the Session of Congress, shall, without the Consent of the other, adjourn for more than three days, nor to any other place than that in which the two Houses shall be sitting.

Rights of Members

Section 6   The Senators and Representatives shall receive a Compensation for their Services, to be ascertained by Law, and paid out of the Treasury of the United States. They shall in all Cases, except

---

[4]Modified by the 17th Amendment

[5]Changed by the 20th Amendment

Treason, Felony and Breach of the Peace, be privileged from Arrest during their Attendance at the Session of their respective Houses, and in going to and returning from the same; and for any Speech or Debate in either House, they shall not be questioned in any other Place.

No Senator or Representative, shall, during the time for which he was elected, be appointed to any civil Office under the Authority of the United States, which shall have been created, or the Emoluments whereof shall have been encreased during such time; and no Person holding any Office under the United States, shall be a Member of either House during his Continuance in Office.

LEGISLATIVE POWERS: BILLS AND RESOLUTIONS

Section 7   All Bills for raising Revenue shall originate in the House of Representatives; but the Senate may propose or concur with Amendments as on other Bills.

Every Bill which shall have passed the House of Representatives and the Senate, shall, before it becomes a Law, be presented to the President of the United States; if he approve he shall sign it, but if not he shall return it, with his Objections to that House in which it shall have originated, who shall enter the Objections at large on their Journal, and proceed to reconsider it. If after such Reconsideration two thirds of that House shall agree to pass the Bill, it shall be sent, together with the Objections, to the other House, by which it shall likewise be reconsidered, and if approved by two thirds of that House, it shall become a Law. But in all such Cases the Votes of both Houses shall be determined by yeas and Nays, and the Names of the Persons voting for and against the Bill shall be entered on the Journal of each House respectively. If any Bill shall not be returned by the President within ten Days (Sundays excepted) after it shall have been presented to him, the Same shall be a Law, in like Manner as if he had signed it, unless the Congress by their Adjournment prevent its Return, in which Case it shall not be a Law.

Every Order, Resolution, or Vote to which the Concurrence of the Senate and House of Representatives may be necessary (except on a question of Adjournment) shall be presented to the President of the United States; and before the Same shall take Effect, shall be approved by him, or being disapproved by him, shall be repassed by two thirds of the Senate and House of Representatives, according to the Rules and Limitations prescribed in the Case of a Bill.

Powers of Congress

Section 8   The Congress shall have Power To lay and collect Taxes, Duties, Imposts and Excises, to pay the Debts and provide for the common Defence and general Welfare of the United States; but all Duties, Imposts and Excises shall be uniform throughout the United States.

To borrow Money on the Credit of the United States;

To regulate Commerce with foreign Nations, and among the several States, and with the Indian Tribes;

To establish an uniform Rule of Naturalization, and uniform Laws on the subject of Bankruptcies throughout the United States;

To coin Money, regulate the Value thereof, and of foreign Coin, and fix the Standard of Weights and Measures;

To provide for the Punishment of counterfeiting the Securities and current Coin of the United States;

To establish Post Offices and post Roads;

To promote the Progress of Science and useful Arts, by securing for limited Times to Authors and Inventors the exclusive Right to their respective Writings and Discoveries;

To constitute Tribunals inferior to the supreme Court;

To define and punish Piracies and Felonies committed on the high Seas, and Offences against the Law of Nations;

To declare War, grant Letters of Marque and Reprisal, and make Rules concerning Captures on Land and Water;

To raise and support Armies, but no Appropriation of Money to that Use shall be for a longer Term than two Years;

To provide and maintain a Navy;

To make Rules for the Government and Regulation of the land and naval Forces;

To provide for calling for the Militia to execute the Laws of the Union, suppress Insurrections and repel Invasions;

To provide for organizing, arming, and disciplining, the Militia, and for governing such Part of them as may be employed in the Service of the United States, reserving to the States respectively, the Appointment of the Officers, and the Authority of training the Militia according to the discipline prescribed by Congress;

To exercise exclusive Legislation in all Cases whatsoever, over such District (not exceeding ten Miles square) as may, by Cession of particular States, and the Acceptance of Congress, become the Seat of the Government of the United States, and to exercise like Authority over all Places purchased by the Consent of the Legislature of the State in which the Same shall be, for the Erection of Forts, Magazines, Arsenals, dock-Yards, and other needful Buildings;—And

To make all Laws which shall be necessary and proper for carrying into Execution the foregoing Powers, and all other Powers vested by this Constitution in the Government of the United States, or in any Department or Officer thereof.

Powers Denied to Congress

Section 9   The Migration of Importation of such Persons as any of the States now existing shall think proper to admit, shall not be prohibited by the Congress prior to the Year one thousand eight hundred and eight, but a Tax or Duty may be imposed on such Importation, not exceeding ten dollars for each Person.

The privilege of the Writ of Habeas Corpus shall not be suspended, unless when in Cases of Rebellion or Invasion the public Safety may require it.

No Bill of Attainder or ex post facto Laws shall be passed.

No Capitation, or other direct, Tax shall be laid, unless in Proportion to the Census or Enumeration herein before directed to be taken.[6]

No Tax or Duty shall be laid on Articles exported from any State.

No Preference shall be given by any Regulation of Commerce or Revenue to the Ports of one State over those of another; nor shall Vessels bound to, or from, one State, be obliged to enter, clear, or pay Duties in another.

No Money shall be drawn from the Treasury, but in Consequence of Appropriations made by Law; and a regular Statement and Account of the Receipts and Expenditures of all public Money shall be published from time to time.

No Title of Nobility shall be granted by the United States; And no Person holding any Office of Profit or Trust under them, shall, without the Consent of Congress, accept of any present, Emolument, Office, or Title, of any kind whatever, from any King, Prince, or foreign State.

Powers Denied to the States

Section 10   No State shall enter into any Treaty, Alliance, or Confederation; grant Letters of Marque and Reprisal; coin Money; emit Bills of Credit; make any Thing but gold and silver Coin a Tender in Payment of Debts; pass any Bill of Attainder, ex post facto Law, or Law impairing the Obligation of Contracts, or grant any Title of Nobility.

No State shall, without the Consent of the Congress, lay any Imposts or Duties on Imports or Exports, except what may be absolutely necessary for executing its inspection Laws: and the net Produce of

---

[6]Modified by the 16th Amendment

all Duties and Imposts, laid by any State on Imports or Exports, shall be for the Use of the Treasury of the United States; and all such Laws shall be subject to the Revision and Controul of the Congress.

No State shall, without the Consent of Congress, lay any Duty of Tonnage, keep Troops, or Ships of War in time of Peace, enter into any Agreement or Compact with another State, or with a foreign Power, or engage in War, unless actually invaded, or in such imminent Danger as will not admit of Delay.

ARTICLE II—THE EXECUTIVE ARTICLE

Nature and Scope of Presidential Power

Section 1   The executive Power shall be vested in a President of the United States of America. He shall hold his Office during the Term of four Years and, together with the Vice President, chosen for the same Term, be elected as follows:

Each State shall appoint, in such Manner as the Legislature thereof may direct, a Number of Electors, equal to the whole Number of Senators and Representatives to which the State may be entitled in the Congress: but no Senator or Representative, or Person holding an Office of Trust or Profit under the United States, shall be appointed an Elector.

The Electors shall meet in their respective States, and vote by Ballot for two Persons, of whom one at least shall not be an Inhabitant of the same State with themselves. And they shall make a List of all the Persons voted for, and of the Number of Votes for each; which List they shall sign and certify, and transmit sealed to the Seat of the Government of the United States, directed to the President of the Senate. The President of the Senate shall, in the Presence of the Senate and House of Representatives, open all the Certificates, and the Votes shall then be counted. The Person having the greatest Number of Votes shall be the President, if such Number be a Majority of the whole Number of Electors appointed; and if there be more than one who have such Majority and have an equal Number of Votes, then the House of Representatives shall immediately chuse by Ballot one of them for President; and if no person have a Majority, then from the five highest on the List the said House shall in like Manner chuse the President. But in chusing the President, the Votes shall be taken by States, the Representation from each State having one Vote; A quorum for this Purpose shall consist of a Member or Members from two thirds of the States, and a Majority of all the States shall be necessary to a Choice. In every Case, after the Choice of the President, the person having the greatest Number of Votes of the Electors shall be the Vice President. But if there should remain two or more who have equal Vote, the Senate shall chuse from them by Ballot the Vice President.[7]

The Congress may determine the Time of chusing the Electors, and the Day on which they shall give their Votes; which Day shall be the same throughout the United States.

No Person except a natural born Citizen, or a Citizen of the United States, at the time of the Adoption of this Constitution, shall be eligible to the Office of President; neither shall any Person be eligible to that Office who shall not have attained to the Age of thirty five Years, and been fourteen Years a Resident within the United States.

In Case of the Removal of the President from Office, or of his Death, Resignation, or Inability to discharge the Powers and Duties of the said Office, the same shall devolve on the Vice President, and the Congress may by Law provide for the Case of Removal, Death, Resignation, or Inability, both of the President and Vice President, declaring what Officer shall then act as President, and such Officer shall act accordingly, until the Disability be removed, or a President shall be elected.[8]

[7]Changed by the 12th and 20th Amendments
[8]Modified by the 25th Amendment

The President shall, at stated Times, receive for his Services, a Compensation, which shall neither be encreased nor diminished during the Period of which he shall have been elected, and he shall not receive within that Period any other Emolument from the United States, or any of them.

Before he enter on the Execution of his Office, he shall take the following Oath or Affirmation:—"I do solemnly swear (or affirm) that I will faithfully execute the Office of President of the United States, and will to the best of my Ability, preserve, protect and defend the Constitution of the United States."

Powers and Duties of the President

Section 2 The President shall be the Commander in Chief of the Army and Navy of the United States, and of the Militia of the several States, when called into the actual Service of the United States, he may require the Opinion, in writing, of the principal Officer in each of the executive Departments, upon any Subject relating to the Duties of their respective Offices, and he shall have the Power to grant Reprieves and Pardons for Offences against the United States, except in Cases of Impeachment.

He shall have Power, by and with the Advice and Consent of the Senate to make Treaties, provided two thirds of the Senators present concur; and he shall nominate, and by and with the Advice and Consent of the Senate, shall appoint Ambassadors, other public Ministers and Consuls, Judges of the supreme Court, and all other Officers of the United States, whose Appointments are not herein otherwise provided for, and which shall be established by Law: but the Congress may by Law vest the Appointment of such inferior Officers, as they think proper, in the President alone, in the Courts of Law, or in the Heads of Departments.

The President shall have Power to fill up all Vacancies that may happen during the Recess of the Senate, by granting Commissions which shall expire at the End of their next Session.

Section 3 He shall from time to time give to the Congress Information of the State of the Union, and recommend to their Consideration such Measures as he shall judge necessary and expedient; he may, on extraordinary Occasions, convene both Houses, or either of them, and in Case of Disagreement between them, with Respect to the Time of Adjournment, he may adjourn them to such Time as he shall think proper; he shall receive Ambassadors and other public Ministers; he shall take Care that the Laws be faithfully executed, and shall Commission all the Officers of the United States.

Section 4 The President, Vice President and all civil Officers of the United States, shall be removed from Office on Impeachment for, and Conviction of, Treason, Bribery, or other High Crimes and Misdemeanors.

ARTICLE III—THE JUDICIAL ARTICLE

Judicial Power, Courts, Judges

Section 1 The judicial Power of the United States, shall be vested in one supreme Court, and in such inferior Courts as the Congress may from time to time ordain and establish. The Judges, both the supreme and inferior Courts, shall hold their Offices during good Behaviour, and shall, at stated Times, receive for their Services, a Compensation, which shall not be diminished during their Continuance in Office.

Jurisdiction

Section 2 The judicial Power shall extend to all Cases, in Law and Equity, arising under this Constitution, the Laws of the United States, and Treaties made, or which shall be made, under their Authority;—to all Cases affecting Ambassadors, other public Ministers and Consuls;—to all Cases of admiralty and maritime Jurisdiction;—to Controversies to which the United States shall be a Party;—to Controversies between two or more States; *between a State and Citizens of another*

State;[9]—between Citizens of different States;—between Citizens of the same State claiming Lands under Grants of different States, and between a State, or the Citizens thereof, and foreign States, Citizens, or Subjects.

In all Cases affecting Ambassadors, other public Ministers and Consuls, and those in which a State shall be Party, the supreme Court shall have original Jurisdiction. In all the other Cases before mentioned, the supreme Court shall have appellate Jurisdiction, both as to Law and Fact, with such Exceptions, and under such Regulations as Congress shall make.

The Trial of all Crimes, except in Cases of Impeachment, shall be by Jury; and such Trial shall be held in the State where the said Crimes shall have been committed; but when not committed within any State, the Trial shall be at such Place or Places as the Congress may by Law have directed.

Treason

Section 3   Treason against the United States, shall consist only in levying War against them, or in adhering to their Enemies, giving them Aid and Comfort. No Persons shall be convicted of Treason unless on the Testimony of two Witnesses to the same overt Act, or on Confession in open Court.

The Congress shall have Power to declare the Punishment of Treason, but no Attainder of Treason shall work Corruption of Blood, or Forfeiture except during the Life of the Person attainted.

ARTICLE IV—INTERSTATE RELATIONS

Full Faith and Credit Clause

Section 1   Full Faith and Credit shall be given in each State to the public Acts, Records, and judicial Proceedings of every other State. And the Congress may by general Laws prescribe the Manner in which such Acts, Records and Proceedings shall be proved, and the Effect thereof.

Privileges and Immunities; Interstate Extradition

Section 2   The Citizens of each State shall be entitled to all Privileges and Immunities of Citizens in the several States.

A person charged in any State with Treason, Felony or other Crime, who shall flee from Justice, and be found in another State, shall on Demand of the executive Authority of the State from which he fled, be delivered up, to be removed to the State having jurisdiction of the Crime.

No person held to Service or Labour in one State, under the Laws thereof, escaping into another, shall, in Consequence of any Law or Regulation therein, be discharged from such Service or Labour, but shall be delivered up on Claim of the Party to whom such Service or Labour may be due.[10]

Admission of States

Section 3   New States may be admitted by the Congress into this Union; but no new State shall be formed or erected within the Jurisdiction of any other State; nor any State to be formed by the Junction of two or more States, or Parts of States, without the Consent of the Legislatures of the States concerned as well as of the Congress.

The Congress shall have Power to dispose of and make all needful Rules and Regulations respecting the Territory or other Property belonging to the United States; and nothing in this Constitution shall be so construed as to Prejudice any Claims of the United States, or of any particular State.

Republican Form of Government

Section 4   The United States shall guarantee to every State in this Union a Republican Form of

---

[9]Modified by the 11th Amendment

[10]Repealed by the 13th Amendment

Government, and shall protect each of them against Invasion; and on Application of the Legislature, or of the Executive (when the Legislature cannot be convened) against domestic Violence.

ARTICLE V—THE AMENDING POWER

The Congress, whenever two thirds of both Houses shall deem it necessary, shall propose Amendments to this Constitution, or, on the Application of the Legislatures of two thirds of several States, shall call a Convention for proposing Amendments, which, in either Case, shall be valid to all Intents and Purposes, as Part of this Constitution, when ratified by the Legislatures of three fourths of the several States, or by Conventions in three fourths thereof, as the one or the other Mode of Ratification may be proposed by the Congress; Provided that no Amendment which may be made prior to the Year One thousand eight hundred and eight shall in any Manner affect the first and fourth Clauses in the Ninth Section of the first Article; and that no State, without its Consent, shall be deprived of its equal Suffrage in the Senate.

ARTICLE VI—THE SUPREMACY ACT

All Debts contracted and Engagements entered into, before the Adoption of this Constitution, shall be as valid against the United States under the Constitution, as under the Confederation.

This Constitution, and the Laws of the United States which shall be made in Pursuance thereof; and all Treaties made, or which shall be made, under the Authority of the United States, shall be the supreme Law of the Land; and the Judges in every State shall be bound thereby, any Thing in the Constitution or Laws of any State to the Contrary notwithstanding.

The Senators and Representatives before mentioned, and the Members of the several State Legislatures, and all executive and judicial Officers, both of the United States and of the several States, shall be bound by Oath or Affirmation, to support this Constitution; but no religious Test shall ever be required as a Qualification to any Office or public Trust under the United States.

ARTICLE VII—RATIFICATION

The Ratification of the Conventions of nine States, shall be sufficient for the Establishment of this Constitution between the States so ratifying the Same.

Done in Convention by the Unanimous Consent of the States present the Seventeenth Day of September in the Year of our Lord one thousand seven hundred and Eighty seven and of the Independence of the United States of America the Twelfth *In Witness whereof We have hereunto subscribed our Names.*

AMENDMENTS

The Bill of Rights

[The first ten amendments were ratified on December 15, 1791, and form what is known as the "Bill of Rights."]

AMENDMENT 1—RELIGION, SPEECH, ASSEMBLY, AND POLITICS

Congress shall make no law respecting an establishment of religion, or prohibiting the free exercise thereof; or abridging the freedom of speech, or of the press; or the right of the people peaceably to assemble, and to petition the government for a redress of grievances.

AMENDMENT 2—MILITIA AND THE RIGHT TO BEAR ARMS

A well regulated Militia, being necessary to the security of a free State, the right of the people to keep and bear Arms, shall not be infringed.

AMENDMENT 3—QUARTERING OF SOLDIERS

No Soldier shall, in time of peace be quartered in any house, without the consent of the Owner, nor in time of war, but in manner to be prescribed by law.

AMENDMENT 4—SEARCHES AND SEIZURES

The right of the people to be secure in their persons, houses, papers, and effects, against unreasonable searches and seizures, shall not be violated, and no Warrants shall issue, but upon probable cause, supported by Oath or affirmation, and particularly describing the place to be searched, and the persons or things to be seized.

AMENDMENT 5—GRAND JURIES, SELF-INCRIMINATION, DOUBLE JEOPARDY, DUE PROCESS, AND EMINENT DOMAIN

No person shall be held to answer for a capital, or otherwise infamous crime, unless on a presentment or indictment of a Grand jury, except in cases arising in the land or naval forces, or in the Militia, when in actual service in time of War or public danger; nor shall any person be subject for the same offence to be twice put in jeopardy of life or limb; nor shall be compelled in any criminal case to be a witness against himself, nor be deprived of life, liberty, or property, without due process of law; nor shall private property be taken for public use, without just compensation.

AMENDMENT 6—CRIMINAL COURT PROCEDURES

In all criminal prosecutions, the accused shall enjoy the right to a speedy and public trial, by an impartial jury of the State and district wherein the crime shall have been committed, which district shall have been previously ascertained by law, and to be informed of the nature and cause of the accusation; to be confronted with the witnesses against him; to have compulsory process for obtaining Witnesses in his favor, and to have the Assistance of Counsel for his defense.

AMENDMENT 7—TRIAL BY JURY IN COMMON LAW CASES

In Suits at common law, where the value in controversy shall exceed twenty dollars, the right of trial by jury shall be preserved, and no fact tried by a jury shall be otherwise re-examined in any Court of the United States, than according to the rules of the common law.

AMENDMENT 8—BAIL, CRUEL AND UNUSUAL PUNISHMENT

Excessive bail shall not be required, nor excessive fines imposed, nor cruel and unusual punishments inflicted.

AMENDMENT 9—RIGHTS RETAINED BY THE PEOPLE

The enumeration in the Constitution, of certain rights, shall not be construed to deny or disparage others retained by the people.

AMENDMENT 10—RESERVED POWERS OF THE STATES

The powers not delegated to the United States by the Constitution, nor prohibited by it to the States, are reserved to the States respectively, or to the people.

AMENDMENT 11—SUITS AGAINST THE STATES

[Ratified February 7, 1795]

The Judicial power of the United States shall not be construed to extend to any suit in law or equity, commenced or prosecuted against one of the United States by Citizens of another State, or by Citizens or Subjects of any Foreign State.

AMENDMENT 12—ELECTION OF THE PRESIDENT

[Ratified June 15, 1804]

The Electors shall meet in their respective states, and vote by ballot for President and Vice-President, one of whom, at least, shall not be an inhabitant of the same state with themselves; they shall name in their ballots the person voted for as President, and in distinct ballots the person voted for as Vice-President, and they shall make distinct lists of all persons voted for as President, and of all persons voted for as Vice-President, and of the number of votes for each, which lists they shall sign and certify, and transmit sealed to the seat of the government of the United States, directed to the President of the Senate;—The President of the Senate shall, in presence of the Senate and House of Representatives, open all the certificates and the votes shall then be counted;—The person having the greatest number of votes for President, shall be the President, if such number be a majority of the whole number of Electors appointed; and if no person have such majority, then from the persons having the highest numbers not exceeding three on the list of those voted for as President, the House of Representatives shall choose immediately, by ballot, the President. But in choosing the President, the votes shall be taken by states, the representation from each state having one vote; a quorum for this purpose shall consist of a member or members from two-thirds of the states, and a majority of all states shall be necessary to a choice. And if the House of Representatives shall not choose a President whenever the right of choice shall devolve upon them, *before the fourth day of March next following*, then the Vice-President shall act as President, as in the case of the death or other constitutional disability of the President.[11] The person having the greatest number of votes as Vice-President, shall be the Vice-President, if such a number be a majority of the whole numbers of Electors appointed, and if no person have a majority, then from the two highest numbers on the list, the Senate shall choose the Vice-President; a quorum for the purpose shall consist of two-thirds of the whole number of Senators, and a majority of the whole number shall be necessary to a choice. But no person constitutionally ineligible to the office of President shall be eligible to that of Vice-President of the United States.

AMENDMENT 13—PROHIBITION OF SLAVERY

[Ratified December 6, 1865]

Section 1   Neither slavery nor involuntary servitude, except as a punishment for crime whereof the party shall have been duly convicted, shall exist within the United States, or any place subject to their jurisdiction.

Section 2   Congress shall have power to enforce this article by appropriate legislation.

AMENDMENT 14—CITIZENSHIP, DUE PROCESS, AND EQUAL PROTECTION OF THE LAWS

[Ratified July 9, 1868]

Section 1   All persons born or naturalized in the United States, and subject to the jurisdiction thereof, are citizens of the United States and of the State wherein they reside. No State shall make or enforce any law which shall abridge the privileges or immunities of citizens of the United States; nor shall any State deprive any person of life, liberty, or property, without due process of law; nor deny to any person within its jurisdiction the equal protection of the laws.

Section 2   Representatives shall be apportioned among the several States according to their respec-

---

[11]Changed by the 20th Amendment

tive numbers, counting the whole number of persons in each State, excluding Indians not taxed. But when the right to vote at any election for the choice of electors for President and Vice President of the United States, Representatives in Congress, the Executive and Judicial officers of a State, or the members of the Legislature thereof, is denied to any of the male inhabitants of such State, being twenty-one[12] years of age, and citizens of the United States, or in any way abridged, except for participation in rebellion, or other crime, the basis of representation therein shall be reduced in the proportion which the number of such male citizens shall bear to the whole number of male citizens twenty-one years of age in such State.

Section 3 No person shall be a Senator or Representative in Congress, or elector of President and Vice President, or hold any office, civil or military, under the United States, or under any State, who, having previously taken an oath, as a member of Congress, or as an officer of the United States, or as a member of any State legislature, or as an executive or judicial officer of any State, to support the Constitution of the United States, shall have engaged in insurrection or rebellion against the same, or given aid or comfort to the enemies thereof. But Congress may by a vote of two-thirds of each House, remove such disability.

Section 4 The validity of the public debt of the United States, authorized by law, including debts incurred for payment of pensions and bounties for services in suppressing insurrection or rebellion, shall not be questioned. But neither the United States nor any State shall assume or pay any debt or obligation incurred in aid of insurrection or rebellion against the United States, or any claim for the loss or emancipation of any slave; but all such debts, obligations and claims shall be held illegal and void.

Section 5 The Congress shall have power to enforce, by appropriate legislation, the provisions of this article.

AMENDMENT 15—THE RIGHT TO VOTE

[Ratified February 3, 1870]

Section 1 The right of citizens of the United States to vote shall not be denied or abridged by the United States or by any State on account of race, color, or previous condition of servitude.

Section 2 The Congress shall have power to enforce this article by appropriate legislation.

AMENDMENT 16—INCOME TAXES

[Ratified February 3, 1913]

The Congress shall have power to lay and collect taxes on incomes, from whatever source derived, without apportionment among the several States, and without regard to any census or enumeration.

AMENDMENT 17—DIRECT ELECTION OF SENATORS

[Ratified April 8, 1913]

The Senate of the United States shall be composed of two Senators from each State, elected by the people thereof, for six years; and each Senator shall have one vote. The electors in each State shall have the qualifications requisite for electors of the most numerous branch of the State legislatures.

When vacancies happen in the representation of any State in the Senate, the executive authority of such State shall issue writs of election to fill such vacancies: *Provided*, That the Legislature of any State may empower the executive thereof to make temporary appointment until the people fill the vacancies by election as the legislature may direct.

---

[12]Changed by the 26th Amendment

This amendment shall not be so construed as to affect the election or term of any Senator chosen before it becomes valid as part of the Constitution.

AMENDMENT 18—PROHIBITION

[Ratified January 16, 1919. Repealed December 5, 1933 by Amendment 21]

Section 1   After one year from the ratification of this article the manufacture, sale, or transportation of intoxicating liquors within, the importation thereof into, or the exportation thereof from the United States and all territory subject to the jurisdiction thereof for beverage purposes is hereby prohibited.

Section 2   The Congress and the several states shall have concurrent power to enforce this article by appropriate legislation.

Section 3   This article shall be inoperative unless it shall have been ratified as an amendment to the Constitution by the legislatures of the several states, as provided in the Constitution, within seven years from the date of the submission hereof to the States by the Congress.[13]

AMENDMENT 19—FOR WOMEN'S SUFFRAGE

[Ratified August 18, 1920]

The right of the citizens of the United States to vote shall not be denied or abridged by the United States or by any State on account of sex.

Congress shall have power, by appropriate legislation, to enforce the provision of this article.

AMENDMENT 20—THE LAME DUCK AMENDMENT

[Ratified January 23, 1933]

Section 1   The terms of the President and Vice President shall end at noon on the 20th day of January, and the terms of the Senators and Representatives at noon on the 3rd day of January, of the years in which such terms would have ended if this article had not been ratified; and the terms of their successors shall then begin.

Section 2   The Congress shall assemble at least once in every year, and such meeting shall begin at noon on the 3rd day of January, unless they shall by law appoint a different day.

Section 3   If, at the time fixed for the beginning of the term of the President, the President elect shall have died, the Vice President elect shall become President. If a President shall not have been chosen before the time fixed for the beginning of his term, or if the President elect shall have failed to qualify, then the Vice President elect shall act as President until a President shall have qualified; and the Congress may by law provide for the case wherein neither a President elect nor a Vice President elect shall have qualified, declaring who shall then act as President, or the manner in which one who is to act shall be selected, and such person shall act accordingly until a President or Vice President shall have qualified.

Section 4   The Congress may by law provide for the case of the death of any of the persons from whom the House of Representatives may choose a President whenever the right of choice shall have developed upon them, and for the case of the death of any of the persons from whom the Senate may choose a Vice President whenever the right of choice shall have devolved upon them.

Section 5   Sections 1 and 2 shall take effect on the 15th day of October following the ratification of this article.

Section 6   This article shall be inoperative unless it shall have been ratified as an amendment to the Constitution by the legislatures of three-fourths of the several States within seven years from the date of its submission.

---

[13]Repealed by the 21st Amendment

AMENDMENT 21—REPEAL OF PROHIBITION

[Ratified December 5, 1933]

Section 1   The eighteenth article of amendment to the Constitution of the United States is hereby repealed.

Section 2   The transportation or importation into any State, Territory, or Possession of the United States for delivery or use therein of intoxicating liquors, in violation of the laws thereof, is hereby prohibited.

Section 3   This article shall be inoperative unless it shall have been ratified as an amendment to the Constitution by conventions in the several States, as provided in the Constitution, within seven years from the date of the submission hereof to the States by the Congress.

AMENDMENT 22—NUMBER OF PRESIDENTIAL TERMS

[Ratified February 27, 1951]

Section 1   No person shall be elected to the office of the President more than twice, and no person who has held the office of President, or acted as President, for more than two years of a term to which some other person was elected President shall be elected to the Office of the President more than once. But this Article shall not apply to any person holding the office of President when this article was proposed by the Congress, and shall not prevent any person who may be holding the office of President, or acting as President, during the term within which this Article becomes operative from holding the office of President or acting as President during the remainder of such term.

Section 2   This Article shall be inoperative unless it shall have been ratified as an amendment to the Constitution by the legislatures of three-fourths of the several states within seven years from the date of its submission to the States by the Congress.

AMENDMENT 23—PRESIDENTIAL ELECTORS FOR THE DISTRICT OF COLUMBIA

[Ratified March 29, 1961]

Section 1   The District constituting the seat of Government of the United States shall appoint in such manner as the Congress may direct:

A number of electors of President and Vice President equal to the whole number of Senators and Representatives in Congress to which the District would be entitled if it were a State, but in no event more than the least populous State; they shall be in addition to those appointed by the States, but they shall be considered, for the purposes of the election of President and Vice President, to be electors appointed by a State; and they shall meet in the District and perform such duties as provided by the twelfth article of amendment.

Section 2   The Congress shall have power to enforce this article by appropriate legislation.

AMENDMENT 24—THE ANTI-POLL TAX AMENDMENT

[Ratified January 23, 1964]

Section 1   The right of citizens of the United States to vote in any primary or other election for President or Vice President, for electors for President or Vice President, or for Senator or Representative in Congress, shall not be denied or abridged by the United States or any State by reason of failure to pay any poll tax or other tax.

Section 2   The Congress shall have power to enforce this article by appropriate legislation.

AMENDMENT 25—PRESIDENTIAL DISABILITY, VICE PRESIDENTIAL VACANCIES

[Ratified February 10, 1967]

Section 1   In case of the removal of the President from office or his death or resignation, the Vice President shall become President.

Section 2 Whenever there is a vacancy in the office of the Vice President, the President shall nominate a Vice President who shall take the office upon confirmation by a majority vote of both houses of Congress.

Section 3 Whenever the President transmits to the President pro tempore of the Senate and the Speaker of the House of Representatives his written declaration that he is unable to discharge the powers and duties of his office, and until he transmits to them a written declaration to the contrary, such powers and duties shall be discharged by the Vice President as Acting President.

Section 4 Whenever the Vice-President and a majority of either the principal officers of the executive departments, or of such other body as Congress may by law provide, transmit to the President pro tempore of the Senate and the Speaker of the House of Representatives their written declaration that the President is unable to discharge the powers and duties of his office, the Vice President shall immediately assume the powers and duties of the office as Acting President.

Thereafter, when the President transmits to the President pro tempore of the Senate and the Speaker of the House of Representatives his written declaration that no inability exists, he shall resume the powers and duties of his office unless the Vice President and a majority of either the principal officers of the executive departments, or of such other body as Congress may by law provide, transmit within four days to the President pro tempore of the Senate and the Speaker of the House of Representatives their written declaration that the President is unable to discharge the powers and duties of his office. Thereupon Congress shall decide the issue, assembling within forty-eight hours for that purpose if not in session. If the Congress, within twenty-one days after receipt of the latter written declaration, or, if Congress is not in session, within twenty-one days after Congress is required to assemble, determines by two-thirds vote of both houses that the President is unable to discharge the powers and duties of his office, the Vice President shall continue to discharge the same as Acting President; otherwise, the President shall resume the powers and duties of his office.

AMENDMENT 26—EIGHTEEN-YEAR-OLD VOTE

[Ratified July 1, 1971]

Section 1 The right of citizens of the United States, who are eighteen years of age, or older, to vote shall not be denied or abridged by the United States or by any State on account of age.

Section 2 The Congress shall have power to enforce this article by appropriate legislation.

AMENDMENT 27—CONGRESSIONAL SALARIES

[Ratified May 7, 1992]

No law, varying the compensation for the services of the Senators and Representatives, shall take effect, until an election of Representative shall be intervened.

NOTES

CHAPTER 1

1. John Bale and Joseph Maguire, *The Global Sports Arena: Athletic Talent Migration in an Interdependent World.* (Frank Cass Publishers, 1994).
2. George Lopez, Jackie Smith, and Ron Pagnucco, "The Global Tide," *The Bulletin of the Atomic Scientists,* July/August 1995, pp. 33-39.
3. Francis A. Beer. *Peace Against War: The Ecology of International Violence* (Freeman, 1981), p. 165.
4. Ambrose Bierce, *The Devil's Dictionary* (Dell Publishing, 1991).
5. "Interview with Ted Williams," *USA Today,* February 21, 1992.
6. Ted Williams, *The Science of Hitting* (Fireside Books, 1986).

CHAPTER 2

1. Jeffrey Gedmin, ed., *The Germans: Portrait of a New Nation* (American Enterprise Institute Press, 1996).
2. "The World's Richest Billionaires," *Forbes Magazine,* July, 1996.
3. Pekka Korhonnen, *Japan and the Pacific Free Trade Area* (Routledge, 1994).
4. John M. Hamilton, *Entangling Alliances: How the Third World Shapes Our Lives* (Seven Locks Press, 1992).
5. Julia Waterlow, *The Nile* (Rivers of the World Series, 1993).
6. Samuel P. Huntington *Political Development and Political Decay* (Irvington Books, 1993).
7. Brian Beedham, "Islam and the West, the Next War, They Say," *Economist,* August 6, 1994, pp. 3–6.
8. Howard Rheingold, *The Virtual Community: Homesteading on the Electronic Frontier* (Addison-Wesley, 1993).
9. Joshua Quittner, "Mr. Rheingold's Neighborhood," *Time,* 25, November 1996, 99.
10. John Lennon, "Imagine," Maclen Music (1970).
11. Dave Barry, *Dave Barry in Cyberspace* (Crown, 1996).
12. Jerel A. Rosati, *The Carter Administration's Quest for Global Community: Beliefs and Their Impact on Behavior* (University of South Carolina Press, 1991).
13. Martin Ira Glassner, *Political Geography* (John Wiley and Sons, 1993), pp. 10–13.
14. Robert Ardrey, *The Territorial Imperative* (Atheneum Books, 1966).
15. Mel Gurtov, *Global Politics in the Human Interest* (Lynne Reinner, 1994).

16. Kalevi J. Holsti, *Peace and War: Armed Conflicts and International Order* (Cambridge University Press, 1994), p. 283.
17. Gerald R. Pitzl, "The Northern Territories Controversy: A Four-Decade Stalemate Between Japan and Russia" (Georgetown University: Pew Case Studies in International Affairs, 1995); H. J. DeBlij and Peter O. Muller, *Geography: Realms, Regions, and Concepts* (John Wiley and Sons, 1994), pp. 159–60, 237.

CHAPTER 3

1. Joseph Brownowski, *The Ascent of Man* (Little, Brown, and Company, 1973), p. 30.
2. "Human Origins: Tootin' the Neanderthal Tusk," *Discover: The World of Science,* April 1997, p. 19.
3. "DNA Shows Neanderthal Difference," *Associated Press Release,* July 13, 1997.
4. Thomas Maugh II, "Seeds Show Farming Began in Mexico 10,000 Years Ago," *Pittsburgh Post-Gazette,* May 9, 1997, p. A-5.
5. Deborah Scoblionkov, "The Beer that Made Sumerians Famous," *The New York Times,* March 24, 1993, p. 2.
6. Robert C. Bannister. *Sociology and Scientism: The American Quest for Objectivity, 1880-1940* (University of North Carolina Press, 1987), p. 3.
7. Max Weber, *Roscher and Kneis: The Logical Problems of Historical Economics* (Free Press, 1975), p. 107.
8. Dorothy Ross, *The Origins of American Social Science* (Cambridge University Press, 1991), p. xiv.
9. Peter T. Manicas. *A History and Philosophy of the Social Sciences* (Basil Blackwell, 1987), p. 210.
10. Dorothy Ross, *The Origins,* pgs. 55, 394.
11. Robert C. Bannister, *Sociology and Scientism,* p. 3.
12. Kenneth R. Hoover. *The Elements of Social Scientific Thinking* (St. Martin's Press, 1980), p. 8.
13. Bernard Berelson and Gary Steiner, *Human Behavior: An Inventory of Scientific Findings* (Harcourt, Brace, and World, 1970), p. 11.
14. Stuart Chase, *The Proper Study of Mankind* (Harper and Row, 1975), p. 9; John and Erna Perry, *Contemporary Society* (HarperCollins, 1994), p. 3; Paul Weisz, *The Science of Biology* (McGraw-Hill, 1967), p. 14; Hoover, *The Elements,* p. 3.
15. Carlo Lastrucci. *The Scientific Approach* (Schenkman, 1967).
16. Earl Babbie. *The Practice of Social Research* (Wadsworth, 1995), pgs. 20-21.
17. F. J. Roethlisberger and W. J. Dickson. *Management and the Worker* (Harvard University Press, 1939).

18. John Darnton, "Scientists Confirm Identification of Bones as Tsar's," *The New York Times,* July 10, 1993, p. 9; "Anastasia," Nova (PBS video), 1995.

19. Brian Bergstein, "Class Project Frees Murder Convicts," Associated Press, June 15, 1996.

20. "The Disappearance of Helle Crafts," The Learning Channel, April 21, 1996.

21. Mark C. Carnes, Ed. *Past Imperfect: History According to the Movies* (Henry Holt, 1995), p. 7.

22. Stanislav Andreski, *Social Science as Sorcery* (St. Martin's Press, 1973), p. 11.

23. Elie Weisel, interview on "The Charlie Rose Show," PBS, November 10, 1995.

24. Stanley Milgram. *Obedience to Authority* (HarperCollins, 1974); Philip Meyer, "If Hitler Asked You to Electrocute a Stranger, Would You?" *Esquire* (1970); Kenneth Hoover. *The Elements of Social Scientific Thinking* (St. Martin's Press, 1980), pp. 125-26.

25. Douglas Pasternak and Peter Cary, "Tales from the Crypt: Medical Horror Stories from a Trove of Secret Cold War Documents," *U.S. News and World Report,* September 18, 1995, pp. 70-82.

26. Abraham Kaplan, *The Conduct of Inquiry* (Chandler, 1970), p. xv.

27. Hayward R. Alker, *Rediscoveries and Reformulations: Humanistic Methodologies for International Studies* (Cambridge University Press, 1996), p. 1.

CHAPTER 4

1. Harold Lasswell, *Who Gets What When and How?* (Peter Smith, 1990).

2. Austin Ranney, *Governing: An Introduction to Political Science* (Prentice Hall, 1996), p. 4.

3. James N. Rosenau, *Turbulence in World Politics: A Theory of Change and Continuity* (Princeton University Press, 1990), pp. 4–6.

4. Martin Griffiths, *Realism, Idealism, and International Politics: A Reinterpretation* (Routledge, 1995).

5. Henry A. Kissinger, *Diplomacy* (Simon & Schuster, 1994).

6. Woodrow Wilson, address at Sioux Falls, South Dakota, September 8, 1919.

7. Woodrow Wilson, *War Message*, 65th Congress, Senate document no. 5 (Government Printing Office, 1971), pp. 3–8; David Callahan, *Between Two Worlds: Realism, Idealism and Foreign Policy after the Cold War* (HarperCollins, 1994); Martin Griffiths, *Realism, Idealism and International Politics* (Routledge, 1995).

8. Fred W. Riggs, "Thoughts about Neoidealism vs. Realism: Reflections On Charles Kegley's ISA Presidential Address," *International Studies Notes*, 19, no. 1 (Winter 1994), 1.

9. Eschel M. Rhoodie, *Cultures in Conflict: A Global Survey of Ethnicity, Sectarianism and Nationalism, 1960–1990* (McFarland, 1993); Walter Connor, "Nation-building or nation-destroying," in Fred A. Sondermann, David S. McClellan, and William C. Olson, Eds., *The Theory and Practice of International Relations* (Prentice Hall, 1979).

10. James N. Danziger, *Understanding the Political World: A Comparative Introduction to Political Science* (Longman, 1996), pp. 136–38.

11. Seyom Brown, *New Forces, Old Forces, and the Future of World Politics* (HarperCollins, 1995).

12. Hendrik Spruyt, *The Sovereign State and Its Competitors: An Analysis of Systems Change* (Princeton University Press, 1994).

13. John T. Rourke, *International Politics on the World Stage* (Dushkin, 1995), pp. 35–42; John H. Herz, "The Rise and Demise of the Territorial State," *World Politics,* 9 (1959), 473–93; Karl Deutsch, *Tides among Nations* (Free Press, 1979).

14. William Eckhardt, "War-Related Death Since 3000 B.C.," *Peace Research*, 23 (1991), 80–85.

15. George C. Kohn, *Dictionary of Wars* (Anchor Doubleday, 1994).

16. Walter Jones, *The Logic of International Relations* (HarperCollins, 1995).

17. Eschel M. Rhoodie, *Cultures in Conflict: A Global Survey of Ethnicity, Sectarianism and Nationalism: 1960–1990* (McFarland, 1993).

18. "Two Million Kids Killed in Decade of Wars," *Associated Press Release,* December 10, 1995.

19. Karl von Clausewitz, *On War* (Princeton University Press, 1976), p. 147.

20. Hans J. Morgenthau, *Politics among Nations: The Struggle for Power and Peace* (Knopf, 1978), p. 42.

21. Matthew 5:38–46, *The New Testament*, trans. Edgar J. Goodspeed (University of Chicago Press, 1948).

22. Seyom Brown, *The Causes and Prevention of War* (St. Martin's Press, 1987), p. 125.

23. SIPRI *Yearbook*, 1985, pp. 44 and 52.

24. "The Atomic Cafe," Thorn EMI Video, 1982.

25. Richard Rosecrance, "Stuffing the Genie Back In," *Institute on Global Conflict and Cooperation*, Fall 1995, pp. 4–5.

26. Francis Fukuyama, *The End of History and the Last Man* (Free Press, 1992).

27. Rex Brynen, Bahgat Korany, and Paul Noble, Eds., *Political Liberalization and Democratization in the Arab World* (Lynne Rienner, 1995).

28. Joe Hagan, "Domestic Political Systems and War Proneness, *Mershon International Studies Review*, 38, no. 2 (October 1994); David Lake, "Powerful Pacifists: Democratic States and War," *American Political Science Review*, March 1992, p. 62; Dina A. Zinnes and Richard L. Merritt, "Democracies and War," in Alex Inkeles, Ed., *On Measuring Democracy: Its Consequences and Concomitants* (Transaction Books, 1991).

29. Bruce Russett, *Controlling the Sword* (Harvard University Press, 1990), p. 123.

30. Max Singer and Aaron Wildavsky, *The Real World Order: Zones of Peace, Zones of Turmoil* (Chatham House, 1993).

31. Michael E. Brown, Sean Lynn-Jones, and Steven Miller, Eds., *Debating the Democratic Peace* (MIT Press, 1996).

32. John Mueller, *Retreat from Doomsday* (Addison-Wesley, 1993), p. 214.

33. John Mueller, *Quiet Cataclysm: Reflections of the Recent Transformation of World Politics* (HarperCollins, 1995), p. 1.

34. Anatol Rapoport, *Peace: An Idea Whose Time Has Come* (University of Michigan Press, 1992).

35. Ralph E. Lapp, "The Einstein Letter that Started It All," *The New York Times Magazine*, August 2, 1964.

36. Robert Elias and Jennifer Turpin, Eds., *Rethinking Peace* (Lynne Rienner, 1994).

37. Donald Snow, *National Security: Defense Policy for a New International Order* (St. Martin's Press, 1994), p. 4.

38. Evan Thomas, "Here We Go Again," *Newsweek*, September 26, 1994, pp. 20–24; Jennifer Lin, "Carter Again Comes to the Rescue of Clinton's Foreign Policy Team," Knight-Ridder/Tribune News Service, September 18, 1994.

39. "Intelligence Report," *Parade*, November 26, 1995, p. 14.

40. Roger Fisher et al., *Beyond Machiavelli: Tools for Coping with Conflict* (Harvard University Press, 1995); Jacob Bercovitch, Ed., *Resolving International Conflicts: The Theory and Practice of Mediation* (Lynne Rienner, 1995).

41. James N. Rosenau, "The Relocation of Authority in a Shrinking World," *Comparative Politics*, 24, no. 3 (April 1992), 266.

42. John T. Rourke, *International Politics on the World State* (Dushkin, 1995), pp. 142–44.

43. Randall Forsberg, "Wasting Billions," *Boston Review*, April/May, 1994.

44. Richard Falk, *On Human Governance: Toward a New Global Politics* (Penn State University Press, 1995).

45. Interview with Pierre Salinger, former press secretary to President Kennedy, "Biography: Khrushchev," *Arts and Entertainment Television*, July 26, 1995.

46. Gabrielle Brussel, "Cuban Missile Crisis: U.S. Deliberations and Negotiations at the Edge of the Precipice," *Pew Case No. 334.* Washington, DC: Georgetown University, 1993); James G. Blight and David A. Welch, *On the Brink: Americans and Soviets Reexamine the Cuban Missile Crisis* (Noonday, 1996).

CHAPTER 5

1. Union of International Associations, *Yearbook of International Organizations,* vol. 4 (K. G. Saur, 1994).

2. The Stanley Foundation, "The UN System and NGOs: New Relationships for a New Era?" (25th United Nations Issues Conference, 1994), p. 1.

3. David Cortright, *Peace Works: The Citizen's Role in Ending the Cold War* (Westview Press, 1993); David C. Korten, *Getting to the 21st Century: Voluntary Action and the Global Agenda* (Kumarian Press, 1990).

4. Annetta Miller, "Teaching an Old Fish New Tricks," *Newsweek,* August 16, 1993, p. 68; Ronald Powell, "Tuna Fleet's Departure Is Still Bitter Tale," *The San Diego Union-Tribune,* August 28, 1994, p. B–1; "Today's Debate: Tuna vs. Dolphins," *USA Today,* December 28, 1996, p. 12A.

5. Peter James Spielmann, "French Navy Seizes Greenpeace Ship Near Nuclear Test Site in Pacific," Associated Press Release, July 11, 1995; Bob Ostertag, "Greenpeace Takes over the World," *Mother Jones,* March/April 1991; Robert Hunter, *Warriors of the Rainbow: A Chronicle of the Greenpeace Movement* (Holt, Rinehart, Winston, 1979); Kenneth W. Stiles, "Greenpeace," in Stiles, *Case Histories in International Politics* (HarperCollins, 1995).

6. Rachel Schucker, "NGO Helps Relieve Distress of Women's Reproductive Health in Uzbekistan," *Surviving Together,* Winter 1994, pp. 37–38.

7. Eugene Linden, "Tigers on the Brink," *Time,* March 28, 1995, pp. 44–51; Vicki Allen, "The U.S. Announces Sanctions on Taiwan for Tiger Trade," *Reuters,* April 11, 1994.

8. Thomas Jewell, "Local Activist Makes *Time* Magazine," *Wheeling News-Register,* December 9, 1994, p. 1.

9. Thomas Jewell, "Woman Appreciates Environmental 'Nobel,'" *Wheeling News-Register,* May 3, 1997, p. 1.

10. Craig N. Murphy, *International Organization and Industrial Change: Global Governance Since 1850* (Oxford University Press, 1994).

11. Union of International Associations, *Yearbook of International Organizations,* 1994.

12. David Mitrany, *A Working Peace System* (Quadrangle Books, 1964).

13. Neill Nugent, *The Government and Politics of the European Union* (Duke University Press, 1994).

14. Mark Lawrence, "Bureaucratic War Waged over Meaning of 'Chocolate,'" Associated Press Release, November 23, 1995.

15. Richard Z. Chesnoff, "A Conversation with Boutros Boutros- Ghali," *U.S. News and World Report,* June 26, 1995, p. 44.

16. Enid Schoettle et al., *An Agenda for Funds: The United States and the Financing of the United Nations* (Council on Foreign Relations Press, 1995); Max Jakobsen, *The United Nations in the 1990s: A Second Chance* (United Nations Publications, 1993); Wendell Gordon, *The United Nations at the Crossroads of Reform* (Mitchell E. Sharp, 1994); "Who Are the UN Peacekeepers?" *Parade,* January 8, 1995, p. 18; Robert H. Reid, "Debts Challenge UN's Future," Associated Press Release, October 24, 1995; Charles J. Hanley, "UN Event Produces Few Answers," Associated Press Release, October 25, 1995.

17. Cathal J. Nolan, *The Longman Guide to World Affairs* (Longman Publishers, 1995), pp. 248–49.

18. David C. Korten, "Sustainability and the Global Economy: Balancing Market and Community Interests," *Surviving Together,* Winter 1994, pp. 3–5; David C. Korten, *When Corporations Rule the World* (Kumarian Press, 1995).

19. *Fortune,* July 25, 1994; "Ford Motor Corporation Circles the World," *The New York Times,* April 22, 1994, p. D1; John T. Rourke, *International Politics on the World Stage* (Dushkin, 1995), pp. 68–69, 498–99.

20. Ian Clarke, *The Spatial Organization of Multinational Corporations* (Croom Helm, 1985); Charles Kegley and Eugene Witkopf, Eds., *World Politics: Trends and Transformation* (St. Martin's Press, 1993), Table 6.1; James N. Danziger, *Understanding the Political World: A Comparative Introduction to Political Science* (Longman, 1996), pp. 366–67.

21. John-Thor Dahlburg, "Littlest Laborers Find Ally," *The Los Angeles Times,* January 4, 1994, p. A1.

22. Amelia A. Necomb, "Protection of the World's Young: Clocking Out on Child Labor," *Christian Science Monitor,* November 16, 1994, p. 1; Martin C. Evans, "Passages to a New India," *The Orange County Register,* February 8, 1994, p. C1; "Child Labor Reportedly Rising," Associated Press News Service, April 12, 1994.

23. FNS Regular Package Broadcast Interview, "The MacNeil Newshour Interview with Lewis Preston," Federal News Service, July 22, 1994.

24. Michael S. Serrill, "The Making of El Presidente," *Time,* August 22, 1994, p. 38; Christopher Palmeri, "The Best of Times, The Worst of Times," *Forbes,* June 20, 1994, pp. 198–99; Manfred Borchert and Rolf Schinkle, Eds., *International Indebtedness* (Routledge, 1990); World Bank, *World Development Report* (Oxford University Press, 1994).

CHAPTER 6

1. Joan Ferrante, *Sociology: A Global Perspective* (Wadsworth Publishing, 1995), p. 21.

2. Joseph J. Tobin, David Wu, and Dana Davidson, *Pre-School in Three Cultures: Japan, China, and the United States* (Yale University Press, 1989), p. 94.

3. Ralph Linton, *The Study of Man: An Introduction* (Appleton-Century-Crofts, 1936).

4. Gerhard and Jean Lenski, *Human Societies: An Introduction to Macrosociology* (McGraw-Hill, 1987).

5. Nelson H. Graburn, *Eskimos Without Igloos* (Little, Brown, 1969), pp. 188–200.

6. Carol and Melvin Ember, *Cultural Anthropology* (Prentice Hall, 1996), pp. 186–87.

7. Syed Zubair Ahmed, "What Do Men Want?," *The Times of India,* January 28, 1994.

8. Melvyn C. Goldstein, "When Brothers Share a Wife," *Natural History,* March, 1987, p. 39.

9. Émile Durkheim, *The Elementary Forms of Religious Life* (Collier Books, 1961).

10. Edward B. Tylor, "Animism," in William A. Lessa and Evon Z. Vogt, Eds., *Reader in Comparative Religion: An Anthropological Approach* (Harper and Row, 1979), pp. 9–18.

11. Bronislaw Malinowski, *Magic, Science, and Religion, and Other Essays* (Doubleday, 1948), pp. 50–51.

12. Gary H. Gossen, "Temporal and Spiritual Equivalents in Chamula Ritual Symbolism," in Lessa and Vogt, Eds., *Reader in Comparative Religion,* pp. 116–28.

13. H. J. De Blij and Peter O. Muller, *Geography: Realms, Regions, and Concepts* (John Wiley and Sons, 1994), pp. 271–73.

14. John E. Yellen, "The Transformation of the Kalahari !Kung," *Scientific American,* April, 1990, pp. 96–105; Richard B. Lee, *The !Kung San: Men, Women, and Work in a Foraging Society* (Cambridge University Press, 1979); "Safari Operator Working to Save Spirit of Bushmen," United Press International, April 12, 1987.

15. "The African American Experience in Japan," produced and directed by Regge Life, Film Library, 1994.

16. Stuart Chase, *The Proper Study of Mankind* (Harper and Brothers, 1956), pp. 84–85; George Peter Murdock, "The Common Denominator of Cultures," in Ralph Linton, Ed., *The Science of Man in the World Crisis* (Columbia University Press, 1945), pp. 123–142.

CHAPTER 7

1. Mattei Dogan and Dominique Pelassy, *How to Compare Nations: Strategies in Comparative Politics* (Chatham House, 1984), p. 5.

2. Robert C. Christopher, *The Japanese Mind* (Fawcett Columbine, 1984), p. 17.

3. Judith Valente, "They Steal from the Devastated," *Parade Magazine,* June 4, 1995, p. 5.

4. Illustrative of cultural differences between Japan and America is the PBS video *Baseball in Japan* (Bowling Green State University Films, 1994).

5. Nathaniel B. Thayer and Stephen E. Weiss, "The Changing Logic of a Former Minor Power," in H. Binnendijk, Ed., *National Negotiating Styles* (U.S. Department of State, 1987), pp. 45–74.

6. U.S. Department of Education, *Japanese Education Today* (1987), p. vi.

7. Edwin O. Reischauer, *The Japanese Today: Change and Continuity* (Harvard University Press, 1988).

8. *Human Development Report 1994: United Nations Development Programme* (Oxford University Press, 1994). The HDI uses fifty-two human development indicators to arrive at a composite ranking of 173 countries.

9. Michio Morishima, *Why Has Japan Succeeded? Western Technology and the Japanese Ethos* (Cambridge University Press, 1984).

10. Josha A. Fogel, *The Cultural Dimension of Sino-Japanese Relations* (Mitchell E. Sharpe, 1994).

11. Jay and Linda Matthews, *One Billion: A China Chronicle* (Random House, 1983).

12. Susan V. Lawrence, "The Legacy of the Red Guards," *U.S. News and World Report,* May 20, 1996, p. 40.

13. Joan Ferrante, *Sociology: A Global Perspective* (Wadsworth Publishing, 1995), pp. 265–273.

14. Brigham Young University, "Culturgram '95: People's Republic of China." (David Kennedy Center for International Studies, 1995); United Nations Development Programme, *Human Development Report 1995* (Oxford University Press, 1995), p. 155.

15. David Brown, "Song of the Steppe," *The Washington Post National Weekly Edition,* January 22–28, 1996, p. 38; R. Emmert and Y. Minegishi, Eds., *Musical Voices of Asia* (Harmony, 1991).

16. Hedrick Smith, *The Russians* (Ballantine Books, 1976), pp. 138–39.

17. Murray Feschbach, *Ecocide in the U.S.S.R.* (HarperCollins, 1989).

18. Brigham Young University, "Culturgram '95: Russia" (David Kennedy Center for International Studies, 1995); United Nations Development Programme, *Human Development Report 1995* (Oxford University Press, 1995), p. 155.

19. Daniel Rancour-Laferriere, *The Slave Soul of Russia: Moral Masochism and the Cult of Suffering* (New York University Press, 1995).

20. Winston Churchill, radio broadcast, October 11, 1939.

21. See Judith Miller, "The Challenge of Radical Islam," *Foreign Affairs,* 72, no. 2 (Spring 1993); Steve Coll and David Hoffman, "Islam's Violent Improvisers," *The Washington Post,* August 9–15, 1993, pp. 6–7; Robin Wright, *Sacred Rage: The Wrath of Militant Islam* (Simon & Schuster, 1985); Martin Kramer, "Islam vs. Democracy," *Commentary,* 95, no. 1 (January 1993); Mark Juergensmeyer, *The New Cold War? Religious Nationalism Confronts the Secular State* (University of California Press, 1993).

22. Mir Zohair Husain, *Global Islamic Politics* (HarperCollins, 1995), p. xi.

23. H. J. DeBlij and Peter O. Muller, *Geography: Realms, Regions, and Concepts* (John Wiley and Sons, 1994), p. 353.

24. Ibid., p. xii.

25. John L. Esposito and John Voll, *Islam and Democracy* (Oxford University Press, 1996).

26. Brigham Young University, "Culturgram '95: Morocco" (David Kennedy Center for International Studies, 1995).

27. "The Tribe that Time Forgot," produced and directed by John Miles for PBS, *Nova* (1994).

28. Brigham Young University, "Culturgram '92: Brazil" (David M. Kennedy Center for International Studies, 1992), p. 2.

29. DeBlij and Muller, *Geography,* pp. 336–49.

30. The World Bank, *World Development Report 1990* (Oxford University Press, 1990).

31. United Nations Development Programme, *Human Development Report 1995* (Oxford University Press, 1995), p. 155.

32. Manuel G. Mendoza and Vince Napoli, *Systems of Society* (D.C. Heath, 1995), pp. 565–73.

33. C. Wright Mills, *The Sociological Imagination* (Oxford University Press, 1959).

34. United Nations Development Programme, *Human Development Report 1995* (Oxford University Press, 1995), p. 156.

35. "Baka: People of the Rainforest," PBS Video, *Nova* (1990).

36. L. Robert Kohls, *Survival Kit for Overseas Living* (Intercultural Press, 1984), pp. 21–26; adapted from Florence Kluckhohn and Fred Strodtbeck, *Variations in Value Orientations* (Row, Peterson, 1961), chap. 1.

CHAPTER 8

1. Brian Jones, Bernard Gallagher, Joseph M. Falls, *Sociology: Micro, Macro, and Mega Structures* (Harcourt, Brace, 1995), p. 209.

2. Robert H. Clarke, "Lest Ye Be Judged: Ethnocentrism or Cultural Relativism," in Frank Zulke, Ed., *Through the Eyes of Social Science* (Waveland Press, 1995), p. 238.

3. Joan Ferrante, *Sociology: A Global Perspective* (Wadsworth Publishing, 1995), p. 129.

4. Carol and Melvin Ember, *Cultural Anthropology* (Prentice Hall, 1996), p. 16.

5. Dorothy Lee, *Valuing the Self: What We Learn from Other Cultures* (Waveland Press, 1995).

6. From "Words of Domon Sage, Ogotemmeli," in Marcel Griaule, *Diew d'Eau,* trans. R. Clarke (Librairie Artheme Fayard, 1966).

7. Jomo Kenyatta, *Facing Mt. Kenya* (Secker and Warburg, 1953) pp. 153–54.

8. Sophronia Gregory, "At Risk of Mutilation," *Time,* March 21, 1994, p. 45.

9. Robin Morgan and Gloria Steinem, "The International Crime of Genital Mutilation," *MS,* March 1980, p. 98.

10. Ellen Goodman, "Setting a Precedent to Protect Little Girls from Mutilation," United Press Release, March 31, 1994.

11. Steve Mufson, "Economic Crime Explodes as China Prospers," *The Washington Post,* October 3, 1994, p. A12; "Amnesty International Reports Human Rights Abuses in 151 Nations," Kyodo News International, July 7, 1994.

12. George Ritzer, *The McDonaldization of Society* (Pine Forge Press, 1995).

13. David Rieff, "The Culture that Conquered the Earth," *World Policy Journal,* October 1994, p. 3.

14. Martin Tolchin, "Japan-Bashing Becomes a Trade Bill Issue," *The New York Times,* February 28, 1988; Willis Witter, "Intelligence Officers Face Pro-Toshiba Heat," *The Washington Post,* March 4, 1988; Willis Witter, "CIA Aide Tells of Toshiba Deliveries," *The Washington Post,* March 9, 1988; Eduardo Lachica, "Tampering by CIA with Toshiba Affair Gets It into Trouble with Policy Makers," *The Wall Street Journal,* March 21, 1988.

CHAPTER 9

1. David Gelman, "Why We All Love to Hate," *Newsweek*, August 28, 1989, p. 62.

2. Peter T. Manicas, *History and Philosophy of the Social Sciences* (Basil Blackwell, 1987), p. 294.

3. Dennis Coon, *Introduction to Psychology: Exploration and Application* (West Publishing, 1995), pp. 2, 6.

4. Keith E. Stanovich, How to Think Straight about Psychology (HarperCollins, 1996), p. xiii.

5. Coon, *Introduction to Psychology*, p. 714.

6. Manicas, *History and Philosophy of the Social Sciences*, p. 171.

7. Geoffrey Masson, *The Making and Unmaking of a Psychotherapist* (Addison-Wesley, 1990).

8. Stanovich, *How to Think Straight about Psychology*, p. 1.

9. Aristotle, *Nichomachean Ethics*, Book III, chap. 3.

10. David Elkind, "Erik Erikson's Eight Ages of Man," *The New York Times Company*, 1970.

11. Coon, *Introduction to Psychology*, p. 13.

12. Peter D. Kramer, *Listening to Prozac* (Penguin Books, 1993).

13. Blema S. Steinberg, *Shame and Humiliation: Presidential Decison Making on Vietnam* (University of Pittsburgh Press, 1996), p. 6.

14. John G. Stoessinger, *Crusaders and Pragmatists: Movers of American Foreign Policy* (Norton, 1985).

15. Sam Keen, *Faces of the Enemy*, documentary film (Catticus Corporation, 1986).

16. See Robert Jervis, "Hypotheses of Misperception," *World Politics*, XX (1968), pp. 454–79; Kenneth Boulding, *The Image: Knowledge in Life and Society* (University of Michigan, 1956); Ole R. Holsti, Robert North, and Richard Brody, "Perceptions and Actions in the 1914 Crisis," in J. David Singer, Ed., *Quantitative International Politics* (Free Press, 1968); Otto Klineberg, *The Human Dimension in International Relations* (Free Press, 1969).

17. Demosthenes, *Third Olynthiac*, section 19.

18. John T. Rourke, *International Politics on the World Stage* (Dushkin, 1995), pp. 139–40.

19. Walter S. Jones, *The Logic of International Relations* (HarperCollins, 1991), pp. 225–30.

20. Ibid.

21. "The U.S. Drops the Atomic Bomb on Japan, August 1945," *Intercom #106*, March 1985, p. 14.

22. Sam Keen, *Faces of the Enemy: Reflections of the Hostile Imagination* (Harper and Row, 1986).

23. "Thatcher Urges the Press to Help 'Starve' Terrorists," *The New York Times*, July 16, 1985, p. 3.

24. Walter Reich, *Origins of Terrorism: Psychologies, Ideologies, States of Mind* (Cambridge University, 1990).

25. John Dickerson, "Four for One," *Time*, March 14, 1994, p. 33; Laurie Mylroie, "Saddam and Terrorism: The WTC Bombing," *Newsweek*, October 17, 1994, pp. 30–32; Terence Samuel, "Man Said to Be Key to World Trade Center Bombing Pleads Not Guilty, but Blames Attack on Iraq," Knight-Ridder/Tribune News Service, February 9, 1995.

26. Jill Smolowe, "Enemies of the State," *Time*, May 8, 1995, p. 61.

27. Christopher John Farley, "America's Bomb Culture," *Time*, May 8, 1995, p. 56.

28. Biography, "Timothy McVeigh," *Arts and Entertainment*, April 20, 1996; "McVeigh Believes Millions Share His Views," Associated Press Release, April 22, 1996.

29. Rochelle Olson, "*Turner Diaries* Author: Dangerous or Revolutionary?" Associated Press Release, June 9, 1996.

30. Robert Jay Lifton, interviewed in Sam Keen's film *Faces of the Enemy* (1987).

31. Christine Gorman, "Calling All Paranoids," *Time*, May 8, 1995, p. 69; James Coates, *Armed and Dangerous: The Rise of the Survivalist Right* (Hill and Wang, 1996).

32. Otto Klineberg, in foreword to Marshall H. Segall, *Cross-Cultural Psychology: Human Behavior in Global Perspective* (Brooks/Cole, 1979), p. v.

33. Carol and Melvin Ember, *Cultural Anthropology* (Prentice Hall, 1996), pp. 284–90.

34. Donald E. Brown, *Human Universals* (Temple University Press, 1991).

35. Margaret Mead, *Coming of Age in Samoa* (Morrow, 1961).

36. Alice Schlegel and Herbert Barry, III, *Adolescence: An Anthropological Inquiry* (Free Press, 1991), p. 44.

37. Ember and Ember, *Cultural Anthropology*, pp. 284, 289.

CHAPTER 10

1. Felix Oppenheim, *The Place of Morality in Foreign Policy* (Lexington Books, 1991).

2. William Korey, *The Promises We Keep: Human Rights, the Helsinki Process, and American Foreign Policy* (St. Martin's Press, 1993).

3. Cathal J. Nolan, Ed., *Ethics and Statecraft: The Moral Dimension of International Affairs* (Praeger Publishers, 1995).

4. George A. Lopez and Drew Christiansen, Eds., *Morals and Might: Ethics and the Use of Force in Modern International Affairs* (Westview Press, 1996).

5. NBC White Paper, "The Decision to Drop the Bomb," *NBC News* (1965), 16 mm film; Michael J. Hogan, *Hiroshima in History and Memory* (Cambridge University Press, 1996); Donald Kagan, "Why America Dropped the Bomb," *Commentary*, September 1995; John Rawls, "Fifty Years after Hiroshima," *Dissent*, Summer 1995.

6. Joel H. Rosenthal, "Fighting the Oxymoron Problem: The Study and Teaching of Ethics and International Affairs," *Forum*, Spring 1994, p. 3.

7. The Learning Channel, "The Gene Hunters," *Science Frontiers*, March 9, 1996.

8. George F. Kennan, "Morality and Foreign Policy," *Foreign Affairs* 64 (1986), 217.

9. Thomas Patterson and Dennis Merrill, Eds., *Major Problems in American Foreign Relations* (D.C. Heath, 1995), p. 29.

10. Larry Berman, *Planning a Tragedy* (Norton and Company, 1982); George C. Herring, *America's Longest War* (John Wiley and Sons, 1979); Doris Kearns, *Lyndon Johnson and the American Dream* (New American Library, 1976).

11. Paul Keal, Ed., *Ethics and Foreign Policy* (Paul and Company, 1995).

12. Kenneth Thompson, "The Ethical Dimensions of Diplomacy," *Review of Politics*, 1984, p. 387.

13. John T. Rourke, *International Politics on the World Stage* (Dushkin, 1995), p. 207.

14. Douglas Johnston, Ed., *Religion, the Missing Dimension of Statecraft* (Oxford University Press, 1994); David R. Smock, *Perspectives of Pacifism: Christian, Jewish and Muslim Views on Nonviolence and International Conflict* (U.S. Peace Institute of Peace, 1995).

15. Mary Lean, *Bread, Bricks and Belief: Communities in Charge of Their Future* (Kumarian Press, 1995).

16. Bruce W. Nelan, "Diplomacy of Terror," *Time*, May 31, 1993, p. 46; "Clinton's Meeting with Rushdie, Remarks Criticized," *Tehran Voice of the Islamic Republic*, December 2, 1993; "Commentary Views Rushdie Visit to the U.S.," *Tehran Jomhuri-Ye Eslami*, December 8, 1993; Peter Millership, "Five Years after Fatwa, Rushdie Still in Hiding," *Reuters America*, February 12, 1994; "EC May Ask Iran to Lift Rushdie Death Sentence," *Reuters America*, December 20, 1993.

17. Kendall W. Stiles, "Nationalism in the Caucasus," *Case Histories in International Politics* (HarperCollins, 1995), pp. 257–77.

18. Irving Aballa and Harold Troper, *None Is Too Many* (Random House, 1983), pp. v, 280.

19. Jack Donnelly, *International Human Rights* (Westview Press, 1993), p. 66.

20. Human Rights Watch, *Human Rights Watch World Report 1995* (Human Rights Watch, 1994), p. xiii.

21. Donnelly, *International Human Rights*, p. 104.

22. Donnelly, *International Human Rights*, pp. 32–39.

23. Bilahari Kausikan, "Asia's Different Standard," *Foreign Policy*, Fall 1993; Aryeh Neir, "Asia's Unacceptable Standard," *Foreign Policy*, Fall 1993; John T. Rourke, *Taking Sides: Clashing Views on Controversial Issues in World Politics* (Dushkin, 1995), pp. 350–51; Terry Nardin and David R. Mapel, Eds., *Traditions of International Ethics* (Cambridge University Press, 1996).

24. United Nations Development Programme, *Human Development Report 1995* (Oxford University Press, 1995), p. 2.

25. Joan and Melvin Ember, *Cultural Anthropology* (Prentice Hall, 1996), p. 162.

26. Brian J. Jones, Bernard Gallagher III, and Joseph A. McFalls, Jr., *Introductory Sociology: Micro, Macro, and Mega Structures* (Harcourt Brace College, 1995), *p. 414.*

27. Paul Gauguin, *Noa Noa: The Tahitian Journal* (Dover, 1919 and 1985), pp. 19–20.

28. Betty Reardon, "Feminist Concepts of Peace and Security," in Paul Smoker et al., Eds., *A Reader in Peace Studies* (Pergamon Press, 1990), p. 136.

29. Joan Ferrante, *Sociology: A Global Perspective* (Wadsworth, 1995), p. 411.

30. *Human Development Report*, pp. 50–71.

31. *Human Rights Watch World Report 1995* (Human Rights Watch, 1995), pp. 252–53.

32. Amnesty International, "Women in the Middle East: Human Rights Under Attack" (Amnesty International, 1995), p. 3.

CHAPTER 11

1. Dorothy R. Ross, *The Origins of American Social Science* (Cambridge University Press, 1991), p. xix–xx.

2. Fred Gottheil, *Principles of Macroeconomics* (South-Western, 1996), p. 226–27.

3. Charles Hampden-Turner and Alfons Trompenaars, *The Seven Cultures of Capitalism* (Doubleday, 1993).

4. Cathal J. Nolan, *The Longman Guide to World Affairs* (Longman Publishers, 1995), p. 237.

5. *Current Population Reports: Money Income of Households, Families, and Persons in the U.S.* (1990), p. 202.

6. Gottheil, *Principles of Macroeconomics*, p. 117.

7. Anders Aslund, *How Russia Became a Market Economy* (Royal Institute of International Affairs, 1995).

8. Richard Robison and David Goodman, *The New Rich in Asia: Mobile Phones, McDonalds, and Middle Class* (Routledge, 1996).

9. Richard Stubbs and Geoffrey Underhill, Eds., *Political Economy and the Changing Global Order* (St. Martin's Press, 1994).

10. Sven Groennings, "The Changing Need for an International Perspective: The Global Economy and Undergraduate Education," *International Studies Notes,* Winter 1989, pp. 64–68; "Black Monday: What Really Ignited the Market's Collapse After Its Long Climb," *The Wall Street Journal,* December 16, 1987, p. 1

11. Hedrick Smith, "Challenge to America" (Films for the Humanities, 1994).

12. Jagdish Bhagwati and Hugh T. Patrick, Eds., *Aggressive Unilateralism: America's 301 Trade Policy and the World Trading System* (University of Michigan Press, 1990).

13. Robert S. Walters, "U.S. Negotiations of Voluntary Restraint Agreements in Steel, 1984," *Pew Case Studies in International Affairs,* Case 107 (Georgetown University, 1988), p. 1.

14. Donald P. Clark, "Recent Changes in Non-Tariff Measures Used in Industrial Nations," *International Trade Journal,* 1992, pp. 311–22.

15. Gary Hufbauer and Kimberly Elliott, *The New York Times,* November 12, 1993, p. D1.

16. Fred W. Frailey, "Ralph Wanger Inside Interview," *Kiplinger's Personal Finance Magazine,* February 1995, pp. 100–105; Kevin Kelly, "The Rumble Heard Round the World," *Business Week,* May 24, 1993, p. 58; Jon Krakauer, "A Hog Is Still a Hog, but the 'Wild Ones' Are Tamer," *Smithsonian* November, 1993, pp. 88–90; Gary Slutzker, "Hog Wild," *Forbes,* May 24, 1993, pp. 45–46; Clint Willis, "Cash In on Companies that Are Hammering the Japanese," *Money,* April 1992, pp. 69–70.

17. Michael J. Boskin, "Pass GATT Now," *Time,* December 12, 1994, p. 137; Susan Dentzer, "Global Trade Meets James Bond," *Christian Science Monitor,* July 25, 1994, p. 45; Emil Innocenti, "GATT Could Destroy the Future of Small Business," *Newsweek,* November 21, 1994, p. 20; Amy Kaslow, "US Congress Dims Future of GATT," *Christian Science Monitor,* October 5, 1994, p. 1; Jeremy Rabkin, "Trading in Our Sovereignty?" *National Review,* June 13, 1994, p. 34.

18. Howard Banks, "Strong Trade Up North," *Forbes,* January 2, 1995, p. 35.

19. Richard Lacayo, "Clinton to Tokyo: No Deal," *Time,* February 21, 1994, p. 41; Richard Lacayo, "Take That! And That!" *Time,* February 28, 1994, p. 39; Amy Kaslow, "US–Japan Trade War Averted, but Auto Dispute Still Looms," *The Christian Science Monitor,* October 3, 1994, p. 6.

20. Sheila Tefft, "US, China Trade Clash Worsens," *The Christian Science Monitor,* January 3, 1995, p. 9; Maria Shao, "China for Sale," *The Boston Globe,* (January 15, 1995), p. 1; Martin Crutsinger, "US Proposes to Impose Sanctions on Chinese Trade," *Associated Press Release,* January 1, 1995.

21. James R. Gaines, "Welcome to the Wild East," *Time,* April 11, 1994, p. 86; James Walsh, "Peace: Finally at Hand," *Time,* February 14, 1994, pp. 34–36.

22. A. A. Berle, Jr., *Economic Power and the Free Society* (Fund for the Republic, 1958), p. 14.

23. Carolyn Henson, "Survey: U.S. Leading the World Competitively," Associated Press Release, May 27, 1996.

CHAPTER 12

1. Steven L. Spiegel, *World Politics in a New Era* (Harcourt Brace, 1995), pp. 284–85, 340–41.

2. Rondo Cameron, *A Concise Economic History of the World from Paleolithic Times to the Present* (Oxford University Press, 1993), pp. 163–90.

3. Robert Gilpin, *The Political Economy of International Relations* (Princeton University Press, 1987), p. 31.

4. Cameron, *A Concise Economic History*, p. 279.

5. Steven Spiegel, *World Politics in a New Era,* pp. 308–9.

6. Spiegel, *World Politics in a New Era,* p. 287.

7. Charles Kindelberger, *The World in Depression, 1929–1939* (University of California Press, 1973), p. 132.

8. Steven Husted and Michael Melvin, *International Economics* (HarperCollins, 1995), p. 227.

9. H. Richard Friman, "Dancing with Pandora: The Eisenhower Administration and the Demise of GATT," unpublished manuscript, 1992.

10. Kala Krishna, "What Do VERs Do?" in Ryuzo Sato and Julianne Nelson, Eds., *Beyond Trade Friction: Japan–US Economic Relations* (Cambridge University Press, 1989), pp. 75–76.

11. Husted and Melvin, *International Economics*, p. 189.

12. Robert Crandell, "Import Quotas and the Automobile Industry: The Costs of Protectionism," *Brookings Review*, 1984.

13. Robert Feenstra, "Voluntary Export Restraint in U.S. Autos, 1980–81," in *The Structure and Evolution of Recent U.S. Trade Policies*, Eds. Robert Baldwin and Anne Krueger (University of Chicago Press, 1984).

14. Rami Khouri, "The Spread of Banking for Believers," *Euromoney,* May 1987; Zubair Iqbal and Abbes Mirakhor, "Islamic Banking," IMF Occasional Paper No. 49, Washington, DC, 1987.

15. Spiegel, *World Politics in a New Era,* pp. 294–300.

16. S.M. Chiu, *China: The Next Economic Superpower* (Westview Press, 1996).

17. John Leger, "The Boom: How Asians Started the 'Pacific Century,'" *Far Eastern Economic Review*, November 24, 1994.

18. "Trade Winds, Trade Wars," *Seapower and Trade* (PBS series).

19. Herman Schwartz, *States Versus Markets* (St. Martin's Press, 1994), p. vii.

20. Jeremy Brecher and Tim Costello, *Global Village or Global Pillage: Economic Reconstruction from the Bottom Up* (South End Press, 1994).

21. "Chainsaw Self-Portrait: Slash-and-Burn Executive Tells All," *USA Today,* August 30, 1996, pp. B1–2.

22. Diana Jean Schemo, "U.S. Pesticide Kills Foreign Fruit Pickers' Hopes," *New York Times International*, December, 6, 1995.

23. Michael Ryan, "They Call Their Boss a Hero," *Parade Magazine,* September 8, 1996, p. 4.

24. John T. Rourke, *International Politics on the World Stage* (Dushkin, 1995), pp. 514–16.

25. Richard Falk, "What Went Wrong with Henry Kissinger's Foreign Policy," *Alternatives I,* 1975, p. 99.

26. Joseph Szlavik, "GOP Majority in Congress Means Less for Africa," Associated Press Release, March 22, 1995.

27. Richard Mansbach, *The Global Puzzle: Issues and Actors in World Politics* (Houghton Mifflin, 1994), pp. 344–51.

28. Carol Lancaster, "An Irresistible Force Meets an Immovable Object: The U.S. at UNCTAD I," *Pew Case Studies in International Affairs* (Georgetown University, 1988).

29. Lancaster, "An Irresistible Force," p. 14.

30. "To Understand the World, Listen to Its People" (Panos Institute, 1994).

31. Richard Lacayo, "The Promises and Perils of an Anti-trust Chief," *Time*, February 27, 1995, p. 33.

32. Walter Jones, *The Logic of International Relations* (HarperCollins, 1995), pp.67–94.

33. *Toronto Globe and Mail*, February 20, 1992.

34. Robert Alexander, "Import Substitution in Latin America in Retrospect," in *Progress Toward Development in Latin America: From Prebisch to Technological Autonomy*, Eds. James L. Dietz and Dilmus D. James (Lynne Rienner, 1991).

35. Spiegel, *World Politics*, p. 373.

36. Spiegel, *World Politics*, pp. 370–71.

37. Paul Kennedy, "Preparing for the 21st Century: Winners and Losers," in *The New York Review of Books*, February 11, 1993, pp. 32–44.

38. Husted and Melvin, *International Economics*, p. 281.

39. United Nations Development Programme, *Human Development Report 1995* (Cambridge University Press, 1995), p. 155.

40. Kennedy, "Preparing for the 21st Century," pp. 193–227.

CHAPTER 13

1. Aristotle, *Parts of Animals*, Book I, chapter 5.

2. World Wildlife Fund, "Southeast Asian Haze," Associated Press Release, September 28, 1997.

3. Jack Anderson and Jan Moller, "Once a Bonanza, Tiny Pacific Island Has Become an Ecological Disaster," *Wheeling News-Register*, May 6, 1997, p. 3.

4. Anthony R. Orme, *Ireland* (Aldine Publishing, 1970), pp. 150–53; Susan Hardwick and Donald Holtgrieve, *Patterns on Our Planet: Concepts and Themes in Geography* (Macmillan, 1990), pp. 383–86.

5. Robin Knight, "Irishness, She Will Tell You, Is Global," *U.S. News and World Report*, June 17, 1996, p. 24.

6. William F. Allman, "A Sense of Where You Are," *U.S. News and World Report*, April 15, 1991, pp. 58–60.

7. In the late 1980s many governmental and private-sector reports criticized the lack of international knowledge possessed by U.S. citizens at a time of global interdependence. Most cited geographic information as especially lacking. The Association of American Geographers believes that geography contributes to international understanding and a global perspective by emphasizing:

    a. The relationships of societies, cultures and economies around the world to specific combina-

tions of natural resources and of the physical and biological environment.

    b. The importance of location of places with respect to one another, as depicted on appropriate maps.

    c. The diversity of the regions of the world.

    d. The significance of ties of one country with another through the flow of commodities, capital, ideas, and political influence.

    e. The world context of individual countries, regions, and problems.

Source: H. J. De Blij and Peter O. Muller, *Geography: Realms, Regions, and Concepts* (Wiley, 1994), p. 51.

8. "Another Casualty of El Niño: Amazon Rainforests," Associated Press Release, October 9, 1997.

9. Hardwick and Holtgrieve, *Patterns on Our Planet*, p. 296.

10. Melinda Bell, "Is Our Climate Unstable?" *Earth Magazine*, January, 1994, pp. 24–31.

11. United Nations Development Program, *Human Development Report 1995* (Oxford University Press, 1995), p. 155.

12. Hardwick and Holtgrieve, *Patterns of Our Planet*, pp. 285–89.

13. John P. LeDonne, *The Russian Empire and the World, 1700–1917: The Geopolitics of Expansion and Containment* (Oxford University Press, 1997).

14. Mikhail Lyubimov, interviewed by the author on June 28, 1995.

15. Allen F. Chew, *An Atlas of Russian History: Eleven Centuries of Changing Borders* (Yale University Press, 1970); M. K. Dziewanowski, *A History of Soviet Russia* (Prentice Hall, 1994), chap. 1: "The Geopolitical Personality of Russia"; James Gregory, *Russian Land, Soviet People* (Pegasus, 1968).

16. John L. Allen, *Student Atlas of World Politics* (Dushkin, 1994), p. v.

17. Robert McCrum, William Cran, and Robert MacNeil, *The Story of English* (Viking Penguin, 1986); James M. Rubenstein, *The Cultural Landscape: An Introduction to Human Geography* (Merrill Publishing, 1989).

18. George J. Demko and William B. Wood, Eds., *Reordering the World: Geopolitical Perspectives on the Twenty-first Century* (Westview Press, 1994).

CHAPTER 14

1. Donald T. Wells, *Environmental Policy: A Global Perspective for the Twenty-First Century* (Prentice Hall, 1996), p. ix.

2. Julian L. Simon, *The Ultimate Resource* (Princeton University Press, 1996).

3. Hilary F. French, "Can the Environment Survive Industrial Demands?" *USA Today Magazine*, January, 1994.

4. Lester R. Brown, *The State of the World 1995* (W.W. Norton, 1995).

5. Garrett Hardin, "The Tragedy of the Commons," *Science*, Winter 1968, pp. 1241–48; Garrett Hardin, *Living Within Limits* (Oxford University Press, 1993).

6. Dennis Meadows, Donnella Meadows, Jorgen Randers, and William Behrend, III, *The Limits to Growth* (Universe Books, 1972).

7. George Sessions, Ed., *Deep Ecology for the Twenty-First Century* (Random House, 1996).

8. Sessions, Ed., *Deep Ecology*.

9. *Titanic: The Legend Lives on*, Arts and Entertainment Channel, September 21, 1996.

10. Gareth Porter and Janet Welsh Brown, *Global Environmental Politics* (Westview Press, 1996), p. 16.

11. Edith Brown Weiss, "Intergenerational Equity: Toward an International Legal Framework," in Nazli Choucri, Ed., *Global Accord: Environmental Challenges and International Responses*, MIT Press, 1993, p. 334.

12. "Introducing Huge Foreign Toad to U.S. a Big Mistake," Associated Press Release, September 21, 1996.

13. Daniel Sitarz, "Agenda 21: Toward a Strategy to Save Our Planet," in Charles W. Kegley and Eugene R. Wittkopf, Eds., *The Global Agenda: Issues and Perspectives* (McGraw-Hill, 1995), p. 364.

14. William K. Stevens, "Humanity Confronts Its Handiwork: An Altered Planet," *The New York Times*, May 5, 1992, p. B5.

15. Facts reported under each global issue taken from these sources: Robert M. Jackson, Ed., *Annual Editions: Global Issues, 95/96* (Dushskin, 1995); Paul Kennedy, *Preparing for the Twenty-First Century* (Random House, 1993), pp. 95–121; Charles W. Kegley and Eugene R. Wittkopf, Eds., *The Global Agenda: Issues and Perspectives* (McGraw-Hill, 1995), Part 4, "Ecology and Politics," pp. 331–455; Wesley M. Bagby, *Introduction to Social Science and Contemporary Issues* (Nelson Hall, 1995), pp. 144–60; John T. Rourke, "Sustainable Development," in chap. 18 *International Politics on the World Stage* (Dushkin, 1995), pp. 587–625; Hoyt Purvis, *Interdependence* (Harcourt Brace Jovanovich, 1992), pp. 307–33.

16. Porter and Brown, *Global Environmental Politics*, p. 7.

17. Wells, *Environmental Policy*, p. 50.

18. Robert S. Stern et al., "Risk Reduction for Nonmelanoma Skin Cancer with Childhood Sunscreen Use," *Archives of Dermatology*, 12, no. 5 (May 1986).

19. Wells, *Environmental Policy*, pp. 44–48.

20. Wells, *Environmental Policy*, p. 162.

21. Jean-Paul Malingreau and Compton J. Tucker, "Large Scace Deforestation in the Southeastern Amazon Basin of Brazil," *Ambio*, 17 (1988), 49; World Resources Institute, *World Resources, 1992–93* (Oxford University Press, 1994), pp. 118–19.

22. Edward O. Wilson, "Threats to Biodiversity," *Scientific American*, 261, no. 3 (1989), 112.

23. Wells, *Environmental Policy*, p. 63.

24. The 20th Century, "Black Tide: Nightmare Oil Spills," *Arts and Entertainment Network*, December 13, 1995.

25. Garry D. Brewer, "Environmental Challenges and Managerial Responses," in Nazli Choucri, Ed., *Global Accord: Environmental Challenges and International Responses* (MIT Press, 1993), p. 300.

26. Porter and Brown, *Global Environmental Politics*, p. 111.

27. Kennedy, *Preparing for the Twenty-First Century*, 96.

28. Factual information taken from the following sources: Nafis Sadik, *The State of the World Population* (U.N. Population Fund, 1990); Kennedy, *Preparing for the Twenty-First Century*, pp. 21–46; John L. Allen, *Student Atlas of World Politics* (Dushkin, 1995), pp. 41–54; *1993 World Population Data Sheet* (Population Reference Bureau, 1993); *The New York Times*, April 30, 1992, p. A12; Paul R. Ehrlich and Anne H. Ehrlich, *Population, Resources, Environment* (W.H. Freeman, 1970), p. 1; Charles W. Kegley and Eugene R. Wittkopf, "Population Pressures and the Global Habitat," in *The Global Agenda*, pp. 367–80; Robert E. Jackson, Ed., *Annual Editions: Global Issues 95/96* (Dushkin, 1995), pp. 36–80, "Population"; John T. Rourke, *Taking Sides: Clashing Views on Controversial Issues in World Politics* (Dushkin, 1995), pp. 308–27; Steven L. Spiegel, *World Politics in a New Era* (Harcourt Brace College, 1995), pp. 437–43; *Popline*, vol. 16 (World Population News Service, March-April 1994).

29. Kegley and Wittkopf, "Population Pressures and the Global Habitat," in *The Global Agenda*, p. 370.

30. Kennedy, *Preparing for the Twenty-First Century*, p. 22.

31. Eugene Linden, "Megacities," *Time*, January 11, 1993, pp. 28–38.

32. Paul Lewis, "U.N. Sees a Crisis in Overpopulation," *The New York Times*, April 30, 1992, p. A6.

33. Boyce Rensberger, "Damping the World's Population," *The Washington Post Weekly*, September 12–18, 1994, pp. 10–11.

34. Anne Nadakavukaren, "The Elusive Quest for ZPG: India's Family-Planning Program," *Our Global Environment: A Health Perspective* (Waveland Press, 1993), pp. 110–12.

35. Timothy C. Weiskel, "Vicious Circles: African Demographic History as a Warning," *Harvard International Review*, Fall, 1994, pp. 12–16.

36. Factual information on food derived from these sources: Nabil Megalli, "Hunger Versus the Environment: A Recipe for Global Suicide," *Our Planet*, 1992; Orville L. Freeman, "Agriculture and the Environment: Meeting Global Food Needs," *The Futurist*, 1993; James Lee Ray, *Global Politics* (Houghton Mifflin, 1995), pp. 566–67; Barry B. Hughes, *World Futures* (Johns Hopkins University Press, 1985); Bruce Stutz, "The Landscape of Hunger," *Audubon*, Spring 1993, pp. 54–63; John Bongaarts, "Can the Growing Human Population Feed Itself?" *Scientific American*, March, 1994, pp. 36–42; "UN Food and Agriculture," *FAO Yearbook, 1991* (FAO, 1992), pp. 237–38; *Hunger 1993: Uprooted People* (Bread for the World, 1993), pp. 172–73; Purvis, *Interdependence*, pp. 307–18; Neal Spivack and Ann Florini, *Food on the Table* (United Nations Association, 1986), pp. 24–53; Peter G. Brown and Henry Shue, Eds., *Food Policy:*

The Responsibility of the U.S. in the Life and Death Choices (Free Press, 1977); Kennedy, *Preparing for the Twenty-First Century*, pp. 65–81; Allen, *Student Atlas*, pp. 55–62; Rourke, *International Politics on the World Stage*, pp. 597–601; Dan Morgan, *The Merchants of Grain* (Viking Penguin, 1979); B. Johnstone, "Fading of the Miracle," *Far East Economic Review*, December 1988, pp. 72–75.

37. Robin Wright, "Hunger in the World: An Overview," in Scott Barbour, Ed., *Hunger* (Greenhaven Press, 1995), p. 12.

38. Bruce Stutz, "The Landscape of Hunger," *Audubon*, Spring 1993, p. 54.

39. Orville L. Freeman, "Agriculture and the Environment: Meeting Global Food Needs," *The Futurist*, Winter 1993.

40. Descriptive information concerning energy extracted from these sources: Daniel Yergin, *The Prize: The Epic Quest for Oil, Money and Power* (Simon & Schuster, 1991); Edward Carr, "Energy: The New Prize," *The Economist*, June 18, 1994; Dan Halacy, "Harvesting the Sun," *The Rotarian*, September 1992, pp. 18–21; Amy Martin, "Petro-Chemical Alternatives," *Garbage*, November/December 1991, pp. 44–49; Barry B. Hughes et al., *Energy in the Global Arena* (Duke University Press, 1985); Dennis Pirages, *Global Technopolitics* (Brooks/Cole, 1989); Frederick Pearson and J. Martin Rochester, *The Global Condition in the Late Twentieth Century* (McGraw-Hill, 1992), pp. 539–41; William Chandler, "Increasing Energy Efficiency," in Lester R. Brown et al., *The State of the World 1985* (Norton, 1985); Spiegel, *World Politics in a New Era*, pp. 485–91; Charles W. Kegley and Eugene R. Wittkopf, "Fueling Growth: Oil, Energy and Resource Power," in *World Politics: Trend and Transformation* (St. Martin's Press, 1995), pp. 333–68; Joseph Stanislaw and Daniel Yergin, "Oil: Reopening the Door," *Foreign Affairs*, September–October 1993, pp. 81–93.

41. Yergin, *The Prize*, p. 2.

42. Nigel Hawkes et al., *Chernobyl: The End of the Nuclear Dream* (Vintage Books, 1987); Christopher Flavin, "Reassessing Nuclear Power: The Fallout from Chernobyl," Worldwatch Paper 75 (Worldwatch Institute, 1987); Richard F. Mould, *Chernobyl: The Real Story* (Pergamon Press, 1988); "Chernobyl: Ten Years After," Sixty Minutes, CBS News, April 27, 1996.

CHAPTER 15

1. Marvin S. Soroos, "The Tragedy of the Commons in Global Perspective," in Charles W. Kegley and Eugene R. Wittkopf, Eds., *The Global Agenda: Issues and Perspectives* (McGraw-Hill, 1995), p. 424.

2. Associated Press Release, June 4, 1994, p. 2.

3. Daniel Sitarz, "Agenda 21: Toward a Strategy to Save Our Planet," in Kegley and Wittkopf, *The Global Agenda*, p. 355.

4. Harry C. Blaney, *Global Challenges: A World at Risk* (Franklin Watts, 1979), pp. 170–75.

5. James N. Rosenau, *Turbulence in World Politics: A Theory of Change and Continuity* (Princeton University Press, 1990), p. 11.

6. Timothy Swanson, *The International Regulation of Extinction* (New York University Press, 1994).

7. Sylvia Nasar, "It's Never Fair to Just Blame the Weather," *The New York Times*, January 17, 1993.

8. Marvin S. Soroos, "The Tragedy of the Commons," pp. 429–32.

9. Donald Wells, *Environmental Policy: A Global Perspective for the Twenty-First Century* (Prentice Hall, 1996), pp. 9, 15.

10. Yusef J. Ahmed, Salah El Serafez, and Ernst Lutz, Eds., *Environmental Accounting for Sustainable Development* (The World Bank, 1989).

11. B. Devall, *Simple in Means, Rich in Ends: Practicing Deep Ecology* (Peregrine Smith, 1988).

12. Anne Nadakavukaren, *Our Global Environment* (Waveland, 1995), pp. 649–51.

13. Gareth Porter and Janet Welsh Brown, *Global Environmental Politics* (Westview Press, 1996), p. 144.

14. Paul Kennedy, *Preparing for the Twenty-First Century* (Random House, 1993), p. 339.

15. Terry Forrest Young and Vicki L. Golich, "Debt-for-Nature Swaps: Win–Win Solution or Environmental Imperialism?" *Pew Case Studies in International Affairs* (Georgetown University, 1993).

16. John Vandermeer and Ivette Perfecto, *Breakfast of Biodiversity: The Truth about Rainforest Destruction* (Food First Book, 1995), p. 14.

17. Vandermeer and Perfecto, *Breakfast of Biodiversity*, p. 1.

CHAPTER 16

1. Stephen Jay Gould, *Full House: The Spread of Excellence from Plato to Darwin* (Harmony Books, 1996), p. 30.

2. Benjamin Barber, *Jihad versus McWorld: How Globalism and Tribalism Are Reshaping the World* (Ballantine Books, 1996), p. 9.

3. Barber, *Jihad versus McWorld*, p. 215.

4. Benjamin Barber, "Jihad vs McWorld," *The Atlantic*, March 1992, p. 53.

5. Barber, *Jihad versus McWorld*, p. 293.

6. Barber, *Jihad versus McWorld*, p. 8.

7. Barry B. Hughes, *International Futures: Choices in the Creation of a New World Order* (Westview Press, 1996), pp. 2–3.

8. Gould, *Full House*, p. 31.

9. Dick Kirschten, "No Refuge," *National Journal*, September 10, 1994, pp. 2068–73; Myron Weiner, *The Global Migration Crisis* (HarperCollins, 1995); U.N. High Commisioner for Refugees, *The State of the World's Refugees* (Oxford University Press, 1995).

10. John Barry, "Future Shock," *Newsweek*, July 24, 1995, pp. 36–37; Michael T. Klare, *Rogue States and Nuclear Outlaws: America's Search for a New Foreign Policy* (Hill and Wang, 1996).

11. Charles W. Kegley and Eugene R. Wittkopf, *World Politics: Trend and Transformation* (St. Martin's Press, 1996), pp. 94–95.

12. Charles Krauthammer, "The Unipolar Moment," *Foreign Affairs*, 70, no. 1 (1991): 23–33.

13. Henry Kissinger, *Diplomacy* (Touchstone Books, 1995).

14. Charles W. Kegley and Gregory A. Raymond, "Preparing Now for a Peaceful 21st Century," *USA Today Magazine*, September 1994, p. 22.

15. Hans W. Singer and Javed A. Ansari, *Rich and Poor Countries* (Unwin Hyman, 1988).

16. Max Singer and Aaron Wildavsky, *The Real World Order: Zones of Peace, Zones of Turmoil* (Chatham House, 1993), p. 22.

17. Barber, *Jihad versus McWorld*, p. 139.

18. Ben H. Bagdikian, *The Media Monopoly* (Beacon, 1994).

19. Ben H. Bagdikian, "The Lords of the Global Village," *Nation*, June 12, 1989, p. 807.

20. Herbert J. Schiller, *Information Inequality* (Routledge, 1996), p. 113.

21. Schiller, *Information Inequality*, p. xiv.

22. "Infectious Disease Rise Linked to Human Growth," *Popline*, 18 (March-April 1996), 3.

23. Dennis Pirages, "Microsecurity: Disease Organisms and Human Well-Being," *The Washington Quarterly*, Autumn 1995, pp. 5–12.

24. Michael D. Lemonick, "The Killers All Around," *Time*, September 12, 1994, pp. 62–69.

25. Pirages, "Microsecurity," p. 5.

26. Roger Ebert, *A Century of Cinema* (Andrews and McMeel, 1996).

27. Barber, *Jihad versus McWorld*, p. 88.

28. Barber, *Jihad versus McWorld*, p. 307.

29. Derek Elley, "Co-productions: Who Needs Them?" *Variety International Film Guide* (Samuel French Trade, 1993), p. 19.

30. Richard Rosecrance, "Economics and National Security: The Evolutionary Process," in Richard Schultz et al., *Security Studies for the Twenty-First Century* (Brassey's, 1997).

31. Joseph S. Nye, *Bound to Lead: The Changing Nature of American Power* (Basic Books, 1990).

GLOSSARY

A-bomb The atomic bombs dropped on Hiroshima and Nagasaki were nuclear fission bombs of twenty kilotons each and served as the precursors of the more potent H-bombs to follow.

Absolute advantage As related to the global division of labor, the ability of either a nation or a firm to produce goods or services below the level of all competitors.

Acid rain Precipitation depositing nitric or sulfuric acids, often adversely affecting ecosystems far downwind from the coal-fired power plants that contributed to these acids.

Acute hunger The most severe form of hunger, in which death from an absolute shortage of food is imminent.

Advertising limits A type of nontariff barrier constructed by an importing country that prevents a low-cost exporter from marketing its goods as fully as it would like to do.

Affirmative action Liberal reform programs undertaken during the 1960s in the United States intended to provide competitive advantages for racial minorities previously discriminated against by American society. Many critics in the 1990s consider such well-intentioned programs to result in reverse discrimination. Global advocates of the NIEO (New International Economic Order) argue for something akin to affirmative action.

Agribusiness A hybridized form of massive farming, resulting from the melding of economies of scale from big business operations with high demand for increased production of agricultural products.

Androgyny Exhibiting characteristics considered both female and male; being a hermaphrodite.

Animism Belief of hunters and gatherers that natural objects make up part of a spiritual world of which the sun and moon often played roles as reverential objects to be worshiped.

Anthropomorphism Assigning humanlike characteristics to supreme religious beings.

Anticipatory thinking The antithesis of waiting until the last minute to address a particular problem. The urgency of many modern global issues, like environment or population, suggests that humans need to think further ahead as a means of devising more timely solutions.

Anxiety A sense of personal dread, panic, or inordinate fear, which represents one of the most commonly reported disorders among individuals suffering from psychological pain.

Applied discipline Putting theories of a particular discipline into practice. While some academic disciplines have relatively few opportunities for use in real-world situations, psychology is not one of those disciplines, and many theories developed in its subfields are put into practice on a regular basis.

Arable Descriptive of land fit for cultivation and capable of supporting crops.

Arms control An approach to peace popular among idealists who believe that humans tend to use what weapons are available to them, and therefore, that efforts should be made to regulate levels and types of weapons in order to reduce temptations which might lead nations to initiate wars.

Arranged marriage A system in simple societies where families often play the lead role in choosing a spouse for prospective husbands or wives. In these cases, match-making is not left to random chance or to the vagaries of young love, but is intended to promote the interests of the family.

Asylum Different forms of this legal status exist for various circumstances, but all refer to some form of safe haven accorded persons who have fled their native country and seek sanctuary elsewhere.

Atheism The belief that no god or supreme being exists and that monotheistic religions conjured up visions of a prime mover bearing the human countenance.

Austerity measures Severely restricted living conditions whereby developing countries tighten their economic belts as a condition for loans granted by international lending institutions. Such steps often seem self-evidently necessary as purely economic measures, but they prove politically difficult to implement because of their unpleasantness.

Autarkical Describing an economic policy of self-sufficiency bordering on national isolation.

Autarky A condition of economic self-sufficiency of a nation, achieved by being isolated from international contacts.

Balance-of-payments An annual accounting device used by nations as a ledger to assess all transactions undertaken with the outside world, including trade, investments, and payments.

Balance of Power The traditional belief that peace and security result from the relatively equitable distribution of power between two or more flexible international alliances which countervail one another, precluding domination by any potential aggressor.

Balance of Terror A play on words derived from the traditional concept of balance of power in world affairs, except that in the upside-down era of nuclear weapons the global balance of forces intended to deter aggression is based on the bizarre mutual suicide pact known as mutually assured destruction.

Bartering The act of exchanging goods or services directly, that is, without the use of money.

Behaviorism The school of psychology emphasizing the rigorous scientific study of environmental forces shaping human behavior.

Bretton Woods Conference The U.S.-dominated meeting held in New Hampshire in 1944 to plan the institutions and procedures that would govern the international economy in the postwar world. These institutions came to be known as the Bretton Woods System.

Brezhnev Doctrine The Soviet Union's Cold War policy of interventionism in the affairs of Eastern Europe countries. It was enunciated by Soviet head Leonid Brezhnev in his justification for sending tanks in to crush Czechoslovakia's liberal reforms known as the Prague spring in 1968.

Brinkmanship Taking some of its cues from the game of "chicken," this policy is based on the belief that one's national interests are maximized in an international bargaining situation by bluffing as a means of encouraging an opponent to back down.

British Corn Laws A series of protectionist measures passed by the English Parliament prior to 1846 aimed at limiting the importation of grain, which could compete with that grown by the English landed aristocracy.

Bucharest World Population Conference The first major global town meeting held on this issue, in 1974 in Rumania; it did not produce any major agreements.

Budget deficit A national economy's shortfall of taxes and revenues as measured against its expenditures, either during a given year or computed cumulatively.

Business cycle The pattern of total economic output over time of the national economy in a capitalist system; it tends to rise and fall rather regularly as a normal part of the expansion and contraction of business activity.

Cairo World Population Conference Held in Egypt in 1994, this was the largest and most important global town meeting ever convened to address population issues. It managed to come up with a detailed "Program of Action."

Capital Manufactured goods created by human labor.

Capitalism An economic system favoring free market forces, competition, and private (as opposed to public) ownership of the means of production.

Capitalist model The prevalent approach among modern developed economies, in which competitive market forces play the key role in producing, distributing, and consuming goods and services.

Carrying capacity The finite amount of life that can be supported by any ecosystem.

Cartel An organization of producers interested in limiting competition and establishing high prices by manipulating shortages via low production quotas among members.

Case study Quantitative studies of human behavior are sometimes criticized for sterile number crunching at the expense of in-depth analysis of real world events. The case study speaks to this point by concretely grounding concepts and theories in historical situations, providing lessons generalizable to other similar contexts.

Caudillismo Related to the concept of machismo in Latin cultures, but more specifically tied to the glorification of the rugged strongman capable of consolidating unbridled power by whatever means necessary.

Choice mating A system in complex societies whereby they provide considerable leeway for marriageable individuals to pick their prospective spouses according to personal values and desires.

Christians The largest grouping of religionists in the world, believing in a monotheistic God whose messages were expressed in the person of Jesus Christ nearly 2,000 years ago.

Chronic hunger A serious but not life-threatening form of hunger in which subjects receive food inadequate to support human growth and health.

Civilization After the agricultural revolution, those settled communities capable of reading and writing began to create cultures. Some ancient civilizations, like those of Greece and Rome, contributed mightily to the content of modern Western civilization.

Class As the term is generally used in sociological parlance, a social grouping based on shared attributes. In Marxist thought, however, it invariably identifies a group shaped by the prevailing mode of economic exploitation—for example, the *bourgeoisie* over the *proletariat*.

Clinically insane A medical diagnosis specifying certain dysfunctional mental or emotional characteristics suggesting abnormalities serious enough to render subjects exhibiting these symptoms as not responsible for, or in control of, their unusual behavior.

Collective bargaining The process by which labor unions in capitalist countries were able to improve the lot of their workers by speaking for large numbers of rank-and-file laborers in negotiations with management in quest of a mutually beneficial contract.

Collective security The proactive approach to international peace and stability which holds that only if a preponderance of power is available to the world community can aggressive behavior by maverick nations be prevented. After failing badly with the League of Nations after World War I, this theory was given a new lease on life with the post-World War II construction of the United Nations.

Colonialism The social, political, and economic domination of an indigenous people by an external power, which historically was often associated with the imperial expansion of a powerful nation.

Command economy Another name for a socialist economic system—one in which the means of production are owned by the state, necessitating central planning as an alternative to the market forces shaping the direction of capitalist economic systems.

Command model An approach, developed as a socialist alternative to capitalist economies, which emphasizes central planning, governmental ownership, and production quotas for producers.

Communications gap A failure in the sending or receiving of informational content or emotion between two or more communicants. In the modern age of narrowly trained specialists, the potential for miscommunication in professional discourse is considerable.

Communist economies Theories of socialist equality spawned in the nineteenth century, which ironically contributed to revolutions in thirteen countries during the twentieth century, each resulting in a monolithic system of repression.

Communitarian capitalism A variation on the theme of the market economy which combines the traditional individualism long associated with the capitalist model with an indigenous sense of social cohesion and social responsibility, as in Japan or Germany.

Comparative advantage The theoretical underpinning of free trade which states that any nation's economy benefits from engaging in trade where it has a relative (not absolute) advantage in efficiently producing some good or service.

Compellence A variation on the theme of deterrence in which coercive diplomacy is backed by a credible threat to use overwhelming force to convince a nation to act in a desired manner.

Complex societies Large, heterogeneous, and literate social groups with surplus economies and more secondary relationships than simple societies have. Often referred to as *Gesellschaft* societies.

Concepts Abstract (rather than concrete) building blocks of explanation, less general than theories but more general than facts.

Conditioned response The conduct of humans motivated by rewards and sanctions, according to the belief of behavioral psychology.

Conference on Security and Cooperation in Europe (CSCE) A loosely structured organization containing most nations of Western, Central, and Eastern Europe as well as North America, established by the Helsinki Accords of 1975 to promote respect for human rights and peaceful resolution of disputes.

Confucianism A conservative ideological perspective emphasizing strong family ties, stressing respect for the elderly, and calling for the individual to rise above trying social conditions. Long influential in Chinese culture, derived from the writings of Confucius (551–479 B.C.), it also advocates solid education and meritocracy as the basis for advancement.

Containerization The creation of steel containers used in commercial shipping, greatly enhancing the efficiency, safety, and cost-effectiveness of long-distance shipping, especially from east Asia to North America.

Containment The backbone of U.S. foreign policy during the Cold War, the belief that, like a malignant cancer, communism had to be opposed wherever it threatened to spread. As first formulated by career diplomat George Kennan in 1947, containment assumed that communism's inner contradictions would cause it to rot from within if it were prevented from expanding its power in the world.

Content analysis A rigorously statistical approach to studying modern human behavior by examining both oral and written statements, especially those by elites representing crucial actors such as nation–states. Subtext patterns indicating the state of mind of leaders are sought through sophisticated means of analysis.

Conventional theory An interpretation of the causes and cures for poverty among less-developed countries: it sees the causes stemming from domestic practices and attitudes, and the cures emanating from international investment and assistance.

Conventions Agreements entered into by nation–states that are less binding under international law than treaties.

Convertible currency A nation's money that can be exchanged freely at market rates in the transactions of international commerce.

Cooperative global endeavors Attempts worldwide to solve problems through holistic and complementary avenues. For centuries, the competitive nature of the nation-state system has ingrained the value of pursuing self-interest via conflict into the human psyche. Modern global issues have forced the world to explore these cooperative endeavors.

Corporate culture Intangible factors like camaraderie, loyalty, communication, and creativity that make up part of a firm's personality and also affect productivity.

Corporation A type of firm that is owned and ultimately controlled by stockholders and in which the management functions are delegated to a board of directors. A corporation constitutes a legal entity having many rights and duties that are usually associated with individual persons.

Cost-push inflation Increased inflation rate resulting when rising prices stemming from limited supply of certain goods or services in turn contribute to increased demand.

Country The spatial designation of territory dovetailing with a nation and a state. Theoretically, nation, state, and country coincide to create the nation–state, but in actuality the fit between these real-world entities rarely blends together so neatly.

Crusades A series of holy wars fought between the two giant monotheistic giants—Roman Catholicism and Islam—between the eleventh and thirteenth centuries, with the holy city of Jerusalem as one of the key symbolic areas of contention.

Cultural anthropology A subfield of social science that looks at both past and present cultures, studying the language, religion, work habits, and other aspects of life—that is, culture—of a people handed down generation to generation.

Cultural genocide A concerted effort, often violent, by one society to destroy the integrity of another society's cultural practices.

Cultural imperialism Nonmilitary, subtler forms of domination of one nation by another via the potent messages conveyed by its infotainment industries. Actual military control is less common now than during most of the nineteenth and twentieth centuries.

Cultural mythology A shared sense of historical distortion characteristic of some large group (e.g., a society) unable or unwilling to deal with the psychic scars associated with some traumatic national event.

Cultural relativism The fair-minded attitude that cultures are not better or worse—merely different—and that other cultures have a right to exist and to be viewed within the confines of their own circumstances.

Cultural universals Aspects of lifestyle commonly found in all societies, such as the pivotal institutions of the family, religion, and education.

Culture The substantive lifestyle content transmitted from one generation to the next via the socialization process. Culture provides the substance to match society's institutions.

Culture shock The experience of personal disorientation or dislocation reported by many people who travel to a given foreign culture for the first time.

Data Often quantitative but sometimes qualitative information crucial to testing hypotheses in scientific inquiry.

Dawes Plan An elegant response to post-World War I demands for reparations, it recycled payments from Germany to Britain and France, and then to the United States in the form of war debt payments, and back to Germany as loans.

Decolonization The process whereby colonial mother countries—largely European—shed their former possessions, creating an influx of newly independent countries.

Deep ecology The philosophical view that nature, both flora and fauna, has an inherent right to fight for its continued existence, above and beyond the question of what it may do to influence the plight of humans.

Dehumanization The psychological process whereby group A comes to consider the members of group B as animals, monsters, vermin, or some other despicable group qualitatively different from itself.

Demand The amount of a commodity that people will buy at a given price at a given time.

Demand-pull inflation Rising prices resulting from high demand for certain goods or services acting to pull up the inflation rate.

Democracy A governmental system that provides its citizens with some form of direct or indirect voice in the decision-making process known as politics. For much of the twentieth century, democracies found themselves competing with authoritarian systems on the world stage.

Democratization Since the 1970s a wave of democratic government that has swept over many Latin American, Asian, and Eastern European nations that previously had been victimized by repressive authoritarian regimes.

Depression A dysfunctional condition in which someone feels inexplicably hopeless or sad for an extended period of time.

Deregulation The process of cutting down governmental oversight of economic activity, begun during the 1980s in the United States and Britain and spread to other countries looking for ways to unleash market forces.

Determinism The belief that human behavior results from some objective forces, as opposed to free will. Social scientists frequently find themselves grappling with explanations that juxtapose the forces of determinism and free will.

Deterrence The standard strategy followed during the bipolar Cold War in which both sides discouraged a military attack by escalating the subsequent costs for the aggressor.

Development In a world divided into haves and have-nots, rich and poor countries, growth model followed by the more-developed countries as the path to a higher standard of living, a growth that the less-developed countries generally wish to emulate.

Deviance Behavior that runs against the grain of social norms and is seen as undesirable by majority in a given society.

Devolution A passing down through successive stages from a higher, more general level to lower, more local stages.

Direct foreign investment Investment by a corporation based in a home country into a corporation in another country, usually either by buying an extant enterprise or by investing capital in starting a new one.

Disarmament A long-existing small movement that seeks future agreement among nation- states to go beyond arms control to the actual elimination of complete categories of weapons of mass destruction.

Discrimination One of the core elements of Christian just war doctrine, which demanded that civilians be excluded from the acts of war perpetrated against combatants.

Distributive justice A concept critical of great inequities in the global allocation of wealth between North and South as ethically indefensible.

Downsizing The common contemporary practice whereby corporations attempt to enhance their international competitiveness and the value of their stock by firing significant portions of their workforce, especially middle managers.

Dumping The practice of selling a product in an export market at a price below the cost of production, often with some form of governmental subsidy that enables the firm to engage in what under normal circumstances would seem to constitute self-defeating behavior.

Earth Summit The United Nations Conference on Environment and Development (UNCED), hosted by Brazil in 1992, known popularly as the Earth Summit because it was the most important global town meeting to address environmental issues.

Earthwatch A monitoring program which compiles vast amounts of environmental data as an early warning system for the United Nations Environmental Programme (UNEP).

Ecological approach A view based on an integrative set of assumptions underlying our intellectual understanding of the great global issues inherently linked together.

Ecological global issues Those worldwide problems revolving around humanity's relationship to the physical world, such as environmentalism, population, food, and energy.

Economic development The Western model of progress as expanded productivity, based on the assumption that a higher material standard of living is desirable. Most southern hemisphere less-developed countries today emulate this path earlier followed by the more-developed countries of the North.

Economic hegemon A dominant world power able to establish the rules of trade and other aspects of the international economic game.

Economic idealism Also called economic liberalism, a philosophy that emphasizes free trade and a laissez faire preference for little governmental interference in economic affairs.

Economic Marxism A philosophy based on economic determinism, in which all other aspects of social, political, cultural, and philosophical life are believed to emanate from the underlying causal influences of the economic substructure.

Economic realism A philosophy grounded in the realist belief that nations will act to maximize their interests by seeking power; it rationalizes the utility of protectionism, which fostered the development of mercantilism in Europe prior to the nineteenth century.

Economic sectors Different parts, or segments, of a national economy used to compare and contrast measurable performance characteristics—for example, the agricultural, service, finance, labor, and manufacturing sectors that are used to examine the U.S. economy.

Economics The social science that studies the basic social institution known as the economy, wherein the production, distribution, and consumption of goods and services transpires.

Economic wants The highly elastic human capacity to desire more and more goods and services to satisfy our wishes.

Economies of scale The inherent profitability of large-scale production as a basic premise stemming from the advances made by the Industrial Revolution. The more units of any commodity you produce, the less the cost to you per unit, and thus the greater your profit margin.

Ecosystem A biological process of interactions involving a community of organisms and their surrounding environment.

Efficacy In the social sciences this means the ability of human actors, individually or in concert with others, exercising meaningful direction and control over their personal destinies.

Ego In Freudian psychoanalysis this refers to the calculating, rational, and balancing part of the human personality trying to mediate between the id and the superego.

Embargo Suspension of foreign trade for one or more commodities, usually as a form of punishment against a nation–state deemed to have violated international norms.

Enlightenment The eighteenth-century commitment to rationalism and belief in the progressive nature of human history. It led to the diminution of religious explanations of human behavior and the rise of critical social, political, and economic analysis among European scholars.

Entrepreneurship A form of risk taking inherent in the process of undertaking any new commercial enterprise in a market setting.

Environmental accounting An accounting method that assigns value to resources like forests, minerals, and water,

based on modern understanding that the cost of depleting natural resources and degrading nature ought to be computed into national accounts.

Environmental profligacy Wild, extravagant, or wasteful misuse of some ecological resource.

Environmental space A new concept used by southern, less-developed countries in their criticisms of profligacy on the part of northern, more-developed countries. It adds a physical dimension (space) to measuring the consequences of wasteful abuse of resources and pollution.

Epistemology One of the branches of philosophy concerned with the question of how we know what we think we know, that is, with the origins and methods underpinning knowledge.

Equilibrium price Another name for the market price of a commodity, since supply and demand act to countervail one another at the market price.

Ethical Having to do with normative questions of moral behavior for individuals or groups of people.

Ethnicity A form of social identity transmitted from one generation to the next as part of a culture. The glue that binds people in this manner may or may not consist of tangible characteristics like race, religion, and historical memory.

Ethnocentrism A self-centered attitude judging the customs of other cultures by the standards of one's own culture, contributing to the view that others are inferior.

Ethologists Biologists who specialize in studying human behavior as deriving in part from traits attributable to the fact that humans are animals.

European Coal and Steel Community (ECSC) One of the early (1954) building blocks contributing to the evolution of the European Union. The ECSC began with Germany and France cooperating in the production of coal and steel.

European Commission on Human Rights The European agency that investigates private complaints against governments and works as a mediator seeking settlement of disputes as an alternative to their going to the European Court of Human Rights. No other world region has done as much as Europe to supplement global human rights protections.

European Community (EC) See European Union (EU).

European Union (EU) The successor organization to the European Community's four-decade struggle to create economic and political cooperation among the democracies on the European continent.

Exclusion rule A requirement that any German political party receive at least 5 percent of the popular vote before gaining official representation in the Bundestag (parliament).

Expansion model The blueprint equating progress with growth that has characterized human intellectual history—bigger is seen as invariably better.

Experimental design A rigorous research method that seeks to emulate the tightly controlled laboratory conditions prevalent in the natural sciences. When human beings become the object of experimentation, however, difficulties often arise in applying such a theoretically attractive model to real-life research.

Exponential growth A very rapid form of numerical expansion characterized by the shortening of doubling times, as in the case of world population growth.

Export-led industrialization A strategy for economic expansion among less-developed countries, designed to expand foreign markets for a nation's manufactured goods by growing domestic export industries.

Extended family Family structure comprised of many possible combinations of individuals linked by blood ties, found most frequently in simple societies. An example would be parents, children, and grandparents living together.

Extrapolation An inference or estimate based on a process of extending or projecting known information.

Fact A statement whose truth or falsity can be established through either empirical verification (synthetic proof) or logical analysis (analytic proof); as distinct from subjectively derived statements such as opinions or beliefs.

Factors of production Those resources committed to the creation of goods and services, consisting of two human resources (labor and entrepreneurship) and two nonhuman resources (land and capital).

Fallacy A thesis inconsistent with either fact or logic, making its conclusions invalid.

Fascism A totalitarian political ideology devoid of democratic norms which glorifies the state and its dictator and romanticizes militarism and racial intolerance.

Female empowerment Changes in laws, codes, or discriminatory attitudes enabling or facilitating the execution of control by women over their own destinies, either individually or collectively.

Femininity Female gender role considered typical in a given culture: the weak, passive, right-brained female good at such subjects as literature and foreign languages is the stereotype in North American culture. Biology and culture both contribute to human sexuality.

Feudalism The prevalent economic system in Europe during the Middle Ages, relying on labor-intensive agriculture conducted by peasants tied to the land owned by their feudal lords.

Financial aid Funds in the form of bank loans and buying of bonds to finance development projects. Since poor countries are short of the funds needed to develop economically, they generally look to the rich countries (and their financial institutions) for such funds. Just how much aid of this type the more-developed countries should be giving to the less-developed countries remains controversial.

Finiteness The idea of limits; though a simple idea, it also proved a revolutionary one as applied to the carrying capacity of global ecosystems.

Firm That unit participating in the national economy as a decisional unit motivated by profit via the production of goods and services using the factors of production.

First World A Cold War era designation of the first tier of affluent and democratic countries, led by North America, Western Europe, and Japan.

Fiscal policy Economic intervention whereby the government uses its tax and spend powers in an effort to combat problems like recession or inflation.

Fixed exchange rate system Also called maintaining parity, this is a mechanism whereby governments agree to set the prices of their currencies at preestablished levels vis-à-vis a marker currency or vis-à-vis gold.

Floating exchange rate system An agreement between governments to allow the relative value of their currencies to be determined by the natural market forces of supply and demand.

Food and Agricultural Organization (FAO) The largest of the U.N. specialized agencies, intended to develop and promote improvements in the production of foodstuffs, including relief, research, education, and advisory functions.

Fordism The model of mass production using economies of scale as the means to low cost per unit that was popularized by Henry Ford's auto company.

Foreign Originating in or pertaining to life in a society other than one's own, usually suggesting the presence of significant differences inherent in divergent cultures.

Fourth World A controversial category of nations considered the poorest of the poor in the southern hemisphere. If the Third World refers to developing countries, then the Fourth World consists of what some have labeled the "never to be developed."

Free rider An actor who threatens the stability of any agreement to share finite ecological resources by taking advantage of the restraint of others to maximize its own short-term profits via overconsumption.

Free trade The antithesis of protectionism, this perspective argues that the greatest good for the greatest number flows from allowing free market forces of competition to play themselves out in the absence of governmental intervention into the process of international trade.

Functionalism A school of sociological thought arguing that all cultural characteristics found in a society serve some useful purpose, thus accounting for their existence.

Gender role Socially conditioned role of either masculinity or femininity which is tied into the subjective experience of how we think and feel about ourselves.

General Agreement on Tariff and Trade (GATT) The organization created at the 1944 Bretton Woods conference to facilitate free trade globally.

General Agreement on Tariffs and Trade (GATT) Set up in 1947 at the instigation of the United States, this global organization set out to reduce trade barriers, reflecting the post-war consensus on free trade. It was superseded in 1995 by the more ambitious World Trade Organization (WTO).

Geopolitics The legitimate study of how climate, natural resources, and other physical features affect the power of nations became distorted during the late-nineteenth and early-twentieth centuries. A highly deterministic pseudoscience became subverted to the political agendas of dictators looking to rationalize their expansionist policies.

Global Not national or regional in scope, but rather having a worldwide reach. This concept represents a relatively new way of looking at problems connected to humans' relationship to the environment.

Global Environment Facility (GEF) Set up in 1991, a World Bank-run organization which funds environmental protection activities and coordinates cooperation between donors to the facility.

Globalism A broad-gauged paradigm emphasizing the importance of seeing the big picture of the world as a whole as an antidote to the limitations of parochialism.

Global issues Those problems defying effective solution which influence not only individual nations or regions, but the world as an interdependent system—for example, environment, the nuclear dilemma, drug trafficking, or human rights.

Global resources Referes to the view common among more-developed countries from the northern hemisphere that the Earth's bounty of natural treasures belong to humanity and to the world community, not to the countries in which they happen to be located.

Global town meetings The popular name given to the multitude of international conferences—usually held under U.N. auspices—addressing the great global issues of the day, such as food, environment, and population.

Gold standard A fixed exchange rate system in which the values of different currencies are set in terms of gold.

Golden Rule The ethical principle of reciprocity advocated widely around the world which argues that you should do unto others as you would have them do unto you.

Government Institutions set up by societies to order their public affairs. As a decisional unit participating in the national economy, government consists of authoritative institutions capable of intervening in the economy in a variety of ways with the intention of benefiting it.

Grass roots Pertaining to efforts undertaken by individuals or small groups from below, often at the local level, and at least partly the result of spontaneous initiatives, as opposed to carefully orchestrated control from above.

Great Depression While any depression signifies prolonged and severe economic decline, the Great Depression of the 1930s witnessed such falling production, mass unemployment, and business failure as to raise fundamental questions about the viability of the capitalist model itself.

Great Society Program When Lyndon Johnson took over the presidency in 1963 he focused his energies on getting through Congress these initiatives intended to help the poor and the disadvantaged in America.

Green consumerism Grass-roots activism for voluntary simplicity on the part of shoppers aimed at punishing corporations that pollute or degrade the environment or that encourage excessive waste of natural resources.

Greenhouse gases Gases such as carbon dioxide, ground-level ozone, chlorofluorocarbons, methane, or nitrous oxide, which, when built up in the atmosphere, contribute to the heating effect known as global warming.

Green justice An ethic of the global ecosystem. Truth and fairness are seen as having primacy over other values in formulating the appropriate starting point for this ethic.

Green Revolution Significant increases in food production that occurred in parts of the Third World (e.g., Asia and India) in the 1950s and 1960s, owing to the use of hybrid grains and advanced forms of fertilizer.

Greens The popular name given to the group of environmentalists in Germany that grew sufficiently in the 1980s to become a bona fide parliamentary political party.

Gross domestic product (GDP) The monetary value of what is produced as goods and services in a given year within the borders of a nation.

Gross national product (GNP) The monetary value of what the citizens of a nation produce as total output of goods and services in a given year.

Group of Seven (G-7) An annual summit conference for leaders of the world's seven leading industrial nations: Canada, France, Germany, Great Britain, Italy, Japan, and the United States. The G-7 became the G-8 with the admission of Russia in 1994.

Group of 77 (G-77) As distinguished from the G-7 industrial powers, these less-developed countries from the southern hemisphere may be poor, but their loose organization represents a majority of the world's nations. In fact, their ranks have swelled from 77 members when they began meeting in the 1970s to more than 125 nations today.

H-bomb Hydrogen bombs developed in the early 1950s, based on nuclear fusion. Most of those developed were in the 3–5–10 megaton range, although the Soviets tested one in 1954 that measured 50 megatons.

Heretic An outcast banished from a religious organization because of failure to adhere to the doctrine of the sect as defined by those who hold power. The quasi-religious ferocity of the Cold War led to true believers' on both sides of the Iron Curtain branding opponents as heretics.

Hidden hunger A covert rather than overt, and long-term rather than short-term, form of hunger characterized by shortened life expectancy because of deficient dietary intake.

Hindus Native to India, a polytheistic religion emphasizing reincarnation and the need for individuals to rise spiritually above their earthly tribulations.

Historicism An excessive attachment to historico-philosophical methods, producing broad analytical themes resulting in unrealistic expectations concerning the assumed validity of conclusions traditionally reached in this manner. Historicism fails to recognize the legitimate contributions of the scientific method to the study of humans.

Holistic Eschewing atomistic, piecemeal explanations in favor of more comprehensive understanding of the complexities of human behavior.

Homogeneous Unified, cohesive, or exhibiting sameness; social groupings, like societies, are often classified according to extent of homogeneity (unity) versus heterogeneity (diversity).

Household The consuming portion of the national economy living as families and acting as discrete decisional units.

Human Development Index (HDI) Beginning in the 1990s, the United Nations began measuring quality of life issues such as life expectancy, literacy, and income in all countries of the world and publishing the results in a summary index.

Humanistic psychology Alternative theory of personality and therapies developed in the United States during the late 1960s, which rejected the Freudian and behaviorist notions that humans have little control over their lives; humanistic theories held that personality changes over the course of a lifetime and that the direction of such change can be shaped by the individual person.

Humanitarian Characterizing the idealist belief that we all have a responsibility to do what we can to assist fellow humans who may be less fortunate than we.

Human rights A movement stemming from the belief that simply by virtue of being human all persons share certain inalienable rights which governments cannot violate. This is a relatively recent contention, emerging from the Nazi Holocaust of World War II, after which the world community expressed the sentiment, "never again." The international human rights movement has been at the vanguard of challenges to traditional international law's bedrock concept of national sovereignty.

Hyperfactualism Extreme reliance on specifically verifiable data to the exclusion of potentially relevant qualitative information.

Hyperinflation An alarming rate of price and wage increases deemed perilous to a nation's economy because it undermines its currency and encourages wild speculation.

Id In Freudian psychoanalysis this refers to primal urges craving satisfaction in the human personality's struggle between competing forces.

Idealism An optimistic approach to the world based on the belief that human reason can find ways to avert war and promote peaceful cooperation by finding common elements uniting all peoples.

Ideal types An archetype, model, or standard of perfection used in social science discourse to portray an image of some abstract concept.

Ideology A coherent set of ideas helping to form a social, political, religious or similar outlook for a group of people. This involves both descriptive (what is) and prescriptive (what should be) elements serving as simplifying lenses to make a complex world more comprehensible.

Imam In the Islamic religion, a Muslim scholar or prayer leader.

Import quota A form of nontariff barrier that arbitrarily limits the number of units that a foreign producer can export to another country.

Import substitution A strategy for economic expansion among less-developed countries that emphasizes economic nationalism and protectionism. Its track record in countries that have tried it has been dismal.

Indigenous people Native inhabitants of areas colonized or otherwise dominated by Western nations.

Individualistic capitalism A variation on the theme of the market economy that favors an entrepreneurial style of personal risk taking and self-reliance, as in the United States or the United Kingdom.

Individual proprietorship The name given to a business enterprise owned by the person(s) who operate that enterprise.

Indo-European Belonging to the group of languages that derived from the Proto-Indo- European language. Among current Indo-European languages are Germanic, Celtic, Slavic, Greek, Iranian, and Italic.

Industrial Revolution First in Britain around 1750 and then throughout Europe, a class of industrial owners replaced the feudal landed aristocracy as they accumulated wealth by means of power-driven machinery replacing hand tools used for labor.

Infant industries New, high-risk entrepreneurial endeavors deemed by some economists as exceptional enough for them to overlook their traditional opposition to protectionism.

Inflation An undesirable economic condition of rising prices and eroding purchasing power in which demand usually is growing faster than supply.

Institution A patterned, regularized set of behaviors and operations constructed by societies to satisfy basic human needs—for example, the economy as a vehicle for dealing with the problem of scarcity.

Intellectual property Property other than goods and services. This piece of the international trading pie has become more important as the monetary value of expressions of human creativity (such as popular music, feature films, and computer software programs) has skyrocketed in recent years.

Interdependence The multifaceted concept describing ways in which the modern world is shrinking. Economic linkages and shared fate over global issues (like environmentalism or the nuclear dilemma) represent two such indicators of modern interdependence.

Intergenerational equity The argument that humanity has a responsibility to future generations to act as stewards of planetary trust in bequeathing to them a viable environment.

Intergovernmental Describes the sharing of something—such as information, decision making, or accountability—among different levels of governmental (e.g., local, state, federal) authority.

Intergovernmental organizations (IGOs) Public institutions established by groups of nation–states to solve some common tasks, such as defense (NATO) or free trade (NAFTA).

International Describing varied forms of intercourse occurring between the nation–states comprising humanity's venue for organizing its public affairs for more than three centuries.

International Bill of Human Rights The codification of global rights specified collectively in the Universal Declaration of Human Rights, the Covenant on Economic, Social, and Cultural Rights, and the International Covenant on Civil and Political Rights.

International Covenant on Civil and Political Rights In 1966 this document was written by the U.N. General Assembly. It strengthened the Universal Declaration of Human Rights by spelling out more specific areas of protection concerning freedom of expression and the right to participate in public discourse.

International Covenant on Economic, Social, and Cultural Rights In 1966 this document was written by the U.N. General Assembly. It strengthened the Universal Declaration of Human Rights by spelling out more specific areas of protection relating to human dignity and material sufficiency.

International Energy Agency (IEA) Following closely on the heels of sharp price increases by the OPEC producers in 1973, this U.S.-inspired organization brought together the major oil-consuming nations in a cooperative effort to counter OPEC's limitation of the oil supply.

International financial institutions (IFIs) Global and regional organizations constructed under the 1944 Bretton Woods system led by the United States and aimed at stabilizing monetary policy, stimulating development lending, and expanding free trade.

International Fund for Agricultural Development (IFAD) One of the specialized U.N. agencies, which operates under the auspices of the Economic and Social Council (ECOSOC) to provide food assistance to victims of famines; it was created by the 1974 Rome Conference.

International law The body of formal and informal codes, norms, and rules accumulated by the world community over time in hopes of exercising a salutary influence over the behavior of the various actors (especially nation–states) at work on the world stage.

Irredentism A territorial claim made by country A, claiming that country B's possession of some disputed land is illegitimate.

Islam The world's second largest religion, with one billion believers who follow the teachings of their seventh-century prophet, Muhammad, as embodied in the holy book called the Koran.

Isolationism The viewpoint that it is in a country's interests to avoid the world's problems as much as possible in order to concentrate on the home front; it was prominent in the interwar period and has arisen in the post-Cold War debate over the aims of U.S. foreign policy.

Just cause One of the core elements of Christian just-war doctrine, which demanded that the reasons for undertaking an act of war to redress national grievances be valid and warranted by the facts.

Just war A distinction drawn in all major monotheistic religions between legitimate and illegitimate resort to force. In each case, ethical principles are established for the identification of a just war, but problems often arise when political elites manipulate this concept for reasons of expediency.

Kiloton A unit of measurement employed in the nuclear weapons field, equivalent to one thousand tons of TNT.

Labor Skills sold, by those who perform work, to managers and owners as their contribution to the production process.

Land Primary products extracted from the earth, such as forests, minerals, and property.

Learning Psychology The school of thought relying extensively on rewards and punishments as inducements to desired human behaviors.

Less-developed countries (LDCs) Those poor, mostly former colonial possessions in the southern hemisphere now struggling to improve their economic prospects. Also sometimes called the Third World or developing countries.

Level-of-analysis An aspect of analysis in the social sciences, where scholars may be studying human behavior from the micro (individual) to the macro (national) to the mega (global) level, we try to maintain awareness of the different social milieus characteristic of each level in order to avoid overgeneralizing from one level to another.

Life chances Opportunities for success. Sociologists studying social stratification point out the ways in which people from various classes experience different opportunities for success, even in self-described egalitarian societies.

Like-minded countries A small number of affluent, moderate international powers that placed a commitment to global human rights at the top of their foreign policy agendas during the 1980s.

Machismo A cultural attitude, deriving from the Iberian societies of Spain and Portugal, which idealizes the image of the strong, proud, and respected dominant male in Latin America.

Managed economy Neomercantilist policies, which originated in Japan, whereby limited and selective governmental intervention into the economy assists domestic companies by limiting free trade. This is a new concept requiring adjustment to the traditionally simple concept of capitalism as a system of free enterprise and competition.

Market Economic exchanges driven by competition between firms in the absence of governmental interference, so that the forces of supply and demand determine the pricing of goods and services.

Masculinity Male gender role considered typical in a given culture: the strong, active, left-brained male good at studying natural sciences is the stereotype in North American culture. Biology and culture both contribute to human sexuality.

Materialism A strong attachment to the importance of physical possessions as a determinant of self-worth and success, an attitude often found in complex societies; the opposite of spiritualism.

Megaton A unit of measurement employed in the nuclear weapons field equivalent to one million tons of TNT.

Mercantilism The belief common during the first 200 years of the nation–state system that the main function of the economy was to aggrandize wealth for the state.

Merchandise trade That sector comprised of tangible manufactured goods exchanged in international commerce, as distinguished from trade in services.

Mexico City World Population Conference A global town meeting convened in 1984 during the conservative presidency of Ronald Reagan in the United States. It was most noteworthy for U.S. participation, despite Reagan's opposition to most international family planning programs.

Middle Ages A period of roughly a thousand years in the history of Western civilization from the fall of the Roman Empire in 476 A.D. to the Renaissance, which began about 1500.

Militarismo Related to the concept of machismo in Latin cultures but more specifically based on a historical tradition of strong military men serving as political leaders.

Militias Those hard-core adherents of the ideology of the patriot movement who go beyond mere quarreling over the federal government's proper powers and organize themselves into militant cells of armed resistance preparing for what they consider to be an inevitable fight with the Feds. Many of them fear a global conspiracy they see trying to use the United Nations as a tool for stealing American sovereignty.

Minority group Literally, a subgroup consisting of less than half of a larger (majority) social identity. As the term is used by sociologists, however, more crucial to minority status than mere numbers is being disadvantaged; thus even women as a group with majority numbers can be considered a minority.

Mixed-market economy Economic systems combining elements from the theories of both capitalism and socialism, as in most advanced industrialized countries in the world today.

Model A term used by social scientists to refer to an ideational structure, similar to a theory, as a means to explain the relationship between variables or hypotheses.

Momentum factor in population The phenomenon whereby the population surge in the less-developed countries,

resulting partly from high birth rates and declining death rates, makes for high proportions of young people of childbearing age relative to their elders, creating a large population bubble that will burst forth in the future.

Monetary policy Managing the size of a nation's money supply so as to encourage investment and economic growth. Also called monetarism.

Money Currency issued by a government that acts as a means of exchange in establishing the price of goods and services.

Monitoring In the area of international human rights this refers to professional activities undertaken by non-governmental organizations to check on the compliance of nation–states to international legal standards.

Monogamy The marital pattern prevalent in Western civilization that calls for union between only one man and one woman at any one time.

Monopoly A market situation in which sale of a given commodity is controlled by a single seller, coupled with the presence of multiple buyers, leading to an absence of competitive dynamics.

Monotheism Belief in one supreme being, as in Christianity, Judaism, and Islam.

Monroe Doctrine Famous dictum issued in 1823 by President James Monroe warning European powers to stay out of the affairs of Latin America. Although the United States was relatively weak at the time, it worked well since European countries had their hands tied by balance-of-power commitments which prevented them from engaging in adventurism in the Americas.

Montreal Protocol Multinational treaty intended to cut production levels of substances that eat away at the atmosphere's protective ozone layer. The Protocol was reached in 1937 among 37 leading industrialized nations, because of the health and environmental risks associated with the depletion of the ozone layer.

More-developed countries (MDCs) Wealthy nation–states found mostly in the North, who united with their peers in opposition to many of the demands made by poor countries for development aid.

Most-Favored-Nation (MFN) Trade Status Somewhat of a misnomer, MFN status actually describes the normal rules of the game between international trading partners. Many countries have used either the granting or denying of MFN as a carrot or stick in efforts to influence the behavior of another nation.

Multilateralist Name given to a state willing to act in concert with other countries in order to work toward some mutually beneficial endeavor.

Multinational Corporations (MNCs) Large profit-making corporations like General Motors, IBM, and Microsoft, who are based mostly in the North but invest and build around the world.

Muslims The second-largest monotheistic religion, with about one billion adherents, whose God, Allah, is believed to have expressed himself through the prophet Muhammad in 692 A.D.

Mutually assured destruction (MAD) The deterrence strategy that recognizes each nuclear nation's capability to unleash a massive retaliation, even if the enemy has struck first. Its logic is based on the rational calculation that nuclear weapons are usable only for purposes of deterrence, not for actual attack.

Narcissism An excessive fixation upon oneself. The term is derived from Greek mythology, where a young male rejected in love pines away at his own image in a pool of water. In psychoanalysis it means an arresting of development resulting in an unhealthy need for external love and adulation.

Nation According to a sociological concept, a sizable group of people identifying with one another, usually on the basis of some shared ethnic, religious, or racial characteristics.

National balance The relationship between a nation's incoming and outgoing monies, which result from its participation in international trade and investment. Nations annually compute this relationship to determine their national balance of payments.

Nation–states Nations of peoples officially represented by goernment, and commonly referred to as countries. Despite operating as the most potent actors on the world stage for three and a half centuries, the sovereign authority of countries is being challenged today on many fronts. Their numbers have also proliferated to about 200 nation–states worldwide.

Naturalist School An approach to human rights that contends that in the natural state of human affairs, preceding any societal arrangements, certain untouchable personal freedoms must be respected in order to maintain a condition of human dignity.

Natural Rights The belief that immutable laws of nature preceding societies establish eternal guarantees of certain protections under international law.

Nature versus nurture One of the most vexing questions about human behavior, concerning whether who we are as individuals is shaped more by genetic inheritance (nature) or more by social experiences and cultural learning (nurture).

Neoclassical school The advocacy of minimal governmental intervention in the economy coupled with a reduction of taxes. This approach, also known as supply-side economics, developed at the University of Chicago in the 1970s and influenced the thinking of U.S. President Ronald Reagan.

Neocolonialism While the old colonial order has largely disappeared from the world, southern hemisphere critics of the prevailing international economic system charge that many vestiges of unfairness and inequality continue to exist under the guise of this newer, more subtle colonialism.

Neomercantilism Under traditional mercantilism, the prime function of trade was to aggrandize wealth for the state, and government was considered justified in protecting its domestic producers against foreign competition. A newer variant using managed trade, especially as practiced by Japan, has led to criticisms of anti-free trade policies as neomercantilist.

Net national product (NNP) The monetary value of what a nation produces as total output of goods and services in a given year, less deductions made for depreciation of the machinery used for production.

New International Economic Order (NIEO) A coalition of less-developed countries whose criticisms of the international economic system created pressure, beginning in the 1970s, for reforms intended to give poor countries some concessions to enable them to compete in the world economy.

Newly industrialized countries (NICs) Countries that have used the relative freedom of contemporary world trade to boost their economies by selling manufactured goods abroad. Their recent economic success stories have unfolded mostly in east Asia.

Nongovernmental organizations (NGOs) Actors on the world stage, not tied to governments, that often serve as global lobbyists trying to influence nation–states, intergovernmental organizations, and multinational corporations in specific issue areas.

Nonintervention One of the basic tenets of the traditional international legal concept of sovereignty which argues that nation–states should not meddle in the internal affairs of other nation–states.

Nontariff barriers (NTBs) Any of the varied means of protecting domestic industries from foreign competition other than excise taxes.

Norms Codes of social behavior set by society which influence us in both formal and informal contexts.

North American Free Trade Agreement (NAFTA) A comprehensive agreement among the United States, Canada, and Mexico aimed at 99 percent tariff reductions within fifteen years of its inception in 1994.

North Atlantic Treaty Organization (NATO) A military body, established in 1949 by North American and Western European allies, intended to deter potential Soviet aggression in the European theater.

Nuclear family A family structure consisting exclusively of a married couple and their children, typically found in many complex societies.

Nuclear meltdown An atomic energy worst-case scenario in which the core of a nuclear reactor is exposed and creates dangerous heat and radiation. The Three Mile Island accident in 1979 raised fears of nuclear meltdown and sidetracked nuclear power in the United States.

Nuclear Non-Proliferation Treaty (NNPT) The original 25-year treaty signed in 1970 to prevent the spread of nuclear weapons to non-nuclear states. The NNPT was extended indefinitely in 1995 after a major push by the Clinton administration for its approval and ratification.

Nuclear proliferation The process whereby states not previously having nuclear weapons come to possess them. In the post-Cold War the possible spread of nuclear weapons to rogue states like Iraq or Libya has supplanted fear of war between nuclear superpowers as the anxiety of choice for the world community.

Obsessive-compulsive disorder An inability on the part of a person to break free from repetitive habits which can range from merely being annoying to completely disrupting the individual's ability to function normally.

Oil shock Name given to periodic shortages (and subsequent price increases) in the global supply of petroleum that have stunned the more-developed countries that depend on oil as their economic lifeblood.

One country, one vote An equal voice for all nations in the voting procedures of international financial organizations. In forums like the New International Economic Order (NIEO), southern less-developed countries have unsuccessfully argued in favor of this system.

Option of last resort One of the core elements of Christian just war doctrine, which demanded that all reasonable alternatives to war be exhausted prior to resort to war.

Overkill One of those terms owing its existence to the excessive nature of military capabilities developed during the frenzied competition of the Cold War. Specifically, the extraordinary ability by the two superpowers to destroy each other via nuclear weapons not just once, but many times over.

Ozone layer A concentration of the gas ozone in the stratosphere, about ten to thirty miles above the Earth's surface.

Pacifist A person of peace who adheres to the tradition of turning the other cheek, thus refusing to meet violence with counterviolence.

Pacifist civil disobedience A form of nonviolent resistance; protest against governmental policies or social norms that are considered by the resistor to be so ethically repugnant as to warrant noncompliance.

Paradigm The prevailing analytical framework used by scholars to explain some natural, social, or intellectual phenomenon. Scientific inquiry requires the willingness to abandon comfortable old paradigms when new data disprove previously accepted hypotheses.

Paranoia A state of excessive mental agitation stemming from a grossly exaggerated fear that someone very threatening is out to harm the person afflicted. Popular misuse of this term has led to distortions of its meaning.

Participant observation A "hands-on" approach to social research in the post-World War I era, pioneered by anthropological field studies of distant cultures. The risk, of course, is that the researcher may become so integrated into the culture examined as to sacrifice objectivity and analytical acuity.

Partnership A form of individual proprietorship distinguishable from sole proprietorship by virtue of ownership being shared by persons sharing risks and rewards.

Patriots A label used by contemporary right-wing extremists in the United States who claim loyalty to the ideals of a historical American nation based on a strict construction of the powers granted to the federal government by the Constitution. They consider the national government as presently constituted abusive and unworthy of their loyalty or obedience.

Peace of Westphalia The 1648 treaty ending the bloody religious struggles in Europe known as the Thirty Years War. The modern nation–state system emerged from this treaty's legitimization of secular political authority independent of the Papacy.

Per capita GDP (gross domestic product) The monetary value of what is produced as goods and services in a given year within the borders of a nation, divided by the total number of citizens.

Per Capita GNP (gross national product) The monetary value of what a nation produces as total output of goods and services in a given year, divided by the total number of citizens.

Perception Refers to the selective and imperfect process of internalizing environmental stimuli by the human brain. The subjective dimension of human experience involves intangible processes of interest to psychologists because they affect our motivation and behavior.

Perceptual analysis An approach to the study of human behavior which emphasizes the relevance of subjective factors (like attitudes, values, beliefs, and perceptions) involved in human motivation.

Permafrost An area of subsoil that remains frozen year-round, as in polar regions.

Personalismo The reciprocally useful relationship between the dominant feudal *patron* and the submissive *peon* in Latin cultures.

Petrodollars U.S. currency held by oil-producing countries. This term was used widely in the 1970s when huge profits among OPEC nations led to the recycling of petrodollars to Western financial institutions.

Physical anthropology A major subfield of the discipline of anthropology with a strong biological bent to its inquiries. These social scientists want to know about the emergence of humans and our evolution, and about why modern human populations differ biologically from one another.

Pollution Agents that render an ecosystem unable to cleanse itself of environmental irritants introduced by humans—generally involving either air, land, or water.

Polyandry The rarer of two forms of polygamy in which one woman is married to more than one man at a time.

Polygamy The plural marital pattern found in many southern hemisphere societies in which union with more than one spouse at a time is considered acceptable.

Polygyny The more common of two forms of polygamy in which one man is married to more than one woman at a time.

Polytheism The recognition of numerous gods without considering any one as supremely ordained over the others. It was characteristic of many ancient civilizations.

Popular culture A colloquial phrase meaning that which is not high-level or sophisticated cultural expression, but rather common, folk, or lower cultural expression.

Positive-sum game Any contest in which gains or wins are not restricted to a particular side, so that two or more participants may emerge from a transaction as winners; also called win–win situations.

Positivist School An approach to human rights that argues that questions of individual rights do not exist in a social vacuum and should be weighed against the collective rights of societies. Asian countries have often taken a cultural relativism position based on positivist philosophy in defending themselves against claims of human rights abuses emanating from Western human rights groups.

Power The ability of A to get B to do something that B would not otherwise do. Power and influence are the stuff of politics, which involves competition for scarce resources—particularly scarce in the international arena.

Primary economy An undiversified national economic system based on the extraction of products from the earth and usually not very competitive in the international economy.

Primary group Those close associates with whom one interacts frequently and intimately, comprising a fairly small group of people. The family constitutes the essential intrinsically valuable primary group.

Primary product In economics, resources extracted from the earth, including natural resources such as petroleum and agricultural products such as coffee. Many poor southern hemisphere countries remain bogged down in this relatively unproductive type of economic activity.

Private Belonging to an independent person or persons, not to a public institution like a government.

Privatization The sale of government-owned industry to the market sector of the economy. This trend has been discernible in the United States and globally beginning around 1980. It has been aided by a parallel trend of reduced governmental regulation of the economy.

Proportionality The demand that retaliation against acts of aggression be in-kind or at a comparable level to the initial injury suffered. This is one of the core elements of Christian just war doctrine.

Protectionism An ideology that holds that the national government should act to shelter its domestic industries from foreign competition via measures like tariffs, import quotas, and subsidies.

Protestant Reformation The sixteenth-century rebellion against the Catholic church. Early Renaissance critical thinking received a major boost when a dissident monk named Martin Luther posted his ninety-five theses on the door of the Wittenberg cathedral, a pivotal catalyst unleashing the force of individualism in its battle against the Roman Papacy.

Pseudo-science A pejorative label used by critics to deride poorly conceived, shabbily executed, or badly misinterpreted studies employing quantitative scientific research methods.

Public Belonging to a collectivity, such as a government, as opposed to private citizens.

Quality standards A form of nontariff barrier that relies on stringent health or safety criteria for the admission of imported goods into a country.

Quasi-Darwinian Partially or somewhat reminiscent of the evolutionary model of survival of the fittest, explicated in the nineteenth century by the pioneering natural scientist Charles Darwin.

Quiet diplomacy As distinguished from more assertive forms of publically trying to influence the behavior of another country, this is a reliance on subtler, behind-the-scenes personal contacts in trying to affect a rival nation–state.

Radical theory An interpretation of the causes and cures for poverty among less-developed countries that considers the causes deriving from international exploitation by more-developed countries and the cures requiring self-reliance and severance of ties with exploitative countries.

Rationalism During the Renaissance, the increased use of reason or critical thinking in explaining the meaning of life in our world, rather than the religious doctrine dominant during the Middle Ages.

Realism A sober, hard-headed theory of world affairs placing a premium on competitive national interest defined in terms of power and suspicious of utopian visions of cooperative endeavors among different nations.

Recession A short-term decline in national business, less severe than a depression. It is officially identified by the absence of economic growth for three consecutive quarters.

Reductionism An intellectual fallacy in which the genuine subtleties of some complex concept or theory is sacrificed in order to achieve an overly facile explanation of questionable value.

Refugees Twenty-six million people dislocated from their countries of origin by war, civil disturbances, and natural disasters, who remain adrift as they seek legal acceptance into other countries, many of which have begun tightening requirements both for initial entry and for possible long-term citizenship.

Regulated capitalism A contemporary term used to describe mixed-market economies, like that of the United States, that lean toward the competitive forces of the free market but also accommodate some degree of governmental intervention.

Renaissance Coming from the French word for "rebirth," the rebirth of ancient Greek and Roman knowledge in Europe from about 1500 to the end of the seventeenth century.

Reparations Money or goods demanded to redress an international grievance often associated with an illegal action by a state. Frequently victors have demanded these types of indemnities from the vanquished after a war.

Response (R) A learned reaction to an environmental stimulus considered by behaviorist psychology as the observable and measurable behavioral result of the milieu known as conditioned response.

Role The action orientation of a social status: What does a person do who carries out a given status? What behaviors does someone perform who fills the role of a gardener or an electrician?

Rome World Food Conference A 1974 global town meeting held in Italy and resulting in the creation of the World Food Council (WFC).

Scientific law A generalization deemed valid through observation of repeated events using rigorous means of verification.

Scientific theory An explanatory postulate whose methodologies are grounded in science.

Scientism The excessive attachment to the foundations of scientific thinking and scientific methods, resulting in unrealistic expectations concerning the extent to which quantification and experimentation can be applied to the study of human beings. Conversely, scientism fails to recognize the legitimate contributions of humanism to the social sciences.

Secondary economy An economy that is advanced beyond the resource extraction of the primary economy, relying largely on the production of manufactured goods for export.

Secondary group As juxtaposed with a primary group, this set of people consists of many acquaintances, useful as instrumental means to an end and usually of short duration only. For example, fellow students would represent a secondary group.

Second World A Cold War-era designation of the second tier of thirteen less affluent and less democratic communist countries led by the Soviet Union.

Sectoral Relating to the divisions, segments, or parts of some greater whole, such as the military sector, economic sector, financial sector.

Security Individual and group safety. During the long Cold War, security meant the military integrity of the nation–state in the face of challenges from other powerful nations. Since then, it has taken on broader connotations related to quality-of-life issues like ecological, economic, and social security.

Selective perception The tendency of the mind to focus on those stimuli that fit most comfortably with what we already believe to constitute reality and with the way we want things to be, rather than to take in stimuli randomly.

Self-determination The right of nations to shape their own destinies independently, a logical extension to the international arena of the bedrock principles of liberty and independence sparked by the French and American revolutions. Woodrow Wilson was the first to make this idea resonate.

Serf A member of the lowest feudal class in medieval Europe, who was bound to the land owned by a lord.

Services trade That sector comprised of intangibles (e.g., tourism, banking) exchanged during international commerce, as distinguished from trade in tangible goods.

Sex The genetically determined fact of biological life which establishes a sex status of either male or female.

Sexual double standard A general tendency in many societies for males to enjoy greater freedom in the realm of sexual expression than their female counterparts.

Shiite Muslim A minority sect of the Islamic religion, diverging from Sunni Muslims in believing that the prophet Muhammad's son-in-law, Ali, is the rightful successor to Muhammad.

Simple societies Small, homogeneous, preliterate social groups which rely on hunting and gathering or agriculture as means of survival and in which the extended family is central. Sometimes called *Gemeinschaft* societies.

Slavic An ethnic designation of social identity comprised of an eastern group which includes the Russians, western peoples like the Poles, and a southern branch to which the Serbians belong.

Slavophilism A form of conservative nationalism prevalent throughout Russian history in which Slavic cultural values are idealized as spiritually superior to their principal alternative—rampant materialism from the West.

Social Darwinism Charles Darwin's nineteenth-century theories which revolutionized our understanding of biological evolution. However, when premises like "natural selection" were carried over to analyze human affairs, they proved ripe for misuse.

Social institutions Repetitive patterns of predictable cultural activities intended to meet basic human needs. The family, religion, education, government, and the economy are especially crucial ones.

Socialism An economic theory based on governmental ownership of the means of production and a planned economy. In the nineteenth century this emerged in European thought as a major challenge to capitalism's deep inequalities.

Socialization The social process whereby one generation educates the next generation about how to live, think, and believe. Values as well as data are transmitted during this lengthy journey.

Society The highest level of social organization. When humans moved from nomadic hunter–gatherers to settled communities, they began forming societies, characterized by the creation of institutions to meet their needs. Society provides the structure to match culture's content.

Sovereign property The belief expressed by many southern hemisphere less-developed countries that the earth's natural resources belong to the countries where they exist.

Sovereignty The key legal concept supporting the 350-year old nation–state system which asserts that countries are independent actors solely responsible for what transpires within their borders.

Spatial Referring to geographic markers like place, location, and space—the physical realities of human interaction with the natural environment—useful in solving the intellectual puzzles that captivate social scientists.

START treaties The popular name given to the two Strategic Arms Reduction Treaties signed in 1991 and 1993 by which the

United States and U.S.S.R. agreed—for the first time—to go beyond mere limitations of nuclear weapons to significant reductions in superpower nuclear arsenals.

State A legal or juridical concept reserved for entities entitled to certain international rights and duties stemming from recognition by their peers that they are legitimate players in the diplomatic game.

State economic monopoly The characteristic of all communist countries whereby ownership of the means of production rested not with citizens or firms, but rather with an authoritarian government.

Status The level of social esteem or prestige accorded to individuals or groups. Such rankings reveal values of the groups doing the mental ranking.

Stimulus (S) A potent event or circumstance in the environment which behaviorist psychology considers crucial to understanding the conditioned behavioral response of a human subject.

Strategic industries Firms producing goods deemed essential to national defense, constituting circumstances exceptional enough for economists to overlook their traditional opposition to protectionism.

Study abroad The increasingly common phenomenon of students completing part of their academic careers in foreign lands, which is symptomatic of rapid globalization.

Subculture A group distinguishable from the main societal culture within which it exists without taking on the confrontational posture of a counterculture.

Subsidy Monetary grant made by a government to a domestic producer to enhance its competitiveness with foreign companies.

Suffrage Movement in the United States roughly 100 years ago advocating the right of women to vote. Female advocates of this movement were labeled suffragettes.

Sunni Muslim The overwhelming majority of the world's one billion Muslims, they consider the first four caliphs as the legitimate successors to their prophet Muhammad.

Superego In Freudian psychoanalysis, the ethical component of the human personality which absorbs society's values in the form of a conscience separating right from wrong.

Supernatural A force believed to be neither human nor subject to the laws of nature, usually entailing an image of some supreme spiritual being; it is found in nearly all societies.

Supply The amount of a commodity needed to match demand or to be sold at a certain price.

Supply-side economics Sometimes called neo-classicism, or the Chicago school, this theory posits that lowering taxes can encourage consumer spending and investment, eventually leading to increased governmental revenues.

Surrogates Local proxies (surrogates) supported by opposing sides in many regional military conflicts. During the long Cold War no direct military confrontation erupted between the two superpowers because of surrogates.

Survey research Canvassing of a large number of people via questionnaires, which allows social scientists to generate a statistically significant sample of opinion or information at a given time. Quantifiability and ease of data gathering make this a valued method of research.

Sustainable development The idealistic philosophy, elevated to a global goal by the 1992 Rio Earth Summit, that the demands for environmental protection emanating from northern countries and the demands for economic development emanating from southern nations can be compatible demands.

Tariff A tax placed by government on goods imported into its country, usually either to raise revenue or to protect domestic industries.

Technetronic A hybrid word derived from the modern-day merger of computer technology and electronics. Similar to the concept of the sophisticated tertiary economy—relatively few postindustrial societies using information as a source of soft power.

Technical aid Assistance characterized by its technical quality. Since the gap is widening between rich North and poor South in an age of expanding technical sophistication (e.g., computers), one of the issues of controversy relates to the proper amount and quality of high-tech assistance to be transferred from the more-developed countries to the less-developed countries.

Terms-of-trade problem The relationship between the value of a country's imports and the value of its exports. Nations relying on exporting primary products suffer declining terms of trade when prices of their imports rise faster than prices of their exports.

Territoriality The controversial contention, advanced by ethologists, that animals, including humans, fight instinctively to protect territory seen as essential to survival.

Tertiary economy Economic system found in those relatively few postindustrial countries that rely on the fruits of the high-tech information revolution; this represents the most sophisticated example of economic evolution to date.

Theocracy A nonsecular form of government ruled by persons believed to be wise by virtue of their holiness. Theocracy was common a few centuries ago but is rare today.

Theories Explanatory models of high-level generality forming the basis of scholarly analysis in the natural sciences, social sciences, and humanities.

Third World The 100-plus poor and often nonaligned countries of the southern hemisphere. The First (U.S.) and Second (Soviet) worlds competed during the Cold War for their loyalty.

Third World diversification The effort in behalf of poor countries to develop more varied goods and services for export. The basic economic disadvantage inherent in reliance on one or two primary products for exportation leads many economists to overlook their traditional opposition to protectionism when it involves poor counrties trying to diversify.

Thirty Years War Central European war in 1618–1648 between pro-Catholic and pro-Protestant forces, resulting in the diminution of religious authority and expansion of secular power under the emerging nation–state system. The war ended with the Peace of Westphalia.

Totalitarianism A repressive type of political system in which a dominant party directs the government, which in turn controls most aspects of the lives of its citizens.

Trade balance The ratio between a country's imports and its exports. No nation's exports and imports exactly equal one another; therefore, at the end of the year nations have either a trade surplus or a trade deficit. Heated political debate has existed since the mid-1980s when Japan began running high trade surpluses with the United States.

Trade brinkmanship The concept of going to the precipice as a means of diplomatic leverage; it was first used in the 1950s in conjunction with the nuclear confrontation and has been employed similarly in the 1990s as a tool in trade wars.

Trade deficit The unfavorable condition that exists during a year when a national economy imports goods more valuable than the goods it exports.

Trade surplus The favorable condition that exists during a year when a national economy exports goods more valuable than the goods it imports.

Traditional model An approach to the institution of the economy based on simple exchanges of goods and services through bartering, a system common among preindustrial societies.

Tragedy of the Commons An educational tool used to illustrate the concept of finiteness via a metaphor involving overuse of a medieval grazing pasture.

Transnational Literally, private contacts *across* borders rather than public ones *between* nation–states, as with international contacts. Transnational activities, which have grown rapidly in recent years, involve one or more private, nongovernmental actors in communication with like-minded persons in other countries.

Transplants Manufacturing plants built in a foreign country. In order to reduce the effects of voluntary export restraints and other forms of nontariff barriers that limit the ability of an exporting country to sell its products in an importing country, some exporting countries resort to building their own plants within the resistant importing country.

Treaties International agreements that bind signatory nations to obligations and responsibilities in much the same manner as contracts do in domestic legal practice. Sometimes called conventions or pacts.

Trend A direction of movement; a course or a flow suggesting the way some phenomenon is proceeding.

Underground economy That portion of a nation's economy that goes unreported to the official economy, generally as a means of avoiding the payment of taxes.

Unilateralist Descriptive of a country preferring to act as a maverick, or alone, in world affairs. The United States is no stranger to this label.

United Nations Commission on Human Rights A body charged with investigating private complaints against governmental human rights violations. It tended to look the other way until strong lobbying from global nongovernmental organizations around 1970 spurred it to start taking complaints more seriously.

United Nations Conference on Environment and Development (UNCED) Also known as the Earth Summit, the largest global town meeting ever held. It met in Brazil during 1992 to address the set of environmental and economic issues revolving around sustainable development as an international goal.

United Nations Environmental Programme (UNEP) A forum created in 1972 to coordinate U.N. environmental matters.

United Nations Population Fund One of the specialized bodies of the U.N. system that studies demographic matters and issues its findings in annual reports.

Universal Declaration of Human Rights The bedrock 1948 United Nations human rights document that explicated rights of customary law a person possesses simply by virtue of being human, and that attempted to limit the ability of governments to infringe upon these rights.

Upscaling A method whereby an exporting country (like Japan) counteracts import quotas enacted by an importing country (like the United States) by shifting to producing more expensive goods so that its profit margin per unit is increased.

Uruguay Round The eighth round of GATT (General Agreement on Tariffs and Trade) negotiations, begun in 1986 and concluded in 1993, which brought agriculture, services, and intellectual property under the GATT's trading rules for the first time.

Utopia Theoretical perfect communes or other groupings of egalitarian relationships conceived by some idealists, known as utopian socialists, as alternatives to life as they witnessed it. These nineteenth-century European idealists chafed at the gross inequalities and insensitivities of capitalism under the Industrial Revolution.

Validity As related to scientific method, validity refers to measuring in fact that which you purport to measure. This issue takes on special significance in social sciences, where it is more difficult to delineate the influence of causal variables than in studies conducted by natural scientists.

Values Assessments of others that are more abstract than concrete in revealing at a subtext level what is considered good and bad by those making the judgments. Individuals have values which contribute to their unique personalities, but individuals also share common values that bind them with their larger cultures.

Videology The potent visual images conveyed by film and video and their subtext of cultural messages which, in recent years, have pushed American consumerism as the standard of global culture.

Virtual community In the computer age of instantaneous global communications and simulated realities, the term virtual has come to mean nearly real or a reasonable experiential facsimile thereof. Virtual community is meant to suggest that neither distance nor location any longer precludes the creation of binding social identities.

Voluntary export restraints (VERs) Bilateral agreements aimed at protecting a domestic industry, ostensibly volitional in nature but usually concealing coercive threats by the protectionist country against a low-cost exporter. In effect, they amount to protectionism without technically engaging in protectionism.

Wars Organized mass violence conducted by societies. Wars represent the dark side of human civilization, since they have been the rule rather than the exception during recorded history. Under traditional international law, war to redress national grievances was legitimate, but modern legal principles enunciated since 1945 challenge the legality of modern warfare.

Weighted voting In many international financial organizations, the practice of wealthy nation-states (like the United States) to tilt the decision-making process in their favor by giving themselves a greater number of votes than poorer countries have.

Westernization The name given to recurrent, though minority, threads in Russian intellectual history advocating reform to emulate European cultures as being more advanced than that of backward Russia.

World Bank One of the global economic institutions set up by the Bretton Woods system in 1944. Also called the International Bank for Reconstruction and Development (IBRD). Its prime function is to serve as a global lending agency. Its initial mission was to finance European rebuilding after 1945. Later it focused on development lending to poor countries.

World Energy Conference A global town meeting on energy, convened in 1981 after the two "oil shocks" of the 1970s. It failed to create the institutions or long-term commitment characteristic of many of the other global issue-areas.

World Food Council (WFC) A 1975 creation of the World Food Conference in Rome, which empowered the WFC to act as the main coordinating body for all U.N. food-related efforts.

World Trade Organization (WTO) The organization that succeeded the General Agreement on Tariff and Trade (GATT) in 1995 as the main global forum for reducing barriers to international trade.

Xenophobic Excessively fearful of foreigners.

Yin and yang The opposite, but complementary, passive and active elements central to classical Chinese dualistic philosophy.

Yom Kippur War The fourth Arab–Israeli conflict, begun by Egypt in 1973 and accompanied by a concerted Arab boycott of oil to the West, leading to the heady days of the OPEC cartel's brief starring role of the world stage in the 1970s.

Zero Population Growth (ZPG) The goal of replacement-level fertility now characteristic of highly affluent countries, but quite elusive in less-developed countries.

Zero-sum game Any contest in which the losses by one side in a conflict are matched by the gains of the opposing side, so that the net result, or sum, equals zero; also called win–lose situations.

PHOTO CREDITS

CHAPTER 1   Courtesy of IBM, 2; Jeff Greenberg/Visuals Unlimited, 3; Jeff Christensen/Gamma-Liaison, Inc., 4; NASA Headquarters, 10.

CHAPTER 2   Carolyn Brown/The Image Bank, 30; Lawrence Migdale/PIX.

CHAPTER 3   Cabisco/Visuals Unlimited, 41; Hulton Getty Picture Collection, 44; American Philosophical Society, 47 (left); Corbis-Bettmann, 47 (right); The Granger Collection, 48; Jane Thomas/Visuals Unlimited, 52; Sean Sprague/Stock Boston, 56; George Bellerose/Stock Boston, 61.

CHAPTER 4   UPI/P. Skingley/Corbis-Bettmann, 67; UPI/Corbis-Bettmann, 76; Reuters/Win McNamee/Archive Photos, 78; Bouvet/Hires/Merillon/Piel/Gamma-Liaison, Inc., 80; AP/Wide World Photos, 84.

CHAPTER 5   Richard Hutchings/PhotoEdit, 93; Hulton Getty Picture Collection/Tony Stone Images, 94; UPI/Corbis-Bettmann, 99 (left); UPI/Corbis-Bettmann, 99 (right); Marleen Daniels/Gamma-Liaison, Inc., 109.

CHAPTER 6   Miranda/Uniphoto Picture Agency, 117; David Hiser/Tony Stone Images, 118; Givliano Colliva/The Image Bank, 122; Jerry Howard/Stock Boston, 123; Gregory Bull/AP/Wide World Photos, 126; John Bishop/Media Generation, 129.

CHAPTER 7   Charles Gatewood/Stock Boston, 136; AP/Wide World Photos, 140; Charles Gatewood/Stock Boston, 145; George Steinmetz/George Steinmetz Photography, 151.

CHAPTER 8   Jens Dige, 157; Tan Ah Soon/AP/Wide World Photos, 161; Philip & Karen Smith/Tony Stone Images, 164.

CHAPTER 9   Hulton Getty Picture Collection/Tony Stone Images, 170; Martin Benjamin/The Image Works, 183; Alex Brandon/AP/Wide World Photos, 185; AP/Wide World Photos, 187; James Sawders, 190; Eddie Adams/AP/Wide World Photos, 191.

CHAPTER 10   UPI/Corbis-Bettmann, 195; Hulton Getty Picture Collection/Tony Stone Images, 197; Hulton Getty Picture Collection/Tony Stone Images, 203; Demetrio Carrasco/Tony Stone Images, 204; Hulton Getty Picture Collection, 212; National Women's Party/AP/Wide World Photos, 218.

CHAPTER 11   Chromosohm/Sohm/Uniphoto Picture Agency, 228; The Stock Market, 229; Hulton Getty Picture Collection/Tony Stone Images, 232; Gamma-Liaison, Inc., 234; Cliff Schiappa/AP/Wide World Photos, 244.

CHAPTER 12   UPI/Corbis-Bettmann, 261; Michael Hirsch/Gamma-Liaison, Inc., 264; Adam Nadel/AP/Wide World Photos, 273; Elise Amendola/AP/Wide World Photos, 275; Sean Sprague, 276.

CHAPTER 13   Hulton Getty Picture Collection/Tony Stone Images, 291; Warner Bros./Ron Batzdorff/AP/Wide World Photos, 294; Natalie Fobes/Tony Stone Images, 300; The University of Reading, 301; UPI/Corbis-Bettmann, 302.

CHAPTER 14   Ricardo Beliel/Gamma-Liaison, Inc., 309; Steve Allen/The Image Bank, 320; Stephen Ferry/Gamma-Liaison, Inc., 322; Bernd Wittich/Visuals Unlimited, 325; Schiller/The Image Works, 333.

CHAPTER 15   Antonio Ribeiro/Gamma-Liaison, Inc., 344; Jane Thomas/Visuals Unlimited, 347; Granitsas/The Image Works, 350; Languna Photo/Gamma-Liaison, Inc., 353.

CHAPTER 16   Robert Nickelsberg/Gamma-Liaison, Inc., 360 (left); Laurent Sasy/Gamma-Liaison, Inc., 360 (right); Reuters/Corbis-Bettmann, 364; Bruce Ayres/Tony Stone Images, 371; The Image Works, 373.

INDEX

A

A-bomb (atomic bomb), 76
  Truman's decision to use, 196–99
  U.S. and Japanese textbooks compared, 182–84
  See also Nuclear weapons
Abkhazians, 17
Abortion, 92, 158, 329, 345
Absolute advantage, 262
Acheson, Dean, 84, 87
Acid rain, 315, 320
Adrianople (Turkey), 294
Advertising limits, 265
Affirmative action, 28
Afghanistan, 55, 146, 247, 374
AFL-CIO, 245
Africa, Sub-Saharan:
  Baka tribe of, 150–54
  deforestation in, 315
  democratization of, 80
  food production in, 332
  Kalahari !Kung of, 128–30
  nation–state in, 71
  origin of humans in, 40
  projected population growth of, 327
  women in, 220
  clitoridectomy, 159
  as world region, 20–21, 30
African American Experience in Japan, The (Life), 131
African Wildlife Foundation, The, 96
Agency for International Development (AID), 353
Agenda 21, 314, 345
Agriculture:
  Brazilian, 150
  in Japan, 137
  in Latin America, MNCs and, 354
  prehistoric revolution in, 41–42, 119–20, 124, 371
  in Russia, 299
  in U.S., 252
  See also Food
AIDS, 370
Air pollution and emissions, 315, 318
Alaska, pipeline in, 323
Alcott, Louisa May, 217
Alexander, Robert, 283

Alexander II (tsar), 143
Algeria, 80, 146, 208, 221, 222
Al-Ghazali, 145
Alker, Hayward, 61, 62
Allen, Woody, 172
Alliance for GATT Now, 246
Alternative sources of energy, 337, 346
Amazon basin, 24, 321
American Academy of Political and Social Science, 49
American Association of Sociologists, 115
American Automobile Labeling Act of 1994, 3
American Economic Association, 49
American Express, 244, 250
American Forestry Association, 346
American Political Science Association, 49
American Psychological Association (APA), 49, 59, 170, 172
American Revolution, 46, 49, 189
American Sociological Society, 49
Amerika (film), 186
Amin, Idi, 79
Amnesty International, 160, 206, 212, 214, 222
Anasazi Amerindians, 158
Anastasia, 54–55
Anderson, Anna, 54–55
Anderson, Rudolph, 85
Andorra, 27, 296
Andreesen, Marc, 5, 31
Andreski, Stan, 57
Andrews, Thomas, 311
Anglo-America, as world region, 24–25
Angola, 55, 129, 71
Animals:
  domestication of, 42, 371
  See also Endangered species
Animism, 148
Annas, George, 201
Anthropology:
  cultural, 116
  definition and scope of, 7, 39–40, 116–17
  holistic perspective of, 158
  origin of, 115
  physical, 116
  psychological universals questioned by, 190

Anthropomorphism, 124
Antibiotics, 370, 371
Anticipatory thinking, 343
Apes, bonobos, 40
Aral Sea, 95, 316, 321
Arapesh, 217
Arara tribe, 147–48, 151–54
Archer Daniels Midland, 230
Ardrey, Robert, 32
Argentina, 21, 33, 78, 94, 211, 233, 282
Aristide, Bertrand, 82
Aristotle, 45, 174, 209, 289
Armenia, 296
  war between Azerbaijan and, 17, 208–9
Arms control, 83
Arnett, Peter, 368
Asia as world region, 18–20
Aspirin, 321
Association of American Geographers, 49
Astrology in matchmaking, 123
Asylum, political, 362
Ataniyazova, Oral, 95
Atheism, 204
Athletes, international, 3–4
Atomic Cafe (film), 76
Attenborough, Richard, 195, 212
Attila, 43
Augustine, St., 171
Austerity measures, 110
Australia, 20, 30, 79, 91, 124, 177, 270, 289
Austria, 213
Autarky, 262, 282
Authority, electric-shock experiment on, 58–59
Automatic teller machines (ATMs), 252
Automobiles:
  air pollution and smog from, 315, 321
  California emission controls on, 264
  Japanese and U.S., 242, 248, 264–95
  transplant, 265
  upscaling of, 265
  whether foreign- or U.S.-made, 3
Azerbaijan, war between Armenia and, 17, 208–9
Aztecs, 126–27, 128